qualitative educational research

readings in reflexive methodology and transformative practice

edited by
wendy luttrell

Routledge
Taylor & Francis Group
NEW YORK AND LONDON

First published 2010
by Routledge
270 Madison Ave, New York, NY 10016

Simultaneously published in the UK
by Routledge
2 Park Square, Milton Park, Abingdon, Oxon OX14 4RN

Routledge is an imprint of the Taylor & Francis Group, an informa business

Typeset in Minion by RefineCatch Limited, Bungay, Suffolk
Printed and bound in the United States of America on acid-free paper by
Sheridan Books, Inc.

Library of Congress Cataloging-in-Publication Data
Qualitative educational research : readings in reflexive methodology
and transformative practice / edited by Wendy Luttrell.
     p. cm.
  1. Education—Research—United States—Methodology.
  2. Qualitative research—United States.   I. Luttrell, Wendy.
  LB1028.25.U6Q83 2009
  370.7′2–dc22

                             2009012017

ISBN10: 0–415–95795–8 (hbk)
ISBN10: 0–415–95796–6 (pbk)

ISBN13: 978–0–415–95795–3 (hbk)
ISBN13: 978–0–415–95796–0 (pbk)

qualitative educational research

Qualitative Educational Research is a comprehensive anthology designed to deepen education students' thinking about their qualitative research purposes, questions, and decision-making. Focusing on various epistemological, intellectual, and ethical conflicts in doing social analysis, this volume invites researchers-in-training to explore why, from what perspective, for whose benefit, and with what stakes are research questions being posed. Drawing from her wealth of expertise executing and teaching qualitative research methods, scholar Wendy Luttrell has selected essays that focus specifically on the challenges of qualitative inquiry as they pertain to the field of education. These essays present multiple paradigms and perspectives in qualitative inquiry, including interpretivism, critical theory, cultural studies, feminist theories, critical psychology, and critical race theory. Reflexive writing assignments at the end of the volume expand readers' understanding of the essays and guide students through developing their own research design.

Wendy Luttrell is Professor of Urban Education at the Graduate Center, City University of New York.

This book is dedicated to my HGSE advisees who trusted me with their ideas and vulnerabilities so that I could learn to be a better listener and guide.

Contents

Acknowledgements

In the fall of 1999 I arrived at the Harvard Graduate School of Education with an institutional charge to redesign the qualitative research methods courses for doctoral students. This volume represents a piece of what became a resource-rich and rewarding learning and teaching experience, inspired by HGSE's greatest treasure—its students.

I was drawn to the vibrant interdisciplinary environment, if not a bit daunted by the demands. The range of students' interests and backgrounds was simply amazing.

My biggest surprise was a quiet angst (sometimes spoken, sometimes not) that hung in the air about what it meant to shift from one's familiar identity—for example, as a teacher, community activist, clinician, or visual artist—to becoming an educational researcher. I too was going through an identity crisis of sorts, identified as a "educational qualitative methodologist" after years of knowing myself as a feminist sociologist interested in gender, race, and class relations in school settings. My students and I grew into our new identities together, and I am forever grateful for their kindness, wisdom, and burning questions. I hope this reader pays tribute to these bonds.

Students who generously commented on drafts of the introduction and/or reflexive writing exercises helped me more than they can know: Abdi Ali, Liz Blair, Sherry Deckman, Bilal Malik, Corinne McKamey, Radhika Rao, Debby Saintil Previna, Carla Shalaby, Folashade Solomon, and Jennifer Zeuli. I am especially thankful that former advisees Rhoda Bernard, Cleti Cervoni, Charlene Desir, and Corinne McKamey agreed to revise a much longer paper about their experience as an interpretive community so that it would fit within the volume, but even more, for their willingness to take risks.

I wish to acknowledge my predecessor, Joe Maxwell, whose courses on qualitative research were legendary. I quickly embraced his thoughtful book *Interactive Qualitative Research Design* as a guide for my task. Colleagues who directly participated in the redesign of the qualitative research courses deserve recognition: Mary Casey, Gil Conchas, John Diamond, Ellie Drago-Severson, Vanessa Fong, Helen Haste, Jim Holland, Vivian Louie, Eileen McGowan, Mica Pollock, and Mark Warren. And I wish to thank those who showed good will toward the effort: Eleanor Duckworth, Bob Kegan, Jerry Murphy, Susan Moore Johnson, Mike Nakkula, Sara Lawrence-Lightfoot, Dick Murnane, Donna San Antonio, Marcelo and Carola Suarez-Orozco, Terry Tivnan, Carol Weiss, and John Willett. I owe special thanks to Julie Reuben for her extraordinary listening skills over many years, and her leadership when updating the qualitative research course offerings. Thanks to Veronica Boix-Mansilla for her friendship and bountiful knowledge of interdisciplinarity. My debt to Annie Rogers is the most far-reaching: her example as a scholar released my imagination.

Over the years, many teaching fellows generously gave their time and energy to my course, *Logics of Qualitative Research*; they all afforded me new sets of lenses through which to engage students in qualitative research. It was a joy and privilege to "grow" the course with Jim Holland through co-teaching. Special thanks are due to Debby Saintil Previna and Bilal Malik for the care and deep thinking they put into collaborative course planning and discussion during the preparation of the book.

I had the good fortune to teach a feminist methodology course in the *Women, Gender, and Sexuality* program at Harvard, which allowed me to try out new articles and reflexive writing strategies. I thank Alice Jardine for this opportunity and the undergraduate students who enriched my life and learning.

Several people read draft versions of the introduction with knowledge and sage advice: Susan Chase, Lisa Dodson, Marj DeVault, Catherine Riessman, and Kathleen Weiler. Their charitable feedback and general encouragement of me, my work, and this project came at a crucial time in my life; their support was invaluable. And in this same vein, I am indebted to Naomi Quinn for shoring me up when I have most needed it; she is a gift in my life that just keeps giving.

Catherine Bernard, my editor at Routledge showed empathy and patience when family health problems turned my world and schedule upside down. I appreciate her steadfast belief in the value of this project. I thank Georgette Enriquez who provided crucial and timely assistance that made things work smoothly.

Jenya Murnikov holds a special place in my heart for her assistance, good humor, and calm intelligence. And were it not for the tireless labors of Kimberly McMahon, this volume would still be sitting in my office.

Finally, I am ever grateful to Robert Shreefter for sustaining my life passions and indulging my work pre-occupations. The artwork for the cover of the book is Robert's. As he created this piece, I marveled at his patience and persistence in winning my aesthetic heart—which he did, and has done throughout our years together. Finally, bottomless thanks to my children Mikaela, Liam, and Emma for being a loving life force beyond all measure.

Introduction

The Promise of Qualitative Research in Education

> Because education is a moral endeavor, educational researchers should be scientists as well as citizens who are committed to promoting democratic ideals.
>
> Banks (this volume: 52)

To advance an agenda of social critique, social justice, and opportunity through educational research is no small task. Nor is it a neutral pursuit.[1] This volume champions qualitative research as a means toward these ends.

As a mode of inquiry, qualitative research holds high expectations of its practitioners, not the least of which is its profound humanism. Qualitative research insists upon a face-to-face, heart-felt encounter between knowing subjects, a recognition that each of us is unique in our effort to make sense of ourselves and the world around us. To approach another as a knowing subject—to care about a person's integrity, joys, sufferings, and self-definition—takes intellectual and moral courage, scientific risk-taking, and artful representation of what one has learned. There is no clear-cut path of discovery in qualitative research, but there are principles and procedures that enable the journey.

This volume is designed to support qualitative researchers-in-the-making as they take up a journey that can be unsettling—filled with false starts, impasses, and surprises. The selected readings and writing exercises open up pedagogical, practical, and theoretical discussion about the contours of qualitative research—the knowing, doing and telling—that it requires. Making these three interrelated parts of qualitative research more visible to aspiring researchers is the main purpose of this volume.

The volume does not provide a neat, generic methodological "tool kit" that can be deployed, because, given the nature of our craft, such a kit could not exist. Moreover, if educational research is going to serve democratic ideals and make a difference in people's lives, it will need to be inventive in its approach to problem solving and social analysis.[2] It is my hope that the volume will serve to strengthen novice researchers' confidence to adapt and refine existing theories and methods for their own research ends, and to reflect on the larger interests and values served by their projects.

No single discipline or field owns qualitative research—it is a broad and diffuse practice. I take its central features to be the following: qualitative research is defined by an effort to highlight the meanings people make and the actions they take, and to offer interpretations for how and why. Qualitative research is committed to participants using their own words to make sense of their lives; it places an importance on context and process; it rests on a dialectic between inductive and deductive reasoning; and uses iterative strategies to comprehend the relationship between social life and individual subjectivities. Doing qualitative research involves a healthy skepticism about whether "to see is to know," and instead calls upon us to look at people (including ourselves as investigators), places, and events through multiple and critical lenses.

Certain enduring concerns of qualitative research in education imbue it with "transformative" promise (Banks 2006: xii).[3] These concerns include (but are not limited to) a focus on (*multi*)cultural sense-making, status maintenance, and inequality; attention to how those with institutional authority exercise their power and control, and how those without it adapt and resist; and an allowance for participant engagement. *Transformative* research is part of a family of terms—advocacy, critical, oppositional, activist, transgressive, decolonizing, and emancipatory—used by researchers who wish to leverage social change through their scholarship. I have made an effort to select articles by a mix of scholars of feminism, critical race theory, poverty work, disability studies, indigenous research, and queer theory to demonstrate the field's vibrancy spanning several decades. However, no single volume could possibly be inclusive enough to do justice to the vast array. Instead, I sought an eclectic and suggestive mix of readings that would historize, problematize, and concretize qualitative research practices. Still, the choices reflect my sociological background and the limits of my training. Hopefully the volume will spur a "need to know" attitude and jump-start a meaningful dialogue among practitioners within an ever-evolving qualitative research tradition.[4]

On Knowing

What Counts as Knowledge?

In recent years, qualitative research in education has been put on the defensive. Driven by federal legislation such as the No Child Left Behind Act of 2001 and the Education Sciences Reform Act of 2002, federal regulation of educational research has increased, and the government has exerted more control over what counts as evidence and quality. Many people have criticized the narrow definition of science that is promoted by the National Research Council report, "Scientific Research in Education" (Shavelson and Towne 2002)— a definition that mischaracterizes science and marginalizes qualitative research. These critiques will not be reviewed here, but I encourage readers to become familiar with them (Eisenhart 2005; Eisenhart and Towne 2003; Erickson 2005; Erickson and Guteirrez 2002; Lather 2004; Maxwell 2004a and 2004b). Among the supporters of qualitative research, there is a continuum of perspectives. I join with those who are not willing to "cede the term 'science' to quantitative, variable-oriented approaches" (Maxwell, 2004a: 36) and with those who reject any single, "objective" or "value-free" definition of science.

Meanwhile, I do not think the division between social science and humanities is productive within educational scholarship. Elsewhere I have written about ethnographic research as a "social art form" (borrowing from anthropologist Karen McCarthy Brown 1991) that can bridge art and science, spontaneity and discipline, emotional engagement and detached analysis.[5] Most important, in my mind, is that the "science wars" a) deflect attention from the urgent social issues that we need to be investigating; and b) curb the methodological diversity and creativity our investigations demand.

Since its inception, what counts as educational science has been fractured by a so-called "theory–practice gap."[6] Given the continuing gendered division of labor that organizes and sustains the institution of education (Griffith and Smith 2005), we should not be surprised that educational research remains split-off from the more devalued, female-dominated practice of teaching. As historian Ellen Lagemann (2000) points out, much like what emerged between medical doctors and nurses, educational research was initially formulated "apart from its elaboration in practice" and assumed "a false sense of superiority" over those whose knowledge of practice was marginalized (234).[7]

The "theory–practice" divide has only been made worse by a trend in educational scholarship to "separate theory and research" (Anyon 2009).[8] Indeed, I have found that students struggle more with their *theoretical frameworks* than with their methodology. I believe there are several reasons for this, including the fact that much of the critical theory in education avoids empirical grounding and is pitched at a level of abstraction that can be hard to translate into appropriate units of analysis, research questions, methods, data collection, and analysis (Fine and Weis, this volume). Another reason is that students in education are either not afforded the time to read social theory or have not been exposed to a wide enough range of it. I refer to theories about culture, identity, power, resistance, social movements, domination and subordination, and knowledge production that are such central and enduring topics in our field. Connected to this is the separation between "theory" and "methods" coursework, which can leave aspiring educational researchers with the impression that their sole concern is to appropriately align their research questions with their methods (i.e. making sure that the data one collects will answer one's research questions) without enough consideration for how one's theory is embedded in the formulation of one's question.[9] Equally important, in my view, is to consider how one's research questions and methods shape relationships between researcher and researched, and the knowledge that is produced as a result.

A colleague once observed that dissertations tend to fall into one of two types: those that are "data rich" and "theory poor" and those that are "theory rich" and "data poor"— only in exceptional cases, he argued, are qualitative researchers-in-the-making able to find the right mix. The capacity to creatively fold together research questions and research relationships, theory-testing and theory-building, methods and ethics, and educational practice and politics, rather than splitting off and devaluing any one of these at the expense of the other, is what I believe can transform the field of education—if we can only support the next generation of scholars to do so.

Reflexive Knowing

In my view, the preeminent skill for conducting qualitative research is reflexivity. Tom Schwandt, in *Qualitative Inquiry: A Dictionary of Terms* (2001), defines reflexivity as a) "the process of critical self-reflection on one's biases, theoretical predispositions, preferences"; b) an acknowledgment that "the inquirer is part of the setting, context, and social phenomenon he or she seeks to understand"; and c) a means for critically inspecting the entire research process" (224). Reflexivity has been especially prized in qualitative research because the investigator is understood to be the "instrument" of data gathering and analysis. Thus, qualitative researchers are encouraged to acknowledge and account for their social backgrounds, relationship to the field site, theoretical and political leanings, and to develop critical self-reflection skills. Understanding one's "self" and stake in one's project is crucial for knowing both the limitations and the strengths of the "instrument."[10]

In some circles, reflexivity has come to be associated with unnecessary confessionals and narcissism on the part of the researcher—perhaps best captured in the familiar joke about the anthropologist conversing with her informant: "Enough about me, tell me what *you* think about me."[11] But those who overlook the necessity of researcher reflexivity do so at the risk of producing "bad data." *For reflexivity is about much more than researcher self-conscious awareness.* It is about making the research process and decision making visible at multiple levels: personal, methodological, theoretical, epistemological, ethical, and political. The reflexive practitioner attends to all levels.

Theoretically speaking, reflexivity means questioning the already *pre-conceived* categorization of the "researched."[12] For example, in my own research this has meant a critical examination of a) how a category of persons—"adult literacy learners" or "pregnant teens" or "immigrant children"—come to stand out as a "problem" population in the first place; and b) how members of each culturally defined, stigmatized group perceive themselves and their schooling in relation to others. Reflexive knowers consider the ways in which their projects rest on *taken for granted* problems, categories, concepts and theories that are themselves created by systems of power, privilege, and patterns of inequality (McDermott and Varenne, this volume).

Ethically speaking, reflexivity means extending one's concerns beyond university Institutional Review Boards' (IRB) rules and regulations pertaining to the protection of human "subjects" and the principle of "do no harm." Ethical reflexivity is an on-going process, not a once-and-for-all accomplishment, as in securing consent forms. Ethical reflexivity is about negotiating unequal distribution of power in the production of knowledge. In addition to finding ways to "give back" as much as one "takes" from those with whom one works, ethical reflexivity means searching for ways to incorporate human subjects as "*thinkers* in research about their lives rather than data producers for experts" (Dodson and Schmalzbauer, this volume: 324).

Reflexive qualitative researchers seek clarity and transparency about each decision made at every stage of the process—beginning with what questions to ask; what design to craft, data collection methods to employ, and analyses to conduct; who and what to include/exclude, and at what levels; and how best to represent what one learns. Reflexive researchers also maintain an awareness of underlying philosophical assumptions, epistemological tensions, and ethical concerns that shape the relationship between what we see and what we know. With each choice (no matter how small or large), something is lost and something is gained; and these trade-offs are the nitty-gritty of reflexivity within qualitative research (Luttrell, this volume). Knowing why we make the decisions we do is what lends our research validity and credibility.

On Doing

Design in the Doing

Developing a solid research design is the linchpin of qualitative research. But by design, I do not mean a blueprint that is drawn up in advance and set in stone. Rather, it is a plan that follows an ongoing set of principles that guide decision making throughout a qualitative study. Qualitative research is "designed in the doing," and "leaves room for, indeed insists on, individual judgment" (Becker 1993: 219). This feature of qualitative research may be anxiety-producing for researchers-in-training who might wish for a "researcher-proof" plan (analogous to "teacher-proof" curriculum).

As a child, I can remember my father, a building contractor, coming home cursing architects and their designs. He insisted that their plans did not take account of the complexities and conflicts of a contractor's life—whether in terms of finding the right building materials or coping with unexpected weather. In his view, architects lived in a world of abstract theory and were ignorant of the "feel" of wood that characterized his prized knowledge as a builder. He swore that if any of his children became architects he would disown us.

I have brought his frustration, if not his wisdom, into my thinking about qualitative research designs. I am suspicious of plans that do not take into account all manner of contingencies—practical, theoretical, and political. I find myself giving students the following advice: a) It takes more than a set of skills and tools to get a qualitative research job done—it takes a "feel" for people, their settings, and their local knowledge. b) Qualitative research is conflict-ridden (in good ways). That is, researchers must reconcile the abstract and the concrete, and be prepared to resolve glitches and dilemmas they encounter in the field. c) Finally, qualitative researchers need to anticipate that their research will take more time than expected. A colleague once told me that the fieldwork rule of thumb is that you double the time spent doing fieldwork to determine how long it may take to write up what you have learned.

It is important to clarify that social science disciplines—sociology, anthropology, psychology—have different research design and evaluation cultures. These nuances are important for educational researchers to understand because we borrow heavily from these traditions. These disciplines also vary in their embrace of constructivist and positivist epistemologies (see Greene, this volume, for discussion of these terms), their emphasis on description, interpretation and explanation, and the degree of consensus about the value and prominence of qualitative research methods.[13]

Moreover, each of these disciplines prepares students to conduct qualitative research in distinctive ways. Indeed, the term qualitative research is not even used among anthropologists because ethnography serves as the preeminent methodology for the study of culture.[14] Among psychologists, qualitative research is often referred to as narrative research (Rogers 2003) or interpretive (Tolman and Brydon-Miller, 2001). For sociologists, qualitative research can span several traditions—from symbolic interactionism and fieldwork methods (Blumer 1969; Mead 1934), to intensive, in-depth interview studies utilizing grounded theory (Charmaz, this volume:), to narrative inquiry (Chase, this volume), to historical studies, and content analyses.[15]

Despite disciplinary differences, researchers utilizing qualitative methods (and for that matter those who use quantitative methods), share the following standards for study design:

- Articulate a clear research question.
- Situate the project and its relevance within theoretical and methodological literature, and demonstrate the intellectual, practical, social, or political significance of the project—explain why it matters.
- Define key concepts being used.
- Make sure the type and source of data being gathered will answer the research question(s) being posed.

- Gather data systematically, and when possible, collect multiple data types and sources so these data can be "triangulated"—in other words, where multiple perceptions can be used to clarify and verify an observation or interpretation.
- Pay close attention to how you might be wrong in the conclusions you draw.

Apart from these, there are some principles, standards and concerns that are unique to qualitative research, as the following questions from students that I most frequently hear indicate:

What is my research question? Formulating good research *question(s)* is the touchstone of any research project. Nothing takes more time, thought, or consideration because our questions reveal our tacit assumptions, theory, purpose, and scope. Your research question is like the "North Star" in that it orients you to where you are and what direction you are traveling—but it is not your destination. Your destination is your research *story*—stories, actually, in that qualitative research includes the perspectives/stories of those who are the participants, the researcher's own story/interpretation, and in some cases, a third story created by a meeting of these minds. But you cannot get to the research stor*y/ies* without orienting questions. *In qualitative research, questions typically evolve along the way.*

Meanwhile, until researchers-in-training can come up with a good reason for why they need to know the answer to their questions, as well as the larger issue of whose interests are served by the investigation, it can be hard to move forward. There is a litany of familiar axioms: Don't ask questions you already know the answer to; don't ask questions that you don't want to know the answer to; don't ask questions that don't matter; don't be afraid to ask questions that do matter; expect that your questions will change as you learn more; research questions are not the same as interview questions; and so on.

Learning how to translate research questions into research action is exacting; it is accomplished over time and through a process of observation, conversation, and analysis—it does not happen in one fell swoop. The endless attention to what might at first seem as trivial or self-evident often comes as a surprise to novice qualitative researchers—e.g. you say you wish to interview "high school drop outs" to understand their perspective on school, but why does this population stand out to you? Where will you find these students? How will you introduce yourself? What will you say is the purpose of your study? Why will these students want to talk with you? Are these question better asked in a face-to-face interview or on a survey instrument, and why do you think so? "God is in the details"—by which I mean that the clarity and success of a research project depends on its smallest and most mundane details.[16]

How do I know how many? Case selection and sampling is a crucial issue in qualitative research. I advise students that they should be more concerned with assessing *which ones*, than how many. The point is to provide a clear explanation for why particular sites, participants, events, or cases have been chosen and why data being gathered will be significant beyond these particulars. There is no magic number that ensures rich or accurate data. Moreover, one single case can throw new light on an existing or well-accepted theory.

How do I know which ones? Purposive rather than random sampling procedures predominate in qualitative research. These "purposes" vary and include wanting to ensure demographic and theoretical variety among the selected participants. For example, in my research about adult literacy learners' schooling experiences, I chose to select mothers with children living at home after learning from a larger survey that one of the reasons respondents gave for returning to school was to "become better mothers." In order to explore this more deeply I made sure to interview mothers at different ages, those who were married and unmarried, employed and unemployed, those with different levels of educational attainment, and so on. Purposive procedures are important for accessing "hard-to-reach" populations or convincing "elite" members to participate through a snowball technique, or identifying "exemplary" cases through referral sampling. The goal of sampling strategies is to yield systematic, relevant, rich, accurate, and complete data. And people who might otherwise avoid participating in research are often more likely to agree to participate if they are recruited by someone they know, respect, and trust. In any case, the point is to make the procedures visible.

I want my study to be generalizable; can I still use qualitative research? This question always gives me pause. First, I want to know what the student means—generalizable to what, for whom, and for what purpose? Does the student want to generalize beyond the particular findings to a *population*? For example, in the previous example, does the researcher want to identify characteristics shared by all students who fall into this category of "high school dropouts"? Or does she or he want to generalize about *processes*—types of *interaction* or *institutional* practices (e.g. student disciplinary codes) that may be operating to create such a population? Answering these questions means returning to the aims of the study. Second, the attention paid to particulars should be understood as a strength, not a weakness, of qualitative research. The ability to discern whether patterns, regularities, or themes identified in one context or setting may be similar to those found in other contexts or settings depends upon the criteria you have used to select your site, case, and participants (see Chase, "The Particular and the General," this volume: 225).

At the end of the day, I often wonder whether at the root of this question is a greater concern about whether one's research will have relevance and be useful to others. This is a conversation for another time.

The Four "I's" of Qualitative Research

If qualitative research is designed in the doing and depends on individual judgment, how is this learned? What habits of mind, apart from maturity and self-awareness, guide the process? I offer the following guidelines:

1. Make explicit what is *implicit*. All empirical research has an implicit set of purposes, assumptions, concepts, and beliefs about knowledge and what counts as evidence. In addition, researchers bring implicit commitments, ethics, and frequently, if not always, unexamined assumptions about their topic. Your research design should make these visible.
2. Know that the elements of your research design are *interactive* in two senses. First, each part of your research plan depends upon another to make a coherent whole. Second, qualitative research requires an interaction between the researcher and the researcher's surroundings, matching up the design elements, data gathering strategies, and analysis through ongoing interaction with research participants.

   Joseph Maxwell (2005) makes an important distinction between a qualitative research *design* and a *proposal*. Design is the "logic and coherence" of all the component parts of a project. The proposal is the "*document* that communicates and justifies this design to a particular audience" (xii). I like this distinction because until you have figured out all the component parts and their proper alignment, planned on possible contingencies, and assessed where the holes are, it is hard to make a convincing *argument* on behalf of your research.

3. Plan for your research process to be *iterative*, tacking back and forth rather than being linear. Anthropologist Michael Agar (1996) provides an especially good description of the ethnographic cycle of research:

> . . . you learn something ("collect some data"), then you try and make sense out of it ("analysis"), then you go back and see if the interpretation makes sense in light of new experience ("collect more data"), then you refine your interpretation ("more analysis"), and so on. The process is dialectic, not linear. (62)

Also plan for *research relationships* to be iterative—a negotiation of shared interests, knowledge, intentions and stakes for both the researcher and the researched. For example, in my own research with women literacy learners this negotiation began when I realized that what the women wanted to talk about (their life stories) was different from what I initially wanted to investigate (their reasons for seeking a high school diploma). It began when my open-ended question— "What do you remember about being in school?"—was routinely greeted with the same refrain, "You want to know about my childhood? I could write a book about my life. . . ." A string of stories—from descriptions of early work experiences (what at first seemed to me like "tangents"); to detailed accounts of the distinction between being "school smart" and having "common sense," and why they claimed the latter; to vivid recollections of why they had or had not been chosen as teachers' pets—all served to redirect my attention. Tracing the topics the women chose to bring up without me asking, which topics they avoided, and in turn, which topics I shied away from, and systematizing these conversational twists and turns, enabled me to explore how the women made meaning within the constraints of different school contexts settings and relationships of power and privilege (Luttrell 1997 and this volume).

4. Finally, know that qualitative research draws on *imagination*—the ability to form images, ideas, and concepts of things both seen and unseen—of forces not experienced directly. Imagination comes into play in multiple ways. Making sense of the relationship between data and theory—the concrete and the abstract—requires imagination, not flights of fancy or wishful thinking, but the ability to synthesize and recognize patterns, significance, and meaning in data. Data—whether in the form of words, numbers, or visual images—do not "speak for themselves," despite claims to the contrary.

It is imagination that allows us to connect micro and macro levels of social life that do not often get connected. To borrow from sociologist C. W. Mills (1959), imagination is required to see the links between private troubles and public affairs. He puts it this way:

> The sociological imagination enables us to grasp history and biography and the relations between the two within society . . . For that imagination is the capacity to shift from one perspective to another—from the political to the psychological; from the examination of a single family to comparative assessment of the national budgets of the world; . . . from the most impersonal and remote transformations to the most intimate features of the human self—and to *see* the relations between the two. (12, 14)

In a similar spirit, anthropologist Paul Willis (2001) identifies the role of imagination in ethnography:

> Ethnography is the eye of the needle through which the threads of imagination must pass. Imagination is thereby forced to try to see the world in a grain of sand, the human social genome in a single cell. (viii)

It is *imagination* that also enables us to make sense of research relationships. Imagination "makes empathy possible" as teachers and researchers "cross the empty spaces between ourselves and those we . . . have called 'other' over the years" (M. Greene 1995: 3). Philosopher Maxine Greene invites educational scholars to "release the imagination" because

> of all the cognitive capacities, imagination is the one that permits us to give credence to alternative realities. It allows us to break with the taken for granted, to set aside familiar distinctions and definitions. (3)

Above all, recognize that *imagination* does not reside solely in the realm of the researcher, but in the hearts and minds of the researched. Imagination is, according to anthropologist Arjun Appadurai (1996), "central to all forms of agency, and is itself a social fact, and is the key component of the new global order" (31). The educational researcher who is both scientist and citizen plans for her or his research to acknowledge and promote the agency of all those involved in the investigation.

On Telling

Most of us have been trained not to write until we have decided what we want to say. Qualitative researchers-in-the-making need to unlearn this lesson and engage the writing process in new ways. Indeed, qualitative data collection and analysis depends upon different genres of writing. For example, writing field notes requires attention to systematic and detailed descriptions, whereas in journal writing researchers take note of their reactions and responses to events in the field. Writing analytic memos where bits of data are connected, concepts are formed, and theories are deployed is quite different from writing "chapters" where arguments are presented.

For most qualitative researchers, myself included, the last phase of authorship is the most problematic. The burdens of representation weigh heavily, as well they should. How does one draw the line in using research participants' words and life experiences for one's own purpose as an author? Who benefits, in what ways, and according to what rules of fairness or relations of power? These concerns cannot be fully resolved but can be made more transparent through our writing.

Writing to Learn

> What anthropologists and other qualitative researchers term reflexivity, composition and rhetoric scholars term writing-to-learn (see for example, Emig, 1977; McLeod, 1988). Writing-to-learn makes thinking visible. When thinking becomes visible, it can be inspected, reviewed, held up for consideration, and viewed as a set of data.
>
> Kleinsasser (2000: 158)

Writing makes your thinking visible, which is why I have included reflexive writing exercises as part of this book. I believe that most graduate students do not have ample support for developing a "writer" identity, in addition to their "researcher" identity, and that this results in a spate of academic writing that is not only uninteresting to read, but too often inaccessible to those for whom it matters.

I encourage students to establish writing groups or interpretive communities (see Bernard et al., this volume) and to read their written work aloud. Reading aloud serves two purposes: First, as the author, when you hear your spoken words, the tone and timbre of your voice may add emphasis and meaning that you were not originally aware of. Second, when you hear others read aloud, without the benefit of the written text in front of you, and with the author's criteria for feedback in mind, it sharpens your ability to be an active and attentive listener—a key skill for qualitative researchers.

For many of us, writing is a process that remains mysterious or fraught with "history coursing through us" (Gordon 1995: 429). We all write within specific contexts, for particular audiences, and with different demons or spirits hovering in the wings. We write for ourselves and for others; with our heads and hearts; and with pleasure and pain. bell hooks (1999) puts it best, "I have not yet found words to truly convey the intensity of this remembered rapture—that moment of exquisite joy when necessary words come together and the work is complete, finished, ready to be read" (xvi).

How to Use this Book

The book is organized into three sections of readings and a final section of writing exercises, but readers should not feel compelled to go through them in sequence. As I have argued, qualitative research is not a linear process—it is dynamic, unfolding over the course of time, and is contingent on multiple and sometimes unpredictable factors. Think of the readings in each section as providing common ground from which you can begin to chart your own path of discovery, critique, and social action.

Section One: On Knowing

Readings in this section focus on historical, epistemological, and ethical premises of qualitative research. Bogdan and Biklen provide a comprehensive account of the different disciplinary traditions, social movements and theoretical perspectives that have shaped the field since the turn of the twentieth century, emphasizing how qualitative research has been used to investigate "real world" problems in the past. The articles by Banks and Becker enrich this account in two ways. Banks specifies how *researchers' own cultural identities, personal biographies, and political values* shape the knowledge they produce through his examination of the lives and legacies of selected social scientists studying race relations in the mid-twentieth century (Kenneth B. Clark, John Hope Franklin, Franz Boas, Ruth Benedict, Otto Kleinberg, and Thomas Pettigrew). Becker highlights *institutional forces within public education* (e.g. standardization and rationalization) that shape the kind of knowledge that is legitimized within the field. Written over 25 years ago, Becker's proposition that the education establishment has favored methods and theories that serve to "prove that they [are] being fair, in the face of substantial and obvious evidence that they [are] not" (this volume: 57) resonates with current debates and skepticism about qualitative research.

The next set of readings considers different orientations to understanding the nature of knowledge—its grounds, limits, and the connections between knowledge and power—otherwise referred to as epistemology. Each excerpt tackles what is often considered an overly abstract and irresolvable set of questions—including what counts as a "fact"; whether something is objective, or value-free, or not and why; and whether we accept some "truths" to be the result of "natural laws," "cultural constructions," or illusions that maintain power. I appreciate the position that Greene takes on these debates—that the "self-conscious and often rarified discourse" about epistemology *really does matter*, and that despite those who might consider these debates tangential to getting research done, "epistemological integrity does get meaningful research done right" (64). Her essay introduces readers to three epistemological perspectives—postpositivism, interpretivism, and critical theory, and aligns each perspective with a different researcher stance: researcher as social engineer, storyteller, and catalyzer of political action, respectively. To bring some levity to these perspectives and stances, I tell students the following joke first told to me by Jim Holland, one of my doctoral advisees and then co-instructor of my course on the "Logics of Qualitative Research." The joke goes something like this: There are three umpires discussing their job of calling balls and strikes, and their philosophy about what they do. The first umpire says, with great assurance, "I call 'em as they are." The second umpire says, "Well, I'm not so sure, but I call 'em as I see 'em." The third umpire looks steadily at both of them and says, "They ain't nothing 'til I call 'em." What I like about this metaphor is that part of the thrill of baseball as a spectator sport, is the way in which fans relish the tension created by umpire "calls." And, while umpires strive for objectivity, fans anticipate the inevitability that an umpire's perspective may be partial, and that some "calls" may have more consequences than others in determining who wins the game. I encourage students to align each "umpire" with one of the three perspectives, without having to swear their own allegiance to one or the other, as a way to establish a spirited dialogue.

I include essays by feminist scholars Sprague and Tuhiwai Smith to augment theories of knowing. Sprague introduces "standpoint" epistemology and four standpoint theorists who have had a major impact on feminist social science: Nancy Harstock, Donna Haraway, Dorothy Smith, and Patricia Hill Collins. Tuhiwai Smith's article introduces "indigenous" research and researchers—not simply as the victim of colonial/outsider/Western science (although that history is told), but as a form of resistance and activism in which members of indigenous communities are increasingly engaging in research related to their own interests. Her article sets the stage for a discussion of the quandaries of research ethics and codes of conduct that extends beyond the enforcement of institutional requirements and professional society guidelines to include a "human rights" perspective.[17]

Two articles follow to buttress these ideas. Haney and Lykes discuss the evolution of ethical guidelines in one such professional society, the American Psychological Association (APA). Halse and Honey chart their ethical dilemmas and uneasy resolutions in preparing an ethics application for an interview study with "anorexic" teenage girls that the researchers had hoped would not privilege clinical diagnoses over girls' own perspectives and accounts of their experiences. Their blow-by-blow description of each step and its double-binds—from labeling the population of study, to recruitment strategies, to consent forms—sheds important light on how a research context and institutional regulations can undermine sensitivity, collaboration, and the advancement of knowledge.

The section ends with the tips and trade secrets of sociologists—C. W. Mills and Marj DeVault—as a means to help readers think about themselves as researchers, their research topics, and the development of provisional research questions.

Section Two: On Doing

This section begins with two qualitative research design models—Maxwell's *interactive* model and my own *reflexive* model (see p. 161). The readings that follow help to flesh out three component parts of research design.

McDermott and Varenne's article, "Culture, Development, Disability" demonstrates why it is important to know what theoretical perspective you bring to your research design (what I refer to as a *knowledge framework* and Maxwell refers to as a *conceptual framework*). The authors discuss three different frameworks for understanding the educational struggles of ten-year-old Adam, who has been assigned the label of *LD* (learning disabled), highlighting the competing definitions of and assumptions about culture, development, and disability that are embedded in each framework. The authors also show clear contrasts between each framework and its methodological implications—starting with the unit of analysis. One framework features Adam's *individual* traits and competencies from which conclusions about his deficiency or difference can be drawn (the individual is the unit of analysis). Another framework features the different *contexts* in which Adam tackles different learning tasks, from which the conclusions drawn are more about the structure of activities than about Adam (these contexts and activities are the unit of analysis).

The next four articles focus on methods and inquiry frameworks. The readings by Charmaz and Chase each provide an example of an *inquiry framework*—grounded theory and narrative inquiry respectively. These readings were selected *not* because these inquiry frameworks have any more merit than other branches of qualitative research (e.g. ethnography or participatory action research), but because in my view, each article does a particularly good job presenting the connections between *little-m methods* (i.e. the techniques of data collection and analysis); *Big-M methodology* (i.e. the theories and assumptions that underlie what researchers are doing when they use various techniques); and epistemological tensions (also see Riessman 1993, 2008).

The chapters by Naomi Quinn and myself are in dialogue about a family of *little-m methods* of data collection and analysis of discourse. There are many research strategies that get labeled "discourse analysis," and this can be confusing. Again, the point is not to advocate one kind over another, but to provide an example of how a scholar provides a rationale for using specific procedures (Quinn) and how these procedures can evolve over the course of an actual research project (Luttrell).[18]

The final set of chapters focuses on questions of validity. Maxwell, Mishler, and Dodson and Schmalzbauer offer varying answers to the question, How might I be wrong in the conclusions I draw? Each author could be said to represent a different epistemological perspective (postpositivism, interpretivism, and critical theory), and hence they suggest different and invaluable strategies for ensuring validity in qualitative research.

To provide an exemplar of how a research design and these component parts are represented *after* a project has been completed—in book, rather than proposal, form—I selected Ann Arnett Ferguson's opening chapter to *Bad Boys: Public Schools in the Making of Black Masculinity.*

Section Three: On Telling

This section features what I consider to be the core of qualitative research: negotiating research relationships. It includes stories told by selected researchers who complicate notions of *culture, identity, voice,* and *participation*—dimensions of a continuum (not a set of dichotomies) along which research relationships may be assessed.

By *culture and identity*, I am referring to the oft-noted "insider–outsider" debate in qualitative research. As France Winddance Twine (2000) describes the history of this debate in sociology, what began as an effort to improve research methodologies so that white university researchers could get valid and reliable information from members of "minority" groups, became an effort to "democratiz[e] the social scientific community by opening it up to scholars of color" (8). Since that time, a new set of *culture and identity* questions abound which are explored by contributors in this section. Villenas, Henry, Gallagher, Foster, and Talburt each examine a different set of power relations, contingencies, and constraints within which they could adequately represent themselves and research participants.

By *voice*, I am referring to the degree to which research subjects are considered to be authorities or experts on their own lives. There has been an explosion of research that claims to "give voice" to disenfranchised or "silenced" populations, but how that voice is produced, whose voice it represents, and toward what ends is not always made explicit in research reports. Several pieces in this book challenge a naïve concept of "voice" and the ethical challenges it raises. Thorne's (this volume) work was groundbreaking in this regard, eloquently describing the paradox of voice. She writes that despite all her best intentions, by the "very act of documenting [*children's*] autonomy, [*she*] undermined it, for [*her*] gaze remained, at its core and in its ultimate knowing purpose, that of a more powerful adult" (418).

By *participation*, I am referring to the degree to which research subjects are involved in ongoing research activities—from setting the research agenda, to collecting and analyzing data, to writing up the results. Ulichny and Schoener describe their collaboration as teacher and researcher—a fieldwork relationship that has been and continues to be imbalanced and conflict-ridden, but need not be so.[19] Finally, scholars Fine and Weis (this volume) reflect on their research and writing dilemmas, bringing readers full circle, so to speak, by calling for a transformative practice of qualitative research that will "serve local struggles, rather than merely . . . document them" (464).

Section Four: Reflexive Writing Exercises

The writing exercises offered in this volume are designed to make your thinking visible and to help release your imagination. These exercises can serve as tools for thinking about your research while you are conducting it—at all stages. I have included an excerpt from writing workshop leaders Peter Elbow and Pat Belanoff in their useful book, *Sharing and Responding*. They outline 11 different ways of responding to writing (481–484), and you should feel free to develop your own. Identifying the type of feedback you wish from your audience is a key step in owning the writing process.

I think it is regrettable that within doctoral education there are not enough occasions for students to engage their written work outside the specter of grades and evaluation. Participating in an interpretive community or writing group can change this as we learn to use our writing to build relationships and think more reflexively. The final piece by former students Rhoda Bernard, Cleti Cervoni, Charlene Desir and Corinne McKamey provides one such example.

At the end of the day, I hope the readings and writing exercises will assure novice researchers that "perfection is professionally unobtainable" in our craft (Fine 1993: 290). We can strive to "get it right" and to "do justice" to what we have seen, heard and learned (Behar 1996: 9), but it won't be complete—something will be lost for each something gained. Yet, if we have done our job well, intellectual labor, life, social action, and justice will be brought into closer relation.

Notes

1. See Ladson-Billings and Tate (2006) for a variety of perspectives on the social, moral, and political parameters necessary for educational research at this time of widening economic instability and deepening poverty.
2. I am grateful to Bilal Malik (personal communication) for reminding me to qualify my assertion about the relationship between qualitative research and democratic ideals. He writes, "One of the great contributions of qualitative research, especially within anthropology, has been to recuperate and 'humanize' non-democratic forms of life—the illiberal, the authoritarian, the patriarchal, the religious, the traditional. Qualitative research has helped uncover the implicit normative assumptions that have crept into scholarship, assumptions that have had the effect of dehumanizing whole swathes of the earth's population (i.e. precisely because 'liberalism' has become so dominant so as to go unquestioned when it is woven into our analytics used to describe our research participants)." See Mahmood (2001); Ewing (1994); and S. F. Harding (1987) as examples that show how qualitative research can help push the limits of existing frameworks within social science—the first about liberalism and the others about secularism.
3. Banks defines transformative research as research that "challenges mainstream and institutionalized findings, interpretations, and paradigms" (2006: xii).
4. A most succinct account of the qualitative research tradition is offered by Denzin and Lincoln (2000: 12–18) in which they define "seven moments" of qualitative research: the traditional, modernist, blurred genres, the crisis of representation, a triple crisis of representation, the post-experimental, and the future.
5. See Luttrell (2003: 165).
6. A slightly different version of this divide can be seen among sociologists and anthropologists, as in the distinction between those who do "applied" versus "academic" scholarship. In recent years, each discipline has made strides to renegotiate the terms of the divide by calling for a "public" sociology and anthropology (see Burawoy, 2004; 2005 for discussion of public sociology).
7. To bridge the "gap" is no small task, especially when the divides—theory versus practice; reason versus emotion; "hard" versus "soft" findings—are culturally associated with male domination and female subordination (see Patti Lather's (2004) critique, where she ties the redefinition of educational "science" to masculinist logic and linguistics). See Bordo (1987); Keller (1985); S. G. Harding (1987); Smith (1987, 1990); Haraway (1998); Collins (1990); Bhavnani (1993); Stanley and Wise (1993) for discussions of the relationship between patriarchy and systems of scientific thought.
8. Anyon notes that an exception in the field of education is psychological research driven by theories like those of Piaget or Vygotsky.
9. See Luttrell (2005) for more discussion of this separation.
10. I want to clarify the distinction between reflection and reflexivity. (Self) reflection is a means of looking back or looking more deeply to gain greater insight, like looking at oneself in the mirror. But reflexivity is a process of (self) awareness and scrutiny that is bi-directional; it demands an "other" through which we develop a more self-conscious awareness. To be reflective does not require engaging with or investigating an "other."

11. Despite almost four decades of new research, I still recommend that students read the work of Jean Briggs (1970) and Barbara Myerhoff (1978) whose pioneering reflexive fieldwork set a gold standard for generations that followed.

12. See *An Invitation to Reflexive Sociology* (Bourdieu and Wacquant 1992). This emphasis on careful examination of the value presuppositions that underline one's research and assessment of social events harkens back to what Max Weber called value discussion.

13. See the recent "Standards for Reporting on Empirical Social Science Research in AERA Publications," in *Educational Researcher*, Vo. 35, No. 6: 33–40 for a discussion of expected standards of empirical work within the field of education, whether quantitative or qualitative.

14. George Spindler (2000), a founding father of educational ethnography, writes that the concept of 'ethnography' as a methodology within anthropology is relatively recent, and that before the 1970s ethnography was simply what anthropologists did, and not a set of codified practices.

15. See Kleinman, Stenross and McMahon (1994) for a helpful discussion about the distinct identities and practice within sociology between "fieldwork" and "interview" studies.

16. Truth be told, I used to use the negative version, "the devil is in the details," before I googled the phrase. I was surprised to learn that this phrase is a variation of "God is in the details", generally attributed to Gustave Flaubert (1821–80), who is quoted as saying, 'Le bon Dieu est dans le detail'. Other attributions include Michelangelo, the architect Ludwig Mies van der Rohe, and the art historian Aby Warburg. http://www.phrases.org.uk/bulletin_board/24/messages/694.html

17. Also see Connell (2007) for her critique of hegemonic academic knowledge production.

18. For other examples of strategies of discourse analysis see Davies and Harré (1990); Gilligan et al. (2003); Gee (1999); and Rogers (2007), to name a few.

19. See Jon Wagner (1997) for his useful rubric of researcher–practitioner cooperation in educational research.

References

AERA. 2006. *Educational Researcher* 35(6): 33–40.

Agar, M. 1996. *The Professional Stranger: an informal introduction to ethnography.* San Diego, CA: Academic Press.

Anyon, J. 2009. "Introduction: critical social theory, educational research, and intellectual agency." In J. Anyon (with M. J. Dumas, D. Linville, K. Nolan, M. Perez, E. Tuck, and J. Weis (eds.) *Theory and Educational Research: toward critical social explanation.* New York: Routledge, 1–24.

Appadurai, A. 1996. *Modernity at Large: cultural dimensions of globalization.* Minneapolis, MN: University of Minnesota Press.

Banks, J. 2006. "Series Foreword." In G. Ladson-Billings, and W. F. Tate (eds.) *Education Research in the Public Interest: social justice, action, and policy.* New York: Teachers College Press, ix–xiv.

Becker, H. 1993. "Theory: the necessary evil." In D. Flinders and G. Mills (eds.) *Theory and concepts in qualitative research: perspective from the field.* New York: Teacher's College Press, 218–229.

Behar, R. 1996. *The Vulnerable Observer: anthropology that breaks your heart.* Boston, MA: Beacon Press.

Bhavnani, K. 1993. "Tracing the contours: feminist research and feminist objectivity." *Women's Studies International Forum* 16: 95–104.

Blumer, H. 1969. *Symbolic Interactionism: perspective and method.* Englewood Cliffs, NJ: Prentice-Hall.

Bordo, S. 1987. *The Flight to Objectivity: essays on cartesianism and culture.* Albany: State University of New York Press.

Bourdieu, P. and Wacquant, L. 1992. *An Invitation to a Reflexive Sociology.* Chicago: University of Chicago Press.

Briggs, J. 1970. *Never in Anger: portrait of an Eskimo family.* Cambridge, MA: Harvard University Press.

Brown, K. M. 1991. *Mama Lola: a Vodou priestess in Brooklyn.* Berkeley, CA: University of California Press.

Burawoy, M. 2004. "Public sociologies: contradictions, dilemmas, and possibilities." *Social Forces* 82: 1603–1618.

—— . 2005. "For public sociology." *American Sociological Review* 70: 4–28.

Collins, P. H. 1990. *Black Feminist Thought: knowledge, consciousness, and the politics of empowerment.* Boston, MA: Unwin Hyman.

Connell, R. 2007. *Southern Theory: the global dynamics of knowledge in social science.* Cambridge: Polity Press.

Davies, B. and Harré, R. 1990. "Positioning; the discursive production of selves." *Journal for the Theory of Social Behavior* 21: 393–407.

Denzin, N. and Lincoln, Y. 2000. "Introduction: the discipline and practice of qualitative research." In N. Denzin and Y. Lincoln (eds.) *Handbook of Qualitative Research*, 2nd edn. London: Sage, pp. 1–28.

Eisenhart, M. 2005. "Science plus: a response to the responses to scientific research in education." *Teachers College Record* 107(1), 52–58.

Eisenhart, M. and Towne, L. 2003. "Contestation and change in national policy on scientifically based education research." *Educational Researcher* 32(7), 31–38.

Emig, J. 1977. "Writing as a mode of learning." *College Composition and Communication* 28: 122–128.

Erickson, F. 2005. "Arts, humanities and sciences in educational research and social engineering in federal education policy." *Teachers College Record* 107(1), 4–9.

Erickson, F. and Gutierrez, K. 2002. "Culture, rigor, and science in educational research." *Educational Researcher* 31(8): 21–24.

Ewing, K. 1994. "Dreams from a saint: anthropological atheism and the temptation to believe." *American Anthropologist* 96(3): 571–583.

Fine, G. A. 1993. "The ten lies of ethnographic research." *Journal of Contemporary Ethnography* 22(3): 267–294.

Gee, J. P. 1999. *An Introduction to Discourse Analysis.* New York: Routledge.

Gilligan, C., Spencer, R., Weinberg, M. K. and Bertsch, T. (2003). "On the listening guide: a voice-centered relational method." In P. M. Camic, J. E. Rhodes, and L. Yardley (eds.) *Qualitative Research in Psychology: expanding perspectives in methodology and design.* Washington, DC: American Psychological Association Press, 157–172.

Gordon, D. 1995. "Border work: feminist ethnography and the dissemination of literacy." In R. Behar and D. Gordon (eds.) *Women Writing Culture.* Berkeley, CA: University of California Press.

Griffith, A. and Smith, D. 2005. *Mothering for Schooling.* New York: Routledge.

Greene, M. 1995. *Releasing the Imagination: essays on education, the arts, and social change.* San Francisco: Jossey Bass.

Haraway, D. 1988. "Situated knowledges: the science question in feminism and the privilege of partial perspective." *Feminist Studies* 14(3): 575–599.

Harding, S. 1987. *Feminism and Methodology: social science issues.* Bloomington, IN: Indiana University Press.

Harding, S. 1987. "Convicted by the Holy Spirit: the rhetoric of fundamental Baptist conversion." *American Ethnologist* 14(1): 167–181.

hooks, b. 1999. *Remembered Rapture: the writer at work.* New York: Henry Holt.

Keller, E. F. 1985. *Reflections on Gender and Science.* New Haven, CN: Yale University Press.

Kleinman, S., Stenross, B. and McMahon, M. 1994. "Privileging fieldwork over interviews: consequences for identity and practice." *Symbolic Interaction* 17(1): 37–50.

Kleinsasser, A. 2000. "Researchers, reflexivity, and good data: writing to unlearn." *Theory into Practice* 39(3): 155–162.

Ladson-Billings, G. and Tate, W. F. (eds.) 2006. *Education Research in the Public Interest: social justice, action, and policy.* New York: Teachers College Press.

Lagemann, E. 2000. *An Elusive Science: the troubling history of education research.* Chicago, IL: Chicago University Press.

Lather, P. 2004. "This is your father's paradigm: government intrusion and the case of qualitative research in education." *Qualitative Inquiry* 10(1): 15–34.

Luttrell, W. 1997. *School-Smart and Mother-Wise: working-class women's identity and schooling.* New York: Routledge.

——. 2003. *Pregnant Bodies, Fertile Minds: gender, race and the schooling of pregnant teens.* New York: Routledge.

——. 2005. "Crossing anxious borders: teaching across the quantitative–qualitative 'divide'." *International Journal of Research & Method in Education* 28(2): 183–195.

McLeod, S. H. 1988. "Translating enthusiasm into curricular change." In McLeod, S.H. (ed.) *Strengthening Programs for Writing across the Curriculum* (pp. 5–12) *New Directions for Teaching and Learning.* No. 36. San Francisco: Jossey-Bass.

Mahmood, S. 2001. "Feminist theory, embodiment, and the docile agent: some reflections on the Egyptian Islamic revival." *Cultural Anthropology* 6(2): 202–236.

Maxwell, J. 2004a. "Reemergent scientism, postmodernism, and dialogue across differences." *Qualitative Inquiry* 10(1): 35–41.

——. 2004b. "Causal explanation, qualitative research, and scientific inquiry in education." *Educational Researcher* 33(2): 3–11.

——. 2005. *Qualitative Research Design: an interactive approach.* Thousand Oaks, London, New Delhi: Sage Publications.

Mead, George Herbert. 1934. *Mind, Self and Society.* Chicago: University of Chicago Press.

Mills, C. W. 1959. *The Sociological Imagination.* New York: Oxford University Press.

Myerhoff, B. 1978. *Number Our Days: a triumph of continuity and culture among Jewish old people in an urban ghetto.* New York: Simon and Schuster.

Riessman, Catherine Kohler. 1993. *Narrative Analysis.* Newbury Park, CA: Sage Publication.

——. 2008. *Narrative Methods for the Human Sciences.* Los Angeles, London, New Delhi, Singapore: Sage Publications.

Rogers, A. 2003. "Qualitative research in psychology: teaching an interpretive process." In R. Josselson et al. (eds.) *Up Close and Personal: the teaching and learning of narrative research.* Washington, DC: American Psychological Association: 49–60.

——. 2007. "The unsayable, Lacanian psychoanalysis, and the art of narrative interviewing." In J. Clanindin (Ed.) *Handbook of Narrative Inquiry Methodologies.* Thousand Oaks: Sage: 99–119.

Schwandt, Thomas, 2001. *Dictionary of Qualitative Inquiry.* Thousand Oaks, London, New Delhi: Sage Publications.

Shavelson, R. and Towne, L., (eds.) 2002. *Scientific Research in Education.* Washington, DC: National Academy Press.

Smith, D. 1987. *The Everyday World as Problematic: a feminist sociology.* Boston, MA: Northeastern University Press.

——. 1990. *The Conceptual Practices of Power: a feminist sociology of knowledge.* Boston, MA: Northeastern University Press.

Spindler, G. 2000. *Fifty Years of Anthropology and Education, 1950–2000: a Spindler anthology*. Mahwah, NJ: Erlbaum Associates.

Stanley, L. and Wise, S. 1993. *Breaking Out Again: feminist ontology and epistemology*. London: Routledge.

Tolman, D. and Brydon-Miller, M. (eds.) 2001. *From Subjects to Subjectivities: a handbook of interpretive and participatory methods*. New York: New York University Press.

Twine. F. W. 2000. "Racial ideologies and racial methodologies." In F. W. Twine and J. Warren *Racing Research, Researching Race: methodological dilemmas in critical race studies*. New York: New York University Press, pp. 1–34.

Wagner, J. 1997. "The unavoidable intervention of educational research: a framework for reconsidering researcher–practitioner cooperation." *Educational Researcher* 26(7): 13–22.

Willis, P. 2001. *The Ethnographic Imagination*. Cambridge, UK: Polity Press.

Section One
On Knowing

1

Foundations of Qualitative Research in Education

Robert C. Bogdan and Sari Knopp Biklen

[. . .]

Traditions of Qualitative Research in Education

The history of qualitative research in education in the United States, is rich and complex. It is rooted in early sociology and anthropology in the United States, but it also has ties to English and French intellectual traditions. Its development cannot be understood by looking only at academe, since larger social changes and upheavals have influenced it, as well as colonialism. In this section, we discuss the history of qualitative research in education, exploring disciplinary, continental, and ideological and political influences. They are intertwined, and we will try to keep them so in this discussion.

Disciplinary Traditions

Anthropologists and sociologists have always collected data in the field, attempting to understand how the particular peoples they studied made sense of their worlds. Bronislaw Malinowski was the first cultural anthropologist to really spend long periods of time in a non-western village to observe what was going on (Wax, 1971). He was also the first professional anthropologist to describe how he obtained his data and what the fieldwork experience was like. He laid the foundation for interpretive anthropology by his emphasis on grasping what he called the "native's point of view" (Malinowski, 1922, p. 25).

Malinowski insisted that a theory of culture had to be grounded in particular human experiences, based on observations and inductively sought. Malinowski's field approach, interestingly, seems to have developed accidentally. When he arrived in New Guinea with an extremely limited budget, World War I immediately broke out. His travel was curtailed, forcing him to remain in Australia and on the islands until the end of the war in 1918. This shaped the direction "fieldwork" would take.

Perhaps the earliest substantive application of anthropology to U.S. education was made by the anthropologist Margaret Mead (see, especially, Mead, 1942, 1951). Concerned particularly with the school as an organization and the role of the teacher, she employed her fieldwork experiences in less technological societies to dramatize the fast-changing educational scene in the United States. Mead examined how particular contexts—the kinds of schools she categorized as the little red schoolhouse, the city school, and the academy—called for particular kinds of teachers and how these teachers interacted with students. She argued that teachers needed to study, through observations and firsthand experiences, the changing contexts of their students' socialization and upbringing in order to become better teachers. The field research of anthropologists was an important source for the model of what is known as *Chicago sociology* (Douglas, 1976; Wax, 1971).

Chicago Sociology

The *Chicago School*, a label applied to a group of sociological researchers teaching and learning at the sociology department of the University of Chicago in the 1920s and 1930s, contributed enormously to the development of the research method we refer to as qualitative. While the sociologists at Chicago differed from each other, they shared some common theoretical and methodological assumptions. Theoretically, they all saw symbols and personalities emerging from social interaction (Faris, 1967). Methodologically, they depended on the study of the single case, whether it was a person, a group, a neighborhood, or a community (Wiley, 1979).

They also relied on firsthand data gathering for their research. W. I. Thomas, an early graduate, analyzed letters that Polish immigrants wrote to develop an insider's perspective on immigrant life (Thomas & Znaniecki, 1927; Collins & Makowsky, 1978). *The Polish Peasant in Europe and America* (Thomas & Znaniecki, 1927) concentrated on "the qualitative analysis of personal and public documents" and "introduced new elements into research and new techniques to study these elements which were not standard to empirical investigations in the traditional sense" (Bruyn, 1966, p. 9).

Robert Park, a leading figure in the Chicago School, came to the University after careers as a reporter, and a public relations representative focusing on issues of race for Booker T. Washington. Park brought some of journalism's practices, such as the importance of being on site, to bear on research practices, moving the role of personal observation to the forefront (Faris, 1967; Hughes, 1971; Matthews, 1977; Wax, 1971).

Chicago sociologists also emphasized city life. Whatever they studied, they did so against the backdrop of the community as a whole, what Becker has called "the scientific mosaic". Studies from Chicago sociologists illustrate both the interest in different aspects of ordinary life and an orientation to the study of ethnicity; publications on the Jewish ghetto (Wirth, 1928), the taxi-dance hall (Cressy, 1932), the boys' gang (Thrasher, 1927), the professional thief (Sutherland, 1937), the hobo, *The Gold Coast and the Slum* (Zorbaugh, 1929), and the delinquent (Shaw, 1966; first published in 1930). In this emphasis on the intersection of social context and biography lies the roots of contemporary descriptions of qualitative research as "holistic." As a Chicago sociologist put it, "behavior can be studied profitably in terms of the situation out of which it arises" (Wells, 1939, p. 428). In addition, especially in the life histories Chicago School sociologists produced, the importance of seeing the world from the perspective of those who were seldom listened to—the criminal, the vagrant, the immigrant—was emphasized. While not using the phrase, they knew they were "giving voice" to points of view of people marginalized in the society.

This perspective emphasized the social and interactional nature of reality. Park, for example, in his introduction to a study of the methodology of a race relations survey on "Oriental-Occidental" relationships in California, suggested that the study was important because of its recognition "that all opinions, public or private, are a social product" (Bogardus, 1926). Many of the informants shared their perspectives on the difficulties they faced as Asian Americans:

> I thought I was American. I had American ideals, would fight for America, loved Washington and Lincoln. Then in high school I found myself called Jap, looked down on, ostracized. I said I did not know Japan, could not speak the language, and knew no Japanese history or heroes. But I was repeatedly told I was not American, could not be American, could not vote. I am heart sick. I am not Japanese and am not allowed to be American. Can you tell me what I am? (Bogardus, 1926, p. 164)

They not only emphasized the human dimension but studied those who had been pushed to the margins of society.

The Sociology of Education

The discipline of the sociology of education was predominantly quantitative except for the work of Willard Waller. Faculty in education were always concerned about the legitimacy of the field, and were concerned with such questions as, "Is educational sociology a science or can it become a science?" To become scientific, an editorial from the *Journal of Educational Sociology*, explained, research in educational sociology must become experimental. This view of the scientific school measurement movement reflected education's dominant concern of the times. This was "the heyday of empiricism" (Cronbach & Suppes, 1969, p. 43). The "scientific method" in education became identified with quantification.

While quantification represented the dominant school of thought in educational sociology, exceptions did appear, notably in the work of Willard Waller. Waller had studied for a master's degree under Ellsworth Faris in the Chicago Sociology Department, and his orientation to educational sociology was empirical but anti-quantitative, based on firsthand involvement with the social world and concerned with how parts related to the whole.

In *Sociology of Teaching* (1932), Waller relied on in-depth interviews, life histories, participant observation, case records, diaries, letters, and other personal documents to describe the social world of teachers and their students. For Waller, the starting point of his book was his belief that "children and teachers are not disembodied intelligences, not instructing machines and learning machines, but whole human beings tied together in a complex maze of social interconnections. The school is a social world because human beings live in it" (Waller, 1932, p. 1). Waller called upon the methods of the "cultural anthropologist," the "realistic novelist," and what we would now describe as the qualitative researcher. His goal was to help teachers develop insight into the social realities of school life. For Waller, insight informed the scientific method, not the reverse.

The importance of Waller's discussion of the social life of schools and their participants rests not only on the strength and accuracy of his description, but also on the sociological concepts on which he depended. Among the foremost of these was W. I. Thomas's "definition of the situation" (Thomas, 1923), a clearly interactional concept that suggests people examine and "define" situations before they act on them. These "definitions" are what make situations real for us.

European Connections and the Social Survey Movement

Work in Britain and France, as well as other parts of Europe, during the nineteenth and twentieth centuries, reflected qualitative approaches to understanding people's lives, as researchers studied groups of people by living with them and trying to understand their perspectives. During the late 1800s, the Frenchman Frederick LePlay studied working-class families through the method that social scientists writing in the 1930s labeled "participant observation" (Wells, 1939). LePlay himself called it "observation" and employed it to seek a remedy for social suffering. As participant observers, LePlay and his colleagues lived with the families they studied; they participated in their lives, carefully observing what they did at work, at play, at church, and in school. Published as *Les Ouvriers Européens* (the first volume of which appeared in 1879), they described in detail the life of the working-class family in Europe.

Henry Mayhew's *London Labor and the London Poor*, published in four volumes between 1851 and 1862, consisted of reporting, anecdote, and description about conditions of workers and the unemployed. Mayhew presented life histories and the results of extensive, in-depth interviews with the poor.

The research of Charles Booth, a statistician who conducted social surveys of the poor in London beginning in 1886 (Webb, 1926), followed on the heels of a new urban literature. Booth's undertaking was of incredible proportions, lasting for seventeen years and filling as many volumes. His chief purpose was to discover how many poor there were in London and the condition of their lives. While his major concern was to quantitatively document the extent and nature of poverty in London, his work contained extensive and detailed descriptions of the people he studied. These descriptions were collected during the periods Booth lived, anonymously, among the people he surveyed. His goal was to experience firsthand the lives of his subjects (see Taylor, 1919; Webb, 1926; Wells, 1939).

One of the workers on Booth's colossal project was Beatrice Webb (nee Potter) who, along with her husband, went on to become a major figure in the Fabian socialist movement. A lifelong investigator of the sufferings of the poor and of social institutions, Webb's sympathy, commitment, and understanding arose from her first fieldwork experience. For the first time, she then understood what Roy Stryker (of the Farm Security Administration's "Photography Unit"), another documentarian of the poor, was later to write, "Individuals make up a people" (Stott, 1973, p. 53):

> I never visualized labor as separate men and women of different sorts and kinds. Right down to the time when I became interested in social science and began to train as a social investigator, labor was an abstraction, which seemed to denote an arithmetically calculable mass of human beings, each individual a repetition of the other, very much in the same way that the capital of my father's companies consisted, I imagined, of gold sovereigns identical with all other gold sovereigns in form, weight and color and also in value. (Webb, 1926, p. 41)

What were once abstractions became flesh and blood for Beatrice Webb through firsthand involvement with the subjects of her research. The Webbs later published a description of their methodology, which was widely read in the United States (Wax, 1971), and appears to be the first practical discussion of the qualitative approach (Webb & Webb, 1932). The lives of poor people in the United States at this time, particularly in urban centers, were also to be documented in similar ways.

On this side of the Atlantic, W. E. B. Du Bois undertook the first social survey in the United States. Published in 1899 as *The Philadelphia Negro*, this survey represented almost a year and a half of close study, including interviews and observations with informants living primarily, though not completely, in the city's Seventh Ward. The purpose of the research was to examine "the condition of the forty thousand or more people of Negro blood now living in the city of Philadelphia" (Du Bois, 1899 [1967], p. 1).

One of the most prominent social surveys was the Pittsburgh Survey, undertaken in 1907. While commentators at the time emphasized the statistical nature of these surveys (see, for example, Devine, 1906–1908; Kellogg, 1911–1912), the results of the Pittsburgh Survey, for instance, suggest that this emphasis may have reflected more on their emphasis of the "scientific method" than on the content of the actual reports. While the Pittsburgh Survey presents quantities of statistics on issues ranging from industrial accidents to weekly incomes, from the types and location of "water closets" to school attendance, it also bulges with detailed descriptions, interviews, portraits (sketched by artists in charcoal), and photographs.

Description ranged from educational planning—"School buildings in this city," said one of the experienced school officials of Allegheny, "are first built, then thought about" (North, 1909)—to problems that "duller" children encountered in school because of a first-grade teacher's approach to tracking. This teacher

> had 128 pupils one year and 107 the next. She divided the children into two classes. The brighter children came in the morning and were allowed to go on as fast as they could, "getting through" six to nine books in a year; the backward, a smaller number, came in the afternoon. They were worn out with play, the teacher was also worn, and the afternoon session was but two hours; so these children usually got through but one book a year. (North, 1909, p. 1189)

The students ended up dropping out to join the "ranks of uneducated industrial workers" (North, 1909).

All of these researchers on both sides of the Atlantic addressed from various standpoints (socialist, liberal, progressive muckraker) a variety of social concerns in the fields of education, human services, poverty, social welfare and urban life. Some of those who conducted this research were academics, anxious to distinguish their work from social welfare workers, but others were activists and social reformers. The work of both groups contributed, however, to including the perspectives or voices of traditionally under-represented constituencies in the dialogue. When Frances Donovan (1920/1974) studied waitresses, for example, she did not undertake a work of social change, but indirectly contributed to representing a marginalized group of women's perspectives. Du Bois, on the other hand, did his work on the Philadelphia Negro in order to help effect social change. Ideological and political issues were also central to the traditions of the qualitative approach.

Ideological and Political Practices

In addition to disciplinary and geographic histories in the development of the qualitative approach as we talk about it today, there are ideological influences as well. That is, the doing of qualitative research reflects particular relationships to how power is distributed in a society. Who is studied? Who studies? What kinds of research project get funded? How do funding and publishing patterns shift over time? What kinds of things carry social interest, and what strategies do researchers use to develop interest in particular areas? In the history of doing qualitative work, researchers have both extended the power of some groups over others, and resisted this power. There are, we would argue, a number of contradictions in the historical relationships of qualitative methods to progressive social change. On the one hand, some of the method's practices and representational strategies have been developed and exercised in the context of dominance and control, as enacted through educational and other institutions, of western countries over so-called third world countries, and, hence, connected to repressive practices. This charge has been directed, with some foundation, particularly at the field of anthropology. On the other hand, at least in the United States, there are strong indications that over the years, qualitative methods have been useful for and attractive to researchers who have been excluded from, or who are studying the perspectives of people excluded from, the mainstream. Groups such as women, African Americans, gays, and lesbians have been attracted to qualitative research because of the democratic emphasis of the method, the ease with which the method attends to the perspectives of those not traditionally included in mainstream research studies, and the strengths of the qualitative approach for describing the complexities of social conflicts.

Our account emphasizes what some might call the *transgressive* possibilities of qualitative methods. Connections between qualitative studies, especially abroad and within the discipline of anthropology, and the discourses of colonialism and post-colonialism have been discussed elsewhere (see for example, Vidich & Lyman, 1994; Pratt, 1985; Thomas, 1994; Clifford & Marcus, 1986). This discussion has been important in describing how western ethnographic studies of indigenous peoples have made them the "other" (Fabian, 1983; Bhaba, 1986). This history is particularly important for anyone interested in doing critical ethnography (Carspecken, 1996). Here, we attend to the contributions of qualitative methods to democracy and justice.

Ideologies and Social Change

The Depression in the United States created overwhelming and visible problems for a majority of citizens, and many scholars, including those hired by government agencies, turned to a qualitative approach to document the nature and extent of these problems. The Work Projects Administration (WPA), for example, produced informant narratives. *These Are Our Lives* contained oral biographies, life histories of black and white southern workers in three states (Federal Writers' Project, 1939). The authors were not social scientists; they were writers who needed work, but the method is sociological. Other forerunners of what we now call oral history included a folk history of slavery, a series of interviews with former slaves, collected in the mid-thirties (Botkin, 1945) and a collection of letters from union members to their union officers. "The Disinherited Speak: Letters from Sharecroppers," published in 1937 on behalf of the Southern Tenant Farmers' Union (Stott, 1973). This collection relied on the same kind of documents that Thomas & Znaniecki (1927) used for their mammoth study, *The Polish Peasant in Europe and America*.

Documentary photography examined the dimensions of suffering of dispossessed American people (see, for example, Evans, 1973; Gutman, 1974; and Hurley, 1972). The Roosevelt administration hired photographers who were out of work, and sent them all over the country to take pictures of daily life. Lewis Hine, Dorothea Lange, Russell Lee, Walker Evans, Jack Delano, Marion Post Wolcott, and John Collier were some of these photographers. When they wrote about their work, they described how they established rapport, worked to present the perspectives of those they photographed, and developed their interview methods (Collier, 1967; O'Neal, 1976; Stryker & Wood, 1973). Wolcott, for example, wrote about the importance of making "people believe you are not trying to ridicule them nor expose them or their living conditions" (O'Neal, 1976, p. 175). Americans were attracted to naturalistic approaches during this period, whether in literature, journalism, photography, or non-academic research, because it documented in personal, particular detail what the Depression meant for most Americans—the southern share-cropper, the northern worker, the homeless Okie.

Qualitative researchers also took up asymmetrical relations of power in gender relationships. In the 1940s, the sociologist, Mirra Komarovsky, completed a study of women in higher education that was to become an important document of feminist movement in the early 1970s. She conducted eighty in-depth interviews with women who were students at Barnard College and studied how cultural values intersected with women's sex role attitudes, noting the difficulty women described in being both "feminine" and "successful" (Komarovsky, 1946).

The 1960s brought national focus to educational problems, revived interest in qualitative research methods, and opened up educational research to this approach. During this period, educational researchers stopped depending completely on sociologists and anthropologists, and began to show interest in these strategies themselves. Their interest was supported by federal agencies which started to fund qualitative research.

The sixties were also characterized by upheaval and social change. Educators' focus turned to the experiences minority children encountered in schools. One reason for this was political: As cities burned and as leaders searched for ways to prevent future protests, they associated poor educational performance with black people's insistence that they receive inadequate services. Spokespeople within the civil rights movement insisted that the perspectives of those who suffered discrimination needed to be represented.

People wanted to know what the schools were like for the children who were not "making it," and many educators wanted to talk about it. A number of autobiographical and journalistic accounts of life in ghetto schools appeared (for example, Decker, 1969; Haskins, 1969; Herndon, 1968; Kohl, 1967; Kozol, 1967). These writers spoke from the "front lines," attempting to capture the quality of the daily lives of the children they taught.

Federal programs, recognizing how little we really knew about the schooling of different groups of children, funded some research on these issues which used what is now generically labeled ethnographic methods. Qualitative research methods began to catch people's imagination.

Project True, undertaken in 1963 at Hunter College to understand different aspects of life in urban classrooms, relied on interviews with principals, teachers, parents, members of the Board of Education, and the community to examine school integration and the experiences of new teachers in urban schools (Eddy, 1969; Fuchs, 1966, 1969). They used participant observation to examine individual classroom experiences (Roberts, 1971), elementary schools (Moore, 1967), and the urban school in the context of the community. As a group, the researchers worked from the standpoint that education had failed poor children, that the cities were in crisis, and that these old problems demanded to be studied in new ways.

Two other important qualitative studies addressed inequality and injustice. Eleanor Leacock (1969) investigated the meanings school authorities in different communities made of students' behaviors. The other major study on racial issues in education that used fieldwork methods was a project directed by Jules Henry which studied elementary schools in St. Louis (see Gouldner, 1978; Rist, 1970, 1973). Through his involvement in this project, Ray Rist, an influential researcher in the 1970s and 80s, began his research.

The audience for qualitative research in education grew in the 1960s. Not yet firmly established as a legitimate research paradigm, its status caused many graduate students to face major hurdles if they chose to study a problem from this perspective. But qualitative approaches kindled excitement. Why did qualitative research begin to emerge from its long hibernation in education at this particular historical period?

First, the social upheaval of the sixties indicated to many that we did not know enough about how students experienced school. Popular accounts exposed for education what nineteenth-century muckraking revealed about social welfare.

Second, qualitative methods gained popularity because of their recognition of the views of the powerless and the excluded—those on the "outside." The qualitative emphasis on understanding perspectives of all participants at a site challenges what has been called "the hierarchy of credibility" (Becker, 1970): the idea that the opinions and views of those in power are worth more than those of people who are not. As part of their typical research process, qualitative researchers studying education solicited the views of those who had never felt valued or represented. Qualitative research methods represented the kind of democratic impetus on the rise during the sixties. The climate of the times renewed interest in qualitative methods, created a need for more experienced mentors of this research approach, and opened the way for methodological growth and development.

Politics and Theory in the Academy

The academic disciplines of sociology and anthropology were in transition. Anthropologists found that fewer non-western communities were willing to allow them to conduct their research; funding for such studies diminished. The number of peoples that had not been significantly changed by contact with the west had declined, undermining the mandate to describe the cultures of the world before they were "spoiled." Anthropologists increasingly turned to studying urban areas and their own culture. Meanwhile, the political upheaval around issues of rights and privilege challenged the idea of studying "unspoiled" societies.

During the 1960s, the field of sociology, which for twenty years had been dominated by the ideas of structural-functionalist theory, turned to the writings of phenomenologists. Groups of researchers began doing what they came to call *ethnomethodology*. Others organized around the more established symbolic interaction tradition. Interest in qualitative methods was kindled by the publication of a number of theory and methods books. (Bruyn, 1966; Glaser & Strauss, 1967; Filstead, 1970; McCall & Simmons, 1969).

During the 1970s ideological conflicts also developed over the style and orientation of qualitative methods. One stylistic difference lay in the tension between the cooperative versus conflictual approach to research. Those researchers who belonged to the cooperative school generally believed that fieldworkers should be as truthful as possible with the subjects they studied. They held to the basic and optimistic assumption that people will grant access to a research site if they can. Followers of this perspective were those who tended to see themselves as descendants of the Chicago School (see Bogdan & Taylor, 1975). On the other hand, practitioners of the conflictual approach assumed that many subjects would want to cover up what they do; truthful and overt researchers would get less information. Particularly if he or she wanted to penetrate the world of big business, organized crime, or groups that were labeled deviant, a researcher should use covert means and not speak truthfully in explaining his or her presence. This perspective was clearly articulated by Douglas (1976).

Another stylistic difference is reflected in the attitude of the researcher toward informants or subjects under investigation. One group, again descendants of the Chicago School, might be said to have had an *empathic* perspective: that is, they called for sympathy and understanding toward those whom they studied. Hence, many of their research publications showed readers humanity in lives that at first glance seemed to make little sense. Proponents of this perspective were, in fact, charged with identifying too closely with those they studied, whether they were deviants, outcasts, or powerbrokers. At the other end of this continuum were those whose position seems to have reflected the view that "the sociology of everything is ridiculous." This perspective is reflected most clearly in the group called the ethnomethodologists (see, for example, Garfinkel, 1967; Mehan & Wood, 1975). Ethnomethodologists study how people negotiate the daily rituals of their lives, and in the process often put people's feelings on the sidelines. At the same time, ethnomethodological contributions to the study of gender have been significant, particularly in the construct of "doing gender" (e.g. West & Zimmerman, 1987).

Other ideological strands of the qualitative approach include *feminism, postmodernism* and *critical theory*. Feminist theory and practice intersected qualitative research starting in the late seventies and early eighties. First, feminism influenced the subjects that (feminist) qualitative researchers studied. Gender, constructed from a feminist perspective, emerged as a central topic in many qualitative research projects (Warren, 1988; Lesko, 1988; Lareau, 1987). Using participant observation, document analysis, life history research, and in-depth interviewing, qualitative researchers took seriously actors and categories of behavior that had previously received little, if any, attention. Feminism affected the content of the research, then, as researchers studied how informants made sense of how gender constructed their worlds as female teachers (Biklen, 1987, 1985, 1993; 1995; Middleton, 1987, 1993; Weiler, 1988; Foster, 1992, 1993, 1994), as food providers (DeVault, 1990), as students in female punk subcultures (Roman, 1988), as readers of romance novels (Radway, 1984), and as consumers and interpreters of medical knowledge about the body and reproduction (Martin, 1987). Additionally, qualitative researchers in education have more recently focused on the experiences of girls in middle schools (Finders, 1997; Research for Action, 1996), masculinity (Mac An Ghaill, 1994), adolescence (Fine, 1988, 1993) and sexuality (Tierney, 1994). Feminists have been important in developing emotion and feeling as topics for research (Hochschild, 1983). In addition, feminist approaches to qualitative methods are apparent in texts not specifically on gender, such as Oyler's study of a teacher changing her classroom pedagogy (1996), and in research on multiculturalism (e.g. Sleeter, 1993).

Second, feminism has affected methodological questions as well. Some of these effects emerged from a general questioning about the nature of feminist research methods in the sciences and social sciences (Harding, 1987; Reinharz, 1993), but practice also affected change. Oakley (1981), for example, worried about power in the interview relationship. Smith (1987) developed "institutional ethnography" as a feminist research strategy to foster a sociology for women instead of a sociology of women. We will discuss some of these issues in Chapter 3.

No matter what avenue one uses to approach the intersection of feminism and qualitative research, mutual influences are significant. Feminists have moved the field of qualitative research toward greater concern with the relationships between researchers and their subjects (DeVault, 1990), as well as toward increased recognition of the political implications of research.

Rivaling feminist contributions to qualitative research in significance in the eighties and nineties—in some cases allied and in other cases antagonistic (Mascia-Lees, Sharpe, & Cohen, 1989) were those of the postmodernist sociologists and anthropologists (Marcus & Cushman, 1982; Marcus & Fischer, 1986; Clifford, 1983, 1988; Clifford & Marcus, 1986; Van Maanen, 1988; Denzin, 1989; Dickens & Fontana, 1994, Denzin & Lincoln, 1994; Brown, 1995). *Postmodernism* represents an intellectual position that claims we are living in a "post" modern period. "Post" carries at least two different meanings. The first is that the postmodern period is an actual historical time that differs from modernism. The second meaning is critical of the ideas represented by modernism. During modernism, beliefs in human progress through rationalism and science; the idea of a stable, consistent, and coherent self; and positivist approaches to knowing—beliefs that have held sway in the West since the enlightenment—were seen to explain the human condition. Postmodernists argue, however, that these foundations are no longer in place. The rise of the nuclear age, the growing gap between the rich and the poor, and the global threat to the environment have stripped away the possibility of human progress based on rationalism and caused people in many different areas of human life to question the integrity of progress. Architecture, art, fashion, and scholarship have all been shaped by the postmodern.

Postmodernists argue that you can only know something from a certain position. This assertion challenges the possibility of knowing what is true through the proper, that is, scientific, use of reason. It is a rejection of what Donna Haraway (1991) called "the view from nowhere." People do not reason or conceptualize outside of the self's location in a specific historical time and body; hence, this perspective emphasizes interpretation and writing as central features of research. Clifford and Marcus (1986), for example, called their collection on the poetics and politics of ethnography *Writing Culture*. Postmodernism has influenced qualitative methodologists to shift their focus to the nature of interpretation and the position of the qualitative researcher as interpreter. Rather than taking writing in the form of text in papers, manuscripts, articles, and books for granted, postmodern qualitative researchers make it an object of study. Postmodernists take the idea of a work as "scientific" and make that problematic, questioning what conventions and attitudes make a certain way of looking at the work, the discourse of science, scientific. In

Getting Smart, for example, Patti Lather insisted that she could not use one explanation or story to account for the resistance of her students to a women's studies class (Lather, 1991). Instead, drawing on Van Maanen (1988) she told four stories, or tales. We will examine the implications of this position more fully in Chapter 6.

The third important recent ideological influence on qualitative methods is critical theory. Critical theory, as the phrase implies, is critical of social organization that privileges some at the expense of others. Tracing a tradition to the Frankfurt School, it is less "a theory" than a group of theories which emphasize some similar features. First, critical theorists believe that research is an "ethical and political act" (Roman & Apple, 1990, p. 41) that always benefits a specific group. Critical theorists would rather benefit those who are marginalized in the society because they believe that the current way society is organized is unjust. Along these lines, critical theorists agree that their research should "empower the powerless and transform existing social inequalities and injustices" (McLaren, 1994, p. 168). Hence critical theorists who do qualitative research are very interested in issues of gender, race and class because they consider these the prime means for differentiating power in this society.

Qualitative researchers influenced by critical theory are interested in either how social values and organization get reproduced in schools and other educational institutions, or how people produce their choices and actions in the society (Weiler, 1988). Those studies whose emphasis is on reproduction examine how educational institutions sort, select, favor, disenfranchise, silence or privilege particular groups of students or people. Eckert (1989), for example, studied how schools reproduce social divisions among students based on social class so that some students were seen as "jocks," or good students, while others became "burnouts," or bad students. Those studies whose emphasis is on production are interested in how people negotiate these reproductive structures, how they act as agents in their own lives, sometimes resisting discrimination, sometimes setting up oppositional cultures, or wending their way through the maze of restrictions. Weis (1990) studied how working-class high school students negotiated an economic landscape without jobs, as well as how white working-class men think about whiteness and privilege when they no longer have access to industrial work (Weis, Proweller & Centrie, 1997). Some studies draw from both feminism and critical theory (e.g., Weiler, 1988), and postmodernism has influenced, to some degree, most discussions of method, objectivity, and power.

Qualitative research is influenced by these ideological perspectives in different degrees. Some have incorporated critical theory into the theory itself and called it *critical ethnography* (Carspecken, 1996). Other researchers have called on postmodernism to enable them to engage in *experimental ethnography* (e.g., Ellis, 1995). And others go about their work because they are interested in specific issues and pay less attention to the methodological debates that are raging on campuses. The tremendous expansion of qualitative methods in education insures that it will engender even more methodological discussion.

Theoretical Underpinnings

The concern qualitative researchers have for "meaning," as well as other features we have described as characteristic of qualitative research, leads us to a discussion of the theoretical orientations of the approach. People use the word theory in many ways. Among quantitative researchers in education its use is sometimes restricted to a systematically stated and testable set of propositions about the empirical world. Our use of the word is much more in line with its use in sociology and anthropology and is similar to the term "paradigm" (Ritzer, 1975). A *paradigm* is a loose collection of logically related assumptions, concepts, or propositions that orient thinking and research. When we refer to a "theoretical orientation" or "theoretical perspective," we are talking about a way of looking at the world, the assumptions people have about what is important and what makes the world work. (Examples of theories other than those associated with qualitative research include: structural-functionalism, exchange theory, conflict theory, systems theory, and behaviorism.) Whether stated or not, whether written in what we have come to think of as theoretical language, or not, all research is guided by some theoretical orientation. Good researchers are aware of their theoretical base and use it to help collect and analyze data. Theory helps data cohere and enables research to go beyond an aimless, unsystematic piling up of accounts. In this section, we briefly examine the most influential theoretical underpinnings of qualitative approaches.

Most research approaches (other than qualitative research) trace their roots to positivism and the great social theorist, Auguste Comte. They emphasize facts and causes of behavior. While there are theoretical differences between qualitative approaches and even within single schools (Gubrium, 1988; Meltzer, Petras & Reynolds, 1975), most qualitative researchers reflect some sort of phenomenological perspective. There are many debates concerning the use of the word *phenomenology* and we use it in the most general sense. We start our discussion of theory by presenting the phenomenological perspective and clarifying some issues it raises. Next we discuss symbolic interactionism, a well-established particular type of phenomenological framework used extensively in sociology. We move on to talk of "culture" as an orientation, the interpretation of which is the undertaking of anthropologists. We also briefly introduce another sociological approach to the qualitative scene, ethnomethodology. Finally, we review contemporary trends in theory, those approaches that have more recently informed the work of many qualitative researchers and are influencing the direction of the methodology. Here we look at "feminist theory," "cultural studies," "textual and discourse analysis" and various trends that can be categorized as "postmodern." Our discussion does not exhaust the types. We have picked the most widely used and those most closely aligned with phenomenology (for further discussion see Guba & Lincoln, 1994; Kincheloe & McLaren, 1994; Olesen, 1994; Schwandt, 1994). Each of these theoretical positions interacts with the phenomenology so central to the qualitative approach.

Phenomenological Approach

At the scene of a car accident a conversation occurred that illustrates two approaches people use to understand what happens around them. At an intersection where all the roads faced stop signs, two cars collided. The drivers were discussing what had happened when a police officer arrived on the scene. One driver took the position that the other had not made a full stop, while the other driver said that he had indeed stopped and that he had the right of way anyway. A reluctant witness was drawn into the debate who, when asked by one of the drivers for her account of the incident, said that it was hard to tell exactly what had happened from where she was standing. Phrases such as, "How could you say that?" "It happened right before your eyes." "Facts are facts. You didn't stop!" "You were looking the other way," were bantered about. The police officer was asked how she reconciled conflicting accounts. Her response was that contradictions occur all the time and that the parties involved were not necessarily lying since "it all depends on where you are sitting, how things look to you." The approach the police officer took to understand the situation is reflective of qualitative approaches that depend on a phenomenological point of view. They require a set of assumptions that are different from those used when human behavior is approached with the purpose of finding "facts" and "causes."

Some might argue, and we would too, that there are facts in such an accident case. If someone said that there were no stop signs, such an assertion could be checked on location. Some viewers' renderings are more accurate than others. If the accident resulted in a trial where one party was charged with causing the accident, we could garner evidence in support of guilt or innocence. Qualitative researchers would not say that this way to approach the situation is wrong; the legal system works on such logic. They would assert that such an approach is just one way of understanding the situation. Further, they would remind us that such an approach is only a partial telling of the occurrence. If you were interested in the dynamics of the encounter, in the behavior at accidents, in the ways people make sense of such incidents, and in the arguments they construct in explaining them, the "just the facts" approach would not be very illuminating.

Researchers in the phenomenological mode attempt to understand the meaning of events and interactions to ordinary people in particular situations. Phenomenological sociology has been particularly influenced by the philosophers Edmund Husserl and Aflred Schutz. It is also located within the Weberian tradition, which emphasizes *verstehen*, the interpretive understanding of human interaction. Phenomenologists do not assume they know what things mean to the people they are studying (Douglas, 1976). "Phenomenological inquiry begins with silence" (Psathas, 1973). This "silence" is an attempt to grasp what it is they are studying. What phenomenologists emphasize, then, is the subjective aspects of people's behavior. They attempt to gain entry into the conceptual world of their subjects (Geertz, 1973) in order to understand how and what meaning they construct around events in their daily lives. Phenomenologists believe that multiple ways of interpreting experiences are available to each of us through interacting with others, and that it is the meaning of our experiences that constitutes reality (Greene, 1978). Reality, consequently, is "socially constructed" (Berger & Luckmann, 1967).

While there are various brands of qualitative research, all share to some degree this goal of understanding the subjects from participant perspectives. When we examine this proposition carefully, though, the phrase "participant perspectives" presents a problem. This problem is the rather fundamental concern that "participant perspectives" is not an expression informants use themselves; it may not represent the way they think of themselves. "Participant perspectives" is a way that people who do this kind of research approach their work; it is thus a research construct. Looking at subjects in terms of this idea may, consequently, force informants' experiences of the world into a mode that is foreign to them. This kind of intrusion of the researcher on the informants' world, however, is inevitable in research. After all, the researcher is making interpretations, and must have some conceptual scheme to do this. Qualitative researchers believe that approaching people with a goal of trying to understand their point of view, while not perfect, distorts the informants' experience the least. There are differences in the degree to which qualitative researchers are concerned with this methodological and conceptual problem as well as differences in how they come to grips with it. Some researchers attempt to do "immaculate phenomenological description"; others show less concern and attempt to build abstractions by interpreting from the data on "their point of view." Whatever one's position, qualitative analysis has to be self-conscious in regard to this theoretical and methodological issue.

While qualitative researchers tend to be phenomenological in their orientation, most are not radical idealists. They emphasize the subjective, but they do not necessarily deny a reality "out there" that stands over and against human beings, capable of resisting action toward it (Blumer, 1980). A teacher may believe he can walk through a brick wall, but it takes more than thinking to accomplish it. The nature of the wall is unyielding, but the teacher does not have to perceive "reality" as it is. He may still believe that he can walk through the wall, but not at this time, or that he had a curse put on him and, therefore, cannot walk through the wall. Thus reality comes to be understood to human beings only in the form in which it is perceived. Qualitative researchers emphasize subjective thinking because, as they see it, the world is dominated by objects less obstinate than walls. And human beings are much more like "The Little Engine That Could." We live in our imaginations, settings more symbolic than concrete.

If human perception is so subjective, one might ask, how do qualitative researchers justify saying they are researchers? Are not they subjective too? Most qualitative researchers believe there are people out there in the world who say and do things which the qualitative researcher can record. These records, or fieldnotes, are data. While they would not claim that the data they collect contain "the truth" or the only way of recording the empirical world, they do claim that their renderings can be evaluated in terms of accuracy. That is, there can and should be a correspondence with what the researcher said happened and what actually occurred. (If the researcher said informants were present and said something, they were in fact present and said these things.) Further, they strive to have their writing be consistent with the data they collect—not that they claim their assertions are "true," but that they are plausible given the data. In this sense qualitative researchers see themselves as empirical researchers. While this is true, most qualitative researchers see what they produce, research reports and articles, not as a transcendent truth, but as a particular rendering or interpretation of reality grounded in the empirical world. They believe that the qualitative research tradition produces an interpretation of reality that is useful in understanding the human condition. That is the logic in their claim to legitimacy.

Symbolic Interaction

As a review of history suggests, symbolic interaction has been around a long time. It was present in the Chicago School approach to research in the early part of this century. John Dewey, the pragmatist philosopher and educator, was at Chicago during the formative years of this theoretical perspective, and his writings and personal contact with such people as Charles Horton Cooley, Robert Park, Florian Znaniecki, and, most importantly, George Herbert Mead, contributed to its development. Mead's formulation in *Mind, Self, and Society* (1934) is the most cited early source of what is now called *symbolic interaction*. No agreement exists among social scientists about the use or importance of its various concepts. Most use it synonymously with qualitative research, but there are a few social scientists calling themselves symbolic interactionists who do quantitative research (i.e., the Iowa School of symbolic interaction). In our discussion we draw heavily on students of Mead's work: Herbert Blumer and Everett Hughes, and their students Howard S. Becker and Blanche Geer.

Compatible with the phenomenological perspective and basic to the approach is the assumption that *human experience is mediated by interpretation* (Blumer, 1969). Objects, people, situations, and events do not posses their own meaning; rather, meaning is conferred on them. Where the educational technologist, for instance, will define a television and VCR as devices to be used by the teacher to show instructional videos relevant to educational objectives, the teacher may define them as objects to entertain students when she runs out of work for them to do or when she is tired. Or, place the television with people who have had not contact with western technology and it may be defined as a religious icon to be worshipped (until the technology specialist arrives bringing, perhaps, new perceptions and possibly influencing some definitions). The meaning people give to their experience and their process of interpretation are essential and constitutive, not accidental or secondary to what the experience is. To understand behavior, we must understand definitions and the processes by which they are manufactured. Human beings are actively engaged in creating their world; understanding the intersection of biography and society is essential (Gerth & Mills, 1978). People act, not on the basis of predetermined responses to predefined objects, but rather as interpreters, definers, signalers, and symbol and signal readers whose behavior can only be understood by having the researcher enter into the defining process through such methods as participant observation.

Interpretation is not an autonomous act, nor is it determined by any particular force, human or otherwise. Individuals interpret with the help of others—people from their past, writers, family, television personalities, and persons they meet in settings in which they work and play—but others do not do it for them. Through interaction the individual constructs meaning. People in a given situation (for example, students in a particular class) often develop common definitions (or "share perspectives" in the symbolic interactionist language) since they regularly interact and share experiences, problems, and background; but consensus is not inevitable. While some take "shared definitions" to indicate "truth," meaning is always subject to negotiation. It can be influenced by people who see things differently. When acting on the basis of a particular definition, things may not go well for a person. People have problems and these problems may cause them to forge new definitions, to discard old ways—in short, to change. How such definitions develop is the subject matter for investigation.

Interpretation, then, is essential. Symbolic interaction, rather than internal drives, personality traits, unconscious motives, needs, socioeconomic status, role obligations, cultural prescriptions, social-control mechanisms, or the physical environment, becomes the conceptual paradigm. These factors are some of the constructs social scientists draw upon in their attempts to understand and predict behavior. The symbolic interactionist also pays attention to these theoretical constructs; however, they are relevant to understanding behavior only to the degree that they enter in and affect the defining process. A proponent of the theory would not deny, for example, that there is a drive for food and that there are certain cultural definitions of how, what, and when one should eat. They would deny, however, that eating can be understood solely in terms of drives and cultural definitions. Eating can be understood by looking at the interplay between how people come to define eating and the specific situations in which they find themselves. Eating comes to be defined in different ways: The process is experienced differently, and people exhibit different behaviors while eating in different situations. Teachers in a school come to define the proper time to eat, what to eat, and how to eat very differently from students in the same location. Eating lunch can be a break from work, an annoying intrusion, a chance to do some low-key business, a time to diet, or a chance to get the answers to questions on an examination. (We are not suggesting that these are mutually exclusive.) Some people's meals, for example, may serve as benchmarks for specific developments in their day. Here, eating takes on significance by providing an event by which one can measure what has or has not been accomplished, how much of the day one may still have to endure, or how soon one will be forced to end an exciting day.

Eating lunch has symbolic meaning with which concepts like drives and rituals cannot deal. The theory does not deny that there are rules and regulations, norms, and belief systems in society. It does suggest that they are important in understanding behavior only if, and how, people take them into account. Furthermore, it is suggested that it is not the rules, regulations, norms, or whatever that are crucial in understanding behavior, but how these are defined and used in specific situations. A high school may have a grading system, an organizational chart, a class schedule, a curriculum, and an official motto that suggests its prime purpose is the education of the "whole person." People act, however, not according to what the school is supposed to be, or what administrators say it is but, rather, according to how they see it. For some students, high school is primarily a place to meet friends, or even a place to get high; for most, it is a place to get grades and amass credits so they can graduate—tasks they define as leading to college or a job. The way students define school and its components determines their actions, although the rules and the credit system may set certain limits and impose certain costs and thus affect their behavior. Organizations vary in the extent to which they provide fixed meanings and the extent that alternative meanings are available and created.

Another important part of symbolic interaction theory is the construct of the "self." The self is not seen lying inside the individual like the ego or an organized body of needs, motives, and internalized norms or values. The self is the definition people create (through interacting with others) of who they are. In constructing or defining self, people attempt to see themselves as others see them by interpreting gestures and actions directed toward them and by placing themselves in the role of the other person. In short, people come to see themselves in part as others see them. The self is thus also a social construction, the results of persons perceiving themselves and then developing a definition through the process of interaction. This loop enables people to change and grow as they learn more about themselves through this interactive process. This way of conceptualizing the self led to studies of the self-fulfilling prophecy and provided the background for the "labeling approach" to deviant behavior (Becker, 1963; Erickson, 1962; Rist, 1977).

A Story

To sum up our discussion of theory from the phenomenological and symbolic interactionist perspective, we end with an anecdote. If we had to give it a title, we would call this story "Forever."

One night at a dinner party a group of university faculty, including the dean of the law school, a physics professor, and a geology professor, all distinguished in their fields, began discussing the concept of "forever." The conversation began with someone making reference to the practice of having property leases drawn up in periods of ninety-nine years. Someone asked the dean of the law school whether the phrase wasn't the convention of the legal profession to refer to "forever." The dean said, "Yes, more or less, that's what it means." The geology professor suggested that in her field, "forever" refers to something quite different—the concept had more to do with how long the earth was expected to exist. The physics professor chimed in with the comment that in his field, "forever" really meant "forever."

Many children's stories end with the phrase, "And they lived happily forever after," another interpretation. Sometimes when children are waiting for their parents to take them somewhere, they complain that they have been waiting "forever." We have not exhausted all the possibilities, but the point is clear. Looked at from a number of perspectives, the word is rich in connotations. Each person referred to uses of the idea of "forever" in a very different world view. The child who says, "I have been waiting forever," finds it difficult to see the world from the point of view of a physicist, and the physicist dismisses the child's use of the concept with a knowing adult smile.

Some might attempt to resolve the discrepancy between the views of various users of the concept by calling for a more precise definition of the term—in other words, to create consensus by deciding on "real" definitions of the term. In discussion groups or in board meetings, this method might forestall misunderstanding, but qualitative researchers attempt to expand rather than confine understanding. They do not attempt to resolve such ambiguity by seeing the differences as "mistakes" and so attempt to establish a standard definition. Rather, they seek to study the concept as it is understood in the context of all those who use it. Similarly, when going to study an organization, one does not attempt to resolve the ambiguity that occurs when varied definitions of the word *goal* arise, or when people have different goals. The subject of the study focuses instead on how various participants see and experience goals. It is multiple realities rather than a single reality that concern the qualitative researcher.

Culture

Many anthropologists operate from a phenomenological perspective in their studies of education. The framework for these anthropological studies is the concept of *culture*. The attempt to describe culture or aspects of culture is called *ethnography*. While anthropologists often disagree on a definition of culture, they all count on it for a theoretical framework for their work. Several definitions help expand our understanding of how it shapes research. Some anthropologists define culture as "the acquired knowledge people use to interpret experience and generate behavior" (Spradley, 1980, p. 6). In this scheme, culture embraces what people do, what people know, and things that people make and use (Spradley, 1980, p. 5). To describe culture from this perspective, a researcher might think about events in the following way: "At its best, an ethnography should account for the behavior of people by describing what it is that they know that enables them to behave appropriately given the dictates of common sense in their community" (McDermott, 1976, p. 159). Researchers in this tradition say that an ethnography succeeds if it teaches readers how to behave appropriately in the cultural setting, whether it is among families in a African American community (Stack, 1974), in the school principal's office (Wolcott, 1973), or in the kindergarten class (Florio, 1978).

Another definition of culture emphasizes *semiotics*, the study of signs in language, and maintains that there is a difference between knowing the behavior and lingo of a group of people and being able to do it oneself (Geertz, 1973). From this perspective, culture looks more complicated and somewhat different: "As interworked systems of construable signs (what, ignoring provincial usages, I would call symbols), culture is not a power, something to which social events, behaviors, institutions, or processes can be causally attributed; it is a context, something within which they can be intelligibly—that is, thickly—described" (Geertz, 1973, p. 14). In this sense, there is interaction between culture and the meanings people attribute to events. The phenomenological orientation of this definition is clear.

Geertz borrowed the term "thick description" from the philosopher Gilbert Ryle to describe the task of ethnography. Geertz uses Ryle's example of a person blinking one eye, and examines the different levels on which such an act can be analyzed. Blinking can be represented as twitching, winking, pretending to wink (and so putting an audience on), or rehearsing winking. How and at what level one analyzes these behaviors constitutes the difference between thin and thick description:

> Between the ... "thin description" of what the researchers (parodist, winker, twitcher ...) is doing ("rapidly contracting his right eyelid") and the "thick description" of what he is doing ("practicing a burlesque of a friend faking a wink to deceive an innocent into thinking a conspiracy is in motion"), lies the object of ethnography: a stratified hierarchy of meaning structures is terms of which twitches, winks, fake winks, parodies, rehearsals of parodies are produced, perceived, and interpreted, and without which they would not (not even the zero-form twitches, which as a cultural category are as much non-winks as winks are non-twitches), in fact exist, no matter what anyone did or didn't do with his eyelids. (Geertz, 1973, p. 7)

Ethnography, then, is "thick description." When culture is examined from this perspective, the ethnographer is faced with a series of interpretations of life, of common-sense understandings, that are complex and difficult to separate from each other. The ethnographer's goals are to share in the meanings that the cultural participants take for granted and then to depict the new understanding for the reader and for outsiders. The ethnographer is concerned with representations.

A third conceptual handle on culture is suggested by the anthropologist Rosalie Wax (1971). In a discussion of the theoretical presuppositions of fieldwork, Wax discusses the tasks of ethnography in terms of understanding. Understanding, according to Wax, is not some "mysterious empathy" between people; rather, it is a phenomenon of "shared meaning." And so the anthropologist begins outside, both literally in terms of his or her social acceptance and figuratively in terms of understanding:

> Thus, a field worker who approaches a strange people soon perceives that these people are saying and doing things which they understand but he does not understand. One of the strangers may make a particular gesture, whereupon all the other strangers laugh. They share in the understanding of what the gesture means, but the field worker does not. When he does share, he begins to "understand." He possesses a part of the "insider's view." (Wax, 1971, p. 11)

An ethnographic study of a kindergarten class (Florio, 1978) examines how children entering kindergarten become insiders, that is, how they learn kindergarten culture and develop appropriate responses to teacher and classroom expectations.

Sociologists use culture as well to theoretically inform their qualitative studies. Becker's description of culture also relies on shared meanings. Using the metaphor of a dance band, Becker suggests that if a group of individual musicians is invited to play in a dance band at a wedding, and if they show up and, having never met, can play the song in the key the leader announces (with the audience never guessing that they have never met), then they are relying on culture to do so. Becker suggests that culture is what enables people to act together.

It is the framework of culture, whatever the specific definitions, as the principal organizational or conceptual tool used to interpret data that characterizes ethnography. Ethnographic procedures, while similar if not identical to those employed in participant observation, do rely on a different vocabulary and have developed in different academic specialities. Recently, educational researchers have used the term *ethnography* to refer to any qualitative study, even within sociology. While people do not agree on the appropriateness of using *ethnography* as the generic word for qualitative studies, there is some evidence to suggest that the sociologist and the anthropologist are coming closer in the ways they conduct their research and the theoretical orientation that underlies their work. As early as 1980 a well-known ethnographer declared that "the concept of culture as acquired knowledge has much in common with symbolic interaction" (Spradley, 1980). Some declare that the concept of "culture" as used by anthropologists asserts a structure, continuity, and pervasiveness of meaning among people that symbolic interactionists do not embrace. For symbolic interactionists meaning is much more to be found in the particular situation rather than in the group studied.

Ethnomethodology

Ethnomethodology does not refer to the methods researchers employ to collect their data; rather, it points to the subject matter to be investigated. As Harold Garfinkel tells the story, the term came to him while he was working with the Yale cross-culture area files which contained words like ethnobotany, ethnophysics, ethnomusic, and ethnoastronomy. Terms like these refer to how members of a particular group (usually tribal groups in the Yale files) understand, use, and order aspects of their environment; in the case of ethnobotany, the particular subject is plants. Ethnomethodology thus refers to the study of how people create and understand their daily lives—their method of accomplishing everyday life. Subjects for ethnomethodologists are not members of non-western peoples; they are citizens in various situations in modern society.

Garfinkel, giving what he calls a shorthand definition of the work of ethnomethodologists, says: "I would say we are doing studies of how persons, as parties to their ordinary arrangements, use the features of the arrangements to make for members the visibly organized characteristics happen" (Garfinkel, in Hill & Crittenden, 1968, p. 12). Ethnomethodologists try to understand how people go about seeing, explaining, and describing order in the world in which they live (Garfinkel, 1967). Ethnomethodologists have studied, for example, how people "do" gender (West & Zimmerman, 1987).

A number of educational researchers have been influenced by the approach. While their work is sometimes difficult to separate from the work of other qualitative researchers, it tends to deal more with micro-issues, with the specifics of conversation and vocabulary, and with details of action and understanding. Researchers in this mode use phrases such as "common-sense understanding," "everyday life," "practical accomplishments," "routine grounds for social action," and "accounts." After a period of increasing popularity in the late 1960s and through the 1970s interest in ethnomethodology fell off in the 1980s. Many current theoretical critiques and concerns of empiricism raised by postmodernists were originally voiced by ethnomethodologists (Holstein & Gubrium, 1994). There is some evidence of a resurgence of interest in its application to education (Lynch & Peyrot, 1992). One issue to which ethnomethodologists have sensitized researchers is that research itself is not a uniquely scientific enterprise; rather, it can be studied as "a practical accomplishment." They have suggested that we look carefully at the common-sense understandings under which data collectors operate. They push researchers working in the qualitative mode to be more sensitive to the need to "bracket" or suspend their own common-sense assumptions, their own world view, instead of taking it for granted.

The Current Theoretical Scene: Cultural Studies, Feminisms, Postmodernism, and Critical Theory

Many researchers who are not primarily phenomenologists also do qualitative research but situate their work in a different conceptual framework. These frameworks include cultural studies, feminisms, postmodernism, and critical theory.

We discussed some of the premises of these theoretical approaches in the historical section. Here, we describe some of the differences between these and phenomenological approaches.

Most qualitative researchers who identify as feminists, critical theorists, or postmodernists reject the idea that the world is "directly knowable"; it "cannot empirically present itself" as phenomenological accounts would suggest (Willis, 1977, p. 194). The world is not directly knowable for several reasons. First, all social relations are influenced by power relations that must be accounted for in analyzing informants' interpretations of their own situations. While the phenomenologist might say that a researcher can never assume how much one's position in the power structure is influential, these perspectives insist that power must always be taken into account to some degree, whether it is the informant's power or lack of it, or the researcher's. These groups may or may not be particularly interested in specific kinds of power. While feminists tend to be interested in the power of gender, including masculinity and femininity (Mac An Ghaill, 1994; Finders, 1997), for example, critical theorists and postmodernists may be as well, so the theoretical orientation of the researchers cannot be identified by the subject of their research (see McRobbie, 1994).

Second, they maintain that all research is informed by some theoretical understanding of human and social behavior; hence, it is not accurate to describe the analytical process as inductive. Researchers have ideas about, for example, race, or gender, before they enter the field, and these ideas are influential. They are not, however, binding. Roman and Apple (1990), for example, suggest that the "prior theoretic and political commitments" of the researcher are "informed and transformed by the lived experiences of the group she or he researches" (p. 62). These views, then, suggest that when qualitative researchers do research they engage in a kind of dialogue with their informants. Their own theoretical and ideological views are powerful, but these perspectives are also shaped by what they learn from their informants.

We have described these theoretical perspectives as if they were only different from each other, but that is somewhat artificial. People describe themselves as feminist postmodernists or as critical feminists, or even as feminist phenomenologists. While there may be some tension between these views, there are also similarities even between these different theories and symbolic interaction. Furthermore, all qualitative researchers are connected to the empirical world, since we must all deal with data. Theory emerges in published studies that, to different degrees, depend on data. Theory influences how we talk about our relationship to data and to the empirical world as well as what we imagine to be significant in what we understand. . . .

References

Becker, H. S. (1963). *Outsiders: Studies in the sociology of deviance.* New York: The Free Press.

Becker, H. S. (1970). *Whose side are we on? Sociological work.* Chicago: Aldine.

Berger, P., & Luckmann, T. (1967). *The social construction of reality.* Garden City, NY: Anchor Books.

Bhaba, H. (1986). The other question: Difference, discrimination, and the discourse of colonialism. In F. Barker, P. Hulme, M. Iversen, & D. Loxley (Eds.), *Literature, politics, and theory.* London: Methuen.

Biklen, S. (1985). Can elementary school teaching be a career? *Issues in Education 3:* 215–231.

Biklen, S. (1987). School teaching, professionalism and gender. *Teacher Education Quarterly 14:* 17–24.

Biklen, S. (1993). Mothers' gaze through teachers' eyes. In S. K. Biklen, & D. Pollard (Eds.), *Gender and education.* National Society for the Study of Education Yearbook. Chicago: University of Chicago Press.

Biklen, S. (1995). *School work: Gender and the cultural construction of teaching.* New York: Teachers College Press.

Blumer, H. (1980). Comment, Mead and Blumer: The convergent methodological perspectives of social behaviorism and symbolic interaction. *American Sociological Review 45:* 409–419.

Bogardus, E. (1926). *The new social research.* Los Angeles: Jesse Ray Miller.

Bogdan, R., & Taylor, S. (1975). *Introduction to qualitative research methods.* New York: Wiley.

Botkin, B. A. (Ed.). (1945). *Lay my burden down: A folk history of slavery.* Chicago: University of Chicago Press.

Brown, R. H. (Ed.). (1995). *Postmodern representations: Truth, power, and mimesis in the human sciences and public culture.* Urbana, IL: University of Illinois Press.

Bruyn, S. (1966). *The human perspective in sociology.* Englewood Cliffs, NJ: Prentice-Hall.

Carspecken, P. (1996). *Critical ethnography in educational research.* New York: Routledge.

Clifford, J. (1983). On ethnographic authority. *Reflections 1*(2): 118–146.

Clifford, J. (1986). Introduction: Partial truths. In J. Clifford & G. Marcus (Eds.), *Writing culture: The poetics and politics of ethnography.* Berkeley: University of California Press, pp. 1–26.

Clifford, J. (1988). *The predicament of culture.* Cambridge, MA: Harvard University Press.

Clifford, J., & Marcus, G. E. (Eds.). (1986). *Writing culture: The poetics and politics of ethnography.* Berkeley: University of California Press.

Collier, J., Jr. (1967). *Visual anthropology: Photography as a research method.* New York: Holt.

Collins, R., & Makowsky, M. (1978). *The discovery of society* (2nd ed.). New York: Random House.

Cressy, P. (1932). *The taxi-dance hall.* Chicago: University of Chicago.

Cronbach, L., & Suppes, P. (Eds.). (1969). *Research for tomorrow's schools.* New York: Macmillan.

Decker, S. (1969). *An empty spoon.* New York: Harper & Row.

Denzin, N. K. (1989). *Interpretive biography.* Newbury Park, CA: Sage.

Denzin, N. K., & Lincoln, Y. S. (1994). Introduction. In N. K. Denzin & Y. S. Lincoln (Eds.), *Handbook of qualitative research.* Thousand Oaks, CA: Sage, pp. 1–17.

DeVault, M. L. (1990). Talking and listening from women's standpoints: Feminist strategies for interviewing and analysis. *Social Problems 37*(1): 96–116.

Devine, E. T. (1906–1908). Results of the Pittsburgh survey. *American Sociological Society: Papers and Proceedings 3:* 85–92.

Dicken, D. R., & Fontana, A. (Eds.). (1994). *Postmodernism & social inquiry.* New York: Guilford.

Donovan, F. (1920/1974). *The woman who waits.* New York: Arno Press.

Douglas, J. (1976). *Investigative social research.* Beverly Hills, CA: Sage.

Du Bois, W. E. B. (1967/1899). *The Philadelphia negro: A social study.* New York: Benjamin Blom, distributed by Arno Press.

Eckert, P. (1989). *Jocks & burnouts: Social categories and identity in the high school.* New York: Teachers College Press.

Eddy, E. (1969). *Becoming a teacher.* New York: Teacher's College Press.

Ellis, C. (1995). The other side of the fence: Seeing black and white in a small southern town. *Qualitative Inquiry 1*(2): 147–167.

Erikson, K. (1962). Notes on the sociology of deviance. *Social Problems 9:* 307–314.

Evans, W. (1973). *Photographs for the Farm Security Administration, 1935–1938.* New York: Da Capo Press.

Fabian, J. (1983). *Time and the other: How anthropology makes its object.* New York: Columbia University Press.

Faris, R. E. L. (1967). *Chicago sociology, 1920–1932.* Chicago: University of Chicago Press.

Federal Writers' Project (1939). *These are our lives.* Chapel Hill, NC: University of North Carolina.

Filstead, W. (Ed.). (1970). *Qualitative methodology.* Chicago: Markham.

Finders, M. (1997). *Just girls: Hidden literacies and life in junior high.* New York: Teachers College Press.

Fine, M. (1988). Sexuality, schooling, and adolescent females: The missing discourse of desire. *Harvard Educational Review 58*(1): 29–53.

Fine, M. (1993). Over dinner: Feminism and adolescent female bodies. In S. Biklen & D. Pollard (Eds.), *Gender and education.* 92nd Yearbook of the National Society of the Study of Education. Chicago: University of Chicago Press, pp. 126–154.

Florio, S. E. (1978). Learning how to go to school: An ethnography of interaction in a kindergarten/first grade classroom. Unpublished doctoral dissertation, Harvard University.

Foster, M. (1992). African American teachers and the politics of race. In K. Weiler (Ed.), *What schools can do: Critical pedagogy and practice.* Albany, NY: State University of New York Press, pp. 93–127.

Foster, M. (1993). Self-portraits of black teachers: Narratives of individual and collective struggle against racism. In W. Tierney & D. McLaughlin (Eds.), *Naming silenced lives: Personal narratives and the process of educational change.* New York: Routledge, pp. 155–175.

Foster, M. (1994). The power to know one thing is never the power to know all things: Methodological notes on two studies of Black American teachers. In A. Gitlin (Ed.), *Power and method: Political activism and educational research.* New York: Routledge, pp. 129–145.

Fuchs, E. (1966). *Pickets at the gates.* New York: The Free Press.

Fuchs, E. (1969). *Teachers talk.* Garden City, NY: Doubleday.

Garfinkel, H. (1967). *Studies in ethnomethodology.* Englewood Cliffs, NJ: Prentice-Hall.

Geertz, C. (1973). Thick description: Toward an interpretive theory of culture. In *The interpretation of cultures.* New York: Basic Books.

Gerth, H., & Mills, C. W. (1978). *Character and social structure.* New York: Harcourt Brace.

Glaser, B., & Strauss, A. L. (1967). *The discovery of grounded theory: Strategies for qualitative research.* Chicago: Aldine.

Gouldner, H. (1978). *Teachers' pets, troublemakers, and nobodies.* Westport, CT: Greenwood Press.

Greene, M. (1978). *Landscapes of learning.* New York: Teachers College Press.

Guba, E. G., & Lincoln, Y. S. (1994). Competing paradigms in qualitative research. In N. K. Denzin, & Y. S. Lincoln (Eds.), *Handbook of qualitative research.* Thousand Oaks, CA: Sage, pp. 105–117.

Gubrium, J. (1988). *Analyzing field reality.* Beverly Hills, CA: Sage.

Gutman, J. M. (1974). *Lewis Hine, 1974–1940: Two perspectives.* New York: Grossman.

Haraway, D. (1991). Situated knowledges: The science question in feminism and the privilege of partial perspective. In *Simians, cyborgs, and women.* New York: Routledge.

Harding, S. (Ed.). (1987). *Feminism and methodology.* Bloomington, IN: Indiana University Press.

Haskins, J. (1969). *Diary of a Harlem schoolteacher.* New York: Grove Press.

Herndon, J. (1968). *The way it spozed to be.* New York: Simon & Schuster.

Hill, R. J., & Crittenden, K. (1968). *Proceedings of the Purdue symposium on ethno-methodology.* Lafayette, IN: Institute for the Study of Social Change, Purdue University.

Hochschild, A. R. (1983). *The managed heart: Commercialization of human feelings.* Berkeley: University of California Press.

Holstein, J., & Gubrium, J. (1994). Phenomenology, ethnomethodology and interpretive practice. In N. Denzin & Y. Lincoln (Eds.), *Handbook of qualitative research.* Thousand Oaks, CA: Sage, pp. 262–272.

Hughes, E. C. (1971). *The sociological eye.* Chicago: Aldine.

Hurley, F. J. (1972). *Portrait of a decade: Roy Stryker and the development of documentary photography in the thirties.* Baton Rouge, LA: Louisiana State University Press.

Kellogg, P. (1911–1912). The spread of the survey idea. *Proceedings of the Academy of Political Science 2*(4): 475–491.

Kincheloe, J. L., & McLaren, P. L. (1994). Rethinking critical theory and qualitative research. In N. K. Denzin & Y. S. Lincoln (Eds.), *Handbook of qualitative research.* Thousand Oaks, CA: Sage, pp. 138–157.

Kohl, H. (1967). *36 children.* New York: New American Library.

Komarovsky, M. (1946). Cultural contradictions and sex roles. *American Journal of Sociology 52:* 184–189.

Kozol, J. (1967). *Death at an early age.* New York: Bantam.

Lareau, A. (1987). Social class and family-school relationships: The importance of cultural capital. *Sociology of Education 56* (April): 73–85.

Lather, P. (1991). *Getting smart: Feminist research and pedagogy with/in the postmodern.* New York: Routledge.

Leacock, E. (1969). *Teaching and learning in city schools.* New York: Basic Books.

Lesko, N. (1988). *Symbolizing society: Rites and structure in a Catholic high school.* London: Falmer Press.

Lynch, M., & Peyrot, M. (1992). A reader's guide to ethnomethodology. *Qualitative Sociology 15*(2): 113–122.

Mac An Ghaill, M. (1994). *The making of men: Masculinities, sexualities and schooling.* Buckingham, UK: Open University Press.

Malinowski, B. (1922). *Argonauts of the western Pacific.* New York: Dutton.

Marcus, G. E., & Fisher, M. M. (1986). *Anthropology as cultural critique: An experimental moment in the human sciences.* Chicago: University of Chicago Press.

Marcus, G. M., & Cushman, D. (1982). Ethnographies as texts. *Annual Review of Anthropology 11:* 25–69.

Martin, E. (1987). *The woman in the body.* Boston: Beacon Press.

Mascia-Lees, F. E., Sharpe, P., & Cohen, C. B. (1989). The postmodernist turn in anthropology: Cautions from a feminist perspective. *Signs 15*(1): 7–33.

Matthews, F. (1977). *Quest for an American sociology: Robert E. Park and the Chicago school.* Montreal: McGill-Queens University Press.

McCall, G. J., & Simmons, J. L. (Eds.). (1969). *Issues in participant observation.* Reading, MA: Addison-Wesley.

McDermott, R. (1976). Kids make sense: An ethnographic account of the interactional management of success and failure in one first grade classroom. Unpublished doctoral dissertation, Stanford University.

McLaren, P. (1994). *Life in schools.* 2nd Edition. New York: Longman.

McRobbie, A. (1994). *PostModernism and popular culture.* London: Routledge.

Mead, M. (1942). An anthropologist looks at the teacher's role. *Educational Method 21:* 219–223.

Mead, M. (1951). *The school in American culture.* Cambridge, MA: Harvard University Press.

Mehan, H., & Wood, H. (1975). *The reality of ethnomethodology.* New York: Wiley.

Meltzer, B., Petras, J., & Reynolds, L. (1975). *Symbolic interactionism: Genesis, varieties and criticism.* London: Routledge and Kegan Paul.

Middleton, S. (1987). Schooling and radicalization: Life histories of New Zealand feminist teachers. *British Journal of Sociology of Education 8*(2): 169–189.

Middleton, S. (1993). *Educating feminists: Life histories and pedagogy.* New York: Teachers College Press.

Moore, G. A. (1967). *Realities of the urban classroom.* Garden City, NY: Anchor.

North, L. V. (1909, March 6). The elementary public schools of Pittsburgh. *Charity and the Commons 21:* 1175–1191.

Oakley, A. (1981). Interviewing women: A contradiction in terms. In H. Roberts (Ed.), *Doing feminist research.* London: Routledge and Kegan Paul, pp. 30–61.

Olesen, V. (1994). Feminisms and models in qualitative research. In N. K. Denzin & Y. S. Lincoln (Eds.), *Handbook of qualitative research.* Thousand Oaks, CA: Sage, pp. 158–169.

O'Neal, M. H. (1976). *A vision shared.* New York: St. Martin's.

Pratt, M. L. (1985). Scratches on the face of the country; Or, What Mr. Burrow saw in the land of the Bushmen. *Critical Inquiry 12* (Autumn): 119–143.

Psathas, G. (Ed.). (1973). *Phenomenological sociology.* New York: Wiley.

Radway, J. (1984). *Reading the romance.* Chapel Hill, NC: University of North Carolina Press.

Reinharz, S. (1993). Neglected voices and excessive demands in feminist research. *Qualitative Sociology 16*(1): 69–75.

Research for Action (1996). *Girls in the middle.* Washington, DC: American Association of University Women.

Rist, R. (1970). Student social class and teacher expectations: The self-fulfilling prophecy in ghetto education. *Harvard Educational Review 40:* 411–451.

Rist, R. (1973). *The urban school: A factory for failure.* Cambridge, MA: Massachusetts Institute of Technology Press.

Rist, R. (1977). On understanding the processes of schooling. In J. Karabel, & A. H. Halsey (Eds.), *Power and ideology in education.* New York: Oxford University Press.

Ritzer, G. (1975). *Sociology: A multiple paradigm science.* Boston: Allyn & Bacon.

Roberts, J. (1971). *Scene of the battle.* Garden City, NY: Doubleday.

Roman, L. G. (1988). Intimacy, labor, and class: Ideologies of feminine sexuality in the punk slam dance. In L. G. Roman & L. C. Christian-Smith with E. Ellsworth (Eds.), *Becoming feminine: The politics of popular culture.* London: Falmer Press, pp. 143–184.

Roman, L., & Apple, M. (1990). Is naturalism a move away from positivism? Materialist and feminist approaches to subjectivity in ethnographic research. In E. Eisner & A. Peshkin (Eds.), *Qualitative inquiry in education: The continuing debate.* New York: Teachers College Press, pp. 38–73.

Schwandt, T. A. (1994). Constructivist, interpretivist approaches to human inquiry. In N. K. Denzin & Y. S. Lincoln (Eds.), *Handbook of qualitative research.* Thousand Oaks, CA: Sage, pp. 118–137.

Sharpe, J. (1993). *Allegories of Empire: The figure of women in the colonial text.* Minneapolis, MN: University of Minnesota Press.

Shaw, C. (1966). *The jack roller* (2nd ed.). Chicago: University of Chicago Press.

Sleeter, C. (1993). How white teachers construct race. In C. McCarthy & W. Crichlow (Eds.), *Race, identity and representation in education.* New York: Routledge, pp. 157–171.

Smith, D. (1987). *The everyday world as problematic.* Boston: Northeastern University Press.

Spradley, J. P. (1980). *Participant observation.* New York: Holt, Rinehart & Winston.

Stack, C. (1974). *All our kin: Strategies for survival in a black community.* New York: Harper & Row.

Stott, W. (1973). *Documentary expression and thirties America.* New York: Oxford University Press.

Stryker, R. E., & Wood, N. (1973). *In this proud land, America 1935–1943 as seen in the FSA photographs.* Greenwich, CT: New York Graphic Society, Ltd.

Sutherland, E. (1937). *The professional thief.* Chicago: University of Chicago Press.

Taylor, C. (1919). *The social survey. Its history and methods.* Columbia, MO: University of Missouri. (Social Science Series 3).

Thomas, N. (1994). *Colonialism's culture: Anthropology, travel and government.* Princeton, NJ: Princeton University Press.

Thomas, W. I. (1923). *The unadjusted girl.* Boston: Little, Brown.

Thomas, W. I., & Znaniecki, F. (1927). *The Polish peasant in Europe and America.* New York: Knopf.

Thrasher, F. (1927). *The gang.* Chicago: University of Chicago Press.

Tierney, W. (1994). On method and hope. In A. Gitlin (Ed.), *Power and method.* New York: Routledge, pp. 97–115.

Van Maanen, J. (1988). *Tales of the field: On writing ethnography.* Chicago: University of Chicago Press.

Vidich, A. J., & Lyman, S. M. (1994). Qualitative methods: Their history in sociology and anthropology. In N. K. Denzin & Y. S. Lincoln (Eds.), *Handbook of qualitative research.* Thousand Oaks, CA: Sage, pp. 23–59.

Waller, W. (1932). *Sociology of teaching.* New York: Wiley.

Warren, C. A. B. (1988). *Gender in field research.* Newbury Park: CA: Sage.

Wax, R. (1971). *Doing fieldwork: Warning and advice.* Chicago: University of Chicago Press.

Webb, B. (1926). *My apprenticeship.* New York: Longmans, Green & Co.

Webb, S., & Webb, B. (1932). *Methods of social study.* London: Longmans, Green & Co.

Weiler, K. (1988). *Women teaching for change.* South Hadley, MA: Bergin Garvey.

Weis, L. (1990). *Working class without work: High school students in a de-industrializing economy.* New York: Routledge.

Weis, L., Proweller, P., & Centrie, C. (1997). Re-examining "a moment in history": Loss of privilege inside white working-class masculinity in the 1990s. In M. Fine, L. Weis, L. Powell, & L. M. Wong (Eds.), *Off white: Readings on race, power, and society.* New York: Routledge, pp. 210–226.

Wells, A. F. (1939). Social surveys. In F. C. Bartlett, M. Ginsberg, E. S. Lindgren, & R. H. Thouless (Eds.), *The study of society.* London: Kegan Paul, Trench, Trubner & Co, pp. 424–435.

West, C., & Zimmerman, D. (1987). Doing gender. *Gender and Society 1*(2): 125–151.

Wiley, N. (1979). The rise and fall of dominating theories in American sociology. In W. Snizek, E. Fuhrman, & M. Miller (Eds.), *Contemporary issues in theory and research, a metasociological perspective.* Westport, CT: Greenwood, pp. 47–80.

Willis, P. (1977). *Learning to labor.* New York: Columbia University Press.

Wirth, L. (1928). *The ghetto.* Chicago: University of Chicago Press.

Wolcott, H. (1973). *The man in the principal's office.* New York: Holt, Rinehart & Winston.

Zorbaugh, H. (1929). *The gold coast and the slum.* Chicago: University of Chicago.

2

The Lives and Values of Researchers
Implications for Educating Citizens in a Multicultural Society
James A. Banks

[. . .]

The Values of Researchers

Social scientists are human beings who have both minds and hearts. However, their minds and the products of their minds have dominated research discourse in the United States and throughout the Western world. The hearts of social scientists exercise a cogent influence on research questions, findings, concepts, generalizations, and theories. I am using "heart" as a metaphor for values, which are the beliefs, commitments, and generalized principles to which social scientists have strong attachments and commitments. The value dimensions of social science research was largely muted and silenced in the academic community and within the popular culture until the neutrality of the social sciences was severely challenged by the postmodern, women's studies, and ethnic studies movements of the 1960s and 1970s (King, 1995; Ladner, 1973; Rosenau, 1992).

Social science research has supported historically and still supports educational policies that affect the life chances and educational opportunities of students. The educational policies supported by mainstream social science and educational researchers have often harmed low-income students and students of color. Yet, as I will document in this article, the values of social scientists are complex within a diverse society such as the United States. Social science and educational research in the United States, over time and often within the same era, have both reinforced inequality and supported liberation and human betterment.

[. . .]

Case Studies of the Lives of Researchers

The case studies that follow examine the lives and values of a select group of researchers who have done race relations research that has important implications for education. I will describe critical incidents in their biographical journeys that are related to their values, to race relations research, and to educational policy. The lives of these individuals exemplify and support the observations and conceptual distinctions I make in the theoretical discussion and in the typology described in Table 2.1.

I will use African American culture as the basis for classifying the scholars and researchers. I will first describe the lives and works of the psychologist Kenneth B. Clark

Table 2.1 A Typology of Crosscultural Researchers

Type of researcher	Description
The indigenous-insider	This individual endorses the unique values, perspectives, behaviors, beliefs, and knowledge of his or her indigenous community and culture and is perceived by people within the community as a legitimate community member who can speak with authority about it.
The indigenous-outsider	This individual was socialized within his or her indigenous community but has experienced high levels of cultural assimilation into an outsider or oppositional culture. The values, beliefs, perspectives, and knowledge of this individual are identical to those of the outside community. The indigenous-outsider is perceived by indigenous people in the community as an outsider.
The external-insider	This individual was socialized within another culture and acquires its beliefs, values, behaviors, attitudes, and knowledge. However, because of his or her unique experiences, the individual rejects many of the values, beliefs, and knowledge claims within his or her indigenous community and endorses those of the studied community. The external-insider is viewed by the new community as an "adopted" insider.
The external-outsider	The external-outsider is socialized within a community different from the one in which he or she is doing research. The external-outsider has a partial understanding of and little appreciation for the values, perspectives, and knowledge of the community he or she is studying and consequently often misunderstands and misinterprets the behaviors within the studied community.

and the historian John Hope Franklin, individuals who may be considered indigenous-insiders within the African American community for most of their careers. I will then discuss the lives and works of a group of social scientists who were external to the African American community but who did work that was empowering and liberating for African Americans. These researchers were, to varying extents, external-insiders in reference to the African American community. They are Franz Boas and two of his students, Ruth Benedict and Otto Kleinberg, and the social psychologist Thomas F. Pettigrew, who did pioneering research on race relations and school desegregation.

Kenneth B. Clark and Research on Race

The research, scholarship, and actions of the psychologist Kenneth B. Clark (b. 1914) illustrate the ways in which personal experiences, perspectives, and values influence scholarship and how scholarship influences action. Clark's work also epitomizes the role of the socially responsible scholar in a democratic, pluralistic society. Throughout his career, Clark consistently opposed institutionalized structures that promoted racism and inequality and constructed scholarship that challenged existing knowledge systems and paradigms.

The values and perspectives that underlie Clark's scholarship, research, and action were developed early in his life. His mother taught him, by her examples, to strongly oppose racial discrimination. She and her two children emigrated from the Panama Canal Zone to New York City when Clark was 5. She took a job as a seamstress in a sweatshop, helped organize a union in the shop, and became a steward for the International Ladies Garment Workers Union (Moritz, 1964).

Clark's early experiences with racial discrimination and his mother's decisive action against it strongly influenced his perception of race in America; the research questions, issues, and people he studied; and his commitment to act both as a scholar and a citizen to help create a more just society. Clark and his mother were refused service at Childs restaurant when he was 6 years old. His mother reacted with "verbal hostility" and "threw a dish on the floor" (Clark, 1993, p. 3). When he was in the ninth grade, Clark again witnessed his mother's strong reaction to discrimination when his White guidance counselor told him that he should attend a vocational high school. Writes Clark, "I again saw the anger on my mother's face that I had seen at Childs restaurant. She said, 'You will not go to a vocational high school. You are going to an academic high school'" (p. 5).

The lessons that Clark's mother taught him were reinforced by his personal experiences and by his professors at Howard University, the historically Black university where he earned his bachelor's and master's degrees. Clark's professors at Howard included the philosopher Alain Locke and the political scientist Ralph Bunche. When Clark was a senior at Howard, he and a group of students demonstrated inside the U.S. Capitol because African Americans were not served in the Capitol's restaurant. When the president of Howard and the disciplinary committee wanted to suspend or expel the students for "threatening the security of the university" (Clark, 1993, p. 8), Ralph Bunche strongly defended the students and threatened to resign if the students were disciplined.

Bunche and the students won the day; the students were not punished. This incident taught Clark important lessons about contradictions in American society. He writes:

> Howard University was the beginning of the persistent preoccupation I have had with American racial injustice. . . . At this stage in my personal development, I became engrossed in the contradictions which exist: the eloquence of American "democracy" and academic hypocrisy. These members of the Howard faculty I respected all became my mentors against American racism. *My life became dominated by an ongoing struggle against racial injustice.* . . . These outstanding professors made it very clear to me that under no circumstances should I ever accept racial injustice. (Clark, 1993, p. 7, italics added)

Clark's research on racial attitudes and their effects on the personality development of African American children, for which he became widely known, was an extension of work originally done by Mamie Phipps Clark for her master's thesis at Howard University. The Clarks, who met at Howard, were married in 1938. From 1939 to the 1950s, they conducted a series of important and influential studies on the racial awareness, preference, and racial self-identification of African American children (Clark & Clark, 1939, 1940, 1947, 1950).

John Hope Franklin's Experiences With Race

The historian John Hope Franklin (b. 1915), a specialist in Southern history, grew up in the South at a time when it was tightly segregated by race. Franklin's view of history, of America, and of the efforts that it will take to create a just society in the United States have been strongly influenced by his early socialization in his native Oklahoma. "Two factors," writes Franklin, "plagued my world of learning for all my developing years. One was race, the other was financial distress; and each had a profound influence on every stage of my development" (1991, p. 352).

Franklin was born in Rentiesville, Oklahoma, the all-Black town to which his parents moved after his father, a lawyer, was expelled from court by a White judge because he was Black. Franklin's parents strongly believed that they should not accept any form of racial segregation. They moved to an all-Black town to escape racial discrimination. The move made a lasting impression on their son, the future historian. The family later moved to Tulsa to seek better work, educational, and recreational opportunities. While living in Tulsa, Franklin's parents refused to attend any events that were racially segregated, including the concerts at Convention Hall that greatly appealed to their son. However, they allowed their son to attend the concerts.

As a college student at Fisk University in Nashville (a historically Black university), Franklin had a number of powerful and memorable personal experiences with racial discrimination that left their marks. When he bought a streetcar ticket with the only money he had—a $20 bill—the clerk screamed racial epithets and gave him $19.75 change in dimes and quarters. The 16-year-old Franklin was shocked and stunned by the incident. Three years later, a young Black man, Cordie Cheek, was taken by a gang of Whites from a Fisk-owned house and lynched on the edge of campus.

Franklin did not acquire a monolithic view of Whites during his coming of age in the South. Approximately half of the Fisk faculty was White. Franklin admired and respected most of his Fisk professors. He changed his lifelong ambition to follow his father's footsteps and become a lawyer because of the exciting lectures given by his White history professor, Theodore S. Currier. Currier became Franklin's mentor when he decided to become a historian. He borrowed $500 and gave it to Franklin so that he could attend Harvard University.

Franklin and the Reconstruction of American History

Franklin's important work to reconstruct and reinterpret American history with African Americans in visible and significant roles draws on and extends the research of African American historians who were his predecessors—such as Carter G. Woodson, Charles H. Wesley, W. E. B. Du Bois, and Luther B. Jackson. Franklin published the first edition of *From Slavery to Freedom: A History of Negro Americans* in 1947. This influential book is now in its seventh edition (Franklin & Moss, 1994). At the time of the publication of the first edition of the book, African Americans were largely invisible in most mainstream school and college textbooks. When they did appear, they were often stereotyped as happy slaves who were loyal to their masters. Ulrich B. Phillips's (1966) view of slavery dominated textbooks as well as mainstream intellectual discourse about slavery. Although Franklin's textbook received a warm reception in predominantly Black colleges and universities when it was first published, it was not until the civil rights movement of the 1960s and 1970s that Franklin's work began to significantly permeate mainstream textbooks and scholarship. Prior to the 1960s, scholars such as Woodson, Du Bois, and Franklin worked primarily in the margins of their disciplines to construct the history of African Americans and to reconstruct mainstream American history.

Franklin has written a score of scholarly books, monographs, and articles that reinterpret Southern history and the role of African Americans in the development of the

United States. In some of his most insightful writings, Franklin (1989) describes how the Founding Fathers and the Constitution played a significant role in racializing the United States.

Throughout his long and impressive career, Franklin has been viewed by most members of the African American community as an indigenous-insider. He is also highly respected by the mainstream scholarly and public communities. He is a former president of each of the major national historical professional associations. He was appointed by President Clinton to chair the Advisory Board for the President's Initiative on Race and Reconciliation in 1997.

The Anti-Racism Project of Anthropologists

The rise and spread of Nazism in Europe and racial conflicts and riots in the United States stimulated a rich period of race relations research and writings during World War II and the postwar period. A number of the books published during this period became classics including *An America Dilemma: The Negro Problem and Modern Democracy* by Gunnar Myrdal (1944), the Swedish economist; *Man's Most Dangerous Myth: The Fallacy of Race* by Ashley Montagu (1942); *The Authoritarian Personality* by Theodor W. Adorno et al. (Adorno, Frenkel-Brunswik, Levinson, Sanford, & Nevitt, 1950); and *The Nature of Prejudice* by Gordon Allport (1954). Much of the work published during the 1940s and 1950s was born out of the hope of stemming the tide of Nazism and anti-Semitism.

Franz Boas (1858–1942) of Columbia University and the anthropologists he trained initiated a major project to discredit scientific racism, which was widespread and institutionalized when Boas arrived in the United States in 1887 (Stocking, 1974). Boas immigrated to the United States from Germany because of the limited opportunities for Jewish scholars in his homeland (Barkan, 1992). The anti-racist work done by Boas and his former students was very important in countering racist scholarship and knowledge. Boas and other anthropologists became involved in an anti-racist project for a number of reasons. Some of Boas's Jewish students, such as Otto Klineberg and Melville Herskovits, realized that a racist ideology not only victimized African Americans but other groups as well, including Jewish Americans.

The anti-racism project initiated by Boas and his colleagues benefited African Americans as well as other racial, ethnic, and cultural groups. Much of their research and writing opposed and deconstructed racist ideologies that argued that African Americans were genetically inferior to Whites (Klineberg, 1935). The work of Boas and his anthropology colleagues indicates that outsiders may identify with and promote equality for a studied community in part because they view the interests of the studied community and their own personal and community interests as interconnected. By opposing racist theories directed against African Americans, Boas and Klineberg were pursuing the interests of their own cultural communities while promoting the public good.

Otto Klineberg (1899–1992), a former Boas student who did significant and influential work that challenges and undercuts scientific racism, was of Canadian-Jewish descent. He believed that his professional training with Boas and a chance visit to an American Indian community were the major factors that motivated his work on racial and ethnic issues. He minimized the role that his personal ethnic experiences played in his desire to study race and to oppose scientific racism.

While visiting an Indian community in Washington state, Klineberg (1973) conducted a study and found that the Indian students took longer to complete an intelligence test but made fewer errors than did the White students. He concluded that the conception and use of time in Indian and White cultures, rather than differences in intelligence, explained variations in performance on the test. He felt that the results of this study "entirely vindicated" Boas's views on the influence of culture and learning on intelligence test performance (Klineberg, 1973, p. 41).

Boas's experience with anti-Semitism and Klineberg's work with Boas and research experience in an American Indian community are important factors that help to explain their race-related work and the values exemplified in their research. Other researchers who become involved in race relations research and who become anti-racists are mainstream Americans who pursue research and exemplify values that are often oppositional to those institutionalized within their cultural communities. In his study of scholars who specialized in race relations research during the 1950s and 1960s, Stanfield (1993) found that White men of Southern and/or Jewish origin were among the most prominent of these scholars. Ruth Benedict and Thomas F. Pettigrew are two mainstream scholars who did influential race relations work.

Ruth Benedict and Anti-Racism Work

Ruth Benedict (1887–1948) was a former Boas student who later became his colleague at Columbia University. The focus of her work was the study of culture, not race. She became involved in race relations work reluctantly, in part because she realized she was not an expert in the field. In 1940, she published *Race: Science and Politics*. In popular language, Benedict described both the scientific facts and the myths about race. She (1940/1947) wrote, "[R]acism is an *ism* to which everyone in the world is exposed; for or against, we must take sides. And the history of the future will differ according to the decision which we make" (p. 5). In 1943, Benedict published (with Gene Weltfish) the *Races of Mankind* for a popular audience (1940/1947). Both *Race: Science and Politics* and *The Races of Mankind* were widely disseminated and influential. Benedict and a high school teacher in 1941 wrote a teaching unit, *Race and Cultural Relations: America's Answer to the Myth of the Master Race*.

Benedict became involved in Boas's anti-racism project for several reasons. First, anti-racism work was an extension of her earlier research on the characteristics of culture. A key assumption of Benedict's (1934) cultural project was the need for people to view outside cultures as similar to their own. Benedict's family experiences are another factor that compelled her interest and participation in the antiracist project. These experiences caused her to be interested in other cultures, to reach beyond her own cultural world, and to study cultural and racial differences.

According to her biographers, Benedict felt alienated and marginalized within the Anglo-American culture into which she was socialized (Caffrey, 1989; Mead, 1974; Modell, 1984). Writes Mead (1974), "[S]he often spoke of how she had come to feel, very early, that there was little in common between the beliefs of her family and neighbors and her own passionate wondering about life, which she learned to keep to herself" (p. 6). Fleming (1971) also describes Benedict's alienation and sense of marginalization within her family and community culture. He writes, "She had been estranged from what she took to be the inevitable nature of life; she now asked if she might have been more at home in another time and culture, say in ancient Egypt" (p. 130).

Benedict also became involved in Boas's anti-racism project because of her high personal regard for him. She greatly admired and respected her influential mentor, friend, and colleague. Becoming involved in his race relations project was an expression of loyalty to Boas, which he appreciated and expected from his former students.

Pettigrew and School Desegregation Research

Thomas F. Pettigrew (b. 1931), of Scottish-American descent, grew up in Richmond, Virginia, in the 1930s and 1940s. He witnessed racial discrimination and often challenged it when he was a youth. Pettigrew (1993) attributes the development of his progressive racial attitudes and his interest in race relations research to his family and Mildred Adams, his family's African American housekeeper.

Pettigrew was expelled from school several times for calling his seventh-grade teacher a bigot because she praised Hitler's anti-Semitism and used derogatory names when referring to African Americans. His mother and grandmother went to the principal's office and defended his actions each time he was expelled. Pettigrew (1993) was deeply influenced by the harsh racial discrimination that Mildred Adams had experienced, which she shared with him. He writes:

> Once a "white" movie theater refused us admission, although she had taken care to dress in an all-white uniform. By the time I was 10 years old, the many psychological defenses that blind most white Americans to the racial injustice that surrounds them were no longer available to me. (p. 160)

Other factors influenced Pettigrew's decision to become a social psychologist and specialize in race relations research. These included a social psychology class he took at the University of Virginia, his professor's suggestion that he do graduate work at Harvard and study with Gordon Allport, and Allport's (1954) work in race relations. Allport (1954) was writing *The Nature of Prejudice*, which became a classic, when Pettigrew was doing graduate work with him.

Pettigrew has made major contributions to race relations research. He has summarized research on the intellectual abilities of African Americans that refutes theories of Black inferiority (Pettigrew, 1964) and has been a major researcher and activist scholar supporting school desegregation. Pettigrew was the chief investigator of the massive study of race and education sponsored by the U.S. Commission on Civil Rights in response to a request made by President Lyndon B. Johnson in 1965. The report, *Racial Isolation in the Public Schools* (U.S. Commission on Civil Rights, 1967), concluded that racial isolation in the public schools was extensive and that it harmed the nation's students.

Intellectual Leadership and Action

The researchers discussed in this article were transformative scholars and intellectual leaders (Banks, 1993, 1995); they were researchers who also had value aims, which they pursued through action to influence public and educational policies (Burns, 1978).

Klineberg, Clark, and Franklin supported, in various ways, the plaintiffs in the *Brown v. Board of Education* Supreme Court case. Pettigrew was an outspoken advocate of school desegregation during the 1960s and 1970s. He challenged Coleman's "White flight" thesis, which stated that large school districts risked losing White students and parents when desegregation took place under certain conditions. Benedict was a minor participant in the intercultural education movement (Caffrey, 1989).

Scholars who become intellectual leaders have many opportunities to make a difference in their communities and in the nation. However, they also experience conflicts, dilemmas, and problems. Scholars, especially those who work within marginalized communities and who promote policies and practices that conflict with those institutionalized within the mainstream academic community, experience a number of academic risks when they become intellectual leaders. They are open to charges by mainstream researchers that they are political, partisan, and subjective. Mainstream scholars who promote policies consistent with those institutionalized within the mainstream academic community are less subject to these risks; their normative-oriented work is more likely to be viewed as "objective and neutral."

[. . .]

The Need for Committed and Caring Researchers

[. . .]

Because education is a moral endeavor, educational researchers should be scientists as well as citizens who are committed to promoting democratic ideals. In other words, they should be intellectuals. The political scientist James McGregor Burns (1978) defines intellectuals as researchers who pursue normative ends. He writes, "[T]he person who deals with analytical ideas and data alone is a theorist; the one who works only with normative ideas is a moralist; the person who deals with both and unites them through disciplined imagination is an intellectual (p. 141). Intellectuals should be knowledgeable about the values that are exemplified in their research and be committed to supporting educational policies that foster democracy and educational equality. Kenneth B. Clark (1974) argues that the intellectual must seek the truth, but this quest must be guided by values. Clark believes that "The quest for truth and justice [is] meaningless without some guiding framework of accepted and acceptable values. These terms—truth and justice—have no meaning independent of a value system" (p. 21). Clark (1965) incorporates a value commitment into his beliefs as a social scientist:

> An important part of my creed as a social scientist is that on the grounds of absolute objectivity or on a posture of scientific detachment and indifference, a truly relevant and serious social science cannot be taken seriously by a society desperately in need of moral and empirical guidance in human affairs. (p. xxi)

Social scientists cannot be "neutral on a moving train" (Zinn, 1994) because the fate of researchers is tightly connected to the fate of all of the nation's citizens. James Baldwin (1971), in an open letter to Angela Davis, wrote, "If we know, then we must fight for your life as though it were our own—which it is—and render impassable with our bodies the corridors to the gas chamber. For if they come for you in the morning, they will be coming for us that night" (p. 23).

Note

I am grateful to the following colleagues for helpful comments on an earlier draft of this article that enabled me to strengthen it: Cherry A. McGee Banks, Carlos E. Cortés, Christine E. Sleeter, and Walter G. Stephan.

References

Adorno, T. W., Frenkel-Brunswik, E., Levinson, D. J., Sanford, R., & Nevitt, R. N. (1950). *The authoritarian personality.* New York: Norton.

Allport, G. (1954). *The nature of prejudice.* Reading, MA: Addison-Wesley.

Baldwin, J. (1971). An open letter to my sister, Angela Y. Davis. In A. Y. Davis & Other Political Prisoners (Eds.), *If they come in the morning* (pp. 19–23). New York: Signet.

Banks, J. A. (1993). The canon debate, knowledge construction, and multicultural education. *Educational Researcher, 22*(5), 4–14.

Banks, J. A. (1995). The historical reconstruction of knowledge about race; Implications for transformative teaching. *Educational Researcher, 24*(2), 15–25.

Barkan, E. (1992). *The retreat of scientific racism: Changing concepts of race in Britain and the United States between the world wars.* New York: Cambridge University Press.

Benedict, R. (1947). *Race: Science and politics* (Rev. ed., with *The races of mankind* by R. Benedict & G. Weltfish). New York: Viking. (Original work published 1940)

Burns, J. M. (1978). *Leadership.* New York: Harper & Row.

Caffrey, R. (1989). *Ruth Benedict: Stranger in this land.* Austin: University of Texas Press.

Clark, K. B. (1965). *Dark ghetto: Dilemmas of social power.* New York: Harper.

Clark, K. B. (1974). *Pathos of power.* New York: Harper & Row.

Clark, K. B. (1993). Racial progress and retreat: A personal memoir. In H. Hill & J. E. Jones Jr. (Eds.), *Race in America: The struggle for equality* (pp. 3–18). Madison: The University of Wisconsin Press.

Clark, K. B., & Clark, M. P. (1939). The development of consciousness of self and the emergence of racial identification in Negro preschool children. *Journal of Social Psychology, 10,* 591–599.

Clark, K. B., & Clark, M. P. (1940). Skin color as a factor in racial identification and preference in Negro children. *Journal of Negro Education, 19,* 341–358.

Clark, K. B., & Clark, M. P. (1947). Racial identification and preference in Negro children. In T. M. Newcomb & E. L. Hartley (Eds.), *Readings in social psychology* (pp. 169–178). New York: Holt, Rinehart & Winston.

Clark, K. B., & Clark, M. P. (1950). Emotional factors in racial identification and preference in Negro children. *Journal of Negro Education, 19,* 341–350.

Franklin, J. H. (1989). *Race and history: Selected essays 1938–1988.* Baton Rouge: Louisiana State University Press.

Franklin, J. H. (1991). A life of learning. In H. L. Gates Jr. (Ed.), *Bearing witness: Selections from African-American autobiography in the twentieth century* (pp. 351–368). New York: Pantheon Books.

Franklin, J. H., & Moss, A. A., Jr. (1994). *From slavery to freedom: A history of Negro Americans* (7th ed.). New York: McGraw-Hill.

King, J. L. (1995). Culture-centered knowledge: Black studies, curriculum transformation, and social action. In J. A. Banks & C. A. M. Banks (Eds.), *Handbook of research on multicultural education* (pp. 265–290). New York: Macmillan.

Klineberg, O. (1935). *Race differences.* New York: Harper & Brothers.

Klineberg, O. (1973). Reflections of an international psychologist of Canadian origin. *International Social Science Journal, 25,* 39–54.

Ladner, J. A. (Ed.). (1973). *The death of White sociology.* New York: Vintage.

Mead, M. (1974). *Ruth Benedict.* New York: Columbia University Press.

Modell, J. (1984). *Ruth Benedict: Patterns of a life.* London: Hogarth Press.

Montagu, M. F. A. (1942). *Man's most dangerous myth: The fallacy of race.* New York: Harper.

Moritz, C. (Ed.). (1964). Clark, Kenneth Bancroft. *Current biography* (pp. 80–83). New York: H. W. Wilson Company.

Myrdal, G. (1944). *An American dilemma: The Negro problem and modern democracy.* New York: Harper and Row.

Pettigrew, T. F. (1964). *A profile of the Negro American.* Princeton, NJ: Van Nostrand.

Pettigrew, T. F. (1993). How events shape theoretical frames: A personal statement. In J. H. Stanfield (Ed.), *A history of race relations research: First-generation recollections* (pp. 159–178). Newbury Park, CA: Sage Publications.

Rosenau, P. M. (1992). *Post-modernism and the social sciences.* Princeton, NJ: Princeton University Press.

Stanfield, J. H. (Ed.). (1993). *A history of race relations research: First-generation recollections.* Newbury Park, CA: Sage Publications.

Stocking, G. W., Jr. (1974). *A Franz Boas reader: The shaping of American anthropology, 1883–1911.* Chicago: The University of Chicago Press.

U.S. Commission on Civil Rights. (1967). *Racial isolation in the public schools* (2 Vols.). Washington, DC: U.S. Government Printing Office.

Zinn, H. (1994). *You can't be neutral on a moving train: A personal history for our times.* Boston: Beacon Press.

3

Studying Urban Schools

Howard S. Becker

The following is a slightly revised version of an invited address presented at the "Ethnography in Education Research" Forum, Graduate School of Education, University of Pennsylvania, March 1983. In the article, the author reflects on the reasons that ethnographic studies are, and probably will continue to be, suspect in the field of education. Appreciation is expressed to Francis A. J. Ianni for help in preparing this paper. ETHNOGRAPHY OF SCHOOLING; EVALUATION; SCHOOL FAILURE.

People have been studying schools and education ethnographically for a long time. Anthropologists, following the lead of Margaret Mead and others, have made the socialization of children into a culture a major concern, and what happened to children in contemporary Western schools could be seen as an example of that process. Sociologists likewise long have been interested in schools. In fact, Willard Waller's classic, *The Sociology of Teaching*, is probably the first ethnography of a contemporary American school.

Waller was not very careful about his methods. He had not really done ethnography so much as he had been the classic participant-as-observer, making the best of his job as schoolteacher by noting the interesting phenomena occurring around him. But his work had one hallmark of good ethnography. He saw and reported a fact, central to the institution he was observing, the existence of which no one there would admit: He said that children did not want to go to school and that adults forced them to, so that the natural state of social relations in the school was conflict. That seems obviously true, today as then, and yet the people who take that statement and its implications seriously (e.g., the writings of Holt or Herndon) still create controversy. Waller did work of the kind Erving Goffman, in his posthumous presidential address to the American Sociological Association ("The Interaction Order," *American Sociological Review*, 48), specified as the proper mode of sociological inquiry:

> unsponsored analyses of the social arrangements enjoyed by those with institutional authority—priests, psychiatrists, school teachers, police, generals, government leaders, parents, males, whites, nationals, media operators, and all the other well-placed persons who are in a position to give official imprint to versions of reality (p. 17).

In many ways, that aspect of Waller's work, and its reception and use, relates to a problem I want to focus on here. Ethnographic studies of schools, and perhaps especially of urban schools, have a paradoxical quality. On the one hand, the ethnographic study of schools has a long and honorable pedigree. Waller published his book in 1932, and work in the tradition has never stopped. Community studies usually pay attention to schools and education, and many researchers have spent years in close unfettered observation in schools. On the other hand, ethnographic studies of schools always have been suspect in the field of education, if not in the fields of anthropology and sociology in which the tradition originated. Ethnographic studies have been suspect even though they frequently produce results the face validity of which is apparent, and even though they do not have the obvious flaws of other styles of research common in schools.

Suspicion toward ethnography shows up in many ways. The most obvious—at least the way it most often comes to my attention—is the defensive posture of people in education who do such work. They are not neurotically and unrealistically defensive, either; they are defensive because they are always being attacked. Ethnographers of education do not receive the professional courtesy that allows unavoidable and irremediable flaws in one's methods to go unchallenged. Every version of research on schools has such problems, yet most of it gets done. But examining committees approve experimental research designs with well-known but conventionally accepted flaws, while balking at students' proposals to do ethnographic research. So I get a lot of phone calls from students and young faculty in education who are looking for legitimation for what they want to do; I'm sure that most people in the field get similar calls all the time. Our flaws have to be accounted for and justified every time—unless we meet among ourselves, and even then much of our attention is devoted to the attacks we will face when we get home.

Why should ethnographic research in education produce good results and still have such a bad reputation? This paradox has two major causes. One is the way scientific research in education came to be used to justify the failures and discriminatory results of the operation of educational institutions. The other is the inability of ethnographic research to be useful, in that or any other way, to educational practitioners.

Anthropology Isn't Psychology

Education, as a field of professional scholarly activity and as a public institution, was captured early by the field of psychology. The premise was that education consisted of putting information and skills into the heads of children and other ignorant people. It thus needed a science of learning and, secondarily, of teaching (as opposed, for instance, to a science of school organizations or educational situations). The science that could provide the knowledge on which to base methods of teaching was psychology, the science of the inside of people's heads. This coincided with psychology's decisive turn toward scientism, experimental modes of thought and procedure, and quantification. I'm not familiar enough with the history of psychology to know why this happened, or how and when it did, but it certainly happened. And education people, looking for theories and methods to justify a "professional" approach to their own work, found everything they needed there.

We all know what followed. First came the enormous growth and success of the testing industry, which quickly assumed authority in areas of major educational concern. Psychological scientists devised tests, some allegedly measuring native ability, others allegedly measuring achievement. As a further consequence, scientific students of the process and institutions of education began their never-ending discoveries of "how best to" do whatever someone who ran schools and similar institutions thought ought to be done. They discovered, for instance, how best to teach children to read. The only thing wrong with these discoveries was the rapidity with which they were replaced by new, contradictory discoveries. In this, education resembled the entire field of child development on which it has always been parasitical. As we all know from our own experiences as children, if not as parents, child development is the field that for decades alternately has advised everyone, on the basis of good scientific evidence, to feed their babies on demand or on a schedule.

Why did the institutions and leaders of education accept the authority of such a patently fallible group of authorities? I want to develop a hypothesis here, although I have not done the work required to verify it. Briefly, the idea is that increasingly over the decades institutions of education found themselves in a situation in which they had to prove that they were being fair, in the face of substantial and obvious evidence that they were not. In that situation, quantitative scientific psychology provided the required proof. I'll begin the argument by noting that education's swoon into the arms of quantitative scientific psychology coincided with the broad democratization of public education. State and federal governments began to believe that every child was entitled to an education provided free of charge by the state and that every child was capable of profiting from such an education.

I accept the first of those propositions philosophically, and I believe that the second one is empirically true, but contingent. Every child *can* learn what an education is supposed to give, but not all children can learn it taught in the same way, nor can they all learn it on the same schedule. The routinization of education that came with its growth as an industry—its development of standardized methods to be applied *en masse* to batches of students (to hark back to another theme of Erving Goffman's)—meant that everyone who came to school had to be equipped physically, mentally, culturally, and in every other way not just to learn but to learn something presented in just *one* of the many ways it might have been presented. People who could have learned something taught in "way X" are out of luck if it is only taught in "way Y" in their school. Similarly, someone who could have learned a body of material in 15 weeks may fail if it comes in a 10-week package.

(The latter point sticks in my mind because of my daughter's experience some years ago, when she switched from San Francisco State College [as it was then known] to the University of California at Berkeley. She reported that, while the courses in calculus in both places covered the same material from the same book, the Berkeley class covered it in 10 weeks while State took 15. I will leave it as an elementary exercise for the reader to work out the arguments by which Berkeley faculty might then have "proved" that this difference made Berkeley a better school. Anyone who wants extra credit also can assess the logical basis and adequacy of those arguments.)

If an institution purports to do a job uniformly over an entire population, basing its claim for financial and other support on the successful doing of that job, and then fails to do it, the people responsible for the institution (and thus for its failures) have some explaining to do. Suppose public health officials had guaranteed to wipe out an epidemic disease like polio by following a procedure of universal innoculation. Suppose, further, that they succeeded in wiping it out in that portion of the population with the highest income, but that rates, while coming down some, were still high in poorer classes. Insofar as they had guaranteed universal results, they would have a big public relations problem.

The proponents of public health might have explained their failure by some characteristic of the people they had not been able to protect—a genetic flaw, perhaps, which made a vaccine not work. That is just what educators did. Rather than ask why their methods did not work universally, as they had claimed, they "found" that certain measurable characteristics of students accounted for their ability to learn. As for the others—well, either you have it or you don't, and they just don't have it. Too bad! I am, of course, caricaturing a complex matter here and making unnecessarily cruel fun of serious and well-intentioned people. Or . . . is that really the gist of that argument?

Whatever the fairness of my caricature, educators did have a problem. They had promised the moon but could not deliver it. It might have been better not to promise the moon, but they were stuck with that. So, as the saying goes, they blamed the victim. But many people will not accept that diagnosis, most of all the representatives of the people who have been characterized as wanting. How can you persuade skeptics to accept your diagnosis? That is where the scientific psychology of the 1920s and beyond becomes useful. Almost everyone accepts, as a practical matter, what seem patently obvious facts of everyday life, no more than common sense: some people are smarter than others and that is why some people fail in school and others don't.

But how can we tell who is smarter and who is dumber, so that we can see if that is true? More to the point, how—if we are running a school system—can we make those distinctions in such a way that no one can complain that we are being unfair? This brings us to the heart of my speculation. If we are in perpetual danger of being accused of favoritism, discrimination, or racism, we need to be able to show skeptics, legislators, friends, and enemies, that we reached our conclusions by a method that is fair and defensible. We cannot explain that we are promoting Dick and Jane because they come from good families and are keeping Tom and Harriet back because they don't; not in the America we live in, even if that is the reason, and even if there are plenty of countries in which that explanation might be acceptable.

Which methods are fair and impartial? Bitter experience has shown that almost any method that leaves discretion in the hands of the people using it can be misused in a discriminatory way. Any method that lets a judge's "subjective" judgments come into play may produce a quite improper result, improper in the sense of being offensive to the standards we want to uphold—a discriminatory result instead of a fair one. (I am not talking here about the results of fair methods that produce the results discrimination might have, e.g., the racial segregation produced by a "color-blind" sorting on economic variables.)

So everyone agrees that "objective" methods are better. Objective methods seem most clearly objective when they are quantitative, when the judge seems to be doing no more than laying down a ruler alongside something and nothing where it falls on the ruler's scale; no room for subjective discrimination in that, or not much. If there is unfairness, it is built into the procedure. It is part of the ruler, and that is where it has to be looked for, the way Allison Davis and others looked for it and found it in the construction of intelligence tests. But those discoveries don't have what is called "face validity," and are much less convincing than the obvious parallels between test results and common observation. Kids who test dumb usually look and act dumb in school. That their dumbness may be the result of deep cultural differences between what they know and feel comfortable doing and what the schools require doesn't alter that.

Let me remind you of two well-known cases. Murray and Rosalie Wax and Robert Dumont reported, in their 1964 monograph *Formal Education in an American Indian Community*, that the Native American children who tested dumb, and who also looked and acted stupid in reservation schools, were responding to a setting that systematically devalued what they did know (including the Sioux language) so that they could not display their abilities. They resented it and acted accordingly. Similarly, Jane Mercer reported in *Labeling the Mentally Retarded* (and here I simplify some complex relationships) that mental retardation was a disease children got by going to school. Before they started school, others might (or might not) think them a little slow to catch on to things, but they could perform adequately. When they got to school, however, and were tested, school personnel "discovered" their retardation. Since these children almost always were from groups whose culture differed significantly from that of the school (Hispanic or black), they had the usual problems and looked dumb enough to make the diagnosis seem reasonable.

Because so many children's troubles with schools are based on cultural differences of this kind, the schools are in a particularly difficult position. The children they fail with are often members of political minorities of whom the schools are specially wary. Courts and legislatures alike may want to catch them discriminating. They don't want to be caught doing that. On the other hand, other constituencies want to prevent what they define as "reverse discrimination."

The schools cannot win. What they *can* do is use methods that they can claim are scientific so that the troubles that arise will be visited on someone else. In other words, objective, quantitative, scientific research provides educators with defensible explanations for their failure to deliver on the various and contradictory promises of educators. That prejudices the entire education establishment in favor of such research and against anything else, especially against qualitative research that relies on the sensitivities and seemingly unrestrained judgments of individual researchers.

Ethnographic research therefore runs afoul of a deeply held belief, one embedded in the operations of major institutions. I don't mean to accuse educators of venality. I don't think they say, "Hey, if we let people do this kind of research it will spoil our explanation of why we can't do the job." But I do think that reasons like that are part of what lies behind the religious zeal with which people in the education industry espouse quantitative research. That zeal, in turn, helps account for their difficulties with, and complaints about, ethnography.

Anthropology Studies (and Judges) Everybody

Thus, educators, responsible for the successes and failures of educational institutions, understandably mistrust ethnographic studies that provide no rationale for the instution's failure to produce acceptable results with lower class students. Worse yet, ethnographic research, with its emphasis on understanding social organizations as wholes, makes it impossible to confine research to uncovering the shortcomings of students. If you study schools by giving students tests, you may find out that the students have not learned what they are supposed to, but you will be studying the teachers and administrators only indirectly. Ethnographers, however, routinely study *everyone* connected with the school. Most ethnographers of schools have had to deal with the surprise (and sometimes shock) of teachers and administrators who discover that the ethnographers aren't just going to look at the students or subordinate members of the organization, but regard everyone in it, from top to bottom, as fair game for investigation. "You mean you are going to study us?" That immediately, and always, opens up for them the possibility that we are somehow going to find out that "it" (whatever "it" is) is their fault. They may not know what "it" is, but they can usually see that someone who hangs around long enough, nosing into everything, is bound to find *something* that is their fault. If we insist on sitting in their offices and observing them at work, and not just observing students, we may find out some things they'd rather we didn't.

In fact, we will *always and necessarily* find out those things. Institutions, in the voices of those who lead them and thus are responsible for them to the rest of the world, always lie about how well they do their jobs. "Lie" is a strong word; the people involved probably prefer to think of what I am talking about as statements of goals that somehow turned out not to be as easy to achieve as they had hoped. But people who don't quite live up to their goals year after year perhaps ought to be more cautious, so I'll stick with "lie."

Ethnographers—who hang around forever—are going to see the reality behind the statements of intention. Worse yet, they are going to see that the reality is no accident but is built into the fabric of the organization. Administrators and others involved in an institution do not mind the discovery of "a few bad apples in the barrel." (That is the usual phrasing in complaints about studies of police departments.) But they do mind the conclusion that the barrel makes good apples into rotten ones, and that is what ethnographers always are discovering and saying.

In fact, all research on schools has overtones of evaluation. We can't help that. Even if we don't intend our work to be evaluative, the people we study will take it that way, for the good reason that everyone else does and will hold them responsible for whatever we find out that anyone thinks untoward. The quotation from Goffman cited earlier attests to that. It is hard for any of us to avoid making those grossly evaluative judgments ourselves. When we thus "expose" the inadequacies of one level of an organization, the people at the higher levels don't mind, as long as the results don't suggest that it was *their* fault. Even ethnographies draw boundaries around organizations, leaving some things out of the field of what is to be studied. So long as we leave the higher-ups out, they won't mind a little ethnography. But eventually we almost always get them into the picture and, if we don't, someone else will look at what we have found, take the logical step, and do research at the next higher level. The investigations of the My Lai massacre are a case in point.

Studying higher-ups leads to some funny confrontations that make clear the difference between scientific organization and the bureaucratic hierarchy and self-protectiveness of schools. Years ago, two researchers produced a book that described sociologically the operations of a well-regarded educational program. They had done their research in the town where their university was located. When the book was published and the school principal saw it, he called the chairman of their department and asked, angrily, "Do you let your people publish stuff like this?"

Anthropology Is No Help

Beginning in the 1960s educators lost some of their autonomy, some of their control over their institutions. The giant sums that came to them as a part of the national effort to raise the educational levels of poor people, and especially poor blacks, carried some conditions. The most important for my argument is that the schools got no blank checks. They had to produce results, and it would not do to blame the children for failure. That was exactly why they were getting the new money: to discover or create new ways of teaching that would be successful with children for whom the old ways had failed. The shift from an emphasis on learning—what made learning hard for children—changed to an emphasis on programs and what about programs made them fail to produce the promised results.

Conventional evaluations might say you had failed to do the job, but could not tell you, except in the most indirect and tortured way, what caused the failure. People at various levels of the educational establishment worried about this in different ways. Those who handed out money for experiments that were supposed to produce startling new results worried about being cheated and wondered whether the experiments were being carried out as promised. If there were results, did they come from the new methods that were being touted as producing them, or were they an artifact of the selection of those exposed to the new methods? Were the experimenters "creaming" the population, attributing to new methods results that were really due to the superior ability of those who took part in the experiment? If so, such chicanery proved hard to document. School administrators and educational researchers are skilled manipulators of records. So it seemed like a good idea to observe these programs closely, and to have the observations made by people who were not part of the educational enterprise. Such people might be more "objective," even though they didn't use objective methods.

From another direction, many school people sincerely wanted to do a better job for students with whom they hitherto had failed. They understood and accepted all the liberal arguments. What they needed were new methods that worked. Many of them distrusted "objective" scientific research that evaluated them and found them wanting or that produced yet another in the long list of "innovations" that soon proved no better than those of their predecessors. Conventional psychologically-oriented testing research could not help them, they were convinced, and they saw hope in the "depth" of ethnography, in its unarguable closeness to the facts of everyday school life, in what had to be its relevance to their problems.

Both groups were disappointed, although in different ways. The basis of the disappointment, most generally, was that anthropologists and sociologists remained social scientists, oriented toward their native disciplines rather than toward the discipline and institutions of education. If the people monitoring the new experiments expected anthropologists to police the experiments they were supporting, they were wrong. Anthropologists have good reason to avoid working for the established powers, having been stung on that score before. We all know that we cannot continue to do research if we go around telling bosses that the workers are goofing or stealing. If we tell research administrators that their experiments are phony, we will not do any more research.

I'm not sure how anthropological researchers solved this problem in all the places they encountered it. It was one of the great difficulties. Even when anthropologists were quite firm in their refusal to squeal that way, guilty teachers and local administrators (who often really did have something to hide) worried that they might. If a local administrator received money for an innovation but used it to cover routine expenses and never did the experiment—who should the anthropologists tell about that? This often erupted as an argument over who would be allowed to see the anthropologists' field notes, in which the incriminating evidence likely was to be found. Administrators, concerned with running a tight ship, could not understand why they were denied relevant evidence. Social scientists remained loyal to disciplinary standards, for in the long run they would make their professional lives in social science, not in school organizations. Concerned with the long-range consequences, for themselves and the field, of letting their data be used for nonscientific purposes, they would not cooperate.

Similarly, anthropologists and sociologists were unlikely to produce "solutions" to the problems of educators who wanted to do better. The understanding produced by our research and theory may be fine-grained and detailed enough to produce solutions, but not ones that will meet the criteria that operate in the educational setting. What I mean is this: We often can see what is causing the trouble, why some technique of teaching or administration is having an effect exactly opposite to what people want and hope for. But what we see as the cause is not something the people who look to us for help can do anything about. Or, at least, they can only do something about it at some cost so great that they are not willing to pay it.

Here is an example. When Blanche Geer, Everett Hughes, Anselm Strauss, and I produced a draft of our study of a medical school (eventually published as *Boys in White*), the doctors in that school who read it—the more thoughtful and dedicated teachers—wanted us to make recommendations. For instance, we described (apparently convincingly) how students studied for exams. Student study methods were the usual ones: cram as much factual material as you can into your head just before the test and forget it all afterward. That appalled teachers. They wanted students to take a more professional attitude toward their work. We explained to them that they provoked this sort of studying by the kind of exams they gave, which called for exactly that sort of fragmented factual knowledge. "If you want students to study differently," we said, "you can do it by giving them a different kind of exam. What do you want them to know?" They wanted students to be able to make a physical examination, take a medical history, establish a diagnosis, and plan a course of treatment. Our ethnographic knowledge immediately suggested how this could be done: give each student one or two patients to examine and treat, and then let the teachers evaluate how well they had done it.

The faculty looked glum when we said that. What was wrong? That, one said, would take a lot of time, and they all had their research to attend to and their own patients to take care of. Our solution would work, of course, but it wasn't *practical*. That is the difficulty. What a social scientist identifies as a cause is usually something the people can't do anything about. So we fail the serious educational reformers on the firing line as well.

Why do we produce such useless advice? Because we are loyal to the traditions of our disciplines, which tell us that these are the kinds of answers worth having, the only kind that will work in the long run. (I believe that, but I can see that it means that practitioners are never going to be happy with the results of my research in educational institutions.)

The implication of all this is that ethnographers of education are never going to work their way out of their bad reputation. Not, at least, as long as they keep on doing good work and the schools keep failing at their job. Not as long as we come up with impractical solutions to chronic problems. Some fun!

4

Knowledge Accumulation

Three Views on the Nature and Role of Knowledge in Social Science

Jennifer C. Greene

This chapter examines the perspectives of postpositivism, interpretivism,[1] and critical theory on issues related to social scientific knowledge accumulation. The discussion is spirited by efforts both to honor the paradigmatic pluralism of this era and, given my own strong pragmatic orientation, to question what it all means for the practical import of our work. For each inquiry framework, in turn, honor is paid via an introductory sketch, both the form and the substance of which are intended to be illustrative; a brief review of the paradigmatic assumptions most germane to knowledge issues; and a focused discussion of the nature of knowledge and its links to the form and function of knowledge accumulation. Then, the challenge is offered via a critique of the implications of each paradigm's view of knowledge accumulation for the purpose and role of science in our world, with an emphasis on the interrelationships of theory, research, and practice.

As a baseline for this discussion, the perspectives of the conventional inquiry framework on these knowledge accumulation issues are offered first. Within our long-standing scientific tradition, knowledge has been equated with theory, where theory comprises a precise, testable network of universal, lawlike relationships among clearly defined variables, a network that is determinate, explanatory, predictive, and verifiable. In conventional science, theories are developed, tested, and refined through empirical research. So, research is intentionally cumulative, and hallmarks of good research studies include clearly defined hypotheses derived from existing theory and results that take the form of generalizable theoretical propositions. The task of the scientist is thus to develop theory. Once developed, scientific theories can be used to address problems or advance life quality in the world of practice. In conventional science, that is, there is a "categorical distinction" between research and practice, between the development of scientific theory and applications of this theory to practical problems (Bernstein, 1976, p. 44).

In relationship to this conventional portrayal of knowledge accumulation, three alternative images frame the present discussion. As the paradigm that represents "old uncertainties unthroned, but not abolished" (Cook, 1985, p. 37), postpositivism also embraces a *social engineering* view of the role and purpose of science. Interpretivism, however, seeks not to adjust the conventional framework but to replace it. With its grounding in phenomenology, hermeneutics, and value pluralism, interpretivism's perspective on the role of social science in the world is likened to *storytelling*.

Critical theory rejects both postpositivism and interpretivism as stand-alone paradigms because of their silence on issues of politics, values, and ideology. This critical inquiry framework seeks to make such issues central to science, thereby intertwining the purpose of science with that of *political engagement and action.*

This chapter then concludes by identifying key issues that cut across these diverse images in the spirit of what Gareth Morgan calls "reflective conversation" (Morgan, 1983, p. 374). In this era of paradigmatic pluralism, Morgan urges such conversation as a way of facilitating more thoughtful research practice, and especially greater responsibility among social scientists, for "their role in making and remaking social science as we know it today" (Morgan, 1983, p. 376).

Stances

As one additional set of introductory comments, I believe it is important to share my own predispositions regarding the three paradigms and the knowledge accumulation issues to be addressed. These comprise four main themes. First, regarding my own expertise or my qualifications for this discussion, I can claim modest mastery of the foundations and perspectives of both postpositivism and interpretivism but consider myself more of a novice with respect to critical theory. My discussion of this latter inquiry framework should thus be viewed as more tentative. Second, my paradigmatic loyalties continue to be troublesomely divided. I have substantially rejected the conventional paradigm that initially shaped my identity as a social scientist but, as yet, am unwilling to swear allegiance to a single alternative. I have opinions about various aspects of different paradigms, but, in the main, I remain a learner, intensely curious and eager to continue learning about the multiple inquiry frameworks that abound in this pluralistic era (Lincoln, 1989). Third, I count myself among those "who believe that science is a remarkably different validity-producing social system [say, than the arts or religion] and at the same time are puzzled as to how this can be so" (Campbell, 1988, p. 498). With the nearly universal recognition that values, ideology, and beliefs permeate the very fabric of social science, what then sets the logic and validity of science apart from any other human endeavor? Finally, and perhaps most important, I believe that all of this self-conscious and often rarified discourse about the assumptional bases and coherence of our work really does matter. This is reflected primarily in this chapter's explicit emphasis on the practical significance of social science. Miles and Huberman (1984) have argued that epistemological purity does not get research done. In counterpoint, I would contend that epistemological integrity does get meaningful research done right. The important "evaluation criteria that can be brought to bear on the nature of knowledge ... relate [primarily] to the way knowledge serves to guide and shape ourselves as human beings—to the consequences of knowledge, in the sense of what knowledge does to and for humans" (Morgan, 1983, p. 373).

Postpositivism: Social Science as Social Engineering

Sketch

Thomas Cook's *Postpositivist Critical Multiplism* (1985) is a leading example of postpositivist thought. This approach to inquiry aims to "approximate the ultimately unknowable truth through the use of processes that critically triangulate from a variety of perspectives on what is worth knowing and what is known" (Cook, 1985, p. 57). The multiplism argument is rooted in the classic methodological ideas of multiple operationalism (Campbell & Fiske, 1959) and between-method triangulation (Denzin, 1978; Webb, Campbell, Schwartz, & Sechrest, 1966). But, in direct response to the philosophical attacks on conventional science, Cook proposes such additional forms of *methodological* multiplism as multiple analyses of the same data set. He also extends the triangulation argument to *theory-related* forms of multiplism, including, for example, the testing of multiple explanatory models for a given set of data (rather than assessing the goodness of fit of a single model). Further, to redress the disappointing failure of social science to contribute meaningfully to the reforms of the Great Society era, Cook advances forms of multiplism that acknowledge the *politics and value pluralism* of such policy contexts, for example, the inclusion of multiple and diverse constituencies in formulating the research agenda.

The Nature of Postpositivist Knowledge and Key Underlying Assumptions

Cook's proposal for critical multiplism, in concert with the remarks on postpositivist "myths and realities" by Denis Phillips (1990a) in the present forum, provide a view of the nature of knowledge in postpositivist thought.

Knowledge remains theory in postpositivism, where theory is construed as a "model" (Cook, 1985) or a "huge fishnet" (Phillips, 1990a, p. 36) of complex, mutually interacting casual relationships among specified constructs or variables. That is, postpositivists believe that human phenomena can best be explained in terms of causal relationships. But this causality is assumed to be complex, multiplistic, and interactive. "Human and social relationships are more like pretzels than single-headed arrows from A to B . . . more like convoluted multivariate statistical interactions than simple main effects" (Cook, 1985, p. 25). Moreover, good theories accurately explain and predict human phenomena but may or may not actually correspond to truth. For, given the realist ontological stance of postpositivism—the belief that there is a natural world out there and that our task as scientists is to know and understand it, in order to explain and predict it—truth remains a "regulative ideal" (Phillips, 1987). However, because "no longer can it be claimed there are any *absolutely authoritative foundations* upon which scientific knowledge is based" (Phillips, 1990a; see also Bernstein, 1983), truth is acknowledged as "ultimately unknowable" (Cook, 1985). Hence, theory in postpositivism is more like *small theory* and knowledge claims are concomitantly more modest. "Any return to grand theory in human sciences . . . is a selective and wishful interpretation of social science research" (Overman, 1988, p. xvi).

In fact, postpositivist knowledge claims or theoretical propositions are viewed, from Dewey, as "warranted assertibility" (Phillips, 1990a) or as established regularities or probabilities about human phenomena rather than as universal laws that govern human behavior. Knowledge claims gain warrant when they are supported by carefully marshaled, objective evidence and when their argument is credible, coherent, and consensual, in other words, when they have survived a *critical tradition* of evaluative challenges and unsuccessful refutations (Cook, 1983, 1985; Phillips, 1990b). This notion of a critical tradition, derived from Popper, constitutes the essence of Cook's multiplism proposal; he advocates multiplism precisely to invite open criticism from diverse and pluralistic perspectives. "So long as ultimate truth is not accessible, the process of assigning validity is social and partly dependent upon a consensus achieved in debate" (Cook, 1983, p. 89).

Survival of the critical tradition is similarly integral to the postpositivist conception of objectivity. For all alternative inquiry frameworks, acceptance of Hanson's insight that no observations are theory or value neutral (Phillips, 1987) forces either a reformulation or a rejection of the conventional view of objectivity as freedom from bias. Postpositivists have opted for reformulation, arguing for a view of objectivity as "critical intersubjective verifiability across heterogeneous perspectives" (Cook, 1983, pp. 83–84; see also Campbell, 1984). Knowledge claims so verified are more objective and thus more warranted or more likely to be true. This reconstrual of objectivity also shifts its locus from the individual scientist and the context of discovery to the "community of inquirers" and the context of justification (Phillips, 1990b). "The objectivity of science is not a matter of the individual scientists but rather the social result of their mutual criticism" (Popper, quoted in Phillips, 1990b).

Knowledge Accumulation in Postpositivism

With a view of knowledge as small but convoluted, pretzel-like theory and a belief in truth as a regulative ideal, postpositivism maintains as the goal of empirical research the development of generalizable theoretical propositions, yet views such generalizations as attainable only tentatively and probabilistically. "Most scientific results have the character of hypotheses, i.e., sentences for which the evidence is inconclusive . . . [and which are] liable to be superseded in the course of scientific progress" (Popper, quoted in Campbell, 1984, p. 4). Further, with a commitment to an open critical tradition and a concomitantly muted confidence in methodology, postpositivism's empirical quest for knowledge emphasizes replicability across heterogeneous populations, settings, times, perspectives (see, for example, Cronbach, 1982) and deductive, critical refutation. Scientific generalizations gain warrant only through such replication and criticism. Thus knowledge in postpositivism is accumulated or small theory developed not via the single definitive study but from programs or traditions of empirical research, and past research serves less as the foundation and more as the catalyst for future inquiry.

As Howe (1985) and Phillips (1990a) describe this relationship between research and knowledge growth in postpositivism, empirical evidence can either provisionally confirm a theoretical hypothesis or prove inconsistent with it. If the latter, and the evidence is accepted as credible and thus falsifying, then postpositivists can use this evidence in a variety of ways. No one specific change, i.e., rejection of the given hypothesis, is necessitated (Phillips, 1990a). This is because the empirical test does not apply to this hypothesis alone but to the entire theory within which it is embedded. So, different scientists may decide to modify different portions of the relevant theory or even to make no theoretical modifications, awaiting further evidence. That is, decisions about how to modify theories and thus contribute to knowledge growth require professional judgment; they cannot be made mechanically (Phillips, 1990a). Nonetheless, while acknowledging the role of professional judgment in scientific growth, postpositivists continue to question how such growth can be rationally justified. And on this, Phillips asserts, "there has been much debate, but little consensus" (Phillips, 1990a).

So Why Do Social Science?

The Postpositivist Response

> The ideology of the experimenting society is a method ideology, not a content ideology. That is, it proposes ways of testing and revising theories of optimal political-economic-social organization rather than proposing a specific political and economic system.
>
> Campbell (1984, p. 16)

> [The social scientist's job] is to interpret the world, not to change it; he [or she] interprets it by offering and testing theoretical explanations. . . . Therefore, he [or she] endorses a categorical distinction between theory and practice or action.
>
> Bernstein (1976, p. 44)

These quotes well illustrate the *intended* political and value neutrality of postpositivism and its continued separation from the world of practice. The line demarcating social science from practice is more permeable in postpositivism than in conventional science. For example, Cook argues that social science must interface with the pluralistic politics and values of applied contexts, especially policy contexts, and that social scientists must not just "build the restricted set of assumptions of the powerful into their research" (Cook, 1985, p. 37). Also arguing largely within the context of applied social policy, Campbell (1984, p. 4) quotes Popper as saying, "Practice is not the enemy of theoretical knowledge, but the most valuable incentive to it."

Nonetheless, the postpositivist social scientist's main job is to participate in the critical community of inquirers whose collective task it is to develop warranted scientific knowledge. The individual scientist's participation is marked by his or her own values, theoretical predispositions, and beliefs, thereby generating a critical but not a normative warrant for the community's collective product of theory. This theory then is to be used to enhance or extend the quality of human endeavors in the world of practice. "How people use the theory to guide practice is not a question of science but of politics" (Popkewitz, 1984, p. 39). So, practical action is a potentiality of the theory because the theory contains valued instrumental knowledge about manipulanda (Cook, 1983), but theory and action remain separate. And so, belying its claims for neutrality and consistent with the character of social engineering, postpositivism clearly rests on a value foundation of utilitarianism, efficiency, and instrumentality.

Interpretivism: Social Science as Storytelling[2]

Sketch and Key Interpretivist Assumptions

The constructivist paradigm developed and continuingly nurtured by Yvonna Lincoln and Egon Guba (Lincoln, this volume; see also Guba & Lincoln, 1981, 1987, 1988; Lincoln, 1988, 1989; Lincoln & Guba, 1985, 1986) constitutes a major example of interpretivist thought and a significant influence within contemporary paradigm debates. The following is a brief sketch of this paradigm, drawn largely from Lincoln (1990) in a form that approximates its own voice.

The impersonality of the small conference room—its institutional-beige walls lacking any adornment and its hard, uncomfortable black chairs arranged in neat precise rows like soldiers on a parade ground—only heightened the drama unfolding with the current speaker at the front of the room. She spoke of a constructivist paradigm for social inquiry, a paradigm erected from the rubble that ensued when the tower of conventional science, besieged by the batterings of the new philosophy of science, finally toppled. Constructivism, she argued, is based on an entirely different, synergistic set of assumptions about the world and the manner in which we can know it.

One such assumption is that "reality is a social, and, therefore, multiple, construction" (Lincoln, 1990, p. 67). As social, this reality derives from human interactions aimed at meaning making, comprises intersubjective meanings that "exist only by social agreement or consensus among participants in a [given] context," and thus is multiplistic as well as ever changing. Moreover, "the ways in which [humans] interpret their own actions and those of others are not externally related to, but constitutive of, those actions" and of human beliefs, practices, and institutions more generally (Bernstein, 1976, p. 156). Other constructivist assumptions are that "knower and known are interactive, inseparable" and that "inquiry is value-bound" (Lincoln & Guba, 1985, p. 37). These represent, the speaker noted, not just acceptance of Hanson's insight but actual celebration of it "as an opportunity to be exploited" (Lincoln & Guba, 1985, p. 101) as in maximizing the power of the dialectical interaction between a cooperating respondent and a human inquiry instrument to generate meaningful understanding.

Beyond these bold strokes of scientific philosophy, the other contribution to this drama was the speaker's integration of the personal with the scientific in her presentation. She spoke of her immersion in constructivism as an "enlightening, curious, idiographic, and piquant voyage" (Lincoln, 1990). She shared her struggles to respond to critics along the way and to make whole and coherent *her* vision of social inquiry. As we share many value stances, my vision of constructivism would be similar. But I can't help but imagine that there are constructivists with different personal values, and then I wonder, what do their visions of constructivism look like?

The Nature of Interpretivist Knowledge

From Lincoln and others, interpretivist knowledge comprises the reconstruction of intersubjective meanings, the interpretive understanding of the meanings humans construct in a given context and how these meanings interrelate to form a whole. Any given interpretive reconstruction is idiographic, time- and place-bound; multiple reconstructions are pluralistic, divergent, even conflictual. Hence, interpretivist knowledge resembles more context-specific working hypotheses than generalizable propositions warranting certainty or even probability. But what is the character, the form and substance, of these working hypotheses and thus of interpretivist knowledge?

- Interpretivist knowledge is grounded knowledge, not developed from armchair speculations or elegant deductive reasoning but both discovered and justified from the field-based, inductive *methodology* (Guba & Lincoln, 1988) of interpretivist inquiry.
- Interpretivist knowledge represents emic knowledge or inside understanding of the perspectives and meanings of those in the setting being studied, and it encompasses both propositional and tacit information (see Phillips, 1987, pp. 92–94, for a critique of this claim). That is, the understanding communicated in

interpretivist knowledge comes not only from its words but also from the broadly shared contexts of natural experience within which it is embedded.

- Interpretivist knowledge constitutes not nomothetic models but holistic "pattern theories or webs of mutual and plausible influence" (Lincoln, 1990, p. 77), webs that reflect a hermeneutic intertwinement of part and whole and a view of knowledge that is more "circular" or "amoebalike" than hierarchic and pyramid like (Lincoln, 1990, p. 84).
- Interpretivist understanding also aims for internal consistency and coherence. "Correspondence theories identify truth with a relationship *between* language and reality; coherence theories identify truth with internal consistency among claims *within* a language."
- And interpretivist knowledge is value-bound and hence "conflictual," "problematic and contested . . . locally and politically situated" (Lincoln, 1990, p. 80). Moreover, "from this [interpretivist] perspective, social inquiry is meaningful only because it does involve values" (J. Smith, 1984, p. 47).

Knowledge Accumulation in Interpretivism

As is evident by this portrayal of interpretivist knowledge, interpretivism denies the possibility of universal social laws and empirical generalizations.[3] If all knowledge is socially constructed, value bound, and indeterminate, "only time- and context-bound working hypotheses (idiographic statements) are possible" (Lincoln & Guba, 1985, p. 37). So, interpretivist research generates working hypotheses that are connected not to a priori theory but to a context-specific, often emergent inquiry problem, which may or may not be informed by existing knowledge.

> The evidence generated by interpretive research is much more likely to be of an evocative rather than a comprehensive kind, to be sustained, rejected, or refined through future studies. The conclusions of one study merely provide a starting point in a continuing cycle of inquiry, which may [or may not] over time serve to generate persuasive patterns of data from which further conclusions can be drawn. (Morgan, 1983, p. 398)

Yet, if all knowledge is context-specific working hypotheses and if research studies may or may not be connected to one another, how is knowledge accumulated within this inquiry framework? What is the meaning of interpretivist scientific progress? Two forms of response to these questions will be offered.

First, within interpretivist circles, the challenge of knowledge accumulation has been primarily addressed by the general concept of *transferability*. This concept shifts the inquirer's responsibility from one of demonstrating generalizability to one of providing sufficient description of the particular context studied so that others may adequately judge the applicability or fit of the inquiry findings to their own context. The locus of judgment about transferability thus also shifts from the inquirer to potential users. (See Cronbach, 1982, for similar themes presented for evaluative inquiry.)

Robert Stake's (1983) *naturalistic generalization* is one version of this transferability concept. Stake argues that "naturalistic generalizations develop within a person as a product of experience. They derive from tacit knowledge of how things are . . . [and] seldom take the form of predictions but lead regularly to expectation." Further, the interpretivist case study can provide a basis for such generalizations because it vicariously communicates natural experience as well as tacit knowledge. The importance of communicating "vicarious, 'déjà vu' experience" is also emphasized in Lincoln's formulation of criteria for constructivist case studies (Lincoln, 1988, 1990). And Lincoln and Guba offer transferability (to replace generalizability) as one of their four trustworthiness criteria for the constructivist inquiry process (Lincoln, 1990; Lincoln & Guba, 1985, 1986). Regarding the latter, Lincoln and Guba contend that the inquirer must provide, at minimum, a thick description of the inquiry context and of the transactions or processes observed in that context that are relevant to the inquiry problem (Lincoln & Guba, 1985, p. 362), though they also acknowledge that "it is by no means clear how 'thick' a thick description needs to be" (Lincoln & Guba, 1986, p. 77). Then, "the final judgment [about transferability] . . . is vested in the person seeking to make the transfer" (Lincoln & Guba, 1985, p. 217). Such persons may be interested readers, other researchers, or practitioners, lending multiple meanings to the transferability concept. In short, interpretivist inquirers must provide for the possibility of transferability, but its actualization—in the form of scientific knowledge accumulation or enhanced practice—depends on the interests of potential users.

Second, Lincoln's comments in the present forum openly invite further work on these issues of knowledge accumulation within constructivism. Arguing that we do not yet have a language for talking about forms of knowledge that are not hierarchic or taxonomic, neither do we have a language for conceptualizing connections between nonhierarchic knowledge forms. Maybe, she argues,

> we ought to be talking not about "building blocks of science" but about extended sophistication, or the artistic and expressive process of creatively conjoining elements in ways that are fresh and new. We ought to think of bridging, . . . or of synthesizing, . . . or of some other linkage processes. . . . we have no models for scientific knowledge that account for nonhierarchic learning, and we may have to borrow from the poet, the artist, the madman, the mystic. (Lincoln, 1990, p. 85)

This importance of this challenge is underscored by the problematic character of the relationship of interpretivist knowledge to the world of practice, as discussed next.

So Why Do Social Science?

The Interpretivist Response

As grounded knowledge, interpretivist knowledge is embedded within the world of practice. Being value laden, interpretivist knowledge is not neutral or even critically neutral but *interested* knowledge, embued with the normative pluralism of the world of practice. Being value-laden, interpretivist knowledge is also permeated by the values and interests of the inquirer. Constructivism does aim to monitor and minimize the intrusion of inquirer biases into the inquiry process. When such reflexivity is successful, the inquiry findings represent primarily the meanings and values of respondents, and the inquirer's role becomes one of translator or intermediary among differing communities (Bredo & Feinberg, 1982b, pp. 430–431). Yet, any efforts to mute inquirer interests can be only partially successful at best. As Lincoln observed, the "research process itself [is] a political endeavor" (Lincoln, 1990, p. 70).

Lincoln's interests as an inquirer are oriented around those of inquiry stakeholders and include fairness, action, and empowerment. She is seeking "a mainstream rethinking of the role the social sciences play in everyday, ordinary life" (Lincoln, 1990, p. 83), a role that includes stakeholders as collaborators in inquiry, that fairly presents the constructions and values of all stakeholders in a setting, and that enhances the ability of stakeholders "to take action, to engage the political arena on behalf of oneself or one's referent stakeholder or participant group" (Lincoln, 1990, p. 72). I believe these interests reflect Lincoln's vital immersions in the domains of social policy and program evaluation. And, as noted earlier, I share some of this experience and many of these values. But I believe they are our values as inquirers and not inherently those of the interpretivist inquiry paradigm.

Rather, the interpretivist paradigm must be characterized as value relative. Interpretivist knowledge inevitably reflects the values of the inquirer, even as it seeks to reconstruct others' sense of meaning and supporting beliefs. Further, as argued previously, uses of this knowledge depend on the interests of potential users, whether other researchers, policymakers, practitioners, or social program beneficiaries. So, even though interpretivist knowledge is embedded within the normative, pluralistic world of practice, interpretivist inquiry "is not directly [or necessarily] concerned with judging, evaluating, or condemning existing forms of social and political reality, or with changing the world" but with describing and understanding its constitutive meaning (Bernstein, 1976, p. 169). And so, given its value relativity, common goals of interpretivist inquiry can only be to enrich human discourse, "to bring us in touch with the lives of strangers . . . to converse with them" (Geertz, quoted in Rabinow, 1983, p. 66), "to enlarge the conversation" (J. Smith, 1984, p. 390) with our own understandings and our own stories. That is all?

Critical Science: Social Science as Political Engagement

Sketch

The sketch for the third inquiry framework, critical social science, is presented as a conversation, illustrating the communication and dialog essential to critical science. The setting is a community housing agency that seeks adequate housing for homeless and other low-income individuals in the community. The participants are Elena, an agency staff member for the past five years since her graduation from college, and Bill, a middle-aged, unemployed, temporarily homeless steel worker who is one of the agency's more active and outspoken clients.

Elena: Hi Bill. You wanted to talk with me as soon as possible. What's up?

Bill: Hi Elena. How's the bum-and-crazy business these days? Just kidding. Actually, I wanted to know if you heard Marcia Wilcox's talk last night at the YWCA about her research on housing in this town.

Elena: No, I didn't go. I'm really sick of researchers and their so-called facts and figures.

Bill: Well, Marcia was different. She started with history, saying that since the Depression days in this country, federal policy on low-income housing has never been more than an empty promise, or at most a half-hearted one. Oh

Elena: sure, there have been some good guys—and gals—and some good intentions in the government all along. But, these intentions never really had much of chance, because they were opposed by the development interests of business and industry.

Elena: We all know that, that's nothing new. And, besides, these intentions you mentioned—they're not empty or half-hearted at all. They represent the fundamental ideals and values in this county.

Bill: Yes, I know, and Marcia agreed, too. She talked about these values as underlying the intent of federal housing policy over the years. But, as I was saying, this intent has always been opposed by the development interests. *And,* the way our government is set up automatically favors these interests over our ideals. She said something like, the political structure inherently contradicts the values of social policy intent.

Then, Marcia got local—and here is where you should be interested. She said that the same thing happens at the local level, and that in this town, agencies like yours are part of the problem.

Elena: Part of the problem! I don't understand! Our whole reason for being is affordable housing for low-income people. We also have a good working relationship with the Downtown Business Association. And I've always thought that was good political strategy, you know, like the lamb lying down with the lion.

Bill: Yeah, but lying down with them, you're doing a whole lot more than just resting. As Marcia said, you're buying into what they represent. And you're therefore reinforcing a local political situation that, just like national politics, favors growth and development even without trying to do so. These priorities are built into the whole structure of the political system. So, what's really needed are some challenges to this structure. Without them, low-income housing will always remain but a quadrennial campaign promise.

Elena: Like what kinds of challenges?

Bill: Marcia gave us some good leads on this. I've made some phone calls and a group of us are meeting tonight to talk more about her ideas. Want to join us?

On Critical Social Science

This sketch is intended to illustrate three key knowledge-related attributes of critical social science: its embeddedness in history and ideology; its own ideology, as revealed in the meaning of *critical*; and its dialectical synthesis of historical dualism. (Critiques of these and other tenets of critical social science are offered by Bredo & Feinberg, 1982a, 1982b; Fay, 1987.)

According to Popkewitz (1990) the rules, standards, and logic of science do not have constant meanings, but embody different concepts that are historically constructed and tied to social agendas (see also Popkewitz, 1984). So, varying views of science, as represented by alternative inquiry frameworks, reflect different intellectual traditions that both arise from and embody different interplays of history and ideology. The assumptions, value dispositions, and methodologies of each tradition coherently interrelate to generate its definition of what counts as legitimate scientific knowledge.

The values explicitly promoted by critical social science are well articulated by its concept of critical,[4] and Popkewitz (1990) offers two senses of what is critical about critical social science: (a) an analytic posture by which the logical consistency of arguments, procedures, and language receive continual cross-examination and scrutiny (not unlike the critical tradition of postpositivism), and (b) a lens for this posture that "give[s] focus to skepticism toward social institutions and . . . considers the conditions of social regulation, unequal distribution, and power" (Popkewitz, 1990, p. 48). A critical social scientist would ask, for example, whether observed patterns of relationship "reveal invariant regularities of social action" or "express ideologically frozen relations of dependence" (Bernstein, 1976, pp. 230–231). Critical science also embodies an action-oriented commitment to the common welfare. It "has a [fundamental] practical interest in the fate and quality of social and political life . . . in radically 'improving human existence' " (Bernstein, 1976, pp. 174, 180).

Finally, Popkewitz (1990) describes critical social science as a tradition that exposes the ideological bases and thus the poverty of such dualisms as objectivity and subjectivity, rigor and relevance, discovery and verification, and even ontology and epistemology. For example, "[objectivity and] relativity [are] issues only within the context of foundationalist epistemologies which search for a privileged standpoint as the guarantee of certainty" (Lather, 1988, p. 10). In short, "phenomenology negates positivism, and philosophies of praxis [or practical action] are concerned with negating the dualism thus created" (Morgan, 1983, p. 372; see also Bernstein, 1983).

The Nature of Critical Knowledge

Following directly from these attributes, knowledge in critical social science is, substantively, nonfoundational knowledge about the historical, structural, and value bases of social phenomena as well as about contradictions and distortions therein. Knowledge in critical science is also interested knowledge or knowledge that reflects the values and priorities of a particular intellectual-cultural-social tradition. In the critical theory of the contemporary Frankfurt school, advanced most notably by Jürgen Habermas (1971), legitimate interests include the technical-instrumental and practical-communicative knowledge claims of postpositivism and interpretivism, respectively. But, in part because neither of these informs us how to tell good from bad, their inquiry paradigms are supplemented and superseded in critical theory by one that takes a third emancipatory, action-constitutive interest as fundamental (Bredo & Feinberg, 1982a, p. 275). "An empirical statement [or critical knowledge claim] must be judged by its intentions for the good and true life" (Fischer, 1985, p. 251, from Aristotle via Habermas).

So, critical knowledge is also practical, action-oriented knowledge that enlightens and thereby catalyzes political and social change. Critical knowledge enlightens an audience by revealing the structural conditions of their existence, specifically, how these conditions came about and what distortions or injustices they currently represent. Such enlightenment carries within it an enabling, motivating force to stimulate action, a catalyst for self-reflection toward greater autonomy and responsibility and for strategic political action toward emancipation (Bernstein, 1976). Critical knowledge does not prescribe such action, for that would be action in its merely technical sense. Rather, critical knowledge represents "a genuine unity of theory and revolutionary praxis where the theoretical understanding of the contradictions inherent in existing society, when appropriated by those who are exploited, becomes constitutive of their very activity to transform society" (Bernstein, 1976, p. 182).

Knowledge Accumulation in Critical Social Science

So, how does knowledge—as an interested, emancipatory account of the history and values underlying social phenomena—accumulate in critical social science? As I understand this inquiry framework, the short answer is that it doesn't. Nor is it intended to. As Popkewitz (1990) argues, the belief that scientific knowledge is a progressive development in which evidence continually clarifies and modifies what is known is erroneous. The logic of science is historically formed and changes in a manner that is not necessarily cumulative. From a critical perspective, knowledge accumulation in its building-block sense reifies "the social and historical conditions in which knowledge is produced and transformed" (Popkewitz, 1990, p. 64) rather than respects the ideological and dynamic character of such conditions. With such respect, what counts as knowledge, including critical knowledge, changes with the times. Moreover, knowledge itself, as practical and action oriented, changes the social-political conditions in which it is produced. So, to endeavor to build on prior work is to estrange it from its own social-historical context, to deny, in turn, its impacts on that context and thereby to strip it of meaning.

Popkewitz (1990, p. 65) does say that "we need to understand what others have said and done before us" and that this involves a complex process of interpretation and analysis. Just what this means, however, is not entirely clear.

So Why Do Social Science?

The Critical Science Response

The practical import of critical social science, its role and function in the world of practice, *is* entirely clear and, moreover, is vitally integral to this inquiry framework. Critical social science denies the distinction between *is* and *ought*, between science as theory and research, and practice as normative, ideologically based action. Critical science seeks to reclaim the critical function of theory (Bernstein, 1976); to reassert the scientist's role as an interested observer who speaks with "a critical voice of social consciousness" (Popkewitz, this volume); to have a "practical political impact" (Fay, 1987, p. 2); "to change the world, not to describe it" (Popkewitz, 1984, p. 45).

Critical social science strives to meet these aims via the action-constitutive nature of its knowledge, its "unity of theory and revolutionary praxis" (Bernstein, 1976, p. 182).

> Critical social science is an attempt to understand in a rationally responsible manner the oppressive features of a society such that this understanding stimulates its audience to transform their society and thereby liberate themselves. (Fay, 1987, p. 4)

Causing some disquiet here is my difficulty in giving concrete form to knowledge that inherently but nonprescriptively catalyzes political action. Just what does such knowledge look like?

Concluding Comments

This discussion about the nature and role of social scientific knowledge in postpositivism, interpretivism, and critical science has been with intention minimally comparative and largely descriptive. I endeavored primarily to present the arguments of each inquiry framework with some measure of internal integrity rather than in reference to selected concerns or criteria. I hoped thereby to invite broad participation in the identification of important issues for further conversation. Some people may be most interested, for example, in issues related to causality, others in questions about subjectivity. My own nominations of agenda items for further conversation are reflected in the critiques made of each paradigm's stance on the role and purpose of social science in society. In concluding this discussion, I would like to return to these issues. Their presentation here highlights both the language and the concepts that differentiate the three inquiry frameworks and some of their common challenges.

1. Given the acknowledged, though varied, complexity of and the contextual and/or historical boundaries on social knowledge, can it serve other than local or micro-level interests? Can and should social scientists aspire to serve the common good, or do we need a social scientist in every community?
2. Given that all social knowledge is value bound, value laden, or value based, is all social science fundamentally about human values? Can and should social scientists seek to "recapture moral discourse" (Schwandt, 1989) as our most significant societal role?
3. As social engineers, as storytellers, or as catalyzers of political action, what moral and ethical responsibilities do social scientists have for the consequences of our work?
4. Even as social scientists from quite different perspectives share a commitment to the improvement of social life through our work, we diverge in how this commitment is actualized in the world of practice. Is relativism justifiable in this context? Whose interests should be served by social science?

And now, please, let us converse.

Notes

AUTHOR'S NOTE: My sincere thanks to Cathy Campbell, Charles McClintock, Bill Trochim, Deborah Trumbull, and particularly Egon Guba for their constructive comments on this chapter.

1. Throughout this chapter, the more generic term *interpretivism* is used to include the constructivist inquiry framework set forth by Lincoln (1990) and the terms *paradigm* and *inquiry framework* are used interchangeably.
2. This discussion will focus on the constructivist view of interpretivism, including similar and related views, but excluding dissimilar qualitative traditions (see Atkinson, Delamont, & Hammersley, 1988; Jacob, 1987, 1988; M. Smith, 1987).

3. Here, there is a sharp break between interpretivism (especially as constructivism) and some other qualitative traditions. Ethnography, for example, does address general theories of culture and does acknowledge the possibility of generalizable knowledge (see the references listed in note 2).
4. Bredo and Feinberg (1982b) criticize other inquiry frameworks for not fully acknowledging or justifying their value positions. Critical theory, they say, at least attempts to do so, notably, Habermas's efforts to define the "universal pragmatics" of a theory of communicative competence (Bredo & Feinberg, 1982b, p. 436).

References

Atkinson, P. Delamont, S. & Hammersley, M. (1988). Qualitative research traditions: A British Response to Jacob. *Review of Educational Research* 58: 231–250.

Bernstein, R. (1976). *The restructuring of social and political theory.* Philadelphia: University of Pennsylvania Press.

——— . 1983. *Beyond objectivism and relativism: Science, hermeneutics, and praxis.* Philadelphia: University of Pennsylvania Press.

Bredo, E. & Feinberg, W. (1982a). The critical approach to social and educational research. In E. Bredo & W. Feinberg (eds.) *Knowledge and values in social and educational research.* Philadelphia: Temple University Press, pp. 115–128.

——— . (1982b). Conclusion: Action, interaction and reflection. In E. Bredo & W. Feinberg (eds.) *Knowledge and values in social and educational research.* Philadelphia: Temple University Press, pp. 422–442.

Campbell, D. (1984). Can an open society be an experimenting society? Paper presented at the International Symposium on the Philosophy of Karl Popper, Madrid, Spain.

——— . (1988). A tribal model of the social system vehicle carrying scientific knowledge. In E. Overman (ed.) *Methodology and epistemology for social science: Selected papers, Donald T. Campbell.* Chicago: University of Chicago Press, pp. 489–503.

Campbell, D. & Fiske, D. (1959). Convergent and discriminant validation by the multitrait-multimethod matrix. *Psychological Bulletin* 56: 81–105.

Cook, T. (1983). Quasi-experimentation: Its ontology, epistemology, and methodology. In G. Morgan (ed.) *Beyond method: Strategies for social research.* Philadelphia: Temple University Press, pp. 370–390.

——— . (1985). Postpositivist critical multiplism. In R. Shotland & M. Mark (eds.) *Social science and social policy.* Beverly Hills, CA: Sage, pp. 21–62.

Cronbach, L. (1982). *Designing evaluations of educational and social programs.* San Francisco: Jossey-Bass.

Denzin, N. (1978). *The research act: An introduction to sociological methods.* New York: McGraw-Hill.

Fay, B. (1987). *Critical social science.* Ithaca, NY: Cornell University Press.

Fischer, F. (1985). Critical evaluation of public policy: A methodological case study. In J. Forester (ed.), *Critical theory and public life.* Cambridge, MA: MIT Press, pp. 231–257.

Guba, E. & Lincoln, Y. (1981). *Effective evaluation.* San Francisco, CA: Jossey-Bass.

——— . (1987). The countenances of fourth generation evaluation: Description, judgment, and negotiation. In D. Palumbo (ed.), *The politics of program evaluation.* New Park, CA: Sage, pp. 202–234.

——— . (1988). Do inquiry paradigms imply inquiry methodologies? In D. Fetterman (ed.), *Qualitative approaches to evaluation in education.* New York: Prager, pp. 89–115.

Habermas, J. (1971). *Knowledge and human interests* (J. Shapiro, Trans.) Boston: Beacon.

Howe, K. (1985). Two dogmas of educational research. *Educational Researcher* 17: 10–16.

Jacob, E. (1987). Qualitative research traditions: A review. *Review of Educational Research* 57: 1–50.

Lather, P. (1988). Educational research and practice in a postmodern era. Paper presented at the meeting of the American Educational Research Association, New Orleans.

Lincoln, Y. (1988). The role of ideology in naturalistic research. Paper presented at the meeting of the American Educational Research Association, New Orleans.

——— . (1989). Trouble in the land: The paradigm revolution in the academic disciplines. In E. Pascarella & J. Smart (eds.), *Higher education: Handbook of theory and research.* Vol. 5. 57–133. New York: Agathon.

Lincoln, Y. (1990). The making of a constructivist: A remembrance of transformations past. In E. Guba (ed.) *The paradigm dialog.* Newbury Park, CA: Sage, pp. 67–87.

Lincoln, Y. & Guba, E. (1985). *Naturalistic inquiry.* Beverly Hills, CA: Sage.

——— . (1986). But is it rigorous? Trustworthiness and authenticity in naturalistic evaluation. In D. Williams (ed.), *Naturalistic evaluation (new directions for program evaluation.* San Francisco: Jossey-Bass, pp. 73–84.

Miles, M. & Huberman, A. (1984). *Qualitative data analysis.* Beverly Hills, CA: Sage.

Morgan, G. (1983). Toward a more reflective social science. In G. Morgan (ed.), *Beyond method: Strategies for social research.* Beverly Hills CA: Sage, pp. 368–376.

Overman, E. (1988). Introduction: Social science and Donald T. Campbell. In E. Overman (ed.), *Methodology and epistemology for social science, selected papers, Donald T. Campbell.* Chicago: University of Chicago Press, pp. vii–xix.

Phillips, D. (1987). *Philosophy, science and social inquiry.* Oxford: Pergamon.

Phillips, D. (1990a). Postpositivistic science: Myths and realities. In E. Guba (ed.) *The paradigm dialog.* Newbury Park, CA: Sage, pp. 31–45.

—— . (1990b). Subjectivity and objectivity: An objective inquiry. In E. Eisner & A. Peshkin (eds.) *Qualitative inquiry in education.* New York: Teachers College Press.

Popkewitz, T. (1984). *Paradigm and ideology in educational research: The social functions of the intellectual.* London: Falmer.

Popkewitz, T. (1990). Whose future? Whose past? Notes on critical theory and methodology. In E. Guba (ed.) *The paradigm dialog.* Newbury Park, CA: Sage, pp. 46–66.

Rabinow, P. (1983). Humanism as nihilism. In N. Haan, R. Bellah, P. Rabinow & W. Sullivan (eds.) Social science as moral inquiry. New York: Columbia University Press, pp. 52–75.

Schwandt, T. (1989). Recapturing moral discourse in evaluation. *Educational Researcher* 18: 11–16.

Smith, J. (1984). The problem of criteria for judging interpretive inquiry. *Educational Evaluation and Policy Analysis* 6: 379–391.

Smith, M. (1987). Publishing qualitative research. *American Educational Research Journal* 24: 174–183.

Webb, E. Campbell, D. Schwartz, R. & Sechrest, L. (1966). *Unobtrusive measures.* Chicago: Rand McNally.

5

Seeing through Science
Epistemologies

Joey Sprague

Most researchers think of epistemology as a nonissue—or, more precisely, do not think of epistemology at all. We have learned to equate science with positivist epistemology and, for most people, the assumptions of positivism do not appear to be assumptions—they seem like common sense. Yet a major contribution of feminist and other critical scholarship has been to raise questions about epistemology. These scholars have questioned the assumptions underlying conventional research practices and have found that prevailing ideas about what knowledge is and how it is best produced emerge from relations of social domination and help to continue that domination.

An epistemology is a theory of knowing. It directs us in how to go about understanding a phenomenon. It spells out the grounds on which we can choose one account of that phenomenon over another (Alcoff 1989). Every epistemology, Anthony Genova (1983) says, involves assumptions about three things, which he describes as distinct points of a triad: the knower, the known, and the process of knowing (cf. Hawkesworth 1989). Genova describes the history of epistemological debates over the course of Western philosophy as revolving around this triad, focusing sometimes on the nature of the knower, other times on the nature of reality, and still other times on the process of knowing.

Feminists writing about epistemology identify the same three elements—the knower, the known, and the process of knowing—but in feminist analysis, the focus tends to be on how they are connected (Smith 1990). Epistemologies, from this perspective, are accounts of the knowing subject, the object of study, and the relationship between them.

First I will present two extreme positions in the current discourse on epistemology—on the one hand, the idea that the facts speak for themselves, and on the other, the idea that systematic knowledge of the social world is impossible. I will argue that while both positions have made important contributions, at this point in history they pose false choices, and critical researchers should be satisfied with neither. Later I will turn to two epistemological alternatives that have more potential usefulness for critical social science researchers because each accepts that knowledge is socially constructed and provisional but attainable: critical realism and standpoint theory.

Positivism: Do the Facts Speak for Themselves?

Almost every child who goes to elementary school in the United States encounters positivist epistemology; it permeates early science education and science fairs. Positivism could be described as an epistemology of the fact. Positivists generally believe that the world of experience is an objective world, governed by underlying regularities, even natural laws. Empirical observations, the "facts," are outcroppings of these underlying regularities. Positivists hold that if, and only if, we systematically and dispassionately observe the data of the empirical world, we can detect the lawful patterns of which they are evidence.

At the heart of positivist epistemology is an emphasis on objectivity. Positivism assumes that truth comes from eliminating the role of subjective judgments and interpretations. Good science, from this perspective, can and should be value-free. According to positivist epistemology, subjectivity is an obstacle to knowledge: the observer's personality and feelings introduce errors in observation. The practices of research are designed to minimize, and hopefully erase, any impact of the subjectivity of the researcher on the collection and interpretation of data. Observations are conducted systematically, through the use of precise instruments and countable measures. Interpretations are developed through applying statistical analyses and theories of probability to the quantities into which the data have been organized. Following these systematic procedures makes data collection and interpretation open to replication, and testing by others, a further assurance of objectivity (Barzun and Graff 1970: 222–29).

Thus, in terms of the three elements of epistemology—the knower, the known, and the process of knowing—positivism assumes the possibility of a sharp dichotomy between the knower and the known, and focuses attention on strategies that researchers might use to enforce that dichotomy.

Sociologists know positivism well—this philosophy of science has been linked with sociology from its beginning. Auguste Comte, the mathematician often credited with founding the discipline, and Emile Durkheim, who played a major role in establishing the new discipline's credibility, were enthusiastic about the promise of the precise use of quantitative methods to reveal the natural laws underlying social phenomena. The founders of American sociology were oriented to sociology as a science, as a systematic collection and analysis of data (Oakley 2000). From the beginning many social scientists, both mainstream and critical, have equated positivist epistemological beliefs with quantitative methods. A key argument of this book is that this equation is inaccurate.

The development of positivism offered some clear advantages over the epistemology that prevailed prior to it, an epistemology based on faith and divine revelation, which grounded authority in tradition (Lovibond 1989). Positivism's reliance on empirical evidence and clear, replicable procedures for collecting and interpreting evidence opens up the production of knowledge to many more than a chosen—even literally anointed—few. The emphasis on systematic procedures presents knowledge claims within a context that is open to critique and argument, even refutation. Thus positivist epistemology has generated methods with democratic potential. However, positivism does have its problems, as has been shown by scholars from Mannheim (1936) to contemporary social constructionists who have argued that official knowing as we have inherited it is not the objective, unbiased, apolitical process it represents itself to be.

Observers See through a Cultural Lens

Scholarly paradigms, like other forms of human consciousness, are the expression of specific worldviews. The central criticism of positivism is directed at the notion that scientists can occupy an Archimedean point outside the ongoing swim of the social world, escaping its influence as they develop hypotheses, make their measurements, analyze the data, and draw conclusions (Smith 1987). The "facts" that are the raw material of scientific analysis are themselves the outcome of specific social practices. What we know about the process of human perception undermines the notion that we can detect pure facts outside some theory (see Bechtel 1988). The very first step in the practice of what we usually think of as scientific objectivity involves a social construction: scientists use some framework to carve up the continuity of lived experience to identify objects, or facts, that they then proceed to investigate (Shiva 1993; Smith 1990). Making any observation requires the acceptance of some background assumptions, some system of beliefs to organize what one is seeing. This is why Helen Longino says scientific data are "theory laden" (1989).

For example, the scientific research literature is filled with hypotheses about sex differences, for example, in brain organization, conceptual ability, and ethical development (Bleier 1984; Eagly 1995; Fausto-Sterling 1985; Gilligan 1982; Tavris 1992). All of this research is premised on the background assumption that sex is a naturally occurring dichotomy—that there are two and only two sexes. Yet there seems to be no consistent set of biological criteria by which we can divide the human population into two mutually exclusive and exhaustive categories (Fausto-Sterling 1985; Kessler 1998; Kessler and McKenna 1978). Further, other cultures have apparently observed the "facts" and reached different conclusions on the topic: a number of other cultures accept as natural the existence of three genders, each of which is accorded distinctive characteristics and social roles (Kessler and McKenna 1978; Lorber 1994). Because our culture assumes dichotomous sex, this has been an unquestioned background assumption guiding scientific research. That research has then been used to demonstrate the "naturalness" of dichotomous sex.

Harding (1998) asserts that even the positivist assumption of underlying natural laws governing phenomena is an expression of the imagery of divine law and purpose in European Judeo-Christian religious traditions. Developments like chaos theory in the natural sciences reveal that, even in physics, the idea that there are natural laws is a background assumption that is open to serious challenge.

The Data Do Not Confess

In addition to positivism's failure to recognize the "theory-laden" quality of the data themselves, Longino (1989) identifies another flaw in positivist logic: the assumption that the data directly support the hypotheses. Drawing on the empiricist philosopher Willard Quine, she argues that the data do not say which hypothesis for which they are evidence; that is, theories are "empirically underdetermined" (cf. Alcoff 1989). The same data can be used to support contradictory hypotheses, and which connection gets made depends, again, on the background assumptions being made by the analyst (Longino 1989).

For example, African Americans tend to score lower on intelligence tests than do European Americans. These data can be used to support hypotheses about race inferiority, as the authors of one highly publicized book, *The Bell Curve*, did. However, this conclusion requires that one also make a whole string of other assumptions, including that what the tests measure is intelligence, that test instruments are not class- or race-biased, that race is unrelated to access to decent nutrition, health care, and education, to region, or to exposure to toxic substances in the environment, and that these social and environmental factors have no bearing on performance on intelligence tests (cf. Hauser, Taylor, and Duster 1995). Each and every one of those assumptions is vulnerable to serious challenge.

In summary, when testing any one hypothesis, a scientist is also testing that set of other hypotheses embedded within it—all the background assumptions contributing to the worldview that supports the hypothesis in the first place. Scientific practices are deeply social. Yet, in the conventions of mainstream scientific interpretation and reporting, findings are represented as independent of the context in which they were generated. The social processes that "uncover" scientific facts are hidden from our view (Latour and Woolgar 1979).

The Practice of Science

The Quine-Duhem thesis in the philosophy of science literature illustrates another flaw with positivist assumptions about objectivity. These assumptions are undermined in the way scientists actually do science. If a test of the research hypothesis fails to achieve the expected results, the scientist does not necessarily reject that hypothesis, but rather can and often does tinker with the background assumptions, arriving at a way to make sense of the data while maintaining the original thought or expectation.

For example, early sex-difference researchers believed that men were more intelligent than women and developed a theory that brain size correlated with intelligence, which led them to predict that men would have larger brains. When subsequent research on brain size revealed that women, on average, had larger brains in relation to their body size than did men, researchers did not reject the background assumption that men were more intelligent than women, or even consider the idea that men's and women's brains were essentially comparable. Rather, they moved on to other aspects of the brain that might show a systematic sex difference in the direction that would support the hypothesis of male superiority (cf. Bleier 1984; Fausto-Sterling 1985).

Thus the vision of a pure empirical test of scientific ideas is not realized in practice. As these examples illustrate, we always rely on background assumptions, and these assumptions are based in values, so science is not value-neutral (Alcoff 1989). In ignoring the cultural embeddedness of the knower, and in concentrating instead on the most accurate procedures for detecting the known, positivism is in a sense hiding the relationship between the knower and the known.

Assuming that science is value-free—and that science should be value-free—has serious consequences, according to Harding (1998). By refusing to consider the relationship between science and broader social phenomena, we preclude discussion about the connection between what we do in science and potential benefits or costs to broader communities. Instead, our discussions about science are radically narrowed into purely technical issues, and the "findings" tend to make the current relations of privilege and disadvantage seem natural.

Radical Social Constructionism: Is Knowledge Illusion?

Most of the critiques of positivism reflect the position that knowledge is socially constructed (see Jussim 1991). Any order or perceived regularity in phenomena is not "out there" in the empirical world. We give order to our perceptions through the application of a cultural framework (Mehan and Wood 1975; Weedon 1987/1997). Thus the object of knowledge, the truth, is the creation of the very process that "discovers" it (Alcoff 1989; Foucault 1972; Fraser 1989; Haraway 1988).

Many social constructionists have been influenced by the writing of Michel Foucault (1972, 1975/1979, 1976/1979). Foucault uses the term "Power/Knowledge" to convey the idea that in the modern world, the two are inextricably linked: power is enacted through the organization of knowledge, and knowledge is constructed as a form of domination. For Foucault, even our subjectivity is a social construction: our values and our very sense of having a self are aspects of the way modern power/knowledge works (cf. Fraser 1989). Older forms of power, says Foucault (1975/1979), were directly enacted on people's bodies at intermittent times. The lord of the manor could impose his will on serfs by threatening or actually administering physical punishment, and when the lord was away, the serfs could engage in small acts of resistance. Newer forms of power operate through discourses that circulate through our daily lives and the way these discourses prompt us to construct certain forms of self-awareness and to manage our own behavior, that is, to discipline ourselves.

Social science, according to Foucault, has been an important part of the development of power/knowledge. The social sciences and their practices of classifying, labeling, diagnosing, and treating groups and individuals constitute a system of intensive surveillance. Social scientists turn the diversity of humanity into linearly distributed characteristics with measurable means and standard deviations. Each individual can now be classified in terms of where they fall on multiple distributions of traits. Social sciences create official standards of normality, feeding a whole set of discourses that circulate through the culture, from professional manuals to self-tests in popular magazines. Notions of normality prompt all of us to monitor and discipline one another and, perhaps especially, ourselves to try to conform to those standards (see Fraser 1989).

Intelligence is one example. In an earlier time in U.S. culture, intelligence was a multifaceted concept. People were diverse in their combinations of skills and limitations, and some were "slower" than others in cognitive processing speed (Bogdan and Taylor 1989). With the invention of the IQ test, scientists focused on a specific kind of intelligence—speed and facility with abstract reasoning—making it visible and measurable. Implementation of the IQ test gave us a distribution of scores interpretable in terms of their deviations from the mean, and a mechanism for assigning each individual a place in that distribution. Those who diverge significantly from the center of this distribution were assigned into categories for "special" attention—mentally retarded at one end, and gifted at the other (Woldensburger 1983). A person's categorization is used to determine his or her opportunities and experiences, and, as a consequence, his or her sense of self (Sprague and Hayes 2000). Scientific conceptualization and measurement of intelligence is a key part of a power/knowledge system through which we manage one another and ourselves.

Social constructionism contributes to our understanding of the production of knowledge in at least three ways. First, it keeps the social character of knowledge production in the foreground, providing an analysis of the connection between the organization of knowledge and social domination. Second, it raises important questions for scholars to address, questions about their own embeddedness in a culture and about their own social role in the institutions that produce and distribute official knowledge. Third, social constructionism has developed useful methods for deconstructing ideas, theories, and practices, methods that can reveal the often complex and even contradictory meanings embedded in cultural "facts." However, there are significant divergences among those who would agree with the basic idea that knowledge is socially created, and some significant limitations with the most extreme positions.

Relativism as a Dead End

In the most radical version of constructionist epistemology, every object of knowledge—each phenomenon, every experience—is a text, a bearer of multiple and conflicting meanings (cf. Hawkesworth 1989). "All actual experience is understood as a surface/screen upon which fantasies are projected and displaced, even while experienced in reality" (Clough 1993: 176). It is not that mass-mediated discourses impose ideologies on the reader or writer; they engage and shape "unconscious mechanisms of wish-fulfillment, denial . . . and resistance" (Clough 1993: 178). The very idea that we have a distinct self that can observe and interpret anything is a creation of discourse. Thus we cannot talk about the discourses and people's subjectivities separately—they are inextricably bound up together and are "all but indistinguishable in the subject position of discourse" (Clough 1993: 178). Knowledge, then, is itself a narrative, another text, even an act of faith based on cult membership (Haraway 1988). Each person's interpretation of the text that is experience is an equally valid and equally limited reading—there is no privileged or definitive interpretation (Fraser 1989).

Ironically, this most radical form of social constructionism's construction of the knower, the known, and the process of knowing is in a sense the mirror image of positivism's. While positivism dissolves the subject into the object, radical social constructionism dissolves the object into the subject. If positivism is the epistemology of fact, then this radical version of constructionism is an epistemology of fiction.

The timing and popularity of this radical form of constructivist response to positivist epistemology are worth considering. In an earlier day when the institutions that organize official knowledge production were homogeneously white, male, and upper-class, the dominant epistemology claimed an objective observer, who disinterestedly pursued the discovery of naturally existing laws. Just when increasing numbers of those previously marginalized or even excluded from the ranks of knowledge producers—women, people from the working class, and people who are not white or from the West—begin to enter these institutions and demand a voice in creating knowledge, another epistemology emerges and gains substantial support, one that asserts that no one has a claim to the truth.

It is easy to imagine the effects of such a relativist stance on struggles to overcome personal and collective oppression. As Mary Hawkesworth notes, when things are unequal, "relativist resignation reinforces the status quo" (1989: 557). Intentional action is premised on an analysis of what is and what might be. Social change takes social action, usually coalitions among diverse groups who recognize mutual interests and shared goals. When analyses of experiences are considered mere texts or individual readings, the potential for supporting meaningful social change is eroded (Mascia-Lees, Sharpe, and Cohen 1989). Scholarship separated from action can devolve into a form of intellectual game conducted by a privileged class of knowledge producers with no relevance to most everyday actors. Haraway's term for the impact is "epistemological electro-shock therapy" (1988: 578).

But the choice between a blind trust in the facts and a radical rejection of them is a false choice, one that would be rejected by many of those who believe in science and/or social constructionism. There are two approaches to epistemology that take as a given that knowledge is socially constructed, without losing the possibility of developing knowledge at all: critical realism and standpoint theory.

Critical Realism

Critical realist epistemology holds that the world exists independently of our thinking about it, there are patterns to the way it works, and our perceptions of it are varied (Bhaskar and Norris 1999; Collier 1994; Cook and Campbell 1979). The world is complex: an effect may be the consequence of multiple causes, some causal links are two-way, and both natural and social systems are open and changing (Cook and Campbell 1979). This means that "science . . . [is] a process in motion attempting to capture ever deeper and more basic strata of a reality at any moment of time unknown to us and perhaps not even empirically manifest" (Bhaskar and Norris 1999). Thus causal laws are imperfect; they leave things out and have to be understood as probabilistic (Cook and Campbell 1979). Even if we will never be able to develop a perfect knowledge of the world, through science and the application of human rationality we can approximate the regularities in phenomena (Bhaskar and Norris 1999).

Sylvia Walby (2001), a feminist proponent of this approach, suggests that we see science as a loosely integrated collection of networks of scholars who often disagree, thus pushing the process of knowledge-building forward through a continual quest for further information and better understandings. Scientific understandings change over time, and, in the process, knowledge is improved, Walby asserts. Sometimes change happens in dramatic ways, with a complete shift of paradigms, as when Einstein's theory of relativity overthrew Newtonian physics. But much more often, change in knowledge is gradual, the result of continued rational and empirical effort—gathering more evidence, reexamining what evidence exists, and reconsidering interpretations in dialogue with other researchers. In Walby's words, "Science is not a mirror of nature, but neither is it a mirror of culture" (2001: 485).

Thus, Hawkesworth says, we should adopt "a minimalist standard of rationality that requires that belief be apportioned to evidence and that no assertion be immune from critical assessment" (1989: 556). On these grounds, she maintains, we will be able to claim superior knowledge "from the strength of rational argument, from the ability to demonstrate point by point the deficiencies of alternative explanations" (Hawkesworth 1989: 557).

For critical realists, the knower is socially constructed, shaped by the discourses of culture and science. The known is complex and changing, including in response to social action. Thus the relationship between the knower and the known is mediated by discourse but amenable to adjustment and increasing refinement, though the known will never be more than an increasingly accurate approximation of reality.

Critical realist epistemology is appealing. It steps back from positivism's most problematic assumptions by recognizing that the data do not speak for themselves, that some person is using an interpretive framework to organize them. And, unlike more radical forms of constructionism, critical realism retains an epistemological grounding for doing science, for working to maximize the adequacy of our understandings, and thus a basis for taking informed action. For critical realists, the relationship between the knower and the known is culturally organized, but every knower has the same potential access to the known, or at least there is nothing systematically organizing the relationship of groups of knowers to the known. This last point is the main source of disagreement between critical realists and the other important application of social constructionism to epistemology, standpoint theory.

Standpoint Theory

Standpoint epistemology argues that all knowledge is constructed in a specific matrix of physical location, history, culture, and interests, and that these matrices change in configuration from one location to another (Harding 1998). A standpoint is not the spontaneous thinking of a person or a category of people. Rather, it is the combination of resources available within a specific context from which an understanding might be constructed. Standpoint theorists reject positivism's pretense of creating a view from nowhere in favor of the postulate that subjects are specific, located in a particular time and place. This locatedness gives access to the concrete world. Thus a knower has a particular vantage point with regard to the object. Knowing is not relative, as radical constructivists maintain; it is partial, local, and historically specific (Haraway 1988; Harding 1998; Hartsock 1983).

In most versions of standpoint theory, there are certain social positions from which it is possible to develop better understandings. Marxist epistemology generally privileges the standpoint of an undifferentiated working class (Bar On 1993; Lukacs 1971). In feminist standpoint theory, epistemic privilege is often accorded to the standpoint of women, who are themselves diverse in location in systems organizing race, class, nation, and other major relations of social domination. I will outline the arguments of four standpoint theorists who have had a major impact on feminist social science: Nancy Hartsock (1983, 1985), Donna Haraway (1978, 1988, 1990, 1993), Dorothy Smith (1979, 1987, 1990), and Patricia Hill Collins (1986, 1989, 2000). Not all of these scholars agree on every point, but they do give a good sense of the general logic of the argument and several ways it can be applied to reveal systematic biases built into the way mainstream knowledge: is constructed.

Nancy Hartsock: Standpoints on Power

Nancy Hartsock (1983, 1985), a political scientist who pioneered the notion of standpoint, carefully distinguished a standpoint from the spontaneous thinking of social actors. A standpoint, she says, is "achieved rather than obvious, a mediated rather than immediate understanding" (1985: 132). To illustrate the contrasts in the kinds of knowledge that are accessible from distinct standpoints, Hartsock uses the example of varying ways political scientists have developed a conceptualization of power.

Beginning with the experience and interests of capitalists, those who own the means of production, leads scholars to focus on exchanges in the market because capitalists are removed from the concrete circumstances of producing goods and services, including their relationship with workers. Taking the standpoint of capitalists, Hartsock says, provides resources for understanding power as a thing, a commodity that a person has more or less of, something that can be exchanged, taken, or given away. The predominant notion of power in political science, and in our culture more broadly, Hartsock says, is developed by taking the capitalist standpoint.

On the other hand, scholars who begin from the practical experience of workers are more likely to foreground the capitalist/worker relationship. Workers must sell their labor to capitalists, do their work in coordination with the labor of other workers, and earn wages that are lower than the market value of the goods that they produce. The workers' standpoint offers resources for understanding power as a relationship of domination, in which one party, by virtue of its control over wealth, is able to take advantage of and extract compliance from, that is, has "power over," the other. Marxists, for example, have built their analysis of power from the standpoint of workers.

But, Hartsock argues, there is a third construction of power, one that becomes available by taking the standpoint of women. The sexual division of labor in our culture makes women responsible for domestic labor in the home, doing the work of transforming commodities into food, clothing, and other things that meet people's needs. Beginning from the position of those who do the work of nurturing makes it possible to develop a notion of power as capacity or potential, as in the word *empower*. Hartsock argues that the standpoint of women offers unique resources for developing the notion of power as "power to."

Donna Haraway: Vision Is Embodied

Donna Haraway (1978, 1988, 1990, 1993), an anthropologist, criticizes positivism for violating one of its own assumptions. Positivism is based, Haraway notes, on the primacy of data, that is, information that is detectable directly through the senses. Positivist epistemology is, then, logically grounded in the materiality of people's bodies. Yet positivism denies the presence of these bodies in making its claims to validity. For example, the bodies of those dominating the production of knowledge have for the most part been in specific social locations in systems of race (white), class (privileged), gender (male), and nation (Western), and yet there is no consideration of how their observations might have been shaped by their social position. Haraway agrees with positivist and critical realist arguments that it is through our sensory experience, our bodies, that we have access to the world; however, she maintains that this empirical grounding is both the basis of valid knowledge and a limit on it. She uses the term "embodied vision" to emphasize that our vision is located in some specific social and physical place, that our knowledge is "situated," and thus partial.

How can we compensate for the partiality of any perspective? Haraway says that the best way to gain a critical perspective on one's situated view is to get a sense of how things look from a different position. Access to contrasting perspectives on a phenomenon reveals the limits and constructedness of each view. Because each of us experiences life and our selves in multiple facets that are "stitched together imperfectly" (586), we can partially identify with another, empathy is possible, and through it, two knowers can make a partial connection. By translating across distinct perspectives and connecting ever-shifting situated knowledges, it is at least theoretically possible to rationally build some collective, if provisional, agreement on the whole. Of course, differences in social power can obstruct such collaboration.

Dorothy Smith: Sociology versus Everyday Life

Dorothy Smith (1979, 1987, 1990), a sociologist, analyzes the standpoint of sociology and of knowledge institutions more broadly. Like Foucault, Smith argues that social science has been part of the practices by which we are all organized and managed. She agrees that knowledge is socially constructed, but in contrast with radical constructionism Smith argues that society has material, knowable reality. What is real is people acting in concert, taking one another's practices into account, within webs of social power and domination that Smith calls "relations of ruling." The sexual division of labor in our society has created a bifurcation of human experience: those who develop knowledge about society are separated from the actual practices that sustain everyday (and everynight) life. The result, Smith says, is a sociology (and by extension, a social science) that is alienated from social life.

The men who dominate the conceptual realm in knowledge institutions are free, if they choose, to almost ignore their bodily existence in every sphere of their lives. This has been possible only because women have been taking care of the practical activities for them: providing for their human needs and for those of their children outside the workplace, and doing the material work of implementing their abstract conceptualizations—clerical work, interviewing, taking care of patients, and so on—in the workplace. The better these women are at their work, the more invisible that work is to the men who benefit from it, allowing them to take women's work for granted and to have their own authority and contribution bolstered in the process.

While Smith draws a sharp male/female division here, in actuality race and class inter-act with gender in sorting people on both sides of this divide. Racially and economically privileged men are most likely to be in positions of power in the realm of the conceptual, but some privileged women, particularly those who are not directly engaged in the prac-tices of sustaining life, gain significant power. On the other hand, women with children, and/or women who are not from racially and economically privileged backgrounds, are the most likely to do the most hands-on practical activities, though some men are also engaged in these activities.

Mainstream scientific research only superficially overcomes the split between official knowledge and practical existence, because scholars work from the standpoint of the managers, the powerful. Researchers reach out through their conceptual frameworks to pluck bits of the empirical world, and retreat to their offices to organize the data to fit their abstract frameworks. Then they cycle this ordering through what Smith describes as a "textually-mediated virtual reality," creating a new order. They reassemble the facts into a construction of their view of "what actually happened," and use that reconstructed version as a lens through which to reexamine lived experience. Sociological practices like these "convert what people experience directly in their everyday/everynight world into forms of knowledge in which people as subjects disappear and in which their perspectives on their own experience are transposed and subdued by the magisterial forms of objectifying discourse" (1990: 4).

Smith argues that sociologists need to make everyday/everynight life our problematic, the place from which we start, the puzzle for us to solve. We need to unpack the "facts" and the conventional abstractions describing them and see what lies behind them, because the concerted activity of specific people in concrete circumstances sustains these "facts" on a daily basis.

Women sociologists, especially those with caretaking responsibilities for children or relatives, tend to cross and recross the boundary between the conceptual and the practical realms. They experience on a daily basis both the sociological virtual reality and the concrete work of meeting human needs, coordinating with child care and schools, finding medical resources, and so on. The standpoint of women within sociology provides an opportunity to drive a wedge through the breach between the means by which we develop our understandings of social life and the concrete work of keeping social life going. It gives us the opportunity to discover ways that sociology constructs a knowledge that mystifies lived experience, thereby playing a role in the relations of ruling.

Patricia Hill Collins: Black Feminist Epistemology

Patricia Hill Collins (1986, 1989, 2000) argues that anyone who reflects on his or her practical experience is an intellectual, a creator of knowledge. She analyzes how the social construction of Black women's standpoint offers a distinctive basis for developing knowledge. First of all, Black women have the experience of oppression and an interest in struggling against it. Second, their work has brought them into contact with dominant groups, but in a marginalized way, for example as domestics in the households of the affluent and, more recently, as outsiders within the academy.

This marginalization is an epistemic advantage because it distances Black women from hegemonic thought and practices, facilitating the development of a critical attitude. Further, segregation brought Black women together (although these days, class divergences are breaking that up a bit), giving them safe spaces in which to construct their own analysis of their experiences. Black women have also historically had access to alternative discourses to use to interpret their situations, including West African tradition and even though they were blocked from participating in formal knowledge production, they found other channels to communicate with one another, including blues music. Thus, while Black women have been subjected to and have internalized the derogating images of them in the dominant culture, they have also found collective ways to resist.

Black women's knowledge has been systematically invalidated, because the validation of knowledge, Collins argues, is a political process involving epistemological gatekeeping, influenced by the standpoint of the existing community of experts applying their standards of credibility, and also by the way the larger culture defines certain groups as more credible than others (2000: 203–4). She uses positivism to illustrate epistemological gatekeeping (2000: 205). The goal of positivist criteria is to decontextualize the observer to produce objective observations via certain rules of method. These include distancing the

researcher/subject from the "object" of study, suppressing emotions, defining considerations of values and ethics as outside the process, and preferring the use of adversarial
debates in order to choose among contending claims to the truth. Each of these rules,
Collins observes, gives the advantage to those with social privilege.

The standpoint of Black women presents alternative criteria for validating knowledge
claims, criteria that contrast starkly with those that dominate the academy. First, Collins
says, the hegemonic view constructs a dichotomy between science and common people's
understandings, with the latter clearly discredited. In Black Feminist epistemology, on the
other hand, concrete experience and the wisdom developed through it are valued as
resources in evaluating knowledge claims. People's use of stories from their lives or of
passages from the Bible to communicate some insight is a cue to the wisdom developed
through practical everyday experience.

Second, the organization of official knowledge is hierarchically controlled by an elite
and distributed to the populace. In Black Feminist epistemology, in contrast, knowledge
claims are not hierarchically imposed by an elite, but rather are worked out through
dialogue with everyday social actors. The validation of truth claims by the common
people is crucial. Knowledge, in this perspective, is not the vision of individuals. It is
rather a form of communication and connection, a search for harmony in a community.

Third, the official approach to knowledge constructs rationality as the opposite of
emotionality. Black Feminist epistemology, on the other hand, incorporates emotions
such as empathy and attachment into the notion of intellect, holding that feeling and
caring can usefully guide knowers in asking and answering questions. Further, because
each individual is unique, emotional identification with and empathy for the other is an
important vehicle for understanding another's position.

Finally, in hegemonic knowledge, claims to truth stand on their own, to be judged
independently of their human source. On the other hand, Collins says, in Black Feminist
epistemology the character and biography of the person advancing an idea are legitimately used to interpret and evaluate the truthfulness of the idea. "Every idea has an owner
and . . . the owner's identity matters" (Collins 2000: 218). For example, Collins tells of
how students in a class discussion of the work of a Black scholar wanted to know about his
life before deciding how to evaluate his claims regarding Black feminism. A biography that
reveals a knower who is not living according to an ethic of caring undermines that
knower's credibility.

Collins asserts that because all knowledge is situated, and thus partial, all knowledge
claims should be open to critique, and this critique should integrate multiple perspectives.
She quotes Alice Walker: "Each writer writes the missing parts to the other writer's story.
And the whole story is what I'm after" (2000: 38–39). Collins's model for reaching the
truth is based on dialogue and consensus building. We need to pivot the center from one
standpoint to another, she says. In the process, people who don't own their own position
when making knowledge claims are less credible. "Everyone must listen and respond to
other voices in order to be allowed to remain in the community" (2000: 236–37). Those
ideas that are validated by multiple standpoints "become the most 'objective' truths"
(2000: 236).

In sum, standpoint epistemology integrates assumptions about the socially constructed
character of subjects and also of the things we seek to understand with the materiality of
the world and people's practical activity in it. Knowers are specifically located in
physical spaces, in systems of social relations, within circulating discourses. Knowing, the

relationship between the knower and the object of knowledge, is, as Jennifer Ring (1987) says, dialectical.

The Choice: Critical Realism or Standpoint Theory?

Both critical realists and standpoint theorists see the relationship between the knower and the known as socially mediated. They disagree over whether there is anything systematic in the biases created in the way that relationship is organized, depending on the social location of the knower. Do we think of the knower as a universal human subject, as multiple individual subjects, or as categories of subjects? Do some knowers relate to the known in qualitatively different ways than do others?

We do not have to resolve the choice between standpoint theory and critical realism in the abstract—there are data for us to consider. Official knowledge producers in the tradition of Western thought have been overwhelmingly racially and economically privileged men who are not engaged in the gendered (in race- and class-specific ways) work of nurturing life (Sprague 1996). We can compare what feminists have identified as distinctive in the worldview associated with this privileged social location to see if there are parallels with the patterns in the knowledge they produce.

Psychoanalysis and (Privileged) Male Consciousness

There are a variety of accounts of the ways that the experience of privileged men in the social organization of white-supremacist, capitalist, patriarchal society has prompted the development of a distinct form of consciousness. The analyses of Nancy Chodorow (1978, 1991) and Mary O'Brien (1981, 1989) operate within distinctly different theoretical traditions and methodological approaches—psychoanalysis and historical materialism. Yet they display a remarkably strong consensus about the object of analysis: the parameters of hegemonic masculine consciousness.

Psychoanalysis analyzes how our selves are formed in the process of trying to meet basic human needs, for example, the need to connect emotionally and physically with other people and the need to exercise some control over our lives, within the context of social constraints. The most pivotal relationships in the formation of the self are our earliest relationships. Chodorow (1978, 1991) observes that in contemporary Western society, these relationships are organized by gender in two crucial ways: men are relatively uninvolved in nurturing, and we learn to use a person's gender as a key indicator of how to treat one another. Thus the nature of these early relationships and their psychic consequences are qualitatively different for boys and for girls. Boys are likely to develop their selves in an "opposite-sex" relationship, while girls do so in a relationship defined as "same-sex." Distinctions in boys' and girls' early experiences lead to the development of gender differences in the sense of self and relationship to others: men develop a highly individuated sense of self in opposition to others and an abstract orientation to the world; for them, connection threatens the loss of identity. Women develop a connected sense of self embedded in concrete relationships; they see themselves in relationship to others.

Chodorow's analysis, like many in feminist theory, gives little attention to the dynamics of class. Her clinical data are heavily biased toward the affluent and highly educated clientele of psychoanalysis, which no doubt explains her analytic focus on the male breadwinner/female housewife nuclear-family form (see Lorber, Coser, Rossi, and Chodorow 1981 for critiques). Though the limits of her analysis imply that caution should be used in extending it beyond the relatively privileged, those same biases make Chodorow's work particularly useful for identifying the consciousness of the privileged.

Her findings parallel those of researchers who study how class organizes consciousness. Scholars in this tradition also use words like *individualistic* and *abstract* to refer to the worldview of capitalists, in contrast with a more collective and concrete orientation in the working class (e.g., Bulmer 1975; Mann 1973; Mueller 1973; Ollman 1972). Integrating Chodorow's view with Marxist perspectives, we see an argument that the consciousness of economically privileged European American men is more likely to be abstract and individuated than the worldviews of men from less-privileged classes and races and most women.

Historical Materialism and Reproductive Consciousness

Mary O'Brien (1981, 1989) uses a historical materialist approach to argue that differences in consciousness are the product of differences in the ways men and women have historically taken intentional action regarding the material imperative to reproduce. To assert social control over a process in which they are marginalized biologically, men in the European traditions she is describing have historically dominated reproduction from the outside, by creating and controlling the public sphere. Men's flight from involvement in the work of reproduction poses a challenge to the legitimacy of their control over the process, a challenge that is addressed by according the male role as much social significance as possible. This, O'Brien argues, is why the dominant patriarchal worldview of reproduction emphasizes intercourse and male potency and overlooks the value of the work of nurturing.

Having distanced themselves from the concrete community of people who do the work of caring, O'Brien says, men have created an abstract community in the public sphere. Alienated from the concrete history of human continuity across generations, men have constructed and sanctified a history of abstractions and ideas. Maintaining privilege through constructing a public/private dichotomy, they tend to see things in terms of opposition and dichotomy. The cultural and social structure they have reproduced encourages the development of a consciousness that is abstract, oppositional, and discontinuous. O'Brien's analysis shares major themes with class-based studies of consciousness. The structuring of work under capitalism leads those in privileged class locations to be more individualized and to have a more abstract orientation to the world (Hartsock 1985; Lukacs 1971).

In summary, whether looking through the lens of psychoanalysis or historical materialism, feminist scholars identify a privileged masculine consciousness, at least in this narrow social historical window, that is highly abstract, individualistic, organized in terms of oppositions, removed from the concrete world of meeting people's needs, and oriented to control.

Social Science and the Standpoint of Privileged Men

Feminists have argued that sociology in particular and social science in general are detached, both intellectually and emotionally, from the daily work of keeping life going, from the people whose lives we study, and from popular political discourse. The organization of knowledge production, from their perspective, seems more oriented to manage people, particularly people on the downside of social hierarchies, than to nurture them. Conceptual frameworks depend heavily on dichotomy, operate at high levels of abstraction, and tend to be organized in framing devices that talk of dominance and control.

The terms of the feminist critique roughly parallel the description of contemporary Western privileged masculine consciousness. The emphasis on detachment and control is the expression of a specific kind of masculine psychology, one that is threatened by all things culturally defined as feminine, including empathy and emotional connection, and by the loss of individuality through connection with another. The hegemonic masculine response to this threat is to maintain control of relationships—to connect through domination (Hartsock 1985; Keller 1982). This is striking evidence in support of Smith's (1990) claim that if sociology has a subject, it has been a (privileged) male subject.

In the end, the choice between critical realism and standpoint theory has to do with how we understand the knower. Are we looking at knowers as abstract individuals sharing the same culture that shapes their paradigms, as critical realism implies? Or are we seeing knowers as people who are located in specific positions in the social relations, organizing inequalities by race, class, gender, and nation, with all that implies for conflicting material interests, access to interpretive frameworks, and admission to effective participation in the dominant discourses?

Critical realist epistemology accepts the notion that knowledge is not a perfect mirror of reality (Walby 2001), that the culturally informed subjectivity of knowers shapes their construction of knowledge. But, in my view, stopping there is just not being critical—or realistic—enough, at least at this moment in history. Standpoint theory calls us to ask if there is something systematic and social to the nature of the biases in knowledge. Many feminist scholars working in this tradition have shown us over and over again that if we actually consider the data—the kind of knowledge that gets produced and accepted as "good"—we find systematic biases toward the interests, experience, and forms of subjectivity of the privileged. Given the choice between critical realist and standpoint approaches, the more careful choice for now is to adopt a standpoint epistemology.

Standpoints, Knowing, and Truth

The world, including humanity, is socially constructed, which is not to say that it is not real, but rather that it is the product of human activity. Human activity in the world is real, and so are the structures that humans devise to meet the challenges they face. If socially constructed categories are used to direct human social action, those categories are real because we are making them real: race, gender, class, and nation are real in their consequences (cf. Thomas and Thomas 1928). Nonetheless, if something is socially constructed, then it is not the durable, detached web of lawlike operations that positivism conjures up. It is—and we are—historically specific and changeable. Rational knowledge is open-ended because the world is open-ended.

Our methodology must center on "the dynamic between human experience and the material world" and must assume "constant change, that is, human history." Truth emerges out of the interplay between intentional, critical subjects and their social action in the world. We will attain truth, she says, when we have finally eliminated the conflicts between subjects and object, expressed as the oppositions of ideas to material reality, of consciousness to history, of thought to action. That is, truth is the outcome of people acting in concert in the world, freely, consciously, and intentionally. Since knowers are specifically situated in distinct locations, truth implies a working consensus on practical activity. Since human activity changes the world, truth is always historically specific and changeable.

Standpoint approaches raise the stakes of the discussion of epistemological choices by pointing to the political character of the project of making assumptions about the knower, the known, and the relationship between them. As Collins puts it, the concerns of epistemology are not "benign academic issues"—they are about "which version of truth will prevail and shape thought and action" (2000: 203). What does that mean for how sociologists should actually go about implementing research methods? Feminists have not yet agreed.

References

Alcoff, L. (1989). Justifying feminist social science. In N. Tuana (ed.) *Feminism & science.* Bloomington: Indiana University Press, pp. 85–103.

Bar On, B.-A. (1993). Marginality and epistemic privilege. In L. Alcoff & E. Potter (eds) *Feminist Epistemologies.* New York: Routledge, pp 83–100.

Barzun, J. & H. F. Graff. (1970). *The modern researcher.* New York: Harcourt Brace.

Bechtel, W. (1998). *Philosophy of mind: An overview for cognitive science.* Hillsdale, NJ: Erlbaum.

Bhaskar, R. & C. Norris. (1999). Roy Bhaskar interviewed. Questions by Christopher Norris. *The Philosopher's Magazine* 8. www.philosophers.co.uk/issue8.htm. Accessed July 7, 2003.

Bleier, R. (1984). *Science and gender: A critique of biology and its theories on women.* New York: Pergamon Press.

Bogdan, R. & S. J. Taylor. (1989). Relationships with severely disabled people: construction of humanness. *Social Problems* 36(2): 135–148.

Bulmer, M. (1975). *Working-class images of society.* London: Routledge and Kegan Paul.

Chodorow, N. (1978). *The reproduction of mothering: psychoanalysis and the sociology of gender.* Berkeley, CA: University of California Press.

——. (1991). *Feminism and psychoanalytic theory.* New Haven, CT: Yale University Press.

Clough, P. T. (1993). On the brink of deconstructing sociology: Critical reading of Dorothy Smith's standpoint of epistemology. *Sociological Quarterly* 34(1): 169–182.

Collier, A. (1994). *Critical realism: An introduction to the philosophy of Roy Bhaskar.* London: Verso.

Collins, P. H. (1986). Learning from the outsider within: The sociological significance of Black Feminist thought. *Social Problems* 33: 514–530.

——. (1989). The social construction of Black Feminist thought. *Signs: Journal of Women in Culture and Society* 14: 745–773.

——. (2000). *Black Feminist thought: Knowledge, consciousness, and the politics of empowerment,* 2nd edn. New York: Routledge.

Cook, T. D. & D. T. Campbell. (1979). *Quasi-experimentation: Design and analysis issues for field settings.* Boston: Houghton Mifflin.

Eagley, A. H. (1995). Connecting method and epistemology: A white woman interviewing black women. *Women's Studies in International Forum* 13(5): 477–490.

Fausto-Sterling, A. (1985). *Myths of gender: Biological theories about women and men.* New York: Basic Books.

Foucault, M. (1972). *Power/Knowledge: Selected interviews and other writings, 1972–1977.* C. Gordon. Ed. New York: Pantheon.

——. (1975/1999). *Discipline and punish.* New York: Random House.

——. (1976/1979). *The history of sexuality.* Trans. Robert Hurley. New York: Pantheon Books.

Fraser, N. (1989). *Unruly practices: Power, discourse and gender in contemporary social theory.* Minneapolis: University of Minnesota Press.

Genova, A. C. (1983). The metaphysical turn in contemporary philosophy. *Southwest Philosophical Studies* 9: 1–22.

Gilligan, C. (1982). *In a different voice*. Cambridge, MA: Harvard University Press.

Haraway, D. (1978). Animal sociology and a natural economy of the body politic. Part 1: A political sociology of dominance. *Signs: Journal of Women in Culture and Society* 4: 21–36.

——— . (1988). Situated knowledges: The science question in feminism and the privilege of partial perspective. *Feminist Studies* 14: 575–599.

——— . (1990). A manifesto for cyborgs: science, technology, and social feminism in the last quarter. In L. Nicholson. ed. *Feminism and postmodernism*, New York: Routledge, pp. 580–671.

——— . (1993). The biopolitics of postmodern bodies: determinations of self in immune system discourse. In L. S. Kauffman, ed. *American Feminist Thought at Century's End: A Reader*, Cambridge, MA: Blackwell, pp. 199–233.

Harding, S. (1998). *Is science multicultural? Postcolonialisms, feminisms, and epistemologies*. Bloomington, IN: Indiana University Press.

Hartsock, N. C. M. (1983). The feminist standpoint: Developing the ground for a specifically feminist historical material-ism. In S. Harding & M. B. P. Hintikka, eds *Discovering reality: feminist perspectives on epistemology, metaphysics, methodology and philosophy of science*, Dordrecht, The Netherlands: D. Reidel, pp. 283–310.

——— . (1985). *Money, sex, and power: Toward a feminist historical materialism*. Boston, MA: Northeastern.

Hauser, R. M., H. F. Taylor & T. Duster. (1995). The bell curve. *Contemporary Sociology* 24(2): 149–161.

Hawkesworth, M. E. (1989). Knowers, knowing, known: feminist theory and claims of truth. *Signs: Journal of Women in Culture and Society* 14(3): 533–557.

Jussim, L. (1991). Social perception and social reality: A reflection-construction model. *Psychological Review* 98: 54–73.

Keller, E. F. (1982). Feminism and science. *Signs: Journal of Women in Culture and Society* 14: 42–72.

Kessler, S. (1998). *Lessons from the intersexed*. New Brunswick, NJ: Rutgers University Press.

Kessler, S. & W. McKenna. (1978). *Gender: An ethnomethodological approach*. New York: Wiley.

Latour, B. & S. Woolgar. (1979). *Laboratory life: The social construction of scientific facts*. New York: Sage.

Longino, H. E. (1989). Feminist critique of rationality: Critiques of science of philosophy of science? *Women's Studies International Forum* 12: 261–269.

Lorber, J. (1994). *Paradoxes of gender*. New Haven, CN: Yale University Press.

Lorber, J. R. L. Corser, A. S. Rossi, and N. Chodorow. (1981). On the reproduction of mothering: A methodological debate. *Signs: Journal of Women in Culture and Society* 6: 482–514.

Lovibond, S. (1989). Feminism and postmodernism. *New Left Review*, 178 (Nov/Dec.).

Lukacs, G. (1971). *History and class consciousness*. Cambridge, MA: MIT Press.

Mann, M. (1973). *Consciousness and action among the western working class*. New York: Humanities Press.

Mannheim, K. (1936). *Ideology and Utopia*. New York: Harcourt Brace.

Mascia-Lees, F. E., P. Sharpe, & C. B. Cohen. (1989). The postmodern turns in anthropology: Cautions from a feminist perspective. *Signs: Journal of Women in Culture and Society* 15: 7–33.

Mehan, H., & H. Wood. (1975). *Reality of ethnomethodology*. New York: Wiley.

Mueller, C. (1973). *The politics of communication: A study in the political sociology of language, socialization, and legitim-ation*. New York: Oxford University Press.

Oakley, A. (2000). *Experiments in knowing: Gender and method in the social sciences*. New York: The New Press.

O'Brien, M. (1981). *The politics of reproduction*. Boston: Routledge and Kegan Paul.

——— . (1989). *Reproducing the world: Essays in feminist theory*. Boulder, CO: Westview.

Ollman, B. (1972). Toward class consciousness: Next time: Marx and the working class. *Politics & Society* 3: 1–24.

Shiva, V. (1993). Reductionism and regeneration: A crisis in science. In M. Mies & V. Shiva, eds. *Ecofeminism*. London: Zed Books, pp. 22–35.

Smith, D. E. (1979). A sociology for women. In J. A. Sherman & E. T. Beck, eds. *The prism of sex: Essays in the sociology of knowledge*, Madison, WI: University of Wisconsin Press.

——— . (1987). *The everyday world as problematic: A feminist sociology*. Boston: Northeastern University Press.

——— . (1990). *The conceptual practices of power: A feminist sociology of knowledge*. Boston: Northeastern University Press.

Sprague, J. (1996). Seeing gender as social structure. Paper presented at the annual meeting of the American Sociological Association, New York (August).

Sprague, J. & J. Hayes. (2000). Self-determination and empowerment: A feminist standpoint analysis of how we talk about disability. *American Journal of Community Psychology* 28(5): 671–795.

Tavris, C. (1992). *The mismeasure of woman*. New York: Simon & Schuster.

Thomas, W. I., & D. S. Thomas. (1928). *The child in America: behavior problems and programs*. New York: Knopf.

Walby, S. (2001). Against epistomological chasms: The science question in feminism revisited. *Signs: Journal of Women in Culture and Society* 26(2): 485–509.

Weedon, C. (1987/1997). *Feminist practice and poststructuralist theory*. 2nd edn. Oxford: Basil Blackwell.

Woldensberger, W. (1983). Social role valorization: A proposed new term for the principles of normalization. *Mental Retardation* 21(6): 234–239.

6

On Tricky Ground

Researching the Native in the Age of Uncertainty

Linda Tuhiwai Smith

[. . .]

Indigenous Research and the Spaces From Which It Speaks

Indigenous peoples can be defined as the assembly of those who have witnessed, been excluded from, and have survived modernity and imperialism. They are peoples who have experienced the imperialism and colonialism of the modern historical period beginning with the Enlightenment. They remain culturally distinct, some with their native languages and belief systems still alive. They are minorities in territories and states over which they once held sovereignty. Some indigenous peoples do hold sovereignty, but of such small states that they wield little power over their own lives because they are subject to the whims and anxieties of large and powerful states. Some indigenous communities survive outside their traditional lands because they were forcibly removed from their lands and connections. They carry many names and labels, being referred to as natives, indigenous, autochthonous, tribal peoples, or ethnic minorities. Many indigenous peoples come together at regional and international levels to argue for rights and recognition. In some countries, such as China, there are many different indigenous groups and languages. In other places, such as New Zealand, there is one indigenous group, known as Mâori, with one common language but multiple ways of defining themselves.

There are, of course, other definitions of indigenous or native peoples, stemming in part from international agreements and understandings, national laws and regulations, popular discourses, and the self-defining identities of the peoples who have been colonized and oppressed (Burger, 1987; Pritchard, 1998; Wilmer, 1993). The category of the native Other is one that Fanon (1961/1963) and Memmi (1957/1967) have argued is implicated in the same category as the settler and the colonizer. As opposing identities, they constitute each other as much as they constitute themselves. Rey Chow (1993) reminds us, however, that the native did exist before the "gaze" of the settler and before the image of "native" came to be constituted by imperialism, and that the native does have an existence outside and predating the settler/native identity. Chow (1993) refers to the "fascination" with the native as a "labor with endangered authenticities." The identity of "the native" is regarded as complicated, ambiguous, and therefore troubling even for those who live the realities and contradictions of being native and of being a member of a colonized and minority community that still remembers other ways of being, of knowing, and of relating to the world. What is troubling to the dominant cultural group about the definition of "native" is not what necessarily troubles the "native" community. The desires for "pure," uncontaminated, and simple definitions of the native by the settler is often a desire to continue to know and define the Other, whereas the desires by the native to be self-defining and self-naming can be read as a desire to be free, to escape definition, to be complicated, to develop and change, and to be regarded as fully human. In between such desires are multiple and shifting identities and hybridities with much more nuanced positions about what constitutes native identities, native communities, and native knowledge in anti/postcolonial times. There are also the not-insignificant matters of disproportionately high levels of poverty and underdevelopment, high levels of sickness and early death from preventable illnesses, disproportionate levels of incarceration, and other indices of social marginalization experienced by most indigenous communities.

There are some cautionary notes to these definitions, as native communities are not homogeneous, do not agree on the same issues and do not live in splendid isolation from the world. There are internal relations of power, as in any society, that exclude, marginalize, and silence some while empowering others. Issues of gender, economic class, age, language, and religion are also struggled over in contemporary indigenous communities. There are native indigenous communities in the developed and in the developing world, and although material conditions even for those who live in rich countries are often horrendous, people in those countries are still better off than those in developing countries. There are, however, still many native and indigenous families and communities who possess the ancient memories of another way of knowing that informs many of their contemporary practices. When the foundations of those memories are disturbed, space sometimes is created for alternative imaginings to be voiced, to be sung, and to be heard (again).

The genealogy of indigenous approaches to research and the fact that they can be reviewed in this chapter is important because they have not simply appeared overnight, nor do they exist—as with other critical research approaches—without a politics of support around them or a history of ideas. This chapter speaks from particular historical, political, and moral spaces, along with a set of relationships and connections between indigenous aspirations, political activism, scholarship, and other social justice movements and scholarly work. Indigenous communities and researchers from different parts of the globe have long and often voiced concern about the "problem of research" and represented themselves to be among the "most researched" peoples of the world. The critique of research came to be voiced in the public domain in the 1970s, when indigenous political activism was also reasserting itself (Eidheim, 1997; Humphery, 2000; Langton, 1981; L. T. Smith, 1999). The history of research from many indigenous perspectives is so deeply embedded in colonization that it has been regarded as a tool only of colonization and not as a potential tool for self-determination and development. For indigenous peoples, research has a significance that is embedded in our history as natives under the gaze of Western science and colonialism. It is framed by indigenous attempts to escape the penetration and surveillance of that gaze while simultaneously reordering, reconstituting, and redefining ourselves as peoples and communities in a state of ongoing crisis. Research is a site of contestation not simply at the level of epistemology or methodology but also in its broadest sense as an organized scholarly activity that is deeply connected to power. That resistance to research, however, is changing ever so slightly as more indigenous and minority scholars have engaged in research methodologies and debates about research with communities (Bishop, 1998; Cram, Keefe, Ormsby, & Ormsby, 1998; Humphery, 2000; Pidgeon & Hardy, 2002; Worby & Rigney, 2002). It is also changing as indigenous communities and nations have mobilized internationally and have engaged with issues related to globalization, education systems, sovereignty, and the development of new technologies.

Indigenous peoples are used to being studied by outsiders; indeed, many of the basic disciplines of knowledge are implicated in studying the Other and creating expert knowledge of the Other (Helu Thaman, 2003; Said, 1978; Minh-ha, 1989; Vidich & Lyman, 2000). More recently, however, indigenous researchers have been active in seeking ways to disrupt the "history of exploitation, suspicion, misunderstanding, and prejudice" of indigenous peoples in order to develop methodologies and approaches to research that privilege indigenous knowledges, voices, experiences, reflections, and analyses of their social, material, and spiritual conditions (Rigney, 1999, p. 117). This shift in position, from seeing ourselves as passive victims of all research to seeing ourselves as activists engaging in a counterhegemonic struggle over research, is significant. The story of that progression has been told elsewhere in more depth and is not unique to indigenous peoples; women, gay and lesbian communities, ethnic minorities, and other marginalized communities have made similar journeys of critical discovery of the role of research in their lives (Hill Collins, 1991; Ladson-Billings, 2000; Mies, 1983; Moraga & Anzaldaua, 1983; Sedgwick, 1991). There have been multiple challenges to the epistemic basis of the dominant scientific paradigm of research, and these have led to the development of approaches that have offered a promise of counterhegemonic work. Some broad examples of these include oral history as stories of the working class, the range of feminist methodologies in both quantitative and qualitative research, the development of cultural and anti/postcolonial studies, critical race theory, and other critical approaches within disciplines (Beverley, 2000; Ladson-Billings, 2000; McLaren, 1993; Mohanty, 1984; Reinharz, 1992; Spivak, 1987; Stanley & Wise, 1983). Critical theorists have held out the hope that research could lead to emancipation and social justice for oppressed groups if research understood and addressed unequal relations of power. Feminism has challenged the deep patriarchy of Western knowledge and opened up new spaces for the examination of epistemological difference. Third World women, African American women, black women, Chicanas, and other minority group women have added immensely to our understandings of the intersections of gender, race, class, and imperialism and have attempted to describe what that means for themselves as researchers choosing to research in the margins (Aldama, 2001; Elabor-Idemudia, 2002; Hill Collins, 1991; Ladson-Billings, 2000; Mohanty, 1984; Moraga & Anzaldua, 1983; Te Awekotuku, 1999). Indigenous women have played important roles in exploring the intersections of gender, race, class, and difference through the lens of native people and against the frame of colonization and oppression (Anderson, 2000; Maracle, 1996; Moreton-Robinson, 2000; L. T. Smith, 1992; Te Awekotuku, 1991; Trask, 1986).

The decolonization project in research engages in multiple layers of struggle across multiple sites. It involves the unmasking and deconstruction of imperialism, and its aspect of colonialism, in its old and new formations alongside a search for sovereignty; for reclamation of knowledge, language, and culture; and for the social transformation of the colonial relations between the native and the settler. It has been argued elsewhere that indigenous research needs an agenda that situates approaches and programs of research in the decolonization politics of the indigenous peoples movement (L. T. Smith, 1999). I would emphasize the importance of retaining the connections between the academy of researchers, the diverse indigenous communities, and the larger political struggle of decolonization because the disconnection of that relationship reinforces the colonial approach to education as divisive and destructive. This is not to suggest that such a relationship is, has been, or ever will be harmonious and idyllic; rather, it suggests that the connections, for all their turbulence, offer the best possibility for a transformative agenda that moves indigenous communities to someplace better than where they are now. Research is not just a highly moral and civilized search for knowledge; it is a set of very human activities that reproduce particular social relations of power. Decolonizing research, then, is not simply about challenging or making refinements to qualitative research. It is a much broader but still purposeful agenda for transforming the institution of research, the deep underlying structures and taken-for-granted ways of organizing, conducting, and disseminating research and knowledge. To borrow from Edward Said (1978), research can also be described as "a corporate institution" that has made state-ments about indigenous peoples, "authorising views" of us, "describing [us], teaching about [us], settling [us] and ruling over [us]." It is the corporate institution of research, as well as the epistemological foundations from which it springs, that needs to be decolonized.

> I name this research methodology as Indigenist.
>
> Lester Rigney (1999, p. 118)

Becoming an indigenous researcher is somewhat like Maxine Green's (2002) descrip-tion of how artists from the margins come to re-imagine public spaces. "Through resist-ance in the course of their becoming—through naming what stood in their way, through coming together in efforts to overcome—people are likely to find out the kinds of selves they are creating" (p. 301). Indigenous researchers are "becoming" a research com-munity. They have connected with each other across borders and have sought dialogue and conversations with each other. They write in ways that deeply resonate shared histories and struggles. They also write about what indigenous research ought to be. Australian Aborigine scholar Lester Rigney (1999), emphasizing Ward Churchill's (1993) earlier declarations of indigenist positioning, has argued for an indigenist approach to research that is formed around the three principles of *resistance, political integrity*, and *privileging* indigenous voices. He, like other indigenous researchers, connects research to liberation and to the history of oppression and racism. Rigney argues that research must serve and inform the political liberation struggle of indigenous peoples. It is also a struggle for development, for rebuilding leadership and governance structures, for strengthening social and cultural institutions, for protecting and restoring environments, and for revitalizing language and culture. Some indigenous writers would argue that indigenous research is research that is carried out by indigenous researchers with indigenous communities for indigenous communities (Cram, 2001; Rigney, 1999). Implicit in such a definition is that indigenous researchers are committed to a platform for changing the status quo and see the engagement by indigenous researchers as an important lever for transforming institutions, communities, and society. Other writers state that purpose more explicitly in that they define indigenous research as being a transformative project that is active in pursuit of social and institutional change, that makes space for indigenous knowledge, and that has a critical view of power relations and inequality (Bishop, 1998; Brady, 1999; Pihama, 2001; L. T. Smith, 1991). Others emphasize the critical role of research in enabling peoples and communities to reclaim and tell their stories in their own ways and to give *testimonio* to their collective herstories and struggles (Battiste, 2000; Beverley, 2000; The Latina Feminist Group, 2001). Embedded in these stories are the ways of knowing, deep metaphors, and motivational drivers that inspire the transformative praxis that many indigenous researchers identify as a powerful agent for resistance and change. These approaches connect and draw from indigenous knowledge and privilege indigenous pedagogies in their practices, relationships, and methodologies. Most indigenous researchers would claim that their research validates an ethical and culturally defined approach that enables indigenous communities to theorize their own lives and that connects their past histories with their future lives (Marker, 2003). Indigenous approaches are also mindful of and sensitive to the audiences of research and therefore of the accountabilities of researchers as storytellers, documenters of culture, and witnesses of the realities of indigenous lives, of their ceremonies, their aspirations, their incarcerations, their deaths. (Pihama, 1994; Steinhauer, 2003; Te Hennepe, 1993; Warrior, 1995).

In New Zealand, Mâori scholars have coined their research approach as Kaupapa Mâori or Mâori research rather than employing the term "indigenist." There are strong reasons for such a naming, as the struggle has been seen as one over Mâori language and the ability by Mâori as Mâori to name the world, to theorize the world, and to research back to power. The genealogy of indigenous research for Mâori has one of its beginnings in the development of alternative Mâori immersion-based schooling (Pihama, Cram, & Walker, 2002; G. H. Smith, 1990; L. T. Smith, 2000). Graham Smith (1990) has argued that the struggle to develop alternative schools known as Kura Kaupapa Mâori helped produce a series of educational strategies that engaged with multiple levels of colonization and social inequality. These strategies included engagement with theory and research in new ways. Kaupapa Mâori research has developed its own life, and as an approach or theory of research methodology, it has been applied across different disciplinary fields, including the sciences. It can be argued that researchers who employ a Kaupapa Mâori approach are employing quite consciously a set of arguments, principles, and frameworks that relate to the purpose, ethics, analyses, and outcomes of research (Bishop & Glynn, 1999; Durie, 1992; Johnston, 2003; Pihama, 1993; L. T. Smith, 1991; Tomlins-Jahnke, 1997). It is particular approach that sets out to make a positive difference for Mâori, that incorporates a model of social change or transformation, that privileges Mâori knowledge and ways of being, that sees the engagement in theory as well as empirical research as a significant task, and that sets out a framework for organizing, conducting, and evaluating Mâori research (Jahnke & Taiapa, 1999; Pihama et al., 2002). It is also an approach that is active in building capacity and research infrastructure in order to sustain a sovereign research agenda that supports community aspirations and development (L. T. Smith, 1999). Those who work within this approach would argue that Kaupapa Mâori research comes out of the practices, value systems, and social relations that are evident in the taken-for-granted ways that Mâori people live their lives.

Indigenist research also includes a critique of the "rules of practice" regarding research, the way research projects are funded, and the development of strategies that address community concerns about the assumptions, ethics, purposes, procedures, and outcomes of research. These strategies often have led to innovative research questions, new methodologies, new research relationships, deep analyses of the researcher in context, and analyses, interpretations, and the making of meanings that have been enriched by indigenous concepts and language. To an extent, these strategies have encouraged nonindigenous researchers into a dialogue about research and, on occasion, to a reformulated and more constructive and collaborative research relationship with indigenous communities (Cram, 1997; Haig-Brown & Archibald, 1996; Simon & Smith, 2001; G. H. Smith, 1992). Critical and social justice approaches to qualitative research have provided academic space for much of the early work of indigenous research. Denzin and Lincoln (2000) describe a moment in the history of qualitative research (1970–1986) as the moment of "blurred genres" when local knowledge and lived realities became important, when a diversity of paradigms and methods developed, and when a theoretical and methodological blurring across boundaries occurred. Arguably, an indigenist research voice emerged in that blurred and liminal space as it paralleled the rise in indigenous political activism, especially in places like Australia, New Zealand, Norway, and North America. For indigenous activists, this moment was also one of recognition that decolonization needed a positive and more inclusive social vision and needed more tools for development and self-determination (as an alternative to violent campaigns of resistance). Research, like schooling, once the tool of colonization and oppression, is very gradually coming to be seen as a potential means to reclaim languages, histories, and knowledge, to find solutions to the negative impacts of colonialism and to give voice to an alternative way of knowing and of being. Indigenous research focuses and situates the broader indigenous agenda in the research domain. This domain is dominated by a history, by institutional practices, and by particular paradigms and approaches to research held by academic communities and disciplines. The spaces within the research domain through which indigenous research can operate are small spaces on a shifting ground. Negotiating and transforming institutional practices and research frameworks is as significant as the carrying out of actual research programs. This makes indigenous research a highly political activity that can be perceived as threatening, destabilizing, and privileging of indigeneity over the interests and experiences of other diverse groups. Decolonization is political and disruptive even when the strategies employed are pacifist because anything that requires a major change of worldview, that forces a society to confront its past and address it at a structural and institutional level that challenges the systems of power, is indeed political. Indigenous research presents a challenge to the corporate institution of research to change its worldview, to confront its past and make changes.

[. . .]

Ethics and Research

One area of research being vigorously contested by indigenous communities is that of research ethics and the definitions and practices that exemplify ethical and respectful research. Indigenous researchers often situate discussions about ethics in the context of indigenous knowledge and values and in the context of imperialism, colonialism, and racism (Cram, 1993; 2001; Menzies, 2001; Rigney, 1999). Indigenous understandings of research ethics have often been informed by indigenous scholars' broad experience of research and other interactions with the media, health system, museums, schools, and government agencies. Increasingly, however, research ethics has come to be a focus of indigenous efforts to transform research and institutions (Worby & Rigney, 2002). Research ethics is often much more about institutional and professional regulations and codes of conduct than it is about the needs, aspirations, or worldviews of "marginalized and vulnerable" communities. Institutions are bound by ethical regulations designed to govern conduct within well-defined principles that have been embedded in international agreements and national laws. The Nuremberg Code (1949) was the first major international expression of principles that set out to protect the rights of people from research abuse, but there are other significant agreements, such as the World Medical Association Declaration of Helsinki Agreement of 1964 and the Belmont Report of 1979. National jurisdictions and professional societies have their own regulations that govern ethical conduct of research with human subjects. Increasingly, the challenges of new biotechnologies—for example, new birth technologies, genetic engineering, and issues related to cloning—also have given rise to ethical concerns, reviews, and revised guidelines.

For indigenous and other marginalized communities, research ethics is at a very basic level about establishing, maintaining, and nurturing reciprocal and respectful relationships, not just among people as individuals but also with people as individuals, as collectives, and as members of communities, and with humans who live in and with other entities in the environment. The abilities to enter preexisting relationships; to build, maintain, and nurture relationships; and to strengthen connectivity are important research skills in the indigenous arena. They require critical sensitivity and reciprocity of spirit by a researcher. Bishop (1998) refers to an example of relationship building in the Māori context as whakawhanaun-gatanga, "the process of establishing family (whānau) relationships, literally by means of dentifying, through culturally appropriate means, your bodily linkage, your engagement, your connectedness, and therefore, an unspoken but implicit commitment to other people" (p. 203). Worby and Rigney (2002) refer to the "Five Rs: Resources, Reputations, Relationships, Reconciliation and Research" (pp. 27–28) as informing the process of gaining ethical consent. They argue that "The dynamic relationship between givers and receivers of knowledge is a reminder that dealing with indigenous issues is one of the most sensitive and complex tasks facing teachers, learners and researchers at all levels . . ." (p. 27). Bishop and Glynn (1992) also make the point that relationships are not simply about making friends. They argue that researchers must be self-aware of their position within the relationship and aware of their need for engagement in power-sharing processes.

In *Decolonizing Methodologies* (L. T. Smith, 1999), I also gave some examples of the ways in which my communities may describe respect, respectful conduct, trustworthiness, and integrity at a day-to-day level of practice and community assessment. My concern was to show that community people, like everyone else, make assessments of character at every interaction. They assess people from the first time they see them, hear them, and engage with them. They assess them by the tone of a letter that is sent, as well as by the way they eat, dress, and speak. These are applied to strangers as well as insiders. We all do it. Different cultures, societies, and groups have ways of masking, revealing, and managing how much of the assessment is actually conveyed to the other person and, when it is communicated, in what form and for what purpose. A colleague, Fiona Cram (2001), has translated how the selected value statements in *Decolonizing Methodologies* could be applied by researchers to reflect on their own codes of conduct. This could be described as an exercise of "bottom-up" or "community-up" defining of ethical behaviors that create opportunities to discuss and negotiate what is meant by the term "respect." Other colleagues have elaborated on the values, adding more and reframing some to incorporate other cultural expressions. One point to make is that most ethical codes are top down, in the sense of "moral" philosophy framing the meanings of ethics and in the sense that the powerful still make decisions for the powerless. The discussions, dialogues, and conversations about what ethical research conduct looks like are conducted in the meeting rooms of the powerful.

No one would dispute the principle of *respect*; indeed, it is embedded in all the major ethical protocols for researching with human subjects. However, what is *respect*, and how do we know when researchers are behaving respectfully? What does *respect* entail at a day-to-day level of interaction? To be respectful, what else does a researcher need to under-

Table 6.1 "Community-Up" Approach to Defining Researcher Conduct

Cultural Values (Smith, 1999)	Researcher Guideline (Cram, 2001)
Aroha ki te tangata	A respect for people—allow people to define their own space and meet on their own terms.
He kanohi kitea	It is important to meet people face to face, especially when introducing the idea of the research, "fronting up" to the community before sending out long, complicated letters and materials.
Titiro, whakarongo . . . kôrero	Looking and listening (and then maybe speaking). This value emphasizes the importance of looking/observing and listening in order to develop understandings and find a place from which to speak.
Manaaki ki te tangata	Sharing, hosting, being generous. This is a value that underpins a collaborative approach to research, one that enables knowledge to flow both ways and that acknowledges the researcher as a learner and not just a data gatherer or observer. It is also facilitates the process of "giving back," of sharing results and of bringing closure if that is required for a project but not to a relationship.
Kia tupato	Be cautious. This suggests that researchers need to be politically astute, culturally safe, and reflective about their insider/outsider status. It is also a caution to insiders and outsiders that in community research, things can come undone without the researcher being aware or being told directly.
Kaua e takahia te mana o te tangata	Do not trample on the "mana" or dignity of a person. This is about informing people and guarding against being paternalistic or impatient because people do not know what the researcher may know. It is also about simple things like the way Westerners use wit, sarcasm, and irony as discursive strategies or where one sits down. For example, Mâori people are offended when someone sits on a table designed and used for food.
Kaua e mahaki	Do not flaunt your knowledge. This is about finding ways to share knowledge, to be generous with knowledge without being a "show-off" or being arrogant. Sharing knowledge is about empowering a process, but the community has to empower itself.

stand? It is when we ask questions about the apparently universal value of respect that things come undone, because the basic premise of that value is quintessentially Euro-American. What at first appears a simple matter of *respect* can end up as a complicated matter of cultural protocols, languages of respect, rituals of respect, dress codes: in short, the "p's and q's" of etiquette specific to cultural, gender, and class groups and subgroups. *Respect*, like other social values, embraces quite complex social norms, behaviors, and meanings, as one of many competing and active values in any given social situation. As an ethical principle, *respect* is constructed as universal partly through the process of defining what it means in philosophical and moral terms, partly through a process of distancing the social value and practice of *respect* from the messiness of any particular set of social interactions, and partly through a process of wrapping up the principle in a legal and procedural framework. The practice of *respect* in research is interpreted and expressed in very different ways on the basis of methodology, theoretical paradigms, institutional preparation, and individual idiosyncrasies and "manners."

Similarly, the principle and practice of *informed consent* presents real-world problems for researchers and for the researched. Fine, Weis, Weseen, and Wong (2000) already have discussed the ways in which "the consent form sits at the contradictory base of the institutionalisation of research" (p. 113). The form itself can be, as they argue, a "crude tool—a conscience—to remind us of our accountability and position" (p. 113). They ague that a consent form makes the power relations between researchers and researched concrete, and this can present challenges to researchers and researched alike, with some participants *wanting* to share their stories while others may feel *compelled* to share. The form itself can be the basis of dialogue and mediation, but the individual person who is participating in the research still must sign it. The principle of *informed consent* is based on the right of individuals to give consent to participation once they have been informed about the project and believe that they understand the project. In some jurisdictions, this right does not necessarily apply to children, prisoners, or people who have a mental illness. Nevertheless, the right is an individual one. However, what if participating in a research project, unwittingly or wittingly, reveals collective information to researchers—for example, providing DNA, sharing the making of a medicine, or revealing secret women's or men's business as may occur in societies like Aboriginal Australian communities, where men's knowledge and women's knowledge are strictly differentiated? Researching with children already has opened up the possibility that family secrets, especially stories of abuse, require actions to be taken beyond the simple gathering of data. One concern of indigenous communities about the *informed consent* principle is about the bleeding of knowledge away from collective protection through individual participation in research, with knowledge moving to scientists and organizations in the world at large. This process weakens indigenous collectively shared knowledge and is especially risky in an era of knowledge hunting and gathering. Another concern is about the nature of what it ready means to be informed for people who may not be literate or well educated, who may not speak the language of the researcher, and who may not be able to differentiate the *invitation* to participate in research from the enforced compliance in signing official forms for welfare and social service agencies.

The claim to universal principles is one of the difficulties with ethical codes of conduct for research. It is not just that the concepts of respect, beneficence, and justice have been defined through Western eyes; there are other principles that inform ethical codes that can be problematic under certain conditions. In some indigenous contexts, the issue is framed more around the concept of *human rights* rather than principles or values. However, whether it is about principles, values, or rights, there is a common underpinning. Ethics codes are for the most part about protecting the individual, not the collective. Individuals can be "picked off" by researchers even when a community signals it does not approve of a project. Similarly, the claim to beneficence, the "save mankind" claim made even before research has been completed, is used to provide a moral imperative that certain forms of research must be supported at the expense of either individual or community consent. Research is often assumed to be beneficial simply because it is framed as research; its benefits are regarded as "self-evident" because the intentions of the researcher are "good." In a review of health research literature reporting on research involving indigenous Australians, Anderson, Griew, and McAullay (2003) suggest that very little attention is paid to the concept of benefit by researchers, and even less attention is paid to the assessment of research benefit. A consequence of the lack of guidelines in this area, they argue, is that "in the absence of any other guidelines the values that guide such a judgement will reflect those of the ethics committee as opposed to those of the Indigenous community in which research is proposed" (p. 26).

A more significant difficulty, already alluded to, can be expressed more in terms of "who" governs, regulates, interprets, sanctions, and monitors ethical codes of conduct", "Who" is responsible if things go terribly wrong? And "who" really governs and regulates the behaviors of scientists outside institutions and voluntary professional societies? For example, rogue scientists and quirky religious groups are already competing for the glory of cloning human beings with those whose research is at least held to a acceptable standards because of their employment in recognized institutions. From an indigenous perspective, the "who" on ethical review boards is representative of narrow class, religious, academic, and ethnic groups rather than reflecting the diversity of society. Because these boards are fundamentally supportive of research for advancing knowledge and other high-level aims, their main task is to advance research, not to limit it. In other words, their purpose is not neutral; it is to assist institutions to undertake research—within acceptable standards. These boards are not where larger questions about society's interests in research ought to be discussed; they generally are the place where already determined views about research are processed, primarily to protect institutions. Marginalized and vulnerable groups are not, by and large, represented on such boards. If a marginalized group is represented, its voice is muted as one of many voices of equal weight but not of equal power. Hence, even if a representative of a marginalized group is included on a review board, the individual may not have the support, the knowledge, or the language to debate the issue among those who accept the dominant Western view of ethics and society. These are difficult concerns to resolve but need to be discussed in an ongoing way, as ethical challenges will always exist in societies.

[. . .]

References

Aldama, A. J. (2001). *Disrupting savagism: Intersecting Chicana/o, Mexican immigrant, and Native American struggles for self-representation*. Durham, NC: Duke University Press.

Alexander, M. J., & Mohanty, C. T. (1997). *Feminist genealogies, colonial legacies, democratic futures*. New York: Routledge.

Anderson, K. (2000). *A recognition of being: Reconstructing native womanhood.* Toronto: Sumach Press.

Anderson, I., Griew, R., & McAullay, D. (2003). Ethics guidelines, health research and indigenous Australians. *New Zealand Bioethics Journal, 4*(1), 20–29.

Battiste, M. (Ed.). (2000). *Reclaiming indigenous voice and vision.* Vancouver: University of British Columbia Press.

Beverley, J. (2000). Testimonio, subalternity, and narrative authority. In N. Denzin & Y. S. Lincoln (Eds.), *Handbook of qualitative research* (2nd ed., pp. 555–566). Thousand Oaks: Sage.

Bishop, R. (1998). Freeing ourselves from neo-colonial domination in research: A Mâori approach to creating knowledge. *Qualitative Studies in Education, 11*(2), 199–219.

Bishop, R., & Glynn, T. (1992). He kanohi kitea: Conducting and evaluating educational research. *New Zealand Journal of Educational Studies, 27*(2), 125–135.

Bishop, R., & Glynn, T. (1999). Researching in Mâori contexts: An interpretation of participatory consciousness. *Journal of Intercultural Studies, 20*(2), 167–182.

Brady, W. (1999). Observing the Other. *Eureka Street, 9*(1), 28–30.

Burger, J. (1987). *Report from the frontier: The state of the world's indigenous peoples.* London: Zed Books.

Chow, R. (1993). *Writing diaspora: Tactics of intervention in contemporary cultural studies.* Bloomington: Indiana University Press.

Churchill, W. (1993). I am indigenist. In W. Churchill (Ed.), *Struggle for the land: Indigenous resistance to genocide, ecocide, and expropriation in contemporary North America* (pp. 403–451). Monroe, ME: Common Courage Press.

Cram, F. (1993). Ethics in Mâori research. In L. Nikora (Ed.), *Cultural justice and ethics.* [Proceedings of the Cultural Justice and Ethics Symposium held as part of the New Zealand Psychological Society's annual conference]. Wellington, New Zealand: Victoria University.

Cram, F. (1997). Developing partnerships in research: Pâkehâ researchers and Mâori research. *Sites, 35,* 44–63.

Cram, F. (2001). Rangahau Mâori: Tona tika, tona pono—The validity and integrity of Mâori research. In M. Tolich (Ed.), *Research ethics in Aotearoa New Zealand* (pp. 35–52). Auckland, New Zealand: Pearson Education.

Cram, F., Keefe, V., Ormsby, C., & Ormsby, W. (1998). Memorywork and Mâori health research: Discussion of a qualitative method. *He Pukenga Kôrero: A Journal of Mâori Studies,* 37–45.

Denzin, N., & Lincoln, Y. S. (2000). The discipline and practice of qualitative research. In N. Denzin & Y. S. Lincoln (Eds.), *Handbook of qualitative research* (2nd ed., pp. 128). Thousand Oaks, CA: Sage.

Durie, A. (1992). *Whaia te Ara Tika: Research methodologies and Mâori.* Seminar on Mâori research at Massey University, Palmerston North, New Zealand.

Eidheim, H. (1997). Ethno-political development among the Sami after World War II: The invention of self-hood. In H. Gaski (Ed.), *Sami culture in a new era: The Norwegian Sami experience* (pp. 29–61). Kárásjohka, Norway: Davvi Girji.

Elabor-Idemudia, P. (2002). Participatory research: A tool in the production of knowledge in development discourse. In K. Saunders (Ed.), *Feminist development and thought: Rethinking modernity, post-colonialism and representation* (pp. 227–242). London: Zed Books.

Fanon, F. (1963). *Wretched of the earth* (C. Farrington, Trans.). New York: Grove Press. (Original work published 1961)

Fine, M., Weis, L., Weseen, S., & Wong, L. (2000). For whom? Qualitative research, representations, and social responsibilities. In N. Denzin & Y. S. Lincoln (Eds.), *Handbook of qualitative research* (2nd ed., pp. 107–132). Thousand Oaks, CA: Sage.

Green, M. (2000). Lived spaces, shared spaces, public spaces. In L. Weis & M. Fine (Eds.), *Construction sites: Excavating race, class, and gender among urban youth* (pp. 293–304). New York: Teachers College Press.

Haig-Brown, C., & Archibald, J. (1996). Transforming First Nations research with respect and power. *Qualitative Studies in Education, 9*(3), 245–267.

Helu Thaman, K. (2003). *Re-presenting and re-searching Oceania: A suggestion for synthesis.* Keynote address to the Pacific Health Research Fono, Health Research Council of New Zealand, Auckland.

Hill Collins, P. (1991). Learning from the outsider within. In M. Fonow & J. A. Cook (Eds.), *Beyond methodology: Feminist scholarship as lived research* (pp. 35–57). Bloomington: Indiana University Press.

Humphery, K. (2000). *Indigenous health and "Western research"* (Discussion paper for VicHealth Koori Health Research and Community Development Unit). Melbourne: Centre for the Study of Health and Society, University of Melbourne.

Jahnke, H., & Taiapa, J. (1999). Mâori research. In C. Davidson & M. Tolich (Eds.), *Social science research in New Zealand: Many paths to understanding* (pp. 39–50). Auckland, New Zealand: Longman Pearson Education.

Johnston, P. M. (2003). Research in a bicultural context: The case in Aotearoa/New Zealand. In J. Swann & J. Pratt (Eds.), *Educational research practice: Making sense of methodology* (pp. 98–110). London: Continuum.

Ladson-Billings, G. (2000). Racialized discourses and ethnic epistemologies. In N. K. Denzin & Y. S. Lincoln (Eds.), *Handbook of qualitative research* (2nd ed., pp. 257–278). Thousand Oaks, CA: Sage.

Langton, M. (1981). Anthropologists must change. *Identity, 4*(4), 11.

The Latina Feminist Group. (2001). *Telling to live: Latina feminist testimonios.* Durham, NC: Duke University Press.

Maracle, L. (1996). *I am woman: A native perspective on sociology and feminism.* Vancouver: Press Gang Publishers.

Marker, M. (2003). Indigenous voice, community, and epistemic violence: The ethnographer's "interests" and what "interests" the ethnographer. *Qualitative Studies in Education, 16*(3), 361–375.

McLaren, P. (1993). Border disputes: Multicultural narrative, identity formation, and critical pedagogy in post-modern America. In D. McLaughlin & W. G. Tierney (Eds.), *Naming silenced lives* (pp. 201–236). New York: Routledge.

Memmi, A. (1967). *The colonizer and the colonized.* Boston: Beacon Press. (Original work published 1957)

Menzies, C. (2001). Researching with, for and among indigenous peoples. *Canadian Journal of Native Education, 25*(1), 19–36.

Mies, M. (1983). Towards a methodology for feminist research. In G. Bowles & R. D. Klein (Eds.), *Theories of women's studies* (pp. 117–139). New York: Routledge.

Minh-ha, T. T. (1989). *Woman, native, other: Writing, postcoloniality and feminism.* Bloomington: Indiana University Press.

Mohanty, C. (1984). Under Western eyes: Feminist scholarship and colonial discourses. *Boundary, 12*(3) and *13*(1), 338–358.

Moraga, C., & Anzaldua, G. (Eds.). (1983). *This bridge called my back.* New York: Kitchen Table Press.

Moreton-Robinson, A. (2000). *Talkin' up to the white woman: Indigenous women and feminism.* St. Lucia: University of Queensland Press.

Pidgeon, M., & Hardy, C. (2002). Researching with Aboriginal peoples: Practices and principles. *Canadian Journal of Native Education, 26*(2), 96–106.

Pihama, L. (1993). *Tungia te ururua kia tupu whakarirorito te tupu o te harakeke.* Unpublished master's thesis, University of Auckland.

Pihama, L. (1994). Are films dangerous?: A Mâori woman's perspective on *The Piano, Hecate, 20*(2), 239–242.

Pihama, L. (2001). *Tihei Mauriora: Honouring our voices—mana wahine as a kaupapa Maori theoretical framework.* Unpublished doctoral thesis, University of Auckland.

Pihama, L., Cram, F., & Walker, S. (2002). Creating methodological space: A literature review of Kaupapa Mâori research. *Canadian Journal of Native Education, 26*(1), 30–43.

Pritchard, S. (Ed.). (1998). *Indigenous peoples, the United Nations and human rights.* London: Zed Books.

Reinharz, S. (1992). *Feminist methods in social research.* New York: Oxford University Press.

Rigney, L. (1999). Internationalization of an indigenous anticolonial cultural critique of research methodologies. A guide to indigenist research methodology and its principles. *Wicazo SA Journal of Native American Studies Review, 14*(2), 109–121.

Said, E. (1978). *Orientalism.* London: Vintage Books.

Sedgwick, E. K. (1991). *Epistemology of the closet.* New York: Harvester Wheatsheaf.

Simon, J., & Smith, L. T. (Eds.). (2001). *A civilising mission? Perceptions and representations of the New Zealand Native Schools system.* Auckland, New Zealand: Auckland University Press.

Smith, G. H. (1990). The politics of reforming Maori education: The transforming potential of kura kaupapa Maori. In H. Lauder & C. Wylie (Eds.), *Towards successful schooling* (pp. 73–89). Basingstoke: Falmer.

Smith, G. H. (1992). *Research issues related to Mâori education.* Auckland, New Zealand: Research Unit for Mâori Education, The University of Auckland.

Smith, L. T. (1992). Mâori women: Discourses, projects and mana wahine. In S. Middleton & A. Jones (Eds.), *Women and education in Aotearoa 2* (pp. 33–51). Wellington, New Zealand Bridget Williams Books.

Smith, L. T. (1991). Te rapunga i te ao marama (the search for the world of light): Mâori perspectives on research in education. In T. Linzey & J. Morss (Eds.), *Growing up: The politics of human learning* (pp. 46–55). Auckland, New Zealand: Longman Paul.

Smith, L. T. (1999). *Decolonizing methodologies: Research and indigenous peoples.* London: Zed Books.

Smith, L. T. (2000). Kaupapa Mâori research. In M. Battiste (Ed.), *Reclaiming indigenous voice and vision* (pp. 225–247). Vancouver: University of British Columbia Press.

Spivak, G. (1987). *In other worlds: Essays in cultural politics.* New York: Methuen.

Stanley, L., & Wise, S. (1983). *Breaking out: Feminist consciousness and feminist research.* London: Routledge & Kegan Paul.

Steinhauer, E. (2003). Thoughts on an indigenous research methodology. *Canadian Journal of Native Education, 26*(2), 69–81.

Te Awekotuku, N. (1991). *Mana wahine Mâori.* Auckland, New Zealand: New Women's Press.

Te Awekotuku, N. (1999). Mâori women and research: Researching ourselves. In *Mâori psychology: Research and practice* (pp. 57–63) [Proceedings of a symposium sponsored by the Mâori and Psychology Research Unit, University of Waikato]. Hamilton, New Zealand: University of Waikato.

Te Hennepe, S. (1993). Issues of respect: Reflections of First Nations students' experiences in post-secondary anthropology classrooms. *Canadian Journal of Native Education, 20*, 193–260.

Tomlins-Jahnke, H. (1997). Towards a theory of mana wahine. *He Pukenga Kôrero: A Journal of Mâori Studies, 3*(1), 27–36.

Trask, H.-K. (1986). *Eros and power: The promise of feminist theory.* Philadelphia: University of Pennsylvania Press.

Vidich, A. J., & Lyman, S. M. (2000). Qualitative methods: Their history in sociology and anthropology. In N. K. Denzin & Y. S. Lincoln (Eds.), *Handbook of qualitative research* (pp. 37–84). Thousand Oaks, CA: Sage.

Warrior, R. A. (1995). *Tribal secrets: Recovering American Indian intellectual traditions.* Minneapolis: University of Minnesota Press.

Wilmer, F. (1993). *The indigenous voice in world politics.* Newbury Park, CA: Sage.

Worby, G., & Rigney, D. (2002). Approaching ethical issues: Institutional management of indigenous research. *Australian Universities Review, 45*(1), 24–33.

7

Practice, Participatory Research and Creative Research Designs

The Evolution of Ethical Guidelines for Research

Walter Haney and M. Brinton Lykes

In this chapter we discuss dilemmas we have experienced as researchers within communities of action. We summarize briefly the guidelines and ethical standards for research with human subjects,[1] standards that formed the core of our socialization into the ethics of behavioral research. Until recently, these ethical standards and guidelines have evolved among various occupational groups with relatively little attention to the intersection of research methodology and ethical considerations. We describe how federal guidelines on research with human subjects have evolved and some of the effects these guidelines have had on research within the professions. Our personal experiences with ethical issues in research beyond university walls provide examples for discussing some of the inevitable dilemmas encountered in participatory and action-oriented research for change. Specifically, we explore the meanings of informed consent when one is engaged with communities in struggles for justice and/or in challenges to injustice within dominant institutions on behalf of those who are not being well-served by these institutions. Our experiences suggest limitations in applying abstract ethical guidelines and standards to such cases. We elaborate several dilemmas raised by creative research designs characteristic of much outreach scholarship for ethical standards and guidelines of selected occupational groups.

It is worth noting that ethics, or moral philosophy, is concerned with the conduct and care of morals, that is, the study of principles and methods for distinguishing right from wrong, good from bad, and just from unjust. One of the first uses of the term "ethic," according to the Oxford English Dictionary came from Apol Poetrie (1581). "The Ethicke and politick consideration, with the end of well doing and not of well knowing only." This original use of "ethic" seems to convey much of the current concern for ethical consideration in research with human subjects—the need to balance not just the research aim of contributing to knowledge, but the moral aim of not just well knowing but well doing in one's dealings with other humans. In the work discussed here we are particularly concerned with issues of justice and how justice is articulated within and among diverse communities.

By way of introduction, we acknowledge also that we are not well versed in philosophy or the study of ethics in general. Despite this we hope it will be useful to describe some of what we have learned about the evolution of guidelines in research with human subjects and how contemporary institutional guidelines on research with human subjects stem quite specifically though indirectly from the most unfortunate Tuskegee syphilis study.

After this review we summarize the manner in which we have sought to deal with ethical dilemmas in some of our own research. In particular we describe how we have dealt with issues such as informed consent when work that began as something other than formal research evolved into just that. Also, we describe how we have had to go beyond the normal boundaries of academic inquiry to use research not just to contribute to knowledge, but to effect social change. We hope that our discussion of our own dilemmas, and our perceptions of the limitations of ethical guidelines on research with human subjects, will inform ongoing consideration of ethical issues and future revisions of ethical guidelines.

Ethical Standards Among Occupational Groups

Many professions have developed ethical codes or standards. Apparently the oldest code of ethics for an occupational group is the Hippocratic Oath, with its rules of conduct for physicians. It dates back to the fourth century BC and contains two major sections. The first specifies the duties of the physician to his teachers and his obligations in transmitting medical knowledge. The second provides rules to be observed in the treatment of diseases and is a short summary of medical ethics expressed in general principles. In a 1948 Geneva Convention, a modern version of the oath was drawn up by the World Medical Association and this was amended in 1968, as follows:

At the time of being admitted a member of the medical profession swears:

> I solemnly pledge myself to consecrate my life to the service of humanity; I will give my teachers the respect and gratitude which is their due; I will practice my profession with conscience and dignity; The health of my patient will be my first consideration; I will respect the secrets which are confided in me, even after the patient has died; I will maintain by all the means in my power, the honor and the noble traditions of the medical profession; my colleagues will be my brothers. I will not permit considerations of religion, nationality, race, party politics or social standing to intervene between my duty and my patient; I will maintain the utmost respect for human life from the time of conception; even under threat I will not use my medical knowledge contrary to the laws of humanity. I make these promises solemnly, freely and upon my honour.

In the twentieth century, many professional groups have developed their own codes of ethics; for example, codes of ethics have been developed by the American Psychological Association (APA), the National Educational Association (NEA), the American Federation of Teachers (AFT), and the American Educational Research Association (AERA). The oldest of these modern ethical standards of occupational groups is the ethical standards of psychologists (APA) promulgated in 1953. This original version of APA ethical standards for psychologists was 170 pages long, divided into six sections dealing with public responsibility, client relationships, teaching, research, writing and publishing, and professional relationships. The section dealing with research contained three specific guidelines dealing with the psychologist's responsibility (1) for adequately planning and conducting research, (2) for reporting research results, and (3) for relating to research subjects. The latter guideline outlined the psychologist's responsibility for protecting the subject's welfare, for preventing unauthorized identification of subjects and fulfillment of obligations to subjects. The 1953 APA standards made no mention specifically of informed consent as a general requirement. Specifically, under Principle 4.31–2 the psychologist is justified in withholding information from or giving false information to research subjects only when in his (sic) judgment this is clearly required by his (sic) research problem and when the provisions of the above principles regarding the protection of subjects are adhered to. A parenthetical comment followed this guideline noting that when the danger of serious after-effects exists, research should be conducted only when the subjects or their responsible agents are fully informed of this possibility and volunteer nevertheless (Haney & Madaus, 1990).

Since 1953 the ethical guidelines of the APA have gone through several revisions. In 1958 they were revised and renamed *The Standards of Ethical Behavior for Psychologists*. The 1963 revision was entitled *The Ethical Standards of Psychologists*. It was revised again in 1977, 1981 and 1990. The most recent version of the APA's guidelines, issued in 1992, was called *The Ethical Principles of Psychologists and Code of Conduct*.

By 1981, Principle 9 of the Ethical Principles dealt specifically with research with human subjects and provided a much stronger guideline for informed consent, specifying the obligation of psychologists to gain informed consent of research subjects. Nonetheless, the following standard still held out the possibility of dispensing with informed consent under the following circumstances:

> Before determining that planned research (such as research involving only anonymous questionnaires, naturalistic observations, or certain kinds of archival research) does not require the informed consent of research participants, psychologists consider applicable regulations and review board requirements, and they consult with colleagues as appropriate.[2]

Continuing and increasing concern for ethical issues in research with human beings is reflected in the fact that in late 1998, the APA circulated for public comment a new proposed revision of its ethical guidelines.

In contrast to the APA Ethical Standards, the American Educational Research Association (AERA) has only very recently issued ethical standards. In June 1992, the AERA developed and adopted *The Ethical Standards of the American Educational Research Association*. These standards were intended to be an educational document to "stimulate collegial debate, and to evoke voluntary compliance by moral persuasion. Accordingly it is not the intention of the Association to monitor adherence to the Standards or to investigate allegations of violations of the Code." The 1992 AERA Ethical Standards apprised: "Participants, or their guardians, in a research study have the right to be informed about the likely risks involved in the research and of potential consequences for participants, and to give their informed consent before they participate in research."[3]

Before analyzing some of our own research experiences in which these guidelines proved helpful but problematic, we backtrack to recount the manner in which federal guidelines on research with human subjects evolved. An understanding of this sociohistorical context will contribute to better understanding the limitations of current guidelines.

Federal Guidelines on Research With Human Subjects

As early as mid-century international guidelines for research with human subjects had been established; for example in the Nuremberg Code of 1947 (e.g., the Declaration of Helsinki issued in 1964 and amended in 1975, and the International Guidelines for Biomedical Research Involving Human Subjects proposed in 1982 by the Council for International Organizations of Medical Sciences (CIOMS) and the World Health

Organization (WHO) (LaVertu & Linares, 1990). Increased attention to guidelines on research with human subjects in the United States was prompted in the United States by hearings in 1973 of the Senate Health Committee, then chaired by Senator Edward Kennedy. The Senate Health Committee held these hearings to investigate abuses in research with human subjects. Among the prominent cases dealt with in these hearings was the Public Health Service Tuskegee study in which 400 Black men with syphilis were studied from 1932 to 1972. They participated in this study for 40 years without ever being told that they had the disease or being treated for it, even though penicillin, a cure for the disease, had been discovered in 1943. The Tuskegee Study was terminated only after details of the study were uncovered by an intrepid newspaper reporter. Publicity given to the Tuskegee tragedy and other abuses led quite directly to the promulgation of federal guidelines. In 1974 the National Research Act mandated the National Commission for the protection of Human Subjects of Biomedical and Behavioral Research and the creation of Institutional Review Boards or IRBs in all institutions that were receiving federal research money. In 1975 the Department of Health, Education and Welfare ordered every institution applying for research grants to establish an IRB to evaluate grant submissions.

The 1979 Belmont Report, one of the key documents in the evolution of federal guidelines concerning research with human subjects, set out the Ethical Principles and Guidelines for the Protection of Human Subjects of Research. This was sponsored by the National Institutes of Health (NIH), Public Health Service (PHS), and the Health and Human Services Department (HHS). Specifically, the Belmont Report described the boundaries between research and practice as well as the basic ethical principles undergirding specific guidelines for research, namely respect for persons, beneficence, and justice. The third part of the Belmont report drew out the specific applications or guidelines motivated by these ethical principles: concern for informed consent, an assessment of risks and benefits, and care in selection of subjects. The federal guidelines evolved quite rapidly after this. The Code of Federal Regulations, with provisions dealing with research with human subjects was issued in 1981, March of 1982, July 1989, and again in 1991. Specifically, the June 18, 1991 Federal Register (10 C.F.R. part 27) set forth a common federal policy for protection of human subjects agreed to by sixteen federal agencies. In addition to elaborating standards for review by institutional review boards (IRB), this federal guideline also mandated establishment of procedures for dealing with cases of alleged misconduct. These federal guidelines have resulted in the establishment of IRBs in every research institution receiving or aspiring to receive, federal funding. In essence, Congressional and public outrage over the Tuskegee Study in the early 1970s led indirectly, but quite specifically, to the mandate for IRBs in universities and other research institutions in the 1990s.

Ethical Dilemmas in Applied and Action Research

Like all seasoned researchers working beyond university walls, both of us have had personal ethical quandaries in conducting research. We grapple with our professional guidelines as we work on behalf of people who have been, not subjects, but rather participants in our research. Even more difficult have been situations in which initiatives that began as something other than formal research evolved over an extended period into research. In some instances, for example, we have developed collaborative relationships over years of community-based activism that led us to seek to creatively design participatory research. As human relationships evolve, it is sometimes difficult to distinguish roles of researcher and subject, and hence to apply existing ethical guidelines that presume a clear and unchanging delineation of these roles. In a 1979 *American Psychologist* article Mirvis and Seashore, facing similar experiences within their own organizational research, proposed that role theory was a resource for analyzing such ethical quandaries. Rather than proposing prescriptive roles for the researcher they explored how critique of our own roles, norms that govern our roles and institutions themselves, can inform ethical decision-making within a field research process (Mirvis & Seashore, 1979). Our experiences suggest additional considerations in ongoing efforts to articulate ethical research guidelines.

Within this context, Walt Haney describes two of his experiences in trying to use research to effect social change. Brinton Lykes then discusses her experiences crossing cultural borders employing participatory research methods. What is common about these accounts, drawn from different research traditions and settings, is that they illustrate both the utility and the difficulty in applying abstract ethical guidelines to endeavors which are not just academic research *on* others as subjects but rather inquiry *with* others to improve practice.

Institutions as Objects/Subjects of Inquiry

The first case began in 1991 when I was asked to help a young man who had, in effect, been accused of cheating on the Scholastic Aptitude Test (SAT) and was under threat of having his scores canceled. The young man, to whom I refer as John Smith, had taken the SAT twice. On the March 1990 administration he had received an SAT-Verbal score of 280. On the November 1990 SAT, he had received an SAT-V score of 500. This gain of 220 points, while unusually large, was not of sufficient magnitude to trigger screening by Test Security Office (TSO) of the Educational Testing Service (ETS). However, one of the recipients of John Smith's scores asked ETS about the unusual gain, and that inquiry triggered TSO review of the case. Among other things the ETS investigators compared Smith's answers with those of other test-takers in the same test center. Apparently, the large score gain combined with an unusual agreement of answers apparent in answer sheets of Smith and another test taker prompted ETS to accuse Smith of cheating and threaten to withhold his scores.

After a flurry of correspondence between ETS and Smith, Smith's parents contacted me and, due to my interest in the obscure subject of statistical methods for detecting possible cheating on tests (that is how the topic is often described in published literature, but I prefer to refer to the topic as statistical methods for identifying unusual answer concordance), I decided to look into the case. After a quick literature review, an analysis of the facts in the case, and statistical analyses to try to reproduce ETS's answer concordance results, I concluded that the statistical evidence against Smith was not at all persuasive, and that the manner in which ETS had handled the case was in violation of specific provisions of the 1985 test *Standards.* After a memo summarizing my findings was sent to the ETS Test Security Office by Smith's father, the case against Smith was dropped and his scores were released.

Concerned about what I had learned, I sought Smith's parents' permission to bring my concerns to the attention of top officials at ETS and to circulate a pseudonymous version of my memo. At this point in this story an ethical dilemma arises: A young man whom I had started out trying to help, turned into my research "subject," when I started sharing information (and eventually publishing accounts) about his case. Under the circumstances, I could not obtain informed consent before the research began (though some sort of consent might be imputed from Smith's request for help). As an alternative solution, I showed Smith and his parents my pseudonymous account of the case and obtained their approval before circulating the story.

The larger ethical dilemma occurred afterwards. Though the ETS officials to whose attention I had sought to bring my concerns thanked me for my observations, they left me with little confidence that the procedures I thought were severely flawed would be changed. However, in August 1992, I learned of a second test security case in which a young man named Brian Dalton had challenged ETS test security procedures in a New York court. In a trial lasting two weeks, several ETS security specialists had been called to testify. The trial court concluded that Dalton's legal challenge was meritorious and ordered ETS to release the questioned scores. ETS appealed this decision to a higher court. My reading of the transcripts of the Dalton trial led me to conclude that the TSO procedures were even more flawed than I had suspected from my work on the Smith case. Hence, in connection with a paper under preparation (Haney, 1993a), I formally requested that three professional organizations that had sponsored the 1985 test *Standards* (the American Psychological Association, American Educational Research Association, and the National Council on Measurement in Education) investigate what I suspected to be serious and ongoing violations of professional standards (Haney, 1993a; 1993b). Each organization responded by thanking me for my concerns, but declining to take on my request.

There are a variety of reasons that these organizations may have declined to do anything about my request, but one of the most obvious was that none of these organizations had a mechanism in place for investigating violations of professional standards by organizations as opposed to individuals. Although the APA has developed procedures for investigating violations by individual psychologists, the Association noted that in the case I had raised the alleged violations were the responsibility not of a psychologist but rather of an organization. The response indicated that the APA simply had no precedent or procedures for dealing with ethical transgressions, or alleged ethical transgressions, by an organization. This experience showed that only one of these three professional groups had developed mechanisms for adjudicating alleged transgressions of existing codes. As importantly it showed that while the APA had developed mechanisms to review ethical behavior of individual members of the organization, it had no way of dealing with acts by groups or institutions, such as corporations, government agencies or community-based groups.

The dilemma for me at this point was what to do next. I had tried direct communications with top officials of ETS, and had received in effect a polite "thanks, but no thanks." I had tried appeals to relevant professional organizations, but they told me there was nothing they could do. Instead of letting the matter drop, I decided to "go public" so to speak by writing an opinion/editorial on the topic (Haney, 1993b), and by alerting newspaper reporters to the story, leading to coverage in newspapers such as *USA Today*. Subsequently, ETS did convene an independent panel to review and recommend changes in its test security procedures. Since 1995, ETS's test security procedures have been changed. I suspect that the review and changes were due more to ETS's loss of the Dalton trial (the first of some 20 test security cases the organization had not won) than to my own efforts. As a result of changes in test security procedures at ETS in the mid-1990s, I am hopeful that the concerns I raised about previous procedures, apparent in the Smith and Dalton cases, are no longer germane. However, this experience illustrates a lesson quickly learned by anyone engaged in action research. If one seeks to use research to effect social change, particularly if large organizations are involved, it is almost always necessary to go beyond the normal bounds of scholarly publications and communications.

Using Student Drawings as a Form of Inquiry and Research

Work by Walt Haney and colleagues in the Center for the Study of Testing Evaluation and Educational Research in using student drawings as a form of inquiry has raised two quite different ethical dilemmas: how to contend with informed consent when a project that did not begin as formal research evolves into publishable work; and second, how should researchers help others use innovative but unproven approaches to social inquiry?

Our work with student drawings evolved out of two projects in which we helped middle schools to evaluate the progress of their own ambitious reform efforts (Haney et al., 1998). As a result of our interest in using multiple modes of assessment, we helped schools develop surveys that included both multiple-choice type survey questions and open-ended written questions (e.g., "What is the most important thing you have learned in school this year?" "What do you think should be done to make your school better?"). An additional survey item read as follows: "*Think about the teachers and the kinds of things you do in the classroom. Draw a picture of one of your teachers working in his or her classroom.*"

After the surveys (and other testing) were completed, we met with school staff to present the results and help them make sense of the results. Though we presented a wide range of assessment results (based on multiple-choice tests, written tests and performance assessments, and surveys of student attitudes), from the very first time we used student drawings in 1994, we were struck with how engaging the drawings were for teachers. When teachers discussed students' test results, conversations were typically brief and tended to focus on whether more or less of various subject matters should be taught. However, when stimulated by student drawings, discussions tended to be more extended and to focus not just on what was taught but also on how it was taught.

In 1995, we helped organize student surveys, including the drawing prompt, at five schools in three sites. Again we found that student reflection surveys, and the drawings in particular, were powerful in that they promoted reflection on the part of teachers about their methods of teaching, and analyses of these drawings were a simple but powerful way to document changes in the educational ecology of schools. Subsequent experience leads us to think that student drawings may be a powerful means for promoting reflection on instructional practices not just at school and district levels, but also among teachers and students.

More recently, in 1996 through 1998, we provided technical assistance to urban school districts funded under the Edna McConnell Clark Foundation's Program for Student Achievement. As part of this work we have helped close to three dozen schools undertake survey research, including student drawings. Again, we have often found that the drawings provide an unusually stimulating form of student generated evidence about what is happening in schools. For example, *Corpus on School Administrator* reported:

. . . the survey had provided the most insightful information they had received regarding student perceptions of the academic standards and the strategies utilized by teachers, or the lack of such, in teaching the standards.

. . . Analysis of the drawings and use of the rubric helped teachers to see the classroom through the eyes of students who "tell it like it is." (Lyons, 1997)

Another school principal reported that using drawings has been "especially helpful in allowing us to learn the feelings of our learning disabled students" and added that Middle school kids in general have a difficult time communicating with adults. The drawing lets us get some of the nonverbal communicators to give us their impressions" (quoted in Tovey, 1996, p. 6).

This work raised questions about informed consent stemming from outshift in roles. Our work with schools had begun as technical assistance aimed at helping them to examine their own educational practices. The results of the student surveys were intended primarily for internal school improvement efforts. We had not sought to obtain informed consent from the thousands of students who were being surveyed because we viewed the surveys as a routine form of educational practice with the schools and not formal research intended for external publication. However, as the work with student drawings proceeded with apparent success, we and others became interested in writing about it and including examples of student drawings.

To balance the research goal of contributing to the knowledge base on an important social issue with the need for fairness to one's subjects, we conceived of the subjects to the research more broadly. Since the drawings had been undertaken for the benefit of the schools with which we were working, we decided that it would be fair to reproduce drawings only with the permission of the schools involved. Most schools readily gave us permission, but in a few instances schools requested that none of their students' drawings be reproduced. This balance was justified, in part, because the student surveys, including the drawings, had been undertaken anonymously, leaving us and readers of the research no way to identify individual artists. However, in two instances, when we or an education writer wanted to reproduce individual drawings widely, we sought to track down the identity of individual artists to obtain their permission and potentially give them public credit for their drawings.

A second dilemma in our work with student drawings arose as we tried to help schools make sense of the drawings that are an unusual and unproven form of inquiry. We resolved this dilemma, through candor and full disclosure. For instance, we were often asked whether the drawings might simply represent students' stereotypes of teachers rather than the reality of teaching that students had actually experienced. Candidly, we responded that people in the schools from which drawings originated are in a much better position than we, as outsiders, to discern the meaning of the drawings, and we are uncertain about the meaning of the drawings and the extent to which they represent typical reality of teaching experienced, student stereotypes of teachers, and/or critical or memorable incidents that individual artists may have experienced in their classes. Because we have found the work with student drawings so promising, we have begun a more formal research study into the reliability and validity of drawings as means of documenting and changing the educational ecology of classrooms and schools (Russell & Haney, 1999). After several years' experience working with several dozen schools we are convinced that though unusual, drawings represent an extremely promising means of action research and social inquiry.

Ethical Quandaries in Participatory Action Research

Brinton Lykes has also had multiple experiences involving groups or collectivities of participants in community-based, participatory action research (PAR). PAR refers to a set of processes and practices whereby knowledge and action are produced by and for groups traditionally excluded from power and resources. Consciousness-raising ("a process of self-awareness through collective self-inquiry and reflection," Fals-Borda & Rahman, 1991, p. 6) and sociopolitical action are achieved through genuine collaboration in research and education at the community level. PAR has a long tradition within committed social science and liberationist movement (Fals-Borda & Rahman, 1991; Gaventa, 1991; McTaggart, 1997) and has more recently been applied to work in Western organizations (Whyte, 1991; see also Reason, 1994).

In this research the boundaries between researcher and research participant are often less clear than in traditional research. Moreover, because of the evolving nature of PAR, it is often the case that one may be engaged with individuals in a practice relationship long before the research aims of the collaboration evolve. In these cases, the exact manner by which one might adhere to prevailing ethical standards for informed consent is not altogether clear.

Several specific examples may clarify these points. The first involved an oral history project in which I collaborated with a local research center in Mexico City. The Center hoped to develop popular education pamphlets from the life stories/oral histories that I was gathering with a colleague (Lykes, 1989; 1996). In the design of the informed consent, I was particularly sensitive to power differentials, including language, culture, education, social class and racial/ethnicity. The human subjects review committee at my university underscored their concern that the women I hoped to interview had psychological or counseling resources, should their conversations with me and my colleague elicit negative psychological effects. I sought to "equalize" power, or at least articulate these differentials through the informed consent form, wanting it to reflect my attention to the ethical considerations of all research involving human subject (i.e., respect for persons, concern for beneficence, and justice).

Imagine my surprise when I encountered resistance on the parts of the participants not to the research itself, but to the informed consent form. These experiences (Lykes, 1989, Lykes, 1996) continue to inform how I think about the challenges facing university researchers seeking to collaborate with community-based participants in the co-construction of social inquiry and knowledge. Similar dilemmas have been explored by LaVertu and Linares (1990) in their discussion of the limits of ethical principles of bio-medical research in working in some parts of the Third and Fourth (sic) worlds where concepts of informed consent may be difficult to articulate. This is particularly true in societies wherein the "life of each person assumes meaning in relation to his role in the community" (LaVertu & Linares, 1990, p. 74) and/or wherein the hierarchical relations within the community may dictate that consent is obtained from the local authority rather than the individual participant. The meaning of individuality and "freedom to choose" has cultural variability.

The reciprocal process of developing ties, building trust, and establishing rapport prior to beginning the research constituted "informed consent" and "ethical behavior" from their point of view. The introduction of a form, which required their approval and signature, shifted the developing understandings of power and powerlessness. As Robert

Levine (1982, cited in LaVertu & Linares, 1990) suggested, the purpose served by informed consent and the document used to obtain it are not identical. In hindsight I also realized the extent to which the form itself was inscribed in a process designed to protect the researcher and her institution, not the participants within the developing relationship we were constructing. The very power differentials as researcher-participant that I was seeking to reorganize as we developed our relationships prior to beginning the interviews were thus undermined by the document. Since I authored the form as researcher, rather than co-authoring it with the "subjects", it reflected my voice including *my* voicing of what I anticipated to be *their* concerns. As importantly, I underestimated the complex meanings of asking for a signature rather than "one's word" as a commitment (LaVertu & Linares, 1990), especially among refugees of a war. The collaboration and trust that we developed and that contributed to their willingness to engage with me in the research process did not erase power differences between us. Rather, it enabled each of us to better understand our relative power and resources. Such understanding was critical for the Mayan women to agree to participate in the study organized by a Unitedstatesian researcher, from a country that was arming their government against its people. Yet, the informed consent form neither reflected that newly constructed understanding nor was it sensitive to the developing bonds between participants and researchers who provide many different resources for negotiating power differences.

Ethical Considerations in PAR in Rural Guatemala

The power of differences in the developing relationships among participating researchers became clear when I sought to articulate the ethical considerations for a PAR project in which I have been engaged in rural Guatemala. I had worked with a local women's organization for nearly six years prior to our developing a PAR project. Within that context I had facilitated training workshops on organizational development, women's self-esteem, and the use of creative techniques for psychosocial work with child survivors of war. I had lived with the family of one of the women in the group and come to know many within the community as personal friends. As we worked together I became more and more concerned with the boundaries of what constituted my ethnographic observations of the process we were co-constructing and what was confidential conversation, not for sharing beyond the intimacy of our encounters. The ongoing war and the deeply complicated politics of the peace negotiations (broader social realities within which our relationships had developed) offered additional reasons for maintaining uncharacteristic silence about what I was discovering.

My own increasing concerns for sharing our developing understandings of women and children's lives in war torn countries and the eventual signature of Peace Accords between the URNG (Guatemalan National Revolutionary Unity) and the Guatemalan government at the end of 1996, created a social space in which we were able to begin to collaborate in developing a research project. We sought to enhance our existing relationships in the co-construction of meaning making and action plans for change. I was particularly conscious, from my earlier research experiences with Maya women, to select research methods that enhanced control of the Maya Ixil women participants in both the knowledge construction and subsequent actions we sought to develop within their community and beyond.

The method we adopted to achieve our goals was used successfully in China with non-formally educated women who used their photographs as a tool for influencing local health and education policies (Wang, 1999; Wang, Wu, Zhan & Carovano, 1998). The focus of our work in rural Guatemala includes an analysis and re-presentation of the experiences of violence, displacement, and loss due to the war and their effects on the health and education of women and children now living in this rural town and its surrounding villages. Based on this documentation and subsequent analysis of the data gathered, participants will identify possible responses, communicate these to a wider community, and strategically plan additional community-based programs that they can coordinate to address their articulated needs.

Ethical considerations have been central to this ongoing two-year PAR project at multiple levels. We began the process by clarifying ethical issues that emerge in any research process and discussing parameters and guidelines for a project involving taking pictures of others (e.g., When would you not want to have someone take a picture of you? Should you ask someone permission before you take their photograph?). The methods for data generation and collection involve participation of all members of the team of twenty. In year one the women took multiple rolls of film based on a set of research goals and specific thematic content developed collaboratively through creative workshops. Once pictures were developed each woman told the story of between 5–7 pictures (per roll of 24) and these were recorded. We then met as a group of twenty participants and two technical assistants (including myself as principle investigator and a graduate student from the U.S. who was living in the community for year one). The gatherings were designed: (1) to discuss themes that had emerged, (2) to compare and contrast our initial understandings of what we have selected to photograph and our understandings of the pictures now that we had taken them, and (3) to analyze the reality of women and children based on these representations, (4) to discuss difficulties, and (5) to adapt our process to our developing understandings and needs.

This work draws on Freirian techniques of popular education and analysis (Freire, 1970), on photovoice (Wang, Burris & Ping, 1996), "talking pictures" (Bunster & Chaney, 1989) and participatory strategies we have used over the previous five years involving the use of indigenous creative resources including weaving, dramatization, and storytelling (see, e.g., Lykes, 1994, 1996; Zipes, 1995). This iterative process of data analysis has been completed and we are currently engaged in the selection of photographs and text to develop a published presentation of these stories for a wider public. The methods adapted facilitate collaboration, not only in the co-construction of meaning making and action plans for change, but also in the exercise of more control by Maya Ixil women in the re-presentation of such knowing and doing to a wider public. As importantly, ongoing engagement of leaders among this group of twenty in training workshops to enhance skills in organizational development, accounting, and data management contributes to sharing additional aspects of power within the research process and to the development of ever-more collegial relations (Biggs, 1989). These participatory resources are catalysts for building cooperation, re-threading community, and enhancing problem-solving strategies among the participants, thereby enhancing understanding while also creating opportunities for sharing and for the development of skills and resources to confront some of the individual and collective effects of war, terror and violence. The data gathered and analyzed are the basis from which participants will design health and education programs for women and children in the participating communities. As importantly, they are acquiring skills that will enable them to evaluate these projects and generate new ones as the community develops and its needs change in relation to changing political and social realities. Photovoice offers an important alternative both at the level of the photograph and, more importantly, at the level of analysis. The photograph re-presents the photographer's perspective or point of view but then becomes a stimulus for the group's reflections, discussions, analyses and re-presentations. The fixed image offers a visual stimulus to ever-widening circles of women that can also be widely "read," providing the opportunity for a discussion of the differing views of reality that are present within these Maya Ixil communities.

The processual nature of the development of this PAR experience results in several ongoing ethical considerations. The ethical considerations raised here go far beyond those of the informed consent but suggest strongly that in PAR not only do the borders between who is a researcher and who is a participant easily blur but the multiple categories which inform critical understandings of power and powerlessness also begin to shift. Building relationships over time as one does in many participatory research processes heightens one's sense of mobile identities or multiple selves. For example, although I bring power and resources into this community, as a Unitedstatesian with a doctorate I do not know either the local indigenous language or the local culture and politics. As I begin to learn the latter I gain power and as the participants begin to develop as researchers they gain power. Within the local community their language skills give them access to power and decision making from which I am excluded. Within these continually changing relations, power is transformed and identity claims shift. However these developing relationships are constrained by wider community dynamics which sometimes do not recognize the micro changes within our research relationships and processes.

Significantly, many of these changes can be traced directly to research interventions that are constitutive of all PAR projects. For example, studies of photography in Central America and, more particularly, in Guatemala, reveal a "preference" for more formal rather than informal photographic representations (Parker & Neal, 1982). A picture is something very special for which one must dress appropriately and take on a serious demeanor. Photovoice, in contrast, records everyday experiences and thereby assumes spontaneity and informality on the parts of those being photographed, which may not be common among members of these rural communities. Thus, the methodology functions as a "cultural intervention" despite the fact that it is members of the "home culture" who themselves selected this strategy, thereby introducing the intervention. As the work has proceeded I have come to better understand that the "Western collaborators" and the "indigenous researchers/participants" share multiple concerns about justice, beneficence and respect in the operationalization of this project. However, it is clear that we have differently weighted priorities. Although I want very much to improve the quality of life (and the material resources) of this rural community I am deeply interested in better understanding how knowledge of the war, its effects, and responses to them, is co-constructed and represented at the local level among indigenous women. These latter concerns are deeply constitutive of my ongoing work within this community. They are of increasing interest to the Maya Ixil leadership within the group but of much less concern to young mothers seeking additional resources for feeding and caring for themselves and their children.

Secondly, this brief description illustrates the processual nature of PAR and the ways in which "participant" and "researcher" are mobile categories that re-present the realities of those involved in very differing ways in this process. We shared an articulated vision of the research when we "officially" inaugurated this research project, taping a conversation about our "informed consent" and dialoguing about risks to those within our research group, those whose pictures we would be taking, and those whose stories we would be recording. However, as the research is developing we encounter additional ethical challenges. For example, the costs of developing film and reproducing pictures are particularly noteworthy within a subsistence economy wherein the funding for this project could support many of the community's survival needs. For example, in some rural towns where few own cameras, a single entrepreneur can establish a "photography shop," offering services to photograph special events, including weddings, funerals, etc. Some women in our project with entrepreneurial spirit had hoped to use their cameras "after hours" to establish a similar business opportunity. The local mayor had initially resisted giving initial permission to the women for the project because he feared such a development. The limited financial resources of all participants made the idea of opening a business particularly appealing to many. I resisted the idea, reminding them of our earlier goals of developing a collective effort that would eventually benefit not only the women's organization that had generated the project but the wider community as a whole. Repeated group discussions helped clarify the distinctions between the camera as an individual resource for economic development and the camera as a resource for social change and justice. Together the women decided to suspend further discussion of picture-taking for income until they completed their two year PAR project, at which point the Association would entertain proposals from all of its members as to how best to use the resources of the cameras and their new found skills as photographers to benefit the Association and its members. This decision was made after considerable discussion and after weighing the individual and collective needs of all participants in this rural economy dominated by extreme poverty wherein women particularly have limited access to cash generating activities.

Thirdly, the strength of the photograph is also its weakness. Because it can be "multiply read" once presented to ever widening communities, the story of the women in this town will be multiply interpreted. For women who have been isolated in a rural community for generations this will present new challenges for which they are preparing themselves. As a Euro-American researcher I have found multiple interpretations to be resources for working through a process of meaning making, but the local realities of these communities place other kinds of constraints on that process. As importantly, years of war and armed conflict have created rigid ways of thinking that are frequently accompanied by dualism and rigid attachments to dichotomous thinking (see Martín-Baró, 1994).

Finally, and perhaps most importantly, I share with some local residents a deep concern about the threat posed to them if they photograph and critically analyze the realities of poverty and violence within their communities and re-present them to others outside the community. Similar agency among Maya and rural peasants has been interpreted as "revolutionary organizing" in Guatemala's all too recent past. The peace process within Guatemala is extremely fragile and experiences in many other countries suggest that war and organized violence may re-emerge. As this discussion suggests, ethical concerns are not once and for all decision-making points but rather ongoing processes wherein we encounter and re-encounter each other and ourselves as we are transformed and transform our contexts through the collaborative process.

Challenges from Collaborative Research Processes

The relationship of current ethical guidelines in research with human subjects and actual practice remains unclear. Collaborative forms of inquiry often blur the boundaries between research and practice. As importantly, these are not static relationships in research beyond university walls but processes wherein multiple selves and relationships are enacted. As significantly, organizations that have developed ethical guidelines and standards for research with human subjects often have not developed mechanisms by which they can examine cases of alleged misconduct. The AERA, in particular, has specifically eschewed any aspiration to enforce ethical standards or guidelines. As Arlene Kaplan Daniels has observed, "professional codes do not simply fulfill the function suggested by the professional ideology; rather, they are part of the ideology designed for public relations and justification for the status and prestige which professions assume vis-à-vis more lowly occupations." In a sense this is not surprising for, according to the Oxford English Dictionary, the oldest meaning of the word standard in the English language refers to an emblem or symbol of a person, persons, or group. Thus we must be aware that occupational groups will sometimes promulgate standards not out of any clear-cut strategy for reforming practice but rather as a symbol or emblem of the professional aspirations of that particular occupational group.

Nonetheless, we are heartened by increased attention to issues of research with human subjects. The proliferation of Institutional Review Boards among universities is a sign of this increased concern. But in our experience, ethical standards of research often are not well served by sometimes-bureaucratic requirements of IRBs or other formal review mechanisms. They are better served, we think, through a concern for the underlying principles behind the guidelines for research with human subjects—as long ago as the Hippocratic Oath and, as recently as, the Belmont Report in the 1970s—respect for persons, concern for beneficence, and justice. As suggested in our own practices as researchers and practitioners, these are not static concerns but rather values that inform the multiple contexts in which researchers, practitioners, and participants encounter each other and in which roles and relationships shift over time. As participants in social inquiry we seek to remain faithful to these values while defining and redefining "good practice" within our variously defined communities of research and action. As definitions of what constitutes research and practice are stretched and redefined, criteria for evaluating the ethical aspects of those practices need to be reconsidered.

Notes

1. As social inquiry continues to be transformed by increasingly collaborative relationships between and among "investigators" and the "subjects" of research the labels that had previously been used to describe the various participants are inadequate. Since ethical guidelines for research with human beings continue to refer to participants as subjects we use that term in referencing these guidelines. However we recognize the limitations of this language and use various, alternative terms in describing our own research experiences.
2. The full set of the APA Ethical Standards is available at http://www.apa.org/ethics/code.html.
3. The full set of the AERA Ethical Standards is available at http://aera.net/resource/ethics.html.

References

AERA, APA & NCME (1985). *Standards for Educational and Psychological Testing.* Washington, DC: American Psychological Association.

Biggs, S. (1989). Resource-poor farmer participation in research: A synthesis of experiences from nine national agricultural research systems. OFCOR Comparative Study Paper 3. The Hague: International Service for National Agricultural Research.

Bunster, X., & Chaney, E. M. (1989). Epilogue. In X. Bunster & E. M. Chaney, *Sellers and servants: Working women in Lima, Peru* (pp. 217–233). Granby, MA: Bergin & Garvey Publishers, Inc.

Fals-Borda, O. & Rahman, M. A. (Eds.), (1991). *Action and knowledge: Breaking the monopoly with participatory action research.* New York: Intermediate Technology/Apex.

Freire, P. (1970). *Pedagogy of the oppressed.* New York: Seabury Press.

Gaventa, J. (1991). Toward a knowledge democracy. In O. Fals-Borda & M.A. Rahman (Eds.), *Action and knowledge: Breaking the monopoly with participatory action research.* New York: Intermediate Technology/Apex.

Haney, W. M. (1993a). *Cheating and escheating on standardized tests.* Paper presented at the annual meeting of the American Educational Research Association, Atlanta, Georgia.

Haney, W. M. (1993b). Preventing cheating on standardized tests. *The Chronicle of Higher Education,* p. B3.

Haney, W. (1998). *The value of supplementary evidence in evaluating unusual answer concordance.* Paper presented at the annual meeting of the American Educational Research Association, San Diego, CA.

Haney, W., et al., (1998). Drawing on education: Using student drawings to promote middle school improvement. *Schools in the middle,* Jan./Feb. 1998, 39–43.

Haney, W. & Madaus, G. (1990). Evolution of ethical and technical standards. In R. Hambleton and J. Zaal (Eds.) *Advances in educational and psychological testing: Theory and applications.* Boston: Kluwer Academic Publishers, pp. 395–425.

LaVertu, D. S. & Linares, A. M. (1990). Ethical principles of biomedical research on human subjects: Their application and limitations in Latin America and the Caribbean. *Bulletin of PAHO, 24*(4), 469–479.

Lykes, M. B. (1989). Dialogue with Guatemalan Indian women: Critical perspectives on constructing collaborative research. In R. Unger (Ed.), *Representations: Social constructions of gender* (pp. 167–185). Amityville, NY: Baywood. [Reprinted in Gergen, M., & Davis, S. (Eds.), (1996). *Toward a new psychology of gender: A reader.* New York: Routledge.]

Lykes, M. B. (1994). Terror, silencing and children: International, multidisciplinary collaboration with Guatemalan Maya communities. *Social Science and Medicine, 38*(4), 543–552.

Lykes, M. B. (1996). Meaning making in a context of genocide and silencing. In M. B. Lykes, A. Banuazizi, R. Liem, & M. Morris (Eds.), *Myths about the powerless: Contesting social inequalities* (pp. 159–178). Philadelphia: Temple University Press.

Lyons, P. (1997). Memo to Ed Fierros, July 23, 1997 (personal communication).

Martín-Baró, I. (1994). *Writings for a liberation psychology: Ignacio Martín-Baró.* (A. Aron & S. Corne, Eds.), Cambridge, MA: Harvard University Press.

McTaggart, R. (Ed.). (1997). *Participatory action research: International contexts and consequences.* Albany, NY: State University of New York Press.

Mirvis, P. H. & Seashore, S. E. (1979). Being ethical in organizational research. *American Psychologist, 34*(9), 766–780.

Parker, A. & Neal, A. (1982). *Los ambulantes: The itinerant photographers of Guatemala.* Cambridge, MA: The MIT Press.

Reason, P. (1994). Three approaches to participative inquiry. In N.K. Denzin & Y.S. Lincoln (Eds.), *Handbook of qualitative research* (pp. 324–339). Thousand Oaks, CA: Sage.

Russell, M. & Haney, W. (1999, April). *Validity and reliability of information gleaned from student drawings.* Paper presented at the annual meeting of the American Educational Research Association, Montreal, Canada.

Tovey, Roberta (1996). Getting kids into the picture: Student drawings help teachers see themselves more clearly. *Harvard Education Letter,* Nov./Dec, 5–6.

Wang, C. (1999). Photovoice: A participatory action research strategy applied to women's health. *Journal of Women's Health, 8*(2), 185–192.

Wang, C., Burris, M., and Xiang, Y. P. (1996). Chinese village women as visual anthropologists: A participatory approach to reaching policymakers. *Social Science and Medicine, 42,* 1391–1400.

Wang, C., Wu, K. Y., Zhan, W. T. & Carovano, K. (1998). Photovoice as a participatory health promotion strategy. *Health Promotion International, 13*(1), 75–86.

Whyte, W. F. (Ed.). (1991). *Participatory action research.* Newbury Park, CA: Sage.

Zipes, J. (1995). Creative storytelling: Building community, changing lives. New York: Routledge.

8

Unraveling Ethics

Illuminating the Moral Dilemmas of Research Ethics

Christine Halse and Anne Honey

This essay offers a critical, reflective analysis of some of the sticky moral questions that can entangle feminist researchers as they work to transform a research proposal into an application for ethics committee approval. We write not as philosophers or ethicists but as feminist social scientists reflecting on our struggle to do ethical research and to be ethical researchers in an environment governed by a regulatory model of research ethics. Our story is constructed as two intersecting narratives. In the first section of our essay, "A Narrative about Ethics," we relate our account of how ethical theory plays out in the real world, drawing on our experience of preparing the ethics applications for an interview study with "anorexic" teenage girls and our struggles with two pillars of research ethics policy: defining the research population and eliciting informed consent.[1] In the second section of our essay, "Ethics in Our Narrative," we tease out the implications of the research ethics approval process for the people who participate in research and for those who desire to be ethical and moral researchers.

The enigmatic, gendered character of self-starvation and the unanswered riddle of its cause(s) and maintenance has made anorexia nervosa an alluring subject for scholars in many disciplines and fields (including cultural studies, women's studies, and media studies) using a spectrum of perspectives (social, cultural, and biological) and epistemologies, from positivism to critical poststructuralism. Amid this enormous corpus of published research there is a deafening silence about the ethics of doing research with "sufferers" in general or with teenage girls—the most frequently affected group—in particular.

Our essay seeks to address this glaring gap in the literature while also responding to the invocations from other researchers for empirical data and concrete documentation of the practice and implications of ethical decision making in human research: "the way ethical decisions are actually reached (as opposed to how they should be reached)" (DeVries and Subedi 1998, v).

Our essay also arises from particular, personal agendas: our desire to "do ethics right," in terms of both complying with institutional ethics policy and being morally and ethically responsible to our research participants; our professional commitment to being critically reflexive about the morality of our interactions with research participants and the research ethics process; and a vested interest by one of us, as the chair of an institutional ethics review board, to see research ethics policy and ethics committees foster genuinely moral behavior and ethical research rather than cultivating cultures of counterfeit practice.

In penning this essay, our aim is to make visible, and therefore revisable, the moral dilemmas embedded in research ethics policy and its implementation by ethics committees, and to illuminate some of the implications these dilemmas carry for feminist research and feminist researchers. Michel Foucault ([1973] 1978) points out that even uttering knowledge that diverges from established discourses is a critical activity and an act of resistance. In this sense our essay is explicitly transgressive because it seeks to unravel the morality of the ethics approval process and the ethics of doing research. This is a dangerous but politically necessary conversation. The investments, dilemmas, and implications of researchers' ethical decisions and moral choices are usually secreted away, buried, concealed, and hidden from public scrutiny, thereby crafting an illusion that "good" research is being done by "good researchers." However, it is necessary to make the ethics of research transparent in order to identify the moral crevices of ethics policy and practice and to develop new and better ways of doing feminist research and being ethical feminist researchers.

I. A Narrative about Ethics

Constructing the Indefinable Subject

Anorexia nervosa is a serious social issue and a potentially life-threatening problem affecting approximately 0.5 percent of females, primarily teenagers, and approximately one-tenth as many males (American Psychiatric Association 2000). Treatment for anorexia nervosa is difficult and prolonged. Approximately one-third of sufferers still meet diagnostic criteria five years after initial treatment, and studies report mortality rates of 5–8 percent from starvation or related complications (Polivy and Herman 2002). Even weight-restored anorexics may experience ongoing medical complications and long-term psychological and social problems that have a detrimental impact on their quality of life.

Clinicians and reviewers have criticized the absence of research into the life history and lived experiences of people with eating problems (e.g., Leder 1990). A particular gap is the absence of systematic, qualitative research about the experience of self-starvation from the standpoints of teenage sufferers. Our study sought to redress this silence and to generate understandings that might improve prevention and support programs in schools and in medical contexts.

We were well versed (and well rehearsed) in "getting through ethics" and had an intimate, insider knowledge about the thinking and machinations of ethics committees, accumulated from years of serving on and chairing such committees. We began preparing our ethics applications complacently confident that the task would be painless and pedestrian. But our interview study posed messy moral quandaries that challenged our ideas about the meaning of doing ethical research.

As a multisite study, our research project required ethics approval from several institutional ethics committees. In Australia, where we work, the national guidelines and policies governing research with humans are generated by the National Health and Medical Research Council (National Health and Medical Research Council 1999). Institutional compliance is required by federal law and monitored by the Australian Health Ethics Committee. Compliance is an employment condition for academics and a prerequisite for the receipt of national research grants. Typically, institutional ethics committees follow the national protocols, although local committees may interpret these differently during the review process. The protocols parallel those of other English-language countries. They include an explanation of the aims, rationale, and design of the research; a description of the target population and the procedures for recruiting participants and eliciting informed consent; an explanation of the methods of data collection and analysis; a statement about the risks and benefits for participants, and the strategies for dealing with possible physical or psychological distress; copies of the interview questions/questionnaires; and a letter to participants summarizing the information in the ethics application.

Research ethics policy positions research participants as the "object" of the research and assumes that these "subjects" form an identifiable, knowable constituency whose members share particular characteristics that distinguish them from others. Self-starvation resists such comfortable categorization. Anorexia nervosa is classified as a psychiatric disorder, but both physical and psychological criteria are used in diagnoses, including the maintenance of a very low body weight (less than 85 percent of "normal" for age and height), amenorrhea, fear of fatness, and distorted body image (American Psychiatric Association 2000). But self-starvation has shifting, multiple identities and assumes different guises at different times, ranging from continued noneating to restricted eating with excessive, compulsive exercise to erratic food restriction accompanied by binge eating and purging (Polivy and Herman 2002). Biomedical discourse constructs self-starvation as an organic disorder and a disease, but the origins and causes of anorexia are uncertain and contested. It has been variously explained as a biological pathology, a genetic predisposition, an affective disorder, and a cognitive deficit or dysfunction. Psychodynamic and psychoanalytical discourses, on the other hand, constitute anorexia as an outcome of a variety of family problems or as a self-pathology that is symptomatic of inadequate or unresolved psychosexual and ego development (see Malson 1998, 78–83, for a review).

Biomedical and psychological research explicitly constitutes self-starvation as an embodied entity and a distinct pathology that is located within the individual. The behaviors attributed to anorexia are positioned as abnormal biological and/or psychological problems that mark the anorexic as deviant and different from a generalized population of "normal" teenage girls. Through her constitution as "other," the anorexic is positioned as physically and psychologically unable to act in or to protect her own interests, thereby justifying medical and psychological intervention to ensure a return to "normal" eating behaviors and constructing anorexia as the remit of the medical profession.

Despite the social and cultural power of such discourses, self-starvation has resisted colonization into biomedical and psychological categories. Many of the pathologies attributed to anorexics, such as erratic, disordered eating and obsessive concerns with weight and diet, are typical of many "normal" women; recovered anorexics commonly reject biomedical constructions of self-starvation, and many diagnosed anorexics do not identify as such, refusing diagnostic classification and medical intervention, and only presenting for treatment when pressured by friends or family. Moreover, much of the research used to construct anorexia as a biological or psychological problem has been based on quantitative research that has been criticized as methodologically flawed, as construing causal relationships from correlation analyses, and for generating research findings that are inconclusive and/or contradictory (see Malson 1998).

In contrast, narrative therapy and community psychology constitute anorexia as existing outside the self and as having a distinct identity and agency for independent, autonomous action. Interpolating Cartesian mind/body dualism, it is the anorexia that takes possession and controls the self, rendering the subject powerless in the face of its determined will. The simultaneous disembodiment and personification of anorexia removes "the origins of distress from the interior psychological workings of the individual person [to] the surrounding environment" (Smail 1994, 6; see also Morgan 1999). In this frame the anorexic is constructed as a victim or a casualty of an uncontrollable, mightier force that is external to the physical and psychological self, erasing the stigma of pathology and exonerating sufferers from the blame attached to the condition.

Feminist scholars shed a different light on self-starvation by illuminating the multiple and contradictory ways that culture is entwined with anorexia. The anorexic body is constituted as an expression of social, cultural, political, and gender anxieties; as a metaphor for contemporary sociocultural concerns about consumption, personal display, feminist politics, and individualistic competitiveness; and as a site of cultural and social oppression (e.g., Bordo 1993; Fallon, Katzman, and Wooley 1994). Drawing on feminist perspectives, poststructuralist scholars elucidate how everyday discourses of femininity, body, and identity are implicated in a range of social institutions and discursive practices that conspire to produce women's bodies as anorexic bodies (e.g., Malson 1998).

Defining the research population is an act of category construction with profound intellectual and moral implications. The multiple identities of self-starvation ignited sticky dilemmas about how we should describe anorexia nervosa in our ethics application and in the information letter to participants. Should it be presented as a "real" physical or psychological condition: a problem, disorder, or illness? Or should it be presented as a label or rhetorical device that positions young women as abnormal, deviant, and in need of treatment when they defy socially constructed notions of normal, healthy eating behaviors? In the light of the differing constitutions of anorexia, how could we establish a universal category that neatly defined the participants in our study? Which words should we use to address a girl whom clinicians classified as anorexic but who rejected the assignation of any medical or psychological problem and saw the label of *anorexic* as a (mis)representation by others? Could we invite her to share her experience of living with anorexia if she did not believe that she was anorexic? We were anxious to adhere to the principle of respect for human subjects, but we worried about how to name those who volunteered to participate in our study. To brand a girl anorexic without consent was to deny her selfhood—one of the very issues the study aimed to address. To include only those girls who acknowledged their diagnosis would affect the research by failing to capture the complex spectrum of "anorexic" experiences.

In part, our problem lay in deciding to listen to the different discourses and bodies of research about self-starvation. While our own epistemic faiths might question the merit of some of these, we could dismiss neither their potential as a source of insight into self-starvation nor the fact that they might echo the different ways that girls viewed self-starvation and their "condition."

To help untangle these quandaries, we sought the advice of the institutional ethics officers. In Australia, to protect confidentiality and to prevent coercion of ethics committees, face-to-face discussions between researchers and committees are infrequent. Ethics officers are specialists in research ethics policy whose job is to help researchers "solve" messy problems before an ethics application is reviewed. The ethics officers were empathetic and supportive but uncomprehending: "If you can't lable the population, then the research isn't possible."

We intended to recruit from specialized treatment clinics for eating disorders where many girls had already been diagnosed (labeled) anorexic. The challenge we faced was how to describe the study's population so that it accommodated girls' perspectives and summoned the essential "anorexic" subject that the ethics officers and research ethics policy urged us to find. We considered the possibilities. We could privilege girls' standpoints by limiting the study to girls who self-identified as anorexic and by excluding girls who did not accept their diagnosis. Or we could limit the study to girls diagnosed as anorexic. Option 1 (privileging girls' perspectives) risked including girls whose emaciation and eating problems were the result of another, possibly undiagnosed psychiatric or biological condition and excluded an important group, namely, girls labeled anorexic who rejected the designation. Option 2 (a medical diagnosis) meant privileging the categorization imposed by others (doctors) over girls' individual views and experiences. Further, as researchers familiar with clinical settings, we knew that a medical diagnosis of anorexia nervosa could not create a coherent category of person. Diagnoses were often inconsistent and changeable—they rarely met *all* diagnostic criteria for anorexia nervosa (American Psychiatric Association 2000) and were often revised days or weeks later as more information unfolded about each sufferer's personal history. At its best, a diagnosis of anorexia nervosa was an informed judgment at a particular point in time, but it could not guarantee the definitive, homogenous population that ethics policy and our ethics officers invoked us to find. Both options censored the particularity of some girls' experiences, and both required us to abandon our sensibility and moral responsibility to some potential participants. Both options altered the research focus and our original aim of illuminating the full range of experiences among all "anorexic" girls.

Dissatisfied with these alternatives, we floated the idea of using multiple descriptions to address the particularity and diversity of potential participants. One ethics officer flatly rejected the idea: "That would mean they're different populations. So you'll need separate ethics applications and approvals for each group." The other ethics officers were confused and mystified. They could not see the problem that troubled us. The doctors had made their diagnoses and issued the decree: "The girls are anorexic. The fact that some girls don't *agree* with their diagnosis doesn't mean they're not anorexic."

Of course, the easy way forward was to ignore the questions that troubled us. All we had to do was fill in the standard ethics review application, prepare generic information letters, get the consent forms signed, and start interviewing. While we struggled to construct a more morally acceptable description of the population, our research project stalled, our funders got restless, and our colleagues got fractious. We had secured highly competitive funding for the research, but this imposed constraints: a tight timeline, accountability indicators and reports, the delivery of designated outcomes. Colleagues vented their incomprehension and frustration at the delay: "What's the problem? All you have to do is fill in the forms and do it." There were no easy answers to our moral tussle, and we felt caught in Jacques Derrida's "double bind": an unsolvable dilemma where "one can only unbind one of its knots by pulling on the other to make it tighter" (Derrida 1998, 36).

Such stalemates nurture compliance. Confronted with abandoning either our anxiety or our study, we opted for a compromise by adopting the broadest, most inclusive category available: "girls who have received a medical diagnosis of anorexia nervosa." Our definition satisfied our ethics committees and enabled the project to proceed—albeit with a less inclusive population than we had intended—but it left us uneasy and uncomfortable. Knowing the capriciousness of clinical diagnoses, we worried about the intellectual and moral dishonesty of defining the study's population in this way. We were also conscious that privileging clinical diagnoses over girls' views and accounts affirmed and thereby invisibly reinforced the hegemony of biomedical discourses that construct self-starvation as "other." Our positioning as actively complicit in perpetuating this story undermined our ethical and moral responsibility to our participants and had troubling moral implications for our desired identities as ethical, feminist researchers, although—ironically—the ethics committees with whom we worked did not share our concerns. We hoped the processes for eliciting consent might compensate for the moral difficulties raised by our definition of the population, but informed consent carried its own moral difficulties.

Speaking the Unspeakable: The Unknowability of Informed Consent

Informed consent is a central canon of research ethics policy. The concept of informed consent assumes the transparency of a social and psychological reality that enables researchers to provide full and accurate information about the research to autonomous subjects who are able to make rational, informed choices. In Australia, the national protocol for informed consent involves giving participants (usually through an information letter) full, comprehensive, and accurate details about the research, including the demands, risks, inconveniences, discomforts, and benefits that might be involved. As we prepared our ethics application, complexities emerged about each of the four dimensions of informed consent, namely, the provision of full information about data collection, voluntarism and coercion, physical/psychological distress, and competence to understand and participate in the research.

Our study involved semistructured life-history interviews that sought to illuminate the ways that self-starvation shaped participants' lives, relationships, and subjectivity. To comply with the ethics policy requirement to provide full information, we dutifully prepared a list of interview questions for potential participants. But semistructured interviews are inherently emergent, reflexive, and messy, and the planned focus of an interview can easily shift as new issues and accounts emerge. Like all diligent researchers, we cautioned potential participants in the information letters that an interview could take unexpected turns and that new questions might arise as girls' narratives raised new substantive or theoretical issues. The ethics committees were satisfied that we had fulfilled our ethical obligations and provided full, complete, and accurate information about the research, but we were less convinced. At best, our warning provided a predication of what might happen during an interview. At worst, our assurances were deceptive because they created an illusion of a certainty that we could not guarantee.

The matter of voluntary, noncoercive consent proved trickier than we had imagined. The clinics we planned to recruit through were enthusiastic about the research, but we were advised that institutional ethics clearance and approval to recruit participants would only be granted if the clinicians were coinvestigators in the study. This edict, it was explained, was non-negotiable and necessary on the grounds that the girls were under clinical care and the clinicians would protect the girls' interests.

This unexpected requirement created an awkward political predicament by compromising our position as independent researchers who worked in (rather than with) clinics, and put at risk our capacity to report findings that might be critical of the clinics and/or clinical practice. Another, shorter stalemate ensued while we discussed how to handle this unexpected turn. We could take the moral high ground and refuse to comply with the institutional requirements. Or we could comply and hope to "manage" the situation. Or we could try to negotiate a different arrangement. Option 1 (the moral high ground) seemed likely to lead to our being excluded from the clinics and would seriously threaten the feasibility of the research. Option 2 (compliance) meant collaborating with the clinicians and raised a bevy of uncertainties. Option 3 (negotiation) seemed hopeful but reckless. Colleagues urged us to comply, explaining that the clinicians were busy (men) who would not interfere if we were agreeable and cooperative. Rather than follow this advice and set aside our moral concerns or abandon the potentially positive outcomes of the study, we decided to negotiate. There were lengthy, sometimes tense, but ultimately successful discussions with the clinicians. Together we developed a strategy to minimize the compromises to the study by agreeing that the original team would be responsible for the project design and implementation, and that we would work together to review the data analysis and to develop ways to use girls' perspectives and accounts to inform and to improve clinical practice. The alliance has been productive and mutually supportive and has resulted in valuable changes in clinical practice.

The positive outcome to our political quandary did not remove the implications for participants that might flow from an alliance with the clinicians. A precondition of informed consent is that it is voluntarily and freely given. The concept of free will is premised on an autonomous liberal humanist subject who is able to make rational and independent judgments regardless of her context. Here the ontological difficulties are the presumption of a stable, decontextualized subject and the discounting of the multiple power relations that work visibly and invisibly to constitute the subject and her inter-action with others (Foucault 1977, 1988). We worried whether genuine informed consent was possible given the clinicians' connection with the research. To what extent could girls exercise agency given their subordinate position in the world they cohabited with the clinicians? As patients, might the girls read the clinicians' association with the study as coercive or as an inappropriate incentive to participate? Would girls resist participating in the study to irk the physicians or attribute greater importance to participating out of a misplaced perception that it might please their doctors? Would the girls hesitate to share their stories given the clinicians' involvement? Could girls feel able to voice concerns about their treatment given their subordination to the doctors' authority in the clinic?

The third obligation under the principle of informed consent is to provide information about the potential for psychological distress or discomfort. The risk of distress is generally considered minimal when the probability and magnitude of harm are not greater "than those ordinarily encountered in daily life or during the performance of routine physical or psychological examinations or tests" (Santelli et al. 1995, 274). Yet how individuals experience distress can be uncertain and disguised, and predicting the potential for distress can be difficult (Latvala, Janhonen, and Moring 1998). Although a growing body of evidence suggests that qualitative research poses little risk of distress and that telling your story to an interested listener has emotional and therapeutic value (Kleinman 1988; Corbin and Morse 2003), the individual histories of anorexic girls suggested that the interviews might revive distressing, secreted traumas. These girls were more likely than the general population to have experienced stressful life events such as the death of a close relative or family breakup or to have experienced depression, low self-esteem, and concerns about identity and control. Clinical literature has postulated relationships between anorexia and a range of family problems, including enmeshed, critical, or coercive family environments; insecure attachment; and physical and sexual abuse in families (see Polivy and Herman 2002 for a review). Although some of this research has been questioned (e.g., Eisler 1995), we could not ignore the possibility that the biographies of some girls might encompass complex, difficult family relationships. Nor could we ignore the possibility that distress might be triggered by the accumulation of painful experiences associated with self-starvation: multiple, long-term hospital admissions; repeated, failed clinical interventions; physical self-harm, including attempted suicide; and extended separation from education, work, friendships, and social interaction.

Given the biography of self-starvation, even distributing an interview protocol in the interest of informed consent carried the possibility of resurrecting upsetting or deeply troubling past memories. Yet ethics policy and privacy legislation prevented us from accessing information that might tell us about the best way of interacting with particular participants. Given the situated chronicles of girls' lives, we worried that acquiescing to a "one-size-fits-all" strategy abdicated our moral and social responsibilities to our potential participants.

Self-starvation also problematizes the question of competence to provide informed consent. Under Australian law, young people under the age of majority are considered competent to participate in research without parental consent if they understand the procedures and implications of research. Relevant to any decision about waiving parental consent is the level of risk involved in the research (Brooks-Gunn and Rotheram-Borus 1994; Levine 1995; Rew, Taylor-Seehafer, and Thomas 2000). In practice, ethics committees set nominal ages at which they consider adolescents capable of independently consenting to participate in research. Each of the ethics committees involved with our multisite study set different age barriers for consent, ranging from fourteen to sixteen years.

Age barriers for adolescent consent have been hotly contested (e.g., Brooks-Gunn and Rotheram-Borus 1994; Brody and Waldron 2000). Research indicates that young people (fourteen years and older) have a capacity to understand research and make decisions similar to that of adults (Meade and Slesnick 2002) but may be affected by lack of experience or by emotionality (Dorn, Susman, and Fletcher 1995) and have trouble understanding the different goals of therapy and research (Brody and Waldron 2000). Some evidence also indicates that acute malnutrition can cause temporary cognitive impairment and that anorexic patients below a certain weight are unable to participate effectively in treatment (e.g., Bruch 1988) or, by implication, to provide informed consent. The capacity of adolescents to reason and to make decisions about the risks and benefits of participating in research can also be limited by stress. Hospitalization and the physical and psychological symptoms of anorexia can be stressful, and anorexics have a higher than average likelihood of experiencing problems like anxiety disorders, obsessive-compulsive disorders, and depression that can inhibit the ability to make informed choices about participating in research. These considerations may not be relevant in every case of self-starvation, but the different age limits set by ethics committees obliged us to treat all potential participants under the age of sixteen years (the maximum, nominal age limit identified by our ethics committees) as lacking decision-making capacity and needing parental protection and consent to participate in research.

Parental consent, however, is not a panacea for the ethical difficulties of consent. The tacit assumption underpinning the idea of parental consent is that parents know what is in the best interests of their daughters and are capable of protecting their interests. Parents, however, are likely to be positioned in similar power relations as their daughters with regard to the medical team and could be influenced to provide consent by a hope that participating in the research could help their daughters (Brody and Waldron 2000). Although the imbrication of families in self-starvation is a complex and contested area, difficult family relationships or histories could affect the decision of some parents to give or to withhold consent. Parental consent is a double-edged sword, protecting some girls and erasing other girls' potential for agency by increasing the opportunity for parental coercion.

We presented our case for relinquishing age barriers and parental consent to the institutional ethics officers, but they advised that all ethics committees were immovable on these issues. The concern was not with the legitimacy of the arguments we presented but with the financial threat of a litigious parent or caregiver. With no option but to acquiesce on this count, we circumvented the restrictions imposed by our committees by using a different form of consent involving "ongoing consensual decision-making" (Ramos 1989, 60) before, during, and after the interviews so that participants had repeated opportunities to withdraw or to qualify consent. This strategy could not guarantee the knowability of informed consent or obviate unseen power relations, but it offered a greater degree of empowerment by providing girls with multiple opportunities to qualify and negotiate their involvement in the research.

II. Ethics in our Narrative

The Knotty Problem of Universalism and the Essentialized Subject

The ethics framework that regulates Western research and guides the decision making of ethics committees is based on the concept of a universalized rational subject and an ethic of justice derived from Kantian moral theory. The presumption of the universalized subject takes for granted that the experiences of the dominant social group can be generalized and taken as true for all others. In this frame, consensus about moral behavior and ethical practice is unproblematic because all rational subjects will acknowledge that the agreed universal moral principles are in the interests of all subjects.

Research ethics policy combines Kantian rationalism with the social contract theories of liberal philosophers like Thomas Hobbes, John Locke, and John Rawls. In the contractarian model of social relations any ethical and moral problem can be resolved by using the liberal principles of equality, fairness, and reciprocity, and a public system of rights and responsibilities in the form of laws, procedures, and protocols (Benhabib 1987, 85). Margaret Walker describes the progeny of Kantian rationalism and social contract theory as the theoretical-juridical model of ethical theory, comprising "a set of law-like moral principles or procedures" that are transhistorical, transcultural, and couched in the language of scientific objectivity to appear dispassionate and authoritative (1997, 36).

Ethics committees grew out of a positivist tradition of biomedical research that evolved in tandem with the theoretical-juridical model of ethics. Positivist research takes for granted the existence of a putative knowable reality, and that objective, universal truths can be revealed through empirical scientific data collection and explicit, transparent, experimental research operations and procedures (Harre and Secord 1972). The conceptual foundation of positivism has been widely challenged, but its assumptions continue to underpin the philosophy and processes embedded in regulatory frameworks for research ethics, particularly when biomedical agencies have an influential role in developing and monitoring ethics policy and practice.

The positivist biomedical model of research ethics has had exceptional discursive power and has been taken up and imposed on disciplines such as the social sciences and humanities, even when these disciplines employ radically different epistemic frames and forms of data collection and analysis. The widespread infiltration of the positivist model of research ethics has worked to visibly and invisibly inscribe the management, surveillance, and control of research ethics in ways that appear natural, benign, and eminently reasonable to "any rational subject." Most researchers accept the requirement (if not the desirability) of ethics review before research commences. Yet the biomedical model also casts research ethics in a shroud of scientific neutrality and universal certainty that crafts an illusion that ethics approval means ethical research, begetting a compliance approach to research ethics and to the ways that researchers think through ethical questions.

The presumption of a universalized, rational subject that is at the heart of Kantian moral theory and modern research ethics policy is inherently problematic because it constructs the self as disembedded and disembodied, without sensibilities, history, or physicality. All research projects face the challenge of finding the "generalized subject" who describes the research population. The theoretical and practical difficulties of this task are rarely openly paraded and discussed, and the task is rarely as problematic as in our narrative. Fewer difficulties arise, for example, in defining the population for a research project about the life histories of "schoolgirls." But the embodiment of self-starvation is both profound and ambiguous; different discourses attach conflicting meanings to the anorexic body (and mind), and the biography of self-starvation is singular and diverse at the same time. Our experiences highlighted the difficulties of constructing a definitive, universal category of the anorexic subject and threw into sharp relief the illusion of the universal subject of Kantian discourse.

The problems of consent illuminated the gulf between the embodied singularity of research participants and the disembodied, humanist subject of the ethic of justice and positivist research. An amalgam of legal edicts (e.g., privacy legislation) and local practices by ethics committees (e.g., prohibition of any contact between researchers and participants before written consent is given) curtail researchers' capacity to engage with and learn about research participants before beginning the research. These constraints were designed to protect participants and to prevent coercion. At the same time, they prevent researchers and potential participants from developing the personal relationships that make it possible to address the diverse singularity of research participants in the design of a research project and in research ethics protocols.

Erasing the singularity of research participants has grave moral implications. Public conversations about self-starvation, the anorexic body, and the anorexic subject have been dominated by voices of doctors, psychologists, medical researchers, sociologists, and feminists. Following Carol Gilligan (1982) and Sandra Harding (1987), a primary aim of our study was to bring girls' standpoints into these public discussions and to open up new theoretical possibilities by hearing the voices and silences smothered by the conversations of others. The definition of the research population offered to our ethics committees satisfied their expectations and requirements, but it narrowed the research focus by excluding a range of potential participants (e.g., girls who rejected their diagnosis) and (re)configured the study's aim to illuminate the diversity among all "anorexic" teenage girls. The result was a disconcerting paradox: the act of defining the research population erased the particular and individual differences among potential participants, ignoring "the plurality of modes of being human, and differences among humans" (Benhabib 1987, 81) and, in doing so, disregarded one of the four fundamental principles of humanist research ethics policy—respect for persons.

Power, Politics, and the Embodiment of Self and "Others"

Power and politics are inextricably entwined with research ethics. The legal requirement to receive ethics committee approval to conduct research in ways that are acceptable to ethics committees (and to ethics officers) explicitly subordinates researchers to the authority of research committees. The ethics approval process also creates a hierarchical power relationship between researchers and participants when it constructs researchers as objective, dispassionate scientists with the knowledge and expertise to reveal "truths" about their research "subjects." Bestowing such an identity positions researchers as superior to their participants, who become the less knowledgeable, passive "objects" of the research and of the researcher. In the case of anorexia, assigning a differential status to researchers and participants through the ethics process replicates the power relations, politics, and public discourses that disempower anorexic girls by constituting self-starvation as different, deviant, and other. When researchers acquiesce to the requirements and interpretations imposed by ethics committees, they are drawn into a position that is vulnerable to perpetuating and reinscribing the hegemonic discourses and practices that construct anorexic girls as other. In this way, the ethics process reconfigures the aim of the research in unintended ways and overlooks questions of moral and ethical responsibility to research subjects in favor of conformity with normative protocols and practices.

Historically, feminists have directed their attention to the colonizing power of discourses about gender, race, and class and to the ways these subjugate and exclude particular groups by constituting them as other. For feminists, the priority has been to show how discourses and practices usurp the rights and capacities of "others" to speak (and act) for themselves by authorizing different voices (e.g., fathers, politicians, lawyers and courts, welfare agencies) to speak in their stead. In Australia, Aboriginal Australians, historically the nation's most marginalized social group, have fought hard to be recognized and to be appointed to research ethics committees so that indigenous people have a say in research ethics. Our experiences illuminate the extent to which the ethics process constructs and silences individuals and social groups, and the extent to which the ethics process can shackle researchers' efforts to interrupt or transform the conditions that perpetuate the assignation of particular groups as other.

The (im)possibilities of Becoming an Ethical Researcher

The explicit purpose of ethics policy is to summon into being ethical research and ethical researchers. Yet corridor conversations and conference banter among researchers are often sprinkled with rumblings about ethics committees. A common complaint is that the ethics approval process is an intrusive, onerous obligation that delays (or obstructs) the "real" work of research. In such conversations, ethics committees and researchers are invariably positioned as binary opposites: powerful versus powerless, dictatorial versus subjugated, rigid and dogmatic versus flexible and responsive, methodologically ignorant versus methodologically knowledgeable. Reflective ethics and moral action are forestalled when researchers see "ethics" as a barrier, rather than a facilitator, to ethical research. Researchers' discomfort with the ways that ethics processes can position researchers as other than ethical is evidenced by the imperative researchers feel to find new ways of doing ethical research—implementing post hoc strategies to circumvent difficulties with prescribed ethics procedures, abandoning research that cannot "fit" the rules or interpretations of ethics committees, constructing elaborate justifications for processes that deviate from the interpretation of ethics policy by local committees, or paying only lip service to the ethics review process.

We incorporated strategies in our recruitment and consent procedures to try to address our complicity in the othering of anorexic girls. In itself, this act illustrates the moral circularity of trying to be ethical researchers and comply with the protocols of ethics policy and practice. Developing consent processes that were morally responsive to the singularity of self-starvation meant thinking outside the existing protocols, endeavoring to connect with relational sensibility to the concrete "otherness" of the girls who might be in our study, and *then* recrafting our understanding of the girls in a realist epistemology and language that fit the ethics regulations and the expectations of our ethics committees. Although our ethics committees endorsed the outcome, we were struck by the irony that the intellectual work of caring about participants within an ethic of justice involved (momentarily) relinquishing all conceptual links with formal ethics procedures and expectations.

The positivist biomedical model casts research ethics as a decontextualized set of principles and procedures for all scenarios, in which researchers are seen as disembodied and dispassionate scientists who are disengaged and removed from the ethics process. Yet our narrative showed that research ethics is deeply embedded and implicated in the social context. Factors like project timelines, the requirements of funding bodies, the local practices of different ethics committees, personal relationships in the research setting and with ethics officers and committees, and ethics committees' anxiety about litigation all play a potent, if sometimes mute, role in decisions about ethics. Researchers are embodied in the ethical process: meeting and negotiating with ethics officers and others in the research setting; refining the research design to address ethical issues; writing and rewriting ethics applications; and wrestling with decisions that kindle an array of intersecting emotions, including discomfort, anxiety, relief, anticipation, optimism, and hope. The practice of decontextualizing and disembodying ethics occludes the investments researchers bring to "getting through" the ethics process and the role these processes can play in privileging particular voices and eroding the relationship between participants and researchers.

Our narrative foregrounds some of the tensions researchers encounter in trying to take up an identity as an ethical researcher in a regulated framework of research ethics. The rigid prescription or interpretation of ethics policy can affect the design of research, undermining its value and nurturing inadequate or even poor research. Nor does compliance with the edicts of ethics committees guarantee moral decision making or moral action. Derrida (1990) cautions that unqualified compliance with laws and regulations creates the very thing they were designed to avert: people relating to each other instrumentally. The ethics approval process confronts a similar difficulty because it is "designed in terms of the greatest good for the greatest number. [The ethics process is] useful to refer to, but [it is] not necessarily humane or even just in every situation because [it] perpetuate[s] tension between the universal and the particular" (Byrne Armstrong and Horsfall, forthcoming).

Our experiences suggest that research ethics policy and processes provide guidance but not definitive solutions to questions about ethical research and moral behavior. Rather, formulaic rules and practices are vulnerable to nurturing unethical and amoral behaviors whereby researchers pay lip service to the ethics approval process knowing they have committed to processes that are conceptually flawed or impossible to implement. In such a climate, the ethics process fosters deception and cultures of counterfeit practice, destroying the very thing it seeks to create: ethical research.

Dreaming the (im)possible Dream: Imagining Future Possibilities

The epistemic tensions between the discourses of the universal, rational subject of scientific realism and those of the multidimensional, particular, and social subject of interpretative, qualitative research create messy moral dilemmas. Despite the advances of recent decades, feminist research straddles a prickly divide in trying to craft research to fit ethics policies and practices when ethics committees employ a biomedical model of research and when dialogue between researchers and ethics committees is constrained.

Rather than succumb to the normalizing power of the ethics process, feminists have challenged the notion of research ethics as a codelike set of rules that regulates moral action (e.g., Gilligan 1977; Benhabib 1992), and researchers have urged reform of the processes for approving qualitative research (Parker 1990; Corbin and Morse 2003). Some ethics committees have developed more sophisticated, flexible understandings of interpretive research practice, often as a result of struggles over the kinds of issues we raise and by appointing knowledgeable practitioners of interpretive research to ethics committees. Yet many committees continue to use the same criteria to judge interpretative and positivist research, reluctant to relinquish the (illusionary) comfort that complying with research ethics means ethical research (see Corbin and Morse 2003, 335–36).

Feminists have challenged Kantian rationalism as a basis for ethical and moral action and proposed an ethic of care and responsibility as an alternative to the universal subject and the explicit separation of self and others embedded in an ethic of justice. Gilligan (1977) has argued that an ethic of care involves fundamentally different moral concepts than an ethic of justice. It comprises a morality based on responsibility and relationships rather than rights and rules, is grounded in concrete circumstances rather than abstractions, and is expressed as an "activity of care" rather than as a set of rules.

Despite the challenges posed in our narratives, we are reluctant to relinquish the idea of an ethics approval process given the long history of researchers denying, abusing, or sacrificing the rights and interests of subjects in the name of knowledge, science, and research. We are also hesitant about an ethic of care in the absence of a moral framework. Such a model presumes the knowability of the "other"; is susceptible to being reduced to a vague, unruly form of empathy; and, as Joan Tronto (1999, 113) points out, makes a claim for a morality based on subjectivity that is vulnerable to relativism or solipsism.

Feminists have proposed that discourse ethics offers a way forward through a morality based on the interdependence of a care ethic and justice, whereby specific cases and claims in particular contexts can be considered within a framework of moral principles (Benhabib 1992). Such an approach would draw on justice principles to guide decision making but would accommodate multiple epistemologies; consider the specificity of individual cases in particular contexts; take both difference and a sensibility to the embedded and embodied particularity of participants and researchers as central to ethical decision making; include processes to encourage and nurture dialogue among researchers, participants, and ethics committees; and constitute ethics as an ongoing process of critical reflection, action, and accountability throughout the research rather than as an act of compliance and approval at the beginning of the research.

In our vague imaginings—our partial dream—the research ethics process would become an ongoing collaborative process shaped by dialogue and responsive relationships that are guided (but not dictated) by principles of justice. Thinking of research ethics as a continual process of collaboration would open up opportunities to dissolve the (mis)-conception that ethics approval means ethical research; to erase the differential power relationships among researchers, ethics committees, and participants; and to interrupt the mechanisms that make researchers and research complicit in the "othering" of research participants.

III. Conclusion

The aim of our narratives is to make visible, and therefore revisable, the dilemmas that surround research ethics policies and their implementation by ethics committees and the implications these carry for research participants and for researchers. The multiple constitutions of self-starvation and the embedded and embodied diversity of "anorexic" girls erase the assumptions that a research population is a homogenous constituency and that informed consent is a conceptually coherent or morally painless act. Rather, the universal, rational subject of an ethic of justice is an illusionary desire, and complying with research ethics processes does not necessarily mean that the ethics processes respect the singularity of participants. Our narratives illuminate how sensibility to power relations, biographical pathways and life experiences, and the identities of the researchers and participants—the "others" of ethics policy—can be obliterated in a compliance model of research ethics and how the research context and institutional structures and practices can fashion ethical decisions and moral actions that curtail sensitivity to "others" and constrain the possibility and practice of feminist research.

The dual aims of research ethics policy are to respect and protect research participants, on the one hand, and to cultivate ethical researchers, on the other. Yet when prescribed ethics protocols fail to engage with the concrete lives and work of participants and researchers, the policy and practice of research ethics functions to construct both researchers and participants as contrary to, different from, and other to its aims. Our narratives illuminate that writing an application for ethics committee review is not a simple or straightforward process. It entangles researchers in tricky moral decisions around complying with the ethics process, appearing to be an ethical researcher, and being an ethical researcher. The decision making involved in preparing ethics applications positions researchers in an awkward moral space between compliance and defiance, legal and transgressive action, instrumentality and sensibility to others. In this space, the rules are unclear, but the moral risks are high.

We do not aim or pretend to offer a definitive solution to the concerns raised in our narratives. Nor do we underestimate the difficulties of transforming established, institutionalized ethics processes, particularly if there are vested interests in protecting and preserving the status quo. Our point is political. Despite advances in the theorizing and practice of feminist research, it is easy to underestimate or to fail to see the ways in which the social, organizational, and cultural practices of the research ethics process work as conceptual and concrete barriers that impede feminist research approaches and position feminist researchers in ideologically uncomfortable spaces. It is equally easy to underestimate the extent to which we, knowingly and unknowingly, take up locations in these uncomfortable spaces and, in doing so, become complicit in preserving the very things our work seeks to erode.

Foucault argued that ethics is not based on or constrained by any legal or religious system but evolves from reflectivity and is indivisible from the self and an aesthetic of existence (Dreyfus and Rabinow 1982). The formal conventions of the ethics review process do not exempt researchers from sensibility to the particular, embedded, and embodied "others" or from doing the intellectual work of reflexively analyzing the ethics and morality of their decisions or actions. Nor do they erase the political imperative for feminist researchers to lead the way in developing better processes for ethical decision making and moral action in research.

Notes

Preparation of this article was supported by a research grant from the Australian Research Council, the Centre for Digestive Diseases, and the Children's Hospital Education Research Institute in Sydney, Australia. We would like to thank Desiree Boughtwood, Peter Bansell, Bronwyn Davies, and Anne Gearside for their helpful comments on various drafts of this article. We are also grateful for the insightful suggestions from the two reviewers who read an early version of the article.

1. A major point in our essay is that anorexia is a contested category and *anorexic* is a problematic label, particularly from girls' standpoints. For this reason we are using the terms *anorexic* and *anorexia* provisionally and tentatively, in the absence of better words.

References

American Psychiatric Association. 2000. *Diagnostic and Statistical Manual of Mental Disorders: DSM-IV-TR*. Washington, DC: American Psychiatric Association.

Benhabib, Seyla. 1987. "The Generalized Other and the Concrete Other: The Kohlberg-Gilligan Controversy and Feminist Theory." In *Feminism as Critique: On the Politics of Gender*, ed. Seyla Benhabib and Drucilla Cornell, 77–95. Minneapolis: University of Minnesota Press.

——— . 1992. *Situating the Self: Gender, Community and Postmodernism in Contemporary Ethics*. Cambridge: Polity Press.

Bordo, Susan. 1993. *Unbearable Weight: Feminism, Western Culture, and the Body*. Berkeley: University of California Press.

Brody, Janet, and Holly Waldron. 2000. "Ethical Issues in Research on the Treatment of Adolescent Substance Abuse Disorders." *Addictive Behaviors* 25(2):217–28.

Brooks-Gunn, Jeanne, and Mary-Jane Rotheram-Borus. 1994. "Rights to Privacy in Research: Adolescents versus Parents." *Ethics and Behavior* 4(2):109–21.

Bruch, Hilde. 1988. *Conversations with Anorexics*. New York: Basic.

Byrne Armstrong, Hillary, and Debbie Horsfall. Forthcoming. "Animating Research Ethics: In the Fact of Frank and

Fearless Conversations and Listening Devices." In *Experiencing Qualitative Research*, ed. Joy Higgs, Angie Titchen, Hillary Byrne Armstrong, and Debbie Horsfall. Oxford: Butterworth.

Corbin, Juliet, and Janice M. Morse. 2003. "The Unstructured Interactive Interview: Issues of Reciprocity and Risks When Dealing with Sensitive Topics." *Qualitative Inquiry* 9(3):335–54.

Derrida, Jacques. 1990. "Force of Law: The Mystical Foundation of Authority." Trans. Mary Quaintance. *Cardozo Law Review* 11(5–6):919–1045.

DeVries, Raymond, and Janardan Subedi. 1998. "Preface: Getting Ethical." In *Bioethics and Society: Constructing the Ethical Enterprise*. Upper Saddle River, NJ: Prentice-Hall. Available online at http://www.stolaf.edu/people/devries/socdocs/preface.html. Last accessed December 17, 2004.

Dorn, Lorah, Elizabeth Susman, and John Fletcher. 1995. "Informed Consent in Children and Adolescents: Age, Maturation and Psychological State." *Journal of Adolescent Health* 16(3):185–90.

Dreyfus, Hubert, and Paul Rabinow. 1982. "On the Geneology of Ethics: An Overview of Work in Progress." In *Michel Foucault: Beyond Structuralism and Hermeneutics*, 229–52. Chicago: University of Chicago Press.

Eisler, Ivan. 1995. "Family Models of Eating Disorders." In *Handbook of Eating Disorders: Theory, Treatment and Research*, ed. George Szmukler, Christopher Dare, and Janet Treasure, 155–76. Chichester: Wiley & Sons.

Fallon, Patricia, Melanie A. Katzman, and Susan C. Wooley, eds. 1994. *Feminist Perspectives on Eating Disorders*. New York: Guilford Press.

Foucault, Michel, ed. (1973) 1978. I, Pierre Rivriere, Having Slaughtered My Mother, My Sister, and My Brother . . .: A Case of Parricide in the 19th Century. London: Peregrine.

—— . 1977. *Discipline and Punish: The Birth of the Prison*. Trans. Alan Sheridan. London: Penguin.

—— . 1988. "Technologies of the Self." In *Technologies of the Self: A Seminar with Michel Foucault*, ed. Luther H. Martin, Huck Gutman, and Patrick H. Hutton, 16–49. London: Tavistock.

Gilligan, Carol. 1977. "In a Different Voice: Women's Conceptions of Self and Morality." *Harvard Educational Review* 47(4):481–517.

—— . 1982. *In a Different Voice: Psychological Theory and Women's Development*. Cambridge, MA: Harvard University Press.

Harding, Sandra. 1987. *Feminism and Methodology: Social Science Issues*. Bloomington: Indiana University Press.

Harre, Rom, and Paul Secord. 1972. *The Explanation of Social Behaviour*. Oxford: Blackwell.

Kleinman, Arthur. 1988. *The Illness Narratives: Suffering, Healing, and the Human Condition*. New York: Basic.

Latvala, Eila, Sirpa Janhonen, and Juha Moring. 1998. "Ethical Dilemmas in a Psychiatric Nursing Study." *Nursing Ethics: An International Journal for Health Care Professionals* 5(1):27–35.

Leder, Drew. 1990. "Clinical Interpretation: The Hermeneutics of Medicine." *Theoretical Medicine* 11(1):9–24.

Levine, Paula. 1995. "The Last Word." *International Journal of Eating Disorders* 3(1):92–95.

Malson, Helen, 1998. *The Thin Woman: Feminism, Post-structuralism and the Social Psychology of Anorexia Nervosa*. London: Routledge.

Meade, Melissa A., and Natasha Slesnick. 2002. "Ethical Considerations for Research and Treatment with Runaway and Homeless Adolescents." *Journal of Psychology* 136(4):449–63.

Morgan, Alice, 1999. *What Is Narrative Therapy? An Easy-to-Read Introduction*. Adelaide: Dulwich Centre Publications.

National Health and Medical Research Council. 1999. *National Statement on Ethical Conduct in Research Involving Humans*. Canberra: AusInfo.

Parker, Ian. 1990. "Discourse: Definitions and Contradictions." *Philosophical Psychology* 3(2):189–204.

Polivy, Janet, and C. Peter Herman, 2002. "Causes of Eating Disorders." *Annual Review of Psychology* 53:187–213.

Ramos, Mary. 1989. "Some Ethical Implications of Qualitative Research." *Research in Nursing and Health* 12(1):57–63.

Rew, Lynn, Margaret Taylor-Seehafer, and Nancy Thomas. 2000. "Without Parental Consent: Conducting Research with Homeless Adolescents." *Journal of the Society of Pediatric Nurses* 5(3):131–38.

Santelli, John, Walter Rosenfeld, Robert DuRant, Nancy Dubler, Madlyn Morreale, Abigail English, and Audrey Rogers. 1995. "Guidelines for Adolescent Health Research: A Position Paper of the Society for Adolescent Medicine." *Journal of Adolescent Health* 17(5):270–76.

Smail, David. 1994. "Community Psychology and Politics." *Journal of Community and Applied Social Psychology* 4(1):3–10.

Tronto, Joan. 1999. "Care Ethics: Moving Forward." *Hypatia* 14(1):112–19.

Walker, Margaret. 1997. *Moral Understanding: A Feminist Study in Ethics*. New York: Routledge.

9

On Intellectual Craftsmanship

C. Wright Mills

To the individual social scientist who feels himself a part of the classic tradition, social science is the practice of a craft. A man at work on problems of substance, he is among those who are quickly made impatient and weary by elaborate discussions of method-and-theory-in-general; so much of it interrupts his proper studies. It is much better, he believes, to have one account by a working student of how he is going about his work than a dozen 'codifications of procedure' by specialists who as often as not have never done much work of consequence. Only by conversations in which experienced thinkers exchange information about their actual ways of working can a useful sense of method and theory be imparted to the beginning student. I feel it useful, therefore, to report in some detail how I go about my craft. This is necessarily a personal statement, but it is written with the hope that others, especially those beginning independent work, will make it less personal by the facts of their own experience.

1

It is best to begin, I think, by reminding you, the beginning student, that the most admirable thinkers within the scholarly community you have chosen to join do not split their work from their lives. They seem to take both too seriously to allow such dissoci-ation, and they want to use each for the enrichment of the other. Of course, such a split is the prevailing convention among men in general, deriving, I suppose, from the hollowness of the work which men in general now do. But you will have recognized that as a scholar you have the exceptional opportunity of designing a way of living which will encourage the habits of good workmanship. Scholarship is a choice of how to live as well as a choice of career; whether he knows it or not, the intellectual workman forms his own self as he works towards the perfection of his craft; to realize his own potentialities, and any opportunities that come his way, he constructs a character which has as its core the qualities of the good workman.

What this means is that you must learn to use your life experience in your intellectual work: continually to examine and interpret it. In this sense craftsmanship is the centre of yourself and you are personally involved in every intellectual product upon which you may work. To say that you can 'have experience', means, for one thing, that your past plays into and affects your present, and that it defines your capacity for future experience. As a social scientist, you have to control this rather elaborate interplay, to capture what you experience and sort it out; only in this way can you hope to use it to guide and test your reflection, and in the process shape yourself as an intellectual craftsman. But how can you do this? One answer is: you must set up a file, which is, I suppose, a sociologist's way of saying: keep a journal. Many creative writers keep journals; the sociologist's need for systematic reflection demands it.

In such a file as I am going to describe, there is joined personal experience and professional activities, studies under way and studies planned. In this file, you, as an intellectual craftsman, will try to get together what you are doing intellectually and what you are experiencing as a person. Here you will not be afraid to use your experience and relate it directly to various work in progress. By serving as a check on repetitious work, your file also enables you to conserve your energy. It also encourages you to capture 'fringe-thoughts': various ideas which may be by-products of everyday life, snatches of conversation overheard on the street, or, for that matter, dreams. Once noted, these may lead to more systematic thinking, as well as lend intellectual relevance to more directed experience.

You will have noticed how carefully accomplished thinkers treat their own minds, how closely they observe their development and organize their experience. The reason they treasure their smallest experiences is that, in the course of a lifetime, modern man has so very little personal experience and yet experience is so important as a source of original intellectual work. To be able to trust yet to be sceptical of your own experience, I have come to believe, is one mark of the mature workman. This ambiguous confidence is indispensable to originality in any intellectual pursuit, and the file is one way by which you can develop and justify such confidence.

By keeping an adequate file and thus developing self-reflective habits, you learn how to keep your inner world awake. Whenever you feel strongly about events or ideas you must try not to let them pass from your mind, but instead to formulate them for your files and in so doing draw out their implications, show yourself either how foolish these feelings or ideas are, or how they might be articulated into productive shape. The file also helps you build up the habit of writing. You cannot 'keep your hand in' if you do not write something at least every week. In developing the file, you can experiment as a writer and thus, as they say, develop your powers of expression. To maintain a file is to engage in the controlled experience.

One of the very worst things that happens to social scientists is that they feel the need to write of their 'plans' on only one occasion: when they are going to ask for money for a specific piece of research or 'a project'. It is as a request for funds that most 'planning' is done, or at least carefully written about. However standard the practice, I think this very bad: it is bound in some degree to be salesmanship, and, given prevailing expectations, very likely to result in painstaking pretensions; the project is likely to be 'presented', rounded out in some arbitrary manner long before it ought to be; it is often a contrived thing, aimed at getting the money for ulterior purposes, however valuable, as well as for the research presented. A practising social scientist ought periodically to review 'the state of my problems and plans'. A young man, just at the beginning of his independent work, ought to reflect on this, but he cannot be expected—and shouldn't expect himself—to get very far with it, and certainly he ought not to become rigidly committed to any one plan. About all he can do is line up his thesis, which unfortunately is often his first supposedly independent piece of work of any length. It is when you are about half-way through the time you have for work, or about one-third through, that such reviewing is most likely to be fruitful—and perhaps even of interest to others.

Any working social scientist who is well on his way ought at all times to have so many plans, which is to say ideas, that the question is always, which of them am I, ought I, to work on next? And he should keep a special little file for his master agenda, which he writes and rewrites just for himself and perhaps for discussion with friends. From time to time he ought to review this very carefully and purposefully, and sometimes too, when he is relaxed.

Some such procedure is one of the indispensable means by which your intellectual enterprise is kept oriented and under control. A widespread, informal interchange of such reviews of 'the state of my problems' among working social scientists is, I suggest, the only basis for an adequate statement of 'the leading problems of social science'. It is unlikely that in any free intellectual community there would be and certainly there ought not to be any 'monolithic' array of problems. In such a community, were it flourishing in a vigorous way, there would be interludes of discussion among individuals about future work. Three kinds of interludes—on problems, methods, theory—ought to come out of the work of social scientists, and lead into it again; they should be shaped by work-in-progress and to some extent guide that work. It is for such interludes that a professional association finds its intellectual reason for being. And for them too your own file is needed.

Under various topics in your file there are ideas, personal notes, excerpts from books, bibliographical items, and outlines of projects. It is, I suppose, a matter of arbitrary habit, but I think you will find it well to sort all these items into a master file of 'projects', with many subdivisions. The topics, of course, change, sometimes quite frequently. For instance, as a student working towards the preliminary examination, writing a thesis, and, at the same time, doing term papers, your files will be arranged in those three areas of endeavour. But after a year or so of graduate work, you will begin to reorganize the whole file in relation to the main project of your thesis. Then as you pursue your work you will notice that no one project ever dominates it, or sets the master categories in which it is arranged. In fact, the use of the file encourages expansion of the categories which you use in your thinking. And the way in which these categories change—some being dropped and others being added—is an index of your intellectual progress and breadth. Eventually, the files will come to be arranged according to several large projects, having many sub-projects that change from year to year.

All this involves the taking of notes. You will have to acquire the habit of taking a large volume of notes from any worth-while book you read—although, I have to say, you may get better work out of yourself when you read really bad books. The first step in translating experience, either of other men's writing, or of your own life, into the intellectual sphere, is to give it form. Merely to name an item of experience often invites you to explain it; the mere taking of a note from a book is often a prod to reflection. At the same time, of course, the taking of a note is a great aid in comprehending what you are reading.

Your notes may turn out, as mine do, to be of two sorts: in reading certain very important books you try to grasp the structure of the writer's argument, and take notes accordingly; but more frequently, and after a few years of independent work, rather than read entire books, you will very often read parts of many books from the point of view of some particular theme or topic in which you are interested and concerning which you have plans in your file. Therefore, you will take notes which do not fairly represent the books you read. You are *using* this particular idea, this particular fact, for the realization of your own projects.

[. . .]

4

But, you may ask, how do ideas come? How is the imagination spurred to put all the images and facts together, to make images relevant and lend meaning to facts? I do not think I can really answer that; all I can do is talk about the general conditions and a few simple techniques which have seemed to increase my chances to come out with something.

The sociological imagination, I remind you, in considerable part consists of the capacity to shift from one perspective to another, and in the process to build up an adequate view of a total society and of its components. It is this imagination, of course, that sets off the social scientist from the mere technician. Adequate technicians can be trained in a few years. The sociological imagination can also be cultivated; certainly it seldom occurs without a great deal of often routine work.[1] Yet there is an unexpected quality about it, perhaps because its essence is the combination of ideas that no one expected were combinable—say, a mess of ideas from German philosophy and British economics. There is a playfulness of mind back of such combining as well as a truly fierce drive to make sense of the world, which the technician as such usually lacks. Perhaps he is too well trained, too precisely trained. Since one can be *trained* only in what is already known, training sometimes incapacitates one from learning new ways; it makes one rebel against what is bound to be at first loose and even sloppy. But you must cling to such vague images and notions, if they are yours, and you must work them out. For it is in such forms that original ideas, if any, almost always first appear.

There are definite ways, I believe, of stimulating the sociological imagination:

1. On the most concrete level, the rearranging of the file, as I have already said, is one way to invite imagination. You simply dump out heretofore disconnected folders, mixing up their contents, and then re-sort them. You try to do it in a more or less relaxed way. How often and how extensively you rearrange the files will of course vary with different problems and with how well they are developing. But the mechanics of it are as simple as that. Of course, you will have in mind the several problems on which you are actively working, but you will also try to be passively receptive to unforeseen and unplanned linkages.

2. An attitude of playfulness towards the phrases and words with which various issues are defined often loosens up the imagination. Look up synonyms for each of your key terms in dictionaries as well as in technical books, in order to know the full range of their connotations. This simple habit will prod you to elaborate the terms of the problem and hence to define them less wordily and more precisely. For only if you know the several meanings which might be given to terms or phrases can you select the exact ones with which you want to work. But such an interest in words goes further than that. In all work, but especially in examining theoretical statements, you will try to keep close watch on the level of generality of every key term, and you will often find it useful to break down a high-level statement into more concrete meanings. When that is done, the statement often falls into two or three components, each lying along different dimensions. You will also try to move up the level of generality: remove the specific qualifiers and examine the re-formed statement or inference more abstractedly, to see if you can stretch it or elaborate it. So from above and from below, you will try to probe, in search of clarified meaning, into every aspect and implication of the idea.

3. Many of the general notions you come upon, as you think about them, will be cast into types. A new classification is the usual beginning of fruitful developments. The skill to make up types and then to search for the conditions and consequences of each type will, in short, become an automatic procedure with you. Rather than rest content with existing classifications, in particular, common-sense ones, you will search for their common denominators and for differentiating factors within and between them. Good types require that the criteria of classification be explicit and systematic. To make them so you must develop the habit of cross-classification.

The technique of cross-classifying is not of course limited to quantitative materials; as a matter of fact, it is the best way to imagine and to get hold of *new* types as well as to criticize and clarify old ones. Charts, tables, and diagrams of a qualitative sort are not only ways to display work already done; they are very often genuine tools of production. They clarify the 'dimensions' of the types, which they also help you to imagine and build. As a matter of fact, in the past fifteen years, I do not believe I have written more than a dozen pages first-draft without some little cross-classification—although, of course, I do not always or even usually display such diagrams. Most of them flop, in which case you have still learned something. When they work, they help you to think more clearly and to write more explicitly. They enable you to discover the range and the full relationships of the very terms with which you are thinking and of the facts with which you are dealing.

For a working sociologist, cross-classification is what diagramming a sentence is for a diligent grammarian. In many ways, cross-classification is the very grammar of the sociological imagination. Like all grammar, it must be controlled and not allowed to run away from its purposes.

4. Often you get the best insights by considering extremes—by thinking of the opposite of that with which you are directly concerned. If you think about despair, then also think about elation; if you study the miser, then also the spendthrift. The hardest thing in the world is to study one object; when you try to contrast objects, you get a better grip on the materials and you can then sort out the dimensions in terms of which the comparisons are made. You will find that shuttling between attention to these dimensions and to the concrete types is very illuminating. This technique is also logically sound, for without a sample, you can only guess about statistical frequencies anyway: what you can do is to give the range and the major types of some phenomenon, and for that it is more economical to begin by constructing 'polar types', opposites along various dimensions. This does not mean, of course, that you will not strive to gain and to maintain a sense of proportion—to look for some lead to the frequencies of given types. One continually tries, in fact, to combine this quest with the search for indices for which one might find or collect statistics.

The idea is to use a variety of viewpoints: you will, for instance, ask yourself how would a political scientist whom you have recently read approach this, and how would that experimental psychologist, or this historian? You try to think in terms of a variety of viewpoints and in this way to let your mind become a moving prism catching light from as many angles as possible. In this connexion, the writing of dialogues is often very useful.

You will quite often find yourself thinking against something, and in trying to understand a new intellectual field, one of the first things you might well do is to lay out the major arguments. One of the things meant by 'being soaked in the literature' is being able to locate the opponents and the friends of every available viewpoint. By the way, it is not well to be too 'soaked in the literature'; you may drown in it, like Mortimer Adler. Perhaps the point is to know when you ought to read, and when you ought not to.

5. The fact that, for the sake of simplicity, in cross-classification, you first work in terms of yes-or-no, encourages you to think of extreme opposites. That is generally good, for qualitative analysis cannot of course provide you with frequencies or magnitudes. Its technique and its end is to give you the range of types. For many purposes you need no more than that, although for some, of course, you do need to get a more precise idea of the proportions involved.

   The release of imagination can sometimes be achieved by deliberately inverting your sense of proportion.[2] If something seems very minute, imagine it to be simply enormous, and ask yourself: What difference might that make? And vice versa, for gigantic phenomena. What would pre-literate villages look like with populations of thirty millions? Nowadays at least, I should never think of actually counting or measuring anything, before I had played with each of its elements and conditions and consequences in an imagined world in which I control the scale of everything. This is one thing statisticians ought to mean, but never seem to, by that horrible little phrase about 'knowing the universe before you sample it'.

6. Whatever the problem with which you are concerned, you will find it helpful to try to get a *comparative* grip on the materials. The search for comparable cases, either in one civilization and historical period or in several, gives you leads. You would never think of describing an institution in twentieth-century America without trying to bear in mind similar institutions in other types of structures and periods. That is so even if you do not make explicit comparisons. In time you will come almost automatically to orient your reflection historically. One reason for doing so is that often what you are examining is limited in number: to get a comparative grip on it, you have to place it inside a historical frame. To put it another way, the contrasting-type approach often requires the examination of historical materials. This sometimes results in points useful for a trend analysis, or it leads to a typology of phases. You will use historical materials, then, because of the desire for a fuller range, or for a more convenient range of some phenomenon—by which I mean a range that includes the variations along some known set of dimensions. Some knowledge of world history is indispensable to the sociologist; without such knowledge, no matter what else he knows, he is simply crippled.

7. There is, finally, a point which has more to do with the craft of putting a book together than with the release of the imagination. Yet these two are often one: how you go about arranging materials for presentation always affects the content of your work. The idea I have in mind I learned from a great editor, Lambert Davis, who, I suppose, after seeing what I have done with it, would not want to acknowledge it as his child. It is the distinction between theme and topic.

   A topic is a subject, like 'the careers of corporation executives' or 'the increased power of military officials' or 'the decline of society matrons'. Usually most of what you have to say about a topic can readily be put into one chapter or a section of a chapter. But the order in which all your topics are arranged often brings you into the realm of themes.

A theme is an idea, usually of some signal trend, some master conception, or a key distinction, like rationality and reason, for example. In working out the construction of a book, when you come to realize the two or three, or, as the case may be, the six or seven themes, then you will know that you are on top of the job. You will recognize these themes because they keep insisting upon being dragged into all sorts of topics and perhaps you will feel that they are mere repetitions. And sometimes that is all they are! Certainly very often they will be found in the more clotted and confused, the more badly written, sections of your manuscript.

What you must do is sort them out and state them in a general way as clearly and briefly as you can. Then, quite systematically, you must cross-clarify them with the full range of your topics. This means that you will ask of each topic: Just how is it affected by each of these themes? And again: Just what is the meaning, if any, for each of these themes of each of the topics?

Sometimes a theme requires a chapter or a section for itself, perhaps when it is first introduced or perhaps in a summary statement towards the end. In general, I think most writers—as well as most systematic thinkers—would agree that at some point all the themes ought to appear together, in relation to one another. Often, although not always, it is possible to do this at the beginning of a book. Usually, in any well-constructed book, it must be done near the end. And, of course, all the way through you ought at least to try to relate the themes to each topic. It is easier to write about this than to do it, for it is usually not so mechanical a matter as it might appear. But sometimes it is—at least if the themes are properly sorted out and clarified. But that, of course, is the rub. For what I have here, in the context of literary craftsmanship, called themes, in the context of intellectual work are called ideas.

Sometimes, by the way, you may find that a book does not really have any themes. It is just a string of topics, surrounded, of course, by methodological introductions to methodology, and theoretical introductions to theory. These are indeed quite indispensable to the writing of books by men without ideas. And so is lack of intelligibility.

[. . .]

Notes

1. See the excellent articles on 'insight' and 'creative endeavour' by E. D. Hutchinson in *Study of Interpersonal Relations*, edited by Patrick Mullahy, New York, Nelson, 1949.
2. By the way, some of this is what Kenneth Burke, in discussing Nietzsche, has called 'perspective by incongruity'. See, by all means, Burke, *Permanence and Change*, New York, New Republic Books, 1936.

10

From the Seminar Room

Marjorie L. DeVault

[. . .]

Planning Inclusive Research

Feminist theorizing has grown enormously during the 1980s and 1990s. Theorists have attended more explicitly to the contributions of lesbian feminists. They have insisted on the centrality of African American, Latina, Asian American, Native American, and international perspectives. White, heterosexual feminists have more carefully considered the racism and heterosexism of some feminist theory. And some writers have paid more careful attention to issues of class, disability, and age (though these dimensions of inequality seem less prominent than others in recent theorizing). Most feminists would now agree—at least in principle—that feminist theory must be theorizing about multiple simultaneous oppressions, or what Patricia Hill Collins (1990) calls a matrix of domination. But these ideas, which have been so central in feminist theorizing of the past decade, have entered discussions of feminist methodologies more slowly and unevenly. Working with students in this area, I have come to feel that the development of feminist theory has outpaced our methodological innovations, so that there is often a serious mismatch between the goals of feminist researchers and what we know how to do in our empirical projects. Often, my seminar groups engage in extended abstract conversations about multiple oppressions, but lose these concerns when our talk turns to their developing projects and the challenge of designing a "doable" dissertation. These practical anxieties are important and ought not to be ignored, but observing this slippage has stimulated my interest in devising a variety of strategies for attending to issues of differential location and cross-cutting dimensions of inequality—strategies that can be deployed in any project in order to maintain the visibility of "differences" that are socially significant.

An obvious place to start thinking about this issue is in decisions about "sampling"—who will be included in a study. A 1988 *Gender and Society* article by Lynn Weber Cannon, Elizabeth Higginbotham, and Marianne L. A. Leung (1998) suggests that the qualitative studies favored by feminist researchers are especially likely to include relatively homogeneous samples, as a consequence of techniques like "snowball" sampling and the use of personal networks to recruit volunteer participants. They argue that it is critical to develop fully stratified samples with adequate representation across categories such as race and class. And they acknowledge that this demand calls for special attention to recruitment, and usually, more labor-intensive recruitment strategies.

These authors present one strategy for designing inclusive research projects, using as an illustration their in-depth study of Black and white professional, managerial, and administrative women's well-being. Their relatively large interview study—with two hundred participants—allowed them to build a sample structured by three dimensions of inequality (race and class background of the respondent and the gender composition of her occupation), producing eight cells with twenty-five interviewees in each cell. This approach to sampling allowed them to examine the separate and intersecting effects of race and class, and they point out that had they not done so, class-related differences might have been erroneously identified as racial effects, fueling a "cultural deficit" interpretation of the findings. Their article raises important issues for feminist researchers, and their research design might be taken as a kind of ideal model for attention to multiple inequalities. But it is a strategy that requires a large sample and relies on a logic of variables that may not be so appropriate for ethnographic investigation (or for secondary analysis of survey data, already collected). Reading their article pushed me to consider several additional strategies that may be more practically applied in the conduct of smaller interview studies, ethnographies, and—with appropriate modifications—other kinds of social research.

(1) As one begins to develop any topic, one ought to be acutely conscious of the composition of the group or setting to be studied. Many naturally-occurring groups are relatively homogeneous in terms of race, class, gender, sexuality, and so on; when that is the case, these features of the group ought to be part of the analysis—from the beginning. Researchers can notice the composition of the group they're concerned with and consider why it forms in the communities it does or attracts these members, and whether this group or setting has counterparts in other communities or with differing memberships. The answer to this latter question provides a basis for considering whether it is practical or desirable to seek additional subjects and sites. Are there other settings where it's different?

A key strategy—central to feminist thought—involves attention to what is missing: Where are those we don't see in this group? If they are not in similar sites elsewhere, why not? How does it happen that this group includes these people and not others? In some cases, I believe that this kind of reflection may suggest expanding one's view. Instead of content analysis using only *New York Times* articles, one might look for ethnic newspapers as well; instead of seeking participants only through private physicians, one might make contacts at public clinics as well; and so on. In other cases, exploring such options may suggest that homogeneity is a feature of this type of setting and, therefore, not so much a matter of sampling as a topic for analysis as the study proceeds. One might discover, for example, that formal support groups for family caregivers are rare in African American communities. This kind of discovery mitigates the need to fill a sampling "cell," but it brings other demands: to consider why one finds this kind of ethnic distribution of the activity under study and what kinds of counterparts to the activity one would find in other communities.

(2) Whether one decides to sample varied or homogeneous groups or settings, it seems important to identify carefully, in some detail, who is included. Such identification should take into account the social organization of "marked" and "unmarked" positions. In the routine practice of social research, studies of subordinated groups are nearly always labeled as such, while those of dominant groups are not. Feminists, and others concerned with inequalities, suggest that this practice reproduces dominance. It takes dominance for granted—normalizes and naturalizes it—and sustains a notion of subordination as exceptional and of subordinate identities as "other." By contrast, a more adequate empirically-grounded description assumes that dominance and subordination are always

in play, part of the seen-but-(often)-unnoticed ground for human interaction. At the very least, it seems to me that any empirical study ought to give some substantial attention to identifying the group under consideration and locating it within a national, or even global context. That is, one ought to make readers aware—at least briefly—of how the membership of a particular site compares with the composition of surrounding communities, a wider regional population, and so on. If it accomplishes nothing else, even a minimal discussion of this sort could serve the purpose of highlighting the partiality of the analysis. One objection to this suggestion takes it as a mandate for "politically correct" labeling, and I would agree that a merely mechanical deployment of "identities" such as "white middle-class heterosexual" can simply reify such categories without providing any useful context. Even that is perhaps better than saying nothing, but I do have in mind a more nuanced and thoughtful description.

One relatively straightforward descriptive strategy that moves some distance in this direction is simply to elaborate the most typical identity categories. For example, in describing a group of U.S. "whites," one might say more about their ethnic ancestry and whether and how it is meaningful for them. Rather than simply labeling a neighborhood "middle class," one might say more about its location, history, employment base, and so on. Another strategy for making these descriptions more meaningful would involve keeping them in play as an analysis unfolds. Too often, such identificatory notes appear briefly in remarks that introduce a study and then fall away, so that the analysis appears as generic or universalized.

(3) These strategies of elaborated description lead to a third possibility for improving studies of homogeneous and relatively privileged groups: making privilege itself a topic for analysis. We see some of the possibilities in an emerging group of studies dealing with "whiteness," heterosexuality, and masculinity (e.g., Frankenberg 1993, Ingraham 1994, Messner 1992, Connell 1995, Kimmel and Messner 1998).

(4) Another strategy for making research more "identity-conscious"—a strategy that may or may not show up in the research product—involves reflexive autobiographical work. My assumption here is that learning more about how and why we see things as we do will allow us to understand more about the meanings others make of their (and our) lives, and to locate ourselves (and others) in more complex and meaningful ways rather than only through simplistic identity categories. In the seminar, we read *Yours in Struggle* (Bulkin, Pratt, and Smith 1984), a collection of three variously autobiographical essays that deal with racism and antisemitism among feminists. Each author tells personal stories, searching her own background for clues to the dynamics of oppression that she encounters, resists, and sometimes inadvertently helps to sustain at different moments in her feminist activism. The fact that all three writers are lesbian-feminists deepens their analyses and adds a layered significance to their accounts that is quite useful in the seminar context. For lesbian students, their stories make visible identities more typically obscured in the classroom; for straight students, the stories teach about lesbian lives and resistance to homophobia as well as racism. The essays provide provocative models for reflexive analysis, and they have often inspired seminar participants to undertake autobiographical writing as one of their projects in the course.

Again, I do not mean to suggest that our own realities should be an endpoint in our investigations. The reason for autobiographical investigation and analysis is to understand better where we fit into a larger system and in relation to others. I understand the feminist call for attention to the personal, or for unabashedly partial and located standpoints, as a struggle against the positivist ideal of a neutral, "value-free" stance toward the field of inquiry. This movement has begun to make it possible for researchers to include themselves as part of the picture, and to treat our own realities as one kind of touchstone by which to evaluate our analyses. But this view also suggests that the most illuminating investigations will always be setting a partial reality in a larger context, and considering how others' views would change the picture.

(5) All of these research strategies depend on knowing something about the operation of the major systems of social inequality that structure people's interactions. Thus, they suggest that social researchers, regardless of specialization, have a responsibility for "continuing education" in this arena (especially about groups historically or typically excluded from our accounts of society and about the processes/mechanisms of exclusion). I would also suggest that the project of inclusive scholarship can be moved forward through thoughtful use of existing scholarship and a concern for using related studies to draw out the ways that particular groups are shaped by the wider social processes that produce inequality. Any researcher studying a homogeneous group or setting, it seems to me, ought to be searching for related studies conducted in other groups and communities. Explicit comparison with other work can highlight the operation of processes that might otherwise go unnoticed or unremarked.

Setting Standards of Inclusion

As empirical researchers understand these challenges better, it seems not uncommon—especially for relatively privileged researchers—to feel guilty, "overwhelmed," and defensive about the choices one inevitably makes. One unfortunate response to such feelings is to become too paralyzed to do any investigation; another is to stop hearing the challenge; another might be to pay lip service to "all oppressions" in a rather mechanical way. All these pitfalls seem to me to argue for noticing the kind of attitude we will need in order to keep on trying: a recognition that we won't succeed absolutely (at least as individuals), but that it is crucial to keep the challenge on the agenda.

I focus here on a psychic or emotional part of the research process that isn't usually taken up as an aspect of methodology. Noticing that emotional element, in order to take it into account, seems to me a feminist move in itself—underlining that research is done by actual people, living complex everyday lives suffused with emotion. The issues are not only or primarily psychic, however, but also structural: how to build feminist groups, spaces, actions, and habits of thought that struggle against racism rather than reproducing it. And I would underline that there are four questions here, not just one. *Again, my intention in making that distinction is to focus on dimensions of the research process as lived experience, and the material underpinnings of that experience—aspects of research, that are often left out of abstract and idealized accounts* (emphasis mine).

My argument for attention to feelings is not meant to deflect us from questions about standards. These questions arise, in a graduate seminar, in a raw and somewhat panicky form: What do I have to do? In this setting, they are driven, understandably, by the hurdles of dissertating, mediated by that small and very particular intellectual community—the "dissertation committee." But I urge participants in my seminar to begin thinking beyond these immediate concerns toward wider intellectual communities, recognizing that scholars always choose where and how to locate ourselves, and that by choosing and entering intellectual communities we not only become responsible to them but also shape the standards of work within them. In this context, questions about standards are broader and more broadly consequential: What do we expect from our own work? from work by other feminists? What responsibilities do we have for constructing better standards (and how does that happen)? How do we select the audiences to whom we will make ourselves accountable? When and how do we call others to be accountable?

During the 1990s, it has become increasingly likely that feminists who present unidimensional, universalized gender analysis could expect critique from many other feminists (though not all). Still, the likelihood of encountering this kind of critique varies considerably, depending on the type of setting (conference, dissertation hearing, journal submission) and the identities and politics of those involved in a particular site. Even when these critiques are made—and especially in face-to-face settings—there is a strong norm of "politeness" in professional settings that I have very mixed feelings about; I appreciate its "usefulness" (e.g., in saving people enough face to avert tears and fisticuffs), but I also know that the practice of "politeness" can blunt or deflate strong challenges to racism in our scholarship. It certainly contributes to the maintenance of relatively isolated intellectual "clubs" (as opposed to communities[4]) that rarely communicate across boundaries of identity, interest, and concern.

I suggest that one major contribution feminist methodologies can make to social science research is the idea that general standards for a complete and adequate social analysis should include continuing attention to the structuring effects of major systems of social inequality. How much attention? What kind? Those are questions we are only beginning to address. But we will develop satisfactory answers only if these questions are introduced routinely into our discussions and evaluations of any empirical investigation. One thing I have learned from my seminar is that inclusion depends on making space for these concerns, and then keeping them on the table. These goals, in turn, raise questions about intellectual connections and networks, what we read and attend to, how we listen to others, and the risks of appropriating works that arise from others' interests and positions.

Those who do empirical research will always be doing limited investigations; no one study can include everything, and doing empirical investigation well often means doing it deeply rather than broadly. But the call for inclusive scholarship, as I understand it, is not to do "everything" at once. Rather, it seems to me that every study ought to be conducted and written with an acute consciousness of what's being left out and the implications of omissions for the claims that can be made. That will help readers to see and understand a particular study as one useful piece of a much larger picture, a piece that must be connected with, and interpreted against, studies that explore other experiences and processes.

Advice:
Plan for inclusion, from the beginning of every study.
Recognize that doing "everything" is impossible, but also that one can almost always do much more than immediately comes to mind.

II. Process

Emotion

Once underway, most researchers experience alternating moments of intensely pleasurable engagement and almost paralyzing doubt and depression. Or perhaps I should say, in the interest of accuracy, that this roller-coaster image captures my typical experience. Observation of others, and of the fits and starts through which student projects develop, leads me to believe that I am not alone. I suspect, as well, that these emotions are heightened for oppositional researchers. The conduct of research is, for this group, meant to be more than just a job or an intellectual puzzle, more than a quest for individual success. Research and writing are supposed to contribute to liberation projects, to benefit oppressed communities and lead to change. When these goals seem in reach, our elation is intensified; when we fear failure, we fear the shame of failing our communities; when we suspect that we are only doing a job, or see that we might be rewarded for our achievements, we often feel guiltily hypocritical.

Some may scoff at this seeming excess of emotion, dismissing such feelings as products of unrealistic expectations. But dismissing feelings is usually shortsighted, since they typically persist as muted but powerful barriers to productive work. Recent writing on feminist research has perhaps exacerbated these emotional challenges, by heightening expectations and honing our critical tools to a razor-sharp edge. As an alternative to "dry and distant" objectivist research, the idea of feminist methodology has accumulated an increasingly "rosy glow," with high expectations for cooperation, intimacy, and authenticity. In addition, as feminists (and others) examine the research encounter more and more closely, we understand with ever greater precision the barriers to cooperation and the risks of exploiting those who participate in our research. Shulamit Reinharz (1993) suggests that these developments have produced "excessive demands" for feminist researchers. She worries that discussions calling for intense rapport and strong personal involvement will have the paradoxical effect of inhibiting feminist investigation by setting unattainable goals.

Jane Mansbridge (1995) provides a related structural analysis that illuminates the challenge facing the oppositional researcher and the context that produces such demands. She points out that virtually all feminists work within organizations designed to serve purposes other than feminist ones. They bring feminist commitments into workplaces, voluntary groups, and their encounters in other institutions, and they struggle to find ways of reconciling those commitments with the often conflicting demands of those organizations. Many join with other feminists and develop collective strategies. Sometimes, they find ample room for feminist practice; sometimes, only the tiniest openings for resistant efforts. In either case, it would be unrealistic to assume that feminists in these settings can freely choose and shape their own practices. Their actions are better understood as strategic compromises, worked out day by day as part of the ongoing business of the organization. Feminist teachers may work to diminish hierarchies of authority, for example, but they are required to give grades at the end of the semester; feminist nurses may hold conceptions of care that diverge from those of physicians, but they are also bound by institutional structures of authority; feminist waitresses may resist patrons' objectifying gestures, but in many establishments they must accept sexist treatment in order to hold a job and make a living wage. The pragmatism of these choices does not "spoil" these workers' feminism; rather, it reveals the inevitably rocky terrain of feminism in practice.

The academic disciplines and the settings where oppositional researchers work—colleges and universities, policy organizations, and so on—shape their practices in similar ways. Often, these settings provide considerable autonomy—so much, in fact, that feminist students and academics may lose sight of the real constraints on our work. Our distinctive challenge is to make accurate assessments of the kinds and degrees of freedom we do have—often, more than we might think, but generally not so much that we can expect to achieve an unimpeachable feminist practice. "Realism," then, seems necessary—and yet potentially dangerous, if it means that the oppositional researcher aims for less than she might reasonably accomplish. As a study goes forward, the challenge of finding ambitions that are both worthy and reasonable may produce inflated desires and feelings of intense anxiety, guilt, and despair. Painful as these feelings can be, they are most usefully treated as inevitable and informative aspects of the process of oppositional research.

Expect strong feelings; pay attention, but try not to wallow

Privilege, in Theory and Practice

Many of the worries that beset oppositional researchers revolve around issues of domination. Researchers exercise particular kinds of interpretive and representational power: they define topics, set the boundaries of their investigations, choose participants and control their participation, interpret data, and of course, craft the text that will be taken as authorized "knowledge." Some critics, then, argue that systematic study of others is an objectifying process inimical to liberation and that analytic writing is inevitably a project of mastery (e.g., Clough 1992). Feminist researchers who take such critiques to heart often come to fear that, rather than dismantling systems of domination, we can only add stones to an edifice of power.

The moral dimension of the critique of empirical research gives it an edge that stimulates confession and apology. While these kinds of responses are sometimes informative, they often leave writers stuck in a moment of guilty paralysis. One pitfall is that researchers may spend so much of their analytic energy on possible problems that their solutions to these problems remain underdeveloped (and therefore perpetuate the flaws of standard practice). My hope is that feminist methodologists will continue to study these critiques of empirical research, but also maintain the sense of possibility that allows us to explore opportunities for better practical strategies.

"Practical," here, means more than just "pragmatic" (though my approach does involve a considerable dose of pragmatism, for better or worse). It points to the fact that empirical research is a practice, unfolding in time, in particular places and in concrete interactions. The point may seem too obvious to mention; it is important because it underlines distinctively methodological imperatives and constraints. The tendency to value theory over method appears to lead some researchers to look to theoretical writing as if it could provide fully developed answers to methodological questions. But intriguing and fruitful ideas—Sandra Harding's (1991) suggestion that we "start thought" from lesbian life, for example, or bell hooks' (1984) notion of bringing marginal perspectives to the center of feminism—do not tell researchers, in practical terms, how to proceed. Thus, it may be useful to acknowledge more explicitly a division of labor among feminist thinkers. Theory and method—"sister" elements in empirical investigation—should always intertwine and inform each other. But when I work with students, I encourage them to see, alongside the critiques of feminist theorists, a space for specifically methodological innovation.

In addition, the injunction to examine the researcher's privilege may sometimes have paradoxical effects. The analysis of privilege is an important corrective to a long history of scientific study conducted by the powerful, and it seems extremely useful for researchers to look critically at the actual relations of inequality that precede such research encounters—often, the relations that make them possible—and that persist beyond these encounters. But what does it mean to "examine" privilege? It might usefully mean examining one's daily life, discovering and cataloging unearned advantage (as Peggy McIntosh [1988] does). It might mean reviewing one's biography, following threads of privilege through a personal history (as Minnie Bruce Pratt does [Bulkin, Pratt, and Smith 1984]). It might mean that one would use the knowledge thus gained as a lens toward a clearer-sighted view of daily interactions. And sometimes, one might want to find a way to acknowledge one's privilege explicitly. Unfortunately, in my view, the last response seems most common, both among students and in feminist writing. It is relatively easy to announce that "I am inordinately privileged" and to elaborate this theme; it is considerably more difficult to know how to move productively beyond the announcement. My worry concerns the border where "examination" becomes the arrogant assertion of privilege. When a man faces a woman classmate and states, "Of course, it's easier for me to get my views heard," he intends to unmask but perhaps inadvertently perpetuates male privilege. Similarly, when straight women use seminar time for elaborate confessions of heterosexual privilege, they intend to correct their dominance but may miss opportunities to learn about lives that are different. These kinds of assertive confessions can reproduce relations of dominance in that they define a situation from a single (privileged) point of view and leave little room for mutual conversation.

In face-to-face research relations (as in the small intellectual community of the seminar), disciplines of courtesy and restraint go farther than one might think in constructing more mutual, less exploitative relations across lines of difference and inequality. While it is true that the researcher writes up the study and thereby defines the interaction, research participants will exercise agency, too, if we let them; they decide whether to talk with us, what to say and how, when to withdraw, and so on. Watching carefully for those decisions and respecting them are large steps toward leveling the power relations of the research encounter.

A discipline of restraint might mean recognizing refusal, avoidance, and withdrawal as meaningful responses to privilege and representing these somehow as meaningful data. It might mean accounting for the life circumstances that make participation in research difficult—bringing along to interviews with parents a research assistant to care for participants' children, for instance. It might mean offering opportunities for collaboration in the research, but without insisting on a formal equality of effort that imposes unmanageable burdens on participants. Finally, restraint should imply extremely careful listening to the words and actions of participants and an openness to unexpected meanings. In studies that bridge cultures, researchers sometimes make assumptions about difference and miss subtle responses that challenge those assumptions. (I have noticed in the seminar, for instance, that white students just beginning to explore issues of oppression and privilege can take from the writings of African American feminists a somewhat reductive view of "an African American perspective," and they sometimes seem nonplussed when the comments of African American classmates move in different directions.)

It is also worth mentioning that critical writing on empirical research (and my discussion thus far) focuses almost entirely on the situation of research in communities considered less powerful than the researcher's. The idea of "studying up"—focusing on those who are more powerful—has a venerable but somewhat muted presence in oppositional discourses, and has been quite underdeveloped in feminist methodology. Strategies for studying up would presumably call for a different set of virtues—bold assertion rather than restraint, for example—and these virtues are perhaps less comfortable for many women than solicitous restraint.

Finally, however, neither of these alternatives—studying "up" or "down"—can be adequate by itself. Focusing primarily on oppressed communities risks ignoring the dynamics of power; focusing on the powerful may obscure dynamics of resistance that fall outside the orbit of dominant institutions and ideologies. It seems important in every project, therefore, to attend to connections, aiming for an analysis that shows in some way both the consequences of power and how it is exercised. Working in this way will not eliminate the power and privilege of the analyst, but it can make that power more visible and deploy it in ways that chart systems of privilege and inequality, offering road maps to change in those systems for those working from various locations within them.

> *Privilege cannot be talked away. Therefore, my suggestion for researchers conscious of their unearned advantages: Resist impulses toward elaborate confession; work instead toward projects that demonstrate an awareness of privilege by advancing understandings of its mechanisms and consequences.*

Writing

Usually, students in the seminar are most immediately concerned with writing in a particular genre: they must prepare a dissertation proposal. For some, the moment of producing this "official" text—with such significance for their careers—is a critical turning point. I am often surprised when students who have been articulate, funny, and passionate in the seminar turn in first proposal drafts that are dull and dead—they seem to have lost their voices! I have learned that most often, they are in thrall to some image of the properly "scientific" text, parroting a voice of imagined authority that they hope will sound "important" (as Becker [1986b] reports in his book on teaching writing). I have also learned that even quite simple questions can be helpful in loosening these constraints and encouraging a new start: "But what did you *want* to say? And why didn't you just say *that*?" The point is to encourage students to sit comfortably with their own writing: "You don't have to copy someone else," I might say. "This is your text."

As a teacher and advisor, I often instruct students in the proper use of standard forms, and in many contexts I insist on the rules, quibbling over grammar and footnote form along with the most curmudgeonly of my colleagues. But I try to make the seminar a space for looking beyond rules and indulging in experimentation. I include in our collective reading several texts that are "unusual" in social science—because they are "personal" (Bulkin, Pratt, and Smith 1984), "evocative" (Trinh T. Minh-ha 1989), or "experimental" (Orr 1990). Students often have mixed reactions, and as we discuss these pieces, we talk about both benefits and risks of adopting such writing strategies in social scientific texts.

Sometimes I tell stories of my own writing practices. For example, I sometimes talk about my meditations on words that are especially important and the discoveries that have come from adopting new usages. For several years, I have been experimenting with using the word "family" as an adjective rather than a noun, since the noun form seems only to contribute to a reified and falsely monolithic conceptualization. And I have become extremely interested in the consequences of writing as "I" or as part of a "we" (see DeVault 1997b). I tell about my writing anxieties and the strategies I have developed for managing my inevitable mood swings. And I tell the story of making room for my anger while writing (see the introduction to Part V). These accounts are meant to encourage students to be more conscious of their writing and to prepare them to follow Laurel Richardson's (1994) advice—to treat writing as an "exercise," using it not just to present a finished piece of work, but also to discover and develop new lines of thought.

Following Richardson's lead, I encourage students to use their course papers to try things out rather than to prepare a final and definitive argument. I often propose that students prepare "sampler" papers—practicing different modes of presentation in the same way that embroiderers combine a variety of stitches in a practice piece of work. In addition to longer papers based on their empirical work, I encourage students to undertake shorter autobiographical essays. These projects provide an opportunity to reflect on our discussions about identity and knowledge, and also to try out an unaccustomed mode of writing that still has a scholarly purpose. I emphasize the one guideline that seems to me most important for social scientists: remember that you are telling this story for some intellectual reason; figure out what you want to accomplish and craft your story toward that end (see also DeVault 1997a).

Above all, my aim is to show students a range of possibilities for taking charge of their own writing. If they worry about how readers will respond to a text, I encourage them to be more explicit about how they would like readers to respond, incorporating these instructions for readers into the text. If they wish to adopt some unusual voice or format, I encourage them to explain why as fully as possible, since more conservative readers will need convincing; in addition, the effort helps to ensure that the innovation is motivated by more than fashion alone.

These writing issues also provide opportunities to discuss "professionalism" and changing expectations for academic work. I am always aware of the two contradictory layers of our work in the seminar: we are preparing students for places in their chosen fields and also preparing them for struggles to change those fields. Their research texts are tickets of admission. Students must learn what it means to write a "proper" text, but they need not always do so slavishly. Instead, I try to hone their ability to assess the kinds of professionalism they value, the kinds that are necessary in particular contexts, and the kinds they may decide to resist. I work with them to devise strategies for "performing" professionalism when it seems useful and crafting sound explanations for the moments when they depart from established practice. And I try to help them "see" professionalism, so as not to take it for granted. As the discourses of feminist methodology grow, they are inevitably marked by the dynamics of research as professional activity. Such changes cannot be wished away, but instead must become part of the continuing challenge of oppositional practice.

Write often, thoughtfully, carefully; learn to write flexibly and adapt textual practices to the demands of different occasions.

References

Becker, Howard S. 1986b. *Writing for Social Scientists: How to Start and Finish Your Thesis, Book, or Article.* Chicago: University of Chicago Press.

Bulkin, Elly, Minnie Bruce Pratt, and Barbara Smith. 1984. *Yours in Struggle: Three Feminist Perspectives on Anti-Semitism and Racism.* New York: Long Haul Press.

Cannon, Lynn Weber, Elizabeth Higginbotham, and Marianne L. A. Leung. 1988. "Race and class bias in qualitative research on women." *Gender and Society* 2:449–462.

Clough, Patricia Ticineto. 1992. *The End(s) of Ethnography: From Realism to Social Criticism.* Newbury Park, Calif.: Sage.

Collins, Patricia Hill. 1990. *Black Feminist Thought: Knowledge, Consciousness, and the Politics of Empowerment.* Boston: Unwin Hyman.

Connell, R. W. 1995. *Masculinities: Knowledge, Power, and Social Change.* Berkeley: University of California Press.

DeVault, Marjorie L. 1997a. "Personal writing in social research." In *Voice and Reflexivity.* Edited by Rosanna Hertz, pp. 216–228. Thousand Oaks, Calif.: Sage.

——. 1997b. " 'Are we alone?' " *Qualitative Sociology* 20(4): 499–506.

Frankenberg, Ruth. 1993. *White Women, Race Matters: The Social Construction of Whiteness.* Minneapolis: University of Minnesota Press.

Harding, Sandra. 1991. *Whose Science? Whose Knowledge?: Thinking from Women's Lives.* Ithaca: Cornell University Press.

hooks, bell. 1984. *Feminist Theory: From Margin to Center.* Boston: South End Press.

Ingraham, Chrys. 1994. "The heterosexual imaginary: Feminist sociology and theories of gender." *Sociological Theory* 12(2): 203–219.

Kimmel, Michael S., and Michael A. Messner. 1998. *Men's Lives* (4th ed.). Boston: Allyn and Bacon.

Mansbridge, Jane. 1995. "What is the feminist movement?" In *Feminist Organizations: Harvest of the New Women's Movement.* Edited by Myra Marx Ferree and Patricia Yancey Martin, pp. 27–34. Philadelphia: Temple University Press.

McIntosh, Peggy. 1988. "White privilege and male privilege: A personal account of coming to see correspondences through work in women's studies." No. 189. Wellesley College Center for Research on Women. Wellesley, Mass.

Messner, Michael A. 1992. *Power at Play: Sports and the Problem of Masculinity.* Boston: Beacon.

Orr, Jackie. 1990. "Theory on the market: Panic, incorporating." *Social Problems* 37(4): 460–484.

Reinharz, Shulamit. 1993. "Neglected voices and excessive demands in feminist research." *Qualitative Sociology* 16: 69–76.

Richardson, Laurel. 1994. "Writing: A method of inquiry." In *Handbook of Qualitative Research.* Edited by Norman K. Denzin and Yvonna S. Lincoln, pp. 516–529. Thousand Oaks, Calif.: Sage.

Trinh T. Minh-h. 1989. *Woman, Native, Other: Writing Postcoloniality and Feminism.* Bloomington: Indiana University Press.

Section Two
On Doing

11

Interactive and Reflexive Models of Qualitative Research Design

Wendy Luttrell

Joe Maxwell (1996, 2005) offered an innovative research design model that improved on other models at the time (LeCompte and Preissle 1993; Miles and Huberman 1994; Robson 2002; Rudestam and Newton 1992). It has five components: goals/purposes; conceptual context/frameworks; research questions; methods; and validity.[1]

Each component part is defined below in his own words:

1. *Goals.* Why is your study worth doing? What issues do you want it to clarify, and what practices and policies do you want it to influence? Why do you want to conduct this study, and why should we care about the results?
2. *Conceptual Framework.* What do you think is going on with the issues, settings, or people you plan to study? What theories, beliefs, and prior research findings will guide or inform your research, and what literature, preliminary studies, and personal experiences will you draw on for understanding the people or issues you are studying?
3. *Research Questions.* What, specifically, do you want to understand by doing this study? What do you not know about the phenomena you are studying that you want to learn? What questions will your research attempt to answer, and how are these questions related to one another?
4. *Methods.* What will you actually do in conducting this study? What approaches and techniques will you use to collect and analyze your data? There are four parts of this component of your design: (1) the relationships that you establish with the participants in your study; (2) your selection of settings, participants, times and places of data collection, and other data sources such as documents (what is often called "sampling"); (3) your data collection methods; and (4) your data analysis strategies and techniques.
5. *Validity.* How might your results and conclusions be wrong? What are the plausible alternative interpretations and validity threats to these, and how will you deal with these? How can the data that you have, or that you could potentially collect, support or challenge your ideas about what's going on? Why should we believe your results?

Maxwell's diagram emphasizes the interaction between parts, stressing that each component is closely tied to the other, but is not "linked in a linear or cyclic sequence" (2005: 6). He explains that he imagines the arrows connecting the different components as "rubber

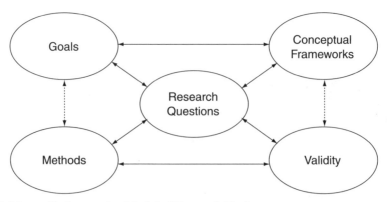

Figure 11.1 Maxwell's Interactive Model of Research Design.

bands" able to "stretch and bend to some extent, but they exert a definite tension on different parts of the design, and beyond a particular point, or under certain stresses, they will break" (ibid.: 6). While not made visible in the model, he stresses that research relationships and ethics should be involved in every aspect of design (ibid.: 7).

My model emphasizes reflexivity as the centerpiece of qualitative research design and process. Thus, the model makes visible the central role that *research relationships* play. Negotiating and representing research relationships—what and how we learn with and about others and ourselves—is at the heart of the research journey.

All manner of contingencies shape the nature of our research relationships—practical, theoretical, ethical, moral, and political—and these must be taken into account, and decisions made along the way. As I have argued, it is the demands placed on qualitative researchers to be aware of our subjectivities (what some people call bias) and to harness our predispositions, imagination, and empathy toward others that distinguishes our craft. To envision these relational and dynamic elements of qualitative research on the flat surface of paper is frustrating, which leads me to offer an origami-like diagram.

Doing qualitative research is like origami—the artful tradition of paper folding that turns a flat and static piece of paper into a three-dimensional representation of an object, such as the well-known Japanese paper crane. Some origami (called action origami) create objects in motion—allowing for the flap of a wing or even putting a paper-folded bird into flight. Similarly, qualitative researchers aim to transform the "object" of their study into multi-dimensional and lively representations of lived experiences, social processes, and complex webs of meanings and values. I am told that in the early days of origami, development of new designs was largely a mix of trial and error, luck, and serendipity. But with advances in origami mathematics the basic structure of a new origami model can be theoretically plotted out on paper before any actual folding even occurs. These two approaches—one based on serendipity and surprise, the other based on prior theoretical plotting—resonate with qualitative research design and reflexive knowing.

Why the star? The point of a research design is to orient your inquiry. Like the North Star, it serves as a sign that you are traveling in the right direction. Unlike other stars in its large constellation, the North Star never changes position, and thus serves as nature's compass for night travelers. Once the guide for slaves seeking freedom, I use it here as emblematic of research in search of social justice. Insofar as qualitative research is a moral endeavor and promotes democratic ideals, the North Star seems like a fitting image.

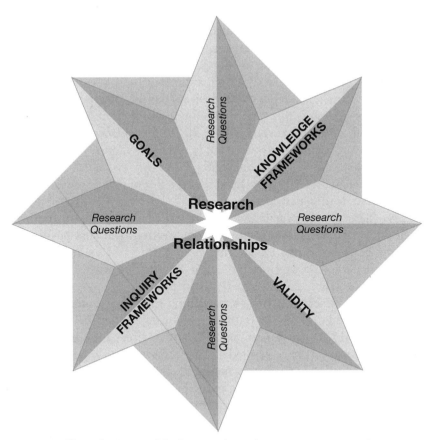

Figure 11.2 Luttrell's Reflexive Model of Research Design.

There are six component parts of the reflexive origami–North Star model I propose. These are defined below:

1. *Research Relationships.* How are you part of the setting, context, and social phenomenon you seek to understand? What is the character/nature of your relationship to research participants? What are the contingencies and constraints within which you and research participants will forge relationships? How will you "name" yourself and others, and what criteria will you use to adequately represent the lives of research participants? What role will research participants have in your investigation? What dilemmas or conflicts (if any) do you anticipate for participants, and how have you taken these into consideration? What specific moral, political, and ethical principles guide your investigation? What guidelines will you follow, including and beyond, "Do no harm?" What criteria of reciprocity, fairness, or justice will you use?

2. *Research Questions.* Because research questions are likely to shift and evolve throughout the process, they appear at many points of the star. Moreover, there are at least four different types of research questions as indicated by each quadrant: including *variance* questions that inquire about differences and correlations; *process* questions; *meaning* questions; and *context* questions. Considering what type of question you are asking can help clarify your thinking.

3. *Knowledge Frameworks.* I have chosen the term "knowledge frameworks" over Maxwell's "conceptual context" for two reasons. First, I want to encourage students to draw upon a wide array of knowledge sources when framing their studies— from social theory, to visual media on one's topic, to personal experiences, practice-based knowledge, and participants' own local knowledge and expertise. Second, I encourage students to think deeply about the epistemologies they are using and consider how this figures into the rest of their design.

4. *Inquiry Frameworks and Methods.* What Big-M *methodology* (the genre of qualitative research, e.g. ethnography, case study, narrative inquiry) have you selected as the best means to investigate your topic? What *little-m methods* (data types, data collection, and analysis strategies) will best enable you to answer the research questions you have formulated, and why?

5. *Validity.* There are many qualitative researchers who are either uncomfortable with or reject this term because it is grounded in positivist and post-positivist claims to truth and certainty. While I share this discomfort, I use it and invite students to make explicit their own epistemological criteria for whether their knowledge claims are sound, well-grounded, and justifiable.

   As a feminist researcher, I think of validity in terms of *authenticity*[2] and *reciprocity* established through my research relationships. I have been concerned about the extent to which the women literacy learners, pregnant teens, and immigrant children with whom I have worked a) have a hand in how their lives and experiences are represented in the research; and b) come to see themselves and others in enhanced ways as a consequence of participating in the research. I have also been concerned that the interests and opportunities of research participants are facilitated by my inquiry and that the social critique I offer integrates participants' perspectives and perceptions. These are some of the criteria I use to establish the validity of my research. To consider other types of validity see Carspecken (2001) and Kvale (1995).

6. *Goals.* Whose interests are being served by your study? Why does your study matter to you—what are your stakes in the project? Why does your project matter for the people involved or affected by your study? What are their stakes in the project and how do these correspond (or not) to yours? What ideals and actions do you wish to promote through your research?

Maxwell's model and my model are but two among many different visual representations of qualitative research design. They are offered to guide and inspire you to display your own thoughts about the research process. Some displays are better than others for conveying your thinking and releasing your imagination. I encourage you to play with line, layout, color, image, and words—and take pleasure in the process.

Notes

1. In Maxwell's 1996 version, he uses the term "purpose" and shifts to the term "goals" in the second edition (2005). Similarly, he originally uses "conceptual context" and shifts to "conceptual framework." For all intents and purposes, these mean the same thing.
2. See Guba, E. G. and Lincoln, Y. S. 1989 for a discussion of authenticity criteria.

References

Carspecken, P. 2001. *Critical ethnography in educational research: a theoretical and practical guide.* New York: Routledge (pp. 55–86).

Guba, E. G., and Lincoln, Y. S. 1989. *Fourth generation evaluation.* Newbury Park, CA: Sage.

Kvale, S. 1995. "The social construction of validity." *Qualitative Inquiry* 1 (pp. 19–40).

LeCompte, M. D., and Preissle, J. 1993. *Ethnography and qualitative design in educational research* (2nd ed.). San Diego: Academic Press.

Maxwell, J. 1996. *Qualitative research design: an interactive approach.* Thousand Oaks, CA: Sage.

—— . 2005. *Qualitative research design: an interactive approach* (2nd ed.). Thousand Oaks, CA: Sage.

Miles, M. B., and Huberman, A. M. 1994. *Qualitative data analysis: an expanded sourcebook* (2nd ed.). Thousand Oaks, CA: Sage.

Robson, C. 2002. *Real world research.* Oxford: Blackwell.

Rudestam, K. E., and Newton, R. R. 1992. *Surviving your dissertation.* Newbury Park, CA: Sage.

12

Culture, Development, Disability

R. P. McDermott and Hervé Varenne

What I liked about anthropology was its inexhaustible faculty for negation, its relentless definition of man, as though he were no better than God, in terms of what he is not.

Samuel Beckett, *Molloy* (1955)

It is always easier to see misfortune rather than injustice in the afflictions of other people. Only
the victims occasionally do not share the inclination.

Judith Shklar, *The Faces of Injustice* (1990)

Cultural Contexts for Disability

In the eighteenth and nineteenth centuries, people on Martha's Vineyard, a small island
off Cape Cod, suffered, or, we might say, were privileged by a high rate of genetically
inherited deafness, approximately one person in every 155. It is easy to use the word
suffered to evoke sympathy for the plight of the "deaf." It is a physical difference that can
count, and it is not unusual for deaf people to suffer terribly for the way it is made to
count in various social settings. Interestingly, the people of Martha's Vineyard did not
share the horror with which most Americans approach deafness. The Vineyard deaf could
not hear, but the community there turned not hearing into something everyone could
easily work with, occasionally work around, and sometimes turn into a strength. In Nora
Groce's *Everyone Here Spoke Sign Language* (1985), we are given a picture of deaf persons
thoroughly integrated into the Vineyard community and the hearing thoroughly integrated into the communicational intricacies of sign. When surviving older members of
the community were asked to remember their deaf neighbors, they could not always
remember who among them had been deaf, for everyone there spoke sign language,
sometimes even the hearing people with other hearing people.

The case of the Vineyard deaf, and it is not the only such case (Kakumasu 1968), raises
interesting questions about the nature of disability, questions that go beyond etiology to
function and circumstance: When does a physical difference count, under what conditions, and in what ways, and for what reasons? When, how, and why: these are deeply
cultural issues, and, depending on how a physical difference is noticed, identified, and
made consequential, the lives of those unable to do something can be either enabled or
disabled by those around them. From Martha's Vineyard, there is good news: it is possible
to organize a culture in which deafness does not have to isolate a person from a full round
in the life of a community; not being able to hear can cut off behavioral possibilities that

can be taken care of in other ways, and, by everyone speaking sign, other possibilities can be explored. There is also bad news: Martha's Vineyard was not an island unto itself, but a peripheral area in a larger social field within which deafness was treated as an appalling affliction.

The easy use of the term *suffer* often carries an invidious comparison of the "disabled" with those seemingly "enabled" by the conventions of a culture. A more principled account of life inside a labeled/disabled community would show, for example, that the abjection with which normals approach the problems of labeled/disabled people is one-sided and distorting. A recent advance in cochlear implants, for example, has deaf children hearing, a seeming advance to researchers, but the source of unrest in the deaf community. Outsiders to the deaf experience are surprised to find that being able to hear is not as important as being a member of the deaf community. Similarly, sighted persons are surprised that lifelong blind persons surgically given the "gift" of sight in their adult years are usually overwhelmed by the drabness of the seen world; "suffering" blindness is minimal compared to "suffering" the depression that follows the recovery of vision (Gregory and Wallace 1963). We must not confuse our ignorance of life with a physical difference for an account of that life; nor should we forget that the particulars of our own ignorance are likely a more crucial determinant of the disabilities manifest in some lives than any differences in the physical makeup of the people.

On Martha's Vineyard in the nineteenth century, people had jobs to do, and they did them. That one person could do them faster or better than another was likely less important than that the jobs got done. In such a world, it was not important to sort out the deaf institutionally from the hearing. By important social measures—rates of marriage and propinquity, economic success, and mastery of a trade—deaf persons were indistinguishable from hearing persons on Martha's Vineyard. There is record of an unbalanced deaf person in the community, but the order to have him committed to an institution did not emphasize his deafness as part of his problem and was, in fact, signed by a deaf person. It is possible to organize a culture in which the deaf play an equal and unremarkable role in most parts of life. On Martha's Vineyard, when it was time to institutionalize a troubled person, a deaf person could be asked to play either side of the culturally constructed divide between the unbalanced and the incarcerator, but not either side of the culturally irrelevant divide between hearing and deaf.

Unfortunately, deaf persons on Martha's Vineyard were not treated well by outsiders who could not sign, and the fortunes of the deaf declined as the island opened up to extensive tourism. That they could not hear was made worse by outsiders who pitied them, wrote them up in Boston newspapers, explained their origin in scientific tracts (one popular claim was that their deafness was a result of a melancholy suffered by their mothers), called for a remedy of their situation, and suggested a eugenics program for their erasure. An irony can be found in the fact that perhaps the people best able on Martha's Vineyard to read such reports were deaf. Although most Vineyarders went to school for only five years, in the late eighteenth century, by mandate of the state educational system, deaf children were supported through ten years of school, and, when faced with a difficult reading and writing task, the hearing would often go to a deaf person for help. This is particularly difficult for participants in contemporary American culture to imagine, as it is now the case that the most difficult task of deaf educators is to get their students past the basic levels of reading and writing.

If the case of the Vineyard deaf suggests that we might want to rethink our understanding of the role of culture in the diagnosis and remediation of developmental disorders, a case study from New York City in the late 1980s can make more specific how that rethinking might develop. First, we can look at the case study of a deaf child at home and school. Then we can take up its implications for how we should think about the very notions of culture, disability, development, and the relations between them.

In a dissertation with the appropriate title "Arrangements for the Display of Deafness," Linda Rosa-Lugo (1989) studied a six-year-old deaf girl at school, where she seemed to be having a difficult time, and at home, where she seemed to be having an easy and highly communicative life. Fortunately, she was born into a fantastic family, albeit with the twin difficulty that she and her older brother were both deaf and their parents were native Spanish speakers in an English-speaking world. A third and middle child could hear. Together, the five members of the family give us a glimpse of a small version of what Martha's Vineyard might have been like for deaf children, namely, a place where people communicated with each other whatever the difficulties, a place where inclusion in family and community was more important than exclusion. In their study of deaf culture in America, Padden and Humphries, themselves deaf, state the basic case: "being able or unable to hear does not emerge as significant in itself; instead it takes on significance in the context of other sets of meaning to which the child has been exposed" (1988: 22). Rosa-Lugo looks at four scenes, or sets of meaning: two at school, where the performance of a communication was understood and evaluated primarily as a pedagogical success or failure; and two at home, where tasks seemingly identical to those tackled at school were woven as a part of a different relational fabric and understood primarily as fun.

The school settings involved the six-year-old Raquel, her mother, a teacher, and an assistant teacher. The three adults worked hard to get Raquel to identify, at different times, in American Sign Language (ASL), in English, or in Spanish, various objects or actions, for example juice, napkin, cup, and to pour. Mostly, Raquel refused, and when she did reply, she sometimes did so incorrectly. The adults were relentless and pushed Raquel to perform just the right word, in just the right code, at just the right time. In her own turn, Raquel mixed together crying, running to her mother, and answering rightly and wrongly on occasion, all apparently in just the right order to get the teachers confused about what questions were being answered or even asked at any given time. In desperation, to organize her attention (or theirs), the teachers would withhold rewards from Raquel until she voiced particular words. The overall tone of the events is unpleasant and perhaps painful to all.

The scene at home is quite different. The naming tasks given to Raquel, even when school related, are attached to quite different social activities. All members of the family use three codes, spoken English, spoken Spanish, and sign, to get done the jobs that come before them. When the mother organizes an activity around Raquel identifying various objects and their colors, her older brother becomes a full participant, holding objects in the air, repeating questions, urging and evaluating answers. Raquel gets some things right and some things wrong, but never stops participating. The confrontation that marked some of the interactions at school never developed. Unlike the school scene in which the teachers insist that answers be spoken, deafness seems not to have been the issue. The answers were accepted for their content, rather than their code. Sometimes Raquel spoke, and sometimes she signed, just like the others in her house, just like what might have happened on Martha's Vineyard.

It is important to note that Rosa-Lugo does not claim to have distinguished all cases of school from all cases of home by producing only two examples from each, and she encourages the reader to imagine how deafness, under the right conditions, could be a strength in school just as it could become a maximum problem in a home where parents did not manage a smooth transition from one code to another. The analysis even produces evidence to the point; note, for example, that Raquel's mother is on the scene at both school and home. The key question concerns the identification of just what kind of thing deafness is in any given interaction. At home, there is evidence that deafness is usually a workable deficit and can even be a plus. The extraordinary event on Rosa-Lugo's tape comes with a display of a fourth communicative code, namely, spoken deafness. While the mother and older brother are working with Raquel on her naming tasks, the middle and hearing child is apparently feeling quite left out of the interaction. She calls her mother often, announces an emergency or two, calls out the answers to some of the questions put to Raquel, and, when all this fails to distract the home lesson, she starts to scream in a good imitation of the way a deaf child pronounces and intones spoken English. She is attended to immediately. On Martha's Vineyard, hearing people sometimes found it easier or more efficient to use sign than to speak, for example, for land-boat communication, for passing secrets around tourists, for intimate conversations in public places like hospitals. In Raquel's house, not only sign, but the high-pitched spoken English of the deaf sometimes had its moment.

Martha's Vineyard and Raquel's family together show how even a difference as definite as not being able to hear in a social world built for the hearing does not have to be a problem. It is one kind of problem to have a behavioral range different from social expectations, and it is another kind of problem to be in a cultural nexus in which that difference is used by others to make one look bad. The argument of this chapter is that the second problem is often the more serious.

Three Ways of Thinking About Culture and Disability

> At the very moment in which this object, "madness," took shape, there was also constructed the subject judged capable of understanding madness. To the construction of the object madness, there corresponded a rational subject who "knew" about madness and who understood it. . . . I tried to understand this kind of collective, plural experience which was defined between the sixteenth and nineteenth centuries and which was marked by the interaction between the birth of "rational" man who recognizes and "knows" madness, and madness itself as an object susceptible of being understood and determined.
>
> Michel Foucault, *Remarks on Marx* (1991)

There are numerous ways to think about the nature of culture, and the terms *disability* and *development* have been defined and debated ad nauseam. Within the variety, there is enough order to show that there are three approaches to using the terms *culture*, *development*, and *disability* and that they differ along a continuum of assumptions about the world, its people, and the ways they learn. In the present section, we contrast the three approaches to highlight the range of assumptions and biases that come with using these terms.[1] The three approaches are discussed in the same order that they developed across the past thirty-five years; the second approach represents an advance over the first, and the third approach, in turn, not only extends the first two but takes them into account as data.

The sequence represents not only a theoretical advance, but ideally an increase in the resources available to the moral order. We are aware, as Judith Shklar has argued, that "the outraged jeremiad is the mark of a moralistic rather than a moral society" (1979: 24), and so it is that in calling for a defense of all against all others, a defense of each of us against our own culture, we run the risk of whining more than actually fixing. We envision no great society where the problems of people being labeled and disabled are forever cured; it is the human situation to create such problems and every generation's responsibility to confront them in their particulars. Many cultures have been harder on its citizens than the United States, but many have been gentler. In pointing to how the very term *disability* has been used to make things harder rather than gentler, and this despite great efforts on the part of our very kindest citizens, we hope to help stem the tide.

The *cultural deprivation* approach takes up the possibility that people in various groups develop differently enough that their members can be shown to be measurably distinct on presumed developmental milestones. This approach is founded analytically on the assumption of a stable set of tasks that can be used to record varying performances across persons and cultures. Low-level performances by members of a group are taken as examples of what the people of the group have not yet developed (for example, certain versions of abstraction, syllogistic reasoning, metacontextual accounts of linguistic behavior, and so on). A crude version of this argument has it, "We have culture, and you don't"; or a little more carefully put, "We seem to have more culture than you do." To unpack the assumptions underlying the argument, consider the following state of the world, its problems, and their consequences:

> The world consists of a set of tasks, some of which are difficult. Development refers to progress up preordained steps to well-defined competencies in handling important tasks. The contrast between the enabled and the disabled can be found in the work people do that shows that some are able to do the most important tasks and that others cannot keep up. The fate of the disabled rests in the easy attitude that institutions can work with those who lag behind, but basically they are out of the running for the rewards that come with a full cultural competence.

By method and style of argument, this approach has been based mostly on psychology and has attracted the intuitive wrath of many anthropologists, who have argued that all cultures, and all languages, however interesting their differences, are essentially equivalent; this has not stopped anthropologists, particularly those working with minorities in their own cultures, from falling for the rhetorical attraction of the deprivation stand and once again finding a "they" who are less than our "we."

The *cultural difference* approach takes up the possibility that people in different groups develop in ways equivalently well tuned to the demands of their culture and that different cultures, though various, offer equivalent roads to complete human development. This approach relies less on predefined tasks and focuses instead on the tasks performed by ordinary people, well beyond the reach of the laboratory, as a matter of course in different cultures. If it is possible to describe the task structure of varying cultures, then it is possible to discern what abilities and disabilities cultures might develop (for example, quantity-estimation skills among Kpelle farmers and Baltimore milk-truck dispatchers, calculation skills among Vai tailors, mnemonic strategies among navigators using the skies for direction). A crude version has it that, "We have culture, and you have a different one." To unpack the assumptions underlying the argument, consider a world similar to the one considered above, but with different problems and consequences:

> The world consists of a wide range of tasks, all of them situated, all of them emerging within a cultural context. Development refers to progress along many roads to task competence, each with its own pace, each with its own price, but all interesting. The contrast between the enabled and the different can be found in the work people do that shows, for any given task, that some achieve full competence, others focus on only parts, and a few seem unable to develop any mastery, all a case of different skills for different wills. The fate of the different as disabled rests in the liberal lament that human variation is wonderful, but those who cannot display required skills in the correct format at the right time are out of the running for the rewards of their culture.

This approach is favored among ethnographically oriented psychologists and anthropologists, particularly those working on school problems among minority populations.

The third approach, the *culture as disability* stand, takes up the possibility that all cultures both socialize and sort and that, indeed, in teaching its members what to aspire to and hope for, every culture also teaches how to notice, handle, mistreat, and remediate those who fall short. As a pattern of institutions, a culture produces a wealth of positions for human beings to inhabit. Each position requires that the person inhabiting it must possess, and must be *known as possessing*, particular qualities that symbolize, and thereby constitute, the reality of their position *to others*. The people in any position may be unable to perform what people in other positions can perform, but the limits on learning what others do is socially not as primary as Americans like to believe. People are only incidentally born or early enculturated into being different. It is more important to understand how they are put into positions for being treated differently. Notice that by this approach, subcultures or otherwise labeled groups do not stand alone, nor even in a simple relation to more dominant other groups, but always in relation to the wider system of which all groups, dominant and minority, are a part.

This approach starts with the question of why any culture, or more likely, any elite group within a culture, would develop an assumed stable set of tasks and a theory of cognition and development against which people of various kinds might be distinguished, measured, documented, remediated, and pushed aside. On what grounds could experts have assumed that the complex worlds of individuals in multiple relationships with each other would stand still enough to be characterized by simplified accounts of either their culture, their cognition, or the ties between whatever culture and cognition are taken to be? One version of the grounds for simplicity is that such theorizing and the methodological assumptions that go with them are part of wider-scale institutional and political agendas, in particular, that it has been handy for modern, ideologically rationalistic, class-divided, industrial- and information-based states to isolate individuals as units of analysis and to record the intimacies of their minds for public scrutiny and control. The contemporary nation state is above all a recordkeeper, much more than it is a container of culture or an organizer of learning (Thomas, Meyer, Ramirez, and Boli 1988). A crude version of this approach has it thus:

> We have a culture, or at least we think we do, and, uh, so do you, well, most likely; but it is difficult to tell the difference between when we are analyzing our culture and when we are living it, and, despite the fact that you people seem to be less than we are, or different enough that you might just as well be less than we are, we are unsure that we have available either the analytic categories or the political awareness to know whether it is we or you who are being most disabled by our situation together.

To unpack the assumptions underlying the argument, consider a variation on the worlds considered above, this time with a third set of problems and consequences:

The world may or may not be a set of well-defined tasks, but it has definitely been shaped by modern societies into a set of measurable tasks of varying difficulty, and task competencies can be impossible to develop or show off at the right time. Development refers to the institutional arrangements by which individual behavior is measured, and individuals made responsible for, progress up the road to task competence, generally without theoretical, methodological, or political attention to the possibility that both the tasks and occasions for their use are conventions at best and political fabrications at worst. The contrast between the enabled and the oppressed can be found in the work people do to show that some display task competence, some hide away at task relevant moments, some isolated from task performance mill about the bottom of the social structure complaining, some only a few task moves better than those on the bottom claim themselves to be lord of all, and only a few disparage the task competencies others have built. The fate of the oppressed as disabled rests on the cynical assumption that, with a severity depending on the conditions of economic and political growth, whatever solutions can be momentarily developed, new kinds of tasks and new kinds of disability can take their place.

Being acquired by a position in a culture is difficult and unending work for all involved—for those being acquired, children, for example, and for those doing the acquiring, their teachers and employers. Every culture invites a delineation and specification not just of what has to be done and who can do it, but of what is difficult, in what ways for whom, and under what circumstances. In fact, even things that do not have to get done on simply functional grounds can be enshrined as the most important measure of the people in a culture. *Cultures are not only occasions for disabilities, they actively organize ways for persons to be disabled.*

By this last approach, culture refers to how we organize our hopes and dreams of how the world should be. The same people, using the same materials and in ways systematically related to our hopes and dreams, also give us our problems. Without a culture we would not know what our problems are; culture, or better, the people around us in culture, help to define the situation-specific, emotionally demanding, and sensuous problems that we must work on today with only the tools we have available here and now. We might just as well say that culture fashions problems for us and, from the same source materials, expects us to construct solutions. It is from life inside this trap that we often get the feeling that working on problems can make things worse.

There is a significant sense in which, or, at the very least, there is much analytic leverage to be gained by thinking as if: without a money system, there is no debt; without a kinship system, no orphans; without a class system, no deprivation; without schools, no learning disabilities; without a working concept of truth, no liars; without eloquence, no inarticulateness. The problems that exist in one culture do not have to exist in another culture, or at least not with the same interpretations and consequences, and the same is true in the same culture at different points of its history or at different levels of its hierarchy. Even a sure physical condition, for example, severe mental retardation, as constraining as it is on any individual's development, is an amazingly different phenomenon in different cultures (Edgerton 1970), across the last century of our own culture (Sarason and Doris 1979), or within different households on the same block of our here and now (Mannoni 1972). For the parents of a retarded child, the situation is culturally complex. Parents are supposed to give birth to fully healthy children who can live out the cultural agenda, and anything less brings two problems to the child's situation: the child must not only suffer from not being able to engage in certain activities, but from being mistreated by those who can. Cultures define what should be the case. They are often explicit, and often unfair, about what mothers should think about their own children and what the rest of us should think about both the children and their mothers; were it not for melancholy, remember, Martha's

Vineyard would not have had so many deaf. If being deaf can go unnoticed in one culture and be a point of torture in another, so it is for being a bastard, a twin, an intersexed person, or even, so simply in a sexist society, a girl.

If cultures define their own problems, can we figure out how they define the ones they claim to have? If a disability corresponds to a situation, just what is our situation that we would have these particular disabilities? From what cultural materials are these problems put together, and from within what institutional and political nexus? And where can we get the tools to confront the system that has given us the problems we have?

If Cultures are Disabling, How Can We Research and Confront Our Situation?

> The search for method becomes one of the most important problems of the entire enterprise of understanding the uniquely human forms of psychological activity. . . . the method is simultaneously prerequisite and product, the tool and the result of the study.
>
> Lev Vygotsky, *Mind in Society* (1978)

> A curious analogy could be based on the fact that even the hugest telescope has to have an eyepiece no larger than the eye.
>
> Ludwig Wittgenstein, *Culture and Value* (1980)

The three approaches to culture, development, and disability have enormous consequences for how one proceeds methodically to research and confront our present situation. A brief account of the differences can focus on the role of context in the organization and subsequent analysis of behavior (see Goodwin and Duranti 1992; Kendon 1990; McDermott 1993). The deprivation approach ignores context as much as possible; the difference approach plays up the importance of context as if the contexts were preestablished sites for people to display their competencies; and the culture as disability approach tries to understand context as a product of the work people do in the course of making sense with each other and the preconstructed materials of their culture, materials filled with the biases and inequalities of their social structure. The approach to context is crucial, because it defines one's unit of analysis and sets limits on the conclusions that can be reached. Without a strong sense of context, research uses the individual for a unit of analysis, and kinds of individuals—the deaf, the learning disabled, the illiterate—are the referents for conclusions. With a dynamic sense of context, the units are usually not individual persons, but their activities as they reach backward and forward in behavioral time; the conclusions then are about the structure of the activities.

These are complex issues, and this section offers only a brief summary of the methodological commitments and habits of each approach.

The deprivation approach places great trust in received and institutionally established categories. The reliance is that we know how to identify tasks in the world and that we can measure the performances of individuals on such tasks. For any hypothesis about how culture figures in the distribution of successful and failing performances, it is equally important that analysts have ways to identify the stable social identity of any group member.

The assumption that there are stable tasks, stable persons with stable social identities, and stable descriptions of stable tasks performed by stable persons with stable and always relevant social identities is not well grounded. The systematic study of persons performing predefined tasks can perhaps tell us a great deal about predefined tasks and the biases of their makers, but it is difficult to show that they have anything to say about what people do when they are not acting within such tasks. There is an old and quite sturdy argument about the danger of operationalizing one's procedures without regard for contextualizing one's results: the argument is that the conditions that operationally define a given object for analysis are only analytically useful while the conditions apply; once the conditions are removed, for example, once a banana is removed from the chemical solution that reacts in a defining way to bananas, then the banana, for analytic purposes, is no longer a banana. There is sometimes reason to abandon this argument, but it must be done carefully and with a forfeit of certainty of conclusion (Bateson 1972; Cole, Hood, and McDermott 1978).

Some argue that performances on tasks predefined by psychologists overlap with stable patterns in the shifting terms of social identity. This should raise questions of believability, despite the fact that we all make such correlations in our daily language; we all assume, for example, that the deaf cannot hear and that is what constitutes their place in the world as deaf persons. The mechanisms that might allow for such a match in reality have not been well explicated, and the correlations that do exist have been claimed by some to be nothing more than a manifestation of how various biases, class and color racist categories, for example, infiltrate, and make relevant, the kinds of tasks developed by schools and developmental psychologists for purposes of measurement. To display what someone knows is analytically difficult, and to display what someone does not know or cannot do, if only because they may be trying to do something else, if only because they may be operating on aspects of the task not well understood by the task definer, may be impossible. Such difficulties and impossibilities have not stopped psychometric and experimental cognitive psychology from becoming the institutional language of schooling and its problems.

The difference approach in principle accepts no categories for analysis, whether of tasks or of persons, until they can be shown to be in use in the behavior of the persons under analysis. Where can we get the categories we need to describe the world in which people live? If we ask the people directly what we would like to know, we will ask them our questions, fully loaded with our assumptions. We need their categories to ask even elementary questions of them. We need, in fact, the questions they ask of each other, or, as phrased three decades ago by Charles Frake (1964), we need notes on their queries, not so much to learn how they talk about each other, but how they actually talk with each other, in their very processing of each other. If every culture has its own categories, its own skills, and its own modes of interpretation, then a description of the people in a culture relies on long-term participation that allows the analyst to derive categories people themselves use to handle their lives with each other. One must look and listen as methodically as possible to discern the sensitivities people use to get around making something of nothing and nothing of something in culturally prescribed ways.

There is a simple epistemology behind this work. The world is likely not available on only your terms and may be more difficult to see and hear than you had thought, but the categories needed to describe the lives of the people you are studying are available upon extended looking and listening. The world is a good place; if you are careful enough, you can understand a part of it; if you are sensitive enough, as the people of Martha's Vineyard were sensitive enough to find the strengths of deaf persons, you can even make the world a better place.

Methodologically, studies based on the possibility that all people make sense and develop fully, albeit in accord with the particulars of the situation, albeit in accord with what David Plath (1980) has called the "idiom of their heritage," have been dedicated to more careful data analyses than insisted on by most anthropologists and to more careful accounts of the contexts with which behavior is organized than is allowed by experimental psychology. At their best, such studies have insisted on both rigor and respect, on both precision and context sensitivity. At their worst, such studies threaten to fail where traditional anthropology failed, in the practical but naive assumption that native categories are simple and stable, that they form uniquely real patterns, and that the best metaphor for the flow of human history is the mosaic, solid and well-bounded bits of color and shape intelligible only to natives. The alternative to this assumption is a focus on culture as an ongoing achievement filled with tensions, disputes, borders, resistances, neuroses, compromises, and repairs (Drummond 1980). Culture, says David Plath (1980), is a "parliament of prodigals," and its every seemingly stable pattern is the product of compromise by all involved.

The culture as disability approach commits us to a constant confrontation with received categories. The categories we need to study our lives are not available for the asking, nor are they available to those who would simply look and listen, no matter how sensitively. The categories we need are not only difficult to come by, they are systematically unavailable; we might just as well say that they are hidden. As Karl Marx once noted (in the third volume of *Capital*), and as Lev Vygotsky (1978; 1986) liked to cite, if the surface of appearances coincided with reality, we would not need science. There is nothing inherently wrong in describing deaf persons as deaf, learning-disabled persons as LD, or people who cannot read as illiterate, but in a social order that is anxious to use disability as a way to stratify and degrade, the categories are in need of constant revision.

This is bad news for more than just the scientist, for it suggests we are all in need of new categories to reorganize our lives. If everyone in a culture thinks that situation X is a problem, it is likely the case that (1) the problem that must be confronted lies elsewhere, and (2) the formulation that situation X is the problem, by keeping the focus on situation X, is in fact part of the problem. By this way of thinking, if deafness appears to be a problem in a community, it is likely the case that the deaf, whom we know from Martha's Vineyard can be complete members of any culture, are put upon by tensions from other sectors of their society. By this way of thinking, if developmental disabilities of various kinds appear to people in the schools to be our problem, then our easy acceptance of their arguments should be one of our first topics of consideration for gaining an understanding of the institutional and cultural contexts of the problem and its consequences.

How then can we get the categories we need to gain a new perspective and to solve our problems? There is no one answer to this, of course, but one place to start is to construct environments that play to people's strengths rather than their weaknesses. We need to create conditions that would make the most rather than the least of disabled persons, of those already disabled by the environments we have available and of those who will meet that fate later in life. We need most of all to construct a world in which the disabled do not have to spend their time arranging to avoid degradation by those around them. Such work will take more than just asking our questions and tallying the answers, and it will take more than figuring out their questions and how they are tied to answers, no matter how sensitive our approach. In addition to figuring out how the members of a disabled minority make sense, there are the even more difficult tasks of showing how they could have been made to look so bad in the eyes of the community and, more importantly, how to change the world enough for them to look sometimes wonderful and sometimes not, just like everyone else. Work on any of these levels can produce categories and research that could make a difference.

The Acquisition of Persons by Culturally Well-Formulated Disabilities

> Research on the psychological essence of childhood presupposes an examination of its social ethos, its internal link with the social demands that are made with respect to the shaping of a person as a main unit of the productive forces.
>
> V. V. Davydov, *Problems of Developmental Teaching* (1988)

Examples of culture as disability may be ubiquitous, but descriptions of disabilities from enough perspectives to allow for a contrast of our three approaches to culture in relation to disability are still rare. The following discussion offers only two examples, the learning-disabled child and the illiterate adult, to complement our introductory example from Martha's Vineyard.

Learning Disabilities (LD)

Deprivation. The school is a set of tasks, and people from the LD subculture, because there is something wrong with them, cannot perform the tasks as quickly or as well as others.

Difference. The school is a set of quite arbitrary tasks not necessarily well tied to the demands of everyday life (consider, for example, phonics, words out of context, digit-span memory), and people from the LD subculture are restricted in various institutional circumstances to operating on tasks in ways that reveal their weaknesses. The performance of LD people on other kinds of tasks, or even the apparent same tasks in other circumstances, can reveal their strengths.

Culture as disability. The world is not a set of tasks, at least not of the type learned, or systematically not learned, at school, but made to look that way as part of political arrangements that keep people documenting each other as failures. Over the past forty years, school performance has become integral to established political arrangements, and, by pitting all against all in the race for measured academic achievement on arbitrary tasks, school has become a primary site for the reproduction of inequality in access to various resources. The use of the term *LD* to describe, explain, and remediate children caught in the system of everyone having to do better than everyone else is a good case in point. Even if used sensitively by good people trying to do the right thing for children apparently disabled, the term has a political life that involves millions of people operating on little information about the social consequences of their work.[2]

The Case of Adam, Adam, Adam, and Adam. A group of us (Michael Cole, Lois Hood, Ray McDermott, and Kenneth Traupmann) worked with Adam and his third- and fourth-grade classmates across a range of settings for over a year (Cole and Traupmann 1981; Hood, McDermott, and Cole 1980; McDermott 1993). The settings included an oral test on experimental and psychometric tasks, classroom lessons, more relaxed after-school clubs, and one-on-one trips around New York City. We knew Adam well enough to notice elaborate differences in his behavior across the four settings that seemed to make up a continuum of competence, arbitrariness, and visibility:

Everyday life   After-school clubs   Classroom work groups   One-to-one tests

The continuum is arranged from left to right and can be conceived as an increase of either (1) task difficulty and cognitive competence (from mastery in everyday life events, at one end, to minimal performance on test materials, on the other); (2) the arbitrariness of the task and the resources the child is allowed to use in the task performance (from everyday life, where tasks are well embedded in ongoing relations among persons and environments and one can use whatever means available to get the job done, at one end, to tasks ripped from their usual contexts and isolated specifically to measure what a child can do with them unaided by anything other than his or her mind); or (3) the social visibility, and often measurability, of the task performance (from invisible as a problem of any kind in everyday life settings to painfully and documentably noticeable on tests). How are we to understand the four Adams who show up in the different contexts? Our three approaches to culture, development, and disability offer a framework for articulating Adam's situation.

By the deprivation approach, Adam is part of a group of people who display particular symptoms in the face of reading and other language-specific tasks. These are persons grouped together by having been diagnosed LD. Adam is often described, by both diagnostic tests and school personnel, as having trouble paying attention and remembering words out of context. His symptoms are easily recognized, and his life in school is one of overcoming his disability. Life in school is particularly difficult, because he is often embarrassed by what he cannot do that other children find comparatively automatic.

By the difference stand, Adam can be understood in terms of what he cannot do only if he is also appreciated for what he can do. One way to understand the continuum of scenes along which his behavior varies is that it moves from unusually arbitrary in its demands on the child to completely open to local circumstance. At the test end of the continuum, one must face each question armed with only what is in one's head; if Adam has to remember a string of digits, he cannot ask for help, look up the information, or even take time to write it down. At the other end of the continuum, in everyday life, whatever one needs to do to get a job done is allowable; if Adam has to remember a telephone number, he is unconstrained in how he can proceed. In focusing on what Adam can do, we can see that he is fine in most of his life, and it is only in response to the arbitrary demands of the school culture that he is shown to be disabled. A careful examination of how he proceeds through life indicates he has a culture in need of respect from those better acculturated to the arbitrary demands of school.

By the culture as disability approach, Adam must be seen in terms of the people with whom he interacts and the ways in which they structure their activities together. Such an approach delivers an account not so much of Adam, but of the people most immediately involved in the production of moments for him to be recognized as a learning problem. It turns out that everyone in his class—the teachers, of course, but all the other children as well—are involved at various times in recognizing, identifying, displaying, mitigating, and even hiding what Adam is unable to do if we include his tutors, the school psychologists, the local school of education where he goes for extra help (and his teachers for their degrees), and the social scientists who show up to study him and the government agencies that finance them, the number of people found contributing to Adam being highlighted as LD grows large. If we add on all the children who do well at school because Adam and others like him fail on standardized tests, then most of the country is involved in Adam being LD. We use the term *culture* for the arrangements that allow so many people to be involved in Adam's being LD, for this allows us to emphasize that, whatever problems Adam may have in his head, whether due originally to genetic or early socialization oddities, these would have had a different impact on his relationships with others if the culture he inhabits did not focus so relentlessly on individual success and failure. The culture that promises equality of opportunity while institutionalizing opportunities for less than half of the people is a culture that invites a category LD and its systematic application within the educational system. Adam is a display board for the weaknesses of the system.

The Illiterate

Deprivation. The world is a text, and some people know how to read better than others. The illiterate are missing what they need to get around the world, and, as a culture and an economy, we are being weighed down with unproductive workers who cannot read. That a high percentage of illiterate persons are in minority groups with a wide range of other problems shows what happens to people who cannot read and write in the modern world.

Difference. Literacy is a complex term covering a wide range of activities that differ from one context or culture to another. Its role in different societies, indeed, even in our society, can vary quite remarkably, and it is not at all clear that it has positive or even uniform effects on a people, their ways of thinking, or their modes of production (Scribner and Cole 1981; Street 1984).

Culture as disability. Illiteracy is a recent term in our lives; it was introduced in England about a century ago and has been gathering increasing attention since that time, to the point where now just about any shift in the definition can leave different portions of the population outside its attributive powers—for example, the computer or mathematically illiterate. The circumstances of the application of the term *illiteracy* to persons then and now have been intensely political more than pedagogical or remedial (Donald 1985; Smith 1986; Varenne and McDermott 1986). The fundamental and powerful assumptions of our culture are that: literacy is inherently good for the individual; mass literacy is good for society; literacy is difficult to acquire; literacy should be transmitted to illiterates through classrooms tasks. There is little comparative evidence to support any of these positions. Worse, and this is the crux of the matter, these positions may be least true in societies in which people believe them: the more people believe that literacy is difficult to acquire, the more they find reasons to explain why some read better than others and, correspondingly, why some do better than others in the economic and political ups and downs of the society; the more people believe that literacy is cognitively and culturally transformative, the more they can find reasons to degrade those without such powers; and the more people believe that literacy is best achieved in classrooms, the more they ignore the various other sources of literacy in the culture, and the more they insist on bringing back into school the persons who have already "failed" to develop literacy in school. The truth does not always bear away the spoils. Even against the facts that literacy can help transform a social and information-processing system and can well be taught in classrooms, the very insistence on the truth of the facts can arrange conditions by which neither is possible.

The Case of Exterminating Literacy. With the help of a union local in New York City, a few of us (Shirley Edwards, David Harman, and Ray McDermott) ran a literacy program for the pest exterminators who service the city's housing projects. Half the exterminators were not fully licensed, and they faced lower pay and job insecurity until they could pass a written exam. The exam was written on an eleventh-grade level, and it would have been easy to find the men simply not knowing enough to work through the materials. If we had simply followed the deprivation approach, there was much at hand to guide our way. Standardized tests were in place, and experts could be hired to handle the many levels of reading ability or spoken-English competence to which the curriculum might be addressed. As lower-level city workers, the exterminators could be understood as missing many of the skills they would need to get through the test; coming from a "culturally deprived culture"—yes, we have culture, but they don't—one could only wonder how they could get through the day.

In our organization of the literacy program, we instead took a difference approach, which, by the counterexample of the exterminators' success in the program, gradually grew into a culture as disability stand. We assumed that the exterminators were not culturally deprived as much as they might be different from those with more education and that such differences were made most manifest on standardized tests. There was some evidence we were right, for the men had been working as exterminators for many years; if nothing else, we reasoned, they must know a great deal about exterminating. If we could appreciate what they could do, we might find a way to focus their skills in ways that could show up even on a difficult paper and pencil test. To maximize their participation and to make best use of their pest-control subculture, we hired exterminators who had passed the tests to teach those who had not. Yes, we have a culture, and so do they. The best way for them to operate in our culture, the reasoning goes, is on their own terms.

After weeks in the exterminator classrooms we had more evidence that the men knew much more than anyone might have imagined, and, even better, they were using it to help each other prepare for the exam. How could we have assumed otherwise? How could we have believed that they did not know? What is it about our culture that would have us systematically believing that we knew better than they did; what is it about our culture that would have us in effect disabled when it came to seeing the knowledge base of the exterminators? One answer to this question is in what happened in the classrooms that enabled the exterminators to become book learners. They already knew exterminating, but they had to organize their knowledge by its test relevance. One practice test opened with the question, "Fumigants do not burn the skin. True or false?" Half the men answered true and the other half, false. A quick look around the room indicated they all knew the answer; they all used fumigants in the field, and they had been careful not to have burned their hands off. Knowing that fumigants burn the skin is not the same has knowing the answer to a test question about whether fumigants burn the skin. The teacher understood their problem and addressed it directly: "Let me help you out with this one. Every time you get a question, true or false, if the question is false, the answer, automatic, is false. Why? Because fumigants burn the skin." His intervention is met with a chorus of affirmation. What is being taught here is an approach to the test, not know-ledge about the world. After answering incorrectly a question about the amount of pesticide in a particular application, "five percent to forty-five percent, true or false," a student was told, "You gonna go by the book, give or take five or ten percent. Don't go by your own ideas." On the job, their ideas rarely had to be within five or ten percent. Tests went by a different and, in terms of exterminator practice, a quite arbitrary standard of precision.

In the union classes, the men used "their" culture to run the classrooms, and they had a way of talking to each other that outsiders might not have managed well. They mobilized their community both in the classroom and beyond. Teachers and students who did not find it easy to operate in a classroom were found helping each other on lunchhours and weekends. Perhaps most exciting, the shop steward often reminded them it was not possible to fail at exterminating literacy forever. One could fail a big test, but one could take it over again and again. Every night they were told that the union would stick with them until they passed. By breaking through the constant threat of failure, they were reorganizing their access to school knowledge, and simultaneously they were showing us how much we were the other half of their failure. As they became more visible as knowing people, our own surprise made more visible to us how much we had invested in not seeing them as knowing people, and this even though we had organized the program to honor what they knew. Yes, culture can be disabling, not just to those labeled, but to those doing the labeling.

By the dictates of the culture, in American education, everyone must do better than everyone else. Of course, this is both logically and social-structurally impossible. Failure is a constant possibility in American schools, and, by the dictates of the normal curve, it absorbs about half the students along the way. Failure is always ready to acquire someone. Our exterminators had for the most part been acquired by school failure. We in turn had been acquired by school success in exact proportion to the difficulties of those designated as failures: we above the norms and they below. It is not easy to get the threat of failure out of the classroom. It keeps some mobilized and some hiding in the corner, but either way, it is difficult to avoid. For a moment, the exterminators were not acquired by failure, and they forced us to see how much we had managed to not see their literacy all along. Of course they could read and write, and they could handle whatever literacy chores came their way in the daily round. Everyday literacy acquires its readers, and this includes the bug exterminators of New York City. Test literacy, on the contrary, is designed to acquire failures, that is, to identify and document illiterates, and this can include the very same bug exterminators. For a brief moment, their union had made it possible for the exterminators to confront their tests and to move beyond. The system will have to make the next test harder if it is to maintain the balance established by the previous test. American education will have its failures. American culture will have its disabilities.

Summary and Conclusion

Men make their own history, but they do not make it just as they please; they do not make it under circumstances chosen by themselves, but under circumstances directly encountered, given and transmitted from the past. The tradition of all the dead generations weighs like a nightmare on the brain of the living.

Karl Marx, *The Eighteenth Brunaire of Louis Bonaparte* (1852)

Unless we move expeditiously and imaginatively in the direction of a systematic response to the needs and rights of the handicapped, it i's we, as a nation, as a people, and as individuals, who shall in the eyes of subsequent history be judged as morally handicapped.

John J. McDermott, *Streams of Experience* (1986)

The terms *culture* and *development* have shared a long history in referring to botanical growth, and it has been easy for analysts to write as if culture were simply a controlled environment, as if a petri dish, for the development of children (see Williams 1977, 1984, for both a history of the terms and a critique of their use). By the logic of the botanical approach, the ethnographic study of development would deliver accounts of how life in different cultures would vary the timing and quality of developmental stages, and the distribution of developmental disabilities across cultures would be one point of focus. This essay has instead pointed to the ethnographic study of disabilities as a resource for rethinking the role of the terms *culture* and *development* in our own lives. The point has been that life in any culture is precarious enough that well-defined identifications of what persons should be, and of how they should develop, are irremediable distortions of the complex persons forced to live inside the limits of the identifications. An analysis of the cultural construction of institutional occasions for the creation and display of various disabilities—deafness, learning disabilities, and illiteracy—reveals not broken persons but inadequate identifications neatly tuned to the workings of institutions serving political and economic rather than educational ends (McDermott 1988).

The term *culture* allows us to talk about patterns in the work people do in organizing their lives together. The term *development* allows us to talk about milestones in the acquisition of individuals by cultural patterns. If in their collective life people find it necessary to arrange differential access to material resources, individuals will be acquired differentially into mainstream cultural identifications. It is a mistake to make believe that any such identifications should be taken as developmental standards. Instead, careful work with those locked out of mainstream identifications, by the ingenuity of the ways they resist being constrained, by the ways they resist being made into less than they could be, or less than they are, helps to reveal our part in the pattern of their development. In the ethnographic study of disability, the subject shifts from them to us, from what is wrong with them to what is wrong with the culture we have organized for them, from what is wrong with them to what is right with them that they can tell us so well about the world we share. They know that "the tradition of all the dead generations weighs like a nightmare," and they know that we risk being "judged as morally handicapped" if we cannot allow a proper social life for those who could be left out, dropped out, and locked out of current arrangements.

In organizing a science of development it may be necessary to begin with the recognition that life in any culture gives us much to fall short of and that we are all disabled often, or at least eventually, in precisely the ways organized by those around us following the dictates of a culturally grounded common sense (Murphy 1987). It is a telling practice that, in the community of physically disabled persons, those who can get around the world of curbs, stairs, and other conveniences built without regard for those who cannot use them are called TABs—the Temporarily Able-Bodied (Halpern 1988). There is an unfortunate certainty in this promise. Age, for sure, can bring on the impossibility of going up stairs or opening food packages. But we do not have to change to become disabled, for the world can do that for us. Just as we can focus on how those not yet labeled are only temporarily, and with the cooperation of others, in command of their situation, so we can focus on the potential strengths in any disability. We end with a case in point.

The young Irish poet Christopher Nolan was born unable to move or even to speak, and until his family discovered that he could communicate by typing messages with an apparatus tied to his head and connected to a keyboard, he was locked away from the wonders of sharing language with others. From such a difficult first fourteen years he emerged with a way of looking to what was possible and a way to express it that was not possible before the English language had spent years unspoken and alone inside his head:

> Century upon century saw crass crippled man dashed, branded and treated as dross in a world offended by their appearance, and cracked asunder in their belittlement by having to resemble venial human specimens offering nothing and pondering less in their life of mindless normality. So [he] mulled universal moods as he grimly looked back on the past, but *reasons never curb but rather create new gleeful designs.* (Nolan 1987: 15; emphasis added)

In all cultures, there may be reasons to identify disabilities and reasons to curb what some are asked to do. But there are no good reasons, whatever the cultural particulars, to inhibit the creation of "new gleeful designs," no good reasons for anyone to be less than they could be, anything less than they are.

Acknowledgment

Eric Bredo, Robbie Case, Paula Fleisher, Laura Kerr, D. C. Phillips, Joseph Reimer, and George Spindler offered helpful corrections on versions of this chapter. Mark Breimhorst offered a particularly powerful critique that will take us years to digest.

Notes

1. To this end, we rely on: Bakhtin 1981, Becker 1971, Garfinkel 1967, Goffman 1963, Pollner 1978, Scheflen 1973, Selby 1976, Wieder 1974, and Williams 1977; and from the study of development and learning: Bateson 1972; Church 1961; Cole 1992; Erickson and Shultz 1982; Frankel, Leary, and Kilman 1987; Goodwin 1990; Lave 1988; Lewin 1951; Mehan 1986; and Vygotsky 1986. Although a diverse group, they all share a point of entry with George Herbert Mead: "In the process of communication, the individual is an other before he is a self. It is in addressing himself in the role of another that his self arises in experience" (1932: 168). One cannot be disabled alone; it takes a culture to make the most of our potential for suffering (see Henry 1963 and Spindler 1974 for accounts of schooling as disability; see Cipolla 1979 and Shiller 1992 for epidemics).
2. See Coles 1987 for a social history of the category of learning disability and its demographics; see the work of Mehan (1986, 1993; and Mehan, Meihls, and Hertweck 1986) for a nicely detailed and theoretically sophisticated account of how children are labeled.

References

Bakhtin, M. 1981. *The Dialogic Imagination*. Austin: University of Texas Press.

Bateson, G. 1972. *Steps to an Ecology of Mind*. New York: Ballantine.

Becker, H. S. 1971. *Outsiders*. 2d ed. New York: Free Press.

Beckett, S. 1955. *Molloy, Malone Dies, The Unnamable*. New York: Grove Press.

Church, J. 1961. *Language and the Discovery of Reality*. New York: Random House.

Cipolla, C. M. 1979. *Faith, Reason, and the Plague: A Tuscon Story of the Seventeenth Century*. Sussex: The Harvester Press.

Cole, M. 1992. "Culture in Development." In *Developmental Psychology: An Advanced Textbook*. Ed. M. Bornstein and M. Lamb, 731–89. Hillsdale, N.J.: Erlbaum.

Cole, M., L. Hood, and R. P. McDermott. 1978. "Ecological Niche Picking: Ecological Invalidity as an Axiom of Experimental Cognitive Psychology." Working Paper no. 14, Laboratory of Comparative Human Cognition, Rockefeller University.

Cole, M., and K. Traupmann. 1981. "Comparative Cognitive Research: Learning from a Learning Disabled Child." In

Aspects of the Development of Competence. Ed. W. A. Collins, 125–54. Minnesota Symposium on Child Psychology, vol. 14. Hillsdale: Erlbaum.

Coles, G. 1987. *The Learning Mystique*. New York: Pantheon.

Davydov, V. V. 1988. "Problems of Developmental Teaching." *Soviet Education* 30: 6–97.

Donald, J. 1985. "How Illiteracy Became a Problem." *Journal of Education* 165: 35–51.

Drummond, L. 1980. "The Cultural Continuum." *Man* 15: 352–74.

Edgerton, R. 1970. "Mental Retardation in Non-Western Societies." In *Sociocultural Aspects of Mental Retardation*. Ed. H. C. Haywood, 523–59. New York: Appleton-Century-Crofts.

Erickson, F., and J. Shultz. 1982. *The Counselor as Gatekeeper*. New York: Academic Press.

Foucault, M. 1991. *Remarks on Marx: Conversations with Duccio Trambadori*. New York: Semiotext(e).

Frake, C. O. 1964. "Notes on Queries in Ethnography." *American Anthropologist* 66: 132–45.

Frankel, R., M. Leary, and B. Kilman. 1987. "Building Social Skills through Pragmatic Analysis." In *Handbook of Autism and Pervasive Developmental Disorders*. Ed. D. Cohen and A. Donnellan, 333–59. New York: Wiley.

Garfinkel, H. 1967. *Studies in Ethnomethodology*. Englewood Cliffs, N.J.: Prentice-Hall.

Goffman, E. 1963. *Stigma*. Englewood Cliffs, N.J.: Prentice-Hall.

Goodwin, C., and A. Duranti. 1992. *Rethinking Context*. New York: Cambridge University Press.

Goodwin, M. 1990. *He-Said-She-Said*. Bloomington: Indiana University Press.

Gregory, R. L., and J. Wallace. 1963. *Recovery from Early Blindness: A Case Study*. Monographs of the *Quarterly Journal of Experimental Psychology*, supp. 2.

Groce, N. 1985. *Everyone Here Spoke Sign Language*. Cambridge, Mass.: Harvard University Press.

Halpern, S. M. 1988. "Portrait of the Artist." *New York Times Book Review*. 30 June, 3–5.

Henry, J. 1963. *Culture Against Man*. New York: Vintage.

Hood, L., R. P. McDermott, and M. Cole. 1980. " 'Let's try to make it a good day'—Some Not So Simple Ways." *Discourse Processes* 3:155–68.

Kakumasu, J. 1968. "Urubu Sign Language." *International Journal of American Linguistics* 34: 275–81.

Kendon, A. 1990. *Conducting Interaction*. New York: Cambridge University Press.

Lave, J. 1988. *Cognition in Practice*. New York: Cambridge University Press.

Lewin, K. 1951 [1935]. *Dynamic Theory of Personality*. New York: McGraw-Hill.

Mannoni, M. 1972. *The Backward Child and His Mother*. New York: Basic Books.

Marx, K. 1963 [1852]. *The Eighteenth Brumaire of Louis Bonaparte*. New York: International Publishers.

McDermott, J. J. 1986. *Streams of Experience: Reflections on the History and Philosophy of American Culture*. Amherst: University of Massachusetts Press.

McDermott, R. P. 1988. "Inarticulateness." In *Linguistics in Context*. Ed. D. Tannen, 37–68. Norwood, N.J.: Ablex.

——— . 1993. "The Acquisition of a Child by a Learning Disability." In *Understanding Practice*. Ed. S. Chaiklin and J. Lave, 269–305. New York: Cambridge University Press.

Mead, G. H. 1932. *The Philosophy of the Present*. Chicago: University of Chicago Press.

Mehan, H. 1986. "The Role of Language and the Language of Role in Institutional Decision Making." In *Discourse and Institutional Authority*. Ed. S. Fisher and A. Todd, 140–63. Norwood, N.J.: Ablex.

——— . 1993. "Beneath the Skin and Between the Ears." In *Understanding Practice*. Ed. S. Chaiklin and J. Lave, 241–69. New York: Cambridge University Press.

Mehan, H., L. Meihls, and A. Hertweck. 1986. *Handicapping the Handicapped*. Stanford: Stanford University Press.

Murphy, R. F. 1987. *Body Silent*. New York: Holt.

Nolan, C. 1987. *Under the Eye of a Clock*. New York: Doubleday.

Padden, C., and T. Humphries. 1988. *Deaf in America: Voices from a Culture*. Cambridge, Mass.: Harvard University Press.

Plath, D. 1980. *Long Engagements*. Stanford: Stanford University Press.

Pollner, M. 1978. "Constitutive and Mundane Versions of Labeling Theory." *Human Studies* 1: 269–88.

Rosa-Lugo, L. 1989. "Arrangements for the Display of Deafness." Ph.D. diss., Columbia University.

Sarason, S., and J. Doris. 1979. *Educational Handicap, Public Policy, and Social Change*. New York: Free Press.

Scheflen, A. E. 1973. *Communicational Structure*. Bloomington: Indiana University Press.

Selby, H. 1976. *Zapotec Deviance*. Austin: University of Texas Press.

Scribner, S., and M. Cole. 1981. *Psychology of Literacy*. Cambridge, Mass.: Harvard University Press.

Shiller, N. 1992. "What's Wrong with This Picture? The Hegemonic Construction of Culture in AIDS Research in the United States." *Medical Anthropology Quarterly* 6: 237–54.

Shklar, J. 1979. "Let's Not Be Hypocritical." *Daedalus* 108: 1–25.

——— . 1990. *The Faces of Injustice*. New Haven, Conn.: Yale University Press.

Street, B. 1984. *Literacy in Theory and Practice*. New York: Cambridge University Press.

Smith, D. 1986. "The Anthropology of Literacy Acquisition." In *The Acquisition of Literacy: Ethnographic Perspectives*. Ed. B. Schieffelin and P. Gilmore, 261–75. Norwood: Ablex.

Spindler, G. D. 1974. "Beth Anne." In *Education and Cultural Process*. Ed. Spindler, 139–53. New York: Holt, Rinehart, and Winston.

Thomas, G., J. Meyer, F. Ramirez, and J. Boli. 1988. *Institutional Structure: Constituting State, Society, and the Individual.* Beverly Hills, Calif.: Sage.

Varenne, H., and R. P. McDermott. 1986. " 'Why' Sheila Can Read." In *The Acquisition of Literacy.* Ed. B. Schieffelin and P. Gilmore, 188–210. Norwood: Ablex.

Vygotsky, L. 1978. *Mind in Society.* Cambridge, Mass.: Harvard University Press.

——— . 1986 [1934]. *Thought and Language.* Cambridge, Mass.: MIT Press.

Wieder, D. L. 1974. *Language and Social Reality.* The Hague: Mouton.

Williams, R. 1977. *Marxism and Literature.* New York: Academic Press.

Williams, R. 1984. *Keywords: A Vocabulary of Culture and Society.* 2d ed. New York: Oxford University Press.

Wittgenstein, L. 1980. *Culture and Value.* Chicago: University of Chicago Press.

13

Grounded Theory
Objectivist and Constructivist Methods
Kathy Charmaz

[. . .]

The Development of Grounded Theory

In their pioneering book, *The Discovery of Grounded Theory* (1967), Barney G. Glaser and Anselm L. Strauss first articulated their research strategies for their collaborative studies of dying (Glaser & Strauss, 1965, 1968). They challenged the hegemony of the quantitative research paradigm in the social sciences. Chicago school sociology (see, e.g., Park & Burgess, 1925; Shaw, 1930; Thomas & Znaniecki, 1918–1920; Thrasher, 1927/1963; Zorbaugh, 1929) had long contributed a rich ethnographic tradition to the discipline. However, the ascendancy of quantitative methods undermined and marginalized that tradition. Scientistic assumptions of objectivity and truth furthered the quest for verification through precise, standardized instruments and parsimonious quantifiable variables. Field research waned. It became viewed as a preliminary exercise through which researchers could refine quantitative instruments before the real work began, rather than as a viable endeavor in its own right. The ascendancy of quantification also led to a growing division between theory and empirical research. Theorists and researchers lived in different worlds and pursued different problems. Presumably, quantitative research tested existing theory as prescribed by the logico-deductive model. However, much of this research remained atheoretical and emphasized controlling variables rather than theory testing.

Glaser and Strauss's (1967) work was revolutionary because it challenged (a) arbitrary divisions between theory and research, (b) views of qualitative research as primarily a precursor to more "rigorous" quantitative methods, (c) claims that the quest for rigor made qualitative research illegitimate, (d) beliefs that qualitative methods are impressionistic and unsystematic, (e) separation of data collection and analysis, and (f) assumptions that qualitative research could produce only descriptive case studies rather than theory development (Charmaz, 1995b). With the publication of *Discovery*, Glaser and Strauss called for qualitative research to move toward theory development.[1] They provided a persuasive intellectual rationale for conducting qualitative research that permitted and encouraged novices to pursue it. And they gave guidelines for its successful completion.

Prior to the publication of *Discovery*, most qualitative analysis had been taught through an oral tradition of mentoring, when taught at all. Glaser and Strauss led the way in providing written guidelines for systematic qualitative data analysis with explicit analytic procedures and research strategies. Glaser applied his rigorous positivistic methodological training in quantitative research from Columbia University to the development of qualitative analysis. Grounded theory methods were founded upon Glaser's epistemological assumptions, methodological terms, inductive logic, and systematic approach. Strauss's training at the University of Chicago with Herbert Blumer and Robert Park brought Chicago school field research and symbolic interactionism to grounded theory. Hence, Strauss brought the pragmatist philosophical study of process, action, and meaning into *empirical* inquiry through grounded theory.

Glaser's 1978 book *Theoretical Sensitivity* substantially advanced explication of grounded theory methods. However, the abstract terms and dense writing Glaser employed rendered the book inaccessible to many readers. Strauss's *Qualitative Analysis for Social Scientists* (1987) made grounded theory more accessible, although perhaps more theoretically diffuse than the earlier methods texts would suggest.

Reformulation and Repudiation

Grounded theory gained a wider audience, a new spokesperson, and more disciples with the appearance of Strauss's 1990 coauthored book with Juliet Corbin, *Basics of Qualitative Research: Grounded Theory Procedures and Techniques.*[2] This book aims to specify and to develop grounded theory methodology. It takes the reader through several familiar analytic steps, illustrates procedures with examples, and stirs a new technical armamentarium into the mix. *Basics* gained readers but lost the sense of emergence and open-ended character of Strauss's earlier volume and much of his empirical work. The improved and more accessible second edition of *Basics* (Strauss & Corbin, 1998) reads as less prescriptive and aims to lead readers to a new way of thinking about their research and about the world. In both editions, the authors pose concerns (1990, p. 7; 1998, p. x) about valid and reliable data and interpretations and researcher bias consistent with "normal science" (Kuhn, 1970). Strauss and Corbin impart a behaviorist, rather than interpretive, cast to their analysis of key hypothetical examples (see 1990, pp. 63–65, 78–81, 88–90, 145–147).[3] Perhaps the scientific underpinnings of the 1990 book reflect both Corbin's earlier training and Strauss's growing insistence that grounded theory is verificational (A. L. Strauss, personal communication, February 1, 1993).[4] Whether *Basics* advances grounded theory methods or proposes different technical procedures depends on one's point of view.

Glaser (1978, 1992) emphasizes emergence of data and theory through the analysis of "basic social processes." Glaser's position (see also Melia, 1996) becomes clear in his 1992 repudiation of Strauss and Corbin (1990). He advocates gathering data without forcing either preconceived questions or frameworks upon it. In *Basics of Grounded Theory Analysis: Emergence vs. Forcing* (1992), Glaser answers Strauss and Corbin's work in *Basics*. Over and over, he finds Strauss and Corbin to be forcing data and analysis through their preconceptions, analytic questions, hypotheses, and methodological techniques (see, e.g., Glaser, 1992, pp. 33, 43, 46–47, 50–51, 58–59, 63, 78, 96–100). For Glaser, the use of systematic comparisons is enough. "Categories emerge upon comparison and properties emerge upon more comparison. And that is all there is to it" (Glaser, 1992, p. 43).

In addition to Glaser's trenchant critique, readers may find themselves caught in a maze of techniques that Strauss and Corbin propose as significant methodological advancements. Linda Robrecht (1995) asserts that the new procedures divert the researcher from the data and result in poorly integrated theoretical frameworks. Glaser declares that Strauss and Corbin invoke contrived comparisons rather than those that have emerged from analytic processes of comparing data to data, concept to concept, and category to category. He views their approach as "full conceptual description," not grounded theory. Glaser argues that the purpose of grounded theory methods is to generate theory, not to verify it. His point is consistent with quantitative research canons in which verification depends upon random sampling and standardized procedures. Strauss and Corbin do not answer Glaser directly, but, as Kath Melia (1996) notes, they do state their view of the essentials of grounded theory in their contribution to the first edition of this *Handbook*, while suggesting that the method will continue to evolve (Strauss & Corbin, 1994). Similarly, Strauss and Corbin do not respond to Glaser's charge that they abandoned grounded theory in favor of full conceptual description in their second edition of *Basics* (1998). However, they do offer an elegant statement of the significance of description and conceptual ordering for theory development (pp. 16–21).

Both Strauss and Corbin's *Basics* and Glaser's critique of it assert views of science untouched by either epistemological debates of the 1960s (Adler, Adler, & Johnson, 1992; Kleinman, 1993; Kuhn, 1970; Lofland, 1993; Snow & Morrill, 1993) or postmodern critiques (Clough, 1992; Denzin, 1991, 1992a, 1996; Marcus & Fischer, 1986). Both endorse a realist ontology and positivist epistemology, albeit with some sharp differences. Glaser remains in the positivist camp; Strauss and Corbin less so. They move between objectivist and constructivist assumptions in various works, although *Basics*, for which they are best known, stands in the objectivist terrain. For example, in their efforts to maintain objectivity, they advocate taking "appropriate measures" to minimize the intrusion of the subjectivity of the researcher into the research (Strauss & Corbin, 1998, p. 43). Both Glaser and Strauss and Corbin assume an external reality that researchers can discover and record— Glaser through discovering data, coding it, and using comparative methods step by step; Strauss and Corbin through their analytic questions, hypotheses, and methodological applications. In their earlier writings, Glaser and Strauss (1967) imply that reality is independent of the observer and the methods used to produce it. Because both Glaser and Strauss and Corbin follow the canons of objective reportage, both engage in silent authorship and usually write about their data as distanced experts (Charmaz & Mitchell, 1996), thereby contributing to an objectivist stance.[5] Furthermore, the didactic, prescriptive approaches described in early statements about grounded theory coated these methods with a positivist, objectivist cast (see Charmaz, 1983; Glaser, 1992; Stern, 1994b; Strauss, 1987; Strauss & Corbin, 1990, 1994).

So who's got the real grounded theory? Glaser (1998) contends that he has the pure version of grounded theory. That's correct—if one agrees that early formulations should set the standard.[6] Different proponents assume that grounded theory essentials *ought* to include different things. Their "oughts" shape their notions of the real grounded theory. Must grounded theory be objectivist and positivist? No. Grounded theory offers a set of flexible strategies, not rigid prescriptions. Should grounded theorists adopt symbolic interactionism? Not always. Emphases on action and process and, from my constructivist view, meaning and emergence within symbolic interactionism complement grounded theory. Symbolic interactionism also offers a rich array of sensitizing concepts. However, grounded theory strategies can be used with sensitizing concepts from other perspectives. Pragmatism? Yes, because applicability and usefulness are part of the criteria for evaluating grounded theory analyses. Should we expect grounded theorists to remain committed to their written statements? Not completely. Published works become separated from the contexts of their creation. Neither their authors' original purpose nor intended audience may be apparent. Authors may write mechanistic prescriptions for beginners to get them started but compose more measured pieces for peers. New developments may influence them. But readers may reify these authors' earlier written words. Strauss and Corbin's (1994) chapter in the first edition of this *Handbook* has a considerably more flexible tone than is found in the first edition of *Basics* (1990), both in describing methods and in positioning grounded theory. For example, they note that future researchers may use grounded theory in conjunction with other approaches, which I argue here. A simplified, constructivist version of grounded theory such as outlined below can supply effective tools that can be adopted by researchers from diverse perspectives.[7]

Grounded Theory Strategies

Regarding Data

Grounded theory methods specify analytic strategies, not data collection methods. These methods have become associated with limited interview studies, as if limiting grounded theory methods *to* interviews and limiting the number *of* interviews are both acceptable practices (see, e.g., Creswell, 1997). Researchers can use grounded theory techniques with varied forms of data collection (for historical analyses, see Clarke, 1998; Star, 1989). Qualitative researchers should gather extensive amounts of rich data with thick description (Charmaz, 1995b; Geertz, 1973). Grounded theorists have been accused, with some justification, of slighting data collection (Lofland & Lofland, 1984). Nonetheless, a number of grounded theorists have gathered thorough data, even those who have relied primarily on interviews (see, e.g., Baszanger, 1998; Biernacki, 1986; Charmaz, 1991, 1995a). Perhaps because grounded theory methods focus on the development of early analytic schemes, data gathering remains problematic and disputed.

Glaser (1992) raises sharp differences with Strauss and Corbin (1990) about forcing data through preconceived questions, categories, and hypotheses. Perhaps both are right, although in different ways. Glaser's comparative approach and emphasis on process provide excellent strategies for making data analysis efficient, productive, and exciting—without formulaic techniques. Every qualitative researcher should take heed of his warnings about forcing data into preconceived categories through the imposition of artificial questions. However, data collecting may demand that researchers ask questions and follow hunches, if not in direct conversation with respondents, then in the observers' notes about what to look for. Researchers construct rich data by amassing pertinent details. Strauss and Corbin's many questions and techniques may help novices improve their data gathering. Glaser (1998) assumes that data become transparent, that we researchers will see the basic social process in the field through our respondents' telling us what is significant. However, what researchers see may be neither basic nor certain (Mitchell & Charmaz, 1996). What respondents assume or do not apprehend may be much more important than what they talk about. An acontextual reliance on respondents' overt concerns can lead to narrow research problems, limited data, and trivial analyses.

Most grounded theorists write as if their data have an objective status. Strauss and Corbin (1998) write of "the reality of the data" and tell us, "The data do not lie" (p. 85).

Data are narrative constructions (Maines, 1993). They are reconstructions of experience; they are not the original experience itself (see also Bond, 1990). Whether our respondents ply us with data in interview accounts they recast for our consumption or we record ethnographic stories to reflect experience as best we can recall and narrate, data remain reconstructions.

As we gather rich data, we draw from multiple sources—observations, conversations, formal interviews, autobiographies, public records, organizational reports, respondents' diaries and journals, and our own tape-recorded reflections. Grounded theory analyses of such materials begin with our coding, take form with memos, and are fashioned into conference papers and articles. Yet our statement of the ideas seldom ends with publication. Rather, we revisit our ideas and, perhaps, our data and re-create them in new form in an evolving process (Connelly & Clandinin, 1990).[8]

Coding Data

How do we do grounded theory? Analysis begins early. We grounded theorists code our emerging data as we collect it. Through coding, we start to define and categorize our data. In grounded theory coding, we create codes as we study our data. We do not, or should not, paste catchy concepts on our data. We should interact with our data and pose questions to them while coding them. Coding helps us to gain a new perspective on our material and to focus further data collection, and may lead us in unforeseen directions. Unlike quantitative research that requires data to fit into *preconceived* standardized codes, the researcher's interpretations of data shape his or her emergent codes in grounded theory.

Coding starts the chain of theory development. Codes that account for our data take form together as nascent theory that, in turn, explains these data and directs further data gathering. Initial or open coding proceeds through our examining each line of data and then defining actions or events within it—line-by-line coding (see especially Glaser, 1978). This coding keeps us studying our data. In addition to starting to build ideas inductively, we are deterred by line-by-line coding from imposing extant theories or our own beliefs on the data. This form of coding helps us to remain attuned to our subjects' views of their realities, rather than assume that we share the same views and worlds. Line-by-line coding sharpens our use of sensitizing concepts—that is, those background ideas that inform the overall research problem. Sensitizing concepts offer ways of seeing, organizing, and understanding experience; they are embedded in our disciplinary emphases and perspectival proclivities. Although sensitizing concepts way deepen perception, they provide starting points for building analysis, not ending points for evading it. We may use sensitizing concepts *only* as points of departure from which to study the data.

Line-by-line coding likely leads to our refining and specifying any borrowed extant concepts. Much of my work on the experience of illness has been informed by concepts of self and identity. The woman whose statement is quoted in Table 13.1 talked of having loved her job as an advocate for nursing-home residents. Through coding her statement line by line, I created the code "identity trade-offs" and later developed it into a category. Line-by-line coding keeps us thinking about what meanings we make of our data, asking ourselves questions of it, and pin-pointing gaps and leads in it to focus on during

Table 13.1   Example of Line-by-Line Coding of an Interview Statement

Line-by-Line Coding	*Interview Statement*[a]
Deciding to relinquish	And so I decided, this [pain, fatigue, and stress accruing during
Accounting for costs	her workday] isn't a way to live. I don't have to work. . . . So it was
Weighing the balance	with great regret, and not something I planned, I turned in my
Relinquishing identity	resignation. It was the best thing I ever did.
Making identity trade-offs	

a. From Charmaz (1995b, p. 671).

subsequent data collection. Note that I kept the codes active. These action codes give us insight into what people are doing, what is happening in the setting.

Generating action codes facilitates making comparisons, a major technique in grounded theory. The constant comparative method of grounded theory means (a) comparing different people (such as their views, situations, actions, accounts, and experiences), (b) comparing data from the same individuals with themselves at different points in time, (c) comparing incident with incident, (d) comparing data with category, and (e) comparing a category with other categories (Charmaz, 1983, 1995b; Glaser, 1978, 1992).

Glaser (1978, 1992) stresses constant comparative methods. Strauss (1987) called for comparisons in his research and teaching—often hypothetical comparisons or, when he was teaching, comparisons from students' lives—at every level of analysis (see also Star, 1997).[9] Strauss and Corbin (1990) introduce new procedures: dimensionalizing, axial coding, and the conditional matrix. These procedures are intended to make researchers' emerging theories denser, more complex, and more precise. Dimensionalizing and axial coding can be done during initial coding; creating a conditional matrix comes later. Schatzman (1991) had earlier developed the concept of dimensionality to recognize and account for complexity beyond one meaning of a property or phenomenon. Strauss and Corbin (1990) build on his notion by urging researchers to divide properties into dimensions that lie along a continuum. In turn, we can develop a "dimensional profile" of the properties of a category. Strauss and Corbin further propose techniques for reassembling data in new ways through what they call "axial coding." This type of coding is aimed at making connections between a category and its subcategories. These include conditions that give rise to the category, its context, the social interactions through which it is handled, and its consequences.

Selective or focused coding uses initial codes that reappear frequently to sort large amounts of data. Thus this coding is more directed and, typically, more conceptual than line-by-line coding (Charmaz, 1983, 1995b; Glaser, 1978). These codes account for the most data and categorize them most precisely. Making explicit decisions about selecting codes gives us a check on the fit between the emerging theoretical framework and the empirical reality it explains. Of the initial codes shown in Table 13.1, "identity trade-offs" was the only one I treated analytically in the published article. When comparing respondents' interviews, I found similar statements and concerns about identity.

Our categories for synthesizing and explaining data arise from our focused codes. In turn, our categories shape our developing analytic frameworks. Categories often subsume several codes. For example, my category of "significant events" included positive events and relieved negative events (Charmaz, 1991). Categories turn description into conceptual analysis by specifying properties analytically, as in the following example:

> A significant event stands out in memory because it has boundaries, intensity, and emotional force.... The emotional reverberations of a single event echo through the present and future and therefore, however subtly, shade thoughts.

In their discussion of selective coding, Strauss and Corbin (1990) introduce the "conditional matrix," an analytic diagram that maps the range of conditions and consequences related to the phenomenon or category. They describe this matrix as a series of circles in which the outer rings represent those conditions most distant from actions and interactions and the inner rings represent those closest to actions and interactions. Strauss and Corbin propose that researchers create matrices to sensitize themselves to the range of conditions conceivably affecting the phenomena of interest and to the range of hypothetical consequences. Such matrices can sharpen researchers' explanations of and predictions about the studied phenomena.

Memo Writing

Memo writing is the intermediate step between coding and the first draft of the completed analysis. This step helps to spark our thinking and encourages us to look at our data and codes in new ways. It can help us to define leads for collecting data—both for further initial coding and later theoretical sampling. Through memo writing, we elaborate processes, assumptions, and actions that are subsumed under our codes. Memo writing leads us to explore our codes; we expand upon the processes they identify or suggest. Thus our codes take on substance as well as a structure for sorting data.

Action codes (e.g., as illustrated above) spur the writing of useful memos because they help us to see interrelated processes rather than static isolated topics. As we detail the properties of our action codes in memos, we connect categories and define how they fit into larger processes. By discussing these connections and defining processes in memos early in our research, we reduce the likelihood that we will get lost in mountains of data—memo writing keeps us focused on our analyses and involved in our research.

Memo writing aids us in linking analytic interpretation with empirical reality. We bring raw data right into our memos so that we maintain those connections and examine them directly. Raw data from different sources provide the grist for making precise comparisons, fleshing out ideas, analyzing properties of categories, and seeing patterns. The first excerpt below is the first section of an early memo. I wrote this memo quickly in 1983 after comparing data from a series of recent interviews.[10]

Developing a Dual Self

The dual self in this case is the *contrast* between the *sick self* and the *monitoring self* (actually *physical* self might be a better term [than *sick self*] since some of these people try to see themselves as "well" but still feel they must constantly monitor in order to maintain that status—they also rather easily sink into self-blame when the monitoring doesn't work).

With Sara S. we see definite conversations held between the physical and monitoring self. Through her learning time or body education, self-taught and self-validated she has not only developed a sense of what her body "*needs*" she has developed a finely honed *sense of timing* about how to handle those needs.

With the dual self, the monitoring self *externalizes* the internal messages from the physical self and makes them concrete. It is as if dialogue and negotiation with ultimate validation of the physical self take place between the two dimensions of the dual self. Consequently, the competent monitoring self must be able to attend to the messages given by the physical self. The learning time is the necessary amount of concentration, trial and error to become an effective monitoring self.

Mark R., for example, illustrates the kind of dialogue that takes place between the monitoring and physical selves when he talks about person to kidney talks and what is needed to sustain that new transplanted kidney in his body.

The dual self in many ways is analogous to the dialogue that Mead describes between the I and the me. The me monitors and attends to the I which is creating, experiencing, feeling. The monitoring me defines those feelings, impulses and sensations. It evaluates them and develops a line of action so that what is defined as needed is taken care of. The physical self here is then taken as an object held up to view which can be compared with past physical (or for that matter, psychological selves), with perceived statuses of others, with a defined level of health or well-being, with signals of potential crises etc.

A consequence of the monitoring self is that it may be encouraged by practitioners (after all, taking responsibility for one's body is the message these days, isn't it?) when it seems to "work," yet it may be condemned when the person's tactics for monitoring conflict with practitioners' notions of reasonable action or are unsuccessful.

The following passage shows how the memo appeared in the published version of the research (Charmaz, 1991). The combination of analytic clarity and empirical grounding makes the memo above remarkably congruent with the published excerpt. Memos record researchers' stages of analytic development. Memo writing helps researchers (a) to grapple with ideas about the data, (b) to set an analytic course, (c) to refine categories, (d) to define the relationships among various categories, and (e) to gain a sense of confidence and competence in their ability to analyze data.

Developing a Dialectical Self

The dialectical self is the contrast between the sick or physical self and the monitoring self. Keeping illness contained by impeding progression of illness, rather than merely hiding it, leads to developing a monitoring self. Developing a dialectical self means gaining a heightened awareness of one's body. People who do so believe that they perceive nuances of physical changes. By his second transplant, for example, Mark Reinertsen felt that he had learned to perceive the first signs of organ rejection.

When people no longer view themselves as "sick," they still monitor their physical selves to save themselves from further illness. To illustrate, Sara Shaw explained that she spent months of "learning time" to be able to discover what her body "needed" and how to handle those needs. She commented, "I got to know it [her ill body]; I got to understand it, and it was just me and mixed connective tissue disease [her diagnosis changed], you know, and I got to respect it and I got to know—to have a real good feeling for time elements and for what my body was doing, how my body was feeling." When I asked her what she meant by "time elements," she replied:

> There's times during the month, during the course of a month, when I'm much more suscep-
> tible, and I can feel it. I can wake up in the morning and I can feel it. . . . So I really learned
> what I was capable of and when I had to stop, when I had to slow down. And I learned to
> like—give and take with that. And I think that's all programmed in my mind now, and I don't
> even have to think about it now, you know; I'll know. I'll know when, no matter what's going
> on, I've gotta go sit down . . . and take it easy, . . . that's a requirement of that day. And so
> consequently, I really don't get sick.

In the dialectical self, the monitoring self externalizes the internal messages from the physical self and makes them concrete. It is as if dialogue and negotiation with ultimate validation of the physical self take place. For example, Mark Reinertsen engaged in "person to kidney" talks to encourage the new kidney to remain with him (see also McGuire & Kantor, 1987). A competent monitoring self attends to messages from the physical self and over time, as Sara Shaw's comment suggests, monitoring becomes taken for granted.

In many ways, the dialectical self is analogous to the dialogue that Mead (1934) describes between the "I" and the "me." The "me" monitors and attends to the "I" that creates, experiences, and feels. The monitoring "me" defines the "I's" behaviors, feel-ings, impulses, and sensations. It evaluates them and plans action to meet defined needs. Here, an ill person takes his or her physical self as an object, appraises it and compares it with past physical selves, with perceived health statuses of others, with ideals of physical or mental well-being, with signals of potential crises and so forth (cf. Gadow, 1982).

The dialectical self is one of ill people's multiple selves emerging in the face of uncertainty. Whether or not ill people give the dialectical self validity significantly affects their actions. For someone like Sara Shaw, the dialectical self provided guidelines for organizing time, for taking jobs, and for developing relationships with others. With jobs, she believed that she had to guard herself from the stress of too many demands. With friends, she felt she had to place her needs first. With physicians, she resisted their control since she trusted her knowledge about her condition more than theirs.

Practitioners may encourage a monitoring self when it seems to "work," yet condemn it when unsuccessful, or when monitoring tactics conflict with their advice (cf. Kleinman, 1988). The development of the dialectical self illuminates the active stance that some people take toward their illnesses and their lives. In short, the dialectical self helps people to keep illness in the background of their lives (Charmaz, 1991, pp. 70–72).

Note the change in the title of the category in the published version. This change reflects my attempt to choose terms that best portrayed the empirical descriptions that the category subsumed. I was trying to address the liminal relationship certain respondents described with their bodies in which they gained a heightened awareness of cues that other people disavow disregard, or do not discern. The term *dialectical self* denotes a more dynamic process that does the term *dual self*.

Although many grounded theorists concentrate on overt actions and statements, I also look for subjects' unstated assumptions and implied meanings.[11] Then I ask myself how these assumptions and meanings relate to conditions in which a category emerges. For example, some people with chronic illnesses assumed that their bodies had become alien and hostile battlegrounds where they warred with illness. Their assumptions about having alien bodies and being at war with illness affected if and how they adapted to their situations. When I developed the category "surrendering to the sick body," I asked what conditions fostered surrendering (Charmaz, 1995a). I identified three: (a) "relinquishing the quest for control over one's body," (b) "giving up notions of victory over illness," and (c) "affirming, however Implicitly, that one's self is tied to the sick body" (p. 672).

Theoretical Sampling

As we grounded theorists refine our categories and develop them as theoretical constructs, we likely find gaps in our data and holes in our theories. Then we go back to the field and collect delimited data to fill those conceptual gaps and holes—we conduct theoretical sampling. At this point, we choose to sample specific issues only; we look for precise information to shed light on the emerging theory.

Theoretical sampling represents a defining property of grounded theory and relies on the comparative methods within grounded theory. We use theoretical sampling to develop our emerging categories and to make them more definitive and useful. Thus the aim of this sampling is to refine *ideas*, not to increase the size of the original sample. Theoretical sampling helps us to identify conceptual boundaries and pinpoint the fit and relevance of our categories.

Although we often sample people, we may sample scenes, events, or documents, depending on the study and where the theory leads us. We may return to the same settings or individuals to gain further information. I filled out my initial analysis of one category, "living one day at a time," by going back to respondents with whom I had conducted earlier interviews. I had already found that people with chronic illnesses took living one day at time as a strategy to maintain some control over their uncertain lives. Only by going back to selected respondents did I learn that this strategy also had consequences for how they viewed the future when they later allowed themselves to think of it. The passage of time and the events that had filled it allowed them to give up earlier cherished plans and anticipated futures without being devastated by loss.

Theoretical sampling is a pivotal part of the development of formal theory. Here, the level of abstraction of the emerging theory has explanatory power across substantive areas because the processes and concepts within it are abstract and generic (Prus, 1987). Thus we would seek comparative data in substantive areas through theoretical sampling to help us tease our less visible properties of our concepts and the conditions and limits of their applicability. For example, I address identity loss in several analyses of the experience of illness. I could refine my concepts by looking at identity loss in other situations, such as bereavement and involuntary unemployment. Comparative analysis of people who experience unanticipated identity gains, such as unexpected job promotions, could also net conceptual refinements.

The necessity of engaging in theoretical sampling means that we researchers cannot produce a solid grounded theory through one-shot interviewing in a single data collection phase. Instead, theoretical sampling demands that we have completed the work of comparing data with data and have developed a provisional set of relevant categories for explaining our data. In turn, our categories take us back to the field to gain more insight about when, how, and to what extent they are pertinent and useful.

Theoretical sampling helps us to define the properties of our categories; to identify the contexts in which they are relevant; to specify the conditions under which they arise, are maintained, and vary; and to discover their consequences. Our emphasis on studying process combined with theoretical sampling to delineate the limits of our categories also helps us to define gaps between categories. Through using comparative methods, we specify the conditions under which they are linked to other categories. After we decide which categories best explain what is happening in our study, we treat them as concepts. In this sense, these concepts are useful for helping us to understand many incidents or issues in the data (Strauss & Corbin, 1990). Strauss (personal communication, February 1, 1993) advocates theoretical sampling early in the research. I recommend conducting it later in order that relevant data and analytic directions emerge without being forced. Otherwise, early theoretical sampling may bring premature closure to the analysis.

Grounded theory researchers take the usual criteria of "saturation" (i.e., new data fit into the categories already devised) of their categories for ending the research (Morse, 1995). But what does saturation mean? In practice, saturation seems elastic (see also Flick, 1998; Morse, 1995). Grounded theory approaches are seductive because they allow us to gain a handle on our material quickly. Is the handle we gain the best or most complete one? Does it encourage us to look deeply enough? The data in works claiming to be grounded theory pieces range from a handful of cases to sustained field research. The latter more likely fulfills the criterion of saturation and, moreover, has the resonance of intimate familiarity with the studied world.

As we define our categories as saturated (and some of us never do), we rewrite our memos in expanded, more analytic form. We put these memos to work for lectures, presentations, papers, and chapters. The analytic work continues as we sort and order memos, for we may discover gaps or new relationships.

Computer-Assisted Analysis

Computer-assisted techniques offer some shortcuts for coding, sorting, and integrating the data. Several programs, including NUD•IST and the Ethnograph, are explicitly aimed at assisting in grounded theory analyses. Hyper-Research, a program designed to retrieve and group data, serves qualitative sociologists across a broad range of analytic applications.[12] Such programs can prove enormously helpful with the problem of mountains of data—that is, data management. Amanda Coffey, Beverly Holbrook, and Paul Atkinson (1996) point out that other advantages of computer coding include the ability to do multiple searches using more than one code word simultaneously and the fact that it enables researchers to place memos at points in the text. Data analysis programs are also effective for mapping relationships visually onscreen. They do not, however, think for the analyst— perhaps to chagrin of some students (see also Seidel, 1991). Nonetheless, Thomas J. Richards and Lyn Richards (1994) argue that the code-and-retrieve method supports the emergence of theory by searching the data for codes and assembling ideas. Further, Renata Tesch (1991) notes that conceptual operations follow or accompany mechanical data management.

Qualitative analysis software programs do not escape controversy. Coffey et al. (1996)

and Lonkila (1995) express concern about qualitative programs based on conceptions of grounded theory methods and their uncritical adoption by users. They fear that these programs overemphasize coding and promote a superficial view of grounded theory; they also note that mechanical operations are no substitute for nuanced interpretive analysis. However, Nigel G. Fielding and Raymond M. Lee (1998) do not find substantial empirical evidence for such concerns in their systematic field study of users' experiences with computer-assisted qualitative data analysis programs.[13] I still have some reservations about these programs for four reasons: (a) Grounded theory methods are often poorly understood; (b) these methods have long been used to *legitimate*, rather than to conduct, studies; (c) these software packages appear more suited for objectivist grounded theory than constructivist approaches; and (d) the programs may unintentionally foster an illusion that interpretive work can be reduced to a set of procedures. Yvonna Lincoln (personal communication, August 21, 1998) asks her students, "Why would you want to engage in work that connects you to the deepest part of human existence and then turn it over to a machine to 'mediate'?" Part of interpretive work is gaining a sense of the whole—the whole interview, the whole story, the whole body of data. No matter how helpful computer programs may prove for managing the parts, we can see only their fragments on the screen.[14] And these fragments may seem to take on an existence of their own, as if objective and removed from their contextual origins and from our constructions and interpretations. Because objectivist grounded theory echoes positivism, computer-assisted programs based on it may promote widespread acceptance not just of the software, but of a one-dimensional view of qualitative research.

Critical Challenges to Grounded Theory

As is evident from the discussion above, recent debates have resulted in reassessments of grounded theory. Objectivist grounded theory has shaped views of what the method is and where it can take qualitative research. Over the years, a perception of how leading proponents have used grounded theory has become melded with the methods themselves. Subsequently, critics make assumptions about the nature of the method and its limitations (see, e.g., Conrad, 1990; Riessman, 1990a, 1990b). Riessman (1990a) states that grounded theory methods were insufficient to respect her interviewees and to portray their stories. Richardson (1993) found prospects of completing a grounded theory analysis to be alienating and turned to literary forms. Richardson (1994) also has observed that qualitative research reports are not so straightforward as their authors represent them to be. Authors choose evidence selectively, clean up subjects' statements, unconsciously adopt value-laden metaphors, assume omniscience, and bore readers.

These criticisms challenge authors' representations of their subjects, their authority to interpret subjects' lives, and their writer's voice, criticisms ethnographers have answered (see, e.g., Best, 1995; Dawson & Prus, 1995; Kleinman, 1993; Sanders, 1995; Snow & Morrill, 1993). These criticisms imply that grounded theory methods gloss over meanings within respondents' stories.[15] Conrad (1990) and Riessman (1990b) suggest that "fracturing the data" in grounded theory research might limit understanding because grounded theorists aim for analysis rather than the portrayal of subjects' experience in its fullness. From a grounded theory perspective, fracturing the data means creating codes and categories as the researcher defines themes within the data. Glaser and Strauss (1967) propose this strategy for several reasons: (a) to help the researcher avoid remaining immersed in anecdotes and stories, and subsequently unconsciously adopting subjects' perspectives; (b) to prevent the researcher's becoming immobilized and overwhelmed by voluminous data; and (c) to create a way for the researcher to organize and interpret data. However, criticisms of fracturing the data imply that grounded theory methods lead to separating the experience from the experiencing subject, the meaning from the story, and the viewer from the viewed.[16] In short, the criticisms assume that the grounded theory method (a) limits entry into subjects' worlds, and thus reduces understanding of their experience; (b) curtails representation of both the social world and subjective experience; (c) relies upon the viewer's authority as expert observer; and (d) posits a set of objectivist procedures on which the analysis rests.[17]

Researchers can use grounded theory methods to further their knowledge of subjective experience and to expand its representation while neither remaining external from it nor accepting objectivist assumptions and procedures. A constructivist grounded theory assumes that people create and maintain meaningful worlds through dialectical processes of conferring meaning on their realities and acting within them (Bury, 1986; Mishler, 1981). Thus social reality does not exist independent of human action. Certainly, my approach contrasts with a number of grounded theory studies, methodological state-ments, and research texts (see, e.g., Chenitz & Swanson, 1986; Glaser, 1992; Martin & Turner, 1986; Strauss & Corbin, 1990; Turner, 1981). By adopting a constructivist grounded theory approach, the researcher can move grounded theory methods further into the realm of interpretive social science consistent with a Blumerian (1969) emphasis on meaning, without assuming the existence of a unidimensional external reality. A con-structivist grounded theory recognizes the interactive nature of both data collection and analysis, resolves recent criticisms of the method, and reconciles positivist assumptions and postmodernist critiques. Moreover, a constructivist grounded theory fosters the development of qualitative traditions through the study of experience from the stand-point of those who live it.

The Place of Grounded Theory in Qualitative Research

Grounded theory research fits into the broader traditions of fieldwork and qualitative analysis. Most grounded theory studies rely on detailed qualitative materials collected through field, or ethnographic, research, but they are not ethnographies in the sense of total immersion into specific communities. Nor do grounded theorists attempt to study the social structures of whole communities. Instead, we tend to look at slices of social life. Like other forms of qualitative research, grounded theories can only portray moments in time. However, the grounded theory quest for the study of basic social processes fosters the identification of connections between events. The social world is always in process, and the lives of the research subjects shift and change as their circumstances and they themselves change. Hence a grounded theorist—or, more broadly, a qualitative researcher—constructs a picture that draws from, reassembles, and renders subjects' lives. The product is more like a painting than a photograph (Charmaz, 1995a). I come close to Atkinson's (1990, p. 2) depiction of ethnography as an "artful product" of objectivist description, careful organization, and interpretive commentary. The tendency to reify the findings and the picture of reality may result more from interpreters of the work than from its author.[18] Significantly, however, many researchers who adopt grounded theory strategies do so precisely to construct objectivist—that is, positivist—qualitative studies.

Grounded theory provides a systematic analytic approach to qualitative analysis of ethnographic materials because it consists of a set of explicit strategies. Any reasonably well-trained researcher can employ these strategies and develop an analysis. The strengths of grounded theory methods lie in (a) strategies that guide the researcher step by step through an analytic process, (b) the self-correcting nature of the data collection process, (c) the methods' inherent bent toward theory and the simultaneous turning away from a contextual description, and (d) the emphasis on comparative methods. Yet, like other qualitative approaches, grounded theory research is an emergent process rather than the product of a single research problem logically and deductively sequenced into a study—or even one logically and inductively sequenced. The initial research questions may be concrete and descriptive, but the researcher can develop deeper analytic questions by studying his or her data. Like wondrous gifts waiting to be opened, early grounded theory texts imply that categories and concepts inhere within the data, awaiting the researcher's discovery (Charmaz, 1990, 1995c). Not so. Glaser (1978, 1992) assumes that we can gather our data unfettered by bias or biography. Instead, a constructivist approach recognizes that the categories, concepts, and theoretical level of an analysis emerge from the researcher's interactions within the field and questions about the data. In short, the narrowing of research questions, the creation of concepts and categories and the integration of the constructed theoretical framework reflect what and how the researcher thinks and does about shaping and collecting the data.

The grounded theorist's analysis tells a story about people, social processes, and situations. The researcher composes the story; it does not simply unfold before the eyes of an objective viewer. This story reflects the viewer as well as the viewed. Grounded theory studies typically lie between traditional research methodology and the recent postmodernist turn. Radical empiricists shudder at grounded theorists' contamination of the story because we shape the data collection and redirect our analyses as new issues emerge. Now postmodernists and post-structuralists castigate the story as well. They argue that we compose our stories unconsciously, deny the oedipal logic of authorial desire (Clough, 1992), and deconstruct the subject. In addition, Denzin (1992a) states that even the new interpretive approaches "privilege the researcher over the subject, method over subject matter, and maintain commitments to outmoded conceptions of validity, truth, and generalizability" (p. 20). These criticisms apply to much grounded theory research. Yet we can use them to make our empirical research more reflexive and our completed studies more contextually situated. We can claim only to have interpreted *a* reality, as we understood both our own experience and our subjects' portrayals of theirs.

A re-visioned grounded theory must take epistemological questions into account. Grounded theory can provide a path for researchers who want to continue to develop qualitative traditions without adopting the positivistic trappings of objectivism and universality. Hence the further development of a constructivist grounded theory can bridge past positivism and a revised future form of interpretive inquiry. A revised grounded theory preserves realism through gritty, empirical inquiry and sheds positivistic proclivities by becoming increasingly interpretive.

In contradistinction to Clough's (1992) critique, ethnographies can refer to a feminist vision to construct narratives that do not claim to be literal representations of the real. A feminist vision allows emotions to surface, doubts to be expressed, and relationships with subjects to grow. Data collection becomes less formal, more immediate, and subjects' concerns take precedence over researchers' questions.

A constructivist grounded theory distinguishes between the real and the true. The constructivist approach does not seek truth—single, universal, and lasting. Still, it remains realist because it addresses human *realities* and assumes the existence of real worlds. However, neither human realities nor real worlds are unidimensional. We act within and upon our realities and worlds and thus develop dialectical relations among what we do, think, and feel. The constructivist approach assumes that what we take as real, as objective knowledge and truth, is based upon our perspective (Schwandt, 1994). The pragmatist underpinnings in symbolic interactionism emerge here. W. I. Thomas and Dorothy Swaine Thomas (1928) proclaim, "If human beings define their situations as real, they are real in their consequences" (p. 572). Following their theorem, we must try to find what research participants define as real and where their definitions of reality take them. The constructivist approach also fosters our self-consciousness about what we attribute to our subjects and how, when, and why researchers portray these definitions as real. Thus the research products do not constitute the reality of the respondents' reality. Rather, each is a rendering, one interpretation among multiple interpretations, of a shared or individual reality. That interpretation is objectivist only to the extent that it seeks to construct analyses that show how respondents and the social scientists who study them construct those realities—*without viewing those realities as unidimensional, universal, and immutable*. Researchers' attention to detail in the constructivist approach sensitizes them to multiple realities and the multiple viewpoints within them; it does not represent a quest to capture a single reality.

Thus we can recast the obdurate character of social life that Blumer (1969) talks about. In doing so, we change our conception of it from a real world to be discovered, tracked, and categorized to a world *made real* in the minds and through the words and actions of its members. Thus the grounded theorist constructs an image of *a* reality, not *the* reality— that is, objective, true, and external.

Objectivist Versus Constructivist Grounded Theory

A constructivist grounded theory recognizes that the viewer creates the data and ensuing analysis through interaction with the viewed. Data do not provide a window on reality. Rather, the "discovered" reality arises from the interactive process and its temporal, cultural, and structural contexts. Researcher and subjects frame that interaction and confer meaning upon it. The viewer then is part of what is viewed rather than separate from it. What a viewer sees shapes what he or she will define, measure, and analyze. Because objectivist (i.e., the majority of) grounded theorists depart from this position, this crucial difference reflects the positivist leanings in their studies.[19]

Causality is suggestive, incomplete, and indeterminate in a constructivist grounded theory. Therefore, a grounded theory remains open to refinement. It looks at how "variables" are grounded—given meaning and played out in subjects' lives (Dawson & Prus, 1995; Prus, 1996). Their meanings and actions take priority over researchers' analytic interests and methodological technology. A constructivist grounded theory seeks to define conditional statements that interpret how subjects construct their realities. Nonetheless, these conditional statements do not approach some level of generalizable truth. Rather, they constitute a set of hypotheses and concepts that other researchers can transport to similar research problems and to other substantive fields. As such, they answer Prus's (1987) call for the development and study of generic concepts. Thus the grounded theorist's hypotheses and concepts offer both explanation and understanding and fulfill the pragmatist criterion of usefulness.

In contrast, objectivist grounded theorists adhere more closely to positivistic canons of traditional science (see Glaser, 1978, 1992; Glaser & Strauss, 1967; Strauss & Corbin, 1990, 1994; Wilson & Hutchinson, 1991).[20] They assume that following a systematic set of methods leads them to discover reality and to construct a provisionally true, testable, and ultimately verifiable "theory" of it (Strauss, 1995; Strauss & Corbin, 1990, 1994).[21] This theory provides not only understanding but prediction. Three extensions of this position follow: (a) Systematic application of grounded theory strategies answers the positivist call for reliability and validity, because specifying procedures permits reproducibility;[22] (b) hypothesis testing in grounded theory leads to confirmation or disconfirmation of the emerging theory; and (c) grounded theory methods allow for the exertion of controls, and therefore make changing the studied reality possible.

Objectivist grounded theory accepts the positivistic assumption of an external world that can be described, analyzed, explained, and predicted: truth, but with a small *t*. That is, objectivist grounded theory is modifiable as conditions change. It assumes that different observers will discover this world and describe it in similar ways. That's correct—to the extent that subjects have comparable experiences (e.g., people with different chronic illnesses may experience uncertainty, intrusive regimens, medical dominance) and viewers bring similar questions, perspectives, methods, and, subsequently, concepts to analyze those experiences. Objectivist grounded theorists often share assumptions with their research participants—particularly the professional participants. Perhaps more likely, they assume that respondents share their meanings. For example, Strauss and Corbin's (1990) discussion of independence and dependence assumes that these terms hold the same meanings for patients as for researchers.

Guidelines such as those offered by Strauss and Corbin (1990) structure objectivist grounded theorists' work. These guidelines are didactic and prescriptive rather than emergent and interactive. Clinton Sanders (1995) refers to grounded theory procedures as "more rigorous than thou instructions about how information should be pressed into a mold" (p. 92). Strauss and Corbin categorize steps in the process with scientific terms such as *axial coding* and *conditional matrix* (Strauss, 1987; Strauss & Corbin, 1990, 1993). As grounded theory methods become more articulated, categorized, and elaborated, they seem to take on a life of their own. Guidelines turn into procedures and are reified into immutable rules, unlike Glaser and Strauss's (1967) original flexible strategies. By taking grounded theory methods as prescriptive scientific rules, proponents further the positivist cast to objectivist grounded theory.

Given the positivist bent in objectivist grounded theory, where might a constructivist approach take us? How might it reconcile both positivist leanings and postmodernist critiques in grounded theory? A constructivist grounded theory lies between postmodernist (Denzin, 1991; Krieger, 1991; Marcus & Fischer, 1986; Tyler, 1986) and postpositivist approaches to qualitative research (Rennie, Phillips, & Quartaro, 1988; Turner, 1981). Researchers no longer provide a solitary voice rendering the dialogue only from their standpoints. Constructivists aim to include multiple voices, views, and visions in their rendering of lived experience. How does one accomplish this?

Constructing Constructivism

What helps researchers develop a constructivist grounded theory? How might they shape the data collection and analysis phases? Gaining depth and understanding in their work means that they can fulfill Blumer's (1969) call for "intimate familiarity" with respondents and their worlds (see also Lofland & Lofland, 1984, 1995). In short, constructing constructivism means seeking meanings—both respondents' meanings and researchers' meanings.

To seek respondents' meanings, we must go further than surface meanings or presumed meanings. We must look for views and values as well as for acts and facts. We need to look for beliefs and ideologies as well as situations and structures. By studying tacit meanings, we clarify, rather than challenge, respondents' views about reality.[23]

A constructivist approach necessitates a relationship with respondents in which they can cast their stories in their terms. It means listening to their stories with openness to feeling and experience. In my studies of chronic illness, several people mentioned that they saw me as someone to whom they could express their private thoughts and feelings. Sometimes, however, researchers frame their questions in ways that cloak raw experience and mute feelings. In studies that tap suffering, we may unwittingly give off cues that we do not welcome respondents' going too deep. Furthermore, one-shot interviewing lends itself to a partial, sanitized view of experience, cleaned up for public discourse. The very structure of an interview may preclude private thoughts and feelings from emerging. Such a structure reinforces whatever proclivities a respondent has to tell only the public version of the story. Researchers' sustained involvement with research participants lessens these problems.

The conceptual level of coding, writing memos, and developing categories likely differ in objectivist and constructivist grounded theory. For example, Strauss and Corbin (1990, 1998) stick close to their depiction of overt data. I aim to understand the assumptions underlying the data by piecing them together. For example, "living one day at a time" is a taken-for-granted explanation of how one manages troubles. Everyone knows what living one day at a time is. But what does it assume? Ill people report living one day at a time or having good days and bad days as self-evident facts. Not until they are asked what these terms mean experientially—that is, how they affect their relating to time, what feelings these experiences elicit, and so on—do they start to define a form and content for "living one day at a time" or "good" and "bad" days.

Objectivist grounded theory studies may offer rich description and make conditional statements, but they may remain outside of the experience. Furthermore, objectivist grounded theory methods foster externality by invoking procedures that increase complexity at the expense of experience. Axial coding can lead to awkward scientistic terms and clumsy categories. Terms and categories take center stage and distance readers from the experience, rather than concentrate their attention upon it. Processual diagrams and conceptual maps can result in an overly complex architecture that obscures experience. Any form of grounded theory can generate jargon. Objectivist grounded theory especially risks cloaking analytic power in jargon.

Making our categories consistent with studied life helps to keep that life in the foreground. Active codes and subsequent categories preserve images of experience. For example, in my discussion of immersion in illness, my categories were "Recasting Life,"

"Facing Dependency," "Pulling In," "Slipping Into Illness Routines," and "Weathering a Serious Episode."[24]

Coding and categorizing processes sharpen the researcher's ability to ask questions about the data.

Different questions can flow from objectivist and constructivist starting points. These questions can be concrete, as described by Strauss and Corbin (1990, 1998), or more abstract. Concrete questions are revealed in their discussion of two categories—pain experience and pain relief: "Who gives pain relief to people with arthritis?" "What gives relief?" "How is the pain experienced and handled?" "How much relief is needed?" "When does the pain occur and when does she institute relief?" "Why is pain relief important?" (1990, pp. 78–79). Here the categories take on an objective, external character—objective because these questions assume answers that reflect "facts"; objective because the answers assume that the researcher discovers what being in pain "really is all about"; objective because the topic of pain now takes on an external character that can be identified, addressed, and managed.

In contrast, I start by viewing the topic of pain subjectively as a feeling, an experience that may take a variety of forms. Then I ask these questions: What makes pain, pain? (That is, what is essential to the phenomenon as defined by those who experience it?) What defining properties or characteristics do ill people attribute to it? When do they do so? These questions lead into a question I share with Strauss and Corbin (1990, 1998): How does the person experience this pain, and what, if anything, does he or she do about it? My questions aim to get at meaning, not at truth. As a result, a constructivist grounded theory may remain at a more intuitive, impressionistic level than an objectivist approach.

My version of grounded theory fosters the researcher's viewing the data afresh, again and again, as he or she develops new ideas. Researchers can code and recode data numerous times (see also Glaser & Strauss, 1967). Posing new questions to the data results in new analytic points. I go back and forth between data and the drafts of chapters or papers many times. I take explicit findings in certain interviews and see if they remain implicit in other interviews. Then I go back to respondents and ask specific questions around the new category. For example, when I returned to a young woman with colitis to ask how the slow, monotonous time of convalescence might seem in memory, she understood my line of questioning immediately and cut in without skipping a beat: "It seems like a wink" (Charmaz, 1991, p. 92).

Every qualitative researcher makes multiple analytic decisions. Foremost among these is how much complexity to introduce. How much is necessary to convey the story with depth and clarity? How much seems like hairsplitting that will irritate or confuse the reader? At what point does collapsing categories result in conceptual muddiness and oversimplification? To achieve the right level of complexity, we must know the potential audience and sense the appropriate style and level at which to write for it.

Rendering Through Writing

The analysis of qualitative data does not cease when the grounded theorist has developed a theoretical framework; it proceeds into the writing (Mitchell & Charmaz, 1996). A grounded theorist's proclivities toward objectivism or constructivism also come through in his or her writing about the research. The image of a scientific laboratory comes to mind with objectivist grounded theory, reflected in carefully organized and stated written reports of concepts, evidence, and procedures. Constructivist grounded theory spawns an image of a writer at a desk who tries to balance theoretical interpretation with an evocative aesthetic. To illustrate how analysis proceeds into writing constructivist grounded theory, I provide several writing strategies and examples from earlier work.

As Laurel Richardson (1990) declares, writing matters. Consistent with the postmodernist turn, I attempt to evoke experiential feeling through how I render it in writing. This means taking the reader into a story and imparting its mood through linguistic style and narrative exposition. This strategy removes the writing from typical scientific format without transforming the final product into fiction, drama, or poetry. I frame key definitions and distinctions in words that reproduce the tempo and mood of the experience:

> *Existing* from day to day occurs when a person plummets into continued crises that rip life apart. (Charmaz, 1991, p. 185)
> Others wait to map a future. And wait. They monitor their bodies and their lives. They look for signs to indicate what steps to take next. They map a future or move to the next point on the map only when they feel assured that the worst of their illness is over. These people map a future or move to the next point when they feel distant enough from illness to release their emotions from it. (p. 191)

Analogies and metaphors can explicate tacit meanings and feelings subsumed within a category (see also Charmaz & Mitchell, 1996; Richardson, 1994):

> Such men and women feel coerced into living one day at a time. They force it upon themselves, almost with clenched teeth. Here, living one day at a time resembles learning an unfamiliar, disagreeable lesson in grammar school; it is an unwelcome prerequisite to staying alive. (Charmaz, 1991, p. 179)
> Drifting time, in contrast [to dragging time], spreads out. Like a fan, drifting time unfolds and expands during a serious immersion in illness. (p. 91)

Simple language and straightforward ideas make theory readable. Theory remains embedded in the narrative, in its many stories. The theory becomes more accessible but less identifiable as theory. Several strategies foster making the writing accessible. Catching experiential rhythm and timing allows the researcher to reproduce it within the writing:

> From embarrassment to mortification. From discomfort to pain. Endless uncertainty. What follows? Regimentation. (Charmaz, 1991, p. 134)
> Days slip by. The same day keeps slipping by. Durations of time lengthen since few events break up the day, week, or month. Illness seems like one long uninterrupted duration of time. (p. 88)

Questions help tie main ideas together or redirect the reader. Sometimes I adopt the role of a chronically ill person and ask questions as she would.

> Is it cancer? Could it be angina? Pangs of uncertainty spring up when current, frequently undiagnosed, symptoms could mean a serious chronic illness. (Charmaz, 1991, p. 32)

Immediacy draws the reader into the story. A story occurring in the present as if now unfolding draws the reader in. I sacrificed immediacy for accuracy by writing about respondents in the past because the events described took place in the past.[25] Where authors place their stories and how they frame them can bring experience to life or wholly obscure it.

A mix of concrete detail with analytic categories connects the familiar with the unfamiliar or even esoteric. Thus I kept material in *Good Days, Bad Days* (Charmaz, 1991) that had been covered before, such as the chapter on living with chronic illness. I took the reader through messy houses, jumbled schedules, pressures to simplify life, fragile pacing, and enormous efforts to function to the relief when remission occurs. This detail gave readers imagery on which to build when I moved into a more elusive analysis of time.

Writers use a linear logic to organize their analyses and make experience understandable. Yet experience is not necessarily linear, nor is it always readily drawn with clear boundaries. For example, experiencing illness, much less all its spiraling consequences, does not fit neatly into one general process. The grounded theory method emphasizes the analysis of a basic process the researcher discovers in the data. Although I pondered over organizing the book around one process, I could not identify an overarching theme. Experiencing illness consists of many processes, not a single process that subsumes others. Further, illness ebbs and flows. Chronically ill people define periods of relative "health" as well as spells of sickness. Thus I chose to collapse time and experience to cover illness.

Written images portray the tone the writer takes towards the topic and reflect the writer's relationships with his or her respondents. I aim for curiosity without condescension, openness without voyeurism, and participation without domination. Maintaining balance is difficult, because I try to portray respondents' worlds and views. Throughout the research and writing of *Good Days, Bad Days*, I tried to go beyond respondents' public presentation of self in illness. Otherwise, the knotty problems, the fear and pain, the moral dilemmas and ambivalent decisions do not come through.

Writers makes moral choices about portraying respondents, designing how to tell their stories, and delineating ways to interpret them. These choices also lead to the researcher's assuming a role as the writer (Krieger, 1991). In my book, I remain in the background as a story-teller whose tales have believable characters, not as an omniscient social scientist. My tone, style, and imagery reduce omniscience. However, because I stayed with the conceptual categories and built the stories around them, my work remains consistent with grounded theory and much social scientific writing.

Revising a manuscript can result in changes in style, possibly even of genre. Carefully crafted grounded theory categories work well as signposts in professional journals. A book editor may delete all the subheadings in one quick read. As signposts go, the narrative style changes. A more straightforward scientific style recedes as a more literary style evolves. Of course, how one sees that style and whether one defines it as scientific or literary depends upon where one stands. The postmodernist may see this style as objectivist, realist, and scientific; the positivist may see it as disconcertingly literary. I agree with Atkinson (1990) that impressionist tales are often embedded in realist accounts. I try to pull readers in so they might sense and situate the feeling of the speakers in the story. Here, what Van Maanen (1988) calls impressionist tales sounds exactly what Clough (1992) calls "emotional realism." Perhaps, however, portraying moods, feelings, and views evokes an aesthetic verisimilitude of them.

Summary and Conclusion

Given the analysis above, what conclusions can we draw about grounded theory studies? What might be the future of grounded theory? First, grounded theory methods evolve in different ways depending upon the perspectives and proclivities of their adherents. I aim to move researchers toward an explicitly constructivist approach. If we examine our epistemological premises, we can acknowledge the limits of our studies and the ways we shape them. In this way, adopting and refining grounded theory methods furthers the study of empirical worlds.

Second, we can reduce or resolve tensions between postmodernism and constructivist grounded theory when we use the former to illuminate and extend the latter. In short, postmodernism can *inform* realist study of experience rather than simply serve as justification for abandoning it. The postmodernist turn has forced renewed awareness of our relationships with and representation of subjects that will long influence qualitative research, possibly longer than the term *postmodernism* itself holds sway. Similarly, the importance of situating qualitative research in historical and cultural context is underscored. We grounded theorists can profit from the current trend toward linguistic and rhetorical analysis by becoming more reflexive about how we frame and write our studies. This trend supports constructivist approaches in grounded theory because it explicitly treats authors' works *as* constructions instead of as objectified products.

Third, the future of grounded theory lies with both objectivist and constructivist visions. Scientific institutions and conventions are unlikely to undergo rapid change. Granting agencies and tenure review committees may long favor objectivist work over constructivist craft. The qualitative revolution has opened up possibilities and potentials, but gatekeepers are likely to reward scholars whose work comes closest to their own. Thus, we can expect to see growing numbers of large studies with small qualitative components and more team projects in multiple sites. Does this mean that constructivist grounded theory will wither and wane? No. The trend toward interpretive study, the quest for understanding, and the challenge to the imagination impel us to take our inquiry into the world. Through sharing the worlds of our subjects, we come to conjure an image of their constructions and of our own.

Notes

1. Lindesmith (1947) and Cressey (1953) both attempted earlier to codify analytic methods for qualitative research through analytic induction. Their work has been preserved in the criminology and deviance literatures but has faded in general methodological discussions.

2. Juliet Corbin has a strong background and a doctorate in nursing science. She has long been a leader in the establishment of qualitative methods in nursing; since the publication of *Basics*, she has attained prominence in the social sciences and other professions as well.

3. To illustrate, when discussing conceptualizing data as the first step in analysis, Strauss and Corbin (1990) provide the following hypothetical example from a restaurant: "While waiting for your dinner, you notice a lady in red. She appears to be just standing there in the kitchen, but your common sense tells you that a restaurant wouldn't pay a lady in red just to stand there, especially in a busy kitchen. Your curiosity is piqued, so you decide to do an inductive analysis to see if you can determine just what her job is. (Once a grounded theorist, always a grounded theorist).

   "You notice that she is intently looking around the kitchen area, a work site, focusing here and then there, taking a mental note of what is going on. *You ask yourself, what is she doing here? Then you label it* watching. Watching what? Kitchen work" (pp. 63–64).

   This example continues in the same vein. It relies on careful observation of the overt behavior of the woman in the restaurant, from the objective observer's viewpoint. It does not take into account what that reality is like from the perspective of the restaurant worker. Nor do the categories develop from comparative study of other restaurants.

4. Anselm Strauss critiqued the draft of my 1995 paper on grounded theory in which I then claimed that grounded theory is not verificational (Charmaz, 1995b). He said that I was wrong.

5. For example, when writing about "mutual pretense," Glaser and Strauss (1965) state: "This particular awareness context cannot exist, of course, unless both the patient and staff are aware that he is dying. Therefore all the structural conditions which contribute to the existence of open awareness (and which are absent in closed and suspicion awareness) contribute also to the existence of mutual pretense. In addition, at least one interactant must indicate a desire to pretend that the patient is not dying and the other must agree to the pretense, acting accordingly" (p. 67). Corbin and Strauss (1987) also adopt a distanced voice in the following passage: "The impact of body failure and consequent performance failure can be measured by the impact that it has on each dimension of the BBC (biographical body conceptions). Since each dimension (biographical time, body, self conceptions) exists in a tightly bound relationship with the other, the consequences of body failure with regard to one aspect are further felt with the other two. It is the combined impact of the three aspects of the BBC that profoundly affects biographical continuity and meaning" (p. 260). Several of Corbin and Strauss's works on chronic illness, such as *Unending Work and Care* (1998), read as if much less distanced than other works. Two factors may contribute to the difference: Strauss's experience with chronic illness and Corbin's direct involvement in data gathering.

6. Stern (1994a) agrees. She sees recent developments in grounded theory methods as eroding the method and the power of the subsequent analyses.

7. For a more developed discussion of how to do constructivist grounded theory, see Charmaz (1995c).

8. Grounded theorists work up and out from data. Not every qualitative researcher does. Rena Lederman (1990) observes that some anthropologists avoid using their field notes when developing their finished work. She writes of how anthropological field notes fulfill different functions for the researcher while he or she is away in the field and later, when the researcher is home. Ethnographers write as both close to and distant from their respondents while in the field, but their loyalties shift to the professional community when they reach home. Then the same field notes that provided a concrete grasp of reality in the field impart a sense of doubt. Lederman argues that conceptions of field notes as fixed and stable data crumble at this point. Instead, field notes can assume multiple meanings and are open to reinterpretation and contradiction.

9. Strauss's remarkably facile mind could not stop making comparisons. He taught students to compare unlikely categories of people, actions, settings, and organizations to tease out the properties of a category (see also Star, 1997).

10. The original memo was considerably longer and contained snippets of data throughout. The more distanced tone of the 1983 memo reflects my earlier socialization in writing and in grounded theory. It also reflects tensions between the relativism I adopted during my first year of graduate school and the objectivism in my grounded theory training (see Charmaz, 1983). By 1990, when *Good Days, Bad Days* went to press, this material reads as less distanced and more constructivist although it is essentially the same as the 1983 memo. In the interim, I came closer to integrating my realist intention to study empirical problems with the relativism inherent in constructivism (see Charmaz, 1990). In addition, I worked on making abstract ideas accessible.

11. I use the term *subjects* not because I view them as subordinate, or subjected to inquiry, but because the term *research participants* is so cumbersome.

12. For guidelines in choosing a data analysis software program, see Weitzman and Miles (1995).

13. However, recent listserv discussions of qualitative computer analysis indicate that some users still view the programs as too mechanical. For example, Aksel Hn Tjorca (MedSoc Listserv, November 17, 1998) found NUD■IST to be useful in sorting data initially but feared that hierarchical categories embedded in the program might work against the relational nature of the data.

14. To gain a sense of the whole on which we are working, we may need to have entire documents, if not the complete data set, before us. Yvonna Lincoln (personal communication, August 21, 1998) tells me that she works with all her data spread out on a large table. That way, she can gain a sense of the whole and, simultaneously, plan how to assemble the parts.

15. There are tensions between the constructivist assumptions of varied and problematic meaning and objectivist assumptions of the world as real, obdurate, external, and predictable. A constructivist grounded theory acknowledges realities of enduring worlds and tries to show how they are socially created through action, intention, and routine.

16. For a detailed report on how diverse scholars have responded to such concerns, see the 1992 debate in the *Journal of Contemporary Ethnography* about reality and interpretation in William Foote Whyte's *Street Corner Society* (Adler et al., 1992). Mariane Boelen (1992) challenges the veracity of Whyte's study and, by doing so, challenges reifications made of it (but not the notion of reifying ethnography itself). The responses to her challenge, however, range from accepting objectivist premises to questioning them (see Denzin, 1992; Orlandella, 1992; Richardson, 1992; Vidich, 1992; Whyte, 1992). Vidich (1992) points out that Boelen assumes only one possible view of reality and that Whyte missed it. Denzin (1992) and Richardson (1992), however, question the objectivist premises that both Whyte and Boelen share.

17. To my knowledge, those who raise these criticisms have not resolved them through using grounded theory. Their recommendations range from abandoning empirical study to moving toward narrative analysis. To the extent that narrative analysis focuses on or drifts into emphasizing the type and structure of the narrative rather than respond-

ents' meanings, I fail to see it as a better alternative than grounded theory studies. Nor do I see recording respondents' statements in one-line stanzas as offering a better frame for meaning than interview excerpts.

18. An author may call attention to an issue, frame a manuscript on it, but assume that the one issue constitutes the entire empirical reality. For example, before my analyses of illness focused squarely on the self, I argued that loss of self is *a* fundamental form of suffering. Readers reified my argument and concluded that I erroneously saw loss of self as the only experience of illness (see Robinson, 1990).

19. Glaser and Strauss (1967; Glaser, 1992; Strauss, 1987) have long stated that the core issues become apparent in the research setting, as if any trained observer will discover them. Similarly, they write as if neither standpoint nor status affects what observers see and find.

20. For a good outline of positivist premises, see Denzin (1989).

21. Strauss and Corbin (1994) call for grounded theory advocates to abandon the quest for truth. However, they also make a strong case for aiming for verification, which assumes a quest for truth. In their 1994 chapter, they also affirm two points I raised earlier, that the researcher's analysis is an interactive product of the views of the researcher and the data, and that the early works are written as if the researcher discovers an external order in the data (see Charmaz, 1983, 1990).

22. Strauss and Corbin (1998) state that exact replication is not possible, but sufficient reproducibility is. They propose that other researchers with similar theoretical premises, data gathering procedures, and research conditions develop similar theoretical explanations.

23. By making our early drafts available to those subjects who wish to read them, we make it possible for them to challenge and correct our views.

24. It is important to distinguish when the actor has agency and when he or she is acted upon. A hazard of any inductive method such as the constructivist approach is overemphasis on the individual. The constructivist approach leads to a style that emphasizes the active, reflective actor. Yet larger social forces also act upon this actor. So the researcher needs to learn how these social forces affect the actor and what, if anything, the actor thinks, feels, and does about them.

25. See, in contrast, Catherine Riessman (1990a) for presenting stories in the present.

References

Adler, P. A., Adler, P., & Johnson, J. M. (1992). New questions about old issues. *Journal of Contemporary Ethnography, 21*, 3–10.

Atkinson, P. A. (1990). *The ethnographic imagination: Textual constructions of reality.* London: Routledge.

Baszanger, I. (1998). *Inventing pain medicine: From the laboratory to the clinic.* New Brunswick, NJ: Rutgers University Press.

Best, J. (1995). Lost in the ozone again: The postmodernist fad and interactionist foibles. In N. K. Denzin (Ed.), *Studies in symbolic interaction: A research annual* (Vol. 17, pp. 125–134). Greenwich, CT: JAI.

Biernacki, P. L. (1986). *Pathways from heroin addiction: Recovery without treatment.* Philadelphia: Temple University Press.

Blumer, H. (1969). *Symbolic interactionism: Perspective and method.* Englewood Cliffs, NJ: Prentice Hall.

Boelen, W. A. M. (1992). *Street corner society:* Cornerville revisited. *Journal of Contemporary Ethnography, 21*, 11–51.

Bond, G. C. (1990). Fieldnotes: Research in past occurrences. In R. Sanjek (Ed.), *Fieldnotes: The makings of anthropology* (pp. 273–289). Ithaca, NY: Cornell University Press.

Charmaz, K. (1983). The grounded theory method: An explication and interpretation. In R. M. Emerson (Ed.), *Contemporary field research* (pp. 109–126). Boston: Little, Brown.

Charmaz, K. (1990). Discovering chronic illness: Using grounded theory. *Social Science and Medicine, 30*, 1161–1172.

Charmaz, K. (1991). *Good days, bad days: The self in chronic illness and time.* New Brunswick, NJ: Rutgers University Press.

Charmaz, K. (1995a). Body, identity, and self: Adapting to impairment. *Sociological Quarterly, 36*, 657–680.

Charmaz, K. (1995b). Grounded theory. In J. A. Smith, R. Harré, & L. Van Langenhove (Eds.), *Rethinking methods in psychology* (pp. 27–49). London: Sage.

Charmaz, K., and Mitchell, R. G. (1996). The myth of silent authorship: Self, substance, and style in ethnographic writing. *Symbolic Interaction, 19*, 285–302.

Clarke, A. E. (1998). *Disciplining reproduction: Modernity, American life sciences, and the problems of sex.* Berkeley: University of California Press.

Clough, P. T. (1992). *The end(s) of ethnography: From realism to social criticism.* Newbury Park, CA: Sage.

Coffey, A., Holbrook, B., & Atkinson, P. (1996). Qualitative data analysis: Technologies and representations. *Sociological Research Online, 1*(1). Available Internet: http://www.socresonline.org.uk/socresonline/1/1/4.html

Connelly, F. M., & Clandinin, D. J. (1990). Stories of experience and narrative inquiry. *Educational Researcher, 19*(5), 2–14.

Conrad, P. (1990). Qualitative research on chronic illness: A commentary on method and conceptual development. *Social Science and Medicine, 30,* 1257–1263.

Cressey, D. R. (1953). *Other people's money. A study in the social psychology of embezzlement.* Glencoe, IL: Free Press.

Creswell, J. W. (1997). *Qualitative inquiry and research design: Choosing among five traditions.* Thousand Oaks, CA: Sage.

Dawson, L. L., & Prus, R. C. (1995). Postmodernism and linguistic reality versus symbolic interactionism and obdurate reality. In N. K. Denzin (Ed.), *Studies in symbolic interaction: A research annual* (Vol. 17, pp. 105–124). Greenwich, CT: JAI.

Denzin, N. K. (1989). *Interpretive interactionism.* Newbury Park, CA: Sage.

Denzin, N. K. (1991). *Images of postmodern society.* Newbury Park, CA: Sage.

Denzin, N. K. (1992). Whose Cornerville is it anyway? *Journal of Contemporary Ethnography, 21,* 120–132.

Fielding, N. G., & Lee, R. M. (1998). *Computer analysis and qualitative research.* London: Sage.

Flick, U. (1998). *An introduction to qualitative research: Theory, method and applications.* London: Sage.

Gadow, S. (1982). Body and self: A dialectic. In V. Kestenbaum (Ed.), *The humanity of the ill.* Knoxville: University of Tennessee Press.

Geertz, C. (1973). *The interpretation of cultures: Selected essays.* New York: Basic Books.

Glaser, B. G. (1978). *Theoretical sensitivity.* Mill Valley, CA: Sociology Press.

Glaser, B. G. (1992). *Basics of grounded theory analysis: Emergence vs. forcing.* Mill Valley, CA: Sociology Press.

Glaser, B. G. (1998). [Contribution to workshop]. In B. G. Glaser & P. Stern (Leaders), *Advanced grounded theory, workshop II.* Workshop conducted at the Qualitative Health Research Conference, Vancouver.

Glaser, B. G., & Strauss, A. L. (1967). *The discovery of grounded theory: Strategies for qualitative research.* Chicago: Aldine.

Glaser, B. G., & Strauss, A. L. (1968). *Time for dying.* Chicago: Aldine.

Kleinman, A. (1988). *The illness narratives: Suffering, healing and the human condition.* New York: Basic Books.

Kleinman, S. (1993). The textual turn. *Contemporary Sociology, 22,* 11–13.

Krieger, S. (1991). *Social science and the self: Personal essays on an art form.* New Brunswick, NJ: Rutgers University Press.

Kuhn, T. S. (1970). *The structure of scientific revolutions* (2nd ed.). Chicago: University of Chicago Press.

Lederman, R. (1990). Pretexts for ethnography: On reading fieldnotes. In R. Sanjek (Ed.), *Fieldnotes: The makings of anthropology* (pp. 71–91). Ithaca, NY: Cornell University Press.

Lindesmith, A. R. (1947). *Opiate addiction.* Bloomington, IN: Principia.

Loftland, L. H. (1993). Fighting the good fight—again. *Contemporary Sociology, 22,* 1–3.

Lofland, J., & Lofland, L. H. (1984). *Analyzing social settings* (2nd ed.). Belmont, CA: Wadsworth.

Lofland, J., & Lofland, L. H. (1995). *Analyzing social settings* (3rd ed.). Belmont, CA: Wadsworth.

Lonkila, M. (1995). Grounded theory as an emerging paradigm for computer-assisted qualitative data analysis. In U. Kelle (Ed.), *Computer-aided qualitative data analysis: Theory, methods and practice* (pp. 41–51). London: Sage.

Maines, D. R. (1993). Narrative's moment and sociology's phenomena: Toward a narrative sociology. *Sociological Quarterly, 34,* 17–38.

Marcus, G. E., & Fischer, M. M. J. (1986). *Anthropology as cultural critique: An experimental moment in the human sciences.* Chicago: University of Chicago Press.

McGuire, M. B., & Kantor, D. J. (1987). Belief systems and illness experience. In J. A. Roth & P. Conrad (Eds.), *Research in the sociology of health care: The experience and management of chronic illness* (Vol. 6, pp. 241–248). Greenwich, CT: JAI.

Mead, G. H. (1934). *Mind, self, and society: From the standpoint of a social behaviorist* (C. W. Morris, Ed.). Chicago: University of Chicago Press.

Melia, K. M. (1996). Rediscovering Glaser. *Qualitative Health Research, 6,* 368–378.

Mitchell, R. G., Jr., & Charmaz, K. (1996). Telling tales, writing stories: Postmodernist visions and realist images in ethnographic writing. *Journal of Contemporary Ethnography, 25,* 144–166.

Morse, J. M. (1995). The significance of saturation. *Qualitative Health Research, 5,* 147–149.

Orlandella, A. R. (1992). Boelen may know Holland, Boelen may know Barzini, but Boelen "doesn't know diddle about the North End!" *Journal of Contemporary Ethnography, 21,* 69–79.

Park, R. E., & Burgess, E. W. (1925). *The city.* Chicago: University of Chicago Press.

Prus, R. C. (1987). Generic social processes: Maximizing conceptual development in ethnographic research. *Journal of Contemporary Ethnography, 16,* 250–293.

Rennie, D. L., Phillips, J. R., & Quartaro, G. K. (1988). Grounded theory: A promising approach to conceptualization in psychology? *Canadian Psychology, 29,* 139–150.

Richards, T. J., & Richards, L. (1994). Using computers in qualitative research. In N. K. Denzin & Y. S. Lincoln (Eds.), *Handbook of qualitative research* (pp. 445–462). Thousand Oaks, CA: Sage.

Richardson, L. (1992). Trash on the corner: Ethics and technography. *Journal of Contemporary Ethnography, 21,* 103–119.

Richardson, L. (1993). Interrupting discursive spaces: Consequences for the sociological self. In N. K. Denzin (Ed.), *Studies in symbolic interaction: A research annual* (Vol. 14, pp. 77–84). Greenwich, CT: JAI.

Richardson, L. (1994). Writing: A method of inquiry. In N. K. Denzin & Y. S. Lincoln (Eds.), *Handbook of qualitative research* (pp. 516–529). Thousand Oaks, CA: Sage.

Riessman, C. K. (1990a). *Divorce talk: Women and men make sense of personal relationships.* New Brunswick, NJ: Rutgers University Press.

Riessman, C. K. (1990b). Strategic uses of narrative in the presentation of self and illness: A research note. *Social Science and Medicine, 30,* 1195–1200.

Robrecht, L. C. (1995). Grounded theory. Evolving methods. *Qualitative Health Research, 5,* 169–177.

Robinson, I. (1990). Personal narratives, social careers and medical courses: Analysing life trajectories in autobiographies of people with multiple sclerosis. *Social Science and Medicine, 30,* 1173–1186.

Sanders, C. R. (1995). Stranger than fiction: In sights and pitfalls in post-modern ethnography. In N. K. Denzin (Ed.), *Studies in symbolic interaction: A research annual* (Vol. 17, pp. 89–104). Greenwich, CT: JAI.

Schatzman, L. (1991). Dimensional analysis: Notes on an alternative approach to the grounding of theory in qualitative research. In D. R. Maines (Ed.), *Social organization and social processes: Essays in honor of Anselm Strauss* (pp. 303–314). New York: Aldine de Gruyter.

Schwandt, T. A. (1994). Constructivist, interpretivist approaches to human inquiry. In N. K. Denzin & Y. S. Lincoln (Eds.), *Handbook of qualitative research* (pp. 118–137). Thousand Oaks, CA: Sage.

Seidel, J. (1991). Method and madness in the application of computer technology to qualitative data analysis. In N. G. Fielding & R. M. Lee (Eds.), *Using computers in qualitative research* (pp. 107–116). London: Sage.

Shaw, C. (1930). *The jack-roller: A delinquent boy's own story.* Chicago: University of Chicago Press.

Snow, D., & Morrill, C. (1993). Reflections upon anthropology's crisis of faith. *Contemporary Sociology, 22,* 8–11.

Star, S. L. (1989). *Regions of the mind: Brain research and the quest for scientific certainty.* Stanford, CA: Stanford University Press.

Star, S. L. (1997). Another remembrance: Anselm Strauss: An appreciation. In N. K. Denzin (Ed.), *Studies in symbolic interaction: A research annual* (Vol. 21, pp. 39–48), Greenwich, CT: JAI.

Stern, P. N. (1994a). Eroding grounded theory. In J. M. Morse (Ed.), *Critical issues in qualitative research methods* (pp. 212–223). Thousand Oaks, CA: Sage.

Stern, P. N. (1994b). The grounded theory method: Its uses and processes. In B. G. Galser (Ed.), *More grounded theory: A reader* (pp. 116–126). Mill Valley, CA: Sociology Press.

Strauss, A. L. (1987). *Qualitative analysis for social scientists.* New York: Cambridge University Press.

Strauss, A. L. (1995). Notes on the nature and development of general theories. *Qualitative Inquiry,* 17–18.

Strauss, A. L., & Corbin, J. (1990). *Basics of qualitative research: Grounded theory procedures and techniques.* Newbury Park, CA: Sage.

Strauss, A. L., & Corbin, J. (1998). *Basics of qualitative research: Techniques and procedures for developing grounded theory* (2nd ed.). Thousand Oaks, CA: Sage.

Tesch, R. (1991). Software for qualitative researchers: Analysis needs and program capacities. In N. G. Fielding & R. M. Lee (Eds.), *Using computers in qualitative research* (pp. 16–37). London: Sage.

Thomas, W. I., & Thomas, D. S. (1928). *The child in America.* New York: Alfred A. Knopf.

Thomas, W. I., & Znaniecki, F. (1918–1920). *The Polish peasant in Europe and America* (5 vols.). Boston: Richard G. Badger.

Thrasher, F. M. (1963). *The gang: A study of 1,313 gangs in Chicago.* Chicago: University of Chicago Press. (Original work published 1927)

Turner, B. A. (1981). Some practical aspects of qualitative data analysis: One way of organizing the cognitive processes associated with the generations of grounded theory. *Quality and Quantity, 15,* 225–247.

Tyler, S. A. (1986). Post-modern ethnography: From document of the occult to occult document. In J. Clifford & G. E. Marcus (Eds.), *Writing culture: The poetics and politics of ethnography* (pp. 122–140). Berkeley: University of California Press.

Van Maanen, J. (1988). *Tales of the field: On writing ethnography.* Chicago: University of Chicago Press.

Vidich, A. J. (1992). Boston's North End: An American epic. *Journal of Contemporary Ethnography, 21,* 80–102.

Weitzman, E. A., & Miles, M. B. (1995). *Computer programs for qualitative data analysis: A software sourcebook.* Thousand Oaks, CA: Sage.

Whyte, W. F. (1992). In defense of *Street corner society. Journal of Contemporary Ethnography, 21,* 52–68.

Wilson, H. S., & Hutchinson, S. A. (1991). Triangulation of qualitative methods: Heideggerian hermeneutics and grounded theory. *Qualitative Health Research, 1,* 263–276.

Zorbaugh, H. (1929). *The Gold Coast and the slum.* Chicago: University of Chicago Press.

14

Narrative Inquiry

Multiple Lenses, Approaches, Voices

Susan E. Chase

During the early 1990s, as I struggled to interpret and represent *as narrative* my interviews with women school superintendents, I relied on a rich interdisciplinary tradition defending the study of individuals in their social and historical context. That tradition includes works as diverse as Thomas and Znaniecki's (1918/1927) *The Polish Peasant in Europe and America*, Garfinkel's (1967) ethnomethodological study of Agnes, and the Personal Narratives Group's (1989) feminist explorations of women's journals, life histories, and autobiographies. In this tradition, researchers begin with the biographical leg of Mills's (1959) famous trilogy—biography, history, and society. Mills called these three "the co-ordinate points of the proper study of man" (p. 143). Of course, I was also writing after the narrative turn, and so Barthes's (1977) dramatic words—"narrative is present in every age, in every place, in every society" (p.79)—had already infiltrated sociological theory. And yet I found few empirical sociological studies based on interview material that could serve as methodological models for the particular way in which I wanted to treat the women's interviews as narratives. Most helpful to me was Riessman's (1990) approach to interview material in *Divorce Talk*.[1]

These days, narrative inquiry in the social sciences is flourishing. Signs of this burgeoning interest include an interdisciplinary journal called *Narrative Inquiry*, a book series on *The Narrative Study of Lives*, and professional conferences specifically showcasing narrative work.[2] Nonetheless, I still get the sense that narrative inquiry is a field in the making. Researchers new to this field will find a rich but diffuse tradition, multiple methodologies in various stages of development, and plenty of opportunities for exploring new ideas, methods, and questions.

In preparation for writing this chapter, I gathered and read as many examples of what might be called narrative inquiry as I could, and I wrestled with various ways of defining the contours of narrative inquiry, both past and present. Although qualitative researchers now routinely refer to any prosaic data (as opposed to close-ended or short-answer data) as "narrative" (Polkinghorne, 1995), I present narrative *inquiry* as a particular type—a subtype—of qualitative inquiry. Contemporary narrative inquiry can be characterized as an amalgam of interdisciplinary analytic lenses, diverse disciplinary approaches, and both traditional and innovative methods—all revolving around an interest in biographical particulars as narrated by the one who lives them.

[. . .]

Pivotal Terms

The terms that narrative researchers use to describe the empirical material they study have flexible meanings, beginning with *narrative* itself. A narrative may be oral or written and may be elicited or heard during fieldwork, an interview, or a naturally occurring conversation. In any of these situations, a narrative may be (a) a short topical story about a particular event and specific characters such as an encounter with a friend, boss, or doctor; (b) an extended story about a significant aspect of one's life such as schooling, work, marriage, divorce, childbirth, an illness, a trauma, or participation in a war or social movement; or (c) a narrative of one's entire life, from birth to the present.

Life history is the more specific term that researchers use to describe an extensive autobiographical narrative, in either oral or written form, that covers all or most of a life. But *life history* can also refer to a social science text that presents a person's biography. In that case, *life story* may be used to describe the autobiographical story in the person's own words (for the complexity of these terms, see Bertaux, 1981; Frank, 2000). Yet some researchers treat the terms *life history* and *life story* as interchangeable, defining both as birth-to-present narratives (Atkinson, 2002). For still others, a life story is a narrative about a specific significant aspect of a person's life, as in the second definition (b) in the preceding paragraph. A life story may also revolve around an epiphanal event (Denzin, 1989) or a turning point (McAdams, Josselson, & Lieblich, 2001) in one's life. Instead of *life story*, some researchers use *personal narrative* to describe a compelling topical narration (Riessman, 2002a). They may use this term to indicate that they are not talking about literary narratives or folklore (but see Narayan & George, 2002, for the intermingling of personal narrative and folklore). *Personal narrative* can also refer in a more generic sense to diaries, journals, and letters as well as to autobiographical stories (Personal Narratives Group, 1989).

Historians use *oral history* to describe interviews in which the focus is not on historical events themselves—historians' traditional interest—but rather on the meanings that events hold for those who lived through them (McMahan & Rogers, 1994; Thompson, 1978/2000). A *testimonio* is a type of oral history, life history, or life story; it is an explicitly political narrative that describes and resists oppression (Beverley, 2000; Tierney, 2000). For the past few decades, *testimonio* has been especially associated with the (usually oral) narratives of Latin American activists in revolutionary movements (e.g., Menchú, 1984; Moyano, 2000; Randall, 1981, 1994, 2003). Finally, a *performance narrative* transforms any oral or written narrative into a public performance, either on stage (Madison, 1998; McCall & Becker, 1990) or in alternative textual forms such as poems and fiction (Denzin, 1997, 2000, 2003; Richardson, 2002).

Sociology and Early Life Histories

The predecessors of today's narrative researchers include the Chicago School sociologists who collected life histories and other personal documents during the 1920s and 1930s.[3] Thomas and Znaniecki's (1918/1927) *The Polish Peasant* is frequently cited as the first significant sociological use of life history. In the final 300 pages of the second volume, Thomas and Znaniecki presented the "life record" of a Polish immigrant, Wladek Wiszniewski, whom they paid to write his autobiography p. 1912). The sociologists' voice preceded the life record with nearly 800 pages on the disorganization and reorganization of social life in Poland as well as the organization and disorganization of social life after immigration to the United States. They also added explanatory footnotes throughout Wiszniewski's life record.

In explaining their interest in life records, Thomas and Znaniecki (1918/1927) stated,

> A social institution can be fully understood only if we do not limit ourselves to the abstract study of its formal organization, but analyze the way in which it appears in the personal experience of various members of the group and follow the influence which it has upon their lives. (p. 1833)

Indeed, they claimed, "Personal life records, as complete as possible, constitute the *perfect* type of sociological material" (p. 1832). In their view, social scientists turned to other materials and methods because of practical difficulties; it is too time-consuming to get sufficient numbers of life records on every sociological issue, and it is too time-consuming to analyze them. Nonetheless, some sociologists, especially in Poland, made the effort. Józef Chalasiński, a follower of Znaniecki, championed the method of using public competitions to solicit hundreds of ordinary people's autobiographies. His research demonstrated that "the formation and transformations of whole social classes (peasants, workers) could be described and understood by analyzing sets of autobiographies" (Bertaux, 1981, p. 3; see also Chalasiński, 1981).[4]

The Polish Peasant was followed by other Chicago School studies based on life histories, especially of juvenile delinquents and criminals (e.g., Shaw, 1930/1966; Sutherland, 1937). These sociologists had some interest in the individual's subjective experience, but they were primarily interested in explaining the individual's behavior as an interactive process between the individual and his or her sociocultural environment. Although studies of urban boys' and men's lives are frequently cited in reviews of the life history method, Hagood's (1939) *Mothers of the South: Portraiture of the White Tenant Farm Woman* also offers an example of early narrative methods.[5]

During the 1940s and 1950s, mainstream American sociology favored abstract theory along with survey and statistical research methods, and the life history method was marginalized. At this point, sociologists were more interested in positivist methods that use single studies to confirm or disconfirm predetermined hypotheses than in research based on the "mosaic" model offered by the Chicago School—studies that may produce no definitive conclusions of their own but that contribute to a larger collective research endeavor (Becker, 1966, pp. viii–ix, xvi–xviii; Bertaux, 1981, p. 1; Denzin, 1970, p. 219).

Anthropology and Early Life Histories

Anthropological use of the life history method emerged early in the 20th century, mostly as a way of recording American Indian cultures that were assumed to be nearly extinct.[6] During the 1920s, life history became a rigorous anthropological method with the publication of Radin's (1926) *Crashing Thunder* (Langness & Frank, 1981, pp. 17–18, 20). Crashing Thunder, a middle-aged Winnebago man in financial difficulty, wrote his autobiography for a fee in two sessions (Lurie, 1961, p. 92). Radin (1926) supplied the cultural context and heavy annotations of the life record.

During the early period, anthropologists gathered life histories as a way of understanding cultural facts, choosing to study people who they assumed were representative of their cultural group (Langness & Frank, 1981, p. 24). By the mid-1940s, under the influence of Edward Sapir, Ruth Benedict, and Margaret Mead, many anthropologists had developed a stronger interest in individuals per se and especially in the relationship between cultural context and distinct personality types (Langness, 1965, pp. 11, 19; see also DuBois, 1944/ 1960; Kardiner, 1945). Anthropologists also used life histories to present insiders' views of culture and daily life, as exemplified by Lewis's (1961) publication of the life stories of the members of one Mexican family in *The Children of Sánchez*. In this and other works, Lewis also developed the controversial concept of "the culture of poverty" (Langness & Frank, 1981, pp. 24–25). Finally, anthropologists have used life histories to study cultural change, as brought about either by contact between different cultural groups or as the result of revolutionary movements (Langness, 1965, p. 16; Langness & Frank, 1981, pp. 24–27). Although the majority of early anthropological life histories were studies of men, some anthropologists—mostly women—used life history methods to study women's lives (Watson & Watson-Franke, 1985, chap. 6).

Feminism and Personal Narratives

The liberation movements of the 1960s and 1970s helped to reinvigorate the life history method. For example, the civil rights movement led to renewed interest in slave narratives, many of which had been collected from 1936 to 1938 by unemployed writers working with the Federal Writers' Project of the Works Project Administration. More than 2,000 oral histories of former slaves had been deposited in the Library of Congress, but only a glimpse of them was available to the public in Botkin's (1945) *Lay My Burden Down: A Folk History of Slavery*. Two and a half decades later, activists and academics returned to these narratives, and sociologist Rawick (1972) published them in their entirety in 18 volumes of *The American Slave: A Composite Autobiography*. In the introductory volume, he offered a beginning toward a social history of black community life under slavery, based on the narratives, countering previous academic treatment of slaves as voiceless victims (p. xiv).[7]

The second wave of the women's movement played a major role in the renaissance of life history methods and the study of personal narratives such as journals and auto-biographies.[8] As feminists critiqued the androcentric assumptions of social science—that men's lives and activities are more important than those of women and/or constitute the norm from which women's lives and activities deviate—they began to treat women's personal narratives as "essential primary documents for feminist research" (Personal Narratives Group, 1989, p. 4). By listening to previously silenced voices, feminist researchers challenged social science knowledge about society, culture, and history (Belenky, Clinchy, Goldberger, & Tarule, 1986; Franz & Stewart, 1994; Gluck, 1979; Gluck & Patai, 1991; Personal Narratives Group, 1989; Reinharz, 1992, chap. 7; Reinharz & Chase, 2002; Watson & Watson-Franke, 1985, chap. 6). Through the influence of working-class feminists and feminists of color (among others), race, ethnicity, nationality, social class, sexual orientation, and disability came to the fore as central aspects of women's lives (for an extensive overview, see Geiger, 1986). The first decade or so of second-wave academic feminism produced many examples of feminist research based on life histories and personal narratives (e.g., Babb & Taylor, 1981; Hunt & Winegarten, 1983; Jacobs,

1979; Ruddick & Daniels, 1977; Sexton, 1981; Sidel, 1978; for an extensive list, see Reinharz, 1992, chap. 7).

The explosion of interest in women's personal narratives was accompanied by feminist challenges to conventional assumptions about research relationships and research methods. Thomas and Znaniecki (1918/1927), and many who followed in their footsteps, had said little about how they gathered their materials, noting only that they motivated people to write their life histories through monetary rewards or public contests (Langness & Frank, 1981; Watson & Watson-Franke, 1985). In addition, despite the early life historians' apparently humanistic bent (e.g., Shaw's [1930/1966] interest in ameliorating the miserable conditions of Stanley's life as a juvenile delinquent and anthropologists' interest in recording what they assumed were disappearing cultures), from a feminist point of view, the people in these life histories appeared as distant "others" or deviant "objects" of social scientist interest. It is important to keep in mind, of course, that the early life historians were writing in positivist times, during which the social sciences were struggling to gain recognition as sciences.[9]

Feminists resisted the idea that life histories and other personal narratives were primarily useful for gathering information about historical events, cultural change, or the impact of social structures on individuals' lives. Rather, they were interested in women as social actors in their own right and in the subjective meanings that women assigned to events and conditions in their lives. Importantly, these feminist lenses opened up new understandings of historical, cultural, and social processes. Furthermore, as feminists approached women as subjects rather than as objects, they also began to consider *their* subjectivity—the role that researchers' interests and social locations play in the research relationship. Whose questions should get asked and answered? Who should get the last say? How does power operate in the research relationship? And as feminists incorporated postmodern influences, they began to ask questions—which are still pertinent today— about voice, authenticity, interpretive authority, and representation. What does it mean to hear the other's voice? In what sense do—or don't—women's life histories and personal narratives "speak for themselves"? How do interactional, social, cultural, and historical conditions mediate women's stories? In what ways are women's voices muted, multiple, and/or contradictory? Under what conditions do women develop "counternarratives" as they narrate their lives? How should researchers represent all of these voices and ideas in their written works? (Anderson & Jack, 1991; McCall & Wittner, 1990; Personal Narratives Group, 1989; Ribbens & Edwards, 1998).

Sociolinguistics and Oral Narratives

The mid-1960s saw the development of another line of inquiry that has influenced contemporary narrative research. At this time, anthropologists, sociologists, and sociolinguists (e.g., Erving Goffman, Harold Garfinkel, John Gumperz, Dell Hymes, Harvey Sacks, Emanuel Schegloff, William Labov) were exploring a "range of subject matters at the intersection of language, interaction, discourse, practical action, and inference" (Schegloff, 1997, p. 98).

A 1967 article by Labov and Waletzky, "Narrative Analysis: Oral Versions of Personal Experience," is often cited as a groundbreaking presentation of the idea that ordinary people's oral narratives of everyday experience (as opposed to full-fledged life histories, written narratives, folklore, and literary narratives) are worthy of study in themselves. In this article, Labov and Waletzky (1967/1997) argued that oral narratives are a specific form of discourse characterized by certain structures serving specific social functions. Using data from individual and focus group interviews, they claimed that narrative discourse consists of clauses that match the temporal sequence of reported events. They also identified five sociolinguistic features of oral narratives: Orientation (which informs listeners about actors, time, place, and situation), Complication (the main body of the narrative—the action), Evaluation (the point of the story), Resolution (the result of the action), and Coda (which returns the listener to the current moment).

In 1997, the *Journal of Narrative and Life History* reprinted Labov and Waletzky's 1967 article along with 47 then-current assessments of how it had influenced linguistically informed narrative inquiry since it was first published. Bruner (1997), for instance, suggested that Labov and Waletzky's "fivefold characterization of overall narrative structure transformed the study of narrative profoundly. It set many of us thinking about the cognitive representation of reality imposed by narrative structure on our experience of the world and how we evaluate that experience" (p. 64). Referring to his own influential distinction between logico-scientific and narrative modes of thought—which he had articulated in *Actual Minds, Possible Worlds* (Bruner, 1986)—Bruner (1997) added, "I happily admit that it set me thinking about narrative not simply as a form of text but as a mode of thought" (p. 64).

Many of the assessments of the 1967 article point to the limits of Labov and Waletzky's narrowly structuralist formulation. For example, Riessman (1997) gave them credit for helping her attend to the fundamental structures and functions of oral narratives in her research on people's experiences of divorce. But she found their definition of narrative much too narrow, and so she developed a typology of narrative genres such as the habitual narrative and the hypothetical narrative (pp. 155–156). These helped Riessman to show how people recount their divorce experiences differently and to discuss the connection between the form and function of their speech.

In a different vein, Schegloff (1997) critiqued Labov and Waletzky's failure to take into account the interactional context in which oral narratives are elicited and received. Over the past three decades, conversation analysts such as Schegloff have explored (among other things) how stories arise and how they function in naturally occurring conversations for an overview, see Holstein & Gubrium, 2000, chap. 7). Other sociolinguistically oriented researchers have investigated the research interview itself as a particular kind of discourse or communicative event in which narratives may be discouraged or encouraged (Briggs, 1986, 2002; Mishler, 1986). Furthermore, although Labov and Waletzky assumed a one-to-one correspondence between a narrative and the events it describes—between narrative and reality—most researchers since then have resisted this referential view of language. A central tenet of the narrative turn is that speakers *construct* events through narrative rather than simply refer to events.[10]

Despite the limitations of the original formulation, the attention that Labov and Waletzky devoted to the linguistic structures and functions of ordinary people's oral narratives served as a launching pad for diverse explorations of the sociolinguistic features of oral discourse. Many contemporary narrative researchers embrace the idea that how individuals narrate experience is as important to the meanings they communicate as is what they say.

Contemporary Narrative Inquiry

Turning to the present, I begin by outlining a set of five analytic lenses through which contemporary researchers approach empirical material. These lenses reflect the influence of the histories just reviewed and, taken as a whole, suggest the distinctiveness of narrative inquiry—how it is different from (if connected to) other forms of qualitative research.

Analytic Lenses

First, narrative researchers treat narrative—whether oral or written—as a distinct form of discourse. Narrative is retrospective meaning making—the shaping or ordering of past experience. Narrative is a way of understanding one's own and others' actions, of organizing events and objects into a meaningful whole, and of connecting and seeing the consequences of actions and events over time (Bruner, 1986; Gubrium & Holstein, 1997; Hinchman & Hinchman, 2001; Laslett, 1999; Polkinghorne, 1995). Unlike a chronology, which also reports events over time, a narrative communicates the narrator's point of view, including why the narrative is worth telling in the first place. Thus, in addition to describing what happened, narratives also express emotions, thoughts, and interpretations. Unlike editorials, policy statements, and doctrinal statements of belief, all of which also express a point of view, a narrative makes the self (the narrator) the protagonist, either as actor or as interested observer of others' actions. Finally, unlike scientific discourse, which also explains or presents an understanding of actions and events, narrative discourse highlights the uniqueness of each human action and event rather than their common properties (Bruner, 1986; Polkinghorne, 1995).

Second, narrative researchers view narratives as verbal action—as doing or accomplishing something. Among other things, narrators explain, entertain, inform, defend, complain, and confirm or challenge the status quo. Whatever the particular action, when someone tells a story, he or she shapes, constructs, and performs the self, experience, and reality. When researchers treat narration as actively creative in this way, they emphasize the narrator's voice(s). The word *voice* draws our attention to what the narrator communicates and how he or she communicates it as well as to the subject positions or social locations from which he or she speaks (Gubrium & Holstein, 2002). This combination of what, how, and where makes the narrator's voice particular. Furthermore, when researchers treat narration as actively creative and the narrator's voice as particular, they move away from questions about the factual nature of the narrator's statements. Instead, they highlight the versions of self, reality, and experience that the storyteller produces through the telling. Although narrators are accountable for the credibility of their stories, narrative researchers treat credibility and believability as something that storytellers accomplish (Holstein & Gubrium, 2000; Lincoln, 2000).

Third, narrative researchers view stories as both enabled and constrained by a range of social resources and circumstances. These include the possibilities for self and reality construction that are intelligible within the narrator's community, local setting, organizational and social memberships, and cultural and historical location. While acknowledging that every instance of narrative is particular, researchers use this lens to attend to similarities and differences across narratives. For example, they emphasize patterns in the storied selves, subjectivities, and realities that narrators create during particular times and in particular places (Brockmeier & Carbaugh, 2001; Bruner, 2002; Hatch & Wisniewski, 1995; Holstein & Gubrium, 2000).

Fourth, narrative researchers treat narratives as socially situated interactive perform-ances—as produced in this particular setting, for this particular audience, for these par-ticular purposes. A story told to an interviewer in a quiet relaxed setting will likely differ from the "same" story told to a reporter for a television news show, to a private journal that the writer assumes will never be read by others, to a roomful of people who have had similar experiences, to a social service counselor, or to the same interviewer at a different time. Here, researchers emphasize that the narrator's story is flexible, variable, and shaped in part by interaction with the audience. In other words, a narrative is a joint production of narrator and listener, whether the narrative arises in naturally occurring talk, an inter-view, or a fieldwork setting (Bauman, 1986; Briggs, 1986, 2002; Mishler, 1986).

Fifth, narrative researchers, like many other contemporary qualitative researchers, view *themselves* as narrators as they develop interpretations and find ways in which to present or publish their ideas about the narratives they studied (Denzin & Lincoln, 2000). This means that the four lenses just described make as much sense when applied to the researcher as they do when applied to the researched. Breaking from traditional social science practice, narrative researchers are likely to use the first person when presenting their work, thereby emphasizing their own narrative action. As narrators, then, researchers develop meaning out of, and some sense of order in, the material they studied; they develop their own voice(s) as they construct others' voices and realities; they narrate "results" in ways that are both enabled and constrained by the social resources and circumstances embedded in their disciplines, cultures, and historical moments; and they write or perform their work for particular audiences. The idea that researchers are narra-tors opens up a range of complex issues about voice, representation, and interpretive authority (Emihovich, 1995; Hertz, 1997; Josselson, 1996a; Krieger, 1991; Tierney, 2002; Tierney & Lincoln, 1997).

Theoretically, it is possible to treat these five analytic lenses as distinct. However, as researchers go about the business of hearing, collecting, interpreting, and representing narratives, they are well aware of the interconnectedness of the lenses. As they do their work, researchers may emphasize one or another lens or their intersections, or they may shift back and forth among the lenses, depending on their specific approaches to empirical narrative material.

Diverse Approaches

Although narrative inquiry as a whole is interdisciplinary, specific approaches tend to be shaped by interests and assumptions embedded in researchers' disciplines. Without claim-ing to be comprehensive or exhaustive in my categories, I briefly outline five major approaches in contemporary narrative inquiry.[11] It is here that we see diversity and multi-plicity in this field of inquiry.

Some psychologists have developed an approach that focuses on the relationship between individuals' life stories and the quality of their lives, especially their psychosocial development.[12] In addition to gathering extensive life stories,[13] these researchers some-times use conventional psychological tests. For example, in a study of adults' narratives about turning points in their lives, McAdams and Bowman (2001) found that those who score high on conventional measures of psychological well-being and generativity (i.e., commitment to caring for and contributing to future generations) are likely to tell "narratives of redemption," that is, to construct negative events as having beneficial consequences. Conversely, those who score low in terms of psychological well-being and generativity are more likely to tell "narratives of contamination," that is, to present good experiences as having negative outcomes. While acknowledging that biographical, social, cultural, and historical circumstances condition the stories that people tell about themselves, narrative psychologists look for evidence (e.g., in a person's score on conventional measures) that the stories that people tell affect how they live their lives. They emphasize "the formative effects of narratives" and propose that some stories cripple, and others enable, an efficacious sense of self in relation to life problems or traumas (Rosenwald & Ochberg, 1992, p. 6).

In their interpretations, these psychological researchers tend to emphasize *what* the story is about—its plot, characters, and sometimes the structure or sequencing of its content. Along these lines, McAdams (1997) argued that the content of a life story embodies a person's identity and that both develop and change over time. This idea was exemplified by Josselson's (1996b) longitudinal study of how women revise their stories *and* their lives as they move through their 20s, 30s, and 40s.

A second approach has been developed by sociologists who highlight the "identity work" that people engage in as they construct selves within specific institutional, organizational, discursive, and local cultural contexts. Unlike the psychologists just described, who conceptualize the life story as distinguishable from—yet having an impact on—the life, these researchers often treat narratives *as* lived experience. Thus, they are as interested in the *hows* of storytelling as they are in the *whats* of storytelling—in the narrative practices by which storytellers make use of available resources to construct recognizable selves. They often study narratives that are produced in specific organizational settings such as prisons, courts, talk shows, human service agencies, self-help groups, and therapy centers (Gubrium & Holstein, 2001; Holstein & Gubrium, 2000; Miller, 1997; Pollner & Stein, 1996). For example, in her study of support groups for women who have experienced domestic violence, Loseke (2001) showed how group facilitators often encourage battered women to transform their narratives into "formula stories" about wife abuse. She found that many women resist the counselors' version of their experience and resist identifying themselves as "battered women," and she suggested that the problem may lie less in women's psychological denial of their victimization and more in the formula story's failure to encompass the complexities of lived experience (p. 122). As part of everyday lived experience, narratives themselves are messy and complex.

A major conceptual touchstone in this sociological approach is the "deprivatization" of personal experience. This approach highlights the wide range of institutional and organizational settings—some more and some less coercive—that shape "the selves we live by." A person's movement across a variety of settings creates further constraints as well as a plethora of options for narrating the self in a postmodern world (Holstein & Gubrium, 2000).

The third approach is also sociological.[14] Here, narrative researchers share the interest in the *hows* and *whats* of storytelling but base their inquiry on intensive interviews about specific aspects of people's lives rather than on conversations in specific organizational contexts. These researchers are interested in how people communicate meaning through a range of linguistic practices, how their stories are embedded in the interaction between researcher and narrator, how they make sense of personal experience in relation to culturally and historically specific discourses, and how they draw on, resist, and/or transform those discourses as they narrate their selves, experiences, and realities.

Examples of this approach include Langellier's (2001) study of how a woman performs the self and resists medical discourse as she comes to terms with breast cancer, Mishler's (1999) exploration of adult identity formation in craft artists' work histories, Foley and Faircloth's (2003) study of how midwives both use and resist medical discourse to legitimize their work, Riessman's (1990) examination of women's and men's divorce stories in relation to discourse about marriage and gender, Bell's (1999) exploration of how diethylstilbestrol (DES)-exposed daughters negotiate tensions between scientific and feminist discourses, Luttrell's (1997) analysis of the gendered and racialized identities of working-class mothers who return to school to get general equivalency diplomas (GEDs), and Lempert's (1994) analysis of how a woman survivor of domestic violence narrates self-transformation in relation to her physical, psychological, social, and cultural environments.

These researchers often produce detailed transcripts to study interactional processes in the interview as well as linguistic and thematic patterns throughout the narrative. A major goal of this sociological approach is showing that people create a range of narrative strategies in relation to their discursive environments, that is, that individuals' stories are constrained but not determined by hegemonic discourses. Another goal is showing that narratives provide a window to the contradictory and shifting nature of hegemonic discourses, which we tend to take for granted as stable monolithic forces.

Anthropologists have led the way in a fourth approach to narrative inquiry. Some call this approach *narrative ethnography*, which is a transformation of both the ethnographic and life history methods. Like traditional ethnography, this approach involves long-term involvement in a culture or community; like life history, it focuses heavily on one individual or on a small number of individuals. What makes narrative ethnography distinct is that both the researcher and the researched "are presented together within a single multivocal text focused on the character and process of the human encounter" (Tedlock, 1992, p. xiii).

Myerhoff's (1979/1994) *Number Our Days* is an early example. In this study of a community of elderly immigrant Jews in California, Myerhoff highlighted the life of Shmuel Goldman, a tailor and one of the most learned members of the community. At the same time, she analyzed her subjectivity as well as her relationship with those she studied. Although Myerhoff presented page after page of Shmuel's life stories "verbatim," she also showed how her questions and interruptions shaped Shmuel's narrative. And she went further. She described her distaste on observing selfish bickering over food at a community lunch, and then—with the help of a dream—she reinterpreted those actions as reflecting the social and psychological conditions of community members' lives (pp. 188–189). When Shmuel died during the course of the study, Myerhoff wrote a conversation that she imagined she and Shmuel would have had about another community member's death (pp. 228–231). Finally, she told her own story of how her grandmother's stories influenced her own life and research (pp. 237–241).

In more recent narrative ethnographies, researchers are even more explicit about the intersubjectivity of the researcher and the researched as they work to understand the other's voice, life, and culture (Behar, 1993/2003; Frank, 2000; Shostak, 2000b). A major goal of narrative ethnography is moving to the center of empirical anthropological work the issues of voice, intersubjectivity, interpretive authority, and representation.

A fifth approach to narrative inquiry is found in *autoethnography*, where researchers also turn the analytic lens on themselves and their interactions with others, but here researchers write, interpret, and/or perform their own narratives about culturally significant experiences (Crawley, 2002; Ellis & Berger, 2002; Ellis & Bochner, 1996; Ellis & Flaherty, 1992). Autoethnographers who share an interest in a topic sometimes engage in collaborative research by conducting interviews with each other, tape-recording conversations with each other, and/or writing separate accounts of their experiences. For example, Ellis and Bochner (1992) narrated separate and joint accounts of their experience of Ellis's unwanted pregnancy and subsequent abortion. And Ellis, Kiesinger, and Tillmann-Healy (1997) used an interactive interviewing method to investigate Kiesinger's and Tillmann-Healy's experiences of bulimia and Ellis's responses to their accounts.

Autoethnographers often present their work in alternative textual forms such as layered accounts (Ellis & Berger, 2002; Ellis & Bochner, 1996), and many have experimented with performing their narratives as plays, as poems, or in various other forms (Denzin, 1997, 2000, 2003; McCall & Becker, 1990; Richardson, 2002). Sometimes autoethnographers resist analysis altogether, leaving interpretation up to the audiences of their performances (Hilbert, 1990). The goal of autoethnography, and of many performance narratives, is to *show* rather than to *tell* (Denzin, 2003, p. 203) and, thus, to disrupt the politics of traditional research relationships, traditional forms of representation, and traditional social science orientations to audiences.[15]

Methodological Issues in Contemporary Narrative Inquiry

The Research Relationship: Narrator and Listener in Interview-Based Studies

All narrative researchers attend to the research relationship, but those whose studies are based on in-depth interviews aim specifically at transforming the interviewer–interviewee relationship into one of narrator and listener. This involves a shift in understanding the nature of interview questions and answers. These researchers often illustrate this shift by telling about how they initially ignored, grew impatient with, or got thrown off track by interviewees' stories—and later realized their mistake (Anderson & Jack, 1991; Mishler, 1986; Narayan & George, 2002; Riessman, 1990, 2002a). For instance, in *Narrating the Organization*, Czarniawska (1997) described how she used to ask questions that encouraged interviewees to generalize and compare their experiences, for example, "What are the most acute problems you are experiencing today?" and "Can you compare your present situation with that of 2 years ago?" She found, however, that most people "would break through my structure" by offering stories about the background of current circumstances. "This used to bring me to the verge of panic—'How to bring them to the point?'— whereas now I have at least learned that this *is* the point" (p. 28).

The moral of Czarniawska's account, and of similar accounts, is that the stories people tell *constitute* the empirical material that interviewers need if they are to understand how people create meanings out of events in their lives. To think of an interviewee as a narrator is to make a conceptual shift away from the idea that interviewees have answers to researchers' questions and toward the idea that interviewees are narrators with stories to tell and voices of their own.

Let me pause to say that this idea need not reflect the romantic notion, critiqued by

Atkinson and Silverman (1997), that "the open-ended interview offers the opportunity for an authentic gaze into the soul of another" (p. 305). Similarly, Gubrium and Holstein (2002) critiqued the notion of a narrator's "own" voice, which implies that narrators' stories are not socially mediated. I contend that conceiving of an interviewee as a narrator is not an interest in the other's "authentic" self or unmediated voice but rather an interest in the other as a narrator of his or her particular biographical experiences as he or she understands them. Although any narration is always enabled and constrained by a host of social circumstances, *during interviews* the narrative researcher needs to orient to the particularity of the narrator's story and voice.

This conceptual shift has consequences for data collection (as well as for interpretive processes, which I will get to next). When researchers conceive of interviewees as narrators, they not only attend to the stories that people *happen* to tell during interviews but also work at *inviting* stories. Although some interviewees tell stories whether or not researchers want to hear them, other interviewees might not take up the part of narrator unless they are specifically and carefully invited to do so.

Paradoxically, assumptions embedded in our "interview society" may discourage interviewees from becoming narrators in the sense that I am developing that idea here. Denzin and Lincoln (2000) suggested that we live "in a society whose members seem to believe that interviews generate useful information about lived experience and its meanings" (p. 633; see also Atkinson & Silverman, 1997; Gubrium & Holstein, 2002). Yet interviewees often speak in generalities rather than specifics, even when talking about their experiences, because they assume (often accurately) that researchers are interested in what is general rather than particular about their experience (Weiss, 1994). As Czarniawska (1997) stated, researchers often "ask people in the field to compare, to abstract, to generalize" (p. 28). Sacks (1989) called these "sociological questions"—questions that are organized around the researcher's interest in general social processes—even though the questions may be couched in everyday language (p. 88). When researchers ask sociological questions, they are likely to get sociological answers—generalities about the interviewee's or others' experiences. The interview questions that qualitative researchers include in appendixes to their studies show how often they encourage interviewees to speak generally and abstractly.[16]

How, then, do narrative researchers invite interviewees to become narrators, that is, to tell stories about biographical particulars that are meaningful to them? I have described this as a matter of framing the interview as a whole with a broad question about whatever story the narrator has to tell about the issue at hand (Chase, 1995b, 2003). This requires a certain kind of preparation before interviewing; it requires knowing what is "storyworthy" in the narrator's social setting, an idea that is most easily grasped through examples from non-Western cultures. Grima (1991), for instance, found that Paxtun women in Northwest Pakistan attributed the most value to stories of suffering and personal hardship and that these stories were intimately connected to an honorable identity. If a woman had no such experiences, she had no story to tell. Similarly, in Rosaldo's (1976) anthropological fieldwork with Tukbaw, an Ilongot man in the Philippines, the researcher told of realizing that he had come close to "assuming that every man has his life story within him" and that the narrator himself "should be the subject of the narrative" (pp. 121–122). Although Tukbaw had plenty of stories to tell, these Western assumptions about narratives were unfamiliar to him.

Although broad cultural assumptions condition narrators' voices and the stories they have to tell, so do specific institutional, organizational, and/or discursive environments (Gubrium & Holstein, 2001). In my study of women school superintendents, for example, the fact that they are highly successful women in an overwhelmingly white- and male-dominated occupation shapes their work narratives and makes them storyworthy in a particular way. Their work narratives revolve around the juxtaposition between their individual accomplishments, on the one hand, and the gendered and racial inequities they face in their profession, on the other, and this juxtaposition makes their work narratives interesting not only to researchers and the general public but also to themselves (Chase, 1995a, pp. 14–15). Once a researcher has a sense of the broad parameters of the story that the narrator has to tell—of what is storyworthy given the narrator's social location in his or her culture, community, and/or organizational setting—the researcher can prepare for narrative interviews by developing a broad question that will invite the other to tell his or her story (Chase, 1995b). The point, of course, is not to ask for a "formula story" (Loseke, 2001); instead, the researcher needs to know the parameters of the story that others similarly situated *could* tell so as to invite *this* person's story.

In some cases, it may be easy to figure out how to frame the interview as a whole; it may be easy to articulate a broad open question that will invite a personal narrative. In my study of women superintendents, the question about their career histories turned out to be pivotal. (I confess that I did not understand it this way at the time and that my coresearcher, Colleen Bell, and I asked plenty of sociological questions along the way.) But it is not always so easy to know what the broad question will be. For example, Sacks (1989), in her ethnographic study of working-class women's militancy and leadership in the workplace, conducted interviews to understand the connection between what women learned from their families and from their workplace militancy. After her sociological interview questions produced dead ends, she finally began to ask "how they learned about work and what it meant to them." She realized that this question invited stories that showed how "family learning empowered women to rebel" (p. 88).

Being prepared to invite a story, however, is only part of the shift in the research relationship. Burgos (1989) described a transformation that may occur when an interviewee takes up the invitation to become a narrator:

> A life story comes off successfully when its narrator exercises her power upon the person who is ostensibly conducting the interview by derealising his interventions, capturing his attention, neutralizing his will, arousing his desire to learn something else, or something more, than what would be allowed by the logic of the narrative itself. (p. 33)

This statement offers a strong version of the narrator's voice as well as of the researcher's listening; in speaking from and about biographical particulars, a narrator may disrupt the assumptions that the interviewer brings to the research relationship. Thus, narrative interviewing involves a paradox. On the one hand, a researcher needs to be well prepared to ask good questions that will invite the other's particular story; on the other hand, the very idea of a particular story is that it cannot be known, predicted, or prepared for in advance. The narrator's particular story is not identical to—and may even depart radically from—what is "storyworthy" in his or her social context.

An example can be found in my own research. As Colleen Bell and I interviewed a woman superintendent who was leaving her job for a less prestigious and less stressful position, she showed us family photographs and began to tell stories about a family member who had a serious physical disability. At the time, I experienced this as a digression from her work narrative, and I waited patiently for her to get back to it. Later, as I reviewed the interview tapes, I realized that her sharing of family photos and stories was integral, not peripheral, to her work narrative; her career move "down," away from the exhausting and very public work of the superintendency, was for her a move toward a more balanced work—family relationship. If I had been open to understanding the family photos and stories as central to her work narrative, I might have prompted for and heard a fuller account of the particular way in which this woman narrated her career history. She was speaking in a different voice, or from a different subject position, from what I had anticipated; she disrupted my assumption about the "logic" of a career narrative.

The Interpretive Process in Interview-Based Studies

When it comes to interpreting narratives heard during interviews, narrative researchers begin with narrators' voices and stories, thereby extending the narrator–listener relationship and the active work of listening into the interpretive process. This is a move away from a traditional theme-oriented method of analyzing qualitative material. Rather than locating distinct themes *across* interviews, narrative researchers listen first to the voices *within* each narrative.[17]

I realized the importance of this shift as I interpreted the women superintendents' interviews. At first, I tried to organize the transcripts into themes about work (e.g., aspirations, competence, confidence) and themes about inequality (e.g., barriers, discrimination, responses). But I soon found that it was difficult to separate a woman's talk about work and her talk about inequality. Finally it dawned on me that there was a connection between a woman's construction of self in one story (e.g., about her individual strength as a competent leader) and her construction of self in other stories (e.g., about her individual strength in fighting discrimination). Thus, I began to focus on connections among the various stories that a woman told over the course of the interview. I used the term *narrative strategy* to refer to the specific way in which each woman juxtaposed her stories about achievement and her stories about gendered and/or racial inequalities, that is, how she navigated the disjunction between individualistic discourse about achievement and group-oriented discourse about inequality (Chase, 1995a, pp. 23–25). The term *narrative strategy* draws attention to the complexity within each woman's voice—to the various subject positions each woman takes up—as well as to diversity among women's voices because each woman's narrative strategy is particular.

Narrative researchers who base their work on interviews use a variety of methods for listening to—for interpreting—complexity and multiplicity within narrators' voices. For example, in their study of adolescent girls "at risk" for early pregnancy and dropping out of school, Taylor, Gilligan, and Sullivan (1995) described an explicitly feminist Listening Guide that requires reading each interview four times. First, they attended to "the overall shape of the narrative and the research relationship"; second, to the narrator's first-person voice—how and where she uses "I"; third and fourth, to "contrapuntal voices"—voices that express psychological development, on the one hand, and psychological risk and loss, on the other (pp. 29–31). In contrast, Bamberg (1997) focused on three levels of narrative positioning: how narrators position self and others (e.g., as protagonists, as antagonists, as victims, as perpetrators), how narrators position self in relation to the audience, and how narrators "position themselves to themselves," that is, construct "a [local] answer to the question 'Who am I?' " (p. 337).

In one way or another, then, narrative researchers listen to the narrator's voices—to the subject positions, interpretive practices, ambiguities, and complexities—*within* each narrator's story. This process usually includes attention to the "narrative linkages" that a storyteller develops between the biographical particulars of his or her life, on the one hand, and the resources and constraints in his or her environment for self and reality construction, on the other (Holstein & Gubrium, 2000, p. 108). Rather than unitary, fixed, or authentic selves, these researchers suggest that narrators construct "nonunitary subjectivities" (Bloom & Munro, 1995), "revised" identities (Josselson, 1996b), "permanently unsettled identities" (Stein, 1997), and "troubled identities" (Gubrium & Holstein, 2001).

Researchers' Voices and Narrative Strategies

Implicit in my discussion of how the researcher listens to the narrator's voice—both during the interview and while interpreting it—is the *researcher's* voice. Here, I return to issues I raised under the fifth analytic lens—issues of voice, interpretive authority, and representation. To sort out a range of possibilities, I develop a typology of three voices or narrative strategies that contemporary narrative researchers deploy as they wrestle with the question of how to use their voice(s) to interpret and represent the narrator's voice(s). My typology is not an exhaustive and rigid classification of every possible narrative strategy; rather, it is a flexible device for understanding the diversity in narrative researchers' voices. In practice, researchers may move back and forth among them.

The Researcher's Authoritative Voice

Many narrative researchers develop an authoritative voice in their writing, including those I just described in the section on interpretive processes in interview-based studies and those I described previously in the section on diverse approaches as taking psychological and sociological approaches (the first three approaches). This narrative strategy connects and separates the researcher's and narrator's voices in a particular way. Sociologists usually present long stretches from narrators' stories or long excerpts of naturally occurring conversation, followed by their interpretations. Psychologists are more likely to offer long summaries of narrators' stories, followed by their interpretations. In each case, in the texts they create, researchers connect or intermingle their voices with narrators' voices.

At the same time, these researchers separate their voices from narrators' voices through their interpretations. They assert an authoritative interpretive voice on the grounds that they have a different interest from the narrators in the narrators' stories. For example, during an interview, both narrator and listener are interested in developing the fullness and particularity of the narrator's story, but when it comes to interpreting, the researcher turns to *how* and *what* questions that open up particular ways of understanding what the narrator is communicating through his or her story. These questions are about narrative processes that narrators typically take for granted as they tell their stories such as their use of cultural, institutional, or organizational discourses for making sense of experience, their development of narrative strategies or narrative linkages in relation to conflicting discourses, their communication of meaning through linguistic features of talk, and/or their reconstruction of psychological issues through particular metaphors or subjugated storylines (Brockmeier & Carbaugh, 2001; Capps & Ochs, 1995; Chase, 1996; Gubrium & Holstein, 1997; Hinchman & Hinchman, 2001; Holstein & Gubrium, 2000; Ochberg, 1996; Rosenwald & Ochberg, 1992).

By writing with an authoritative voice, these researchers are vulnerable to the criticism that they "privilege the analyst's listening ear" at the narrator's expense (Denzin, 1997, p. 249). After all, as narrators work to make sense of their experiences through narration, they do not talk about "the selves we live by," "identity work," "nonunitary subjectivities," "discursive constraints," or "hegemonic discourses." Nor do researchers talk this way as they narrate stories in *their* everyday lives. But I prefer (in part because my work fits here) to understand these researchers as making visible and audible taken-for-granted practices, processes, and structural and cultural features of our everyday social worlds. The socio-logical concepts that researchers develop serve that aim. Ochberg (1996) articulated this point from a psychological perspective: "Interpretation reveals what one [the narrator] might say if only one could speak freely, but we can see this only if we are willing to look beyond what our informants tell us in so many words" (p. 98).

By taking up an authoritative sociological or psychological voice, the researcher speaks differently from, but not disrespectfully of, the narrator's voice. Czarniawska (2002) sug-gested that "the justice or injustice done to the original narratives depends on the attitude of the researcher and on the precautions he or she takes" (p. 743). In discussing "narrative responsibility and respect," she recommended that researchers attend to diversity in the stories that various narrators tell, to dominant and marginal readings of narrators' stories, and to narrators' responses (including opposition) to the researchers' interpretations (pp. 742–744).[18] It bears emphasizing that when these researchers present extensive quota-tions from narrator's stories, they make room for readers' alternative interpretations (Laslett, 1999; Riessman, 2002).

The Researcher's Supportive Voice

At the other end of an imaginary continuum, some narrative researchers develop a sup-portive voice that pushes the narrator's voice into the limelight. This is characteristic of Latin American testimonios. For example, in *I Rigoberta Menchú; An Indian Woman in Guatemala* (Menchú, 1984), the translator, Ann Wright, offered a short preface, and anthropologist Elisabeth Burgos-Debray wrote an introduction in which she described how she conducted and edited the interviews with Menchú. But the majority of the book consists of Menchú's uninterrupted stories. Diana Miloslavich Tupac developed a simi-larly supportive voice as editor and annotator of the work and autobiography of martyred Peruvian activist Maria Elena Moyano (Moyano, 2000). Significantly, these two testi-monios named the narrators—Menchú and Moyano—as the books' authors. Other testimonios, especially those that include two or more narrators, name the researchers as the authors (e.g., Randall, 1981, 1994, 2003).

Researchers who publish oral histories or life histories may also use a muted supportive voice. For instance, in Shostak's (1981/2000a) introduction and epilogue to *Nisa: The Life and Words of a !Kung Woman*, she described her research with Nisa and the !Kung people, and she began each chapter with anthropological commentary. But the majority of the book consists of Nisa's stories (see also Blauner, 1989; Gwaltney, 1980/1993; Terkel, 1995).

When researchers present performance narratives, they may also deploy supportive voices. For example, Madison (1998) described a theatrical performance of the personal narratives of two women cafeteria workers who led a strike for better pay and working conditions at the University of North Carolina. Although the strike took place in 1968, the public performance of the narratives took place 25 years later to a packed audience during the university's bicentennial celebration. Both women were in the audience, and after the performance they received "a thunderous and lengthy standing ovation" (p. 280) as well as attention from the local media. On the occasion of the performance, the researcher's voice as interviewer and editor of the women's narratives was muted; the performance highlighted the women's voices and opened possibilities for political and civic engagement on the part of the women, the audience, and the performers.[19]

In each of these cases—testimonio, oral history, life history, and performance narrative—the researcher (and translator, who is sometimes—but not always—the same person) makes decisions about how to translate and transcribe the narrator's story, which parts of the story to include in the final product, and how to organize and edit those parts into a text or performance. And yet, because the goal of this narrative strategy is to bring the narrator's story to the public—to get the narrator's story heard—researchers do not usually dwell on how they engaged in these interpretive processes. Or if they do, they do so elsewhere. For example, in an article written after *Nisa* was published, Shostak (1989) discussed the complexities of these interpretive decisions, including the way in which she presented three voices in the book: Nisa's first-person voice, Shostak's anthropological voice, and Shostak's voice "as a young American woman experiencing another world" (pp. 230–231). Along somewhat different lines, Madison (1998, pp. 277–278) explained the idea of the "performance of possibilities," which underlies performance narratives and which provides a strong framework during the performance itself.

These researchers may encounter the criticism that they romanticize the narrator's voice as "authentic" (Atkinson & Silverman, 1997). At its best, however, this narrative strategy aims not for establishing authenticity but rather for creating a self-reflective and respectful distance between researchers' and narrators' voices. There is a time and there is a place, these researchers might say, for highlighting narrators' voices and for moving temporarily to the margins the ways in which researchers (along with a host of social, cultural, and historical circumstances) have already conditioned those voices.

The Researcher's Interactive Voice

A third narrative strategy displays the complex interaction—the intersubjectivity—between researchers' and narrators' voices. These researchers examine *their* voices—their subject positions, social locations, interpretations, and personal experiences—through the refracted medium of narrators' voices. This narrative strategy characterizes narrative ethnographies as well as some autoethnographies.

Frank (2000) used this narrative strategy in *Venus on Wheels: Two Decades of Dialogue on Disability, Biography, and Being Female in America*, in which she presented her long-term relationship with Diane DeVries, a woman who was born without arms and legs. Frank not only presented DeVries's stories about living with her disability but also investigated her own interest in DeVries's stories:

> In choosing to write about the life of Diane DeVries, I had to ask myself how it was that, as an anthropologist, I chose not to travel to some remote place, but to stay at home and study one individual, one with a congenital absence of limbs. (p. 85)

Through reflection on her experiences of others' disabilities, her own disabilities, and emotional lack and loss in her own life, Frank realized that "I had expected to find a victim in Diane" but instead found "a survivor" (p. 87).

Interestingly, in *Return to Nisa*, Shostak (2000b) developed the same narrative strategy while moving in the opposite geographic direction. Whereas Frank needed to understand why she chose to "stay at home," Shostak needed to understand why, after being diagnosed with breast cancer, she felt compelled to leave her husband and three young children to spend a month in Botswana with Nisa and the other !Kung people whom she had not seen for 14 years. In *Return to Nisa*, shostak wrote not only about Nisa's life during the intervening years but also about her own complex interest in reconnecting with Nisa, who (among other things) is a well-respected healer.

In narrative ethnographies and autoethnographies, researchers make themselves vulnerable in the text (Behar, 1996; Krieger, 1991). They include extensive discussions of their emotions, thoughts, research relationships, and their unstable interpretive decisions. They include embarrassing and even shameful incidents. Indeed, these researchers are vulnerable to the criticism that they are self-indulgent and that they air dirty laundry that nobody wants to see. Yet they ground these practices in the idea that researchers need to understand themselves if they are to understand how they interpret narrators' stories *and* that readers need to understand *researchers'* stories (about their intellectual and personal relationships with narrators as well as with the cultural phenomena at hand) if readers are to understand narrators' stories. These researchers aim to undermine the myth of the invisible omniscient author (Tierney, 2002; Tierney & Lincoln, 1997).

The Particular and the General

Despite differences in their narrative strategies for interpreting and representing narrators' voices, narrative researchers have in common the practice of devoting much more space in their written work to fewer individuals than do other qualitative researchers. Many anthropologists have written books based on the individual's life story (e.g., Behar, 2003; Crapanzano, 1980; Frank, 2000; Shostak, 2000a, 2000b).[20] And many sociologists, psychologists, and other narrative researchers have based books, book chapters, and articles on a small number of narratives (e.g., Bell, 1999; Bobel, 2002, chap. 1; Capps & Ochs, 1995; Chase, 1995a, 2001; DeVault, 1999, chap. 5; Ferguson, 2001, pp. 135–161; Josselson, 1996b, chaps. 4–7; Langellier, 2001; Lempert, 1994; Liebow, 1993, pp. 251–309; Luttrell, 2003, chap. 4; Mishler, 1999; Riessman, 1990, chap. 3; Rosier, 2000; Stromberg, 1993, chaps. 3–6; Wozniak, 2002, chaps. 2 and 9).

The question of whether and how an individual's narrative (or a small group of individuals' narratives) represents a larger population goes back to *The Polish Peasant*. Thomas and Znaniecki (1918/1927) argued that sociologists should gather life histories of individuals who represent the population being studied (pp. 1834–1835). They defended their extensive use of Wiszniewski's life record by claiming that he was "a typical representative of the culturally passive mass which, under the present conditions and at the present stage of social evolution, constitutes in every civilized society the enormous majority of the population" (p. 1907). In evaluating *The Polish Peasant*, however, Blumer (1939/1979) claimed that Thomas and Znaniecki had failed to demonstrate Wiszniewski's representativeness and that it would have been difficult for them to do so anyway (p. 44).

Contemporary narrative researchers occupy a different social and historical location. Under the auspices of the narrative turn, they reject the idea that the small number of narratives they present must be generalizable to a certain population. Some researchers do this by highlighting the particularity of the narratives they present and by placing them in a broader frame. For example, Shostak's *Nisa* is about one woman's narrative, but Shostak (1989) used the stories of the other !Kung women she interviewed, as well as previous anthropological studies of the !Kung people, to show how Nisa's story is at once unique in some respects and similar to other !Kung women's stories in other ways.

Many contemporary narrative researchers, however, make a stronger break from Thomas and Znaniecki's (1918/1927) positivist stance regarding representativeness. Given "narrative elasticity" and the range of "narrative options" in any particular setting (Holstein & Gubrium, 2000), as well as constant flux in social and historical conditions, these researchers propose that the range of narrative possibilities within any group of people is potentially limitless. To make matters more complex, as Gubrium and Holstein (2002) suggested, "Treating subject positions and their associated voices seriously, we might find that an ostensibly single interview could actually be, in practice, an interview with several subjects, whose particular identities may be only partially clear" (p. 23).

Thus, many contemporary narrative researchers approach *any* narrative as an *instance* of the possible relationships between a narrator's active construction of self, on the one hand, and the social, cultural, and historical circumstances that enable and constrain that narrative, on the other. Researchers often highlight a range of possible narratives to show that no one particular story is determined by a certain social location, but they do not claim that their studies exhaust the possibilities within that context (see, e.g., Auerbach; 2002; Bell, 1999; Chase, 1995a; Mishler, 1999). From this perspective, any narrative is significant because it embodies—and gives us insight into—what is possible and intelligible within a specific social context.[21]

Narrative Inquiry and Social Change

[...]

I now turn to questions about the relationship between narrative inquiry and social change. What kinds of narratives disrupt oppressive social processes? How and when do researchers' analyses and representations of others' stories encourage social justice and democratic processes? And for whom are these processes disrupted and encouraged? Which audiences need to hear which researchers' and narrators' stories?

For some people, the act of narrating a significant life event itself facilitates positive change. In discussing a breast cancer survivor's narrative, Langellier (2001) wrote, "The wounded storyteller reclaims the capacity to tell, and hold on to, her own story, resisting narrative surrender to the medical chart as the official story of the illness" (p. 146; see also Capps & Ochs, 1995; Frank, 1995). Along similar lines, Rosenwald and Ochberg (1992) claimed that self-narration can lead to personal emancipation—to "better" stories of life difficulties or traumas. In these cases, the narrator is his or her own audience, the one who needs to hear alternative versions of his or her identity or life events, and the one for whom changes in the narrative can "stir up changes" in the life (p. 8; see also Mishler, 1995, pp. 108–109).

For other narrators, the urgency of storytelling arises from the need and desire to have *others* hear one's story. Citing René Jara, Beverley (2000) described testimonios as "emergency narratives" that involve a problem of repression, poverty, marginality, exploitation, or simply survival. . . . The voice that speaks to the reader through the text . . . [takes] the form of an I that demands to be recognized, that wants or needs to stake a claim on our attention (p. 556).

But it is not only Latin American testimonios that are narrated with this urgent voice. The stories of many marginalized groups have changed the contemporary narrative landscape—to name just a few, the stories of transgendered people, people with disabilities, and the survivors of gendered, racial/ethnic, and sexual violence. Indeed, "giving voice" to marginalized people and "naming silenced lives" have been primary goals of narrative research for several decades (McLaughlin & Tierney, 1993; Personal Narratives Group, 1989).

If a previously silenced narrator is to challenge an audience's assumptions or actions effectively, the audience must be ready to hear the narrator's story—or must be jolted into listening to it. In writing about empathetic listening, Frank (2000) stated, "Taking the other's perspective is a necessary step in constructive social change" (p. 94). In a similar vein, Gamson (2002) argued that story-telling "promotes empathy across different social locations" (p. 189). Although he was writing about media discourse on abortion, Gamson's argument is relevant to the narrative approaches I have been discussing. Gamson resisted the critique of American popular media (e.g., newspapers, television) that they are too infused with personal narratives. Because an unwanted pregnancy is ultimately a woman's problem, excluding stories about that "existential dilemma" from media and policy discourse silences women in particular. Thus, he argued that "personalization . . . opens discursive opportunities" (p. 189). Gamson had in mind "deliberation and dialogue in a narrative mode," which (unlike abstract argument) "lends itself more easily to the expression of moral complexity." In this sense, "storytelling facilitates a healthy democratic, public life" (p. 197).

During recent years, many narrative researchers have pushed beyond the goal of eliciting previously silenced narratives. Tierney's (2000) description of the goal of life history research applies to other forms of narrative research as well:

> Life histories are helpful not merely because they add to the mix of what already exists, but because of their ability to refashion identities. Rather than a conservative goal based on nostalgia for a paradise lost, or a liberal one of enabling more people to take their places at humanity's table, a goal of life history work in a postmodern age is to break the stranglehold of metanarratives that establishes rules of truth, legitimacy, and identity. The work of life history becomes the investigation of the mediating aspects of culture, the interrogation of its grammar, and the decentering of its norms. (p. 546)

. . . When researchers' interpretive strategies reveal the stranglehold of oppressive metanarratives, they help to open up possibilities for social change. In this sense, audiences need to hear not only the narrator's story, but also the researcher's explication of how the narrator's story is constrained by, and strains against, the mediating aspects of culture (and of institutions, organizations, and sometimes the social sciences themselves). Audiences whose members identify with the narrator's story might be moved by the researcher's interpretation to understand *their* stories in new ways and to imagine how they could tell their stories differently. Audiences whose members occupy social locations different from the narrator's might be moved through empathetic listening to think and act in ways that benefit the narrator or what he or she advocates (Madison, 1998, pp. 279–282).

What if the audience is hostile? DeVault and Ingraham (1999) broached this issue: "A radical challenge to silencing is not only about having a say, but about talking back in the strongest sense—saying the very things that those in power resist hearing" (p. 184). When the audience is both powerful and invested in the status quo—invested in oppressive metanarratives—narrators and narrative researchers may turn to "collective stories," which connect an individual's story to the broader story of a marginalized social group (Richardson, 1990). In discussing the collective stories of sexual abuse survivors and gays and lesbians, Plummer (1995) wrote, "For narratives to flourish, there must be a community to hear. . . . For communities to hear, there must be stories which weave together their history, their identity, their politics. The one—community—feeds upon and into the other—story" (p. 87). In the face of a hostile and powerful audience, narrators strengthen their communities through narratives and simultaneously seek to broaden their community of listeners. Thus, collective stories—or testimonios—become integral to social movements (see also Davis, 2002). However, it is important to heed Naples's (2003) cautionary note. In her analysis of how personal narratives function in the social movement of childhood sexual abuse survivors, she argued that we must determine when and where various strategies of speaking from personal experience are more effective and less effective in challenging oppression (p. 1152).

Although discussion of social movements and testimonios evokes the need for large-scale social change, we also need to consider the role of narratives and narrative research in small-scale, localized social change. For example, in Auerbach's (2002) study of Latino/Latina parent involvement in a college access program for their high school children, she heard many parents tell of poor treatment at the hands of school personnel. Auerbach also observed that the program gave parents some opportunities to share their stories publicly with each other and that sometimes this public performance of their stories led to collective problem solving (p. 1381). Equally important, Auerbach pointed to the need for such programs to create "a third space" that "disrupts the official discourse and scripted behavior that normally dominates school events for parents, just as it does in classrooms for students" (p. 1386). In other words, such programs hold the promise of creating conditions that would allow school administrators, teachers, and counselors to hear parents' narratives so that school staff can be jolted into resisting metanarratives that usually prevail in their work environments—immigrant families of color are uninterested in their children's education, immigrant children of color have limited educational potential, and so forth (see also Rosier, 2000). Auerbach suggested that researchers can help to create public spaces in which marginalized people's narratives can be heard even by those who normally do not want to hear them.

Narrative Inquiry: A Field in the Making

In *my* narrative, I have attempted to give shape to the massive material that can be called narrative inquiry, identifying its contours and complexities and arguing for the idea that it constitutes a subfield within qualitative inquiry even amid its multiplicity. Here I raise some issues—in the form of a set of relationships—that I believe are pivotal to the future of this field.

First is the relationship between theoretical and methodological work within narrative inquiry. Narrative theorists point out that narrative research is embedded in and shaped by broad social and historical currents, particularly the ubiquity of personal narratives in contemporary Western culture and politics—from television talk shows, to politicians' speeches, to self-help groups. Clough (2000) warned, however, that the "trauma culture" we currently inhabit encourages proliferation of personal narratives about trouble and suffering without offering a theory and politics of social change. Along similar lines, Atkinson and Silverman (1997) and Gubrium and Holstein (2002) pointed to the powerful tug of our "interview society," and they warned researchers against the romantic assumption that narrators reveal "authentic" selves and speak in their "own" voices, as if their selves and voices were not already mediated by the social contexts in which they speak. I argued earlier that treating interviewees as narrators does not mean succumbing to those problematic assumptions. Here, however, I suggest that narrative researchers need to do more, collectively, to integrate a critique of the trauma culture/interview society with discussion of methodological issues involved in conducting empirical research (e.g., inviting and interpreting narrators' stories). How do these two activities—one theoretical and the other methodological—support each other and serve a joint purpose? What specific research practices produce narrative research informed by a broad social critique and a politics of social change? Given the centrality of personal narrative in many political, cultural, and social arenas, narrative researchers have much work to do and much to offer by way of empirically grounded analysis and social critique (Crawley & Broad, 2004; Naples, 2003). No one theoretical or empirical project can do everything, of course, but it seems to me that one key lies in more conversation among narrative researchers across theoretical and methodological interests.

Second is the relationship between Western and non-Western narrative theories and practices. Gubrium and Holstein (2002) suggested that the interview society has gone global—that people around the globe know what it means to be interviewed. Even Nisa, a member of the (until recently) hunting and gathering !Kung people, knows how to place herself at the center of a life story (Shostak, 1981/2000a, 2000b). At the same time, narrative researchers need to understand cross-cultural differences more fully. What do Western narrative researchers (and Westerners in general) have to learn from the ways in which non-Westerners narrate the self, narrate group identities, or integrate folklore narratives into personal narratives (Grima, 1991; Narayan & George, 2002; Riessman, 2002b)? If self or identity is not the central construct in (at least some) non-Western narratives (Rosaldo, 1976), what is? What do non-Western narrative researchers have to teach their Western counterparts about the kinds of narratives that need to be heard and about interpretive and narrative strategies for presenting and performing them? What is the relationship among narrative, narrative research, and social change in non-Western societies? For example, what impact do Latin American testimonios have in the local communities from which they arise? I am not suggesting that Western narrative researchers should take up residence in non-Western locales; rather, I am suggesting that we need to understand more fully how our research is imbued with Western assumptions about self and identity. Anthropologists may be ahead of the game here, but much American narrative research remains unreflective about its Western character.

The third issue revolves around the relationship between narrative inquiry and technological innovation. Although it is hard to imagine narrative researchers giving up the domain of face-to-face interviewing and on-site gathering of naturally occurring conversation, some researchers have already moved into the domain of virtual research and many others will follow in their footsteps (Mann & Stewart, 2002). How are e-mail, chat groups, online support groups, and instant messaging changing the meaning of "naturally occurring conversation"? How are they creating new arenas for narrating the self and for constructing identities, realities, relationships, and communities? As narrative researchers explore these new opportunities to hear people converse and to interview individuals and groups, what new risks and ethical issues will they encounter? What new forms of knowledge will emerge?

Fourth, researchers interested in the relationship between narrative and social change need to do more to address the issue of audience (Lincoln, 1997). We need to think more about who could benefit from, and who needs to hear, *our* research narratives. Marginalized people in the communities we study? Power brokers and gatekeepers in the communities we study? Policymakers? Students in our classes? The public at large? Other researchers within our disciplines and substantive fields of study? Equally important, in my view, is the need for narrative researchers to explore the possible points of contact between *narrators'* stories and various audiences who need to hear them. What kinds of stories (and what kinds of research narratives) incite collective action? And to what effect? When do previously silenced narrators jolt powerful—and initially hostile—audiences to join in breaking the stranglehold of oppressive metanarratives? And how can researchers help to create the conditions of empathetic listening across social locations?

Along these lines, what do we have to learn from Ensler's (2001) wildly successful *Vagina Monologues*? How did Ensler transform interviews with women about their bodies into performances that have sparked a massive international movement against violence against women?[22] Similarly, what do we have to learn about writing for the public from Ehrenreich's (2001) best-seller, *Nickel and Dimed: On (Not) Getting By in America*? In this mixture of undercover reporting and narrative ethnography, Ehrenreich wrote both seriously and humorously about her efforts to make ends meet for a month at a time as a waitress in Florida, a house cleaner in Maine, and a Wal-Mart employee in Minnesota. Many of my students claim that this text disrupts their attachment to individualist ideologies in ways that other texts do not. I am not suggesting that we should all aspire to off-Broadway performances or to best-sellerdom for our work; rather, I am suggesting that we need to think more concertedly and broadly about whom we write for and speak to—and how we do so. For many of us, this may mean thinking about how to create public spaces in our local communities where the personal narratives and collective stories of marginalized people can be heard by—and can jolt out of their complacency—those who occupy more powerful subject positions and social locations.

Finally, narrative researchers need to attend to the relationship between our work and that of our social science colleagues who work within other traditions of inquiry. We need to treat other social science scholars as an important audience for our work. We need to demonstrate that immersion in the biographical leg of Mills's trilogy—biography, history, and society—produces new significant concepts and analyses that other researchers in our substantive areas and disciplines *need* to do their work well. For example, Loseke's (2001) concept of the "formula story" of wife abuse, and her analysis of its inadequacy in capturing women's complex stories of domestic violence, is crucial to the work of other social scientists—whether quantitative or qualitative—who study the success or failure of battered women's shelters in helping women to leave abusive partners. Generally speaking, narrative inquiry's contributions to social science have to do with concepts and analyses that demonstrate two things: (a) the creativity, complexity, and variability of individuals' (or groups') self and reality constructions and (b) the power of historical, social, cultural, organizational, discursive, interactional, and/or psychological circumstances in shaping the range of possibilities for self and reality construction in any particular time and place. Narrative researchers need to confidently assert their contributions to, their interventions in, and their transformations of social science scholarship.

As narrative researchers grapple with these and myriad other issues and questions, it is hard to imagine Mills's argument for the joint investigation of biography, society, and history going out of style. What exactly that means, however, will likely undergo many further permutations, disrupting assumptions that many of us now hold dear.

Notes

1. I thank Norman Denzin, Yvonna Lincoln, James Holstein, Ruthellen Josselson, and Catherine Riessman for their comments on earlier drafts of this chapter.
2. The *Journal of Narrative and Life History* was created in 1990, and it became *Narrative Inquiry* in 1998. As just two examples of conferences, in February 2003 the American Educational Research Association held a Winter Institute on Narrative Inquiry in Social Science Research at the Ontario Institute for Studies in Education, and in May 2004 the second biannual Narrative Matters conference was held at St. Thomas University in New Brunswick.
3. For overviews of early life history methods in sociology, see Becker (1966), Bertaux (1981), Denzin (1970), and Plummer (1983).
4. The life history and life story approaches continue to be international in scope. The 2003 Board of Biography and Society, a research committee of the International Sociological Association, included researchers from many European countries as well as from Japan, South Africa, and Russia.
5. In addition to summarizing the interview data that she gathered from 129 women about childbearing, child rearing, marriage, housework, fieldwork, and community participation, Hagood (1939) presented two women's life stories in depth. This allows readers to see the impact on these two women's lives of the social and economic conditions described earlier in the book.
6. For overviews of early life history methods in anthropology, see Langness (1965), Langness and Frank (1981), and Watson and Watson-Franke (1985).
7. Two volumes of *The American Slave* consist of interviews conducted at Fisk University before the Federal Writers' Project was created. During the late 1960s and early 1970s, Lester (1968) and Yetman (1970), among others, were publishing parts of and writing about the slave narratives. After the publication of *The American Slave*, Rawick (1977) and other researchers searched for, found, and published many other slave narratives that had been deposited in state collections and libraries. Not surprisingly, they found evidence that some of the narratives had been tampered with, presumably to suppress negative portrayals of whites.
8. For overviews of early second-wave feminist use of life history and personal narratives, see Armitage (1983), Geiger (1986), Gluck (1979, 1983), Personal Narratives Group (1989), and Reinharz (1992, chap. 7).
9. Even before feminism became a major influence in social science research, there were exceptions to this pattern of methodological indifference and objectification of research participants. For example, in *Mountain Wolf Woman: Sister of Crashing Thunder*, Lurie (1961) addressed many methodological issues and described in detail her relationship with Mountain Wolf Woman.
10. See Mishler (1995, pp. 90–102) on various ways in which narrative researchers connect the "telling" and the "told."
11. Polkinghorne (1995) and Mishler (1995) also made distinctions among types of narrative research in the social sciences, but because they excluded some kinds of work that I want to include (and because they included some kinds that I want to exclude), I construct my own categories here.
12. Because quantitative modes of inquiry are so dominant in psychology, some psychologists treat narrative inquiry as synonymous with qualitative inquiry (Josselson, Lieblich, & McAdams, 2003). Nonetheless, I have tried to separate out a psychological approach that uses the analytic lenses I have articulated and so is not identical to qualitative research in general.
13. For interview guides used by psychological researchers who take a narrative approach, see McAdams and Bowman (2001, pp. 12–13) and Josselson (1996b, pp. 265–272).
14. Some of the researchers I include in this approach are not sociologists. For example, Mishler is a psychologist and Langellier is a communication scholar. Nonetheless, their approach is sociological in the ways described here.
15. Sometimes memoirs, even those not written by social scientists, have autoethnographic characteristics. For example, in *Crossing the Color Line: Race, Parenting, and Culture*, Reddy (1994) investigated her experiences as a white woman married to an African American man and as the mother of two biracial children. She showed how these racialized

relationships disrupted her identity as a white woman and her understanding of racial issues in the social world. The writing itself, however, is not experimental in the same way that much autoethnographic writing is.

16. See Chase (1995b, 2003) for a comparison of sociological interview questions and questions oriented to inviting narratives.

17. The influence of narrative inquiry can be seen in the difference between Rubin's (1976) *Worlds of Pain: Life in the Working Class Family* and Rubin's (1994) *Families on the Faultline: America's Working Class Speaks About the Family, the Economy, Race, and Ethnicity*. In the earlier book, Rubin (1976) presented anonymous excerpts from a range of interviewees to represent various themes. In contrast, Rubin (1994) organized the more recent book around the stories of specific families, beginning and ending the book with the same four families.

18. See also Ochberg (1996) on the ways in which researchers "convert what we have been told from one kind of account into another" (p. 110). In addition, Josselson (1996a) offered an interesting discussion of the anxiety, guilt, and shame that may arise when "writing other people's lives" and sharing interpretations with those people.

19. Ferguson's (2001) *Bad Boys: Public Schools in the Making of Black Masculinity* offers an example of a researcher mixing narrative strategies. For the most part, Ferguson wrote with an authoritative voice. But in the middle of the book, she shifted to a supportive voice when she included a 27-page transcript from an interview with an African American mother whose attempt to discipline her son was itself disciplined by police, courts, and social service agencies. Ferguson stated, "You must read what Mariana had to say aloud. You cannot understand it unless you hear the words" (p. 135).

20. For many other examples, see Koehler (1981, pp. 89–93), Langness and Frank (1981), and Watson and Watson-Franke (1985).

21. Focusing on instances rather than representative cases is not unique to narrative inquiry, but the issue may seem more urgent in narrative research because of the small number of narratives that researchers present. For broader discussions of the relation between the particular and the general, see Blum and McHugh (1984, p. 37), Denzin (1997, p. 245), and Psathas (1995, p. 50).

22. *The Vagina Monologues* was originally an off-Broadway production based on interviews with 200 American women. It has been performed in many cities and communities across the United States as well as around the globe. When performed in conjunction with the "V-day" movement, profits are donated to organizations fighting violence against women.

References

Anderson, K., & Jack, D. C. (1991). Learning to listen: Interview techniques and analyses. In S. B. Gluck & D. Patai (Eds.), *Women's words: The feminist practice of oral history* (pp. 11–26). New York: Routledge.

Atkinson, P., & Silverman, D. (1997). Kundera's *Immortality*: The interview society and the invention of the self. *Qualitative Inquiry, 3*, 304–325.

Atkinson, R. (2002). The life story interview. In J. F. Gubrium & J. A. Holstein (Eds.), *Handbook of interview research: Context and method* (pp. 121–140). Thousand Oaks, CA: Sage.

Auerbach, S. (2002). "Why do they give the good classes to some and not to others?" Latino parent narratives of struggle in a college access program. *Teachers College Record, 104*, 1369–1392.

Babb, J., & Taylor, P. E. (1981). *Border healing woman: The story of Jewel Babb*. Austin: University of Texas Press.

Bamberg, M. G. W. (1997). Positioning between structure and performance. *Journal of Narrative and Life History, 7*, 335–342.

Barthes, R. (1977). *Image, music, text* (S. Heath, Trans.). New York: Hill & Wang.

Bauman, R. (1986). *Story, performance, and event: Contextual studies in oral narrative*. Cambridge, UK: Cambridge University Press.

Behar, R. (1996). *The vulnerable observer: Anthropology that breaks your heart*. Boston: Beacon.

Behar, R. (2003). *Translated woman: Crossing the border with Esperanza's story*. Boston: Beacon. (Original work published in 1993)

Belenky, M. F., Clinchy, B. M., Goldberger, N. R., & Tarule, J. M. (1986). *Women's ways of knowing: The development of self, voice, and mind*. New York: Basic Books.

Bell, S. E. (1999). Narratives and lives: Women's health politics and the diagnosis of cancer for DES daughters. *Narrative Inquiry, 9*, 347–389.

Bertaux, D. (Ed.). (1981). *Biography and society: The life history approach in the social sciences*. Beverly Hills, CA: Sage.

Beverley, J. (2000). Testimonio, subalternity, and narrative authority. In N. K. Denzin & Y. S. Lincoln (Eds.), *Handbook of qualitative research* (2nd ed., pp. 555–565). Thousand Oaks, CA: Sage.

Bloom, L. R., & Munro, P. (1995). Conflicts of selves: Nonunitary subjectivity in women administrators' life history narratives. In J. A. Hatch & R. Wisniewski (Eds.), *Life history and narrative* (pp. 99–112). London: Falmer.

Blum, A., & McHugh, P. (1984). *Self-reflection in the arts and sciences*. Atlantic Highlands, NJ: Humanities Press.

Blumer, H. (1979). *Critiques of research in the social sciences: An appraisal of Thomas and Znaniecki's* The Polish Peasant in Europe and America. New Brunswick, NJ: Transaction Books. (Original work published in 1939)

Bobel, C. (2002). *The paradox of natural mothering.* Philadelphia: Temple University Press.

Botkin, B. A. (Ed.). (1945). *Lay my burden down: A folk history of slavery.* Chicago: University of Chicago Press.

Briggs, C. L. (1986). *Learning how to ask: A sociolin-guistic appraisal of the role of the interview in social science research.* Cambridge, UK: Cambridge University Press.

Briggs, C. L. (2002). Interviewing, power/knowledge, and social inequality. In J. F. Gubrium & J. A. Holstein (Eds.), *Handbook of interview research: Context and method* (pp. 911–922). Thousand Oaks, CA: Sage.

Brockmeier, J., & Carbaugh, D. (Eds.). (2001). *Narrative and identity: Studies in autobiography, self, and culture.* Amsterdam, Netherlands: John Benjamins.

Bruner, J. (1986). *Actual minds, possible worlds.* Cambridge, MA: Harvard University Press.

Bruner, J. (1997). Labov and Waletzky: Thirty years on. *Journal of Narrative and Life History, 7,* 61–81.

Bruner, J. (2002). *Making stories: Law, literature, life.* New York: Farrar, Straus, & Giroux.

Burgos, M. (1989). Life stories, narrativity, and the search for the self. *Life Stories [Récits de vie], 5,* 27–38.

Capps, L., & Ochs, E. (1995). *Constructing panic: The discourse of agoraphobia.* Cambridge, MA: Harvard University Press.

Chase, S. E. (1995a). *Ambiguous empowerment: The work narratives of women school superintendents.* Amherst: University of Massachusetts Press.

Chase, S. E. (1995b). Taking narrative seriously: Consequences for method and theory in interview studies. In R. Josselson & A. Lieblich (Eds.), *Interpreting experience: The narrative study of lives* (pp. 1–26). Thousand Oaks, CA: Sage.

Chase, S. E. (2001). Universities as discursive environments for sexual identity construction. In J. E. Gubrium & J. A. Holstein (Eds.), *Institutional selves: Troubled identities in a postmodern world* (pp. 142–157). New York: Oxford University Press.

Chase, S. E. (2003). Learning to listen: Narrative principles in a qualitative research methods course. In R. Josselson, A. Lieblich, & D. P. McAdams (Eds.), *Up close and personal: The teaching and learning of narrative research* (pp. 79–99). Washington, DC: American Psychological Association.

Clough, P. T. (2000). Comments on setting criteria for experimental writing. *Qualitative Inquiry, 6,* 278–291.

Crapanzano, V. (1980). *Tuhami: Portrait of a Moroccan.* Chicago: University of Chicago Press.

Crawley, S. L. (2002). "They still don't understand why I hate wearing dresses!" An autoethnographic rant on dresses, boats, and butchness. *Cultural Studies, Critical Methodologies, 2,* 69–92.

Crawley, S. L., & Broad, K. L. (2004). "Be your(real lesbian)self": Mobilizing sexual formula stories through personal (and political) storytelling. *Journal of Contemporary Ethnography, 33,* 39–71.

Czarniawska, B. (1997). *Narrating the organization: Dramas of institutional identity.* Chicago: University of Chicago Press.

Davis, J. E. (Ed.). (2002). *Stories of change: Narrative and social movements.* Albany: State University of New York Press.

Denzin, N. K. (1989). *Interpretive biography.* Newbury Park, CA: Sage.

Denzin, N. K. (1997). *Interpretive ethnography: Ethnographic practices for the 21st century.* Thousand Oaks, CA: Sage.

Denzin, N. K. (2000). The practices and politics of interpretation. In N. K. Denzin & Y. S. Lincoln (Eds.), *Handbook of qualitative research* (2nd ed., pp. 897–922). Thousand Oaks, CA: Sage.

Denzin, N. K. (2003). The call to performance. *Symbolic Interaction, 26,* 187–207.

Denzin, N. K., & Lincoln, Y. S. (2000). Introduction: The discipline and practice of qualitative research. In N. K. Denzin & Y. S. Lincoln (Eds.), *Handbook of qualitative research* (2nd ed., pp. 1–28). Thousand Oaks, CA: Sage.

DeVault, M. L. (1999). *Liberating method: Feminism and social research.* Philadelphia: Temple University Press.

DeVault, M. L., & Ingraham, C. (1999). Metaphors of silence and voice in feminist thought. In M. L. DeVault, *Liberating method: Feminism and social research* (pp. 175–186). Philadelphia: Temple University Press.

DuBois, C. (1960). *The people of Alor: A social-psychological study of an East Indian island.* Cambridge, MA: Harvard University Press. (Original work published in 1944)

Ehrenreich, B. (2001). *Nickel and dimed: On (not) getting by in America.* New York: Metropolitan Books.

Ellis, C., & Berger, L. (2002). Their story/My story/Our story: Including the researcher's experience in interview research. In J. F. Gubrium & J. A. Holstein (Eds.), *Handbook of interview research: Context and method* (pp. 849–875). Thousand Oaks, CA: Sage.

Ellis, C., & Bochner, A. P. (1992). Telling and performing personal stories: The constraints of choice in abortion. In C. Ellis & M. G. Flaherty (Eds.), *Investigating subjectivity: Research on lived experience* (pp. 79–101). Newbury Park, CA: Sage.

Ellis, C., & Flaherty, M. G. (Eds.). (1992). *Investigating subjectivity: Research on lived experience.* Newbury Park, CA: Sage.

Ellis, C., Kiesinger, C. E., & Tillmann-Healy, L. M. (1997). Interactive interviewing: Talking about emotional experience. In R. Hertz (Ed.), *Reflexivity and voice* (pp. 119–149). Thousand Oaks, CA: Sage.

Emihovich, C. (1995). Distancing passion: Narratives in social science. In J. A. Hatch & R. Wisniewski (Eds.), *Life history and narrative* (pp. 37–48). London: Falmer.

Ensler, E. (2001). *The vagina monologues: The V-day edition.* New York: Villard/Random House.

Ferguson, A. A. (2001). *Bad boys: Public schools in the making of black masculinity*. Ann Arbor: University of Michigan Press.

Foley, L., & Faircloth, C. A. (2003). Medicine as discursive resource: Legitimation in the work narratives of midwives. *Sociology of Health & Illness, 25*, 165–184.

Frank, A. W. (1995). *The wounded storyteller: Body, illness, and ethics*. Chicago: University of Chicago Press.

Frank, G. (2000). *Venus on wheels: Two decades of dialogue on disability, biography, and being female in America*. Berkeley: University of California Press.

Franz, C. E., & Stewart, A. J. (Eds.). (1994). *Women creating lives: Identities, resilience, and resistance*. Boulder, CO: Westview.

Gamson, W. A. (2002). How storytelling can be empowering. In K. A. Cerulo (Ed.), *Culture in mind: Toward a sociology of culture and cognition* (pp. 187–198). New York: Routledge.

Garfinkel, H. (1967). *Studies in ethnomethodology*. Englewood Cliffs, NJ: Prentice Hall.

Geiger, S. N. G. (1986). Women's life histories: Method and content. *Signs: Journal of Women in Culture and Society, 11*, 334–351.

Gluck, S. (1979). What's so special about women? Women's oral history. *Frontiers: A Journal of Women's Studies, 2*, 3–11.

Gluck, S. B., & Patai, D. (Eds.). (1991). *Women's words: The feminist practice of oral history*. New York: Routledge.

Grima, B. (1991). The role of suffering in women's performance of *paxto*. In A. Appadurai, F. J. Korom, & M. A. Mills (Eds.), *Gender, genre, and power in South Asian expressive traditions* (pp. 78–101). Philadelphia: University of Pennsylvania Press.

Gubrium, J. F., & Holstein, J. A. (1997). *The new language of qualitative method*. New York: Oxford University Press.

Gubrium, J. F., & Holstein, J. A. (Eds.). (2001). *Institutional selves: Troubled identities in a post-modern world*. New York: Oxford University Press.

Gubrium, J. F., & Holstein, J. A. (2002). From the individual interview to the interview society. In J. F. Gubrium & J. A. Holstein (Eds.), *Handbook of interview research: Context and method* (pp. 3–32). Thousand Oaks, CA: Sage.

Hagood, M. J. (1939). *Mothers of the South: Portraiture of the white tenant farm woman*. New York: Greenwood.

Hatch, J. A., & Wisniewski, R. (Eds.). (1995). *Life history and narrative*. London: Falmer.

Hertz, R. (Ed.). (1997). *Reflexivity and voice*. Thousand Oaks, CA: Sage.

Hilbert, R. A. (1990). The efficacy of performance science: Comment on McCall and Becker. *Social Problems, 37*, 133–135.

Hinchman, I. P., & Hinchman, S. K. (Eds.). (2001). *Memory, identity, community: The idea of narrative in the human sciences*. Albany: State University of New York Press.

Holstein, J. A., & Gubrium, J. F. (2000). *The self we live by: Narrative identity in a postmodern world*. New York: Oxford University Press.

Hunt, A. M., & Winegarten, R. (1983). *I am Annie Mae: An extraordinary black Texas woman in her own words*. Austin: University of Texas Press.

Jacobs, R. H. (1979). *Life after youth: Female, forty—What next?* Boston: Beacon.

Josselson, R. (1996a). On writing other people's lives: Self-analytic reflections of a narrative researcher. In R. Josselson (Ed.), *Ethics and process in the narrative study of lives* (pp. 60–71). Thousand Oaks, CA: Sage.

Josselson, R. (1996b). *Revising herself: The story of women's identity from college to midlife*. New York: Oxford University Press.

Josselson, R., Lieblich, A., & McAdams, D. P. (Eds.). (2003). *Up close and personal: The teaching and learning of narrative research*. Washington, DC: American Psychological Association.

Kardiner, A. (1945). *The psychological frontiers of society*. Westport, CT: Greenwood.

Koehler, L. (1981). Native women of the Americas: A bibliography. *Frontiers: A Journal of Women's Studies, 6*, 73–101.

Krieger, S. (1991). *Social science and the self: Personal essays on an art form*. New Brunswick, NJ: Rutgers University Press.

Labov, W., & Waletzky, J. (1997). Narrative analysis: Oral versions of personal experience. *Journal of Narrative and Life History, 7*, 3–38. (Original work published in 1967)

Langellier, K. M. (2001). You're marked: Breast cancer, tattoo, and the narrative performance of identity. In J. Brockmeier & D. Carbaugh (Eds.), *Narrative and identity: Studies in autobiography, self, and culture* (pp. 145–184). Amsterdam, Netherlands: John Benjamins.

Langness, L. L. (1965). *The life history in anthropological science*. New York: Holt, Rinehart & Winston.

Langness, L. L., & Frank, G. (1981). *Lives: An anthropological approach to biography*. Novato, CA: Chandler & Sharp.

Laslett, B. (1999). Personal narratives as sociology. *Contemporary Sociology, 28*, 391–401.

Lempert, L. B. (1994). A narrative analysis of abuse: Connecting the personal, the rhetorical, and the structural. *Journal of Contemporary Ethnography, 22*, 411–441.

Lewis, O. (1961). *The children of Sánchez: Autobiography of a Mexican family*. New York: Random House.

Liebow, E. (1993). *Tell them who I am: The lives of homeless women*. New York: Penguin.

Lincoln, Y. S. (1997). Self, subject, audience, text: Living at the edge, writing in the margins. In W. G. Tierney & Y. S. Lincoln (Eds.), *Representation and the text: Re-framing the narrative voice* (pp. 37–55). Albany: State University of New York Press.

Lincoln, Y. S. (2000). Narrative authority vs. perjured testimony: Courage, vulnerability, and truth. *Qualitative Studies in Education, 13*, 131–138.

Loseke, D. R. (2001). Lived realities and formula stories of "battered women." In J. F. Gubrium & J. A. Holstein (Eds.), *Institutional selves: Troubled identities in a postmodern world* (pp. 107–126). New York: Oxford University Press.

Luttrell, W. (1997). *School-smart and mother-wise: Working-class women's identity and schooling.* New York: Routledge.

Luttrell. W. (2003). *Pregnant bodies, fertile minds: Gender, race, and the schooling of pregnant teens.* New York: Routledge.

Madison, D. S. (1998). Performance, personal narratives, and the politics of possibility. In S. J. Dailey (Ed.), *The future of performance studies: Visions and revisions* (pp. 276–286). Annandale, VA: National Communication Association.

Mann, C., & Stewart, F. (2002). Internet interviewing. In J. F. Gubrium and J. A. Holstein (Eds.), *Handbook of interview research: Context and method* (pp. 603–627). Thousand Oaks, CA: Sage.

McAdams, D. P., Josselson, R., & Lieblich, A. (Eds.). (2001). *Turns in the road: Narrative studies of lives in transition.* Washington, DC: American Psychological Association.

McAdams, D. P. (1997). *The stories we live by: Personal myths and the making of the self.* New York: Guilford.

McAdams, D. P., & Bowman, P. J. (2001). Narrating life's turning points: Redemption and contamination. In D. P. McAdams, R. Josselson, & A. Lieblich (Eds.), *Turns in the road: Narrative studies of lives in transition* (pp. 3–34). Washington, DC: American Psychological Association.

McCall, M. M., & Becker, H. S. (1990). Performance science. *Social Problems, 37*, 117–132.

McLaughlin, D., & Tierney, W. G. (Eds.). (1993). *Naming silenced lives: Personal narratives and processes of educational change.* New York: Routledge.

McMahan, E. M., & Rogers, K. L. (Eds.). (1994). *Interactive oral history interviewing.* Hillsdale, NJ: Lawrence Erlbaum.

Menchú, R. (1984). *I, Rigoberta Menchú: An Indian woman in Guatemala* (with an introduction by E. Burgos-Debray, Ed.; A. Wright, Trans.). London: Verso.

Miller, G. (1997). *Becoming miracle workers: Language and meaning in brief therapy.* New York: Aldine de Gruyter.

Mills, C. W. (1959). *The sociological imagination.* London: Oxford University Press.

Mishler, E. G. (1995). Models of narrative analysis: A typology. *Journal of Narrative and Life History, 5*, 87–123.

Mishler, E. G. (1999). *Storylines: Craft artists' narratives of identity.* Cambridge, MA: Harvard University Press.

Mishler, E. G. (1986). *Research interviewing: Context and narrative.* Cambridge, MA: Harvard University Press.

Moyano, M. E. (2000). *The autobiography of María Elena Moyano: The life and death of a Peruvian activist* (D. M. Tupac, Ed. and Annot.). Gainesville: University Press of Florida.

Myerhoff, B. (1994). *Number our days: Culture and community among elderly Jews in an American ghetto.* New York: Meridian/Penguin. (Original work published in 1979)

Naples, N. (2003). Deconstructing and locating survivor discourse: Dynamics of narrative, empowerment, and resistance for survivors of childhood sexual abuse. *Signs: Journal of Women in Culture and Society, 28*, 1151–1185.

Narayan, K., & George, K. M. (2002). Personal and folk narrative as cultural representation. In J. F. Gubrium & J. A. Holstein (Eds.), *Handbook of interview research: Context and method* (pp. 815–831). Thousand Oaks, CA: Sage.

Personal Narratives Group. (Eds.). (1989). *Interpreting women's lives: Feminist theory and personal narratives.* Bloomington: Indiana University Press.

Plummer, K. (1995). *Telling sexual stories: Power, change, and social worlds.* London: Routledge.

Polkinghorne, D. E. (1995). Narrative configuration in qualitative analysis. In J. A. Hatch & R. Wisniewski (Eds.), *Life history and narrative* (pp. 5–23). London: Falmer.

Pollner, M., & Stein, J. (1996). Narrative mapping of social worlds: The voice of experience in Alcoholics Anonymous. *Symbolic Interaction, 19*, 203–223.

Psathas, G. (1995). *Conversation analysis: The study of talk-in-interaction.* Thousand Oaks, CA: Sage.

Randall, M. (1981). *Sandino's daughters: Testimonies of Nicaraguan women in struggle.* Vancouver, British Columbia: New Star Books.

Randall, M. (1994). *Sandino's daughters revisited: Feminism in Nicaragua.* New Brunswick, NJ: Rutgers University Press.

Randall, M. (2003). *When I look into the mirror and see you: Women, terror, and resistance.* New Brunswick, NJ: Rutgers University Press.

Rawick, G. P. (1977). General introduction. In G. Rawick, J. Hillegas, & K. Lawrence (Eds.), *The American slave: A composite autobiography,* Supplement, Ser. 1, Vol. 1: *Alabama narratives* (pp. ix–li). Westport, CT: Greenwood.

Reddy, M. T. (1994). *Crossing the color line: Race, parenting, and culture.* New Brunswick, NJ: Rutgers University Press.

Reinharz, S. (1992). *Feminist models in social research.* New York: Oxford University Press.

Richardson, L. (1990). Narrative and sociology. *Journal of Contemporary Ethnography, 19*, 116–135.

Richardson, L. (2002). Poetic representation of interviews. In J. F. Gubrium & J. A. Holstein (Eds.), *Handbook of interview research: Context and method* (pp. 877–892). Thousand Oaks, CA: Sage

Riessman, C. K. (1990). *Divorce talk: Women and men make sense of personal relationships.* New Brunswick, NJ: Rutgers University Press.

Riessman, C. K. (1997). A short story about long stories, *Journal of Narrative and Life History, 7*, 155–158.

Riessman, C. K. (2002a). Analysis of personal narratives. In J. F. Gubrium & J. A. Holstein (Eds.), *Handbook of interview research: Context and method* (pp. 695–710). Thousand Oaks, CA: Sage.

Riessman, C. K. (2002b). Positioning gender identity in narratives of infertility: South Indian women's lives in context. In M. C. Inhorn & F. van Balen (Eds.), *Infertility around the globe: New thinking on childlessness, gender, and reproductive technologies* (pp. 152–170). Berkeley: University of California Press.

Rosaldo, R. (1976). The story of Tukbaw: "They listen as he orates." In F.E. Reynolds & D. Capps (Eds.), *The biographical process: Studies in the history and psychology of religion* (pp. 121–151). The Hague, Netherlands: Mouton.

Rosenwald, G. C., & Ochberg, R. L. (Eds.). (1992). *Storied lives: The cultural politics of self-understanding.* New Haven, CT: Yale University Press.

Rosier, K. B. (2000). *Mothering inner-city children: The early school years.* New Brunswick, NJ: Rutgers University Press.

Rubin, L. B. (1976). *Worlds of pain: Life in the working-class family.* New York: Basic Books.

Rubin, L. B. (1994). *Families on the faultline: America's working class speaks about the family, the economy, race, and ethnicity.* New York: HarperPerennial.

Ruddick, S., & Daniels, P. (Eds.). (1977). *Working it out: 23 women writers, artists, scientists, and scholars talk about their lives and work.* New York: Pantheon.

Sacks, K. B. (1989). What's a life story got to do with it? In Personal Narratives Group (Eds.), *Interpreting women's lives: Feminist theories and personal narratives* (pp. 85–95). Bloomington: University of Indiana Press.

Schegloff, E. A. (1997). "Narrative analysis" thirty years later. *Journal of Narrative and Life History, 7,* 97–106.

Sexton, P. C. (1981). *The new Nightingales: Hospital workers, unions, new women's issues.* New York: Enquiry Press.

Shaw, C. R. (1966). *The jack-roller: A delinquent boy's own story.* Chicago: University of Chicago Press. (Original work published in 1930)

Shostak, M. (1989). "What the wind won't take away": The genesis of *Nisa—The life and words of a !Kung woman.* In Personal Narratives Group (Eds.), *Interpreting women's lives: Feminist theory and personal narratives* (pp. 228–240). Bloomington: Indiana University Press.

Shostak, M. (2000a). *Nisa: The life and words of a !Kung woman.* Cambridge, MA: Harvard University Press. (Original work published in 1981)

Shostak, M. (2000b). *Return to Nisa.* Cambridge, MA: Harvard University Press.

Sidel, R. (1978). *Urban survival: The world of working-class women.* Boston: Beacon.

Stein, A. (1997). *Sex and sensibility: Stories of a lesbian generation.* Berkeley: University of California Press.

Stromberg, P. G. (1993). *Language and self-transformation: A study of the Christian conversion narrative.* Cambridge, UK: Cambridge University Press.

Sutherland, E. H. (1937). *The professional thief.* Chicago: University of Chicago Press.

Taylor, J. M., Gilligan, C., & Sullivan, A. M. (1995). *Between voice and silence: Women and girls, race and relationship.* Cambridge, MA: Harvard University Press.

Tedlock, B. (1992). *The beautiful and the dangerous: Encounters with the Zuni Indians.* New York: Viking/Penguin Books.

Thomas, W. I., & Znaniecki, F. (1927). *The Polish peasant in Europe and America* (Vol. 2). New York: Alfred A. Knopf. (Original work published in 1918)

Thompson, P. (2000). *The voice of the past: Oral history* (3rd ed.). New York: Oxford University Press. (Original work published in 1978)

Tierney, W. G. (2000). Undaunted courage: Life history and the postmodern challenge. In N. K. Denzin & Y. S. Lincoln (Eds.), *Handbook of qualitative research* (2nd ed., pp. 537–553). Thousand Oaks, CA: Sage.

Tierney, W. G. (2002). Get real: Representing reality. *Qualitative Studies in Education, 15,* 385–398.

Tierney, W. G., & Lincoln, Y. S. (Eds.). (1997). *Representation and the text: Re-framing the narrative voice.* Albany: State University of New York Press.

Watson, L. C., & Watson-Franke, M-B. (1985). *Interpreting life histories: An anthropological inquiry.* New Brunswick, NJ: Rutgers University Press.

Weiss, R. S. (1994). *Learning from strangers: The art and method of qualitative interview studies.* New York: Free Press.

Wozniak, D. F. (2002). *They're all my children: Foster mothering in America.* New York: New York University Press.

15

The Cultural Analysis of Discourse[1]

Naomi Quinn

This article is about a family of methods, under the rubric of the cultural analysis of discourse, that colleagues and I have been developing over the years, and that are under explicated, under appreciated, and relatively unknown outside of cognitive anthropology. The discussion is directed toward those who are in search of more satisfying analytic methods for investigating cultural understandings embedded in interviews and other kinds of discourse. Readers who want to know more about these methods and the methodological tradition from which they arise, can consult the volume edited by myself, *Finding Culture in Talk* (2005a) and two other key sources of methodological inspiration, Charles Briggs's *Learning How to Ask* (1986), and Charlotte Linde's *Life Stories* (1993). In what follows I will refer liberally to all three volumes.

Two incidents in the course of my routine at my university, juxtaposed in a single week, galvanized me to write about these methods. First, during a committee discussion of a student's proposal for a project I would be supervising in an interdisciplinary program, a biological anthropologist objected that the planned collection and analysis of interviews provided only, in his words, "anecdotal evidence." Later that week, in the discussion following a department talk by a cultural studies scholar that I attended, an audience member asked the speaker how she thought we could ever study "subjectivity." The speaker threw up her hands. These two small and ordinary moments in the course of academic life, happening as they did side by side, made me realize that the methodological tradition of which I was a part was endangered. I saw that the present disciplinary and interdisciplinary climate, with its false dichotomy and unfortunate antagonism between scientific and humanistic approaches, was likely to obliterate the particular methodological contribution that my colleagues and I had made. On the one side stand the methodologically scientistic, who are ready to assume that it isn't systematic evidence if it hasn't been reduced to numbers. On the other side are the methodologically agnostic, who are ready to altogether dismiss systematic data collection as a handmaiden of bad Western imperialist science, and who scorn the very word "data." (For those who would object that I am invoking overdrawn caricatures, both these sentiments have actually been expressed to me in these very terms on one occasion or another.)

Practitioners of the methods I speak of here are committed to systematic—not anecdotal or impressionistic—data collection and analysis.[2] Thus, we are concerned for adequate, representative sampling and adequate, fully disclosed evidence. At the same time, systematicity does not always mean large samples or quantitative findings. Indeed, the cultural analysis of discourse often militates against both, since it is so time-consuming to collect, transcribe, and analyze very large samples of the rich discourse required, and since techniques for quantification may, for all their advantages, also have the disadvantage that they wring meaning, including cultural meaning, out of these data.[3] Thus, in this methodological approach, sample size tends towards the modest and analysis does not involve much counting.[4] The proviso about sample size is true both of the number of speakers sampled and of the number of discourse units and features sampled. (It should be remembered, though, that a small number of speakers can produce a large corpus of discourse and, within that body, a large number of instances of the discourse feature under analysis—instances which, for many analytic purposes, can be treated as independent.)

I will use this article, first, as an opportunity to delineate the common ground upon which practitioners of cultural analyses of discourse stand, a stance that joins us in our commitment to systematic data collection of a certain kind. Then, in the second half, I will explore several of the more significant dimensions of difference across the analytic approaches that fall within this methodological tradition.

A Shared Tradition and its Methodological Implications

The cultural analysis of discourse begins with the assumption that people in a given group share, to greater or lesser extent, understandings of the world that have been learned and internalized in the course of their shared experience, and that individuals rely heavily on these shared understandings to comprehend and organize experience, including their own thoughts, feelings, motivations, and actions, and the actions of other people. Theoretically, this view of culture as shared understandings based on shared experience spans two contemporary subfields of psychological anthropology. It stems most directly from cognitive anthropology, in particular that school of cognitive anthropology known as the *cultural models school* or *cultural schema theory* (see, e.g., D'Andrade 1995; Holland and Quinn 1987; Strauss and Quinn 1997). It has also drawn inspiration from psychoanalytic anthropology (see, e.g., Luttrell 2003; McCollum 2002; Quinn 1997b; Westen 2001). These approaches from cognitive and psychoanalytic anthropology seek, and more and more often collaborate, to illuminate the workings of the human mind, in all its cognitive, emotional, and motivational complexity, and to trace the role of cultural meanings in these complex workings.

Importantly for this brand of research, we who conduct it recognize that these shared, or cultural, understandings are largely tacit, and referentially transparent to those who hold them. How can such cultural knowledge best be recovered or reconstructed from talk? Collective experience has proven that doing cultural analysis of discourse requires a reasonably extended sample of rich discourse. While a majority of practitioners resorted to their own version of the "interview" as the method of choice for gathering such rich talk, some have found it useful to exploit other discursive lodes, such as writings elicited for the purpose, or spontaneously-occurring genres of discourse such as folktales or other narratives. However it is collected, the cultural analysis of talk of all kinds always requires that it be tape recorded and transcribed. I take up each of these aspects of this methodological approach, about cultural analysis, about interviewing, and about tape recording, in turn.

Cultural Analysis

Discourse, rather than other kinds of human activities or behaviors, is the object of investigation for all of us because it is the best available window into cultural understandings and the way these are negotiated by individuals. Culture in this sense of understandings encompasses the largely tacit, taken-for-granted, and hence invisible assumptions that people share with others of their group and carry around inside them, and draw upon in forming expectations, reasoning, storytelling, and performing a plethora of other ordinary everyday cognitive tasks. This internalized side of culture has been the object of study by cognitive anthropologists for half a century now, and for other psychological anthropologists for even longer. In recent years, cognitive anthropologists have developed a schema theoretic account of how these shared understandings are learned and organized in the mind.[5]

A *schema* is a generic version of (some part of) the world built up from experience and stored in memory. The schema is generic because it is the cumulative outcome of just those features of successive experiences that are alike. Although schemas can change, those built on repeated experiences of a similar sort become relatively stable, influencing our interpretations of subsequent experiences more than they are altered by them. To the degree that people share experiences, they will end up sharing the same schemas—having, we would say, the same culture (or subculture). The social world is constructed in just such a way that many of our experiences—the language we speak, for example, or the way we are brought up as children, or the built environment we inhabit—are indeed shared. Hence, many, many of our schemas are cultural ones.[6]

Schemas can include words, but are hardly limited to them. They can include experience of all kinds—unlabeled as well as labeled, inarticulate as well as well-theorized, felt as well as cognized. Schemas, in short, can be as various and complex as the experience from which they are derived. The same is true, of course, for cultural schemas, which do not differ from other schemas except that they are built up from experience that has been shared.

The other side of culture is all the visible, but always partial and often cryptic, manifestations of these shared understandings that people produce. Of all such cultural products, the things people say offer certainly not an unproblematic record of the cultural understandings that people have in mind when they say them, and certainly not the only record of these shared understandings, but simply the fullest and most decipherable record available. As Hill (2005) has put it, rightly drawing our attention to culture's emergent as well as its constraining dimension in any human interaction, discourse "is the most important place where culture is both enacted and produced in the moment of interaction" (159). Hence our attention to discourse. This is certainly not meant to exclude others' efforts to reconstruct culture through the analysis of other patterns of human action and its products.

Cultural analysis, then, refers here to the effort to tease out, from discourse, the cultural meanings that underlie it. These cultural meanings are implicit in what people say, but rarely explicitly stated. In schema theoretic terms, this lack of isomorphism between what people know and what they can state arises because cultural understandings reflect the experience from which they have been learned, and this experience often occurs in nonlinguistic contexts, unattached to language. Only under special circumstances (such as some kinds of formal teaching) does experience come to us codified in language or is it translated into language. So the tacit understandings that underlie discourse must be reconstructed from the clues that this discourse provides. As I have said elsewhere (Quinn 2005b), "I came to see my analytic approach as the reconstruction, from what people said explicitly, of the implicit assumptions they must have in mind to say it" (45). The term *discourse* is used by practitioners of this kind of cultural analysis in the way linguists commonly use it, to mean language in use, either spoken or written, and typically consisting of segments of speech or written text longer than single words or sentences (see Fairclough 1992; Hill 2005). We use *discourse* interchangeably with the less technical term *talk*. Given the popularity of another, narrower, definition of the term "discourse" in contemporary usage, it needs to be added that our usage here could include but is not limited to that other sense: its Foucauldian sense of a way of talking and a set of associated practices, forms of subjectivity, and power relations that together constitute a body of knowledge, identified with members of some subgroup of society—e.g., the medical establishment, or defense intellectuals or educators. Strauss (2005) neatly distinguishes the ways of talking that are a component of Foucauldian "discourses" from other usages of "discourse" by calling the former "social discourses."[7] Nothing, of course, prevents methods of discourse analysis from being used to analyze features of social discourses. Indeed, Fairclough (1992) recommends just such a move. Strauss (2005) suggests further that inconsistency in an individual's ideas can arise from the contradictory social discourses of two different subgroups to which the speaker belongs. She gives the example of an African-American minister who delivered an anti-welfare view in his preacher's voice, using born-again Christian discourse and, in a subsequent interview, expressed a pro-welfare view in a very different, Black Power, discourse. Arising from given subcultural groups as they do, social discourses are certainly one legitimate focus of cultural analysis, and Strauss's example suggests how our appreciation of social discourses and their deployment might benefit from close linguistic analyses such as hers.

At the same time, the focus of this article on *cultural* analysis does distinguish it from the sizeable number and variety of other writings on discourse analysis. It should not be surprising that there are so very many approaches to discourse analysis, since discourse is an exceedingly rich source of data from which many different kinds of information can be retrieved. Other existing approaches may be linguistic, psychological, political, sociological, sociolinguistic, or literary in orientation—that is, examining patterns of linguistic usage in and for themselves; searching for the cognitive and/or motivational bases of this usage; tracing the deployment of power and ideology coded in it; identifying differences in speech due to gender, class, or other social categories; addressing discourse genres that have become established in given literary traditions (see, e.g., van Dijk 1985); or documenting the patterns of conversational exchange that characterize ordinary speech or speech in specialized settings such as the therapeutic or the legal or—the subject of this volume—the pedagogic (Cazden 2001; Erickson 1982, 2004; Heath 1983; Michaels 1981).[8] All of these matters are deserving of study, but they do not constitute the primary subject of this article—the cultural meanings that infuse people's talk.

The cultural analysis of discourse can be thought of as falling along a continuum, from those applications that are more concerned with the way cultural schemas are organized in and of themselves, to those that are more intent on delineating, not entire cultural schemas, but just those aspects of them that form a critical context for the interpretation of individuals' understandings of their lives, motives and identities. My own work (e.g.

Quinn 1997a) is a clear example of the former orientation (how cultural schemas are organized), while Strauss's (e.g., 2005) work presented in the same volume is a clear example of the latter (an individual's use of a cultural schema).[9] Of course, language, power, ideology, gender, class, interpersonal interaction, and other dimensions of social life cannot be disentangled from culture or language, and thus none of these is entirely absent from any cultural analysis of discourse. Nor are our methods for analyzing culture of a type apart from other methods that have been devised by specialists from other fields for studying other aspects of discourse. Quite the opposite. My colleagues and I are not staking claim to a unique methodology. We are trying to bend existing methods to the study of culture, amending and revising these or, when they do not reach all the way to our goal of cultural analysis, inventing our own extensions or entirely new methods.

The Interview

It needs to be said immediately that, in ways that will emerge, the style of interviewing favored by practitioners of the cultural analysis of discourse is far from the traditional kind of social science interviewing in which the researcher asks a set of predetermined questions, establishing a mechanical, "lets-get-this-over-with-as-quickly-as-possible atmosphere" (Strauss 2005: 239). At its most typical, that kind of interviewing is better thought of as face-to-face survey research. (Unable to find a good distinguishing label for our very different kind of "interview," I find myself resorting to surrounding it with scare quotes.)

In the important book I cited at the beginning of this article, anthropologist Charles Briggs (1986) provided a trenchant and important critique of interviewing as it is typically conducted across the social sciences. We would argue that our method of interviewing circumvents two of Briggs' chief concerns. First, he interrogates the common expectation that the interviewer controls the interview, while the interviewee's role is confined to answering questions. Says Briggs (1986), "Indeed, as many writers have argued, interviews are not supposed to be conversations" (26). In contrast, my colleagues and I view the interview as we conduct it as a special form of conversation. What is perhaps most special about this form of conversation is its one-sidedness—that is, the degree to which its control is granted to the interviewee. Secondly, Briggs makes the case that traditional interviewers, intent on amassing as much information on a given topic as possible, foreground the referential content of surface forms to the neglect of the web of meaning on which the interviewee constantly draws (1986), and privilege conscious models and explicit presuppositions over that which is outside the limits of the interviewee's awareness (1986). Our methods of discourse analysis, quite opposite to this characterization, are designed to mine implicit meaning. To draw a very brief example from my own work, here is an interview excerpt that I have partially quoted elsewhere:

> So she picks at him in that way yet I'm sure they must have something good in their marriage or they wouldn't still be together. Who knows? They might be staying together for their little girl's sake but—they—she doesn't seem to be as happy as she could be.

An analysis of the referential content of this passage would likely prompt the interviewer to ask about the way this wife "picks at" her husband, the nature of the marital "something good," the rationale behind married people staying together for the sake of their children, and why the wife doesn't seem to be happy, among other perfectly valid questions. My own analysis of the excerpt (helped by being able to place it in the context of much other causal reasoning on the same subject) extracts from it some underlying reasoning that the speaker is doubtless not even aware of drawing upon, but that depends on a cultural model of marriage that she shares with other Americans (and that would take me too much space to fully explicate here, but see Quinn 2005b)—to wit, that without mutual benefit, a marriage will not last.

I hope, then, that our methods of conducting and analyzing interviews can serve as a model for addressing and surmounting these two serious drawbacks of traditional interviewing—taking control of the interview and foregrounding its referential content—to which Briggs has rightly called attention. Nevertheless, we do interview (and Briggs does not advocate the abandonment of interviewing). There is a good reason why we depend so heavily on the interview for the discourse we subject to cultural analysis, and it is directly tied to our common focus, delineated in the last section, on the cultural understandings underlying discourse. Interviews can provide a density of clues to cultural understandings that is virtually unobtainable in any other way. This is largely because interviews, unlike many naturally occurring conversations, frame the interviewee's task as one of communicating what he or she knows about a given subject to the interviewer.

Performance of the interview task produces a relatively dense frequency of what has been called *expository discourse* (Schiffrin 1987: 17), which would seem to correspond to what Hill terms *argumentative discourse* (2005: 160), and includes what Linde (1993) calls *explanation* (90–94). As Linde (1993) defines it, the explanation is a unit of discourse that "begins with a statement of some proposition to be proved, and then follows it with a sequence of stated reasons (often multiply embedded reasons) why the proposition should be believed" (90). In its fullest form, such a sequence may end with a coda repeating and reinforcing the initial proposition. A particularly well-formed example from my own research on American marriage is the following, which was spoken as one continuous discourse unit, although I have segmented it into proposition, reasoning, and coda for illustrative purposes:

> PROPOSITION: And there isn't any signs [sic] right now that it's not going to be a very s—that our marriage isn't going to be a successful marriage in terms of lasting. Not only just lasting but our wanting it to last and enjoying each other.
> REASONING: I think Rich is very happy. I think Rich is getting affection, and having affection expressed, probably for the first time in his life, really. Really feeling accepted just for being Rich, you know. And he acts it. I mean he says things—he'll say, you know, how happy he is, and I really believe so . . . And some people have said to me that it's really obvious that he feels for me, in the way he acts, sort of thing. And certainly back on my part, I mean it's very nice knowing that I'm loved that much. That is just a tremendous feeling. I—and he spoils me rotten, at times, like when I was sick and on the couch, you know, he always changed the channel on the TV, or turned it up or down, and he still does. I mean—like he—after the seven o'clock news . . . he'll get up, wrap my—the afghans around me, turn down the game shows, turn off the light and kiss me good-night for an hour. I mean, he really does spoil me, and I really like it.
> CODA: So I don't see any reason at this point that anything is going to happen. And I can't imagine it happening. So, maybe we'll be a success.

Often, though, expository discourse is much more attenuated than full-blown explanation, dropping not only the final, finishing coda, but also most or even all of the reasons—when the speaker assumes that the listener already knows and agrees upon these reasons, for example, or when the speaker is intent on making a larger point to which the immediate assertion is subsidiary. Explanation of this kind, full-blown or attenuated, is ideal material for the reconstruction of cultural understandings.

This is not to say that such discourse automatically makes implicit cultural understandings explicit; rather, the expository discourse in interviews provides relatively rich and frequent clues to these tacit understandings. From another perspective, that of the interviewer, D'Andrade (2005) observes that, in general, "it is better not to ask informants directly about their models, but rather to ask something which will bring the model into play; that is, something that will make the person *use* the model" (90). Interviewing as we conduct it is well designed to "bring the model into play." By contrast, in other more ordinary kinds of conversation, participants begin with the assumption of shared cultural understandings. Rather than being "brought into play," these understandings tend to be indexed in passing in the course of some other immediate task, such as mutual problem solving, or gossiping, or reminiscing. Such indexing can result in highly condensed references, often cryptic to outsiders. While such unelaborated referencing is likely to be heightened in talk among familiars on topics that they routinely discuss, it figures more or less prominently in all ordinary conversation between or among those who share a common culture. The interview situation minimizes—though by no means eliminates—the indexing of shared cultural assumptions.

At their best, too, interviews of the sort we conduct encourage those interviewed to be forthcoming. Indeed, interviewers in the tradition I am describing note how crucial it is to actively grant control to the interviewee—encouraging the interviewee to organize the interview (or series of interviews) his or her own way and to pursue his or her own thoughts, conveying the interviewer's openness to the interviewee's own perspective, unique insight, and special knowledge, and being an extraordinarily good listener and a non-judgmental one. It should be clear that our approach to interviewing differs radically from the traditional method of question-asking that Briggs critiques.

Another of Briggs' (1986) major concerns about interviewing, its insensitivity to social context, is not overcome by our method, however. Because the interview is, by definition, a conversation between two people (one of whom, the interviewer, does not normally belong to the immediate social world of the other), and because the logistics of interviewing and taping make it highly impractical to conduct this conversation when and where it might overlap or interweave with ongoing talk that is part of that social world, interviews cannot capture the complexities of social relationships that are often revealed in spontaneously-occurring group conversations. It is not a good method for the investigation of social relationships in process (other than the somewhat contrived one between interviewee and interviewer themselves, of course). Still, as Hill (2005) observes, "interviews may elicit very striking and interesting narratives from people whose voices would not be heard if collection methods were restricted to 'socially-occurring' discourse" (183).[10] And, a psychological anthropologist would want to add, interviews may elicit discourse, and reveal the cultural understandings underlying that discourse, that would not otherwise be voiced by any people under any other circumstances, in any type of discourse. That is to say, some cultural knowledge that we as researchers want to retrieve would remain forever untold if not for the interview as a stimulus to its revelation. Some of my American interviewees mentioned to me that they had never thought about or talked with their spouses about their marriages in the same depth, or come to the same realizations about their marriages, before being interviewed about them.

Interviews as we conduct them also produce longer stretches of uninterrupted discourse, including both exposition and narrative, by one person than are likely to be sustained naturally. In ordinary conversation, participants typically take shorter conversational turns; indeed, in much social interaction, such turn taking is only polite. Too, the discourse produced in interviews is directed to the interview topic, and stays on topic more predictably than in spontaneously-occurring talk. Indeed, interviewers can encourage continuous discourse on the topic of their interest by redirecting an interviewee's attention to the topic at hand, and by subtler conversational maneuvers designed to keep the interviewee on track. Topic-switching in ordinary conversation between or among other parties, by contrast, is out of the researcher's control.

Interviewing also permits the researcher to arrange with a given interviewee to return to the same topic on later occasions. Such long, multiple interviews with each of her interviewees permit Strauss (e.g., 1997a, 1997b) to trace out personal semantic networks and identify inconsistencies of belief that show up only over a great deal of a given interviewee's discourse. More generally speaking, the clues that allow us to reconstruct culture are often widely dispersed and would be difficult or impossible for the researcher to trace across spontaneous conversation.

"Ideally," comments D'Andrade (2005), "one would like to encounter multiple natural situations in which people discuss with each other the relevant topic" (89). Unfortunately, the relevant topic may come up only rarely in natural contexts.[11] A final reason for relying on interviews, then, is the pragmatic difficulty of assembling a sufficient corpus of spontaneously occurring discourse on a given topic. D'Andrade goes on to consider an alternative to the interview—arranging discussions between people, somewhat like focus groups—that would circumvent this last difficulty while arguably coming closer to the ideal of collecting spontaneously-occurring talk on a topic. But it should now be clear that group interviews can have other drawbacks (most of which are addressed by Agar and McDonald 1995) for the cultural analysis of discourse. Most importantly, like the conversation in natural settings that they mimic, they encourage non-expository, highly condensed talk and short conversational turns. As already observed about spontaneous conversation, cultural assumptions in such talk are likely to be referenced only in passing, glossed over or highly abbreviated, subordinate as they are to the main conversational task—in the case of arranged group discussions, the task of debating and reaching clarity, if not agreement, on the topic under discussion. There are other limitations to such arranged discussions as sources of discourse for analysis. Like spontaneously occurring conversations, they may permit some participants to dominate the discussion, and some things to be discussed, while discouraging other participants from saying what they have to say and other things from being spoken. In addition, focus-group-style discussions may curtail the researcher's ability to keep discussion on topic. And they may be difficult to transcribe. In the end, D'Andrade (2005) concludes, "easier to arrange is the standard one-on-one interview" (90). Of course, nothing prevents one-on-one interviews from being supplemented, or perhaps preceded, by group interviews, which, like group conversation of all kinds, do turn up information and insights that might not otherwise emerge. And, in spite of all the logistical difficulties they pose, if spontaneous conversations on the research topic can be depended upon to occur in groups—say, at regular group meetings organized around a particular group interest—they should hardly be rejected as a potential source of rich discourse for cultural analysis (see, e.g., Cain 1991; Mathews 2000).

Having mounted this forceful case for interviews, I must immediately qualify it.

Nothing rules out the cultural analysis of spontaneously occurring discourse, if only that discourse is available in sufficient quantity and is sufficiently extended and rich enough.[12] Some kinds of exposition-rich discourse, such as public debate, dispute settlement, classroom instruction, or therapeutic talk in our society, may occur spontaneously in predictable, accessible settings. There is no reason, too, why interview discourse cannot be supplemented by spontaneously occurring discourse overheard or picked up on tape by the researcher, and that addresses an analytic point—as illustrated by Strauss's (2005) inclusion in her analysis, of short examples from a Thanksgiving dinner conversation she taped and from a published text. Nor is the distinction hard and fast: Somewhere between interviewing and collecting spontaneously-produced discourse lies the strategy of eliciting, for the researcher's purposes, some otherwise "entextualized" discourse—that is, discourse that "has become relatively fixed, shareable, and transmittable" (Hill 2005: 160) in a given speech community. Certain narratives provide a good example. When narratives are told in designated settings or in the course of ordinary conversation, it is feasible to ask them to be retold to the researcher—even if the setting for this retelling and the occasion for it are out of the culturally usual. Such narratives, like interviews but unlike ordinary conversation among multiple participants, can occasion relatively sustained and uninterrupted talk by the narrator, providing lengthy stretches of discourse for analysis. Mathews (2005) adopts this strategy, describing in her volume chapter how she collected and analyzed multiple versions of a folktale that is commonly retold in everyday contexts, most often as a cautionary tale to engaged couples, newlyweds, or those experiencing marital problems. She was interested in alternative male and female versions of a certain Oaxacan folktale that she had come across. She collected some tellings of it that she was lucky enough to be present for, but the tale was simply told too infrequently to make it practical for her to collect a sample of its tellings large enough for her analysis. Mathews was able to capitalize on the entextualization of this folktale to elicit recreations of it told especially for her.

Interestingly, the interview genre itself can come to have an "entextualized" quality to it, posing difficulty for any hard-and-fast distinction between spontaneous and elicited discourse. Interviewees of mine would occasionally tell me, when I showed up for our weekly interview, that they had "saved" some incident or insight to tell me about. In all these cases, the regular interview had taken on a life of its own, as a highly specialized kind of entextualized discourse that occurred in a special setting, within the intimacy of the dyadic relationship that the interviewer had developed with the interviewee.

Charlotte Linde, in the key 1993 book I cited at the beginning of this article, has made a more fundamental proposal, that interviews themselves are a naturally occurring genre of talk. As Linde (1993) comments, "[I]t is a mistake to try to make a sharp distinction between the interview situation and so-called real life, or between the interview situation and non-contrived social interaction" (60). She emphasizes that the interview itself "is part of real life too," that (59) it is "an existing social form used as a technique to achieve all kinds of social purposes"—e.g., doctor-patient, lawyer-client, hairdresser-client, and decorator-homeowner interviews. More generally, interview data are valid, she believes (61), because what people do in interviews—represent themselves and tell their life stories—is something that they do spontaneously in a wide variety of other contexts. That this task of self-presentation makes sense to interviewees—in the context of an interview just as in other, more ordinary contexts—is responsible for their willingness to take charge of the interviewing process and to talk. Further, it accounts for what Luttrell

(1997; in this volume) describes as the "narrative urgency" with which people like the women she interviewed tell their stories and thereby "define and defend their selves and identities" (8).

Of course, Linde and Luttrell interviewed English-speaking Americans. The experiences of anthropologists working in other places suggest that, if the interview cannot be treated as "an existing social form" everywhere in the world, perhaps people everywhere at least practice some form of interlocution that is close enough to the interview so that either this alternative discourse genre can be adapted to the anthropologist's purpose, or the speaker can make the conversion into an interviewee. The presence of interview-like genres in other places should not surprise us, any more than Hill's (2005) conclusion that there is a universal human narrative competence surprises us. Language evolved, after all, for the purpose of communication, and something akin to an "interview" in format appears to be one of the modes of linguistic communication, along with narrative and conversation, granted us within the constraints of human cognition and social life.

Caution is merited before assuming the transferability of this method of data collection, intact, across cultural setting—and across class and educational disparity. How to locate and adapt some other, local, discourse genre that can serve the same purpose may be far from obvious. I will give two examples. In 2007 I returned to my field site, a Mfantse fishing town outside of Cape Coast, Ghana, to interview women about child rearing. Because my Mfantse comprehension is far from good enough for interviewing, I prevailed upon a young Ghanaian friend of mine who spoke Mfantse, Aseye Ame-Bruce, to conduct the interviews, while I listened in as best I could. Things seemed to be progressing splendidly: Many times the speaker grew highly animated, and we were collecting an unimaginable welter of information and opinion. I did notice, however, that in the course of the interviews Aseye was doing her share of the talking, contributing her own experiences and reactions freely. I had always considered it a sign that my American interviewee had taken control of the interviews if they were doing the lion's share of the talking. I asked Aseye about this, and she explained to me that these women expected her to join in the discussion, and would be uncomfortable if she did not. Different discourse rules apparently applied than when interviewing Americans—at least in this context (there are other Mfantse contexts in which people are expected to speechify at length).

An even more striking case is that of Debra Skinner's experience attempting to interview Nepalese women about their lives, summarized in Holland and Lave (2001): "Expecting a narrative, a life story, when she asked them to tell her about their lives, she was surprised when they sang songs for her instead, especially ones that had been collaboratively produced by groups of local women for the Tij festival" (11). One kind of song, *dukha* (hardship, suffering) songs, told by women for an audience of women, vividly depict moving scenes of inequality in the domestic lives of women. Prose stories of actual life events are also told by these rural people from central Nepal; *dukha*, while they may be based on individual women's life stories, are clearly more generic than the life stories of particular individuals (Holland and Skinner 2001).[13] But the songs are just as clearly a significant cultural medium for enunciating women's perspective on, and evaluation of, their lives—a rich resource for the reconstruction of cultural understandings of gendered domestic relationships, and an invaluable one for the interpretation of women's lives themselves. In a comparable way, Mathews (personal communication) reports that she could not get Oaxacans to talk about marital relationships until she happened on the device of presenting them with renditions of the *La Llorona* tale, which unexpectedly opened the floodgates to their discourse on marriage. Researchers working in places where interviewing is an unfamiliar genre must, as Briggs (1986: 59) advises, do early and extensive ethnography of speaking to identify local genres such as *dukha* songs and *La Llorona* tales that can provide entrée into topics or deepen and expand knowledge of them.

Briggs' critique goes further, though. He worries not only that researchers may be inattentive to local discourse genres, but also that we may be insensitive to the local, culturally valued, meta-communicative norms embedded in these genres. And that interviewing may impose our own meta-communicative norms, ones that violate local ones (1986, especially pp. 90–92; Briggs calls this "communicative hegemony"). We claim to have adapted interviewing to one set of local meta-communicative norms, those for conversation among Americans. Can interviewing as we do it be combined with attention to other local genres, and re-adapted to other local norms of communication, in such a way as to lay Briggs' concern to rest? Admittedly, we have not yet demonstrated this. This question will have to be addressed as those who pursue the cultural analysis of discourse attempt to extend it beyond Americans to other, comparative, research settings so important to the cultural anthropological enterprise.

From a different angle altogether, defense of the interview and other "contrived" opportunities to collect discourse is necessary because, in our reliance on it, those of us in the cultural discourse analysis tradition differ sharply from many linguistic anthropologists. As Hill (2005), trained as a linguist, points out, her colleagues strongly prefer to work on narratives, and by extension, other types of discourse, that occur spontaneously "in everyday contexts of family, work, play, religious observation, courtroom procedure, medical treatment, scientific conferences, and the like, that are not elicited or organized by the anthropologist" (161). But this preference ought not to harden into a prejudice against the interviews favored by cultural discourse analysts.

To see that analyses of both kinds of discourse have their place, what must first be appreciated is that linguistic and psychological anthropologists who analyze discourse have different research foci and goals. Linguistic anthropologists, understandably, have their eye on language—a cultural domain in its own right, of course, if a highly specialized one—and have as their goal a better understanding of how language works.[14] This is an enterprise well served by analysis of spontaneous discourse. A good recent example of this focus exclusively on language, and based on spontaneous discourse, is the fine-grained, masterful study by Elinor Ochs and Lisa Capps (2001) of everyday storytelling, or conversational narrative, as this goes around the dinner table and in other family settings. While the authors (Ochs and Capps 2001) subtitle their book *creating lives in everyday storytelling*, and observe early on that "conversation is the most likely medium for airing unresolved life events" (7), it is neither the creation of lives nor the life events aired, as these may be culturally patterned and hence revealing of cultural presuppositions, upon which the authors focus their attention. Instead, and, again, understandably, their focus is on patterns in the structure of such narratives themselves, and in the process of their telling: e.g., what makes them tellable, for instance, or how they get launched, or how their temporal sequencing is managed, or how children, over the course of development, are incorporated into their telling, or how these narratives embody moral assessments, or how their plots are structured. Analysis of the cultural content of these moral messages itself is not the point.

As is typical of psychological and other cultural anthropologists, we practitioners of cultural analysis of discourse are primarily concerned, not with some particular linguistic feature, discourse type, or speech genre, but with some underlying cultural topic, theme, or schema, or a cluster of these—for example, a cultural model of marriage (Quinn 1997a; 1997b), or beliefs about work and welfare (Strauss 2002; 2005: 204–221), or the divided identity conferred by schooling (Luttrell 1997). Because our eye is on that underlying topic of interest, we will organize our presentation around that topic and are likely to be eclectic as to the discourse types and genres we submit to analysis in the pursuit of insight into the cultural question before us. (Conversely, a linguist's eye is likely to be on a discourse type, and to be eclectic as to discourse topic.)

Even within interviews and other relatively rich sources of discourse for cultural analysis, the topics of interest to psychological anthropologists are likely to arise much less frequently than the features of language that are the focus of socio-linguists' and linguistic anthropologists' study. From the point of view of a linguistic anthropologist like Hill (2005), for whom narratives on any subject are grist for the analytical mill, narrative is "extremely common," especially brief narrative embedded in other types of discourse. But from my vantage point (Quinn 2005b: 43–44), narratives on the particular topic of my research—marriage—did not occur commonly enough to be useful for analysis; so I rejected them as an object of analysis in favor of the much more frequently-occurring metaphors interviewees used for marriage and the reasoning embedded in their explanations of it.

Here, then, is the take-home lesson: For those of us who do cultural analysis of discourse, what matters is dishing up a big scoop of language—one we can be relatively certain will contain plentiful, rich clues to the topic under study. And it is because we are intent on reconstructing the presuppositions underlying language, and not with language *per se*, that we are less concerned than are linguistic anthropologists with whether the discourse on which we draw for our analysis has been produced spontaneously in natural settings. The discourse we analyze must conform to a less stringent standard of "naturalness" than that analyzed by linguists; but that doesn't mean that there is no standard. This discourse must be collected in such a way as to minimize distortion to the underlying cultural presuppositions we wish to recover. But the paranoia of some anthropologists—who believe that nothing people tell us is to be trusted because nothing people say is free of distortion—is unjustified. As I elsewhere (Quinn 2005b) point out and illustrate with regard to such features of speech as metaphor use (see also my short example of reasoning earlier in this paper), the invocation of cultural presuppositions in interviews, as in any spoken discourse, is largely beyond the conscious control of the speaker. The corollary to D'Andrade's (2005) observation that speakers typically cannot state cultural assumptions directly, is that they are unaware of using them. These taken-for-granted presuppositions therefore have a good chance of surviving both any foreignness of the interview genre, and any effects on the interview by the interviewee-interviewer relationship. Of course, this caveat does not relieve us of acknowledging, and taking measures to minimize, these two sources of bias. Once again, however, our attention to non-referential assumptions underlying prepositional knowledge, rather than to the latter "information" itself, marks ours as a very different breed of interviewing than the traditional "information-amassing" task that Briggs (1998) critiques.

It should be stressed that these various suggestions for letting the interviewee talk freely and expansively, even to the point of pursuing tangents, do not preclude leading the interviewee back to topic when he or she has strayed altogether too far for too long, or asking questions about matters that the interviewee seems to have forgotten or avoided. A technique used by interviewers is to develop a comprehensive checklist of items that have ever been raised by any interviewee in connection with the topic at hand, or that the researcher thinks may be relevant to the topic, but not asking about these matters until the very end of the series of interviews with each interviewee.[15] In this way, exhaustiveness of inquiry and comparability across subjects do not have to be sacrificed to freeness of form.

Luttrell (this volume) offers suggestions for what she calls *psychoanalytic listening*—actively paying attention to how individuals make sense of their own stories, to their fantasies, images, feelings, and the other associations they make. Luttrell found especially useful those "intruding associations" that initially seem to the interviewer to disrupt the interview and the research focus, but which led, on rethinking, to major breakthroughs in the research process. Equally rewarding for this process was attention to instances of her own reluctance to deal with topics that evoked strong or mixed emotions—"what could be called countertransference in my fieldwork relationships," she says (this volume: 271). Relatedly, Strauss (2005) advises that we should "let interviewees speak in a stream-of-consciousness fashion" (239), which parallels the clinical technique of encouraging free association. There is also my own suggestion (2005a) about making a mental note of, and following up on, cues that an interviewee might have more to say on a given topic; and Luttrell's tip (this volume) about treating interviewees' conversational "tangents" as clues. While interviewees might be culled from an initial telephone survey, as Strauss's originally were, neither she nor any other contributor would suggest anything but face-to-face interviewing, and it should be apparent, from these suggestions for psychoanalytic listening, why not.

Tape Recording

Discourse analysis, including the cultural analysis of discourse, requires some kind of written record of that discourse to work with (see Briggs 1986: 99). Discourse analysts differ as to the types of notational systems they use for transcribing and the level of notational detail these systems require, depending on their analytic purpose.[16] As Catherine Riessman (1993), in her useful discussion of transcribing, recommends, I myself work initially from a very bare-bones transcription, returning to the tapes to listen to selected passages that bear closer analysis, and augmenting their original transcription with further detail. The initial stages of analysis typically require, as Reissman (1993) reports, considerable time spent just scrutinizing one's transcriptions, and going back and forth among them. (At some point in working with mine, I found I had become so familiar with them that I could quote them extensively in my head.) Of course, what and how one transcribes itself reflects the analyst's interests (Ochs 1979).[17] In general, in line with our commitment to ceding control of the interview to the interviewee, my colleagues and I try not to interpose too many transcriptional conventions and devices between the tape recording and the analysis (a point I owe to Holly Mathews, personal communication). And, in line with our interests in underlying cultural meaning, broadly speaking we begin with *what* people are saying, both explicitly and implicitly, and only subsequently and selectively turn to relevant aspects of how they say it—including, e.g., meta-linguistic features of discourse which may not have been captured in the original "bare-bones" transcript. Thus, for example, in her elucidation of interviewees' personal semantic networks, Strauss (2005) initially isolates their usages of a key word—"work"—in her transcripts, and the most frequent associations of that word to other words and phrases, and the recurrent themes surrounding it, and then takes up associated "emotional and motivational hot spots" which may be reflected in "emotional tone," such as the pride or outrage with which memories are reported or opinions given. To take this analysis of "hot spots" one step further, she might find it worthwhile to include tone of voice in the assessment of emotional tone, returning to her tapes to listen for and label this paralinguistic feature of her interviewees' talk.

Whatever their procedures, like other discourse analysts, we rely on close analysis of tape-recorded, transcribed discourse. A cultural anthropologist I know once told me that she didn't need to tape record, because she had such a good memory, which she relied upon to write everything down immediately after an interview. But cultural analysis, we have already seen, does not rely on the manifest or referential content of what is said in an interview. It requires a search for evidence of tacit understandings, and comparison across multiple samples of discourse to find patterns in this evidence. These clues are to be found, for example, in metaphor usage, in the recurrence across varied language of under-lying propositions, in departures from temporal narrative sequencing, in subtle linguistic markers of the cultural standing of ideas, in non-obvious asymmetries between folktales told by men and told by women, or in occasional meta-comments on what had previously been said—to name just a few of the features of discourse that receive attention in cultural analyses of discourse. These features of discourse are so subliminal as not to be noticed by either interviewer or interviewee while the interview is ongoing, never mind remembered after it. Working in another language and culture, and lacking full control of it, the outside analyst will surely want to partner with a local one. Even scrupulous notes taken during the interview will miss these clues. Notes are likely to capture no more than the overall sense of the conversation, along with, perhaps, brief fragments of actual speech. Moreover, such notes are likely to be rendered in the tacit, taken-for-granted, cultural understand-ings of the interviewer—which are not necessarily those of the interviewee. (This is decidedly not to say that tape recording relieves the researcher of keeping separate field notes, which have their own role to play in field research; detailed field notes augment, and are often kept by, researchers conducting cultural analyses of talk.) Finally, it needs to be added, the features of discourse that enter into our analyses are so often tacit, subtle, subliminal, as to require of the analyst native or near-native control over the language and culture of the interviewee. This is undoubtedly another reason why so many of us have worked in our own language and culture.

In linguistics and in most quarters of sociology and the other social sciences in which researchers use the interview or collect other kinds of discourse, the use of tape recorders would require no defense. Today, among cultural anthropologists like my colleague with the good memory, this practice does need defending. Anthropologists who object to tape recording do so on three grounds. The first reason likely to be given is that tape recording may arouse suspicion or occasion outright objection. It is true, certainly, that an historical association of recording equipment of any kind with government surveillance has made people in some nations very jumpy about its use in any context. Certainly, also, the cosmological beliefs of some other groups of people, or their attitudes toward anthropol-ogists, or other concerns, make them resistant to the use of recording devices, cameras as well as tape recorders, for research purposes. It is also the case that some individuals everywhere do not want what they have to say, or some things they have to say, taped because of the potential loss of privacy. Research dependent upon analysis of taped discourse must be limited or redesigned in such circumstances. But it seems to me misguided to make these particular circumstances under which tape recorders cannot be used, into a blanket justification for not using them. The kind of cultural analysis advocated in this article requires tape-recorded discourse. All field researchers who have used this approach have undoubtedly had to explain, initially, the presence of their recorders and had to obtain permission to use them under stipulated conditions. Such explanations and negotiations are well worth making.

A second, related, objection anthropologists commonly bring forward is that the tape recorder is too invasive—too Western, too technological—a research tool. We should remember, though, that all over the world people are becoming more familiar with and more technologically sophisticated about the use of tape recorders (and even their more advanced cousins, video recorders) all the time. But there is a more fundamental problem with this bias against the tape recorder. To single it out as overly invasive is to displace onto it a larger issue—the invasiveness of even paper and pencil as a technology, of participant observation as a method, of the more general Western project of making records of people's talk and other practices and publishing these, along with our interpretations of them, in books.

Thirdly, even if they accept the use of the tape recorder in principle, other anthropologists are primed to assume that these devices will create practical difficulties—like the graduate student I asked whether she intended to take a tape recorder with her to the field, who answered without a blink, "Oh, but tape recorders are sooo intrusive." In my own view, nothing is more intrusive—even, among some groups and in some contexts, rude—than a listener scribbling madly rather than looking at you while you talk (I feel this way about students taking notes in classrooms, where I myself am subjected to it). Tape recorders, in this sense, may well be *less* intrusive than paper and pen or pencil (or their replacement, the laptop), since they free the interviewer to be a good listener and pay attention. They are also small and quiet, so that their presence is almost always quickly forgotten. In my view, anthropologists ought to rethink what may amount to a romantic prejudice against the tape recorder.

This issue is important because audiotapes are an unparalleled source of data. Moreover, the rapid development of audio and video recording and analysis technology will only bring more and better data—as it also increases the welter of this data, raising new problems about how and what to select for transcription (Hill 2005: 161). Perhaps the prospect of so much data to process and analyze is daunting to some. However, if anthropologists today truly want, as we say we do, to make heard the voices of the people we study, and to avoid distorting these voices through the filter of our own meta-narratives, then we ought to welcome use of the tape recorder as an essential aid in that effort.

One Choice Leads to Another

An important question every researcher must begin by asking is this: What does he or she hope to gain from the analysis? In my own case, for instance, I started out by questioning whether there was a set of understandings Americans shared about marriage. More generally, I wished to use this case study to explore the nature of culture, defined as shared understandings. Although the body of discourse with which I worked would have allowed me to explore variation across individuals, marriages, or genders, or variability in the way in which individuals mold the cultural model of marriage to their own personal experience, or manage their personal psychic conflicts with respect to marriage, I have not pursued these lines of inquiry as I explained earlier (but see Quinn 1992). Of course, one choice leads to another, ending in unexpected places. The discovery and delineation of a highly shared cultural model led me to further theorizing about the function of such culturally shared event sequences in reasoning, their role in the production of metaphor in discourse, and the basis of this cultural model in deep motivation. In one way or another, though, these are all questions about how and why cultural sharing arises.

It would be a careless mistake to assume that culture is the only source of constraint on what individuals are free to think, say, or do. Another source, of course, is the individual's own distinctive lifetime of experience, including those early, traumatic, or otherwise signal experiences that give indelible structure to the individual's ongoing concerns—the structure of the personality, if you will. This point about distinctive individual orientations to culturally shared matters is made by Strauss (2005), in her a comparison of the very different personal semantic networks surrounding two interviewees' views of work and welfare, and her speculation about the experiences in each of their lives leading them to these personal webs of meaning. Interestingly, the personal semantic networks of each interviewee may share themes—such as the assumption that work is fulfilling, or the belief that welfare mothers have too many children—with other interviewees, though these themes may bear distinctive resonances, and be more or less central, for each individual. These shared themes point to subcultural clustering.

Strauss works with discourse across interviews taken from the same person at different times, allowing her to better assess the enduringness of given themes across these different tellings by the same individual. That some themes prove to have constancy is not to say that the interviewer is never implicated in the form and content of the interviewee's story. But those who emphasize only how individuals negotiate culture to suit the immediate circumstances of the interview and the interviewee-interviewer relationship, all too often work with isolated pieces of discourse collected from different interviewees. This practice (easy to fall into when the researcher does not use a tape recorder that would allow collection of longer, fuller bodies of discourse) may promote a false sense of the mutability of meanings for individuals.

Moreover, the practice of analyzing a few scattered excerpts of discourse can give no sense at all of the shared understandings that inevitably, in any society or group, frame the ideas and actions of individuals, even when these individuals, as do Strauss's interviewees, draw only selectively on what is widely understood and shape these wider understandings in distinctively personal ways, or reject them altogether. At the other end of Strauss's continuum of cultural standing from what interviewees take for granted or regard as common opinion, are ideas they proffer that they mark as matters of opinion, or even highly controversial. These are matters of opinion or controversy, Strauss stresses, with respect to what the interviewees imagine these widely shared understandings to be. An analysis founded on an inadequate corpus of relevant discourse leaves the impression, and sometimes fuels the claim, that there are no such shared understandings.

A second decision that arises early in any cultural analysis of discourse is what type of discourse to focus on. Practitioners have three broad strategies for selecting discourse types for analysis. Some researchers—e.g., D'Andrade (2005) in his classroom exercise on social inequality, Strauss (2005) in her analysis of people's attitudes toward welfare, and I

(Quinn 2005b) in my analysis of people's understandings of marriage—focus on passages containing *expository discourse*. This consists in propositions stated in the form of explanation, belief, opinion, and the like, and, as I argued in a previous section, *The interview*, is especially rich in linguistic clues to underlying cultural understandings. D'Andrade's (2005) student interviewers asked their interviewee colleagues a series of questions such as, "What does social equality mean to you?" "What are examples of social inequality?" and "Why does this happen?" (90) and probed for clarification and amplification in a way that was well designed to elicit explanations of social equality and inequality. Strauss and I also asked our interviewees questions on our respective topics, but over longer, less tightly focused, interviews that encouraged the interviewees to stray to matters that they perceived to be related.

Others analyze *narrative*. For Hill (2005) the most general point is to demonstrate how culture-full such narratives are, and how this rich cultural meaning is made through narratives, as well as how these cultural meanings can be extracted from them. She chose them to illustrate, more specifically, the structure of narrative and a series of theoretical problems and possibilities in the cultural analysis of narrative sequence, attempts at coherence construction, apparent deviations from narrative structure, the dialogic dimension of narrative, and the embedding of narrative within longer discourse. Mathews (2005) analyzes variants of a widely told folktale, *La Llorona* (The Weeping Woman), for the obvious reason that she was concerned with the domain of gender and this particular folktale—variants of which are widespread in Mexico, and which is a conspicuous part of folk tradition in the Oaxacan Mexican community she studied—is a matchless window onto gendered relationships, particularly marital ones. The tale is used by Oaxacan elders as a dramatic device to inculcate in young men and women certain moral values concerning marriage. Hence it is made up of injunctions about the ideal marital relationship and illustrations of how this relationship can fail.

The work of Luttrell (1997; in this volume) and Strauss (2005) exemplifies yet another option, the analysis of *life stories* (Linde 1993). Strauss (2005) terms these *life histories* to mark the fact that she gathered this life story material by asking interviewees to tell the complete stories of their lives (rather than about some particular part of their lives as, in Luttrell's case, their school experience, which then led to the telling of life stories). These life stories or life histories are larger units of discourse that contain both conversational narrative and explanation (Linde 1993). Notably, they are *stories* rather than *a story*—that is, segments of a longer story of one's life that is told discontinuously at different times, and that is always provisional, being supplemented, updated, and revised over the course of one's life. Even the "complete" life histories collected by Strauss have this selective and unfinished quality shared by all such life stories.

A still different discourse type is the *conversation*. Interviewing as we typically conduct it does not encourage such exchange (but remember my example of interviewing Mfantse women, in which the interview was modified to accommodate the culturally expected back-and-forth). There is, however, a well-established tradition in linguistics of collecting and analyzing spontaneously occurring conversations, and certainly such conversations can be rich in cultural content. Miller and her colleagues (Miller, Fung, and Mintz 1996), for example, demonstrate how co-narratives mothers construct with their children can be mined for culturally distinctive moral messages. Taiwanese mothers use such exchanges as educational opportunities to revisit incidents of their children's bad behavior, shaming them in front of new audiences; while American mothers use co-narratives to praise their children for past actions, building their self-esteem. Conversational exchanges between teacher and student would be another obvious discourse to investigate.

What motivated a researcher's choice of discourse type? This choice depended on a purely pragmatic assessment of the likelihood that exposition, narrative, life story, or conversational exchange would be dense with cultural presuppositions on the topic of study. For example, Mathews (personal communication) decided to elicit tellings of the *La Llorona* folktale after she had heard the tale told in spontaneous conversation and realized that men and women were telling strikingly different versions of this same tale. She also noticed that the tale was sometimes being referenced without being actually told (a good example of cultural knowledge that can be left implicit because already shared by all parties to a conversation), in the context of talk about others' inappropriate spousal behavior or the state of their marriages. She surmised from all this that the folktale would be a rich source of cultural presuppositions about marriage and gender.

For another example, asking people to tell me about their marriages suited my purpose of reconstructing their understandings of marriage, because their marriages are typically an important, richly discussed segment of married Americans' life stories. D'Andrade might have used the same device, asking students about their personal experiences with social inequality as they were growing up and going to school, for instance. But he could not be certain, as I was with regard to adults' marital experiences, that all students would have had or recognized experiences of social inequality, or found them important enough to incorporate into their stories about their lives. He and his student researchers might have failed to pick up, from these stories, a sampling of interviewees' views on social inequality and inequality that would be extensive and comprehensive enough for analysis.

Researchers who are directly interested in the topics of self and identity are most likely to find life stories analytically helpful, since these stories contain such a concentration of presuppositions about one's self and one's identity. It is no accident, then, that Luttrell, setting out to develop a theory of "the links among school structure, culture, identity, and self-understanding" (this volume: 265), chose to analyze life stories. In the end, we all ask about something that will make the speaker use the model under examination. What that model is (e.g., of marriage, social inequality, schooling), and what the discursive contexts and formats are for talking about it, dictate the discourse type most suitable for its reconstruction.

Conclusion

There is no recipe for doing this kind of research. From beginning to end it is an adventure. Where to start? What to do next? What trade-offs have to be made, for example between the scope of the cultural schema(s) captured and the depth of the cultural detail described; between cultural generalizations and individual lives; between reducing data and preserving cultural meanings; between following one cultural lead or another. Meanwhile, how has our research objective shifted as we went along? How must method be adapted, and how has theory evolved? And how is our confidence in the value of the ultimate outcome to survive? The visceral side of this process is the inevitable drudgery, the hesitations and miscues, uncertainties and anxieties, as well as the happy serendipities, and the satisfying moments of discovery that attend analysis.[18]

It should be ultra-clear, then: Researchers should not approach this methodological tradition thinking that they will find just that method or set of methods they can mechanically and unquestioningly apply to their own research. Readers should treat this family of methods, not as a methodological canon, but as a starter methodological repertoire to be expanded and selectively drawn upon according to their own cultural analysis. Each researcher will have to find and create his or her own personal approach. Guided, in each case, by local opportunities for and limitations on collecting discourse, by the nature of the resulting corpus and, in the end most decisively, by the theoretical questions being asked and perspective being taken. I hope readers will treat this article as inspirational reading, providing them with some ideas and some of the self-assurance to help them adapt and invent methods to suit their own diverse research purposes, just as others before them have done. For the most general lesson to be taken away is that the cultural analysis of discourse can be done by anyone with the patience for close, attention-demanding, time-consuming work and an eye for pattern, detail, and nuance.

Notes

1. This chapter has been adapted from the author's Introduction to her edited volume, *Finding Culture in Discourse* (Quinn 2005c).
2. For a penetrating discussion of what such systematicity can involve when the data are interviews, see Luttrell (in this volume: 258–260).
3. See an article by Linda Garro (2000) for a useful comparison of how two kinds of analysis of the same material, one based on cultural models theory and adopting a methodological approach akin to those presented in this volume, the other based on consensus theory and employing methods more amenable to quantification, can be used in collaboration.
4. Although numbers are certainly presented when appropriate. D'Andrade (2005) for example, uses word frequencies to winnow out "gist propositions"; Quinn (2005b) demonstrates that over 400 metaphors fall into just eight categories; and Mathews (2005) tallies male and female versions of the *La Llorona* folktale.
5. See the opening pages of Quinn (2005b) for a brief historical recounting of this theoretical development, and D'Andrade (1995: 122–149) for a fuller account.
6. See Strauss and Quinn (1997).
7. Also see Erickson (2004: 107–133) for his discussion of varying strands of discourse analysis, which he characterizes as top-down and bottom-up.
8. See Cazden (1986) for a review of various strands of discourse analysis within classroom contexts.
9. Another way to put this is that in some work, like my own, the cultural schema is the unit of analysis whereas in other work, like Strauss's, the individual's use of the schema is the unit of analysis.
10. I prefer "spontaneous discourse" or "spontaneously-occurring discourse" to Hill's "socially-occurring discourse," in order to avoid any confusion with Strauss's term, "social discourses," which she uses for an entirely different purpose (see the end of the last section). Further, "socially-occurring" might suggest that interviews themselves were not, as Linde argues they are, social events in their own right.
11. Think, for example, of the difficulties I might have encountered had I tried to collect discourse about marriage as this arose spontaneously in conversations at bars or coffee klatches or mealtimes (I would have had to wait an awfully long time between mentions of my topic); or in intimate conversations between spouses (How would I have gained access to these?); or in marital therapy sessions (even could I have gained access, these would have been tilted in a particular direction and cast in a technical language unlike that of ordinary conversation about marriage).
12. Alexei Yurchak (1997a, 1997b), for one good example, has collected and analyzed Soviet political discourse, including written (textual) materials and spontaneously occurring talk, augmented by his observations of other, non-linguistic, practices.
13. These hardships and suffering include preferential treatment of brothers, displacement by co-wives, abuse by husbands, and the like. The actual stories that find their way into such songs are especially likely to be those told by recently married young women who have returned to their natal villages, sometimes for the first time since marrying out, to attend the annual Tij festival and join in the composition of songs being prepared for the festival (Holland and Skinner 2001).
14. And within the field of education, the goal has been to understand how language works in the service (or not) of student learning and achievement.

15. For example, in my own research on marriage, this checklist (Quinn 2005b) included "every aspect of their marriages and marriage in general that any interviewee had ever raised, including items such as pet names couples had for each other, the kinds of birthday gifts they gave each other, and dreams about their spouses interviewees had had . . . That few interviewees had much to add in response to these checklist questions suggests that the approach of letting them organize and run the interviews, and talk as long as they wanted to, succeeded in eliciting from them all that they did have to say, at that time, about marriage" (41–42).

16. A pointed example is provided by Strauss (2005a), who shifts to a more fine-grained level of analysis than she typically relies on, in order to capture speakers' ambivalence on the topic of welfare. For this purpose Strauss adds line-by-line numbering so that she can readily refer to meta-linguistic features within each line of discourse. She then homes in on what she calls "verbal fumbling"—pauses and hesitations, verbal fillers, disfluencies, sighs—and other linguistic features such as shifts in pronoun from "I" to "you" (e.g., "You think" versus "I think") or hedging ("you could almost say that . . .") or laminating ("If you want to get into a real paranoid view . . ."), all of which mark places in each line where the speaker switches voices. She also describes these different voices, which reflect the speaker's conflicting internal positions about welfare—though she does not, as a linguist might, employ a notation to represent the qualities of the voices.

17. Ochs suggests ways to reduce bias in transcription of child language.

18. The separate accounts of their research by the contributors to Quinn (2005a) give immediacy and passion to this bedeviled research process and the lessons learned along the way.

References

Agar, M. and MacDonald, J. 1995. "Focus groups and ethnography," *Human Organization*, 54:1: 78–86.

Briggs, C. L. 1986. *Learning How to Ask: a sociolinguistic appraisal of the role of the interview in social science research*, Cambridge, UK: Cambridge University Press.

Cain, C. 1991. "Personal stories: identity acquisition and self-understanding in Alcoholics Anonymous," *Ethos*, 19:2: 210–253.

Cazden, C. 1986. "Classroom discourse," in *Handbook of Research on Teaching*, 3rd edn, American Educational Research Association, New York: Macmillan Publishing Co., pp. 432–463.

—— . 2001. *Classroom Discourse: the language of teaching and learning*, Portsmouth NH: Heinemann.

D'Andrade, R. 2005. "Some methods for studying cultural cognitive structures," in N. Quinn (ed.) *Finding Culture in Talk*, New York: Palgrave Macmillan, pp. 83–104.

—— . (1995) *The Development of Cognitive Anthropology*. Cambridge, UK: Cambridge University Press.

Erickson, F. 1982. "Classroom discourse as improvisation: relationships between academic task structure and social participation structure in lessons," in L. C. Wilkinson (ed.) *Communicating in the Classroom*, New York: Academic Press, pp. 153–179.

—— . 2004. *Talk and Social Theory: ecologies of speaking and listening in everyday life*, Cambridge, MA: Polity Press.

Fairclough, N. 1992. *Discourse and Social Change*, Cambridge, England: Polity Press.

Garro, L. 2000. "Remembering what one knows and the construction of the past: a comparison of cultural consensus theory and cultural schema theory," *Ethos*, 28:3: 275–319.

Heath, S. B. 1983. *Ways with Words: language, life, and work in communities and classrooms*, Cambridge, UK: Cambridge University Press.

Hill, J. 2005. "Finding culture in narrative," in N. Quinn (ed.) *Finding Culture in Talk*, New York: Palgrave Macmillan, pp. 157–202.

Holland, D. and Lave, J. 2001 "History in person: an introduction," in D. Holland and J. Lave (eds.) *History in Person: enduring struggles, contentious practice, intimate identities*, Santa Fe, NM: School of American Research Press, pp. 3–33.

Holland, D. and Quinn, N. (eds.) 1987. *Cultural Models in Language and Thought*, Cambridge, UK: Cambridge University Press.

Holland, D. and Skinner, D. 2001. "From women's suffering to women's politics: reimagining women after Nepal's 1990 pro-democracy movement," in D. Holland and J. Lave (eds.) *History in Person: enduring struggles, contentious practice, intimate identities*, Santa Fe, NM: School of American Research Press, pp. 93–133.

Linde, C. 1993. *Life Stories: the creation of coherence*, Oxford: Oxford University Press.

Luttrell, W. 2003. *Pregnant Bodies, Fertile Minds: race, gender and the schooling of pregnant teens.* New York: Routledge.

—— . 1997. *Schoolsmart and Motherwise: working-class women's identity and schooling*, New York: Routledge.

McCollum, C. 2002. "Relatedness and self-definition: two dominant themes in middle-class Americans' life stories," *Ethos*, 30:1/2: 113–139.

Mathews, H. 2005. "Uncovering cultural models of gender from accounts of folktales," in N. Quinn (ed.) *Finding Culture in Talk*, New York: Palgrave Macmillan, pp. 105–155.

—— . 2000. "Negotiating cultural consensus in a breast cancer self-help group," *Medical Anthropology Quarterly*, 14:3: 394–413.

Michaels, S. 1981. "'Sharing time': children's narratives styles and differential access to literacy," *Language and Society*, 10: 423–442.

Miller, P. J., Fung, H., and Mintz, J. 1996. "Self-construction through narrative practices: a Chinese and American comparison of early socialization," *Ethos*, 24:2: 237–280.

Ochs, E. 1979. "Transcription as theory," in E. Ochs and B. B. Schieffelin (eds.) *Developmental Pragmatics*, New York: Academic Press, pp. 43–72.

Ochs, E. and Capps, L. 2001. *Living Narrative: creating lives in everyday storytelling*, Cambridge, MA: Harvard University Press.

Quinn, N. 1992. "The motivational force of self-understanding: evidence from wives' inner conflicts," in R. D'Andrade and C. Strauss (eds.) *Human Motives and Cultural Models*, Cambridge, UK: Cambridge University Press, pp. 90–126.

—— . 1997a. "Research on shared task solutions," in C. Strauss and N. Quinn, *A Cognitive Theory of Cultural Meaning*, Cambridge, UK: Cambridge University Press.

pp. 137–188.

—— . 1997b. "Research on the psychodynamics of shared understandings," in C. Strauss and N. Quinn, *A Cognitive Theory of Cultural Meaning*, Cambridge, UK: Cambridge University Press, pp. 189–209.

—— . 2005a. *Finding Culture in Talk: a collection of methods*. New York: Palgrave Macmillan.

—— . 2005b. "How to reconstruct schemas people share, from what they say," in N. Quinn (ed.) *Finding Culture in Talk*, New York: Palgrave Macmillan, pp. 35–81.

—— . 2005c. Introduction to *Finding Culture in Talk*, N. Quinn (ed.), New York: Palgrave Macmillan, pp. 1–34.

Riessman, C. K. 1993. *Narrative Analysis*, Newbury Park, CA: Sage Publications.

Schiffrin, D. 1987. *Discourse Markers*, Cambridge, UK: Cambridge University Press.

Strauss, C. 1997a. "Partly fragmented, partly integrated: an anthropological examination of 'post-modern fragmented subjects,'" *Cultural Anthropology*, 12: 362–404.

—— . 1997b. "Research on cultural discontinuities," in C. Strauss and N. Quinn (eds.) *A Cognitive Theory of Cultural Meaning*, Cambridge, UK: Cambridge University Press, pp. 210–251.

—— . 2002. "Not so rugged individualists: U.S. Americans' conflicting ideas about poverty," in F.F. Piven, J. Acker, M. Hallock, and S. Morgan (eds.) *Work, Welfare, and Politics: confronting poverty in the wake of welfare reform*, Eugene, OR: University of Oregon.

—— . 2005. "Analyzing discourse for cultural complexity," in N. Quinn (ed.) *Finding Culture in Talk*, New York: Palgrave Macmillan, pp. 203–242.

Strauss, C. and Quinn, N. 1997. *A Cognitive Theory of Cultural Meaning*, Cambridge, UK: Cambridge University Press.

van Dijk, T. (ed.) 1985. *Handbook of Discourse Analysis, Vol. 1: disciplines of discourse*, London: Academic Press.

Westen, D. 2001. "Beyond the binary opposition in psychological anthropology: integrating contemporary psycho-analysis and cognitive science," in C. C. Moore and H. F. Mathews (eds.) *The Psychology of Cultural Experience*, Cambridge, UK: Cambridge University Press, pp. 21–47.

Yurchak, A. 1997a. *The Cynical Reason of Late Socialism: language, ideology and culture of the last Soviet generation*, Ph.D. dissertation, Duke University.

—— . 1997b. "The cynical reason of late socialism: power, pretense, and the *Anekdot*," *Public Culture*, 9: 161–188.

16

"Good Enough" Methods for Life-Story Analysis
Wendy Luttrell

Introduction

Researchers of culture and consciousness who use narrative are caught between the proverbial rock and a hard place. On the one hand, we strive to listen and represent those we study "on and in their own terms." On the other hand, we recognize that our role in shaping the ethnographic encounter is huge; that whether consciously or not, we listen and make sense of what we hear according to particular theoretical, ontological, personal and cultural frameworks and in the context of unequal power relations. There is always the worry that the voices and perspectives of those we study will be lost or subsumed to our own views and interests. Given all this, it is understandable that some researchers see no way out of this dilemma.[1] But I advocate a different way of looking at the problem. I don't believe that researchers can eliminate tensions, contradictions, or power imbalances, but I believe we can (and should) name them. I like the way that feminist researchers Mathner and Doucet (1997) put it:

> The best we can do then is to trace and document our data analysis processes, and the choices and decisions we make, so that other researchers and interested parties can see for themselves some of what has been lost and some of what has been gained. We need to document these reflexive processes, not just in general terms such as our class, gender and ethnic background; but in a more concrete and nitty-gritty way in terms of where, how and why particular decisions are made at particular stages. (138)

I have written elsewhere about how my own background has affected my relationships, identifications, and exchanges with the working-class women and pregnant schoolgirls I have studied (Luttrell 1997, 2003). In this chapter, I focus on key decisions I made during my fieldwork and their consequences for life-story analysis reported in *Schoolsmart and Motherwise: Working-Class Women's Identity and Schooling* (1997).[2] I want to make a case for what I call "good enough" methods, whereby researchers think about their research decisions in terms of what is lost and what is gained, rather than what might be ideal. Accounting for the decisions one makes is the nitty-gritty of researcher reflexivity and the hall-mark of "good enough" research. In this chapter, I discuss my emergent research design and decision-making about choosing methods of discourse analysis that would prove to be most useful in building a theory about school structure, culture and identity.

Tracing the Steps

I entered the field profoundly influenced by the ethnographic study of working-class high school boys by Paul Willis (1977). I was especially intrigued by Willis's analysis of the lads' knowledge—what he called their "cultural penetrations."[3] According to Willis, the lads had insights into their futures as working-class, manual laborers that led them to reject certain school values. These insights were not fully conscious—the lads were not aware that their resistance to school knowledge and values, their rebellious attitudes toward teachers' authority, and their hyper-masculinity were all part of the shop-floor culture for which they were destined. Willis's contribution to the study of culture and consciousness was to suggest that the links between structural determinants, cultural beliefs, and individual agency were far more complicated than first imagined. He represented the lads as being neither dupes of nor rebels against an educational system designed to keep working-class students in their place. Willis's work provoked a flurry of school ethnographies, including my own, in which researchers set out to discover pieces that he had left out, particularly regarding gender and race.[4]

From 1980 to 1983 I observed and interviewed women who were enrolled in a community-based adult education program in Philadelphia. Like Willis, I wanted to learn how the women saw themselves in relation to school, now and in the past. I began the project by conducting short, semi-structured interviews with 200 women asking them why they were returning to school and what getting a high school diploma meant to them. The responses I collected provided a baseline set of issues I wanted to probe with a smaller sample of women. The following issues are some examples: What did it mean when almost every respondent said she wanted a high school diploma so that she could "become somebody"? What did it mean when so many women said that they were returning to school to become "better mothers?" (80 percent of the women offered this as a reason they had enrolled in the program.) And what did it mean when so many women described feeling "uncomfortable" in school? I wanted to understand the connection between education, betterment, and mothering, which was not a topic I had initially planned to study.

As an ethnographer, I believed it was important to investigate the women's responses as part of a larger fabric of social life and cultural beliefs. I had already gathered some clues from previous experience as a teacher in the adult education program. But when I returned to the program as a researcher, I began taking daily field notes about my everyday conversations and interactions with students and staff members in the program, in classroom settings, and in the neighborhood. In all three contexts the women provided me with examples of what might be called a cultural model of education and success—that there are those who are expected to "become somebody" and those who aren't. There are people who do the right thing (finish school, get married, etc.) and those who don't (or can't), which explains who gets ahead and why. There are those with brains, ambition, and drive who can make it in school, while others are lacking in these and therefore can not succeed. In one sense, I understood these beliefs in the context of "American individualism"—the common and unreflected-upon view of the individual as the only or main form of reality; a view of individuals that stresses self-sufficiency and independence as the most salient characteristics of the "free," American, adult subject.[5] But I also noticed that embedded in this shared talk about education and success was a critique of the American model of success and "betterment":

> Just because a person has a college degree doesn't mean he is any better than me, it doesn't give
> him the right to talk down to me with any less respect than a college professor. But I want a high
> school diploma so I can feel like I'm somebody.

I wanted to probe this equivocation, expressed over and over again by the women I spoke with and observed.

I then selected 15 women who would represent (generally speaking) those enrolled in the program.[6] Everyone I asked to participate in the study agreed. These women were all white and had been born and raised in the neighborhood.[7] They had attended local schools (two-thirds went to public school and one-third went to parochial school) and had moved in and out of the labor force as waitresses, factory hands, and clerical workers. Because a relationship between schooling and mothering had emerged so saliently in the short interviews, I decided to interview women who were mothers with children still living at home. I want to emphasize that I did not realize, even when making this sampling decision, that I was taking a theoretical step in my conception of the research as a study of the relationship between mothering and schooling. This realization would come later.

I interviewed each woman at least three times in her home over the span of a year. The "official" portion of the interview lasted from one and a half to three hours, but I was often invited to stay for tea and more discussion after the tape recorder had been packed away. I transcribed the taped interviews and wrote up field notes after each interview, including my own reactions and interpretations.[8]

My interviewing strategy was unstructured and open-ended, interrupted only by clarifying questions. For the first interview, I opened by saying, "tell me what you remember about being in school?" In the second interview, I followed up on issues left over from the first interview (there were always questions I overlooked asking or events about which I needed clarification). In the third interview, we talked about why the women had returned to school, what, if any events had led to their decision and how they would describe their experiences. I tried my best to follow the women's lead, to consider seeming "tangents" as important clues. For example, many of the women talked about their early work experiences when I asked what they remembered about being in school. Rather than redirecting the conversation to discuss school, I pursued these work experiences, which turned out to shed important light on the women's class-, race-, and gender-concepts of knowledge and authority.

In rare cases when a woman did not offer an example to illustrate her point, I would ask for it. For example, one woman said that what she remembered most about school was that teachers treated students like her differently. She said she didn't have much more to say than that school was "boring" and she didn't like being treated differently. I asked, "Can you remember a time when you were treated differently? What happened?" She proceeded to tell a string of stories about the cruel punishments she had suffered, including being locked in a closet. But usually I did not have to prompt the women; they offered up story after story about their life experiences. I came to view the women's passionate storytelling, what I called "their narrative urgency to tell it like it was," as an expression of the emotional salience of school and its formative role in the women's identities and self understandings.

Decision # 1: Collecting Life Stories

I explained to the women selected that I was doing a research project about women's education and was interested in learning about their past experiences as girls, and why they had decided to return to school as women. My request for their school experiences was most often greeted with the refrain, "You want to know about my life? I could write a book about that." I was surprised by this response, but sociolinguist and life-story theorist Charlotte Linde (1993) would not have been. She argues that the life story is a taken-for-granted interpretive device, a discursive category furnished by American culture—the idea that we have a life story to exchange with others. She says, "In order to exist in the social world with a comfortable sense of being a good, socially proper, and stable person, an individual needs to have a coherent, acceptable and constantly revised life story" (1993: 20).[9] Realizing, and then accepting, the fact that the interview material I was collecting was in the form of life stories, changed the course of this project and my career as a researcher. While I hadn't planned my project to be about life stories, the subjects of my research held their own notions of what my project was about and what they wanted from it. I learned two things from this. First, that the extent to which respondents actively shape the research process, while not well documented within scholarly reports, cannot be underestimated. Second, that reconstructing culture from discourse depends upon attending to the richness and variety of discourse types one may encounter. Whereas I began my research expecting to identify "accounts" (one discourse type) about why the women had returned to school, and that these would shed light on their model of schooling and success, I had not been expecting life stories or forms of "personal narrative" (yet another discourse type).[10]

I had been trained as a sociologist in fieldwork methods most closely aligned with symbolic interactionism. From this perspective, the information people give about themselves always serves more than one purpose, and tends to "add up," in one way or another. Borrowing on the language of mathematics, these theorists examined how people "account" for their actions, commonly explaining in advance what others might perceive as unexpected or inappropriate behavior. "Indeed, the giving and taking of accounts in everyday life represents one of the most fundamental characteristics of the social order" (Weinstein 1980: 591). So, while I was prepared to elicit and analyze "accounts," I was not yet aware that collecting, interpreting, and narrating life stories was a common tool in the anthropological kit (it has since gained prominence in both sociology and anthropology since the oft-noted postmodern turn). Falling somewhere between autobiography and biography, the narration of these stories is meant to provide the listener a sense of what life is like or what it means to be a member of a particular culture.[11] James Peacock and Dorothy Holland (1993) divide the use of life-story analysis within anthropology and the social sciences into two types: "One emphasizes the 'life,' the other the 'story'" (1993: 368). As my research evolved, I utilized both types. I elicited the women's life stories to learn something about the women and the structural as well as psychological processes that their stories were presumed to mirror—the "life-focused" approach. I was also using the "story-focused" approach (1993: 370), paying close attention to the structure, coherence, and forms of discourse the women used to tell their stories. This dual approach enabled me to see that the women were constructing their identities and forging social relationships as part of the story-telling process. As I discuss in detail later, I also turned to a psychoanalytic approach to life-story telling and *listening*, to help me understand the divided sense of self I noted in the women's discourse.

Collecting and then transcribing the women's life stories was the most comfortable part of the research for me—it was when I felt most at ease as a researcher listening and responding to what I heard. During this stage I felt that my mistakes could be corrected. If I listened to a taped interview and realized I had not followed through on a topic or missed an opportunity to probe for information and understanding, then I could go back and ask more questions.[12] The next stage of research—the classification and winnowing of the interview material—was more anxiety-ridden for me. I worried about the magnitude of the analytic task (more than 500 pages of transcribed interview material) and the fear that I would "get it wrong." Meanwhile, at this stage of my research, increasing numbers of scholars had begun writing about the highly constructed nature of oral testimony and personal narratives. The more I read, the more I questioned my epistemological premises. I found myself moving between two ways of thinking about life stories. On the one hand, I saw these stories as factual accounts of the women's experiences, views, and values about schooling. On the other hand, I also understood that these stories represented what the women wanted me most to know and what they construed as being worth talking about (which is not to say that these stories were "fictions," but that they were told with particular points in mind). I decided against taking an either/or position on these two forms of life-story analysis—"life" and "story"; realist and reflexive.

While I believe there is an important distinction, I don't believe that researchers must choose to do one or the other. Part of the challenge of my research was finding a way to do both—to make realist claims about school culture and organization, the material conditions of the women's lives and their cultural beliefs, *and* to make reflexive interpretations of the ethnographic exchange between the women I studied and myself.[13] I designed a three-step coding procedure, in part to relieve my anxieties and in part to sustain what I saw as a necessary tension in the analysis of life stories.[14]

Decision #2: Developing the Coding Procedures

I provided each woman a copy of her interview transcript to see whether she wanted to make any changes. Most women told me they weren't interested in reading the transcripts; they wanted to read what I wrote about them (which only increased my anxiety level).[15] After gaining their permission to proceed, I read through each individual woman's set of transcripts and looked for an overall point, the gist of a woman's life story. During this reading I took note of recurring images, words, phrases, and metaphors as each woman talked about growing up. I listened for what sort of person I thought the interviewee wished to present, not just in school, but also at work, in the community, in her family, and to me.

During my second reading of each woman's set of transcripts, I selected out all the passages referring to school and educational views and values—what I called their school narratives. I took note of the sequence of the string of stories the women told (stories about teachers' pets and teachers' discipline routinely came first followed by stories of rebellion or acquiescence). I also looked for any coherence among the stories—what theme(s) tied them together. I paid particular attention to how each woman named her difficulties in school and how she sought resolution. Then I grouped together stories related to these problems.[16] My main aim was to glean insights about how each woman understood herself in school from the stories she told. For example, Doreen described herself having an "attitude problem" in school. I grouped this story together with one she told about being the class clown which won her the respect of her friends but not of her teachers (thus, she was never a teacher's pet). Later she told about having a "problem with authority" and "resenting school rules and regulations," which she explained was part of her decision to leave school when she became pregnant at age 16. She made it a point to say that being pregnant in school was not a problem for her, but the school regulations against pregnancy were. Still later she talked about her dilemma as a mother raising children who she hopes will "speak their minds," but not get in trouble with the teachers. She said she couldn't decide whether to laugh or to cry about some of the disciplinary problems her children bring home from school because "they've been taught to speak up when they think something is unfair." I viewed these stories as being related, tied together by her concern with/conflict about authority relations. Needless to say, a story could fit into more than one category. For example, the class clown story also fit into a string of stories Doreen told about how she often used humor to ease tensions at home or on the job.

During my third reading I looked for patterns across all 15 women's school stories. All 15 women identified three conflicts without any prompting on my part:

1. They all talked about having common sense, but not being "school-smart." This distinction emerged in each woman's narration of her childhood schooling, albeit not in the same way. It was as if my request for school memories was a catalyst for critical self-appraisal. The unstated assumption seemed to be that there was a story to be told, and this story was about comparing oneself to others through school-based eyes, as to who was better, "smarter," and more worthy. At times, the women sounded defensive as they described the gap between having common sense and being school-smart. The women would often make it a point to say that "real intelligence" has nothing to do with schooling (in fact, too much schooling could ruin a person's common sense). The smartest people they knew were those (working-class men) who could "make things work," who were "good with their hands." The fact that the women cited only men as examples of those people with "real intelligence" unsettled me. And as I began to ask more directly about this gap between common sense and "real intelligence" I discovered that gender and class were wedded together in the women's definitions of and values regarding knowledge. The women were aware that they held values about knowledge that differed from what they believed to be school values. But they were not necessarily aware that their explanations of these opposing genres of knowledge (school-smarts and common sense) could be seen as a critique of class and gender relations.[17]

2. All 15 women told stories about teachers' pets, describing why they had or had not been chosen as a pet. Some women could vividly recall the names, demeanors and outfits of the girls who had been chosen as pets. Others told about how they didn't like the girls who "acted cutesie" and that they had refused to join in the pet contest. Each woman also offered her own version of how teachers selected their pets—but all agreed that teachers liked girls who were both smart and submissive. These stories were told with strong feelings of envy and guilt, and sometimes with flashes of embarrassment for expressing so much emotion. In Gloria's words, "I

still remember that girl's name; can you believe all these years and I still can't get over how the teacher treated that girl?" As in their stories about common sense, I heard the women blaming themselves for not being "pet material" and defending themselves against what they felt were unfair school judgments or expectations about working-class femininity. As Debra put it, "you couldn't be prissy and make it on the streets."

3. The third conflict they all mentioned revolved around aspirations. Each woman named the same set of career options that she saw available—"you could either be a secretary, nurse, nun (if you were Catholic), or mother." Nevertheless, each woman told about her childhood dream of "becoming somebody" (such as a judge, fashion model, or lawyer). Each then proceeded to explain difficult and often discriminatory circumstances and events in school that interfered with the realization of these aspirations. For example, one woman talked about having been placed into a vocational track called "kitchen practice—the lowest of the low" despite her success in junior high. She lamented that at the time she had not challenged this school placement.

These conflicts about aspirations and obstacles resonate with Charlotte Linde's observation that "people show enormous zest for discussing their experiences in high school, however horrific the stories they tell may be" (1993: 25). She attributes this zest to the prohibition within American culture against talking about *class* as a legitimate explanation for why people end up in the particular position that they do. Instead, there seems to be an unspoken assumption that important life decisions are made in schools, decisions that people feel compelled to incorporate and explain as part of their life story. The women's stories also echoed the work of Sennett and Cobb (1972), whose interviews with white, working-class men had produced what they called "confessions" and "defensive" stories about the role of formal education.[18]

Symbolic interactionists might have analyzed the women's school stories as "accounts" and looked to explain different face-saving strategies, such as "credentialing" (a strategy for establishing qualifications for one's actions so they won't be viewed negatively) or "disclaimers" (a strategy used to counteract in advance the possibility of being seen as not exercising good judgment).[19] Across the interviews, the women used the same accounting strategies in their school narratives. First, they would explain that, as young girls, they had often thought about going to college, but that financial difficulties had made it impossible to consider seriously (a disclaimer if applying an accounts framework). But the discussion would not stop there. As if an explanation based on lack of financial resources was not enough, each woman would go on to describe how she also did not "feel comfortable" with "those" kinds of students—students who were "real smart" or had money or acted superior because their parents were professionals. These feelings of discomfort were described in unique ways, from feeling a lump in one's throat when walking on a college campus, to being worried about not wearing the "right" clothes or saying the "wrong" things among people with higher class status. Those "other" kinds of people (including me? I wondered) were "different from" them. They felt more affiliated with people who had common sense, who had graduated from the "school of hard knocks" and shared common interests and concerns (a credentialing strategy.)[20]

Paying attention to the women's accounting strategies made me return to the school narratives one more time, taking note of how often the stories were framed in class-based, "us" and "them" terms. For example, knowledge was presented in us–them terms. Thus, being "schoolsmart" was associated with middle-class, "professional" people, who were not necessarily better, just "different from us." In talk about school, middle-class, female teachers from the suburbs (understood as "them") were pitted against working-class girls (understood as "us") who shouldered considerable family and work responsibilities and resented being treated as if they "had nothing to do but go to school" (which also explained why stories about work were salient in their school narratives).[21] These same middle-class teachers only chose those girls as their pets who met traditional standards of femininity (i.e., those who could afford nice clothes, acted "cutesie" and obediently). The teacher's pet contest was an us-against-them struggle—and for the women I interviewed a key conflict was about choosing which side they were on.[22]

It struck me that these us–them stories about school served dual purposes. On the one hand, the stories explained the women's failed social mobility (disclaimers). Yet, at the same time, the stories affirmed their working-class affiliations and identities (credentialing). I argued that the women's accounts served to illustrate their shared class-based views and values about education and success. They shared the view that school is a sorting mechanism, dividing students into class-based, divided types—those who will succeed and those who won't. And they shared a set of personal experiences of school as a place in which they measured themselves against others in terms of divided types: those who were and were not pets; those who were and were not "college material"; those who were and were not "school" smart. But lacking in this explanation was the power of the women's feelings, especially their sense of ambition and envy that I detected in their affirmations of their "common sense," "street-smarts" and "mother-wise knowledge" that set them apart from their teachers. I wrestled with how to write about the emotions these stories evoked, what role schooling played in producing such feelings, and where these emotions fit into a larger argument about the women's gender and class identities and self-understandings.

Decision #3: Designing a Comparative Study

As I wrote about the interview material, I felt torn between reporting individual life stories (which could not so easily be reduced to a main point) and building a case for the patterns I was detecting.[23] It was at this point that I made a decision to focus on patterns and not individuals and something was lost and something else gained. I lost the capacity to see each woman primarily as an individual with her own story to tell, but gained clarity on what I came to understand as links between the social and the psychological in the women's narratives. I think the alternative approach (developing more complete and holistic case studies of individual women) would have had certain benefits. And some might argue that such an approach is more consistent with feminist epistemologies.[24] The trade-off, as I saw it, was that insofar as the women's individuality (the personal context and emotional force of their stories) would be lost, building a theory about the links among school structure, culture, identity, and self-understandings would be gained.

To trace and explain these links, I would need to cast the ethnographic net farther and investigate at least one other kind of school and another group of working-class women. I had moved to North Carolina and was working in a workplace literacy program that presented unique opportunities for a comparative analysis. When I learned that most of the North Carolina literacy students had grown up in rural counties and had attended one-room schoolhouses, I thought the urban–rural contrast of school context would be especially fruitful to examine. Both school contexts were also racially segregated, with the urban school being white-only and the rural school being black-only, and this provided another rich, if not complicated, layer of comparison.

My decision to do a comparative study came at a particularly contentious time in the historical development of feminist anthropology.[25] While some people were focusing on *commonalities* in women's experiences of gender inequality, others were focusing on the *differences* among women, and the context-bound nature of gender inequality. Still others were arguing against using the analytic category "women" altogether. I was taken with Ruth Behar's (1993: 301) observation of the opposing tendencies within feminism—"to see women as not at all different from one another or as all too different." She warned, "to go too far in either direction is to end up indifferent." Meanwhile, as Naomi Quinn (2000) has argued, feminist anthropology had reached an impasse, in part because of academic politics, and in part because of the feminist turn from universalism to particularism. Right at the time when feminist anthropology was close to explaining gender inequality (having identified many "near-universals"), it became unfashionable to develop explanations that could be tested or confirmed. In the context of these debates, my decision to focus on institutional, psychological, and cultural patterns and not individual particularities meant taking a position favoring one side over the other.

My responsibilities directing a workplace literacy program at a North Carolina state university included teaching, curriculum development, and research. This program had traditionally served the predominantly African American housekeeping, landscaping, and maintenance staff, mostly female housekeepers. I followed the same research protocol as in the Philadelphia study. I conducted short interviews with 50 program participants about why they were returning to school. Then I selected 15 women to observe and interview. These women had all been raised in southern rural communities, growing up mostly on tenant farms. Their past schooling had been sporadic, in part because of the demands of farm work and in part because of racial discrimination. The women were all employed as housekeepers; most had also worked as domestics, and some had been waitresses and factory workers.

My decision to label the two groups of women as the Philadelphia and North Carolina women rather than as the white, working-class and the black, working-class women (as I did in an early publication of my research)—was another research decision, one that I write about elsewhere (Luttrell 2000).[26] Here, my focus is on my approach to finding the structural features and cultural meanings embedded in the women's school stories and linking these to their personal conflicts.[27]

Decision #4: Attending to Variations

I used the same three-step procedure to analyze the North Carolina women's interview material, only this time I had the Philadelphia women's stories at the forefront of my mind.[28] I quickly learned that the North Carolina women offered the same skeletal school story as had been offered by the Philadelphia women. They too cast school as a battleground, used us–them terms, and identified a series of divided types who peopled their school stories. Their stories also evoked powerful emotions, including defensiveness, self doubt, and a critical self-appraisal. But there were key variations on the theme that demanded explanation. Paying close attention to these variations enabled me to develop a more nuanced argument about the links between school structure, culture, and identity.

Variation A: Knowledge Types

Like the Philadelphia women, the North Carolina women divided knowledge into two types: common sense (often referred to as mother wit) and school-smarts. The North Carolina women also held those with common sense in high esteem, arguing that being educated was not the same as having "real intelligence." Indeed, "book learning" could not always match the wisdom of those who had actually seen or experienced life events, most especially slavery and the effects of Jim Crow laws. Moreover, the North Carolina women expressed a great deal of suspicion about much that is written in books, newspapers, and other printed material that did not reflect the "truth" of black life in white America. (I returned to the Philadelphia women's interviews to discover a similar distrust of the written word, albeit expressed in different terms. They were suspicious of "forty dollar" vocabulary, either spoken or written, that served to exclude people like themselves from public discourse.) But, unlike the Philadelphia women, the North Carolina women did not privilege the knowledge of men over women, nor did they associate "real intelligence" with skilled manual labor. Their definition of "real intelligence" was more all-encompassing, most often associated with "making ends meet," overcoming natural disasters (e.g., droughts and hurricanes), and avoiding racial conflict. Black men, as often as black women, were identified as having "real intelligence" when they successfully negotiated and survived racism, even when the emotional cost was great. Black women who were self-sufficient and raised a family without the support of a man were held in the highest regard as those having "real intelligence." And, yet, it was black men who could most easily cause a woman to "lose" her common sense, a recurring theme across the North Carolina's life stories. Like the Philadelphia women, the North Carolina women did not seem to be aware that their explanations of these opposing genres of knowledge could be seen as a critique of race, class, or gender relations. Both groups of women described knowledge in terms of divided types of people, not as a set of abstract categories.

Variation B: Teacher Types

Like the Philadelphia women, the North Carolina women pitted their middle-class, black female teachers against students like themselves (in this case, students who had "country ways" and darker skin color). But embedded in these us–them stories were examples of "good" teachers who had treated them with special care and "bad" teachers who had belittled or made them feel ashamed of themselves and/or their parents. These stories had to do with teachers' efforts to either make up for or correct the women's "country ways" (in terms of speech, deportment, or clothing), which I learned was a cornerstone of the "racial uplift" mission of the all-black rural schools the North Carolina women had attended. Teachers were "good" if they provided students the means for uplift (such as clothes, books, hair ribbons, and other traditionally feminine accessories) and "bad" if they made fun of students' deficiencies. The link between the definition of goodness in teachers and the school's uplift mission led me to return to the Philadelphia women's interview material and reexamine what criteria they had used to assess their teachers. I discovered that the Philadelphia women also divided the teachers into good versus bad types. Teachers were "good" if they were strict but fair; teachers were "bad" if they were arbitrary or cruel. In light of the urban-bureaucratic school mission to prepare students for the industrial workforce, this emphasis on discipline made sense.

I began to realize that each school organization and mission had its own forms of authority and discipline and produced its own divided types. In the rural school, black female teachers' knowledge and authority were embedded in a web of community and school relationships, and discipline focused on enforcing "personal" attributes like manners and habits. In the urban school, white, middle-class teachers' authority was more distinct from working-class parental authority, and while these two forms of authority were not necessarily in conflict, they didn't stem from the same source ("if I got in trouble at school, there was no question about what had happened. First I got it from the teacher and then I got it from my mother for getting caught in the first place."). The disciplining practices in the urban school had more to do with rigid rules and imposing "public" (i.e., work) attributes, like punctuality and obedience. Each group of women's critical self-appraisals reflected the disciplinary code of each school context. The North Carolina women characterized their problems in school as stemming from personal deficiencies and described themselves as "slow learners," whereas the Philadelphia women characterized their problems in school as stemming from rigid rules and their own "bad" attitudes toward authority.

Variation C: Feminine Types

The teacher's pet contest was an organizing theme in the North Carolina women's school stories, as it had been in the Philadelphia women's stories. But, rather than seeing themselves as potential competitors for the teacher's approval and affection (as had the Philadelphia women) the North Carolina women said that because of their dark skin color they would not have been chosen as a teacher's pet, even if they had wanted to be. The teachers' pets—the light-skinned girls with the "good" hair and nice clothes and professional parents—were set against dark-skinned girls who were "passed over" by the teachers and made to feel "invisible." The fault lines dividing feminine types were distinctive for each group of women. For the North Carolina women, the color line was tightly woven into definitions of the "ideal" schoolgirl.

The North Carolina women's use of the metaphor of visibility (who was seen and recognized by the teachers) made me look for the metaphors the Philadelphia women had used to describe their relationships to and conflicts with teachers. I discovered a pattern that, again, I had not been attuned to before. When describing their schooling, the Philadelphia women drew upon terms related to voice—how they were "talked down to" by the teachers and how they had a "mouth," and resented not being able to speak their minds, and so on. These contrasting metaphors of visibility and voice provided yet more insight into the relationship between school structure, culture, and identity. One the one hand, these metaphors reflected the grammar of each school context, disciplinary code, and student response. In the case of the rural school context, where "bad" black teachers used public shaming and humiliation to enforce the school mission, making oneself "invisible" was an effective means to defend against personal attack. In the case of the urban school context, being silent in the face of abusively enforced rigid rules could provide protection from even further trouble. On yet a deeper level, these distinct metaphors spoke to a constellation of emotions about self-other relationships that were being forged in school settings.

Decision #5: Turning to Psychodynamic Understandings of Self–Other Relationships

My argument—that each school context produced its own set of divided student identities, critical self-appraisals, and anxieties about measuring up to school standards—was based on an analysis of variations in the themes that organized the women's school narratives. Yet striking similarities in the women's self-narration, especially their split sense of self, deserved examination. Both groups of women made persistent references to feeling torn about how best to present themselves in school. They talked about their different sides—for example the side that could "con" the teacher or "put on the dog" versus the side that resented having to play the game; or the side that wanted the teacher's approval versus the side that sought peers' approval and felt disloyal if chosen by the teacher as a pet. Moreover, it was not easy to resolve these two sides. In Helen's words, "I felt bad because I felt like I had conned them, like it wasn't really me who they (*teachers*) liked."

Initially, I had understood the women's "us versus them" stories about school in terms of class and race conflict. Drawing on a culturalist Marxist tradition, most specifically E. P. Thompson, I argued that the women's "us–them" view of knowledge—their pitting common sense against school knowledge—reflected their class and race consciousness.[29] The women spoke about knowledge in the same way that Thompson defines class consciousness, as the way people "feel and articulate the identity of their interests as between themselves, and as against other men (*sic*) whose interests are different from (and usually opposed to) theirs" (Thompson 1963: 9). I understood the women's notion of class (and race) consciousness to be embedded in relationships that are "embodied in real people in a real context" (Thompson ibid.). Real people and real school contexts were at the heart of the women's stories about knowledge and schooling and the explanations they gave for why they did or did not measure up to whatever they construed as the ideal. But there was another layer of emotionally charged talk that did not seem to fit into this class- and race-consciousness framework. This layer had to do with the women's split sense of self—the tenacious pattern whereby they would break themselves or others into two parts, one side idealized ("good") and the other devalued ("bad"). To help me understand this phenomenon I turned to feminist relational psychoanalysis for guidance.

Splitting is a psychoanalytic concept that is used to explain the meanings we make of and the feelings we attach to our relationships with others. In object-relations terms, it is our earliest experiences with those upon whom we are dependent for survival (usually maternal caregivers) that shape what we take in as meaningful, important, fearful or fanciful about ourselves (introjection) and what we project onto others (projection). These early emotional or fantasy meanings about a person, object, or idea become part of who we are and how we relate to others. Whereas splitting most commonly refers to individual psychic conflicts, I began to reconsider the range and scope of references to splitting throughout the women's self-narrations that were suggestive of personal conflicts *and* larger cultural processes. I took note of just how frequently the women cast aspects of the schooling process in divided, either/or terms, from their relationships to teachers (good versus bad); to the subject matter (academics versus vocational); to the division between school-smarts and street-smarts. And, as a consequence of paying new attention to varied forms of splitting that were embedded in the women's school stories, I realized that there were stories about mothers that I had not previously probed with the same fervor as I had the stories about teachers and students. Taking up a psychodynamic understanding of the women's life stories meant rethinking each speaker's identifications, conflicts and emotions, including those conflicts I might have preferred to avoid for myself. This decision brought me full circle from focusing on individual lives, to focusing on overriding patterns, back to focusing on individual lives (including my own).

Decision #6: A Psychoanalytic Listening to Life Stories

Within psychology, and particularly psychoanalysis, life stories (referred to as case histories) are elicited and tied together by the analyst as insight into a person's development or illness, as clues to both the care and cure of the patient. The foundation for this notion of the life story is that there is a "normal" developmental path against which everyone's life can be evaluated. Many critics of psychoanalysis, including some psychoanalysts themselves, have pointed out the "class-blind, politically pacifying and apparently ahistorical myth of human development" (Phillips 1998: 39). Still, what appeals to me about psychoanalysis is the attention paid to how individuals make sense of their own story of development and how they infuse their life stories with fantasies, images, feelings, and other associations.[30] A description of the psychoanalytic life story I found useful was Juliet Mitchell's:

> [T]he patient comes with the story of his or her own life. The analyst listens; through an association something intrudes, disrupts, offers the "anarchic carnival" back into that history, the story won't quite do, and so the process starts again. You go back, and you make a new history. (1984: 288)

Intruding associations—especially about mothers—disrupted many of my interviews. There were times when the women would be taken back to images and feelings from childhood, realizing that the story would not quite do. In one particular case, Kate, a North Carolina woman, asked that I turn off the tape recorder before telling about a memory that she said still "has a hold on me." In telling her memory Kate tried unsuccessfully to keep from crying, apologizing several times for the fact that she couldn't tell her story without emotion. At the end Kate thanked me for being willing to "hold" her memory, but then said she wished we had tape-recorded it so she could hear it for herself. We agreed that I would return the next week to record the story. Not surprisingly, the taped version took some new turns, but again she focused on her regrets about not having been nicer to her (now-dead) mother. Initially, I filed this entire exchange as tangential—a disruption unrelated to my research topic.

In another case, Tina, from Philadelphia, was remembering an incident at school in which she had felt compelled to make up a story to cover for her mother's negligence. As she was telling the story she started to cry and then angrily said, "why did you make me remember all this? I don't like thinking about my mother this way." Feeling guilty and wanting to avoid conflict, I apologized, turned off the tape recorder and said I knew how much she cared for her mother. I suggested that we should stop for the day. This only made Tina angrier. She turned the tape recorder back on and said she had a lot more to say about her mother and that I wasn't getting off that easily. We talked for over an hour about how certain of her mother's actions still haunt her to this day and how she continues to feel anger and guilt about herself in relation to her mother. At the end, she said that I shouldn't "feel bad if people get angry" and that I shouldn't be "afraid to ask more about mothers." "I'm the first to say that I love my mother and that she did the best to raise me, but. . . ."

Realizing my reluctance to deal with strong emotions and mixed feelings about mothers—what could be called countertransference in my fieldwork relationships—marked a major breakthrough in my thinking and in my research process.[31] Becoming attuned to my feelings about and avoidance of what the women were saying about their mothers made me rethink the practice of ethnography and the role of interpersonal encounters. I like the way Nancy Chodorow puts it:

> There is no psychoanalysis or anthropology apart from the interpersonal encounter, an encounter that draws unavoidably on the investigator's power of empathy as well as observation. Both fields have come increasingly to emphasize the central participatory role and influence of the practitioner, who is no longer seen as a detached scientific observer. They now recognize that what comes to be understood about the subject (culture or psyche) is a product created within a particular encounter or set of encounters. In this encounter, both fields have increasingly emphasized the real emotional effects on the investigator: anthropologists who are not psychologically inclined write of culture shock; those who are psychologically attuned, of anxiety, fear and anger discovered through self observation, introspection, and observation of transferences that emerge in relation to informants or to the culture as a whole; psychoanalysts speak of the widened field of countertransference and the role of the analyst's subjectivity as well as objectivity in the analytic encounter. (1999: 134–135)

I returned again to all the interview material, and with more self-awareness discovered a range of maternal images and mixed feelings that the women had expressed, but that I had minimized in my analysis of the links between school structure, culture, and identity.

A new line of questioning emerged from this finding: Why had the request for school memories evoked these maternal images and conflicts? Feminist relational psychoanalysts would argue that these ever-present, yet varying maternal images and memories reflect women's identificatory struggles in the gender- and self-making process (Chodorow 1978, 1989, 1995; Benjamin 1988, 1994; Flax 1987, 1990).[32] But, what structural or cultural aspects of schooling might produce such associations? And what might be the connection between the women's split sense of self, the particular school context, and their stories about mothers? As D'Andrade (p. 90) points out in this volume, "it is better not to ask informants directly about their models, but rather to ask something that will bring the model into play; that is, something that will make the person *use* the model." What model of schooling was being "brought into play" as a result of these interviews and how might this model address the women's identificatory struggles?

Two theories about the gendered organization of schooling helped me answer these questions. The first was Alison Griffith and Dorothy Smith's (1987) observation that schools are organized around the unacknowledged and devalued work of women (as teachers and mothers). The second was Madeleine Grumet's (1988) observation that teaching and learning are unconsciously associated with mothering despite great efforts on the part of schools, teachers, and students to deny and repress this connection. Both helped to explain why the women might express mixed feelings about the role of women (as mothers and teachers) in their life-story telling. The women's stories, which drew upon a vivid world of women (teachers, mothers, and daughters), revealed a knowledge about how the school world works that the women themselves did not know they knew.[33] One insight to be drawn from their descriptions and associations about school was that each school context had, in its own way, fostered personal conflicts and anxiety about a host of related issues, about school-wise knowledge, about themselves as female objects of desire ("pets"), about their class and race affiliations, and about their future lives as mothers, to name a few.[34] While the process of splitting (specifically the idealization and devaluation of women's work and knowledge) had helped the women deal with these mixed emotions, it had also deflected the women's attention away from the effects of social inequality in their lives.[35]

A psychoanalytic *listening* to women's narratives made me realize how much more mutually engaging and intersubjective the process of fieldwork is, as well as the extent to which my own subjectivity shapes the research.[36] When I entered the field I was best prepared to think about issues of access and rapport, and to negotiate my multiple roles as a researcher, a teacher, and as a mother (I often brought my children to interviews). I saw these multiple roles as positive because I believed they enabled me to tap into the women's life worlds and perspectives.[37] In retrospect, I can also see that I was hearing the women's stories through several layers of identification—not the least of which were my own complicated feelings as a daughter and schoolgirl.[38]

Reducing Researcher Anxieties

The epistemology of social science demands a distinction between researchers and researched, observer and observed, and at the most abstract level, between subject (self) and object (other). But, this distinction need not break down into research relations of domination and submission, or idealization and devaluation, or detachment and (over) involvement.[39] This is why I agree with George Devereux (1967), who has argued that traditional research methods help researchers to overcome threats posed by making connections and relationships with the objects/subjects of their research. For example, he says that methods of detachment are a way for researchers to bind their anxieties and not necessarily a means to discover truth about an "other." Ruth Behar takes this observation one step further:

> Because there is no clear and easy route by which to confront the self who observes, most professional observers develop defenses, namely "methods" that "reduce anxiety" and enable us to function efficiently. . . . This is especially the case for situations in which we feel complicitous with structures of power, or helpless to release another from suffering, or at a loss as to whether to act or to observe. (Behar 1996: 6)

But how do we prepare ourselves to effectively negotiate self-other ethnographic relationships? I propose that we strive to develop "good enough" methods in the same spirit as pediatrician and child psychoanalyst D. W. Winnicott (1965) called for "good enough" mothering. He argued that the perfect mother (like the perfect researcher) is a fantasy, a projection of infantile wishes that cannot be met by any *real* person. Moreover, efforts to attain perfection (either for one's self or for another) can stand in the way of healthy tensioned human relations.

It is possible to be a "good enough" researcher—that is, a person who is aware that she/he has personal stakes and investments in research relationships; who does not shy away from frustrations, anxieties, and disappointments that are part of any relationship; and who seeks to understand (and is able to appreciate) the difference between one's self and another. The "good enough" researcher tries not to get mixed up between fantasies, projections, and theories of who the "others" are and who they are in their own right. "Good enough" researchers accept rather than defend against healthy tensions in fieldwork. And they accept the mistakes they make—errors often made because of their blind spots and the intensity of their social, emotional, and intellectual involvement in and with the subject(s) of their research. These mistakes can be compensated for by the many times that they will do it right.

I believe that students of ethnography during anthropology's "double crisis"—in terms of the challenges to ethnographic writing and feminism—need both reassurance and direction. Students need practice in order to learn how to be attuned to questions of relationship, position, and social complexities, and how to turn resulting tensions into data, analysis, and eventually theories. Being reflexive is something to be learned in terms of degrees rather than absolutes (a "good enough" ethnography is more or less reflexive, not either/or in my view). I think of being reflexive as an exercise in sustaining multiple and sometimes opposing emotions, keeping alive contradictory ways of theorizing the world, and seeking compatibility, not necessarily consensus. Being reflexive means expanding rather than narrowing the psychic, social, cultural, and political fields of analysis.

Applying the "good enough" credo to gathering life stories, I suggest that researchers concentrate on the specifics of life events. Frigga Haug (1987) calls this "memory work" and argues that it is not so much a question of respondents "having a good memory," as practicing it. she writes:

> Once we have begun to rediscover a given situation—its smells, sounds, emotions, thoughts, attitudes—the situation itself draws us back into the past, freeing us for a time from notions of our present superiority over our past selves; it allows us to become once again the child—a stranger—whom we once were. With some astonishment, we find ourselves discerning linkages never perceived before: forgotten traces, abandoned intentions, lost desires and so on. (47)

In this way I side with the "life-focused" side of life analysis, believing that buried memories can be recovered. I have listened countless times to respondents say, "I haven't thought about this in years. Now that we are talking about it I can remember. . . ." and then proceed to describe in rich detail a scene they had long forgotten. The passion with which the women recalled (and in some ways, emotionally relived) their pasts, makes me an advocate for facilitating interviewees' "memory work."

Two listening strategies are particularly useful toward this end. The first is paying attention to and pointing out interviewees' self-evaluative language and second is taking note of interviewees' meta-statements. Examples of the first are statements like, "I guess you could say I just didn't measure up," "I didn't work to my potential," "I didn't try hard enough," "I gave up on myself." Asking for details and examples—that is, "Can you tell me about a time when you felt like you didn't measure up? What happened?"—often opened up the space for the women to draw conclusions about their past selves (e.g., reconsidering what they valued and what they thought others valued, or how they were told to act and how they felt about themselves when they did or did not act that way). Examples of the second, or metastatements, occurred when the women spontaneously commented about what they had just said, as if they were considering their statement from an outsider's (my own?) perspective. It was common for the women to say things like, "I know this might strike you as strange. . . .," or "that was a crazy thing . . .," or "there's no telling why such and such happened." Paying attention to these meta-statements clued me into aspects of the women's model of schooling and knowledge that I might need to probe further (e.g., why I thought it might be strange that a Philadelphia woman chose not to attend an honors program into which she had been selected, a story which opened a storehouse of painful memories about the role her mother played in this decision). The frequency of the women's meta-statements made me realize the extent to which they held their own images of me as the researcher and audience of their stories. Perhaps these meta-statements (ways of hooking me a listener) would not have been necessary had I not been viewed as an outsider, or as a "college-educated" person.[40] Nonetheless, I often found it difficult to ask why they thought I might consider something strange. At times it seemed improper (i.e., not the kind of question a researcher asks) and at other times I felt vulnerable. But if I was to be a narrator of the women's life stories, I felt it was necessary to take the risk to find out who they thought I was. When I began to ask—or perhaps I should say when it became impossible for me not to ask more about how the women were meant to feel about their mothers and how they actually felt (thanks to interviewee Tina who pushed me on this point)—only then was I able to tap into a range of complicated feelings and to connect these feelings to the gendered organization of schooling.

Finally, in collecting the women's life stories I learned to worry less about whether the women were "telling the truth" than in listening for gaps, inconsistencies and associations. Noting these out loud allowed both the women and me to rethink and reconstruct our stories. Here, the psychoanalytic, "story-focused" side of my ethnographer self predominates. For whatever else can be said about it, I believe that ethnographic research and life story analysis is about making meaningful connections with others who may or may not be like us. Karen McCarthy Brown puts it this way:

> Ethnographic research is a form of human relationship. When the lines long drawn in anthropology between participant-observer and informant break down, then the only truth is the one in between; and anthropology becomes closer to a social art form, open to both aesthetic and moral judgment. This situation is riskier, but it does bring intellectual labor and life into closer relation. (1991: 12)

Many things influence how a researcher shapes her/his social art form—one's research questions, study design, and theoretical-explanatory approaches, coupled with one's particular temperament, personality, and intended audience. I strongly endorse the use of a variety of discourse methods (some of which are presented in this volume) to bring intellectual labor and life stories into closer relation. At its core, ethnographic research and cultural discourse analysis is creative, inventive, emotionally charged and fraught; and "good enough" researchers find ways to sustain all these aspects.

Notes

1. Many people have written about different forms of this dilemma. I like the way Behar and Gordon (1995) describe the dilemma in terms of anthropology's "double crisis," which they argue, has its roots in the postmodern turn and critique of the "realist" tradition in ethnographic writing and in the critique of white, middle-class feminist versions of women's experience that lesbians, women of color, and working-class women have been so effective in making. These debates and crises notwithstanding, and despite the fact that there has been much hand wringing and spilt ink over the question of what it means to be an anthropologist "writing culture," I agree with Faye Harrison who has observed that most anthropologists do not want to give up on written representations of culture, nor do we want to refashion ethnography as a "literary enterprise" (Harrison 1993: 403).

2. Another version of this chapter appeared in *Harvard Education Review* 70(4): 499–523 (2000). The initial inspiration to write an article came from Naomi Quinn's invitation to contribute to a methods volume she was editing. As time passed, I decided to submit the article for publication. For this volume, I have revised the chapter to focus specifically on decisions related to methods of discourse analysis rather than the larger issues of research design about which I had already written.

3. The term "penetration" struck me as quite masculinist and I was interested in finding more gender-neutral ways to describe the knowledge people hold about the way the world works that they are not always aware they hold. This is where feminist versions of psychoanalysis would come in handy.

4. Willis was successful in showing that structure, culture and agency are linked, but he did not explain the "how" of these links.

5. See Linde (1993: 200) for her discussion of ontological individualism in American culture.

6. See Luttrell (1997: 132) for a description of how I selected the sample.

7. The neighborhood was known for its stability and yet, was experiencing tumultuous community relations, especially in terms of increasing drug use, racial violence, and domestic abuse. The year I started working in the local Lutheran Settlement House all three issues were on the top of the social service agenda which was the context within which the Women's Program opened its doors.

8. See Kleinman and Copp (1993) for a good discussion of "notes on notes" in which field-workers record their doubts, feelings, and worries, as well as their emerging theories about what they are seeing.

9. Linde defines the life story as consisting "of all the stories and associated discourse units, such as explanations and chronicles and the connections between them, told by an individual in his/her lifetime" (1993: 21).

10. See Luttrell (2003) for a detailed discussion of life story as a taken-for-granted interpretive device. In my research with pregnant schoolgirls I found it particularly difficult to elicit life stories, for a variety of reasons. The girls with whom I worked did not narrate their pasts in light of the present as the older women had. They didn't claim they could "write a book" about all the things that had made them who they are today. Indeed, several girls said they didn't know where to start or what to say. Mostly, their relationship to the past was told in bits and piece, was not unified or linked as the older women's retrospective accounts had been. Thus, my realization of the girls' unique discourse types (including their performative style of storytelling) lead to yet other methods for reconstructing culture from discourse. See Luttrell 2003, chapter 6 for more discussion of these methods.

11. As Naomi Quinn mentions in the introduction, there is, of course, much debate about the use and meaning of life stories collected by anthropologists, particularly when anthropologists bring certain expectations about what should constitute the life story of any particular person. Ruth Behar provides one, among many, examples. She writes that her subject, Esperanza, refused to talk about certain matters, for example sexuality, which is a key subject that we have come to expect to find discussed in women's lives. Behar says, "her life story, as she told it to me, was not a revelation of the 'real truth' of her inner life but an account of those emotional states (which were also often bodily and religious states) that she construed as worth talking about—physical suffering, martyrdom, rage, salvation" (1993: 12).

12. Indeed, this is a stage of research in which getting feedback from more experienced interviewers is key. It is for this reason that I advocate teaching courses in research methods so that ethnographers/interviewers can develop and practice skills before entering the field. I disapprove of the "sink or swim" approach to fieldwork.

13. It is this either—or thinking that has, in my mind, fueled the long-standing debate about whether there can be such a thing as a "feminist ethnography." I think reframing this question to ask, "In what ways is or is not a particular ethnography 'feminist'?" is a more useful approach.

14. I have seen this anxiety in my own students who get to this stage. After collecting extensive and rich interviews, they feel overwhelmed about what to do next, hoping that their coding scheme will ease their worries.

15. Two women did read and comment on their transcripts—the first said she was surprised, if not a bit embarrassed about how much time she had spent talking about her mother and the second asked for an additional interview so that she could fill in the gaps of her life story—events she had "short-shrifted," like how she had met her husband.

16. This was before the availability of computer programs for doing qualitative research. I have yet to become proficient

in the use of such programs and prefer a more "hands-on" approach that includes colored highlighting, cutting and pasting, filing and re-filing.

17. This is an example of the women's "cultural penetration"—a knowledge of the way the world worked that they didn't know they held.

18. Linde discusses the evaluative property of life stories—that life stories have confessional qualities, allowing the narrator to reflect upon whether his or her self is (or was) good, proper, worthy, etc. "Confession may be good for the soul, but it is also excellent for the self-image" (1993: 124).

19. See Arlene McLaren (1985) for her use of the notion of accounts in her study of British working-class women's pursuit of education.

20. See Luttrell (1997: 15) for a discussion of an exchange with a Philadelphia interviewee in which the issue of our class difference was crystallized.

21. In Luttrell (1997) I show that the women spoke "in the voice of" and "in the image of" their peers, often referring to themselves in the plural, as in "we knew what we wanted."

22. Aspirations were also described in us against them terms, as in "We knew we were going to become secretaries. We weren't like those girls who were going to college."

23. "Was my focus on the *women* or on the *schools* they attended?," one kind critic asked after I had completed writing up the Philadelphia study in the form of my dissertation. I wanted to do both, I said, but was not sure how to achieve this.

24. I had this same conversation (about my decision to focus on the Philadelphia women as a group and the patterns that emerged throughout their stories and not on individuals) with some of the Philadelphia interviewees. One interviewee, after hearing me speak about the interview material at a conference, said she wished I had focused more on her individual life story. Another interviewee, who was also at the conference disagreed and said she didn't want me to write her story; if she wanted her personal story told she would write it herself. She preferred her experiences being used to illustrate larger points about "working-class women's lives" (her words). See Luttrell (1997: 17–18) for more discussion of this conversation.

25. See Micaela di Leonardo's introduction to *Gender At the Crossroads of Knowledge* (1991) for an excellent review of the feminist project in anthropology, which she rightly says has "flown under several flags." In this piece she traces the shift from the anthropology of women, to the anthropology of gender, to feminist anthropology, to feminist-inspired anthropological research and writing on gender relations, and how these shifts reflect changes in the academy, political economy and the critique of ethnography (1991: 1–48).

26. See Luttrell (1989).

27. See Nancy Chodorow (1999) for her discussion of the underexamined links between cultural and personal meanings within feminist research on gender identity and within much psychological anthropology on self and identity.

28. It would be interesting to know how my analysis would be different had I conducted the North Carolina study first.

29. I developed this argument in Luttrell 1989.

30. George Rosenwald (Rosenwald and Ochenberg 1992) writes that no other science has paid such close attention to the life story as does psychoanalysis, whatever its limitations. I found the following work on narrative in psycho-analysis most useful: Steedman (1986); Rosenwald and Ochenberg (1992); and Mischler (1986).

31. See Sherryl Kleinman and Martha Copp (1993) for an excellent discussion of emotions and fieldwork, particu-larly the section on researcher identifications with those being researched entitled, "The Costs of Feeling Good." Jennifer Hunt (1989) also writes about the role of transference and countertransference in fieldwork relationship in a way that I found helpful. And Barrie Thorne's (1993) realization that her own memories of being a schoolgirl made her overidentify with a particular girl she was observing also enabled me to rethink my reactions.

32. See Chodorow (1995) for her observation that "guilt and sadness about mother are particularly prevalent female preoccupations and as likely to limit female autonomy, pleasure, and achievement as any culture mandate. . . . Similarly women's shame *vis-à-vis* men, whether of dependence or of discovery in masculine pursuits, is certainly situated in a cultural context in which such pursuits are coded as masculine in the first place. But this shame is also experienced in itself, inflected with many unconscious fantasies that stem from a time in development well before such coding could be known. It is a conflict in itself, and it inflects the general sense of self and gender as well as interacting with specific cultural expectations and meanings" (1995: 540). I argue that the women's stories were tied together by (a) their social/cultural analysis of motherhood and (b) their personal/psychological preoccupation with their own mothers.

33. Again, Willis would call this a cultural penetration. But I am arguing that the women's knowledge stems from psychodynamic processes that fill in a necessary piece of the puzzle about social and cultural reproduction in school settings.

34. See Jenny Shaw (1995) about the relationship between school organization, anxiety, and gender. I have recently written about schools as sites of profound anxiety (Luttrell 2003). I argue that schooling evokes deep-seated personal feelings, and that institutional mechanisms that are often designed to contain such feelings can themselves create more anxiety and disaffection (e.g., depersonalized routines that allow teachers and students to distance

themselves from feelings of failure). The convergence of institutionally created and individually felt emotions has been under-examined in the anthropological and sociological literature on identity.

35. See Luttrell (1997: 91–107) for a full discussion of how the cultural and personal myth of maternal omnipotence and idealized images of the perfect mother work in the context of schooling. Also see Griffith and Smith (2005).

36. In graduate school I had studied symbolic interactionism as a theoretical and methodological approach to fieldwork. While I was fortunate to take courses with Nancy Chodorow, who exposed me to psychoanalysis and feminism, when I entered the field I did not see this perspective as guiding my research questions or approach. It is only in retrospect and in revisiting parts of my field notes that I have been able to see the connections between the theoretical traditions I have just outlined.

37. What I like about this (classical) sociological view of the researcher as negotiator of roles and actor learning a social script, is its emphasis on consciousness and intentionality. Insofar as I made conscious choices and acted in certain ways based on what I learned in the field, then I could extend this notion of consciousness and intentionality to the subjects of my study.

38. See Luttrell (1997: 13–23) for a detailed discussion of my multiple identifications with each group of women. And see Luttrell (2003: 147–170) for a discussion of how my position as a "daughter" was created by the women interviewees, whereas, in my work with pregnant girls, my position as a "mother" was reinforced in ways that imbued my analysis.

39. This is the research version of splitting. See Luttrell (2003) for a more explicit discussion of how ethnographers engage in and defend against feeling "split at the root" in their work.

40. See Catherine Kohler Riessman (1993) for her discussion of the teller-listener relationship in narrative analysis. Her work (and her comments on this chapter) have been very influential in my thinking.

References

Behar, Ruth. 1993. *Translated woman: Crossing the border with Esperanza's story*. Boston, MA: Beacon Press.

—— . 1996. *The vulnerable observer: Anthropology that breaks your heart*. Boston, MA: Beacon Press.

Behar, Ruth and Deborah Gordon. 1995. *Women writing culture*. Berkeley, CA: University of California Press.

Benjamin, Jessica. 1988. *The bonds of love: Psychoanalysis, feminism, and the problem of domination*. New York: Pantheon.

—— . 1994. The omnipotent mother: a psychoanalytic study of fantasy and reality. In *Representations of motherhood*, ed. Donna Bassin, Margaret Honey, and Meryle Mahrer Kaplan, pp. 129–146. New Haven, CT: Yale University Press.

Brown, Karen McCarthy. 1991. *Mama lola: A vodou priestess in Brooklyn*. Berkeley, CA: University of California Press.

Chodorow, Nancy. 1978. *The reproduction of mothering: Psychoanalysis and the sociology of gender*. Berkeley, CA: University of California Press.

—— . 1989. *Feminism and psychoanalytic theory*. New Haven, CT: Yale University Press.

—— . 1995. Gender as personal and cultural construction. *Signs: Journal of Women in Culture and Society* 20(3): 516–544.

—— . 1999. *The power of feelings: Personal meaning in psychoanalysis, gender and culture*. New Haven, CT: Yale University Press.

Devereux, George. 1967. *From anxiety to method in behavioral sciences*. The Hague: Mouton.

di Leonardo, Micaela. 1991. *Gender at the crossroads of knowledge: Feminist anthropology in the postmodern era*. Berkeley, CA: University of California Press.

Flax, Jane. 1987. Postmodernism and gender relations in feminist theory. *Signs: Journal of Women in Culture and Society* 12(4): 621–643.

—— . 1990. *Thinking fragments: Psychoanalysis, feminism, and postmodernism in the contemporary West*. Berkeley, CA: University of California Press.

Griffith, Alison and Dorothy Smith. 1987. Constructing cultural knowledge: mothering as discourse. In *Women and education: A Canadian perspective*, ed. Jane Gaskell and Arlene McLaren, pp. 87–103. Calgary, Alberta: Detselig Enterprises.

—— . 2005. *Mothering for schooling*. New York: Falmer Press.

Grumet, Madeline. 1988. *Bitter milk: Women and teaching*. Amherst, MA: University of Massachusetts Press.

Harrison, Faye. 1993. Writing against the grain: cultural politics of difference in the work of Alice Walker. In *Women writing culture*, ed. Ruth Behar and Deborah Gordon, pp. 233–245. Berkeley, CA: University of California Press.

Haug, Frigga. 1987. *Female sexualization: A collective work of memory*, translated from German by Erica Carter. London: Verso.

Hunt, Jennifer. 1989. *Psychoanalytic aspects of fieldwork*. Newbury Park, CA: Sage Publications.

Kleinman, Sherryl and Martha Copp. 1993. *Emotions and fieldwork*. Newbury Park, CA: Sage Publications.

Linde, Charlotte. 1993. *Life stories: The creation of coherence*. Oxford, England: Oxford University Press.

Luttrell, Wendy. 1989. Working-class women's ways of knowing: effects of gender, race and class. *Sociology of Education* 62(1): 33–46.

——— . 1997. *Schoolsmart and motherwise: Working-class women's identity and schooling.* New York: Routledge.

——— . 2000 "Good Enough" methods for ethnographic research. *Harvard Educational Review* 70(4): 499–523.

——— . 2003. *Pregnant bodies, fertile minds: Gender, race and the schooling of pregnant teens.* New York: Routledge.

Mathner, Natasha and Andrea Doucet. 1997. Reflections on a voice-centered relational method: analysing maternal and domestic voices. In *Feminist dilemmas in qualitative research: Public knowledge and private lives*, ed. Jane Ribbens and Rosalind Edwards, pp. 119–146. London: Sage Publications.

McLaren, Arlene. 1985. *Ambitions and realizations: Women in adult education.* London: Peter Owen.

Mishler, Elliot. 1986. *Research interviewing: Context and narrative.* Cambridge, MA: Harvard University Press.

Mitchell, Juliet. 1984. *The longest revolution: Essays in feminism, literature and psychoanalysis.* London: Virago.

Peacock, James and Dorothy Holland. 1993. The narrated self: Life stories in process. *Ethos* 21(4): 367–383.

Phillips, Adam. 1998. *The beast in the nursery.* London: Faber and Faber.

Quinn, Naomi. 2000. The divergent case of cultural anthropology. In *Primate encounters: Models of science, gender and society*, ed. Shirley Strum and Linda Fedigan, pp. 223–242. Chicago, IL: University of Chicago Press.

Riessman, Catherine Kohler. 1993. *Narrative analysis.* Newbury Park, CA: Sage Publications.

Rosenwald, George C. and Richard L. Ochenberg. 1992. *Storied lives: The cultural politics of self-understanding.* New Haven, CT: Yale University Press.

Sennett, Richard and Jonathan Cobb. 1972. *The hidden injuries of class.* New York: W. W. Norton and Co.

Shaw, Jenny. 1995. *Education, gender and anxiety.* London: Taylor and Francis.

Steedman, Carolyn. 1986. *Landscape for a good woman.* New Brunswick, NJ: Rutgers University Press.

Thompson, E. P. 1963. *The making of the English working-class.* New York: Vintage Books.

Thorne, Barrie. 1993. *Gender play: Girls and boys in school.* New Brunswick, NJ: Rutgers University Press.

Weinstein, R. M. 1980. Vocabularies of motive for illicit drug use: an application of the accounts framework. *Sociological Quarterly* 21: 577–593.

Willis, Paul. 1977. *Learning to labour: How working-class kids get working-class jobs.* Westmead, England: Saxon House, Teakfield.

Winnicott, D. W. 1965. *The maturational processes and the facilitating environment.* New York: International Universities Press.

17

Validity

How Might You Be Wrong?

Joseph A. Maxwell

In the movie *E.T. the Extra-Terrestrial,* there is a scene near the end of the film where the hero and his friends are trying to rescue ET and help him return to his spaceship. One of the boys asks, "Can't he just beam up?" The hero gives him a disgusted look and replies, "This is reality, Fred."

Validity, like getting to ET's spaceship, is the final component of your design. And as with ET's dilemma, there is no way to "beam up" to valid conclusions. This is reality. The validity of your results is not guaranteed by following some prescribed procedure. As Brinberg and McGrath (1985) put it, "Validity is not a commodity that can be purchased with techniques" (p. 13). Instead, it depends on the relationship of your conclusions to reality, and there are no methods that can completely assure that you have captured this.

The view that methods *could* guarantee validity was characteristic of early forms of positivism, which held that scientific knowledge could ultimately be reduced to a logical system that was securely grounded in irrefutable sense data. This position has been abandoned by philosophers, although it still informs many research methods texts (Phillips & Burbules, 2000, pp. 5–10). Validity is a goal rather than a product; it is never something that can be proven or taken for granted. Validity is also relative: It has to be assessed in relation to the purposes and circumstances of the research, rather than being a context-independent property of methods or conclusions. Finally, validity threats are made implausible by *evidence*, not methods; methods are only a way of getting evidence that can help you rule out these threats.

The realist claim that validity can't be assimilated to methods is one of the two main reasons that, in the model presented here, I have made validity a distinct component of qualitative design, separate from methods. The second reason is pragmatic: that validity is generally acknowledged to be a key *issue* in research design, and I think it's important that it be explicitly addressed. Przeworski and Salomon (1988) identified, as one of the three questions that proposal readers seek answers to, "How will we know that the conclusions are valid?" And Bosk (1979) stated that "All fieldwork done by a single field-worker invites the question, Why should we believe it?" (p. 193). A lack of attention to validity threats is a common reason for the rejection of research proposals. Making validity an explicit component of design can help you to address this issue.

The Concept of Validity

I use validity in a fairly straightforward, commonsense way to refer to the correctness or credibility of a description, conclusion, explanation, interpretation, or other sort of account. I think that this commonsense use of the term is consistent with the way it is generally used by qualitative researchers, and does not pose any serious philosophical problems.[1] This use of the term "validity" does not imply the existence of any "objective truth" to which an account can be compared. However, the idea of "objective truth" isn't essential to a theory of validity that does what most researchers want it to do, which is to give them some grounds for distinguishing accounts that are credible from those that are not. Nor are you required to attain some ultimate truth in order for your study to be useful and believable.

Geertz (1973) told the story of a British gentleman in colonial India who, upon learning that the world rested on the backs of four elephants, who in turn stood on the back of a giant turtle, asked what the turtle stood on. Another turtle. And that turtle? "Ah, Sahib, after that it is turtles all the way down" (p. 29). Geertz's point is that there is no "bottom turtle" of ethnographic interpretation, that cultural analysis is essentially incomplete. While I accept Geertz's point, I would emphasize a different lesson: that you do not have to get to the bottom turtle to have a valid conclusion. You only have to get to a turtle you can stand on securely.

As Campbell (1988), Putnam (1990), and others have argued, we don't need an observer-independent "gold standard" to which we can compare our accounts to see if they are valid. All we require is the possibility of *testing* these accounts against the world, giving the phenomena that we are trying to understand the chance to prove us wrong. A key concept for validity is thus the validity *threat:* a way you might be wrong. These threats are often conceptualized as alternative explanations, or what Huck and Sandler (1979) called "rival hypotheses." Validity, as a component of your research design, consists of the strategies you use to identify and try to rule out these threats.

There are important differences between quantitative and qualitative designs in the ways they typically deal with validity threats. Quantitative and experimental researchers generally attempt to design, in advance, controls that will deal with both anticipated and unanticipated threats to validity. These include control groups, statistical control of extraneous variables, randomized sampling and assignment, the framing of explicit hypotheses in advance of collecting the data, and the use of tests of statistical significance. These prior controls deal with most validity threats in an anonymous, generic fashion; as Campbell put it, "randomization purports to control an infinite number of 'rival hypotheses' *without specifying what any of them are*" (1984, p. 8).

Qualitative researchers, on the other hand, rarely have the benefit of previously planned comparisons, sampling strategies, or statistical manipulations that "control for" plausible threats, and must try to rule out most validity threats after the research has begun, using evidence collected during the research itself to make these "alternative hypotheses" implausible. This strategy of addressing particular validity threats *after* a tentative account has been developed, rather than by attempting to eliminate such threats through prior features of the research design, is, in fact, more fundamental to the scientific method than is the latter approach (Campbell, 1988; Platt, 1964). However, this approach requires you to identify the *specific* threat in question and to develop ways to attempt to rule out that particular threat.

This conception of validity threats and how they can be dealt with is a key issue in a qualitative research proposal. Many qualitative proposal writers make the mistake of talking about validity only in general, theoretical terms, presenting abstract strategies such as "bracketing," "member checks," and "triangulation" that will supposedly protect their studies from invalidity. Such presentations often appear to be "boilerplate"—language that has been borrowed from methods books or successful proposals, without any demonstration that the author has thought through how these strategies will actually be applied in the proposed study. These sections of the proposal often remind me of magical charms that are intended to drive away evil; they lack any discussion of how these strategies will work in practice, and their use seems to be based largely on faith in their supernatural powers.

In contrast, the main emphasis of a qualitative proposal ought to be on how you will rule out *specific* plausible alternatives and threats to your interpretations and explanations. Citations of authorities and invocation of standard approaches are less important than providing a clear argument that the approaches described will adequately deal with the particular threats in question, in the context of the study being proposed.

Two Specific Validity Threats: Bias and Reactivity

I argued previously that qualitative researchers generally deal with validity threats as particular events or processes that could lead to invalid conclusions, rather than as generic "variables" that need to be controlled. It clearly is impossible for me to list all, or even the most important, validity threats to the conclusions of a qualitative study, as Cook and Campbell (1979) attempted to do for quasi-experimental studies. What I want to do instead is to discuss two broad types of threats to validity that are often raised in relation to qualitative studies: researcher bias and the effect of the researcher on the individuals studied, often called reactivity.

Researcher "Bias"

Two important threats to the validity of qualitative conclusions are the selection of data that fit the researcher's existing theory or preconceptions and the selection of data that "stand out" to the researcher (Miles & Huberman, 1994, p. 263; Shweder, 1980). Both of these involve the subjectivity of the researcher, a term that most qualitative researchers prefer to "bias." It is impossible to deal with these issues by eliminating the researcher's theories, beliefs, and perceptual "lens." Qualitative research is not primarily concerned with eliminating *variance* between researchers in the values and expectations they bring to the study, but with understanding how a *particular* researcher's values and expectations influence the conduct and conclusions of the study (which may be either positive or negative) and avoiding the negative consequences. Explaining your possible biases and how you will deal with these is a key task of your research proposal. As one qualitative researcher, Fred Hess, phrased it, validity in qualitative research is not the result of indifference, but of integrity (personal communication).

Reactivity

The influence of the researcher on the setting or individuals studied, generally known as "reactivity," is a second problem that is often raised about qualitative studies. Trying to "control for" the effect of the researcher is appropriate to a quantitative, "variance theory" approach, in which the goal is to prevent researcher *variability* from being an unwanted cause of variability in the outcome variables. However, eliminating the *actual* influence of the researcher is impossible (Hammersley & Atkinson, 1995), and the goal in a qualitative study is not to eliminate this influence, but to understand it and to use it productively.

For participant observation studies, reactivity is generally *not* as serious a validity threat as some people believe. Becker (1970, pp. 45–48) pointed out that, in natural settings, an observer is generally much less of an influence on participants' behavior than is the setting itself (though there are clearly exceptions to this, such as situations in which illegal behavior occurs). For interviews, in contrast, reactivity—more correctly, what Hammersley and Atkinson (1995) called "reflexivity," the fact that the researcher is part of the world he or she studies—is a powerful and inescapable influence; what the informant says is *always* influenced by the interviewer and the interview situation. While there are some things you can do to prevent the more undesirable consequences of this (such as avoiding leading questions), trying to "minimize" your effect is not a meaningful goal for qualitative research. As discussed previously for "bias," what is important is to understand *how* you are influencing what the informant says, and how this affects the validity of the inferences you can draw from the interview.

Validity Tests: A Checklist

Although methods and procedures do not guarantee validity, they are nonetheless essential to the process of ruling out validity threats and increasing the credibility of your conclusions. For this reason, I will provide a checklist of some of the most important strategies that can be used for this purpose. Miles and Huberman (1994, p. 262) included a more extensive list, having some overlap with mine, and other lists can be found in Becker (1970), Kidder (1981), Lincoln and Guba (1985), and Patton (1990). What follows is not a complete compilation of what these authors said—I urge you to consult their discussions—but simply what I see as most important (Maxwell, 2004b).

The overall point I want to make about these strategies is that they primarily operate not by *verifying* conclusions, but by *testing* the validity of your conclusions and the existence of potential threats to those conclusions (Campbell, 1988). The fundamental process in all of these tests is looking for evidence that could challenge your conclusions or make the potential threats implausible.

Keep in mind that these strategies work only if you actually *use* them. Putting them in your proposal as though they were magical spells that could drive away the validity threats (and criticism of the proposal) won't do the job; you will need to demonstrate that you have thought through how you can effectively use them in your own study. Not every strategy will work in a given study, and even trying to apply all the ones that are feasible might not be an efficient use of your time. As noted previously, you need to think in terms of *specific* validity threats, and what strategies are best able to deal with these.

1. Intensive, Long-Term Involvement

Becker and Geer (1957) claimed that long-term participant observation provides more complete data about specific situations and events than any other method. Not only does it provide more, and more different kinds, of data, but also the data are more direct and less dependent on inference. Repeated observations and interviews, as well as the sustained presence of the researcher in the setting studied, can help to rule out spurious associations and premature theories. They also allow a much greater opportunity to develop and test alternative hypotheses during the course of the research. For example, Becker (1970, pp. 49–51) argued that his lengthy participant observation research with medical students not only allowed him to get beyond their public expressions of cynicism about a medical career and uncover an idealistic perspective, but also enabled him to understand the processes by which these different views were expressed in different social situations, and how students dealt with the conflicts between these perspectives.

2. "Rich" Data

Both long-term involvement and intensive interviews enable you to collect "rich" data, data that are detailed and varied enough that they provide a full and revealing picture of what is going on[2] (Becker, 1970, pp. 51–62). In interview studies, such data generally require verbatim transcripts of the interviews, not just notes on what you felt was significant. For observation, rich data are the product of detailed, descriptive note taking (or videotaping and transcribing) of the specific, concrete events that you observe (Emerson, Fretz, & Shaw, 1995). Becker (1970) argued that such data counter the twin dangers of respondent duplicity and observer bias by making it difficult for respondents to produce data that uniformly support a mistaken conclusion, just as they make it difficult for the observer to restrict his observations so that he sees only what supports his prejudices and expectations (p. 53).

Martha Regan-Smith's study of medical school teaching relied on lengthy observation and detailed field notes recording the teachers' actions in classes and students' reactions to these. In addition, she conducted and transcribed numerous interviews with students, in which they explained in detail not only what it was that the exemplary teachers did that increased their learning, but how and why these teaching methods were beneficial. This set of data provided a rich, detailed grounding for, and test of, her conclusions.

3. Respondent Validation

Respondent validation (Bryman, 1988, pp. 78–80; Lincoln & Guba, 1985, referred to this as "member checks") is systematically soliciting feedback about your data and conclusions from the people you are studying. This is the single most important way of ruling out the possibility of misinterpreting the meaning of what participants say and do and the perspective they have on what is going on, as well as being an important way of identifying your own biases and misunderstandings of what you observed. However, participants' feedback is no more inherently valid than their interview responses; both should be taken simply as *evidence* regarding the validity of your account (cf. Hammersley & Atkinson,

1995). For a more detailed discussion of this strategy, see Bloor (1983), Bryman (1988, pp. 78–80), Guba and Lincoln (1989), and Miles and Huberman (1994, pp. 242–243).

4. Intervention

Although some qualitative researchers see experimental manipulation as inconsistent with qualitative approaches (e.g., Lincoln & Guba, 1985), informal interventions are often used within traditional qualitative studies that lack a formal "treatment." For example, Goldenberg (1992), in a study of two students' reading progress and the effect that their teacher's expectations and behavior had on this progress, shared his interpretation of one student's failure to meet these expectations with the teacher. This resulted in a change in the teacher's behavior toward the student, and a subsequent improvement in the student's reading. The intervention with the teacher, and the resulting changes in her behavior and the student's progress, supported Goldenberg's claim that the teacher's behavior, rather than her expectations of the student, was the primary cause of the student's progress or lack thereof. In addition, Goldenberg provided an account of the *process* by which the change occurred, which corroborated the identification of the teacher's behavior as the cause of the improvement in a way that a simple correlation could never do.

Furthermore, in field research, the researcher's presence is *always* an intervention in some ways, and the effects of this presence can be used to develop or test ideas about the group or topic studied. For example, Briggs (1970), in her study of an Eskimo family, used a detailed analysis of how the family reacted to her often inappropriate behavior as an "adopted daughter" to develop her theories about the culture and dynamics of Eskimo social relations.

5. Searching for Discrepant Evidence and Negative Cases

Identifying and analyzing discrepant data and negative cases is a key part of the logic of validity testing in qualitative research. Instances that cannot be accounted for by a particular interpretation or explanation can point up important defects in that account. However, there are times when an apparently discrepant instance is not persuasive, as when the interpretation of the discrepant data is itself in doubt. Physics is full of examples of supposedly "disconfirming" experimental evidence that was later found to be flawed. The basic principle here is that you need to rigorously examine both the supporting and the discrepant data to assess whether it is more plausible to retain or modify the conclusion, being aware of all of the pressures to ignore data that do not fit your conclusions. Asking others for feedback is a valuable way to check your own biases and assumptions and flaws in your logic or methods. In particularly difficult cases, the best you may be able to do is to report the discrepant evidence and allow readers to evaluate this and draw their own conclusions.

6. Triangulation

Triangulation—collecting information from a diverse range of individuals and settings, using a variety of methods—reduces the risk of chance associations and of systematic biases due to a specific method, and allows a better assessment of the generality of the explanations that one develops. The most extensive discussion of triangulation as a validity-testing strategy in qualitative research is by Fielding and Fielding (1986).

One of Fielding and Fielding's key point is that it is not true that triangulation automatically increases validity. First, the methods that are triangulated may have the *same* biases and sources of invalidity, and thus provide only a false sense of security. For example, interviews, questionnaires, and documents are all vulnerable to self-report bias. Fielding and Fielding therefore emphasized the need to recognize the fallibility of *any* particular method or data and to triangulate in terms of *validity threats*. As argued previously, you should think about what particular sources of error or bias might exist, and look for specific ways to deal with this, rather than relying on your selection of methods to do this for you. In the final analysis, validity threats are ruled out by *evidence*, not methods.

7. Quasi-Statistics

Many of the conclusions of qualitative studies have an implicit quantitative component. Any claim that a particular phenomenon is typical, rare, or prevalent in the setting or population studied is an inherently quantitative claim, and requires some quantitative support. Becker (1970) coined the term "quasi-statistics" to refer to the use of simple numerical results that can be readily derived from the data. As he argued,

> One of the greatest faults in most observational case studies has been their failure to make explicit the quasi-statistical basis of their conclusions. (pp. 81–82)

Quasi-statistics not only allow you to test and support claims that are inherently quantitative, but also enable you to assess the *amount* of evidence in your data that bears on a particular conclusion or threat, such as how many discrepant instances exist and from how many different sources they were obtained. This strategy is used effectively in a classic participant-observation study of medical students by Becker, Geer, Hughes, and Strauss (1961), which presented more than 50 tables and graphs of the amount and distribution of observational and interview data supporting their conclusions.

8. Comparison

Explicit comparisons (such as between intervention and control groups) for the purpose of assessing validity threats are most common in quantitative, variance theory research, but there are numerous uses of comparison in qualitative studies, particularly in multicase or multisite studies. Miles and Huberman (1994, p. 254) provided a list of strategies for comparison, as well as advice on their use. Such comparisons (including comparisons of the same setting at different times) can address one of the main objections to using qualitative methods for understanding causality—their inability to explicitly address the "counterfactual" of what would have happened *without* the presence of the presumed cause (Shadish, Cook, & Campbell, 2002, p. 501).

In addition, single-setting qualitative studies, or interview studies of a relatively homogeneous group of interviewees, often incorporate less formal comparisons that contribute to the interpretability of the results. There may be a literature on "typical" settings or individuals of the type studied that makes it easier to identify the relevant characteristics and processes in an exceptional case and to understand their significance. In other instances, the participants in the setting studied may themselves have experience with other settings or with the same setting at an earlier time, and the researcher may be able to draw on this experience to identify the crucial factors and the effect that these have.

For example, Martha Regan-Smith's study of how exceptional medical school teachers help students to learn included only faculty who had won the "Best Teacher" award. From the point of view of quantitative design, this was an "uncontrolled" study, vulnerable to all of the validity threats identified by Campbell and Stanley (1963). However, both of the previously mentioned forms of implicit comparison were employed in the research. First, there is a great deal of published information about medical school teaching, and Regan-Smith was able to use both this background and her own extensive knowledge of medical schools to identify what it was that the teachers she studied did in their classes that was distinctive. Second, the students she interviewed explicitly contrasted these teachers with others whose classes they felt were not as helpful. In addition to these comparisons, the validity of her research conclusions depended substantially on a process approach; the students explained in detail not only *what* it was that the exemplary teachers did that increased their learning, but also *how* and *why* these teaching methods were beneficial. Many of these explanations were corroborated by Regan-Smith's own experiences as a participant-observer in these teachers' classes and by the teachers' explanations of why they taught the way they did.

Notes

1.   I present the philosophical argument that informs these statements elsewhere (Maxwell, 1992, 2004c). I also think that the concept of validity presented here is compatible with some "postmodern" approaches to validity (e.g., Kvale, 1989; Lather, 1993; cf. Maxwell, 1995, 2004a).
2.   Some qualitative researchers refer to these sorts of data as "thick description," a phrase coined by the philosopher Gilbert Ryle (1949) and applied to ethnographic research by Geertz (1973). This is not what either Ryle or Geertz meant by the phrase. "Thick description," as Geertz used it, is description that incorporates the intentions of the actors and the codes of signification that give their actions meaning for them, what anthropologists call an *emic* account. It has nothing to do with the amount of detail provided. (For a more detailed discussion of this issue, see Maxwell, 1992, pp. 288–289.)

References

Becker, H. 1970. *Sociological work: Method and substance.* Chicago: Aldine.

Becker, H. & Geer, B. 1957. "Participant observation and interviewing: A comparison." *Human Organization.* 16: 28–32.

Becker, H., Geer, B., Hughes, E. C., & Strauss, A. L. 1961. *Boys in White: Student culture in medical school.* Chicago: University of Chicago Press.

Bloor, M. J. 1983. "Notes on member validation." In R. M. Emerson (Ed.), *Contemporary field research: A collection of readings.* Prospect Heights, IL: Waveland Press. 156–172.

Bosk, C. 1979. *Forgive and remember: Managing medical failure.* Chicago: University of Chicago Press.

Briggs, J. 1970. *Never in Anger: Portrait of an Eskimo family.* Cambridge, MA: Harvard University Press.

Brinberg, D. & McGrath, J. E. 1985. *Validity and the research process.* Beverly Hills, CA: Sage.

Bryman, A. 1988. *Quantity and quality in social research.* London: Unwin Hyman.

Campbell, D. T. 1984. Foreword to *Case study research: Design and methods*, by R. Yin. Beverly Hills, CA: Sage.

———. 1988. *Methodology and epistemology for social science: Selected papers*. Chicago: University of Chicago Press.

Campbell, D. T. & Stanley, J. 1963. "Experimental and quasi-experimental designs for research on teaching." In N. L. Gage (Ed.), *Handbook of research on teaching*. Chicago: Rand McNally. 171–246.

Cook, T. D. & Campbell, D. T. 1979. *Quasi-experimentation: Design and analysis issues for field settings*. Boston: Houghton Mifflin.

Emerson, R. M., Fretz, R. I., & Shaw, L. L. 1995. *Writing ethnographic fieldnotes*. Chicago: University of Chicago Press.

Fielding, N. & Fielding J. (1986). *Linking data: the articulation of qualitative and quantitative methods in social research*. London: Sage.

Geertz, C. 1973. *The interpretation of cultures*. New York: Basic Books.

Goldenberg, C. 1992. "The limits of expectations: A case for case knowledge of teacher expectancy effects." *American Educational Research Journal*, 29: 517–544.

Guba, E. & Lincoln, Y. 1989. *Fourth generation evaluation*. Newbury Park, CA: Sage.

Hammersley, M. & Atkinson, P. 1995. *Ethnography: Principles in practice* (2nd ed.). London: Routledge.

Huck, S. W. & Sandler, H. M. 1979. *Rival hypotheses: Minute mysteries for the critical thinker*. London: Harper & Row.

Kidder, L. H. 1981. "Qualitative research and quasi-experimental frameworks." In M. B. Brewer & B. E. Collins (Eds.), *Scientific inquiry and the social sciences*. San Francisco: Jossey-Bass.

Kvale, S. (Ed.), 1989. *Issues of validity in qualitative research*. Lund, Sweden: Studentlitteratur.

Lather, P. 1993. "Fertile obsession: Validity after poststructuralism." *Sociological Quarterly*. 34: 673–693.

Lincoln, Y. and Guba, E. 1985. *Naturalistic Inquiry*. Beverly Hills, CA: Sage.

Maxwell, J. A. 1992. "Understanding and validity in qualitative research." *Harvard Educational Review*, 62: 279–300.

———. 1995. "Diversity and methodology in a changing world." *Pedagogia* 30: 32–40.

———. 2004a. "Re-emergent scientism, postmodernism, and dialogue across differences." *Qualitative Inquiry*, 10: 35–41.

———. 2004b. "Using qualitative methods for causal explanation." *Field Methods*, 16 (3): 243–264.

Miles, M. B. & Huberman, A. M. 1994. *Qualitative data analysis: A sourcebook of new methods*. Beverly Hills, CA: Sage.

Patton. M. Q. 1990. *Qualitative evaluation and research methods* (2nd ed.), Newbury Park, CA: Sage.

Platt, J. R. 1964. "Strong inference." *Science*, 146: 347–353.

Phillips, D. C. & Burbules, N. 2000. *Postpositivism and educational research*. Lanham, MD: Rowman & Littlefield.

Przeworski, A. & Salomon, F. 1988. *On the art of writing proposals: Some candid suggestions for applicants to Social Science Research Council competitors*. New York: Social Science Research Council.

Putnam, H. 1990. *Realism with a human face*. Cambridge, MA: Harvard University Press.

Ryle, G. 1949. *The concept of mind*. London: Hutchinson.

Shadish, W. R. Cook, T. D. & Campbell, D. T. 2002. *Experimental and quasi-experimental designs for generalized causal inference*. Boston: Houghton Mifflin.

Shweder, R. A. (Ed.), 1980. *Fallible judgment in behavioral research*. San Francisco: Jossey-Bass.

18

Validation in Inquiry-Guided Research
The Role of Exemplars in Narrative Studies

Elliot G. Mishler

The reason why only the right predicates happen so luckily to have become well entrenched is just that the well entrenched predicates thereby become the right ones. (p. 98) . . . The line between valid and invalid predictions (or inductions or projections) is drawn upon how the world is and has been described and anticipated in words.

Goodman (1979/1983, p. 121)

. . . rules are only rules by virtue of social conventions: they are social conventions. . . . That is the sociological resolution of the problem of inductive inference. . . . It is not the regularity of the world that imposes itself on our senses but the regularity of our institutionalized beliefs that imposes itself on the world.

Collins (1985, pp. 145–148)

Acceptance or rejection of a practice or theory comes about because a community is persuaded. Even research specialists do not judge a conclusion as it stands alone; they judge its compatibility with a network of prevailing beliefs.

Cronbach (1988, p. 6)

The individual scientist tends to assume that data replicated by certain of his colleagues are more likely to prove reliable and representative than those of other colleagues. Although there is no logical basis for such decisions, they represent accumulated, practical scientific experience. (p. 108) . . . The fact is that there are no rules of experimental design.

Sidman (1960, p. 214)

When I speak of knowledge embedded in shared exemplars, I am not referring to a mode of knowing that is less systematic or less analyzable than knowledge embedded in rules, laws, or criteria of identification. Instead I have in mind a manner of knowing which is misconstrued if reconstructed in rules that are first abstracted from exemplars and thereafter function in their stead.

Kuhn (1962/1970, p. 192)

Validation: A Reformulation

Those of us in the social sciences who do one or another type of inquiry-guided research have long been aware that the standard approach to validity assessment is largely irrelevant to our concerns and problems.[1] This is not surprising, since the prevailing conception of and procedures for validation are based on an experimental model whereas our studies are designed explicitly as an alternative to that model, with features that differ markedly and in detail from those characteristic of experiments.

These differences in the design of experimental and inquiry-guided studies have not prevented the mis-application of experiment-based criteria and methods of validation to other types of studies, resulting in their being evaluated as lacking scientific rigor.

With failure built in from the start, they are systematically denied legitimacy, and the dominance of the experimental model is assured. A new approach to validation is required that takes into account the distinctive features and problems of inquiry-guided studies and, at the same time, provides alternative, applicable methods for researchers. This article is directed to that task.[2]

Like the fabled Gordian Knot, validation is a mess of entangled concepts and methods with an abundance of loose threads. Sophisticated, technical procedures pulling out and straightening each thread, one at a time, seem to leave the knot very much as it was. The apparent increase in rigor and precision of successive advances in methods have brought us no closer to resolving the special problems faced by inquiry-guided researchers. Alexander the Great's decisive cut through the intractable Knot—a move that dissolved the problem by doing away with it—suggests that we might do better to begin at the beginning with a radical, conceptual recasting of the problem.

In sketching out a new perspective, I will begin by reformulating validation as the social construction of knowledge. With this reformulation, the key issue becomes whether the relevant community of scientists evaluates reported findings as sufficiently trustworthy to rely on them for their own work. I ground this perspective in recent historical and sociological studies of scientific practice. Further, I suggest that this reformulation is compatible with a growing recognition among mainstream validity theorists of the centrality of interpretation in validation, which poses intractable problems for the standard model. Using Kuhn's analysis of the role of exemplars in science, I then examine several instances of how validity claims are made and may be assessed in inquiry-guided, interpretive studies.

Recent studies in the history, philosophy, and sociology of science have seriously damaged the "storybook image of science" (Mitroff, 1974)—an image that has served to legitimate the dominant conception of validation. These new studies, which focus on actual practices of scientists rather than on textbook idealizations, reveal science as a human endeavor marked by uncertainty, controversy, and ad hoc pragmatic procedures— a far cry from an abstract and severe "logic" of scientific discovery. Validation has come to be recognized as problematic in a deep theoretical sense, rather than as a technical problem to be solved by more rigorous rules and procedures. An extended review of these developments is beyond the limits of this paper, but the quotations with which I began may evoke the tenor and thrust of the argument.[3]

Further encouragement for an alternative approach may be found in recent views of some of the principal architects of our current governing conception. A new understanding of validity has evolved gradually over the last 35–40 years, from the first codification of standards by the American Psychological Association (APA, 1954) and the influential paper by Cronbach and Meehl (1955). One of the central features of both statements was the partitioning of validity into four types: content, predictive, concurrent, and construct.[4] This was followed by successive efforts to revise the model, without altering the assumption of different specifiable types, by proposing other typologies.[5]

Each new proposal underscored the fundamentally flawed nature of this model. It became clear that validation, the touchstone of scientific inquiry, could not be achieved by applying a formal algorithm to assess each type of validity. Campbell and Stanley's (1963; see also Cook & Campbell, 1979) elegant and influential analysis of different quasi-experimental designs and their respective threats to one or another validity has turned out, in retrospect, to be a death-blow to the typology approach. There are two reasons for this unanticipated consequence, both reflecting Campbell and Stanley's clear understanding that validity assessments are not assured by following procedures but depend on investigators' judgments of the relative importance of different "threats." First, no general, abstract rules can be provided for assessing overall levels of validity in particular studies or domains of inquiry. Second, no formal or standard procedure can be determined either for assigning weights to different threats to any one type of validity, or for comparing different types of validity. These assessments are matters of judgment and interpretation. And these evaluations depend, irremediably, on the whole range of linguistic practices, social norms and contexts, assumptions and traditions that the rules had been designed to eliminate. To Sidman's (1960) statement that there are "no rules of experimental design," we may now add that there are "no rules" for assessing validity. Investigators of course, follow accepted procedures in their domains of inquiry. However, as will become clear, these "rules" for proper research are not universally applicable, are modified by pragmatic considerations, and do not bypass or substitute for their nonrule-governed interpretation of their data.

Recognition of these unresolvable problems has led to a new perspective in which validity is viewed as a unitary concept with construct validation as the fundamental problem.[6] This, of course, makes issues of meaning and interpretation central. Thus, Cronbach (1984) states that the "end goal of validation is explanation and understanding. Therefore, the profession is coming around to the view that *all* validation is construct validation" (p. 126). Messick (1989), reviewing the history of changing conceptions, argues that validation is essentially a type of "scientific inquiry," and that a validity judgment is an "inductive summary" of all available information, with issues of meaning and interpretation central to the process. He also expands the validation framework to include social values and social consequences of findings as contexts for validity assessments.[7]

This emergent consensus is good news. It acknowledges, albeit implicitly, that the traditional approach has failed and offers an opportunity for exploring alternatives. The new emphasis on interpretation, and on social contexts and values, resonates closely with the detailed findings of historians and sociologists of science. Both developments encourage us to view all types of research as "forms of life" (Wittgenstein, 1953; see also Brenner, 1981) rather than technical exercises governed by an abstract logic of methodological rules. With this understanding, we may be able to move towards a conception of validation that is more relevant not only to inquiry-guided studies but to experimental modes of research as well.

Trustworthiness: Grounds for Belief and Action

As a first step, I propose to redefine validation as the process(es) through which we make claims for and evaluate the "trustworthiness" of reported observations, interpretations, and generalizations.[8] The essential criterion for such judgments is the degree to which we can rely on the concepts, methods, and inferences of a study, or tradition of inquiry, as the basis for our own theorizing and empirical research. If our overall assessment of a study's trustworthiness is high enough for us to act on it, we are granting the findings a sufficient degree of validity to invest our own time and energy, and to put at risk our reputations as competent investigators. As more and more investigators act on this assumption and find that it "works," the findings take on the aura of objective fact; they become "well-entrenched" (Goodman, 1983).

This definition and criterion depart in critical ways from standard doctrine. First, by making validation rather than validity the key term (see Messick, 1989), they focus on the range of ongoing activities through which claims are made and appraised rather than on the static properties of instruments and scores. Second, by adopting a functional criterion—whether findings are relied upon for further work—rather than abstract rules, validation is understood as embedded within the general flow of scientific research rather than being treated as a separate and different type of assessment.[9] In this way, this definition and criterion emphasizes the role played in validation by scientists' working knowledge and experience, aligning the process more closely with what scientists actually do (Collins, 1985; Latour, 1990; Latour & Woolgar, 1979; Lynch, 1985; Ravetz, 1971; Sidman, 1960) than with what they are assumed to be and supposed to do.

Further, focusing on trustworthiness rather than truth displaces validation from its traditional location in a presumably objective, nonreactive, and neutral reality, and moves it to the social world—a world constructed in and through our discourse and actions, through praxis. Since social worlds are endlessly being remade as norms and practices change, it is clear that judgments of trustworthiness may change with time, even when addressed to the "same" findings. Finally, truth claims and their warrants are not assessed in isolation, but enter a more general discourse of validation that includes not only other scientists but many parties in the larger community with different and often conflicting views. (See Latour's 1988 account of shifting conflicts and alliances in the "validation" of Pasteur's microbial theory of infection; also Richards, 1979, on the reception of non-Euclidean geometry in nineteenth-century England.)

Reformulating validation as the social discourse through which trustworthiness is established elides such familiar shibboleths as reliability, falsifiability, and objectivity. These criteria are neither trivial nor irrelevant, but they must be understood as particular ways of warranting validity claims rather than as universal, abstract guarantors of truth. They are rhetorical strategies (Simons, 1989) that fit only one model of science—experimental, hypothesis-testing, and so forth. Used as proof criteria, they serve a deviance-sanctioning function, marking off "good" from "bad" scientific practice. (See Gieryn, 1983, and Prelli, 1989, for case studies of the rhetoric of exclusion.)

Bazerman (1989), reviewing Collins's (1985) studies of replication and induction in science, observes that: "Experimentation is so embedded in forms of life that compelling experimental results are compelling only to those who have already entered in the form of life which generates the result" (p. 115). These warrants have less "rightness of fit" (Goodman, 1978) for interpretive and inquiry-guided forms of research which, in turn, may only be compelling to those who have entered that form of life.[10]

Conflict and controversy are as much a part of "normal science" (Kuhn, 1970) as the shared concepts, procedures, and findings dutifully inscribed in textbooks. All scientific reports—from spare accounts of methods and findings to philosophical analyses—are partisan forays into contested terrain. Nonetheless, the "truths" of normal science are embedded in complex networks of concepts, linguistic and technical practices, and an established framework of norms and values (Collins, 1985; see also Campbell, 1979, on the "tribal model" of scientific knowledge), and it is not surprising that they are markedly resistant to change. New approaches or new discoveries cannot easily be absorbed, nor can their potential threat to the whole system be defused by tinkering with minor details.

For these reasons, I would not expect easy assent to this new formulation of validation. However, by showing that experimentalists are in the same boat as inquiry-guided researchers in that we all rely for the validation of our work on contextually grounded linguistic and interpretive practices, I hope to gain a hearing and perhaps enlist "allies" (Latour, 1988). As Collins (1985) points out, the possibility of changing current practices depends on putting forward "an interpretation of data which has the potential to create some contradictions and reverberate through the social and conceptual web . . . [but] must not appear to be completely unreasonable" (p. 151).

Exemplars: Resources for Inquiry

If validity claims cannot be settled by appeal to abstract, standard rules or algorithms, what would be a useful alternative approach? The indeterminateness of such claims is not a matter of the imprecision of technical methods. Rather, definitions of evidence and rules and criteria for their assessment are embedded in networks of assumptions and accepted practices that constitute a tradition. Recomending new rules for inquiry-guided studies would confront us with the same uncertainties that, as we have seen, undermine the canonical approach. The utility of alternative rules would be limited—as are the standard ones—to their pragmatic function as accounting practices that help researchers monitor, arrange, and order their data in some methodic way.[11] Rather than proposing yet another list of rules and criteria, I will rely on Kuhn's (1970) analysis of "exemplars" to suggest an approach to the problem of how claims for trustworthiness may be made and evaluated.[12]

Kuhn's (1962/1970) concept of paradigms and the role they play in "normal science" has had considerable influence in studies of the history and sociology of science. Responding to criticism about ambiguities in the referents of this term, he replaced it with "disciplinary matrix" for the full set of assumptions, theories, and practices shared within a community of specialists. A critical element of this matrix is the "exemplar":

> By it I mean, initially, the concrete problem-solutions that students encounter from the start of their scientific education, whether in laboratories, on examinations, or at the ends of chapters in science texts. . . . [and] at least some of the technical problem-solutions found in the periodical literature that scientists encounter during their post-educational research careers and that also show them by example how their job is to be done. More than other sorts of components of the disciplinary matrix, differences between sets of exemplars provide the community fine-structure of science. (Kuhn, 1970, p. 187)

Kuhn views "knowledge embedded in shared exemplars" as a "mode of knowing" no less systematic or susceptible to analysis than that of "rules, laws, or criteria" (p. 192), and also recognizes that these "modes" of doing and acting are not acquired simply by "encounters" with textual descriptions. Skilled research is a craft (Ravetz, 1971; see also Polanyi, 1966, on "tacit knowing"), and, like any craft, it is learned by apprenticeship to competent researchers, by hands-on experience, and by continual practice. It seems remarkable, if we stop to think about it, that research competence is assumed to be gained by learning abstract rules of scientific procedure. Why should such "working knowledge" (Harper, 1987; Mishler, 1989) be learned any more easily, or through other ways, than the competence required for playing the violin or blowing glass or throwing pots?

Technical descriptions of methods in themselves, however detailed and precise, are insufficient for replication, the prescribed route to validation. Sidman (1960) observes that it is "common practice in biological science" for researchers to make personal visits to the laboratories of competent users of an experimental procedure to "learn the required skills firsthand" (p. 109). Replication is a routinely uncertain endeavor and, as Collins (1985, pp. 29–78) argues, the usual notion is misleading and does not correspond to how scientists use other studies as springboards for their own work rather than "replicating" them.

Collins documents the "capricious nature" of the transfer of knowledge and concludes that such knowledge "travels best (or only) through accomplished practitioners," that "experimental ability is invisible in its passage," and that the only evidence of the "proper" conduct of an experiment is the "proper" experimental outcome—not the precision with which the work was done. Finally, he observes that although successive failures to replicate might lead scientists to temporarily suspend their belief that following "algorithm-like instructions" make carrying out an experiment a "formality," this belief "re-crystallizes catastrophically upon the successful completion of an experiment" (p. 76). Thus, by concealing their skills and artfulness from themselves—their own craft and tacit knowledge—scientists reaffirm the "objectivity" of their findings and reproduce the assumptive framework of "normal science."

In sum, knowledge is validated within a community of scientists as they come to share nonproblematic and useful ways of thinking about and solving problems. Representing the "community-fine structure of science" (Kuhn, 1970, p. 187), exemplars contain within themselves the criteria and procedures for evaluating the "trustworthiness" of studies and serve as testaments to the internal history of validation within particular domains of inquiry.[13] Developing new exemplars is a complex social process, over which individual investigators have only modest control. To move towards this goal, those of us engaged in inquiry-guided and interpretive forms of research have the task of articulating and clarifying the features and methods of our studies, of showing how the work is done and what problems become accessible to study. Although they cannot serve as "standard" rules, a context-based explication is required of how observations are transformed into data and findings, and of how interpretations are grounded.

In the remainder of this paper, I will focus on studies of narrative, one branch of interpretive research, and propose three different approaches as candidate exemplars. My immediate aim is to demonstrate alternative ways to do such studies that may be useful to other investigators. My broader aim is to promote a dialogue about ways of doing inquiry-guided research so that together we can develop a community with shared exemplars through which we confirm and validate our collective work.

Candidate Exemplars for Interpretive Research

There may be several exemplars, each with its own variants, that achieve legitimacy within a community of specialists sharing a perspective and methodology—"search cells" or "language communities" in Koch's (1976) terms. Together they constitute normal practice—the ordinary, taken-for-granted and trustworthy concepts and methods for solving puzzles and problems within a particular area of work. Legitimacy cannot be legislated in advance. Neither abstract rules nor appeal to an idealized version of *the* scientific method will suffice. Rather, the defining features of exemplars are inferred from the actual practices of working scientists. Like the inductive categories of "natural" objects studied by cognitive psychologists, experiments and types of inquiry-guided studies are both "fuzzy categories" (Mervis & Rosch, 1981; Rosch, 1973, 1978; Rosch & Mervis, 1975). Each includes prototypes—for example, the model experiment, and a range of variants, such as "quasi-experiments."

As a context for discussing the approaches that I am nominating, tentatively, as candidate exemplars, I will first briefly outline some features of the dominant research exemplar as it has been applied to the study of narratives. All of the studies I will examine, though differing in content and theoretical orientation, share certain characteristics that make for useful comparison: each 1) focuses on a piece of "interpretive discourse," 2) takes this "text" as its basic datum, 3) reconceptualizes it as an instance of a more abstract and general "type," 4) provides a method for characterizing and "coding" textual units and 5) specifies the "structure" of relationships among them, and 6) interprets the "meaning" of this structure within a theoretical framework. Interpretive discourse (White, 1989) refers to researchers' understandings of the texts as representing efforts by speakers/authors themselves to describe and interpret their experiences.

As will be seen, the three proposed alternatives share features distinguishing them from the standard approach. Each "displays" the full texts to which the analytic procedures are applied, in contrast to the typical presentation of decontextualized fragments illustrating a coding manual. Further, rather than defining coding "dimensions" that are independent of and isolated from each other, these studies focus on analytic "structures" of relationships among textual features, which then become the basis for theoretical interpretation.

Normal Science and Narrative Research

Many critics of the positivist-based experimental model argue that its assumptions—about, for example, causality and objectivity—are inappropriate for the study of language and meaning (see footnote 2). Their argument would apply to research on "narrative modes of knowing" (Bruner, 1986). Investigators, however, are not governed in their practices by philosophical analyses of their epistemological and ontological assumptions. Skilled researchers working within the standard framework can find ways of adapting and applying their methods to any phenomenon that catches their interest, and narratives have not escaped their net.

Two recent studies (McAdams, 1985; Stewart, Franz, & Layton, 1988) illustrate how this is done. Both use life history narratives to examine issues of personal identity. I will focus on their research practices—on some of the ways they make the dominant exemplar "work" on apparently unsuitable material. Although they warrant their validity claims by an explicit reliance on "standard" methods, it turns out that their success in carrying out their analyses depends fundamentally on their pragmatic modifications of these methods. This is their "practical accomplishment" (Garfinkel, 1967) as researchers. Although I emphasize their research practices in this section, the inappropriateness of their conceptual models for narrative research is an equally important problem that will be addressed at various points. The aim of this brief review of their work is to set the stage for discussion of more appropriate approaches.

These investigators face a difficult task. They must convert voluminous, multi-dimensional, and variable language samples into the types of objects that allow them to apply standard procedures—sampling, measuring, counting, and hypothesis-testing through statistical analysis. To make the problem reasonably tractable, they begin deductively, relying on general theories to specify a few dimensions—power and intimacy motives for McAdams, based on McClelland's model; themes of identity, intimacy, and generativity for Stewart et al. from Erikson's (1950/1959) model of ego development. These concepts—motives and themes—are converted into coding categories that are applied to the original texts: responses to interviews from samples of respondents in McAdams' case and from letters, diaries, and autobiographical memoirs of one person in Stewart et al.'s study. The resultant "scores" are the data for successive stages of description, analysis, and interpretation.

Their competence as researchers is displayed by their success in accomplishing this transformation—from the messy and diffuse narrative texts with which they begin to the quantitative measures that now represent and stand for those texts. The reduction and transformation of source data—that is, initial observations and descriptions—is a necessary feature of all research. However, different rules and strategies of reduction lead to different re-presentations of the phenomena. These new "objects," constructed by researchers, include and emphasize only some features of the originals and exclude others as irrelevant to their interests. Interpretive researchers view the transformations achieved by the standard model as deeply flawed distortions in that they exclude precisely those features of the phenomena that are their essential, defining characteristics. Thus, with reference to narratives, representing them as scores for separate motives or themes, as is done in these two studies, excludes both their structural and sequential features, which are specifically what makes them "narratives" rather than some other type of text.

A principal claim of researchers who follow an experiment-based model is that their use of standard methods and procedures allows others to replicate their studies. Thus, Stewart et al. assert the generalizability of their codes: "The coding definitions were designed for use in coding any verbal text for preoccupation with self-definitional issues" (p. 49). Studies in the history and sociology of science, reviewed earlier, make it clear that "standardization" is not easily achieved and that replication is a function of local, situated practices. The problem may be seen in the ways that "standard" methods are modified in these two studies so that they can be applied to the particular and contingent features of their data.

For example, Stewart et al.'s coding units are "meaningful phrases" defined by the presence of a "codable image" (p. 57), which can include any length of text. Adequate understanding and use of this code depends on this particular study's coders' subculture (Mishler, 1984, p. 37) and, in a strong sense, the coding procedure could not be transferred directly to another research context. McAdams found it necessary to alter coding definitions of power and intimacy for individuals' accounts of their "earliest memories," since these were "rather banal and lacking in feeling tone." Categories were "broadened to include events and actions similar, though perhaps not identical, to the original characterizations" (pp. 173–174). Broadening or narrowing coding categories is, of course, an option open to other researchers, and the question of whether or not they had "replicated" the procedure would then be unanswerable.

Sometimes inconsistencies or contradictions, appearing at one or another stage in an analysis, require a mid-stream change in methods. Looking at summary scores for the "same" themes in different types of documents referring to the same time period, Stewart et al. found themselves "faced with the dilemma that we had not only different accounts of the period, but accounts in which the scores were in fact uncorrelated" (p. 59). Rather than taking this finding as a test of their hypotheses, they decided to "treat these media as alternative expressions" and "took the higher score for a given month, for all subcategories of that stage, regardless of which medium produced it" (p. 59). McAdams found that "the four main themes for power and intimacy did not appear relevant for the coding" of "negative nuclear episodes." He "settled inductively on four new themes for each of the content categories of power and intimacy. In some cases, the new themes bear some resemblance, typically as an opposite, to the original themes used in the analysis of positive nuclear episodes. In other cases, any similarity is lacking" (p. 158).

Similar observations might be made about the situated practices through which any investigator assures the success of his or her work. The main point is that standard methods are poorly standardized, allowing great latitude to researchers in how they specify them, and specification is contextually grounded in the idiosyncracies and exigencies of particular studies. All investigators have to adapt, convert, and translate "standard" methods to solve their practical problems.

McAdam's and Stewart et al.'s on-line, pragmatic decisions are as much a part of normal scientific practice as their use of a coding manual and statistical tests. However, they highlight the problematic nature of their validity claims. Standard procedures—for sampling, coding, and quantifying—are weak and insufficient warrants because when they are actually applied they turn out to be context-bound, nonspecifiable in terms of "rules," and not generalizable. Close examination of the procedures used in any study would reveal a similar gap between the assumption of standardization and actual practices. Other investigators would be unable to determine whether their own versions, or adaptations, of their procedures represented a reasonable equivalent of them. Replication, rather than being assured by these procedures, would be essentially indeterminate.

Alternative Models for Narrative Research[14]

The three studies I will review below depart in significant ways from normal practice. They do not escape the thorny and unavoidable problems of validation. Nonetheless, I hope to show that they provide reasonable grounds for and ways of assessing their claims for trustworthiness, and, also, that they are more adequate and appropriate models for the study of narratives as a type of interpretive discourse.

Life History Narratives and Identity Formation

A life history interview with one artist-furniture maker provides the narrative text that I analyze in my study of adult identity formation (Mishler, in press). Reviewing my work in the context of the preceding discussion of standard studies that also focused on issues of identity will help to clarify differences in our respective research strategies and methods.

Informing and guiding my study is the question of how craftspersons sustain their commitments to and motivations for nonalienating forms of work in an in-hospitable sociocultural and economic environment. Drawing on William Morris's (1883/1966) concept of the "craftsman ideal," which assigns a high value to craft work as creative, varied, and useful, I try to understand how craftspersons balance that "mode of being" with economic, social, and family demands. I define identity formation as the process by which these problems are resolved over the life course.

The concepts of alienated and nonalienated work are not used to derive testable hypotheses but as issues to explore with respondents to learn whether and how they might be relevant to them in their work. My inductive approach contrasts with McAdams' and Stewart's deductive one, and leads to different methods for collecting, describing, analyzing, and interpreting the interviews. For example, my research interviews are relatively unstructured, with respondents controlling the introduction, content, and flow of topics. Informing them of my interest in how craftspersons live and work, I ask them to talk about how they came to be doing the work they're doing and "what's involved in the kind of life you lead that's related to being in the crafts." Within this frame of a research interview, we have a shared task and purpose: to understand how they came to do and how they view their current work. The personal narrative that emerges is a solution to this task, representing the individual's general solution to the task of making sense of his or her life.

I take it for granted that the account produced during the interview is a reconstruction of the past, shaped by the particular context of its telling. A respondent's re-interpretation of his or her work history is the basic "text" for analysis and interpretation. The problem of "distortion" that troubles Stewart et al.—that is, whether the account corresponds to the "real" past—does not arise since I do not rely on a correspondence model of truth, where the earlier "objective" reality serves as a validity criterion for what is being told now. This is not a weakness, but rather a hallmark of interpretive research in which the key problem is understanding how individuals interpret events and experiences, rather than assessing whether or not their interpretations correspond to or mirror the researchers' interpretive construct of "objective" reality. A concern with distortion places the burden of validity claims on the wrong shoulders—it is the investigator's problem, not the respondent's. Instead of assuming a past reality as a criterion, a potential warrant for the validity of my interpretation is whether it makes sense to the respondent.

My text-sampling procedure does not follow a statistical model, but reflects successive steps of the inquiry: interviews with a small, varied group of artist-crafts-persons, repeated listenings to taped interviews and readings of transcripts, discovery of parallel trajectories in their work histories, development and refinement of a model of work history narratives, selection of this respondent as a representative case, and specification of the episodes and structure of his narrative for detailed analysis and interpretation. Thus, the text samples were not drawn randomly but inductively, and chosen as representative of patterns I was finding in the full data set.

Clearly, this form of inquiry-guided or "grounded theory" research (Glaser & Strauss, 1967; Strauss, 1987) involves a continual dialectic between data, analysis, and theory. Its steps are no more mysterious or less attentive to the data than statistical procedures. The latter, as we saw in McAdams' and Stewart et al.'s studies, also require on-line adjustments. This process-dependence of research decisions, though usually viewed as a methodological weakness and a source of contamination and error, is a necessary part of any study.

I view the "personal narratives" that emerge during the interviews as retrospective accounts whose function is to provide a sense of coherence and continuity through life transitions (Cohler, 1982), that is, as representing the formation of a craft identity. My analytic model focuses on respondents' reports of their shifts between types of work, of the reasons for these changes, and of how they achieved their current work identity. It distinguishes between and then links together the two essential dimensions of any narrative—the "non-chronological" or structural one, and the "chronological" or temporal one (Ricoeur, 1981). The structural component locates work identities within social and cultural contexts that define alternatives and limit choices among culturally available types of work for artist-craftspersons: Art, Craft, Type of Craft, and specific Mode of Craft work. Each succeeding choice is constrained by the previous ones. The second component focuses on the temporal ordering of respondents' actual choices within this structure of general categories, which serve as a "code" to classify the narrative episodes, or "units" of the interview.

The structure of hierarchically ordered categories was empirically rather than theoretically derived. Using it as a framework to locate the "identity relevance" of particular choices led to the discovery that the achievement of a current work identity was neither linear nor progressive. In shifting from one job to another, individuals sometimes made moves within the same category and sometimes moved back to a prior one before going on to succeeding ones. I refer to these shifts as "detours," as off the straight path to their achieved identity. Further, they are recognized by the respondents themselves, from their current vantage point and achieved identity, as functioning in this way. This is one criterion for assessing the trustworthiness of the model and my interpretation of the identity relevance of job changes.

For example, my analytic distinction between Art and Craft derives from and can be tracked directly back to respondents' ways of talking about their different types of work. For example, the furniture-maker refers to the distinction as present in "this endless discussion that goes on and on and on in schools and between professionals and all that." As to himself: "I don't consider myself just a craftsperson. I consider myself a designer committed to craftsmanship." For him, "a craftsperson and an artist are synonymous if you're looking at those that you respect as good craftspeople. Not people who are just churning out objects, but people who are doing personal work, and doing progressive work." And further, "It has to do probably with their input into creating the object, rather than being given a design or being given something to copy and produce and just giving with their manual skills as—as opposed to their intellect and creativity."

Further, the episodes that are the plot of his work history narrative, which I constructed from the full interview, include all of the different jobs and transitions that he describes. Thus, he specifies a sequence of changes from entering college as a "chemical engineer," switching to train as an "architect," when he first "became involved in the design world" (an Art choice), and changing again to become a "landscape architect." His first post-college job was as an architect (Art), but then he began to work with a "third-generation craftsman" and "really started to do wood-working" (a Craft choice). After two years, feeling that he was "being locked into Milltown, Indiana, for the rest of my life" and was "wasting" his training in landscape architecture, he moved and "started working as a landscape architect" (a detour back to Art).

He stayed at this for five-and-a-half years, and then, realizing that "it just wasn't what I wanted to do for the rest of my life," he "did a search and, uh, decided to go" to graduate school for training in furniture making: "totally investing myself in—in, ah, the furniture world as a craftsman" (a switch back to Crafts). It is his own evaluation of his work as a landscape architect as off the path to his current work identity that grounds my interpretation of it as a detour. He received a degree in "crafts, treating furniture as an art form," and then began "teaching" furniture making, and setting up a "shop" and "doing some shows and commission work" (his move to his current Mode of Work and his achieved identity as an artist-furniture maker). Note that his transitions between types of work are explicitly marked by such locutions as: "I decided I wanted to do something else," "so at that time . . . I started working as," "so I did a search and, uh, decided to go," "I ended up, um . . . opting to go."

The view of validation that I have advanced suggests that the questions to be asked about my study, and of any study within any research tradition, are: What are the warrants for my claims? Could other investigators make a reasonable judgment of their adequacy? Would they be able to determine how my findings and interpretations were "produced" and, on that basis, decide whether they were trustworthy enough to be relied upon for their own work? I believe these questions have affirmative answers. The primary reason is the visibility of the work: of the data in the form of the texts used in the analysis, with full transcripts and tapes that can be made available to other researchers; of the methods that transformed the texts into findings; and of the direct linkages shown between data, findings, and interpretation.

I am not arguing that my methods and procedures "validate" my findings and interpretations. That would be counter to my basic thesis that validation is the social construction of a discourse through which the results of a study come to be viewed as sufficiently trustworthy for other investigators to rely upon in their own work. Nor does my study escape the difficult problems of "knowledge transmission," of how others might learn how to do this type of work and of what criteria they could use to determine the degree of equivalence between our respective studies. I am arguing, however, that they would be able to make a reasoned and informed assessment about whether or not my validity claims are well warranted.

I used my own study to contrast one type of narrative research with examples of standard practice. Parallels between the studies, particularly their shared focus on identity and their analysis of texts, allowed me to highlight and clarify differences between them in methods for collecting, displaying, analyzing, and interpreting data. The next two candidate exemplars differ from my own in aims, methods, texts, and models of narrative analysis.

Narrativization in the Oral Style

A seven-year-old Black child tells a story about her puppy during "sharing time" in her second grade class (Michaels, 1981). It does not match her teacher's expectations, lacking the standard story structure of sequentially connected episodes. (Michaels refers to it as "topic-associating" rather than "topic-centered.") Finding it difficult to understand and missing the point, the teacher treats it as a sign of the child's inadequate language skills. (See Riessman, 1987, on an interviewer's similar difficulties with a respondent's nonstandard narrative.)

Gee (1985, also 1986) reexamines the story as an instance of an "oral" rather than a "literate" style (Heath, 1982, 1983). Starting with the assumption that, "One of the primary ways—perhaps *the* primary way—human beings make sense of their experience is by casting it in a narrative form" (p. 11), Gee tries to explicate how this child does that. His stylistic analysis reveals that her narrative "shares many features with narratives found throughout the world in oral cultures" (p. 9), with its structure achieved through such "technical devices" as "repetition, parallelism, sound play, juxtaposition, foregrounding, delaying, and showing rather than telling [that] are hallmarks of spoken language in its most oral mode, reaching its peak in the poetry, narratives, and epics of oral cultures" (p. 26).

His route to a description and understanding of the "structures behind her narrative performance" begins with his observation/hearing of a "characteristic prosodic pattern." Her extended stretch of speech consists of "a series of relatively short sequences of words, each sequence having a continuous intonational contour" (p. 12). A fall in pitch does not come until after several such sequences. This contrasts with literate speech, where falling contours tend to mark ends of sentences. Gee suggests that her falling contours have discourse-level rather than syntactic-level functions, and serve to mark the ends of episodes rather than sentences.

Displaying the text in terms of the " 'lines' that L is aiming at," the "idea units" that she expresses as short clauses, "it becomes apparent that L groups her lines together into series of lines—often four lines long—that have parallel structure and match each other in content or topic" (p. 14). Gee calls these groups of lines "stanzas." Using the stanza as the basic structural unit in his analysis, he finds that the sequence of stanzas in her narrative, each representing an episode, are grouped together: there are three main parts to her story, each of which has two sub-parts. The following excerpts illustrate Gee's structural analysis (1985, pp. 34–35).

Part 1: INTRODUCTION
Part 1A: Setting
  1. Last yesterday in the morning
  2. there was a hook on the top of the stairway
  3. an' my father was pickin me up
  4. an I got stuck on the hook up there
  5. an' I hadn't had breakfast
  6. he wouldn't take me down =
  7. until I finished all my breakfast =
  8. cause I didn't like oatmeal either //
Part 1B
  9. an' then my puppy came
  10. he was asleep
  11. he tried to get up
  12. an he ripped my pants
  13. an' he dropped the oatmeal all over

Part 3: RESOLUTION
Part 3A: Concluding Episodes
  . . .
  36. an' last yesterday, an' now they put him asleep
  37. an' he's still in the hospital
  38. (an' the doctor said . . .) he got a shot because
  39. he was nervous about my home that I had
Part 3B: Coda
  . . .

41. an' he could still stay but

42. he thought he wasn't gonna be able to let him go //

The first part of her story takes place in the child's home, the "setting" described first in two four-line stanzas followed by another two four-line stanzas that introduce her puppy and father. The second part involves going to school and being followed by her puppy, "complicating actions" consisting again of two four-line stanzas, with a brief non-narrative "evaluation" section. The last part takes place in a hospital, the "resolution" of the story in two four-line stanzas and a concluding two-line "coda." By using terms for the story components—"setting," "complicating actions," and so forth—from a model for standard, temporally ordered narratives (Labov, 1972; Labov & Waletzky, 1967), Gee is arguing that this story has a structure that serves the usual functions of narratives despite its different surface appearance.

Gee's close analysis of this structure and features of the child's speech uncovers an underlying theme: her sense of being "counterpoised between the world of the puppy and the adult world," where "she must deny her own longings and those of the puppy in turn, so he will not disrupt the discipline of that world" (p. 20). Although her story was not "well-received by her teacher" who found it "inconsistent, disconnected, and rambling," Gee refers to it as a "tour de force" (p. 24). In a "quite sophisticated way" she makes sense of her world through narrativization that both states her problem and its resolution: "why she doesn't have her puppy, why he didn't work out, and ultimately why she must belong to the world of home and school" (p. 24).

Gee's elegant analysis is an important contribution to narrative studies. Further, it provides what we need to assess its trustworthiness—the full text is displayed, as are its "re-presentations" in terms of stanzas and narrative functions: the technical devices that make it work are clearly defined and visible; the underlying structure is specified; and his interpretation is tied directly to the data. These are essentially the same grounds I proposed earlier in describing my study of a life-history narrative as strong warrants for the validity claims that may be made in alternative types of narrative study.

Proust's Narrative Strategy

White (1989) explicates the "narrative strategy" used by Marcel Proust in his *Á la recherche du temps perdue*, by a close textual analysis of one paragraph from this multi-volume novel. He "frames" this brief extract by observing that it appears, on first inspection, as a "descriptive pause" or "interlude" in the action (p. 4). The paragraph relates four successive "characterizations" of a fountain by the narrator, Marcel, as he walks towards it in a garden of the Guermantes' palace where he has been attending a soiree. The text is presented in French because, White argues, translations other than his own blur distinctions that are important for his analysis.

A novel differs in many respects from the narrative texts usually studied by social scientists, such as the life history interviews and stories of personal experience in, respectively, my own and Gee's studies. (However, see Bruner's [1986] argument for studying great works of fiction.) Nonetheless, although White's terms may be unfamiliar, his analysis is generally applicable to other types of texts since he follows a sequence of steps that closely parallel those of more typical "empirical" studies: theoretical formulation of interpretative discourse, selection of a sample text, definition and application of coding categories, redescription of the text in terms of the categories, finding a sequential order of categories, analytic restatement of this finding as a structural model of narration, interpretation of the function of the text in the larger narrative, generalization of the interpretation into a theory of narrative strategy.

White begins by distinguishing "interpretive discourse" from both explanation and description. He refers to interpretation as a "preliminary stage" in efforts to understand an object or event when we are uncertain as to how to "properly" describe or explain it. It is an "effort of deciding, not only *how* to describe and explain such an object, but *whether* it can be adequately described or explained at all" (p. 1). This is White's theoretical category in which he locates Marcel's sequence of descriptions—the passage that is the object for his analysis. He then proposes that the characteristic "modality of discursive articulation" in interpretative discourse is "more *tropical* than logical." That is, it is organized in terms of the meanings and functions of the different tropes and their relation to each other rather than by a series of propositions that are logically or causally connected. It departs from literal or technical language and from relations of "strict deducibility," "giving itself over to techniques of figuration" (p. 2). His analysis focuses on Proust's use of four such "techniques"—familiar tropes of literary criticism: metaphor, metonymy, synecdoche, and irony.[15]

The analytic function of these tropes is the same as the "codes" for self-preoccupations, motives, work spheres, and poetic devices found in the studies described earlier. Although they may be unfamiliar to social scientists, they are drawn from a comprehensive category system, refined through a long tradition of literary criticism and textual analysis. As is true of any coding system, an adequate comprehension of what the tropes "mean" requires more than their definition. We must also understand the conceptual framework within which they are located; that is, we must understand them as linguistic practices within a type of discourse. For White, their significance lies in their relationship to each other as they are deployed in an orderly sequence. Thus, he presents a structural model for the analysis of this passage as a narrative, much as Gee and I did in our respective studies.

These tropes are omnipresent in both fictional and nonfictional narrative accounts. Pointing them out, or counting them, would not tell us very much about Proust's "narrative strategy," which is White's primary concern. To this end, he focuses on their specific sequential placement relative to each other and on the overall function of this "tropical" order. (Note the resemblance between this approach and Gee's emphasis on the discourse—rather than the syntactic-level functions of narrative devices.) White summarizes the "model" of narration, displayed in this passage, as a successive movement of the narrator through the four tropes, as alternative descriptions of the fountain: from an initial "metaphoric apprehension" of it, through a "metonymic" characterization as a "dispersion of its attributes," to a "synecdochic comprehension of its possible 'nature'," to, finally, "an ironic distancing of the process of narration itself" (p. 6).

This "passage" through the four tropes parallels the actual movement of the narrator towards the fountain, with each stage marked explicitly in the text. From afar, the narrator's impression of the fountain is captured in a metaphor as a "pale and quivering plume." Closer, the fountain is "revealed to be 'in reality as often interrupted as the scattering of the fall,' " with new jets of water producing the effect of the "single flow," a metonymic description. At the third stage, the "form" and "content" of the spray are " 'grasped together' as a whole indistinguishable from the parts that constitute it," "in the manner of a synecdoche." The last characterization is:

by turns lyrical-elegiac and playful in tone . . . at once ironical in its structure and radically revisionary with respect to all three of the preceding descriptions. . . . It both radically alters the semantic domain from which its figures of speech are drawn and abruptly, almost violently, undercuts the very impulse to metaphorize by its reminder that the fountain is, after all, *only* a fountain. (pp. 7–11)

The passage ends in this ironic mode.

White observes that the fourth description is not the "most precise, correct, comprehensive, or appropriate" one. The other three cannot be "adjudged in some way inferior." Rather, it gives us, as we near the end of the passage, the "crucial bit of information that allows us suddenly to grasp 'the point of it all.' . . . to discern something like the kind of 'plot' that permits a retrospective correlation of the events of this 'story' as a story of a particular kind—a specifically 'ironic' story" (pp. 11–12).

He then proposes that the trope-sequence structure of this passage, "considered as a *narrational unit* . . . is related to the three scenes of interpretation that precede it by the four figurative modes which constitute the substance of its own form," and, further, that "as a *model of interpretation* itself, the fountain scene provides a paradigm for how to read the three more extensive scenes of interpretation that precede it" (p. 20). That is, each of the preceding scenes and the relationship among them and the key paragraph reveals the same structure of successive tropes—metaphor, metonymy, synecdoche, and irony—with the fountain scene functionally related to each of the others through the same forms of figuration.

Finally, bringing his argument back to the distinction between interpretation and either explanation or description, he states that there is no "logical connection" between the scenes. The relation is "only tropical, which is to say that it is unpredictable, unnecessary, undeductible, arbitrary and so on but, at the same time, functionally effective and retrodictable as a narrative unit *once its tropical relationship to what comes before (and what comes after) it is discerned*" (p. 13). This is his answer to the question of how narration and interpretation

can be endowed with a coherence quite other than the kinds of coherence it may possess at the level of the sentence (grammatical coherence) and the level of demonstration or explicit argument (logical coherence). Obviously, my answer to this question is "figurative coherence," the coherence of the activity of (linguistic) figuration itself. (p. 19)

Can we make a reasonable assessment about the trustworthiness of White's analysis? I think we can, and for the same reasons I gave for the preceding two studies, namely, the visibility of his analysis. That is, he presents the full text of the passage, explicitly defines and links the coding categories to specific words and phrases, and shows us the location and sequential ordering of the different tropes, that is, the structure of the paragraph.

One advantage of choosing a relatively unfamiliar "literary" approach as a candidate exemplar for narrative analysis is that it highlights the problematic nature of validation. Although White has shown us what he did, the "rules" that inform his analysis cannot be applied mechanically. We must have some level of specialized knowledge and skills to assess its adequacy and potential range of application. Minimally, of course, it would be useful to have more than high school mastery of French as well as an understanding of tropes. However, that would only scratch the surface of what we have to know to understand White's research practice as a form of life and, from that understanding, be able to decide whether it would be a productive direction to pursue in our own work. The same requirement applies, of course, to our efforts to assess the validity claims of any study. Since White displays the evidence for his claims, this problem is not his but ours.

I have focused only on the first level of White's analysis—his description of the structure of the paragraph as a sequence of tropes and his interpretation of this structure as a narrative strategy. He expands his interpretation to the larger narrative context of the core paragraph, the three preceding scenes in this chapter, and then to the novel as a whole. How far we would wish to pursue our assessment of his work depends on the aims and scope of our own studies. Different criteria might come into play, depending on our theoretical interests and the range of inferences that we intend. We would, however, have a place to begin these extended explorations.

Conclusion

In this article, I have proposed an approach to the critical assessment of inquiry-guided research that is more appropriate to the features of such studies—ethnographies, case studies, textual analyses—than the standard experiment-based model. These studies, comprising a significant sector of the theoretical and empirical enterprise in psychology and the social sciences, are not designed as experiments, and do not "test" hypotheses, "measure" variation on quantitative dimensions, or "test" the significance of findings with statistical procedures. Criteria and procedures based on the dominant experimental/ quantitative prototype are irrelevant to these studies in the literal sense that there is nothing to which to apply them.[16] When the standard model is misapplied, as it often is, inquiry-guided studies fail the test and are denied scientific legitimacy.

Recognizing this problem, other investigators engaged in these studies have proposed alternative validity criteria and procedures that parallel the standard ones, but take into account the special features of inquiry-guided research. Although these efforts have been useful, particularly in their critique of the standard model, I believe that they do not go far enough. By retaining the dominant model as the implicit ground against which alternative approaches are evaluated, the latter continue to be viewed as inadequate, temporary expedients—useful, perhaps, but only until the time that "real" scientific methods are found.

My proposal moves in a different direction. As a point of departure, I argued that the dominant research model is an abstract idealization that does not correspond to how the work of science gets done. I suggested replacing the "storybook image of science" with an empirically based description of scientific practices, of the ways that working scientists produce, test, and validate their findings. When closely observed, as in studies by historians and sociologists of science, research scientists turn out to resemble craftspersons more than logicians. Competence depends on apprenticeship training, continued practice, and experience-based, contextual knowledge of the specific methods applicable to a phenomenon of interest rather than on an abstract "logic of discovery" and application of formal "rules."

Further, the knowledge base for scientific research is largely tacit and unexplicated, learned through a process of socialization into a particular "form of life." The discovery, testing, and validation of findings is embedded in cultural and linguistic practices. Transmission of the necessary knowledge for replicating other work is an uncertain process, depending primarily on personal contact with researchers and observation of their practices. Even this does not guarantee comparability, as one of Collin's (1985) respondents indicates:

> It's very difficult to make a carbon copy. . . . But if it turns out that what's critical is the way he glued his transducers, and he forgets to tell you that the technician always puts a copy of the *Physical Review* on top of them for weight, well, it would make all the difference. (p. 86)

Within this perspective on science as practice, I proposed a reformulation of validation as the social construction of scientific knowledge. It is evident that the model to which inquiry-guided researchers have been held accountable has little if any reality. Experimental scientists proceed in pragmatic ways, learning from their errors and failures, adapting procedures to their local contexts, making decisions on the basis of their accumulated experiences.

This resemblance between experimental and inquiry-guided studies becomes clear when we shift our attention from single studies to research programs. The typical way of doing experimental work is to conduct a series of successive studies, each building on preceding ones, and this progression is clearly inquiry-guided. The analogue in complex nonexperimental studies is the sequence of different stages—from initial observations, through preliminary coding, through further observations, revisions of coding, and so on—which may viewed as sub-studies building progressively on each other. (This is, of course, an insight we owe to "grounded theory"; see Glaser & Strauss, 1967; Strauss, 1987.)

This discovery—of the contextually grounded, experience-based, socially constructed nature of scientific knowledge—should be cause for celebration rather than despair. It does not dispense with methods for systematic study but locates them in the world of practice rather than in the abstract spaces of Venn diagrams or Latin Squares. Assessments of the validity of any single study are provisional. Following *the* rules of experimental design, quantification and statistical analysis are not truth tests but methodic accounting procedures, and a researcher's documentation of their use is part of the rhetoric of a particular form of scientific life. This perspective does not lead to an empty relativism or to Feyerabend's (1978) anarchic program of an "anything goes" science. Methods are still assessed for their consistency and utility in producing trustworthy findings, and trustworthiness is tested repeatedly and gains in strength through our reliance on these findings as the basis for further work.

The recent convergence among some prominent validity theorists on the primacy of construct validity adds support to the argument I advanced based on studies of scientific practice. Their emphasis on the fundamental importance of theory and interpretation in validation puts the problem beyond the reach of "technical" solutions. Again, this shift away from formal rules and procedures does not mean a retreat from systematic and methodic ways of inquiry. But it does mean that more is involved in these ways (that is, these practices) than was captured by explicit and elaborate lists of types of and threats to validity.

If standard rules will not serve for experiments, neither will they serve for inquiry-guided studies. As an alternative approach, I adopted Kuhn's (1962/1970) concept of exemplars, the "concrete problem-solutions" that show researchers "by example how their job is to be done" (p. 187). In experimental sciences, laboratory exercises do this job. Learning from them depends on more than following a series of outlined steps: heat "*x*" to 80°C and add "*y*." Ravetz (1971) remarks that "one of the things that every schoolboy knows about science is a general property of scientific equipment, which has been given the name of the 'fourth law of thermodynamics': no experiment goes properly the first time" (p. 76). Making an experiment work requires attention to various idiosyncratic features of the laboratory, of instrument errors and artifacts, of the ambient temperature and humidity, and many other factors too numerous and cumbersome to list but easily recognized in practice. Thus, learning from examplars is a process of contextually grounded practice, which brings us full circle to what we have come to understand as scientific research.

An important task for the less well established areas of scientific inquiry is to develop a collection of relevant exemplars.[17] I proposed three studies as candidate exemplars for narrative research, recognizing that they are only a few of the many potential ones. They vary in types of texts, concepts, aims, and methods and were chosen to suggest a range of alternative approaches. However, they are similar in several important respects that I believe make them strong candidates, and, at the same time, differ from the standard model in ways that make them more appropriate for studies of narratives. These are: the display of the primary texts; the specification of analytic categories and the distinctions in terms of discernable features of the texts; and, theoretical interpretations focused on structures, that is, on relations among different categories, rather than on variables.

In each study, the text is available so that other researchers can inspect it and assess the adequacy with which the methods and interpretations represent the data. Further, the availability of the primary data allows for a reasonable judgment, albeit a preliminary one, of whether and how representative it might be of other texts. That is, the question may be addressed, in an empirically grounded way, of the possible generalizability of findings and interpretations, of the "projectibility" (Goodman, 1979/1983) of inferences based on the analyses. Our assessments of trustworthiness are as firmly grounded as those we might make of studies relying on the standard research model.

The central theoretical aim in each of the selected studies is to describe, analyze, and interpret a pattern of relationships within a set of conceptually specified analytic categories. I refer to these patterns as structures, and the studies are instances of different types of structural analysis. These structures represent a significant characteristic of the texts at a more abstract level. Their general theoretical significance depends upon whether or not the particular texts are representative samples of a general class of texts. For example, in my study of an artist-craftsman's narrative, the double structure of hierarchically ordered possible choices among types of work and the temporal ordering of actual choices is viewed as a model for analyses of the work histories of other craftspersons. Gee relates the stanza structure of a child's story, and her use of technical poetic strategies to achieve meaning and coherence, to the typical form of narratives in oral cultures. And White's discovery of the sequential structure of tropes in one paragraph of Proust's novel—from metaphor, to metonymy, to synecdoche, to irony—is interpreted by him as an instance of a general narrative strategy.

In these studies, theory and analysis are in a continuing dialectic with each other and with the data, and the process is open to us. This does not mean that we would necessarily be compelled or persuaded by the findings of any particular study, or agree with a proposed interpretation. But, as I have repeatedly stressed, we are given sufficient information to make a judgment of their trustworthiness and can then decide whether or not to depend on them for further work.

This paper was written for, and from the perspective of, researchers engaged in inquiry-guided and interpretive studies. As a member of that new but growing research community, I have tried to show that we can make a strong claim for the scientific legitimacy of our work. Our collective task, to which I hope this paper has contributed, is to engage each other in vigorous debate about issues of validation as we move towards an alternative form of scientific life.

Notes

1. I use the term "inquiry-guided" research for a family of approaches that explicitly acknowledge and rely on the dialectic interplay of theory, methods, and findings over the course of a study. This includes many variants of "qualitative" and interpretive research—ethnographies, case studies, ethno-methodological and grounded-theory inquiries, and analyses of texts and discourses—that share an emphasis on the continuous process through which observations and interpretations shape and reshape each other. This feature marks their departure from the dominant model of hypothesis-testing experimentation.

2. Frustrated by the misunderstanding and devaluation of their work associated with the standard approach, many nonexperimental researchers either dismiss or ignore issues of validation. Kvale (1989b), for example, notes that discussion of the validity of results in qualitative research is "an exception rather than the rule" (p. 73). Nonetheless, my attempt to deal with the special features of such studies is only one of a number of such efforts, which include Cherryholmes, 1988; Katz, 1983; Kvale, 1989a; Lather, 1986; Lincoln & Guba, 1985; Reason & Rowan, 1981. There are parallels among our approaches, particularly in our respective critiques of the experiment-based model of validation, as well as differences in our proposals. Detailed comparisons of the epistemological and ontological assumptions of the positivist tradition underlying experimental models and alternative "post-positivist" perspectives are provided by several of these authors (see also Carini, 1975; Mishler, 1979; Polkinghorne, 1988) and will not be repeated here.

3. Among the instructive studies and analyses of scientific practice that bear on issues of validation are: Collins, 1985; Gilbert & Mulkay, 1981, 1984; Goodman, 1978, 1979/1983; Kuhn, 1962/1970, 1970/1974a,b; Latour, 1988, 1990; Latour & Woolgar, 1979; Lynch, 1985; Mitroff, 1974a,b; Ravetz, 1971. Useful collections of sociological studies of science are: Barnes & Edge, 1982; Barnes & Shapin, 1979; Knorr, Krohn, & Whitley, 1981; and Simons, 1989.

4. Both "predictive" and "concurrent" validities are "criterion-oriented": the first refers to the relation between a test score and a criterion measure obtained "some time after the test is given," the second to a criterion measure "determined at essentially the same time" (Cronbach & Meehl, 1955, pp. 281–282). Content validity, "ordinarily to be established deductively," involves a systematic sampling of test items from a universal of interest (p. 282): "Construct validation is involved whenever a test is to be interpreted as a measure of some attribute or quality which is not 'operationally defined.' . . . Construct validity is not to be identified solely by particular investigative procedures, but by the orientation of the investigator" (p. 282).

5. Among these revisions are: Campbell and Stanley's (1963) external–internal contrast pair, updated by Cook and Campbell (1979) to statistical conclusion, internal, construct, and external; Katz's (1983) reliability, representativeness, reactivity, and replicability; Lather's (1986) triangulation, face, construct, and catalytic; Levy's (1981) communicability, plausibility, generalizability, and interpretability; Lincoln and Guba's (1985) credibility, transferability, dependability, and confirmability. Rather than partitioning validity, some investigators parse the research process into different steps, each requiring its own validity assessment; for example, Brinberg and McGrath's (1982, 1985) "network of validity concepts," Huberman and Miles's (1983) rules for data display and reduction, Lincoln and Guba's (1985) "audit," and Tagg's (1985) "facet" analysis.

6. This view had early proponents. For example, Cronbach and Meehl (1955) viewed construct validity as the fundamental issue, and Loevinger (1957) asserted that "since predictive, concurrent, and content validities are all ad hoc, construct validity is the whole of validity from a scientific point of view" (p. 636). However, as Angoff (1988) points out, this view did not become generally accepted until the late 1970s. Consensus on this position is, nonetheless, hardly universal. For example, Messick's (1989) proposal of construct validation as a "unifying theme" is harshly criticized by another prominent methodologist who finds his approach "questionable" and his solution unsuccessful since "there is no agreed upon method for determining construct validity" (Green, 1990, p. 850).

7. Cherryholmes (1988), in a parallel expansion, locates validation within larger systems of socio-political discourse: "Construct validation is a pragmatic and socially critical activity because clear-cut distinctions among social research, social theory, and social practice cannot be sustained" (p. 421); "Decisions about construct validity cannot be disentangled from ethico-political decisions" (p. 440).

8. Trustworthiness is the key term in Lincoln and Guba's (1985) analysis of validation in "naturalistic inquiries." They pose the basic issue as: "How can an inquirer persuade his or her audiences (including self) that the findings

of an inquiry are worth paying attention to, worth taking account of?" (p. 290). We share that view of the researcher's task, but I place more emphasis on other researchers' willingness to act on the basis of, as well as pay attention to, a study, and on the continuing social process through which claims are contested, assessed, and warranted.

9. This gives primacy to the "pragmatic" conception of truth in contrast to "correspondence" or "coherence" conceptions, although the latter also enter into our assessments (Enerstvedt, 1989).

10. Only a strong faith in experiments could account for their compellingness, since they are so difficult and time-consuming, and so often fail. Collins (1985) points out that, "Experiments hardly ever work the first time; indeed, they hardly ever work at all" (p. 41). Even the apparently rapid spread of a new experimental procedure or piece of equipment requires trial-and-error and modification to meet local conditions and problems. For example, examination of widespread "replications" of studies of vacuums after Boyle's invention of the air pump shows "that no two pumps are the same and that each transportation through Europe means a *transformation* of the pump" (Latour, 1990, p. 154; see Shapin & Schaffer, 1985). See also Ravetz (1971) on the many "pitfalls" involved in any experiment.

11. Other critics of the standard model are more sanguine about the value of substitute rules tailored to the specific features of inquiry-guided research. For example, Huberman and Miles (1983) provide detailed procedures for data reduction and display, and Lincoln and Guba (1985) offer an elaborate set of axioms, characteristics, and guidelines for "naturalistic inquiries," parallel to those used in experimental studies. Salner (1989) avoids rules but lists nine "qualities and abilities [that] the human researcher needs" (pp. 65–68).

12. The value of exemplars for clarifying and comparing alternative research models has been recognized by, among others, Bredo and Feinberg (1982) for educational research; Dervin, Grossberg, O'Keefe, and Wartella (1989) for communication studies; and Morgan (1983) for organizational research.

13. The social production of knowledge is more visible in the histories of initially marginal lines of inquiry that managed, though their methods deviated from established tenets and prescriptions, to carve out niches in the ecological space of science. Prime examples are psychoanalysis, cognitive stage theory, experimental behaviorism, and ethnomethodology—associated respectively with the names of their originators: Freud, Piaget, Skinner, and Garfinkel. Each made problematic a previously taken-for-granted or ignored phenomenon, respectively, dreams and slips of the tongue, the orderly development of cognitive structures, the dependence of stable behavior on the frequency and timing of contingent reinforcements, and the relationship between social norms and actions as practical accomplishments of actors' routine practices. Further each provided an alternative methodology for its study: free association, process observation and interview, schedules of reinforcement and baselines, norm-violation procedures and conversation analysis.

    Experimental designs, quantitative scales, and tests of significance are notably absent. Learning these new approaches required apprenticeship through, for example, psychoanalytic training, or at the Geneva Institute, in the Pigeon Lab, or in intensive workshops and seminars. With their paths blocked to establishment journals, proponents of these schools of thought founded their own or circulated unpublished documents through their networks, as was the case, for example, with Harvey Sacks's lecture notes on conversation analysis, many of which were published posthumously (Jefferson, 1989). Facing resistance and rejection in their home disciplines, they found allies in others: in literature and history, among teachers and educators, and in the ranks of anthropologists and linguists.

14. The study of narratives has emerged in recent years as a large and diverse area of inquiry. The three models suggested here as candidate exemplars do not and are not intended to represent the variety of approaches. There are many others that might serve as well and that merit attention. For an appreciation of the range of work, see Bruner, 1986, 1990; Labov, 1972; Labov & Waletzky, 1967; Langellier, 1989; McAdams & Ochberg, 1988; Mishler, 1986a, b, in press; Paget, 1983; Polanyi, 1985; Polkinghorne, 1988; Riessman, 1990; Rosenwald & Ochberg, in press; Sarbin, 1986a, b; White, 1987; Young, 1984, 1987; and two issues of *Critical Inquiry*: Vol. 7, 1980, and Vol. 7, 1981.

15. These tropes are "fuzzy categories." Burke (1945) refers to them as the "master tropes," and observes that they "shade into one another. Give a man but one of them, tell him to exploit its possibilities, and if he is thorough in doing so, he will come upon the other three" (p. 503). Briefly, a metaphor involves describing or characterizing something in terms of something else, a metonymy describes a whole by one of its parts or aspects, a synecdoche represents the relationship between the parts and the whole, and irony brings together all the terms or "sub-perspectives" so that they interact with and influence one another in a "total form" (Burke, p. 512).

16. My conjoint term "experimental/quantitative prototype" reflects the prevailing view of an intimate and inherent linkage between statistics and experimentation, a position I have not challenged in this paper. However, the relationship is problematic, and it is worth noting that there is a viable, critical perspective that sees these two "methods" as antithetical to each other. It is expressed forcefully by Lewin and Skinner, who are poles apart on most other issues, but share a negative view of the assumed equivalence between experimental and statistical "controls." Thus, Lewin (1931/1935), observing the "commanding significance of statistics in contemporary psychology," argues that reliance on frequencies of occurrences cannot lead to theoretical "laws," which depend instead on the study of the individual case in all its "concreteness." And Skinner (1961), commenting on "The Flight from the Laboratory," attributes it to a deficiency in graduate school training: "They have taught statistics in lieu of scientific

method. Unfortunately, the statistical pattern is incompatible with some major features of laboratory research" (p. 247). He goes on to point out various "destructive" effects of the emphasis on statistics, such as their leaving the psychologist with "at best an indirect acquaintance with the 'facts' he discovers" and the "inimical" effect on laboratory practice of statisticians' recommendations. A recent, related critique of the tendency in sociological research to assume that statistical controls can be substituted for experimental controls in causal analyses may be found in Lieberson (1985).

17. Many inquiry-guided studies differ not only from the experimental prototype, but from the structural analysis of narrative texts that I have examined. The specific features of, for example, ethnographies or studies of social institutions require different criteria and procedures for assessing their trustworthiness. I hope that other researchers will undertake the task of explicating their methods so that we can build a corpus of exemplars for various types of research.

References

American Psychological Association. (1954). Technical recommendations for psychological tests and diagnostic techniques (Part 2). *Psychological Bulletin, 51*(2).

Angoff, W. H. (1988). Validity: An evolving concept. In H. Wainer & H. I. Braun (Eds.), *Test validity*. Hillsdale, NJ: Erlbaum.

Barnes, B., & Edge, D. (Eds.). (1982). *Science in context: Readings in the sociology of science*. Cambridge: MIT Press.

Barnes, B., & Shapin, S. (Eds.). (1979). *Natural order: Historical studies of scientific culture*. Beverly Hills: Sage.

Bazerman, C. (1989). [Review of *Changing order: Replication and induction in scientific practice* by H. M. Collins (1985)]. *Philosophy of the Social Sciences, 19,* 115–118.

Bredo, E., & Feinberg, W. (Eds.). (1982). *Knowledge and values in social and educational research*. Philadelphia: Temple University Press.

Brenner, M. (1981). *Social method and social life*. New York: Academic Press.

Brinberg, D., & McGrath, J. E. (1982). A network of validity concepts within the research process. In D. Brinberg & L. H. Kidder (Eds.), *Forms of validity in research*. San Francisco: Jossey-Bass.

Brinberg, D., & McGrath, J. E. (1985). *Validity and the research process*. Beverly Hills: Sage.

Bruner, J. (1986). *Actual minds, possible worlds*. Cambridge: Harvard University Press.

Bruner, J. (1990). *Acts of meaning*. Cambridge: Harvard University Press.

Burke, K. (1945). *A grammar of motives*. New York: Prentice-Hall.

Campbell, D. T. (1979). A tribal model of the social system vehicle carrying scientific knowledge. *Knowledge: Creation, Diffusion, Utilization, 1*(2), 181–201.

Campbell, D. T., & Stanley, J. T. (1963). Experimental and quasi-experimental designs for research. In N. L. Gage (Ed.), *Handbook of research on teaching*. New York: Rand McNally.

Carini, P. F. (1975). *Observation and description: An alternative methodology for the investigation of human phenomena* (North Dakota Study Group on Evaluation Monograph). Grand Forks, ND: University of North Dakota Press.

Cherryholmes, C. H. (1988). Construct validity and the discourses of research. *American Journal of Education, 96,* 421–457.

Cohler, B. J. (1982). Personal narrative and life course. In P. B. Baltes & O. G. Brim, Jr. (Eds.), *Life-span development and behavior*. New York: Academic Press.

Collins, H. M. (1985). *Changing order: Replication and induction in scientific practice*. Beverly Hills: Sage.

Cook, T. D., & Campbell, D. T. (1979). *Quasi-experimentation: Design and analysis issues for field settings*. Chicago: Rand McNally.

Critical Inquiry. (1980). On narrative. Vol. 7, pp. 1–236.

Critical Inquiry. (1981). Critical response. Vol. 7, pp. 777–809.

Cronbach, L. J. (1984). *Essentials of psychological testing* (4th ed.). New York: Harper & Row.

Cronbach, L. J. (1988). Five perspectives on validity argument. In H. Wainer & H. I. Braun (Eds.), *Test validity*. Hillsdale, NJ: Erlbaum.

Cronbach, L. J., & Meehl, P. E. (1955). Construct validity in psychological tests. *Psychological Bulletin, 52,* 281–302.

Dervin, B., Grossberg, L., O'Keefe, B. J., & Wartella, E. (Eds.). (1989). *Rethinking communication: Vol. 2. Paradigm exemplars*. Newbury Park, CA: Sage.

Educational Testing Service. (1980). *Test use and validity*. Princeton: Author.

Enerstvedt, R. T. (1989). The problem of validity in social science. In S. Kvale (Ed.), *Issues of validity in qualitative research*. Lund, Sweden: Studentlitteratur.

Erikson, E. H. (1950). *Childhood and society*. New York: Norton.

Erikson, E. H. (1959). Identity and the life cycle [Monograph No. 1]. *Psychological Issues, 1*(1). New York: International Universities Press.

Feyerabend, P. (1978). *Against method.* London: Verso.

Garfinkel, H. (1967). *Studies in ethnomethodology.* Englewood Cliffs, NJ: Prentice-Hall.

Gee, J. P. (1985). The narrativization of experience in the oral style. *Boston University Journal of Education, 167,* 9–35.

Gee, J. P. (1986). Units in the production of narrative discourse. *Discourse Processes, 9,* 391–422.

Gieryn, T. F. (1983). Boundary-work and the demarcation of science from non-science: Strains and interests in the professional ideologies of scientists. *American Sociological Review, 48,* 781–795.

Gilbert, G. N., & Mulkay, M. (1981). Contexts of scientific discourse: Social accounting in experimental papers. In K. D. Knorr, R. Krohn, & R. Whitley (Eds.), *The social process of scientific investigation.* Boston: Reidel.

Gilbert, G. N., & Mulkay, M. (1984). *Opening pandora's box: A sociological analysis of scientists' discourse.* Cambridge: Cambridge University Press.

Glaser, B. G., & Strauss, A. (1967). *The discovery of grounded theory.* Chicago: Aldine.

Goodman, N. (1978). *Ways of worldmaking.* Indianapolis: Hackett.

Goodman, N. (1979/1983). *Fact, fiction, and forecast* (4th ed.). Cambridge: Harvard University Press.

Green, B. F. (1990). [Review of *Educational measurement,* edited by R. L. Linn (1989; 3rd ed.)]. *Contemporary Psychology, 35,* 850–851.

Harper, D. (1987). *Working knowledge: Skill and community in a small shop.* Chicago: University of Chicago Press.

Heath, S. B. (1982). What no bedtime story means: Narrative skills at home and school. *Language in Society, 11,* 49–76.

Heath, S. B. (1983). *Ways with words: Language, life, and work in communities and classrooms.* Cambridge: Cambridge University Press.

Huberman, A. M., & Miles, M. B. (1983). Drawing valid meaning from qualitative data: Some techniques of data reduction and display. *Quality and Quantity, 17,* 281–339.

Jefferson, G. (Ed.). (1989). Harvey Sacks: Lectures 1964–65 [Special issue]. *Human Studies, 12*(3–4).

Katz, J. (1983). A theory of qualitative methodology: The social system of analytic fieldwork. In R. M. Emerson (Ed.), *Contemporary field research.* Boston: Little, Brown.

Knorr, K. D., Krohn, R., & Whitley, R. (Eds.). (1981). *The social process of scientific investigation.* Boston: Reidel.

Koch, S. (1976). Language communities, search cells, and the psychological studies. In W. J. Arnold (Ed.), *Nebraska symposium on motivation, 1975.* Lincoln: University of Nebraska Press.

Kuhn, T. S. (1962/1970). *The structure of scientific revolutions* (2nd ed., enlarged). Chicago: University of Chicago Press.

Kuhn, T. S. (1970/1974a). Logic of discovery or psychology of research? In I. Lakatos & A. Musgrave (Eds.), *Criticism and the growth of knowledge* (3rd impression). Cambridge: Cambridge University Press.

Kuhn, T. S. (1970/1974b). Reflections on my critics. In I. Lakatos & A. Musgrave (Eds.), *Criticism and the growth of knowledge* (3rd impression). Cambridge: Cambridge University Press.

Kvale, S. (Ed.). (1989a). *Issues of valdity in qualitative research.* Lund, Sweden: Studentlit-teratur.

Kvale, S. (1989b). To validate is to question. In S. Kvale (Ed.), *Issues of validity in qualitative research.* Lund, Sweden: Studentlitteratur.

Labov, W. (1972). The transformation of experience in narrative syntax. In W. Labov, *Language in the inner city: Studies in the Black English vernacular.* Philadelphia: University of Pennsylvania Press.

Labov, W., & Waletzky, J. (1967). Narrative analysis: Oral versions of personal experience. In J. Helms (Ed.), *Essays on the verbal and visual arts.* Seattle: University of Washington Press.

Langellier, K. M. (1989). Personal narratives: Perspectives on theory and research. *Text and Performance Quarterly, 9,* 243–276.

Lather, P. (1986). Issues of validity in openly ideological research: Between a rock and a soft place. *Interchange, 17*(4), 63–84.

Latour, B. (1988). *The pasteurization of France.* Cambridge: Harvard University Press.

Latour, B. (1990). Postmodern? No, simply Amodern! Steps towards an anthropology of science. *Studies in the History and Philosophy of Science, 21*(1), 145–171.

Latour, B., & Woolgar, S. (1979). *Laboratory life: The social construction of scientific facts.* Beverly Hills: Sage.

Levy, P. (1981). On the relation between method and substance in psychology. *Bulletin, British Psychological Society, 34,* 265–270.

Lewin, K. (1931/1935). The conflict between Aristotelian and Galilean modes of thought in contemporary psychology. In K. Lewin, *A dynamic theory of personality: Selected papers.* New York: McGraw-Hill.

Lieberson, S. (1985). *Making it count: The improvement of social research and theory.* Berkeley: University of California Press.

Lincoln, Y. S., & Guba, E. G. (1985). *Naturalistic inquiry.* Beverly Hills: Sage.

Loevinger, J. (1957). Objective tests as instruments of psychological theory [Monograph Supplement No. 9]. *Psychological Reports, 3,* 635–694.

Lynch, M. (1985). *Art and artifact in laboratory science: A study of shop work and shop talk in a research laboratory.* Boston: Routledge & Kegan Paul.

McAdams, D. P. (1985). *Power, intimacy, and the life story: Personological inquiries and identity*. Homewood, IL: Dorsey.

McAdams, D. P., & Ochberg, R. L. (Eds.). (1988). Psychobiography and life narratives [Special issue]. *Journal of Personality, 56*(1).

McClelland, D. C. (1984). *Human motivation*. Glenview, IL: Scott, Foresman.

Mervis, C. B., & Rosch, E. (1981). Categorization of natural objects. *Annual Review of Psychology, 32*, 89–115.

Messick, S. (1989). Validity. In R. L. Linn (Ed.), *Educational measurement* (3rd ed.). New York: Macmillan.

Michaels, S. (1981). Sharing time: Children's narrative styles and differential access to literacy. *Language in Society, 10*, 423–442.

Mishler, E. G. (1979). Meaning in context: Is there any other kind? *Harvard Educational Review, 49*, 1–19.

Mishler, E. G. (1984). *The discourse of medicine: Dialectics of medical interviews*. Norwood, NJ: Ablex.

Mishler, E. G. (1986a). *Research interviewing: Context and narrative*. Cambridge: Harvard University Press.

Mishler, E. G. (1986b). The analysis of interview narratives. In T. R. Sarbin (Ed.), *Narrative psychology: The storied nature of human conduct*. New York: Praeger.

Mishler, E. G. (1989). [Review of *Working knowledge: Skill and community in a small shop* by D. Harper (1987)]. *American Craft, 49*(2), p. 22.

Mishler, E. G. (In press). Work, identity, and narrative: An artist-craftsman's story. In G. Rosenwald & R. Ochberg (Eds.), *Storied lives*. New Haven: Yale University Press.

Mitroff, I. (1974a). Norms and counter-norms in a select group of the Apollo moon scientists: A case study of the ambivalence of scientists. *American Sociological Review, 39*, 579–595.

Mitroff, I. (1974b). *The subjective side of science: A philosophical inquiry into the psychology of the Apollo moon scientists*. Amsterdam: Elsevier.

Morgan, G. (Ed.). (1983). *Beyond method: Strategies for social research*. Beverly Hills: Sage.

Morris, W. (1883/1966). Art under plutocracy. In M. Morris (Ed.), *The collected works of William Morris: Vol. XXIII. Signs of change: Lectures on socialism*. New York: Russell and Russell.

Paget, M. A. (1983). Experience and knowledge. *Human Studies, 6*, 67–90.

Polanyi, L. (1985). Conversational storytelling. In T. A. van Dijk (Ed.), *Handbook of discourse analysis* (Vol. 3). London: Academic Press.

Polanyi, M. (1966). *The tacit dimension*. New York: Doubleday.

Polkinghorne, D. E. (1988). *Narrative knowing and the human sciences*. Albany: State University of New York Press.

Prelli, L. J. (1989). The rhetorical construction of scientific ethos. In H. W. Simons (Ed.), *Rhetoric in the human sciences*. Newbury Park, CA: Sage.

Ravetz, J. R. (1971). *Scientific knowledge and its social problems*. New York: Oxford University Press.

Reason, P., & Rowan, R. (Eds.). (1981). *Human inquiry: A sourcebook of new paradigm research*. New York: Wiley.

Richards, J. L. (1979). The reception of a mathematical theory: Non-Euclidean geometry in England, 1868–1883. In B. Barnes & S. Shapin (Eds.), *Natural order: Historical studies of scientific culture*. Beverly Hills: Sage.

Ricoeur, P. (1981). *Hermeneutics and the human sciences: Essays on language, action, and interpretation*. New York: Cambridge University Press.

Riessman, C. K. (1987). When gender is not enough. *Gender and Society, 1*, 172–207.

Riessman, C. K. (1990). *Divorce talk: Women and men make sense of personal relationships*. New Brunswick, NJ: Rutgers University Press.

Rosch, E. (1973). On the internal structure of perceptual and semantic categories. In T. E. Moore (Ed.), *Cognitive development and the acquisition of language*. New York: Academic Press.

Rosch, E. (1978). Principles of categorization. In E. Rosch & B. B. Lloyd (Eds.), *Cognition and categorization*. Hillsdale, NJ: Erlbaum.

Rosch, E., & Mervis, C. B. (1975). Family resemblances: Studies in the internal structure of categories. *Cognitive Psychology, 7*, 573–605.

Rosenwald, G., & Ochberg, R. (Eds.). (In press). *Storied Lives*. New Haven: Yale University Press.

Salner, M. (1989). Validity in human science research. In S. Kvale (Ed.), *Issues of validity in qualitative research*. Lund, Sweden: Studentlitteratur.

Sarbin, T. R. (1986a). *Narrative psychology: The storied nature of human conduct*. New York: Praeger.

Sarbin, T. R. (1986b). The narrative as a root metaphor for psychology. In T. R. Sarbin, *Narrative psychology: The storied nature of human conduct*. New York: Praeger.

Shapin, S., & Schaffer, S. (1985). *Leviathan and the air pump: Hobbes, Boyle, and the experimental life*. Princeton: Princeton University Press.

Sidman, M. (1960). *Tactics of scientific research: Evaluating experimental data in psychology*. New York: Basic Books.

Simons, H. W. (Ed.). (1989). *Rhetoric in the human sciences*. Newbury Park, CA: Sage.

Skinner, B. F. (1961). *Cumulative record*. New York: Appleton-Century-Crofts.

Stewart, A. J., Franz, C., & Layton, L. (1988). The changing self: Using personal documents to study lives. *Journal of Personality, 56*(1), 41–74.

Strauss, A. L. (1987). *Qualitative analysis for social scientists*. New York: Cambridge University Press.

Tagg, S. K. (1985). Life story interviews and their interpretation. In M. Brenner, J. Brown, & D. Canter (Eds.), *The research interview: Uses and approaches.* London: Academic Press.

White, H. (1987). *The content of the form: Narrative discourse and historical representation.* Baltimore: Johns Hopkins University Press.

White, H. (1989). The rhetoric of interpretation. In P. Hernadi (Ed.), *The rhetoric of interpretation and the interpretation of rhetoric.* Durham, NC: Duke University Press.

Wittgenstein, L. (1953). *Philosophical investigations* (3rd ed.). Oxford: Blackwell.

Young, K. (1984). Ontological puzzles about narratives. *Poetics, 13,* 239–259.

Young, K. G. (1987). *Taleworlds and storyrealms.* Boston: Martinus Nijhoff.

This paper reflects an extended dialogue over the past few years with members of my research seminar about problems of validation in inquiry-guided and interpretive research. They responded seriously and constructively to earlier efforts in what may have appeared to them as a quixotic activity. For their fine blend of support and criticism, I wish to thank: Jane Attanucci, Darlene Douglas-Steele, Rosanna Hertz, Roque Mendez, Catherine Riessman, and Stephen Soldz; and Vicky Steinitz for her patient, skeptical, and close readings of various drafts. Although I could not always follow their recommendations, I would like to acknowledge the detailed comments of: Phil Brown, Stuart Hauser, Dorothy Hollingsworth, Robert McCarley, Mike Miller, and the editors of the *Harvard Educational Review.*

19

Poor Mothers and Habits of Hiding
Participatory Methods in Poverty Research

Lisa Dodson and Leah Schmalzbauer

Poor mothers have long-standing habits of hiding their lives in response to punitive authorities and stigma. We identify practices of hiding daily life, and we describe participatory research approaches for and ethical concerns in learning more about poor women's critical insights and survival strategies.

Poor families have long been studied in the United States and even more so recently during the era of welfare reform. Yet, gaining accurate representations of life and learning from people's knowledge in poor or marginalized communities can be challenging because low-income and otherwise vulnerable people hesitate to share their worlds. Experiences with stigmatization (Goffman, 1963), concerns about regulatory scrutiny and abuse (Dodson, 1998; Soss, Schram, Vartanian, & O'Brien, 2001), and experience with punitive authorities (Scott, 1990) all contribute to habits of hiding daily life.

In this article, we frame a theoretical discussion about poor women and habits of hiding that examines how *othered* people exercise caution in speaking about their lives. We identify the context in which poor mothers withhold information that may affect reliability in social research and even preserve distorted images of low-income people, in particular, people of color. We use brief excerpts from our studies to identify particular habits of hiding that we have come to see as endemic in low-income communities. Using scholarship on participative research, we detail our methods in three stages of the inquiry process that include the development of the research design, conducting field research, and interpreting data toward gaining a deeper understanding of family life in contemporary low-income America. We conclude with a discussion about ethical considerations and the difficulties and importance of these research methods.

Background

Poor women have long been called upon to provide detailed information about their families and themselves as they seek income support, access to health care, subsidized food, housing, jobs, and child care (Abromovitz, 1996; Dodson, 2005; Edin & Lein, 1996). Immigrant and undocumented women are often called upon to prove their citizenship status as they seek jobs, education for their children, health care, and income supports to manage their families' daily needs (Chavez, 1998; Coutin, 2000; Schmalzbauer, in press). Beyond interviews with officials in public welfare institutions and employers, mothers, who generally oversee children's everyday needs, are largely responsible for communicating with teachers and school personnel, health care providers, social workers, and others whose focus is the status of children (Arendell, 2000).

For poor people, these public accountings of family matters are never neutral. Low-income mothers, who are disproportionately women of color and immigrant women, enter public interactions haunted by "controlling images" and accusations of childbearing for welfare (Chang, 2000; Collins, 1998). They carry with them histories molded by being known as suspect people, unworthy of public aid, and undeserving of opportunities reserved for true legal or social citizens (Neubeck & Cazenave, 2001; Soss et al., 2001). Still, these treks into suspicious, sometimes hostile, terrain cannot be avoided. Encounters with public assistance officials, immigration authorities, social workers, school administrators, and potential employers are mandatory and may well determine whether poor families will remain intact and be able to manage daily life. Forced to interact with biased authorities to survive, poor women have developed complex and protective strategies. Some scholarship suggests that poor women are "shut up and shut out" (Reid, 1993) or are socialized not to voice their insights and troubles. Yet, withholding information may be a conscious act of self-protection.

Bourdieu (1990) described common strategy to manage everyday life as adaptation to the particular game of the moment that may or may not mean adherence to the rules. "The good player does at every moment what the game requires" presupposing a permanent capacity for "invention" and for a "double game" playing in apparent conformity with the rule yet disobeying (p. 63). Goffman (1963) described "othered" people's efforts to manage stigmatization. He suggested that those who are stigmatized may feel unsure of how the "normals" will identify and receive them (p. 13) and may have to be "self-conscious and calculating about the impressions" that they make (p. 14). Scott (1990) argued that marginalized people learn to code, camouflage, and submerge opinions; a voice lost in the crowd is far safer than a lone speaker (Scott). The work of Du Bois (1903) pointed to double games, not in a universal expression, but rather, as played by endangered people against the stakes of life and death.

Some researchers have recognized that the necessity for double games, improvisation, and information "guarded in whispers" is endemic (Du Bois, 1903, p. 144). Edin and Lein (1996) pointed out that survival for poor families has depended on welfare-reliant mothers' ability to be creative because welfare income was never adequate to sustain a family. Yet, to disclose the ways one barters, swaps, sells informal labor, or accepts gifts to make ends meet, when on public assistance, may be dangerous; acknowledging additional income means losing aid. Dodson (1998) reported that when poor mothers enter the welfare office, they may consciously engage in theater, playing a part to ease the tension of the interrogative process. The necessity of apparent accommodation and acquiescence becomes part of the "welfare culture" (Soss, 2000).

Equally unsettling in managing authorities is the fluidity of rules. Regulations for eligibility for welfare, definitions of "fraud," and eligibility for citizenship are ambiguous, shifting, and discretionary, requiring vigilance to be sure to adhere to the latest iteration (Coutin, 2000; Houppert, 1999; Soss, 2000). Dodson (1998) reported that mothers enter the welfare office acting "like a stone" both to minimize the penetration of disrespect and to avoid interrogation intent on denying eligibility for aid. Immigrant household workers tell of seeking work that minimizes contact with employers, choosing physically more demanding domestic work over nanny work that requires more emotional interaction (Hondagneu-Sotelo, 2002). These lessons in managing stigma and the cultivation of self-protective practices nurture community habits and a "culture of silence" (Freire, 1981).

Fear and Research on Families

Fear of speaking, or, if willing to speak, of saying what is really going on, is a vital if largely ignored force in the development of social research methodology for inquiry into the lives of poor and marginalized people. Social theorists who recognize power and marginality as essential to any representation of social reality point to the critical contribution of the liminal perspective (Anzaldua, 1987; Ladson-Billings, 2000). Indeed, the development of knowledge is always stunted by bias when certain groups are "kept from the table" (Gaventa & Cornwall, 2001, p. 71). But people confined to social margins may be reluctant to tell what they know because they may understand doing so as giving information to the enemy (Scott, 1990).

Lykes (1989), contending with the conventions of social research, challenged the use of *informed consent* when used in a context of clear and entrenched power imbalance. There are "constraints on developing collaboration between subjects in a context of real power imbalances" that a signed piece of paper does not alleviate (p. 177). Heron and Reason (2001) called for *cooperative inquiry* in which researchers and subjects collaborate to promote multiple and discursive versions of social reality. We share a commitment to participative social inquiry and the coproduction of knowledge while recognizing the conditions that stifle the inclusion of low-income people and people of color. In this article, we detail our experiences conducting participatory cooperative inquiry with those who have long been trained into habits of hiding.

Finding Fear in the Field

Between 1990 and 2003 one author and throughout 2001–2003 the other author was engaged in field research with low-income women including documented and undocumented immigrants, women formerly reliant on welfare, and wage-poor mothers. The great majority of the respondents were mothers (the majority, women of color) who were having great difficulty maintaining family stability, seeking social mobility, and even simply ensuring the safety of children. These variables were central to the various studies. The next section of this article identifies three habits of hiding everyday life that emerged in our research on low-income families in contemporary America including staying quiet, agreeable talk, and selective telling. All names are pseudonyms.

Staying Quiet

References to staying silent and guarding information were common in discussions and interviews with low-income mothers. Erika, in Denver (2000), recalled how workers in the welfare office would doubt that she had back problems, assuming that she was just trying to avoid going to work. She found that if she "stayed quiet" and simply let the caseworker behind the desk criticize her, she could curtail the exchange.

In a focus group in Milwaukee (2000), Magdalia explained that it is hard for some mothers to call in to work when they are going to be late or absent. "I know the reason they don't call in . . . cause everyone thinks she just lying. She's just a loser that can't be bothered with coming to work. It is hard to be put down all the time." Magdalia went on to explain that staying silent is self-protective. "I just stay quiet sometimes."

Darna told the same group, "I give my daughter (a four-year-old) some Tylenol and then take her in to the day care center. Then, when it wears off and her fever goes on up, they call me at work. They get my boss . . . and so he hears from *them* that she's sick, so there is nothing about 'oh here she goes again, making an excuse.' " Darna went on to advise silence and cunning when dealing with what she regarded as bigoted authority.

Agreeable Talk and "Telling Them What They Want to Hear"

Just "going along with" the expectations of authorities, including researchers in some cases, was a strategy often mentioned. In 1998, a mother of a 6 year old answered a specific child-care question this way: ". . . my son is watched by my neighbor after school until I come home. . . ." Yet, later, when she described her daily worries in detail, she chose job and child-care conflicts as the major one because, "I just have to leave work early too much 'cause I get so worried with my son there alone for three hours after school everyday . . . I just get up and go." Because she often left work abruptly out of worry for her son, she was on probation at her place of employment. Indeed, child care was frequently reported on in contradictory ways, obliquely referenced as okay but emerging as a source of great anxiety and instability, when mothers described the wider frame of their lives.

In another example, in the spring of 1998, during a focus group that was interpreting previously gathered data, Naylia explained that mothers are afraid that child protective services will remove children from their care so they say, " 'No I don't have childcare problems. . . .' It's like you can't tell the truth 'cause you lose everything if you do.' "

Other respondents acknowledged that they "just tell them what they want to hear" when questioned by welfare caseworkers, social workers, and job supervisors. There is no point in saying what is really going on because, as Annette explained, "The stereotypes society has formed about us, like we are on drugs, lazy, prostitution, we don't have it together" so "you keep your business to yourself."

Arts of Selective Telling: "No One's Going to Tell You . . ."

Immigrants expressed the need to mask or downplay experiences with discrimination in the work-place and unfair if not abusive treatment by employers. In interviews with Honduran immigrants, they reported poor working conditions and long arduous work-days and they sometimes described these experiences with a political analysis. They commonly used words such as "exploitation," "unjust treatment," "fear provoking," and even "fascist" to describe employers and work experiences.

But when asked if they felt there were barriers to economic mobility in the United States, only a couple answered in the affirmative. The majority smiled and said a version of "No, this is a land of opportunities." Respondents in a focus group of Honduran immigrants and Honduran community workers explained the apparent contradiction.

"No one is going to tell you, an American, that there are problems with your country. They may say that their work situations are difficult or that certain individuals are cruel, but they won't attack the system. They would be afraid of looking anti-American," Rosalia, a lay pastor in the community, replied.

"That's for sure," Ignacia asserted. "Even though you work here in the community, you're a *gringa*, and there's fear. People are being deported around here; there are people being deported right now as we're talking. It's scary to speak critically of America to an American even if we're told that they are 'safe.' "

These are a few of many excerpts from our research in which mothers acknowledged that they commonly obscure data of everyday life, which emerged as an important influence in our research. If mothers are unwilling, for example, to accurately represent a lack of child care, the abusive behavior of a cohabitant whose financial contribution is needed, or eroding effects of wages that do not cover basic family needs, critical information about the status of millions of American families is omitted.

Participatory Research Approaches

Over years of conducting research in low-income America, we used and elaborated on a variety of approaches and practices in an effort to promote research interaction in which marginalized people would choose to share accurate information about their lives and perspectives. Our research approaches are consonant with a broad understanding of action research (Reason & Bradbury, 2001), constructivist methods toward expanding the conceptual range of the inquiry while in process (Charmaz, 2000), and a firm belief in the importance of "indigenous knowledge" in social research (Lykes, 1997; Prych & Castillo, 2001). We have been particularly attentive to the questions and challenges raised by Fine, Weis, Weseen, and Wong (2000) pertaining to "What's Safe to Say Aloud—And by Whom?" (p. 121) and the ethical complexity of seeking participation and coproduction of knowledge with people who are racially, economically, ethnically, nationally, and otherwise marginalized. The ethical boundaries of such research stretch wider than simply guarding individual confidentiality. We continuously challenged our work with questions about how to negotiate the borderline between mainstream and underground society, seeking to build knowledge *with* people who live the conditions under study without disrupting their ways of protecting themselves and their families.

Involving community members as a participatory approach has become increasingly popular in qualitative research. Krueger and King (1998) argued that using community members as volunteers assists "outside" researchers in accessing "inside" information that subjects are unlikely to share with strangers. From another perspective, Park (2001) argued that participatory methods are not just a convenient way to gather useful information; they also introduce perspectives of community members into the fabric of the inquiry. Madriz (2000) found that among low-income women and women of color, focus group approaches and *collective testimonies* foster more speaking up than do individualistic methods such as interview formats.

The next section of this article examines the methodological approaches we have incorporated into and expanded upon in our work. In each study, we had a methodological goal (not always met) of the inclusion of community members (Krueger & King, 1998) in every stage of the research process (Fals-Borda & Rahman, 1991; Lykes, 1997).

We drew lessons from participatory action research that, when fully realized, is inquiry designed and controlled by the people under study with research "experts" as available advisors (Freire, 1970). Our participatory efforts, however, are far more modest.

Our approach was to integrate collaborative participative methods into three stages of the inquiry process, including the development of the research design, conducting field research, and interpreting data gathered. We particularly focused on the interpretive stage as the research moment that generally excludes community members. In the following section, we describe this analytical method in detail.

Developing Participatory Research Designs

In the development stage of the various studies, the principal investigators enlisted community members' participation through several approaches. These included one or more of the following: prolonged researcher engagement in local organizations that allowed ongoing participant observations and trust building, meeting repeatedly with community informants and discussing research themes and goals, conducting *theme gathering* or preliminary focus groups, and including research-trained community members on research teams. In all these approaches, principal investigators were responsible for contacting, meeting with, and, in some cases, doing the ongoing work with community members.

Activities to build the links between the research and community participation (such as meetings, field researcher trainings, and focus groups) always took place in the low-income communities. In some cases, community informants who learned of the research efforts (such as a leader in a community center or local service provider) would advise the researchers and lend their space and credibility to promote focus groups, community meetings, or other connections. In other cases, the researchers would simply ask for the opportunity to distribute leaflets publicizing a community discussion or focus group at a local library or community center. In one case, the principal investigator spent a full year working in a community-based nongovernmental organization (NGO) that served immigrants. She became a well known and helpful staff person and was constantly under the scrutiny of local community members. In another case, the principal investigator worked in a city school for 2 years to evaluate a new parent-support program and, on the basis of a request from activist parents, codeveloped a participatory inquiry on low-income parents' role in school structure.

Integral to these participatory approaches was a keen awareness of societal and local conditions and how they change the lives of community members. For example, the level of fear in immigrant communities increased dramatically after the passage of the Patriot Act. Similarly, fear and instability increased among poor families during the era of welfare reform. As the conditions and status of members changed, in turn, so did their everyday priorities, and these were always incorporated into the studies. Although the entire research design did not change as transitions swept through the communities, changing imperatives of the community members were always integrated into the research design, methods, and questions posed.

Central to the design-building phase is establishing a presence within the community whereby members can observe and evaluate trustworthiness and (it is hoped) choose to become involved, or in any case not to obstruct the study. Researchers, in turn, become more enlightened about the local climate, community fears, and local ways of persisting, despite hardship. More conventionally, another goal of this stage is to gain preliminary information, usually through focus groups and observation, toward developing and refining the inquiry (e.g., in designing interview guides) through the data gathered.

Conducting Collaborative Field Research

In the fieldwork or data-gathering phase the studies also sought the inclusion of community members. The most aggressive and well funded effort allowed the inclusion of community members as regular salaried members of the research team. This study included developing a fieldwork training guide, planning conference calls, and a 2-day in-residence training that brought together teams from cities around the country. The training included audio- and videotaping interviews for newly trained field team and local community members. All team and community members involved in the training collectively critiqued the field team "performances" and interview instruments. These field teams then returned to their locales and conducted pilot interviews that were then critiqued collaboratively via conference calls. Through this constructivist and collaborative approach to designing methods and refining themes, developing field practices, and creating instrumentation, the teams entered the field.

In another collaborative approach with a much smaller budget, the single field team was composed of graduate students, former graduate students, and individuals who had previously worked with the principal investigator in conducting field research. Team development included a commitment to develop an interracial/interethnic bilingual team as reflected in the population of low-income mothers in the study, although the team did not include community members. Collaborative approaches to team building and instrumentation were similar to those described, but in only one city, and were managed by the principal investigator and a part-time project coordinator.

In fieldwork that was based on one person gathering data, the principal investigator developed the design, as above, with community leaders and members. In these approaches, rather than building a team in some way composed of community membership, the lone researcher entered into the community for a protracted period as a volunteer in the local NGO, with the intent of designing inquiry into life in that community. Thus, collaboration came not from building a team but from the researcher entering into everyday community life and introducing the study as a peripheral but overt activity.

In seeking collaborative research practice, the characteristics of those who became effective included, above all, a sincere commitment to the central issues under study. This was true for senior researchers, graduate student research associates, as well as for community member research associates who joined the projects. Graduate students seeking grounded participatory research experience frequently approached one author to gain experience in this kind of inquiry. These students often shared some of the socio-economic, racial, or contextual life experiences of the people under study; thus, they would bring this insight into the research. Community members too have approached the authors, once a project was in the field, to learn about the meaning of the work or to join it. In seeking community members as research associates, an additional attribute we sought was that these individuals be known as respectful and trustworthy "neighbors," knowing that they would always be the team members approached first by other community members to "check out" the project and the researchers.

Whether a national multisite study or an individual inquiry, seeking true collaborators in conducting the research demands willingness to adapt and share decision making. Although each project may have a specific design, protocols, and mission, enlisting people to become coinvestigators will affect the inquiry. This mandates a sincere willingness for mutual learning on the part of the "experts" and community members.

Collaborative Interpretation and Coproduction of Knowledge

The interpretive stage of research is conventionally one in which the data become the sole province of the researcher community for analysis and construction of meaning, although some qualitative researchers include participants in this phase. An established approach is that of member checking. This method, undertaken informally or systematically, typically involves asking respondents to review transcriptions or other data to gain confirmation of accuracy (Lincoln & Guba, 1985; Patton, 1990). Janesick (2000) pointed out that reviewing data with respondents is not always feasible; an alternative is sharing data with others who have expertise in the area under study. Central to members' review of data is an effort toward confirmation of, or challenge to, the accuracy of the gathered evidence. Although scholars of qualitative research argue that the concept of *validity* is pertinent to quantitative data, qualitative inquiry seeks experiences and perspectives. These approaches, however, do offer a level of verification of the information gathered.

Our approach is a participatory analysis that emerged over time as an extension of focus groups and a variation on a *member checking approach*. In groups of between 6 and 10 community members, we routinely began to examine data already gathered. Contrasting conventional members' checking, we sought coanalysis, not confirmation, of data previously gathered. Thus, we sought members who had *not* been involved in the data gathering because new participants more readily assumed the role of analyst, rather than respondent. We also found that asking participants to be data interpreters right from the start interrupted the habits of sequestering knowledge; many participants were quite ready to speak on behalf of *other* women and families facing daily conditions they knew so well. Essentially, interpretive focus groups sought a communitarian approach to analysis and *multivocal* representation of the meaning of data (Christians, 2000).

Detailing the Steps of Interpretive Focus Groups

The interpretive focus groups took place in local settings known to be "safe" or to be generally comfortable for the participants. These included community centers, public schools, child-care centers, and churches. Participants were always paid a stipend for their time (between $10 and $20). Whenever resources allowed, children were welcomed and child care was provided in adjacent rooms so mothers could easily check on their children. We also served a meal to mothers and their children when our budgets allowed encouraging a gathering that included social exchange and the presence of family.

Following focus group tradition, each group started with personal introductions. We then explained—and reiterated throughout—the goal of the interpretive focus group as an effort to better understand the data already gathered or "what people had said to us." We stated our commitment to learning "what is really going on" and our recognition of the limitations of our ability to "get it," to know what "it is really like," and "what people face" everyday. In some cases, the principal investigator and/or a coresearcher had relevant shared experience, and this was mentioned in the introductions.

The process then turned to a researcher(s) presenting a brief oral overview of the study from which the data were drawn. We summarized why it was done and who was involved and then summarized the data. During the usual 2-hour discussion, the principal investigator and coinvestigators traded roles of group facilitation, observation of group responses, and taking field notations. The groups always included many pauses and "check-ins" to ask participants if they had questions or comments.

Specific ways of presenting the previously gathered material varied. A common approach was pasting newsprint to walls that could include visualizations such as large pie charts or bar graphs of numeric data gathered, for example, about low-income children's health status, types of child care used, hours of paid employment, rates of welfare case closings, and other variables central to the particular study. The posted newsprint would also include common themes or quotes from transcripts. This approach included asking people to walk around and look at the newsprint. Often, this activity overlapped with getting food that was laid out on tables near the posted newsprint, promoting the data review as a social activity. Researchers too walked around seeking ways to interact with the people and the data to try to ascertain whether the material seemed coherent and meaningful.

Another approach to data presentation was oral reporting of data including readings from transcripts (sometimes involving two team members) or in some cases, listening to a tape-recorded individual or group interview. In one project we summarized case studies orally, including quotations and central themes. The focus of all these approaches to data presentation was to pass information to the participants. We varied the precise method, tempo, or "performance" according to how people were responding.

The questions we used in the various interpretive focus groups were based on the specific variables and themes from each study, and we modified, omitted, or repeated the questions on the basis of participant reaction. All interpretive focus group inquiry, however, included the following underlying guiding questions:

1. Are we hearing what is really going on in these people's lives? Does this sound like what is going on in the lives of people you know?
2. What else do you think is going on, that is not represented here?
3. We do not understand the meaning of what is being said here. Can you explain to us what this means? (List points where clarity is missing.)
4. If you were trying to find out what we are trying to find out about . . . (insert the pertinent variable(s) of interest), what would *you* expect people not to share or talk about? Why would they be hesitant to talk about this? What's at stake?
5. After going over all of the information that we have gathered from our interviews, we have concluded the following. (List and say out loud the preliminary findings and accompanying conclusions.) Do you think we have this right? Are we getting it?

We asked these questions and variations on them in conjunction with any of the above methods of presenting data. For example, while reading from a transcript, we interjected one or several of these questions tailored to the specific example. Or in walking around with participants and talking about the graphics and quotations, we would use some version of these queries. Participant responses (assuming they were said for public hearing) would also be written on newsprint taped on the walls, and participants often corrected or added to what researchers were writing up. Periodically, one of the researchers would read the accumulating comments out loud for general reaction, modification, or elaboration as a collaborative interpretation evolved. When time and enthusiasm allowed, participants would circulate again and add written comments or call a researcher over to advise additions, on a one-on-one basis. In most cases, interpretive discussions were also recorded, transcribed, and integrated into research findings.

It should be noted that we always improvised. Although we would arrive with our pie charts, scripts, and quotes, we would often change course on the basis of how the people were responding. For example, the first time we actually "play-acted" a transcript rather than simply read it out loud was in response to participants' confusion about "who's asking . . . and who's answering?" In the moment, we decided to identify one team member as "interviewer" and the other as "single mother having a hard time." We found that the juxtaposition encouraged deconstruction of the responses and a sharp critique of some of the questions. We continued to use that approach, thereafter. This exemplifies an essential element of this practice: It is a constructivist or evolving approach, not a precise replication of steps or a rigid rendition of questions.

A key challenge of the interpretive focus groups was to engender an environment in which participants assumed the role of data analysts rather than interviewees. Our years of experience have taught us, as discussed above, that many low-income women are accustomed to slipping into habits of self-protection and thus, they may be difficult to engage. We have also learned that sometimes participants are so caught up in their own immediate difficulties that they find it difficult to focus on data presented. Sometimes participants do not seem comfortable talking together or building collaborative analyses. But in most cases, we gained significant insight into the data we had already gathered.

Occasionally, a participant would take on an authoritative role overtly advising the researchers and suggesting better ways to dissect the data, even changing the structure of the focus group discussion. In one such group, for example, a participant pronounced "that's not what that means" regarding a description of child-care data. When she asserted this the rest of the group immediately agreed with her and aggressively deconstructed the themes in the data presented. We found that when participants believed the interaction was open to their knowledge and their critique of our limitations, the most unexpected and revealing commentaries emerged.

Taking It Back to the Community

Each of these studies included various strategies for returning information and analytic discussion to the individuals who participated and to the communities in which the research was done. In each case, participants were asked whether they wanted any or all findings sent to them. When funding permitted, we produced high-quality materials and distributed them for use by community members, organizations, and policymakers. In one study, one of the authors disseminated several thousand booklets that were used extensively by local and collaborating organizations in various efforts to advocate on behalf of low-income families. The authors have also participated in data presentation in local and statewide forums including school meetings, community and health center gatherings, town and city hall events, and, in one case, U.S. congressional committees.

One author, after working for 2 years in a local NGO, completed her doctoral dissertation from study findings. Community members were present at her doctoral defense and provided oral commentary on the importance of the research in their community. The week after her defense, she presented her work to a larger gathering of community members at the field site where she did the majority of her participant research. The other author, who worked in a school for 2 years, provided useful information for a parent-led debate in that neighborhood about school decision making, and she presented findings in a public forum.

Taking the information back to the community developed into more than providing individuals with accounts that ensured them of the trustworthiness of the research. The participatory research practices, designed to draw in community members and engage them to speak when they might otherwise have been silent, invariably called upon the authors to be participatory in turn, speaking their knowledge on behalf of the community collaborators.

Discussion

Daily life in low-income immigrant communities and communities of color is wrapped in protective layers. Pulling those layers back is difficult and questionable ethically. In social research, lines are fairly well drawn in terms of protecting individual confidentiality. Yet, it is far more difficult to understand the ethics of illuminating corners of communities in which camouflaging life is akin to survival. In our work, we are always reflecting on how data would be received, reinterpreted, and transformed into descriptions of low-income America and the likelihood of "becoming part of the negative configuration of poor women and men" (Fine et al., 2000, p. 117). We worked with community members toward an ethical reporting back, a way to provide important insight about the status of millions of wage-poor families without "causing suffering in those already the objects of daily racism" (Hurtado & Stewart, 2001, p. 308). In an interpretive focus group, we were counseled, "You gotta figure out how to tell about it without telling too much" and we are trying.

Why Do It?

Conducting participative research in low-income America is time consuming, expensive, and demands that researchers stretch themselves and the conventions of social research. Over the past five decades, a number of scholars have written in-depth texts offering valuable insight into the lives of low-income women and families (Dodson, 1998; Hays, 2003; Schmalzbauer, in press; Stack, 1974). As these rich texts reflect, many people facing poverty and stigma will share revelations and reflections provided they believe they are safe and their words are recognized as informed representations of their world. Despite these works, social research into the lives of marginalized people seldom explicates the context of risk or the likelihood that people will withhold data. This conventional omission allows researchers to interview, observe, and survey people ignoring the powerful context of marginalization; they may treat all "fields" as neutral territory and all methods as universal.

Further, despite the growing use of creative qualitative methods, rarely are low-income community members incorporated as *thinkers* in research about their lives rather than data producers for experts. Researchers, ourselves included, face constant pressures from academic and peer reviewers to reiterate standards in research "rigor" and pressure from funding sources to produce theoretically sound, practical, and policy-oriented results. Producing, or more to the point, coproducing knowledge in participatory ways may be risky. Becker (2004) pointed to a *hierarchy of credibility* and cautioned, "As sociologists, we provoke the charge of bias . . . by refusing to give credence and deference to an established status order, in which knowledge of the truth and the right to be heard are not equally distributed." He warned that "accusations of bias" will fly when attention to "subordinates" is perceived as a vital element in the inquiry (pp. 24–25). Those drawn to participative research learn quickly that the path is a steep climb.

Seeking accurate accounts of marginalized low-income people and families in contemporary America is essential for an accurate portrait of the nation. As community coinvestigators have pointed out to us, it is easy to pretend people are not suffering or that their suffering is their own fault when *their* testimonies of social reality are absent. Additionally, from a personal perspective, we believe that our methods led to our learning more about the daily lives of families of color and poor and immigrant families. We believe that we heard richer and more accurate descriptions of everyday efforts to try to stay healthy, care for children, cope with poverty wages, meet job demands, and hold onto self-valuing identities. Inaccurate accounts distort low-income communities. Learning what lives beneath silence and omissions is requisite for a national narrative of low-income America.

Equally important, these and other methods break silence, which is requisite to unseat distorted versions of poor women and families. "Stories of the substandard, child of color and poverty" that contrast with "White middle-class expression as the normative," and other tales of deviance may go unchecked in most conventional data gathering (Ladson-Billings, 2000, p. 269). Beyond "writing the wrongs" in ethnographies (Fine & Weis, 1996), we argue that low-income mothers have a critical way of knowing society and can offer "kitchen table policy" (Dodson, 2000). Their recommendations, when freely given, are essential to the advancement of poor and marginalized people. Of equal importance, they "shift the center" (Collins, 1986) just a little toward a more enlightened portrait of the society.

References

Abromovitz, M. (1996). *Regulating the lives of women: Social welfare policy from colonial to present times.* Boston: South End Press.

Anzaldua, G. (1987). *Borderlands, la frontera: The new mestiza.* San Francisco: Spinsters/Aunt Lute.

Arendell, T. (2000). Conceiving and investigating motherhood: The decade's scholarship. *Journal of Marriage and the Family, 62,* 1192–1207.

Becker, H. S. (2004). Whose side are we on? In W. K. Caroll (Ed.), *Critical strategies for social research* (pp. 23–28). Toronto: Canadian Scholar's Press.

Bourdieu, P. (1990). *In other words: Essays towards a reflexive sociology.* Stanford, CA: Stanford University Press.

Chang, G. (2000). *Disposable domestics: Immigrant women workers in the global economy.* Boston: South End.

Charmaz, K. (2000). Grounded theory: Objectivist and constructivist methods. In N. Denzin & Y. Lincoln (Eds.), *Handbook of qualitative research* (pp. 509–535). Thousand Oaks, CA: Sage.

Chavez, L. (1998). *Shadowed lives: Undocumented immigrants in American society.* New York: Harcourt Brace College.

Christians, G. (2000). Ethics and politics in qualitative research. In N. Denzin & Y. Lincoln (Eds.), *Handbook of qualitative research* (pp. 133–155). Thousand Oaks, CA: Sage.

Collins, P. H. (1986). Learning from the outsider within: The sociological significance of Black feminist thought. *Social Problems, 33,* 514–532.

Collins, P. H. (1998). *Fighting words: Black women and the search for social justice.* Minneapolis: University of Minnesota Press.

Coutin, S. (2000). *Legalizing moves: Salvadoran immigrants' struggle for U.S. residency.* Ann Arbor: University of Michigan Press.

Dodson, L. (1998). *Don't call us out of name: The untold lives of women and girls in poor America.* Boston: Beacon Press.

Dodson, L. (2000). At the kitchen table: Poor women making public policy. In N. Hirschmann & U. Liebert (Eds.), *Women & welfare: Theory and practice in the United States and in Europe* (pp. 177–190). New Brunswick, NJ: Rutgers University Press.

Dodson, L. (2005). When there is no time or money: Work, family and community lives of low-income families. In J. Heymann & C. Beem (Eds.), *Unfinished business: Building equality and democracy in an era of working families* (pp. 122–155). New York: New Press.

Du Bois, W. E. B. (1903). *The souls of Black folk.* Millwood, NY: Kraus-Thomson.

Edin, K., & Lein, L. (1996). *Making ends meet: How single mothers survive welfare and low-wage work.* New York: Russell Sage.

Fals-Borda, O., & Rahman, M. A. (1991). *Action and knowledge: Breaking the monopoly with participatory action research.* New York: Intermediate/Apex.

Fine, M., & Weis, L. (1996). Writing the "wrongs" of fieldwork: Confronting our own research/writing dilemmas in urban ethnographies. *Qualitative Inquiry, 2,* 251–274.

Fine, M., Weiss, L., Weseen, S., & Wong, L. (2000). For whom? Qualitative research, representations, and social responsibilities. In N. Denzin & Y. Lincoln (Eds.), *Handbook of qualitative research* (pp. 107–131). Thousand Oaks, CA: Sage.

Freire, P. (1970). *Pedagogy of the oppressed.* New York: Seabury Press.

Freire, P. (1981). *Education for critical consciousness.* New York: Continuum Press.

Gaventa, J., & Cornwall, A. (2001). Power and knowledge. In P. Reason & H. Bradbury (Eds.), *Handbook of action research: Participative inquiry and practice* (pp. 70–80). Thousand Oaks, CA: Sage.

Goffman, E. (1963). *Stigma: Notes on the management of spoiled identity.* Englewood Cliffs, NJ: Prentice-Hall.

Hays, S. (2003). *Flat broke with children: Women in the age of welfare reform.* Oxford, U.K.: Oxford University Press.

Heron, J., & Reason, P. (2001). The practice of co-operative inquiry: Research "with" rather than "on" people. In P. Reason & H. Bradbury (Eds.), *Handbook of action research* (pp. 179–188). London: Sage.

Hondagneu-Soteio, P. (2002). Blow-ups and other unhappy endings. In B. Ehrenreich & A. R. Hochschild (Eds.), *Global woman: Nannies, maids and sex workers in the new economy* (pp. 55–69). New York: Metropolitan Books.

Houppert, K. (1999, October 25). You're not entitled! *The Nation,* 11–14.

Hurtado, A., & Stewart, A. (2001). Through the looking glass: Implications of studying whiteness for feminist methods. In L. Weis, L. Powell Pruitt, L. Burns, & M. Fine (Eds.), *Off white: Readings on race, power and society* (pp. 315–330). New York: Routledge.

Janesick, V. (2000). The choreography of qualitative research. In N. Denzin & Y. Lincoln (Eds.), *Handbook of qualitative research* (pp. 379–400). Thousand Oaks, CA: Sage.

Krueger, R. A., & King, J. A. (1998). *Involving community members in focus groups.* Thousand Oaks. CA: Sage.

Ladson-Billings. G. (2000). Racialized discourses and ethnic epistemologies. In K. Denzin & Y. Lincoln (Eds.), *Handbook of qualitative research* (pp. 257–278). Thousands Oaks, CA: Sage.

Lincoln, Y. S., & Guba, E. G. (1985). *Naturalistic inquiry.* Beverly Hills, CA: Sage.

Lykes, B. (1989). Dialogue with Guatemalan Indian women: Critical perspectives on constructing collaborative research. In R. K. Unger (Ed.), *Representations: Social construction of gender* (pp. 167–185). Amityville, NY: Baywood.

Lykes, M. B. (1997). Activist participatory action research among the Maya of Guatemala: Constructing meanings from situated knowledge. *Journal of Social Issues, 53,* 725–746.

Madriz, E. (2000). Focus groups in feminist research. In N. Denzin & Y. Lincoln (Eds.), *Handbook of qualitative research* (pp. 835–850). Thousand Oaks, CA: Sage.

Neubeck, K. J., & Cazenave, N. A. (2001). *Welfare racism: Playing the race card against America's poor.* New York: Routledge.

Park, P. (2001). Knowledge and participatory research. In P. Reason & H. Bradbury (Eds.), *Handbook of action research: Participative inquiry and practice* (pp. 81–90). Thousand Oaks, CA: Sage.

Patton, M. (1990). *Qualitative evaluation and research methods* (2nd ed.), Newbury Park, CA: Sage.

Prych, T., & Castillo, M. T. (2001). The sights and sounds of indigenous knowledge. In P. Reason & H. Bradbury (Eds.), *Handbook of action research: Participative inquiry and practice* (pp. 379–385). Thousand Oaks, CA: Sage.

Reason, P., & Bradbury, H. (2001). *Handbook of action research: Participative inquiry and practice.* Thousand Oaks, CA: Sage.

Reid, P. T. (1993). Poor women in psychological research: Shut up and shut out. *Psychology of Women Quarterly, 17,* 133–150.

Schmalzbauer, L. (in press). *Striving and surviving: A daily life analysis of Honduran transnational families.* New York: Routledge.

Scott, J. (1990). *Domination and the arts of resistance: Hidden transcripts.* New Haven, CT: Yale University Press.

Soss, J. (2000). *Unwanted claims: The politics of participation in the U.S. welfare system.* Ann Arbor: University of Michigan Press.

Soss, J., Schram, S., Vartanian, T., & O'Brien, E. (2001). Setting the terms of relief: Explaining state policy choices in the devolution revolution. *American Journal of Political Science, 45,* 378–395.

Stack, C. (1974). *All our kin.* New York: Harper and Row.

20

Don't Believe the Hype

Ann Arnett Ferguson

The minute they see me, fear me
I'm the epitome—a public enemy
Used, abused, without clues
I refused to blow a fuse
They even had it on the news
Don't believe the hype
Don't believe the hype.

—Public Enemy, "Don't believe the hype"

Soon after I began fieldwork at Rosa Parks Elementary School, one of the adults, an African American man, pointed to a black boy who walked by us in the hallway.[1] "That one has a jail-cell with his name on it," he told me. We were looking at a ten-year-old, barely four feet tall, whose frail body was shrouded in baggy pants and a hooded sweatshirt. The boy, Lamar, passed with the careful tread of someone who was in no hurry to get where he was going. He was on his way to the Punishing Room of the school. As he glanced quickly toward and then away from us, the image of the figure of Tupac Shakur on the poster advertising the movie *Juice* flashed into my mind. I suppose it was the combination of the hooded sweatshirt, the guarded expression in his eyes, and what my companion had just said that reminded me of the face on the film poster that stared at me from billboards and sidings all over town.

I was shocked that judgment and sentence had been passed on this child so matter-of-factly by a member of the school staff. But by the end of the school year, I had begun to suspect that a prison cell might indeed have a place in Lamar's future. What I observed at Rosa Parks during more than three years of fieldwork in the school, heard from the boy himself, from his teachers, from his mother, made it clear that just as children were tracked into futures as doctors, scientists, engineers, word processors, and fast-food workers, there were also tracks for some children, predominantly African American and male, that led to prison. This book tells the story of the making of these bad boys, not by members of the criminal justice system on street corners, or in shopping malls, or video arcades, but in and by school, through punishment. It is an account of the power of institutions to create, shape, and regulate social identities.

Unfortunately, Lamar's journey is not an isolated event, but traces a disturbing pattern of African American male footsteps out of classrooms, down hallways, and into disciplinary spaces throughout the school day in contemporary America. Though African American boys made up only one-quarter of the student body at Rosa Parks, they accounted for nearly half the number of students sent to the Punishing Room for major and minor misdeeds in 1991–92. Three-quarters of those suspended that year were boys, and, of those, four-fifths were African American.[2] In the course of my study it became clear that school labeling practices and the exercise of rules operated as part of a hidden curriculum to marginalize and isolate black male youth in disciplinary spaces and brand them as criminally inclined.

But trouble is not only a site of regulation and stigmatization. Under certain conditions it can also be a powerful occasion for identification and recognition. This study investigates this aspect of punishment through an exploration of the meaning of school rules and the interpretation of trouble from the youth's perspective. What does it mean to hear adults say that you are bound for jail and to understand that the future predicted for you is "doing time" inside prison walls? What does school trouble mean under such deleterious circumstances? How does a ten-year-old black boy fashion a sense of self within this context? Children like Lamar are not just innocent victims of arbitrary acts; like other kids, he probably talks out of turn, argues with teachers, uses profanities, brings contraband to school. However, I will argue, the meaning and consequences of these acts for young black males like himself are different, highly charged with racial and gender significance with scarring effects on adult life chances.

The pattern of punishment that emerges from the Rosa Parks data is not unique. Recent studies in Michigan, Minnesota, California, and Ohio reveal a similar pattern.[3] In the public schools of Oakland, California, for example, suspensions disproportionately involved African American males, while in Michigan schools, where corporal punishment is still permitted, blacks were more than five times more likely to be hit by school adults than were whites. In the Cincinnati schools, black students were twice as likely to end up in the in-house suspension room—popularly known as the "dungeon"—and an overwhelming proportion of them were male.[4] In an ominous parallel to Cincinnati's dungeon, disciplinary space at Rosa Parks is designated the "Jailhouse."

The School and Neighborhood

I was initiated to Rosa Parks Elementary School in 1989 as a member of an evaluation team for a new intervention program for children diagnosed as "at-risk" of failing in school. The program, Partners at Learning Skills (PALS), included in-school counseling, after-school tutoring and recreation, evening and weekend workshops for parents, and in-service training for teachers. It was just one of hundreds that had been started in schools and communities throughout the United States in response to the erosion of funding and services to urban public schools that had occurred over the previous decade.

The children participating in PALS had been selected by a committee of teachers, school administrators, and a counselor. I was told that the selection committee had had a very difficult time choosing the first group of thirty children since more than three times that number had been proposed by classroom teachers. One of the most difficult questions facing the selection committee, it was said, was whether to choose pupils who might benefit from extra help or to select those who were, in the words of one of the school administrators, "unsalvageable" and on whom precious resources would be wasted. The selection committee could not agree, so they compromised and included both types.

The first time I saw the entire group of children in PALS, they were in the school library taking a pencil-and-paper test designed to measure self-esteem. That was when I first became aware of a disturbing fact: all the children except one were African American, and of those 90 percent were males.[5] I quickly became aware that what was surprising and problematic for me appeared to be taken for granted by the others. No one at the school seemed surprised that the vast majority of children defined as "at-risk" of failing academically, of being future school dropouts, were mostly black and male. My own puzzle over how this raced and gendered pattern had come into being led me to conduct an in-depth study through participant observation at the Rosa Parks School over a three-and-a-half year period from January 1990 to May 1993.

Rosa Parks School is the largest of five intermediate schools (grades 4 through 6) in the school district of Arcadia, a medium-sized city on the West Coast. The city is best known as the home of a large public university whose prestige and reputation has attracted students and faculty from all over the world. Arcadia has operated a complex plan for school desegregation since 1968 that involves citywide busing to produce a racial/ethnic and socioeconomic mix in its schools. Students attending Rosa Parks come from a population where race, household type, and annual income are skewed into three types of neighborhood I have called Heartland, Midland, and the Highlands.[6] Each day the buses bring children, the majority of whom are white, from upper-middle-class professional families in the relatively affluent Midland and the wealthy Highlands to Rosa Parks School, where they join the kids from the predominantly low-income African American families living in the Heartland neighborhood surrounding the school.[7]

The racial balance targeted by the Arcadia desegregation program has never been actually attained because of the "white flight" from the public schools that followed the implementation of the desegregation plan in 1968. The percentage of white students in the K–12 grades of the city's schools declined from 60 percent to 30 percent between 1960 and 1993.[8] For a city with a reputation for being one of the most liberal communities in the country, Arcadia has one of the highest percentages of children attending private schools in the region.[9] Many of the white children who attend private or parochial elementary schools eventually return to attend the Arcadia public high school, where classes are de facto segregated as the result of an elaborate tracking system.

At the time of my study approximately one-half of the Rosa Parks student body was black and one-third was white. Of the remaining students, 10 percent were Asian American, 4 percent Hispanic, and 8 percent were classified as Other. The racial composition of the teaching staff, however, had changed little since desegregation, continuing to be predominately white and female.[10]

Rosa Parks School itself is far from being one of the run-down, resource-poor facilities documented in several recent accounts of urban schools.[11] The freshly painted two-story building and the asphalt playground occupies a full city block. Beautiful old pine trees stand on either side of the walkway leading up to a wide stone porch set in front of the main entrance to the school. The building faces onto a grassy lawn that is green for a short time in the spring and brown by the end of the summer when the school year begins. After school, children play football on the grass or hang around on the wide stone porch.

Inside the front door I am always struck by the calm atmosphere. The hallways are wide, clean, and lined by bulletin boards displaying children's work. The classrooms are filled with light from big windows. These are not rooms that speak of the bare necessities. Rooms are adorned with books, plants, animals, computers, games. Even so, teachers reminisce about better times in the school when the availability of basic school supplies could be taken for granted, when there was a school nurse, when the playground was open for recreation in the afternoons.

Nor is the neighborhood in which the school stands dilapidated or run-down. There is a mix of small, neat, single-family dwellings with older rambling wood-frame houses converted into multiple family units. Some are shabby, some are newly renovated. A few 1960s vintage apartment buildings, home to many of the poorest families, are interspersed throughout the neighborhood.

In spite of the quiet, ordinary feeling of its surroundings, Rosa Parks School is located in the heart of a major drug-trafficking area in the city. The buying and selling of drugs, the symbolic presence of urban poverty, is signaled through the signposts on a number of street corners that warn that police are watching and that the car license numbers of people buying drugs are being recorded. The area accounted for ten of the city's fourteen murders; one-half of the reported rapes; about a third of the robberies, and almost a half of the aggravated assaults in the city, according to 1991 statistics from the Arcadia Police Department.[12]

Doing Fieldwork

Statistics about school trouble and punishment provide a map that delineates a raced and gendered pattern of who gets punished in school and present the big picture of a disturbing phenomenon, but they can tell us very little about the actual processes that give rise to this configuration. So, my fieldwork was designed to explore these processes. Through a combination of participant observation at the school and a wide range of interviews and conversations with kids and adults, I examined the beliefs, the social relationships, and the everyday practices that give rise to a pattern in which the kids who are sent to jailhouses and dungeons in school systems across the United States are disproportionately black and male.

As a participant observer, I roamed the hallways before, during, and after school, hung out in the student cafeteria and the teachers' lounge at lunchtime, attended assemblies, wandered around the playground during recess. I sat in on classes and in the school library. I also tutored in the PALS after-school program.

During my second year, I began sitting in on Mrs. Daly's sixth-grade class. I had chosen this room because Horace, the boy who I was tutoring after school, was in the class.[13] The first few visits, I spent most of my time sitting at a worktable, quietly watching what was going on. But very soon, with Mrs. Daly's encouragement, I began participating in the regular classroom activities. I often worked with small groups of kids who needed help. I observed Horace and his friends "in action" and also got to know several of the African American girls in the class who were considered "challenges" and who also spent time in the Punishing Room. I accompanied the group on several field trips, including a three-day camping trip, the sixth-grade picnic at the end of the school year, and the orientation at the junior high school to which some of the kids would be transferring the following year.

But the most important site of all was observing in what I came to call the Punishing Room as well as in the other spaces connected with the school's discipline system. I would not have discovered the existence of the Punishing Room on my own. Some of the boys whom I was observing in Mrs. Daly's class led me to it because it was a regular stop on their passage through the day. I had already begun following them into more familiar places: their classroom, the playground, the cafeteria. I had begun to sift through their files in the school office and had learned about their scores on reading and math placement tests, whether their vision had been checked, whether they had moved from another school district. But I had never actually followed them down to "Miss Woolley's office" when they got in trouble until one day Mrs. Daly asked me to accompany two boys who had gotten in trouble right after recess for squirting water at each other. "I want to make sure they make it back to class quickly. Not get lost"—this with a significant look at both boys—"on the way back." So I went with them and discovered the function of one of the spaces of the school that up to that point I had only glanced at as I passed by.

After this first visit I asked permission to observe in the Punishing Room. At first the staff of the Punishing Room, all African Americans, were uneasy about my presence. But they were interested in the fact that my research was looking for answers as to why the majority of children getting into trouble and frequenting their office were African American. It turned out that this was a topic that they had theories about themselves. As a result, they not only gave me access, but urged me to look through the discipline records kept on individual children in the filing cabinets in their office.[14]

I spent many hours sitting in the Punishing Room, and my presence became less obtrusive as time went by. After the first few days, during which I felt that the student specialists were consciously bridling their responses to the children, being "softer" because of my presence, I became a taken-for-granted member of the setting. When this happened, verbal harangues, sympathy, even physical intimidation could be expressed without the fear that I was monitoring their activities on behalf of the school district. I became even more "invisible" as I sat copying the data from the discipline files. I would sit there handwriting the contents of referral slips onto a yellow pad while a stream of children came in and out of the room with stories, explanations, complaints. Scathing adult comments and childish declarations of innocence took place as if I were not there at all. Phone calls to parents were made, and families were critically appraised by staff after these conversations. I gained a great deal of insight from these interactions. What I observed confirmed that a trip to the Punishing Room was not necessarily a shameful event but held a variety of meanings for the children. For example, one day a fifth-grade African American boy who was always in trouble saw the file folder with his name on the desk. "I got a lot in there, don't I? Who else got one that big?" he asked. There was awe in his voice at his accomplishment. He had made an important mark on the school.

Troublemakers and Schoolboys

The heart of my research was the time I spent with twenty fifth- and sixth-grade African American boys. These boys had been selected after discussions with school personnel, review of the discipline files, and my own initial observations in and around the school. Ten of the boys, whom I have called *Schoolboys*, had been identified by the school as "doing well," while ten boys, whom I call the *Troublemakers*, were identified as "getting into trouble." I conducted interviews with all and spent time observing, hanging out with, and getting to know a smaller group.

The Troublemakers were no strangers to the Punishing Room. All the members of this group of boys had been suspended at home at least once over the course of the year for school infractions such as fighting, obscenity, bringing toy guns to school. None had ever been charged with illegal acts such as bringing drugs or real guns to school. None were inveterate truants; the vast majority rarely voluntarily missed a day of school and were usually on time. All had been labeled "at-risk" of failing, "unsalvageable," or "bound for jail" by school personnel.

The Schoolboys, on the other hand, had only occasionally been handed a referral slip, and none of them had ever been suspended. At the outset of my study I saw this group as just the opposite of the Troublemakers, as a control group; I wondered how they were different. What could we learn about the attitude, home-life, experiences of a group of boys who were clearly committed to the school's project that would help explain Troublemakers? However, I gradually realized that to see Schoolboys and Troublemakers as fundamentally different was to make a grave mistake. As African American males, Schoolboys were always on the brink of being redefined into the Troublemaker category by the school. The pressures and dilemmas this group faced around race and gender identities from adults and peers were always palpable forces working against their main-taining a commitment to the school project. That is, of course, why schools across the nation witness the continual attrition of the ranks of the "schoolboys" as they join those of the "troublemakers."

All of the boys in the study lived in the neighborhood around the school. All except two of the Schoolboys were from low-income families eligible for the school lunch program.[15] The composition of these households varied greatly from family to family and affected resources available to them in significant ways. Of the Schoolboys, three came from families in which both mother and father lived in the household, four from mother-headed households, one lived with his grandmother, and one lived with both grand-parents. Of the Troublemakers, two were living in families with both parents, four lived in mother-headed households, one was being raised by his father, two were in foster families, and one lived with his sister.[16]

I conducted a series of in-depth, unstructured interviews with the adults who had contact with the boys in the school: classroom teachers, principals, discipline staff, the district truant officer, school psychologists, social workers, school janitors. I also inter-viewed their parents or guardians—usually women, but in two cases fathers—as I explored the disciplinary systems outside of the school that the boys called on to make sense of interactions within the school. I came to know several of these families quite well as they drew me into their lives as a sympathetic ear, a sounding board, a person with resources and credibility in a community in which those currencies were often in short supply. In one instance, I became not just a friend or acquaintance, but was adopted as a member of the family.

Learning from Kids

Though I paid attention to the accounts of a variety of individuals and heard explanations and theories from numerous viewpoints, it is the perspective and the voices of the kids, mostly boys, whom I talked to that animate and bind this text together. I have spotlighted their voices not only because they are the most silenced and the most invalidated in discussions of school trouble and punishment, but also because they provide a critical view that augments significantly our knowledge about the contemporary crisis in education.

How I heard the voices of the boys whom I interviewed and how I listened to what they were saying changed qualitatively over the course of my research. I assumed at the start that I would learn *about* kids; but it was not long before I was obliged to question this premise and begin to learn *from* children. This enabled me to tell their story from a fresh viewpoint.

In my initial research design I had planned to learn about kids through "formal" interviews as well as through observation. My goal was to tape-record in my office at the university conversations about several topics including school, trouble and punishment, friends, heroes, adult careers. The venue of the interview was to set a tone of adult importance and serious business to the engagement that I hoped would have an effect on the quality of the responses that I got from the children.

I explained to the boys that I was writing a book about kids and school and that I wanted to tell the story from their perspective; that I needed their help, what they knew, in order to write something good. Word got around to their friends that I was writing a book, and a few approached me and asked if they could be in it. I was surprised at how savvy they were about the telling of life stories. For one thing, the favorite television program of almost all the kids was the *Oprah Winfrey Show*, which featured the telling of personal stories. One boy asked me what kind of cover the book would have; another seemed disappointed that I would not be using his real name. Most of the boys seemed genuinely pleased to discover that I wanted to talk about things that interested them. Two of them, however, were especially noncommittal during the interview. These two already had to deal with the criminal justice system. One boy had, in fact, been placed in a foster home for several days when his mother was arrested. Their demeanor was by no means hostile but extremely cautious, monosyllabic, noncommittal. After I interviewed each kid, he had a turn to be the interviewer and ask me whatever questions he wanted. Several took me up on the offer. I was asked about my work, my family, and what I spent my money on. Just the kind of questions I might get from social science researchers.

When the formal interviews were over, the reward for the boys was pizza and a visit to nearby video arcades, or a trip up to the lookout deck of the highest building at the university. I found that the spontaneous conversations that I had with them during these outings were often more informative about the topics that I was interested in than the actual interviews. The question-and-answer format, with me in control of the topic and them responding, was not the best one; in this form of dialogue, the kids responded to my questions, but carefully. Too carefully. On the other hand, rich stories of experience in and out of school, observations and theories, bits of advice, flowed out of the ad-lib, spontaneous conversations during the course of our "free" time together. I began to realize how imperative it was to rethink my interviewing strategies. "Free time" was the space in which the kids felt free to talk about what interested and impressed them. So, while I continued with the formal interviews, I began to understand that the time before and after the interviews was even more important.

When I decided to study a group of young people I did not think about how I would gain access to their meaning systems. I admit now with embarrassment that when I began the research my assumption was that my own knowledge and experience would give me the tools necessary to figure out what was going on in the lives of the boys I would interview and observe. I was required to provide a lengthy protocol for the Human Subjects Committee at the university. This procedure was couched in terms of "protecting children," so my efforts in composing the protocol were to assure the committee that my interview questions would not traumatize the "interviewees" in any way. At that point, my unexamined research common sense was that children were substantively different than adults; they were more transparent. They were "natural" subjects whose behavior I would interpret, rather than having to elicit interpretations from the kids themselves. I could observe them in depth—almost as if they were animals in the laboratory—to make sense of what I perceived. They were somehow more accessible because they were less social, more biologically determined. They were not yet totally "human," but were humans-in-the-making. It was me, not them, who was wise.

I was an "adult," beyond biology and development because fully social, and would use my knowledge of the world to interpret what I saw them do and what they told me of their lives. I did not even think about whether the kids would choose to let me into their lives, tell me their stories. They were on the surface: I would not have to plunge deep into another world of experience, meaning, interpretation, learn another language, unscramble new codes and symbols.

For one, I believed that I already knew a great deal about childhood. I am the mother of two sons; I have been a schoolteacher. From these experiences, I assumed that children could be extremely good at keeping, and highly motivated to keep, secrets, so that I would have to work to put them at their ease with me. I planned to draw on the legendary uncanny ability of mothers to ferret out information. But the "omniscient mother" as interviewer kept me locked into a perspective, into strategies of power from which I had to move away. This "extorting information model" offered few surprises.

I had underestimated the enormous chasm of power that separated grown-ups and young people. For one thing, question and answer is the customary form of communicative exchange between powerful and powerless, between adult and child. The young, especially, under the circumstances of being interviewed by an outsider are guarded, cautious. They have been taught to be suspicious of strangers. They have usually learned that almost anything they say can be the "wrong" answer, can get them into trouble. Boys who were already marked as troublesome were often anxious to present themselves in as positive a light as possible. They wanted me to be aware that they knew what was "right" and "wrong" in the context of school. In spite of my pledge prior to the taped interview that what they said would be confidential, they could not be absolutely sure that they could trust me. Why should they? They were in the position of guarding not only themselves but also families and friends from my scrutiny. The interview format also contravened the code against "telling" that adults seek to undermine in the name of "truth." As an interviewer, I too, was asking them to "tell."

Who and where I was in my own life acted both as a barrier and a facilitator to making meaning of their lives. I was an older black woman, not a youth, not male; yet, my life as a graduate student helped to freshen my memory of what it meant to be a "child" in a world of total and arbitrary "adult" power. To be a graduate student was to be "infantilized." I had returned to graduate school after years of working as a teacher, as a social worker, as a university administrator. I had mothered. But the hierarchy of knowledge in the university was one in which my accumulated knowledge counted for nothing; I was expected to start as if I were a blank slate on which would be written the theories, ways of understanding the world that were gleaned from "approved" texts. In seminars, I found that discussions of work, mothering, bureaucracy, and organizations deliberately excluded the personal experience of those around the table from what was considered appropriate, admissible data. Those students who drew on life experience in seminars quickly learned that scholarly discussion moved on over this offering as if it never occurred. I learned that experience was a shameful burden of knowledge acquired "practically," every day, rather than "theoretically" from a distance. This erasure of a particular form of knowing the world by the academy was one aspect of my present life that helped me to listen more respectfully to the children's talk than I might have otherwise. Moreover, it opened me up to consider how the knowledge, experience, and forms of expression that were brought into school by the group of kids that I was studying were excluded.

Research Assistance: Introducing Horace

But it was fundamentally through my relationship with twelve-year-old Horace that I began to be conscious that my research agenda was focused on learning about boys rather than from them. I was assigned to be Horace's tutor in the after-school program the first semester of my fieldwork. Though I wanted to get to know one of the boys "getting in trouble," I worried about whether I would be able to "handle" him. My anxiety had been raised by the reputation he had among school adults as a boy who was difficult and out of control. Horace's name had become the standard against which other children would be judged. For example, in a faculty meeting discussion of another African American boy at the school, Horace's name was invoked as the norm. The adult said, "That child's a problem, but he's not a Horace."

In spite of the bad press that he had gotten from the school adults and my anxiety about working with him, we got along well. I often found him exasperatingly determined to control the conditions of his after-school tutoring sessions. But I recognized that he was leaning on the side of "humanizing" our relationship, while I was bent on making our time together as "productive" as possible. I was out to "teach" him something. He was carefully laying out, testing, and undermining the original terms of our relationship, in which I had all the power and respect and he had none. With his help, I came to see kids not as humans-in-the-making but as resourceful social actors who took an active role in shaping their daily experiences. I began to recognize and appreciate the stresses and strains they faced and the strategies they devised for negotiating and maneuvering within structures of power.

Over the weeks and months that I got to know Horace, I pieced together a shifting portrait of how he was seen by others: his teachers, the student specialists, the principals, his mother and siblings; and how he saw himself. I also listened carefully to the stories Horace told me about what was going on in his life as well as his analysis of relationships in and out of school.

These stories and the time Horace and I spent together confirmed what I had suspected, had gotten glimpses of through observation in the school, through interviews with some of the boys' families. Those who were classified as lazy, belligerent, incorrigible at school could be respectful, diligent, and responsible in other contexts. Horace, who was characterized by school as "volatile," "insubordinate," was also described by others who knew him in different contexts as "a team player," "affectionate," "great with kids." From my observation of Horace, I could see that he tested, resisted, and defied the authority of certain adults. But it became clear that he was also conforming, obedient, and deeply focused in other contexts in school and out.

At the end of my first year of fieldwork at Rosa Parks, I asked Horace to be my research assistant during the summer vacation to help me put together the topics for my interviews with the other boys. He turned out to be an excellent guide to issues on young boys' minds with a remarkable "sociological eye." He saw patterns, relationships, contradictions, and disjunctures. Horace helped me decide—I might say he insisted—on the themes for the interviews I later conducted with the other boys. He was quick to let me know when he thought I was beating a topic to death or asking a question to which the answer seemed obvious. He interviewed *me* on issues such as mothering, school, and money.

Most important of all, he pointed out that I would learn nothing about his peers and himself if I didn't listen to their music. So I tuned in to their favorite radio station listening to the rap music, the DJ talk, the phone-in calls that weaved them together. I listened to the commercials, the advice, the attitudes that were being dished out. I began watching music videos. I became familiar with the names and works of contemporary popular rap artists such as Ice Cube, Ice T, Paris, Naughty by Nature, Pooh Man, Snoop Doggy Dog, Dr. Dre, Queen Latifah, Monie Love, Salt 'n' Pepa. I found that rap lyrics and the accompanying visual images, though sometimes offensive and shocking, and almost ritualistically misogynist, were also witty, ribald, catchy, and often sharpened by a measure of social criticism and political commentary. I was delighted to find that the lyrics articulated some of the very ironies and contradictions that I myself observed as a researcher. I have selected some examples of these as epigraphs to introduce and set the tone for several chapters of this book.

My introduction to this music opened up a cultural space to me that was far more rich and critically innovative than I had expected; it was more than the background noise and mindless escape of the music of my own youth that reproduced simple hegemonic notions of romance and power. Instead, I discovered a potent alternative site of knowledge for youth about bodies and beauty, sexuality, gender relationships, racial identification, authority, justice and injustice, loyalty and friendship, style and address, transmitted through a vehicle that simultaneously engaged pleasure and fantasy.

My brief and intense exposure to and growing familiarity with this cultural production was an indispensable element in alerting me to some key sources that the boys drew on for self-fashioning. Two of these are especially significant for this work. First, as I listened to the music, heard the lyrics, watched the images, I became conscious of the highly controversial, embattled figure of the "gangsta" in gangster rap. Rather than the stigmatized figure of the criminal feared by members of society, the gangster in rap music and videos was a heroic medium for articulating the tragic realities of urban poverty as well as the dangers, pleasures, and privileges of being male. This image led me to consider the multiple ways of incorporating authority figures, rules and laws, transgressive acts and consequences into a worldview. Second, I became aware that the alternative, critical discourse and heightened consciousness about race and racism that some kids brought to school was reflected in the lyrics and images of rap music.

Race Signifies

A structuring element of this text is an examination and analysis of the continuing significance of "race" as a system for organizing social difference and as a device for reproducing inequality in contemporary United States.[17] Race continues to be a ready-made filter for interpreting events, informing social interactions, and grounding identities and identification in school. One racial interpretation infusing several boys' accounts of the school day was that African American boys were singled out for punishment because of their race.

This claim was especially provocative because school adults were visibly uneasy about, and committed to, avoiding public discussions of race that went beyond a recitation of desegregation demographics. While several kids raised the issue of how race made a difference in their experience of school, the adults typically limited their talk about race to matters of numbers and distributions. Officially, race existed in school as the baseline category for classifying and distributing kids throughout the system and into classrooms, but beyond that the public consensus among adults was that distinctions of race were of no further significance. The working assumption was that racial discrimination had come to an end with school desegregation; that in its everyday operations school was race-blind to the differences that had led to the need for busing in the first place. In relation to this study, the position was that children were sent to the Punishing Room not because of who they were, but because of what they did. The institutional discourse was that getting in trouble was not about race but a matter of individual choice and personal responsibility: each child made a choice to be "good" or "bad." The homily "The Choice is Yours" was printed at the top of the list of school rules to emphasize this connection.

However, this discourse of "individual choice" was undercut by a more covert, secretive conversation about race that circulated primarily among African American adults in the school that presumed race to be a continuing force in determining the outcome for children. In public, school people seemed to subscribe to explanations that the "at-riskness" of children was a consequence of apathetic or dysfunctional families; but in private conversations and interviews, black teachers and staff hinted that race, gender, and class made a significant difference in a child's experience of school. They suggested that certain boys got picked on because they were black and came from the neighborhood; that white teachers didn't know how to discipline black kids; that white teachers were "intimidated" by black boys; that some African American teachers had problems working with the neighborhood children, almost all of whom were black and poor. In several of these conversations, individuals seemed to be egging me on to pursue the saliency of race to the phenomena over which I was puzzling.

To jump to the conclusion that racism is a significant component of the problem is, in fact, not all that far-fetched. Up to 1968, when Arcadia schools were desegregated, the observation that black children were being treated differently from white children would have been a mere statement of fact. Racial discrimination sanctioned by law and by custom was the norm across the United States in every sphere. The Arcadia School District had, as did the vast majority of school districts across the United States, an official policy of racial segregation that applied not only to children, but to teachers as well.[18] Race made a vast difference in the treatment that was afforded to black and white students. Segregated schools were organized on the assumption that white students were entitled to a better education than black students. Black children were not being educated to compete with whites for jobs in the adult world of work. Memories of this injustice is still very much alive at Rosa Parks School among faculty and staff. Cyril Wilkins, the African American custodian at Rosa Parks, and a product of Arcadia schools, reminded me of this when he recalled applying for a job as a bus driver in Arcadia in the 1960s and having his application form crumpled up and tossed into a wastebasket right before his eyes by the white man in charge of hiring because those jobs were not open to black people.

Cyril Wilkins's personal experience is a vivid reminder of how the ways for maintaining racial hierarchies in the United States have changed over the past generation as a result of political struggle. The marking of the boundaries of racial difference and the form that racism takes has varied according to the specific social relations and historical context in which they are embedded. Legal and open institutional endorsement of racial discrimination was dismantled as a consequence of the Civil Rights Movement that culminated in the 1960s. Disqualification on the basis of race in the blatant manner that Wilkins describes is now illegal. Yet, in spite of this profound legislative change, "race" continues to be a significant mode for the distribution of power in the society.[19]

For purposes of this study, we need to be aware of two ways that racial inequalities are reproduced today. One is through institutional practices, and the other is through cultural representations of racial difference. Both operate in a covert and informal manner. *Bad Boys* is a study of these two modes: how institutional norms and procedures in the field of education are used to maintain a racial order, and how images and racial myths frame how we see ourselves and others in a racial hierarchy.

Institutional practices continue to marginalize or exclude African Americans in the economy and society through the exercise of rules and purportedly objective standards by individuals who may consider themselves racially unbiased.[20] Punishment is a fruitful site for a close-up look at routine institutional practices, individual acts, and cultural sanctions that give life and power to racism in a school setting that not only produces massive despair and failure among black students, but that increasingly demonizes them.

In this contemporary racial formation the category of race has increasingly been defined through cultural rather than biological difference.[21] Relations of power and inequality are explained as the demonstrated consequence of superior or pathological cultural characteristics. Attitudes, values, behaviors, familial and community practices become the field from which social distinctions derive. Black people, in this form of racism, can only redress their condition by rejecting the cultural modes that make them "different." So, in the school setting, it is assumed that it is the cultural difference kids bring to school that produces the existing pattern of punishment rather than institutional operations themselves.[22] Since a good part of the ideological work of race is to fix meanings and relationships as natural and durable, the racialization of cultural forms and practices not only extracts behaviors and attitudes from the social matrix in which they are embedded but transforms them into immutable racially linked characteristics that produce poverty and bad citizens.

Two cultural images stigmatize black males in the United States today: one represents him as a criminal, and the other depicts him as an endangered species. I found that both of these images were commonly invoked at Rosa Parks School for identifying, classifying, and making punishment decisions by the adults responsible for disciplining the kids.

It is important that we understand human culture differently—not as a set of immutable characteristics that seem to be transmitted through the genes but as a practical, active, creative response to specific social and historical conditions. As such, culture can be a significant mode of defense, of succor, of resistance and recuperation for those with few sources of power in society. A good illustration of this, which I elaborate on in the text, is the way that African American boys use language brought from home and community as a form of self-protection and asserting a group identification in opposition to school.

An example of the multiple meanings and contradictory uses of culture and of cultural representation developed in this study is the way in which a national event acts as a catalyst to both mark "otherness" and heighten racial self-definition. The videotaped beating of Rodney King by Los Angeles police, the trial and acquittal of the men charged with the attack, and the subsequent riots in Los Angeles occurred during my research. Students reacted visibly and vocally to the racism and public discourse emanating from the events. In this way race came into the school to create cultural and racial awareness. School adults, at the same time, drew on the spectacular events as a framework for evaluating the behavior of black kids. This national outpouring also made visible to me the way that traumatic and emotionally disturbing events outside of school directly contributed to children's anger and troubling behavior in school and how unwilling our society is to deal with issues of race as a real, divisive, social problem.

I have organized the text to reflect certain theoretical and methodological considerations of my research. One aim is to join the debate about the relative significance of social structure and personal agency in explaining human behavior.[23] As I was engaged in this project, I found stimulating and compelling arguments on both sides of this discussion.[24] I have found it rewarding to utilize both approaches to demonstrate the interplay between the determining effects of social structure and the creative response of individuals in everyday life that usually reproduces a status quo, but that sometimes produces change. Punishment is an especially fruitful site for this demonstration, as it is a space where educational structures clash with the resistance strategies of individual students. My conviction is, however, that the balance tilts heavily in favor of structural determinants.

The text is, therefore, designed to reveal this interaction between institutional and individual forces. There are two parts. The first part emphasizes structure. In this part I describe and analyze the disciplinary system of the school and the practices of labeling and categorization that construct the boys as individuals with behavioral problems. The second part foregrounds the meaningful actions of individuals as I present the school day from the youths' perspective. Here, I explore how kids recoup a sense of self as competent and worthy under extremely discouraging work conditions. Sadly, they do this by getting in trouble.

Another goal is to elaborate through practical application the theoretical work that challenges the use of the categories of race, class, and gender, as if they are isolated and independent social locations.[25] My analysis foregrounds the technologies of representation of subjects and the experience of subjectivity as a complex, dynamic interaction of race and gender. Sex is a powerful marker of difference as well as race. While the concept of intersecting social categories is a useful analytical device for formulating this convergence, in reality we presume to know each other instantly in a coherent, apparently seamless way. We do not experience individuals as bearers of separate identities, as gendered and then as raced or vice versa, but as both at once. The two are inextricably intertwined and circulate together in the representations of subjects and the experience of subjectivity. Though the racial etiquette of today's form of racism has sent a discourse of racial difference underground, it piggybacks on our beliefs about sex difference in the construction of images. I explore the specific way that black boys are constituted as different from boys-in-general by virtue of the sexing of racial meaning.

I have also structured the text along methodological lines to suggest the interplay between the "raw" form of the data that I collected and my own interpretive and analytical authorial work in framing the documentary evidence as one thing rather than another. Interspersed between the chapters is an example of the types of data that I drew on as I pulled together the strands that became this story: self-reflexive musings, transcriptions of interviews, primary source materials, field notes. These documents are, of course, not mere "examples," but are intentionally chosen to illustrate or to strengthen points that I make in the chapters themselves. Several of these seem to speak for themselves with the richly detailed, complex, often contradictory subjective voices that are the fabric out of which the ethnographer as storyteller tailors a coherent account. I have tried as much as possible to leave these complexities and contradictions in so that you, the reader, can more consciously participate in the critical work of interpretation.

Notes

1. This research was assisted by an award from the Social Science Research Council through funding provided by the Rockefeller Foundation. The names of the city, school, and individuals in this ethnography are fictitious in order to preserve the anonymity of participants.

2. Punishment resulted in suspension 20 percent of the time. Records show that in 1991–92, 250 students, or almost half of the children at Rosa Parks School, were sent to the Punishing Room by adults for breaking school rules, for a total of 1,252 journeys. This figure is based on my count of referral forms kept on file in the Punishing Room. However, it by no means represents the total number of students referred by teachers for discipline. I observed a number of instances where children came into the Punishing Room but the problem was settled by the student specialist on the spot and no paperwork was generated. This seemed especially likely to occur when the adult referring the child had written an informal note rather than on the official referral form, when a parent did not have to be called, or when the infraction was judged by the student specialist to be insignificant. So it is likely that a much larger number of children were sent to the Punishing Room over the year but no record was made as a result of the visit.

3. "Survey: Schools Suspend Blacks More," *Detroit Free Press*, December 14, 1988, 4A; Joan Richardson, "Study Puts Michigan 6th in Student Suspensions," *Detroit Free Press*, August 21, 1990, 1A; Minnesota Department of Children, Families and Learning, *Student Suspension and Expulsion: Report to the Legislature* (St. Paul: Minnesota Department of Children, Families and Learning, 1996); Commission for Positive Change in the Oakland Public Schools, *Keeping Children in Schools: Sounding the Alarm on Suspensions* (Oakland, Calif.: The Commission, 1992), 1; and John D. Hull, "Do Teachers Punish according to Race?" *Time*, April 4, 1994, 30–31.

4. In Oakland, while 28 percent of students in the system were African American males, they accounted for 53 percent of the suspensions. See note 3 for racial imbalance in corporal punishment in Michigan schools ("Survey: Schools Suspend Blacks More"), and the racial discipline gap in Cincinnati (Hull, "Do Teachers Punish?").

5. The one who was not black had a Hispanic surname.

6. Children are bused in from areas of the city that are vastly different in terms of their social and economic characteristics. I compared 1990 census data from two of the most affluent census tracts from which children are bused (Midland and the Highlands) to data from the tract in which the school is located (Heartland). Heartland has a median family income of $20,192, while Midland has a median family income of $66,234, and that of the Highlands is $97,315. Heartland has the highest percentage of blacks and the lowest percentage of whites, while the reverse is true for the Highlands. Race is therefore an excellent predictor of whether a child comes from a family with limited resources. Children in Heartland are also more likely to be living in female-headed households than those bused in. Sixty-one percent of children under eighteen years in Heartland live in female-headed households, compared with 27 percent for Midland and 8 percent for the Highlands. This is significant because female-headed households in the United States are more likely to be poverty households than married-couple households. This is true of Heartland, where women head three-quarters of the families living below the poverty level. Households headed by females in Heartland had a mean income of $15,150 per year, compared to $38,306 for those of married couples. In the Highlands, however, the mean income of female-headed households is $54,388, and those headed by married couples averaged $153,828 annually.

7. About half of the kids in the school are eligible for the subsidized lunch program, while just over one-third come from families that receive AFDC. Almost all of these are neighborhood kids.

8. Arcadia Schools Enrichment Office, "Comparative Racial Census of the Arcadia School District, Grade K–12," 1991.

9. Diana Walsh, "Money Isn't the Only Factor in School Choice," *San Francisco Examiner*, March 7, 1993, 13.

10. There were twenty white, nine African American, and three Asian American teachers, of whom only three classroom teachers were male, one of whom was African American.

11. See, for example, Alex Kotlowitz, *There Are No Children Here* (New York: Doubleday, 1991), and Jonathan Kozol, *Savage Inequalities: Children in America's Schools* (New York: HarperCollins, 1991).

12. Arcadia Police Department statistics as reported in a PALS document.

13. There were twenty-seven children, ten girls and seventeen boys, in Mrs. Daly's class. Fifteen of the children were African American, six were white, three were Hispanic, and three were of Asian descent.

14. The student specialists also turned over to me the referral forms from 1992–93 at the end of the school year. I organized the data from the forms according to grade, race, gender, type of infraction, punishment, and noted any comments by teachers.

15. About half of the kids in the school are eligible for the subsidized lunch program, while just over a third come from families that receive AFDC. Almost all of these students are from the Heartland (see note 7).

16. This pattern is replicated in the 1990 census data for the neighborhood in which a majority of the families are mother-headed households. This is in contrast to the children, mostly white, who are bused to the school from neighborhoods in which the vast majority of the families are two-parent households.

17. I use the concept of race not to mark off essential, fixed differences between groups of humans but to refer to a socially constructed category of human difference and division whose boundaries and meanings have changed over time, but which always is a mechanism for the unequal distribution and allocation of social goods and status. This category, though a social fiction, because it is politically motivated has serious, real consequences for individuals and for social life.

18. No black teacher taught in an Arcadia district white school until the late 1960s.

19. For examples of this in the realm of housing see Douglas S. Massey and Nancy A. Denton, *American Apartheid: Segregation and the Making of the Underclass* (Cambridge: Harvard University Press, 1993); in schooling see Kozol, *Savage Inequalities;* for an overview of some recent studies in business, see chapter 5 of Joe Feagin and Melvin Sikes, *Living with Racism: The Black Middle-Class Experience* (Boston: Beacon Press, 1994).

20. The concept of institutional racism as distinct from individual prejudice and bigotry was elaborated on by Stokely Carmichael and Charles V. Hamilton in *Black Power: The Politics of Liberation in America* (New York: Vintage Press, 1967). On page 5 they argued that "institutional racism relies on the active and pervasive operation of anti-black attitudes and practices. A sense of superior group position prevails: whites are 'better' than blacks; therefore blacks should be subordinated to whites. . . . 'Respectable' individuals can absolve themselves from individual blame: *they* would never plant a bomb in the church; *they* would never stone a black family. But they continue to support political officials and institutions that would and do perpetuate institutionally racist policies. Thus *acts* of overt, individual racism may not typify the society, but institutional racism does—with the support of covert, individual *attitudes* of racism." See also Thomas Pettigrew, ed., *Racial Discrimination in the United States* (New York: Harper and Row, 1975), x, for the following description: "racial discrimination is basically an institutional process of exclusion against an outgroup on largely ascribed and particularistic grounds of group membership rather than on achieved and universalistic grounds of merit."

21. For discussion of historical changes in the racial formation in the United States see Michael Omi and Howard Winant, *Racial Formation in the United States: From the 1960s to the 1980s* (New York: Routledge and Kegan Paul, 1986). Paul Gilroy's work provides important parallels with racial formation in Britain. See, for example, Paul Gilroy, *Small Acts: Thoughts on the Politics of Black Culture* (New York: Serpent's Tail, 1993).

22. An example of this connection between race and culture and how it is used in understanding school trouble is found in the article about the Cincinnati schools by Hull, "Do Teachers Punish?" Teachers and administrators explained the disproportionate number of African Americans who were suspended by stating that "blacks tend to be more boisterous," "black students are much more trouble prone," and "some black males are more physical."

23. For an excellent summary of these positions see chapter 2 of Jay MacLeod, *Ain't No Making It: Leveled Aspirations in a Low-Income Neighborhood* (Boulder, Colo.: Westview Press, 1987); Stanley Aronowitz and Henry A. Giroux, *Education under Siege: The Conservative, Liberal, and Radical Debate over Schooling* (South Hadley, Mass.: Bergen and Garvey, 1985).

24. On the structural determinist side I found the following works most persuasive and insightful: Pierre Bourdieu and Jean-Claude Passeron, *Reproduction in Education, Society, and Culture,* trans. Richard Nice (Beverly Hills: Sage, 1977); Samuel Bowles and Herbert Gintis, *Schooling in Capitalist America: Educational Reform and the Contradictions of Economic Life* (New York: Basic Books, 1976). Some of the work that stressed personal agency and the creative insights and oppositional responses of subjects that I found important included that of Patricia Hill Collins and of John Ogbu. See for example, Patricia Hill Collins, *Black Feminist Thought: Knowledge, Consciousness, and the Politics of Empowerment* (Boston: Unwin Hyman, 1990); and John U. Ogbu, "Class Stratification, Racial Stratification, and Schooling," in *Class, Race, and Gender in American Educational Research: Toward a Nonsynchronous Parallelist Position,* ed. Lois Weis (Albany: State University of New York Press, 1988). The work that most inspired my own thinking in the early phases of my research was that which stressed the active cultural production of resistance and opposition: Paul Willis, *Learning to Labor: How Working Class Kids Get Working Class Jobs* (New York: Columbia University Press, 1977); and Paul Willis, "Cultural Production Is Different from Cultural Reproduction Is Different from Social Reproduction Is Different from Reproduction," *Interchange* 12, nos. 2–3 (1981).

25. For example, see Rose M. Brewer, "Theorizing Race, Class, and Gender: The New Scholarship of Black Feminist Intellectuals and Black Women's Labor," in *Theorizing Black Feminisms: The Visionary Pragmatism of Black Women,*

ed. Stanlie M. James and Abena P. A. Busia (New York: Routledge, 1993). For a discussion and application of the concept of "intersectionality," see Kimberle Crenshaw, "Beyond Racism and Misogyny: Black Feminism and 2 Live Crew," in *Words That Wound: Critical Race Theory, Assaultive Speech, and the First Amendment*, ed. Mari J. Matsuda et al. (Boulder, Colo.: Westview Press, 1993).

Section Three
On Telling

21

The Colonizer/Colonized Chicana Ethnographer
Identity, Marginalization, and Co-optation in the Field
Sofia Villenas

It is not easy to name our pain, to theorize from that location.

hooks (1994, p. 74)

Like a "mojado" [wetback] ethnographer, I attempt to cross the artificial borders into occupied academic territories, searching for a "coyote" [smuggler] to secure a safe passage.

E. G. Murillo Jr. (personal communication, 1995)

What happens when members of low-status and marginalized groups become university-sanctioned "native" ethnographers of their own communities? How is this "native" ethnographer positioned vis-à-vis her own community, the majority culture, the research setting, and the academy? While qualitative researchers in the field of education theorize about their own privilege in relation to their research participants, the "native" ethnographer must deal with her own marginalizing experiences and identities in relation to dominant society. This "native" ethnographer is potentially both the colonizer, in her university cloak, and the colonized, as a member of the very community that is made "other" in her research.

I am this "native" ethnographer in the field of education, a first-generation Chicana born in Los Angeles of immigrant parents from Ecuador. Geographically, politically, and economically, I have lived under the same yoke of colonization as the Chicano communities I study, experiencing the same discrimination and alienation from mainstream society that comes from being a member of a caste "minority."[1] I share the same ethnic consciousness and regional and linguistic experiences. The commonly used terms "Hispanic" and "Latino" do not adequately describe who I am.[2] Racially and ethnically I am *indigena*, a detribalized Native American woman, descendant of the Quechua-speaking people of the South American Andes. Politically I am a Chicana, born and raised in the American Southwest, in the legendary territories of Aztlan.[3] This story is about how these identities came into play in the process of conducting research with an emerging Latino community located in the U.S. South.

The Colonizer/Colonized Dilemma

Rethinking the political and personal subjectivities of researcher and ethnographer has in recent times pushed the boundaries of theorizing about the multiple identities of the researcher within the research context of privilege and power. Qualitative researchers in education have called for a reexamination of the raced, gendered, aged, and classed positions of the researcher with respect to the research participants (Fine, 1994; Lather, 1991; Roman & Apple, 1990). These researchers are also recognizing that they are and have been implicated in imperialist agendas (Pratt, 1986; Rosaldo, 1989) by participating in "othering" (Fine, 1994) and in the exploitation and domination of their research subjects (Roman & Apple, 1990).[4]

In the last decade, ethnographers and qualitative researchers have illuminated the ways in which the researched are colonized and exploited. By objectifying the subjectivities of the researched, by assuming authority, and by not questioning their own privileged positions (Crapanzano, 1986; Fine, 1994; Rosaldo, 1989; Van Galen & Eaker, 1995), ethnographers have participated as colonizers of the researched. Rosaldo (1989) uses the image of the "Lone Ethnographer" who once upon a time "rode off into the sunset in search of his 'natives' " (p. 30). After undergoing arduous fieldwork as his rite of passage, the Lone Ethnographer "returned home to write a 'true' account of the culture" (p. 30). In the texts of classic anthropology, people were depicted as "members of a harmonious, internally homogeneous and unchanging culture" (p. 31), and written about in a way that "normalizes life by describing social activities as if they were always repeated in the same manner by everyone in the group" (p. 42). Rosaldo reminds us that this manner of objectifying people's lives has been the classic norm of ethnography, and that researchers have rarely asked what the researched think about how their lives are being interpreted and described in text.

Researchers are also implicated as colonizers when they claim authenticity of interpretation and description under the guise of authority. In a critique of Geertz's description of the Balinese cockfight, Crapanzano (1986) exposes the ways in which the event described is subverted and sacrificed to "a literary discourse that is far removed from the indigenous discourse of their occurrence" (p. 76). This discourse, according to Crapanzano, is ultimately masked by the authority of the author, "who at least in much ethnography, stands above and behind those whose experiences he purports to describe" (p. 76).

As ethnographers, we are also like colonizers when we fail to question our own identities and privileged positions, and in the ways in which our writings perpetuate "othering." As Fine (1994) explains:

> When we write essays about subjugated Others as if *they* were a homogeneous mass (of vice or virtue), free-floating and severed from contexts of oppression, and as if we were neutral transmitters of voices and stories, we tilt toward a narrative strategy that reproduces Othering on, despite, or even "for." (1994, p. 74)

Moreover, we are like colonizers when, as Van Galen and Eaker (1995) point out, the professional and intellectual gatekeeping structures (e.g., university admissions to graduate studies, journal publication referees) from which we gain our legitimacy and privilege remain "highly inaccessible to those on whose behalf we claim to write" (p. 114).

For example, women teachers of working-class backgrounds are expected to consume a body of literature that emanates from elite universities from which they are excluded, and that thus excludes them from the production of material used for the teaching profession and their own training. Fine (1994) and Van Galen and Eaker (1995) urge ethnographers to probe the nature of their relationship to those they write about.

While we continue to push the borders of the multiple, decentered, and politicized self as researcher, we continue to analyze and write about *ourselves* in a unidirectional manner as imperialist researchers (Rosaldo, 1989) and colonizers (Fine, 1994) in relation to the research participants. Yet, what about the researcher as colonizer *and* colonized? Here is my own dilemma: as a Chicana graduate student in a White institution and an educational ethnographer of Latino communities, I am both, as well as in between the two. I am the coloniz*ed* in relation to the greater society, to the institution of higher learning, and to the dominant majority culture in the research setting. I am the coloniz*er* because I am the educated, "marginalized" researcher, recruited and sanctioned by privileged dominant institutions to write for and about Latino communities. I am a walking contradiction with a foot in both worlds—in the dominant privileged institutions *and* in the marginalized communities. Yet, I possess my own agency and will to promote my own and the collective agendas of particular Latino communities. I did not even consider the multiplicity of self and identity and the nuances of what such consideration meant until I had to confront my own marginality as a Chicana researcher in relation to the dominant majority culture in the research setting. In the research context of power and domination, I encountered what it means to examine closely within myself the intersectedness of race, class, gender, and other conceptual notions of identity.

I am a Chicana doctoral student, and have been conducting research in a small rural community in North Carolina, which I have named Hope City. My research project involved the educational life histories of Latina mothers who were recent immigrants to Hope City. In the telling of their stories, the women defined education—how they experienced it in their lives as learners and teachers in families, communities, and schools, and how they constructed educational models for raising their own children. I spent over two years in Hope City, teaching English as a Second Language (ESL) at the local community college and in an after-school tutorial program for elementary-school-age Spanish-speaking children. I participated in family social gatherings, and in community and church events and meetings. I also had a lot of contact with the English-speaking community of professionals who were servicing Latino families in health care and education, joining them in meetings and informal gatherings. These professionals were also formally interviewed by other colleagues involved in the Hope City project. As a team, we were funded by a child development center to investigate the beliefs about education held by the agencies and schools serving the Hope City Latino community, and by the diverse Latino community members themselves. In my own research, I systematically analyzed the public sphere and the organization of relations of power in Hope City. Through a historiographic analysis of the town's newspaper and through my observations and participant observations within the community of school and agency professionals, I found that the Latino community in Hope City was being framed as a "problem."

At the beginning of the research project, I was aware of the politics and privilege of my researcher role and my relation to the research participants. I was eager to experience the process of constructing meaning with the research participants. By talking with these Latina mothers about their beliefs and philosophies of child-rearing and education, as well as my own, I hoped to engage them in conversations about how they could create a dignified space for themselves and their families in a previously biracial community that was not accustomed to Latinos. I had vague ideas about community projects that I hoped would emerge from the research participants themselves. When I reflected later, these notions seemed arrogant, as if I thought I knew the hopes and aspirations of this Latino community. I realized I had to question all my assumptions about this southern Latino community, such as defining as problems certain aspects of their lives that, to them, were not problematic at all. I was certainly ready to learn from this Latino community, but in the process of seeking to reform my relationship with them, I failed to notice that I was being repositioned and co-opted by the dominant English-speaking community to legitimate their discourse of "Latinos as problem." In the course of working with Hope City's non-Latino school and service professionals, I discovered that while I engaged in a rethinking of my own politics and the processes of empowerment within the Latino community, I was hiding my own marginality in relation to the majority culture. I did not know then that I would have to scrutinize my own lived experiences as a Chicana daughter, mother, wife, and student in confronting the dominant community's discourses of "othering" and of difference.

In this article, I attempt to heed Fine's words in "unearthing the blurred boundaries between Self and Other" (1994, p. 72). Weis (1995) summarizes the discourse on colonialism, which takes as its central point the idea that the colonial "other" and the self (read the "Western White" self) are simultaneously co-constructed, the first being judged against the latter. Furthermore, Weis notes, "this process of 'othering' is key to understanding relations of domination and subordination, historically and currently" (p. 18). This article, then, speaks to the discourses of "othering" that jolted me out of my perceived unproblematic identity and role as a Chicana researcher in education, and into a co-construction of the "Western" self and the Chicana "other." This ongoing story involves my confrontation with my contradictory identities—as a Chicana researcher in the power structures of the dominant discourse of "other," and as a Chicana working with this marginalized Latino community. Through this story, I hope to recontextualize the ways in which qualitative researchers in education have theorized about identity and privilege to include the repositioning and manipulation of identities that can occur, particularly with native ethnographers. This recontextualization problematizes the ways in which qualitative researchers who seek to analyze privilege and the "situatedness" of each ethnographer fail to note that we as ethnographers of education are not all the same "We" in the literature of privileged ethnographers. My standpoint as a Chicana and my historical relation to Latino communities mediate and complicate my "privilege." Unveiling the ways in which the ethnographer is situated in oppressive structures is a critical task for qualitative researchers in the field of education. Even in new positions of privilege, the Chicana ethnographer cannot escape a history of her own marginalization nor her guilt of complicity.

Personal History

My encounter with discourses of difference and of "othering" as a child in Los Angeles neighborhoods and schools intensified my scrutinization of my own identity and role as a Chicana in academia. Growing up in Los Angeles, I was aware of racism. As a child, I acted out the effects of colonization, refusing to speak Spanish, emphasizing that I was South American and not Mexican, as Mexicans were relegated to second-class citizenship. I grew up knowing that my culture and language were not valued, but I did not suffer direct, blatant racism. I found safety in numbers, as there were many other Latinas, Chicanas, and Mexicans with whom I could hang out.

As I grew older, our peer group continually created and celebrated our Chicano/Latino cultures and languages. As an adult, I thought I had overcome the loss of self that comes with second-class relegation of the Spanish language and Latino cultures, and that I did not speak with the voice of a colonized person, one whose culture and language were devalued. Yet I was not as prepared for Eurocentric academia as I thought I was. In community, I had learned to manipulate my identities successfully and did not expect them to be manipulated by others. But such a manipulation is precisely what occurred when I began my professional university training in ethnographic research. At the university, I experienced the dilemma of creating my identity as a Chicana researcher in the midst of Eurocentric discourses of "other." Being an ethnographer made my contradictory position more obvious, complex, and ironic. I recognize this contradiction now, but at the university, the discourse of "othering" did not begin with my research study.

An awakening of sorts occurred for me when I attended a seminar on topics in education. On that particular day, the topic was whether public single-population schools should exist. The readings for that week centered on public and private schools for women only, for gays and lesbians, and schools based on Afrocentric or Chicano-centric curriculum. Most of my fellow classmates argued that people should not be separated, reasoning that students should be integrated so that everybody could come together to talk about societal inequities and find solutions together. They argued that single population schools promoted separatism, and that through integrated schools, the Eurocentric curricula would be challenged. While I agreed that all people need to dialogue about oppression and work together to bring about social justice, and therefore was in favor of integrated schools, I did not agree that Afrocentric or Chicano-centric curricula and schools promoted separatism. In trying to engage in the discussion, however, I began to feel uncomfortable. I tried to explain why I felt that disenfranchised groups had the right to these curricula if they wanted them and, furthermore, why I felt they were important and necessary. I argued that people who have been stripped of their cultures through public schooling need to come together and reclaim their cultures, histories, and languages, but although I believed this, I was nevertheless buying into the discourse of fear of separatism, saying that we needed to have separate spaces before coming together to be a part of the larger group. Of course, implicit in this argument was the idea that as people of color, we were going "to come together" to join the dominant culture and integrate ourselves within it, rather than challenge the notion of a single common culture.

The discourse of this group of fellow students and friends was so powerful that it disabled me. I explained my stance apologetically, acquiescing to the notion that we would have to come back and join a mainstream culture and society rather than challenge it. Everyone else was speaking as if they were detached and removed from the topic, rationalizing the logic of their arguments, but it was different for me. The topic was personal and deeply embedded in my experiences. In this conversation, I was not the subject anymore but the object, the "other." Using Cornell West's words, hooks (1990) writes that people often engage in debates that "highlight notions of difference, marginality, and 'otherness' in such a way that it further marginalizes actual people of difference and otherness" (p. 125). hooks likens these debates to reinscribing patterns of colonization: "When this happens . . . the 'Other' is always made object, appropriated, interpreted, taken over by those in power, by those who dominate" (1990, p. 125).

In this same manner, I felt that my experiences as a Latina going through the Eurocentric curriculum of public schools was being objectified and appropriated through a rationalized logical argument against Chicano- or Afrocentric schools. In the rational, logical arguments in that seminar, no space existed for my deeply passionate personal experience and voice, for me to argue for the right to choose to be with Latinas/os, for us to be educated together and to center our curriculum in our diverse roots and history, to find out about ourselves and to claim ourselves in our own terms. My classmates and I talked against oppressed groups coming together to form their own schools in a way that ignored the existence of race, class, and gender privileges among the class participants. In this discussion, an aura of disinterested, detached, scientific rationalism existed that rendered me voiceless and silenced. Ellsworth (1989) describes the oppression of rational argument as putting as its opposite the irrational "other"—for example, women and people of color. In schools, she said, the rational argument has become the "vehicle for regulating conflict and the power to speak" (p. 303).

After the group dispersed, I was left feeling stripped of my identity and angry with myself for betraying my own voice. I had fallen into the trap of the dominant discourse, trying to convince the group not to worry, that we would eventually come around to integrating ourselves. But into what? I did not know, but it was implied that we would integrate ourselves into some core set of shared social and cultural ideals and belief systems, a core that evidently was the White, middle-class lifestyle. I was reminded again of Ellsworth's (1989) critique of critical pedagogy. She argues that the dialogue emphasized in critical pedagogy assumes that we could all engage in dialogue equally as if we were not raced, gendered, and classed persons with vested interests and different experiences. The seminar participants (including myself) failed to see how, in the process of discussing people of color, we silenced and marginalized the very voices of those who were supposed to have been the subjects and authors of their experiences—the voices of fellow Chicana and African American classmates.

I now realize that something else also occurred that afternoon in our seminar. The topic, as well as the disinterested, detached way in which the discussion was carried out, fueled what I wanted so desperately to express, but could not. I was the only Chicana there, and had to think and speak individualistically rather than collectively. I was without my Latino friends from home who shared the power of our activism in defying the colonization of our identities and of our people. In the absence of that collectivity, I changed my commitment and orientation from the visions my friends and I had shared. Cut off from those who collectively sustained them, I lost those visions of activism and self-determination. Deep inside, I wanted to voice what I was experiencing at that moment—the disempowerment that comes from being cut off from your own. Perez (1991), a Chicana feminist, writes what I wanted to express at that time:

> You attempt to "penetrate" the place I speak from with my Chicana/Latina hermanas. I have rights to my space. I have boundaries. . . . At times, I must separate from you, from your invasion. So call me a separatist, but to me this is not about separatism. It is about survival. I think of myself as one who must separate to my space and language of women to revitalize, to nurture and be nurtured. Then, I can resurface to build the coalitions that we must build to make the true revolution—all of us together acting the ideal, making alliance without a hierarchy of oppression. (p. 178)

Only now, as I am writing these words, do I realize what was happening. It hit me and it hurt me. I felt it in my bones, but I could not articulate it until now. The coalitions referred to by Perez imply groups of empowered and self-identified peoples who do not have to pack neatly and put away their languages and cultures in order to comply with a "standard" way of being. To be Chicanas in the myriad and infinite ways there are of being, to come as we are, poses a threat to integrated schools and to mainstream society. In the absence of collectivity in my graduate seminar, I could not be true to my vision of a Chicana.

Revealing Tension in My Identity as a Chicana Researcher

As I look back, describe, and theorize about my seminar experience, I can articulate the elements that constituted my marginalization and my complicity in the discourses of difference and "othering." The power of the dominant discourse of "other," the objectification of my experiences as the "other" through detached, rational argumentation, and the severing of a collective vision and memory that disabled me and rendered me voiceless, all constituted marginalization and complicity. These elements resurfaced when I started the process of conducting qualitative research with the Latino community in Hope City, North Carolina. There, my dilemma of being a Chicana and a researcher became problematic in ways similar to my experiences in the seminar, that is, as an accomplice to the marginalization and objectification of my identity and experiences as a Chicana, which became embedded in the power structure of the dominant and the disenfranchised.

Going into the field, my intent was to gain access to the Hope City Latino community so that I could interview Latina mothers about their beliefs on child-rearing and education, particularly as their narratives played out in the context of a changing rural southern town. Yet I did not want only to take their stories and leave. I also wanted to become involved in some way with their Latino community, either through bilingual tutoring for children with their mothers or through English as a Second Language (ESL) instruction. As I sought to gain access to the community, I had to speak with numerous English-speaking institutional representatives, including educators in the elementary school, community college, and health department. From the beginning, I felt uncomfortable in my conversations with these community leaders and with their cultural views of Latino families, and of the women in particular. They constructed Latino families as "problems" tending towards violence, sexism, machismo, and low educational aspirations. In their meetings, well-meaning providers talked about showing Latina mothers models of proper child-rearing. A Hope City newspaper headline read, "Program Teaches Hispanics How to Be Better Mothers." Other articles about Latino families carried headlines such as "Literacy Void." Again, the dominant discourse concerning the "other" was powerful and overwhelming—so much so that I found myself, as in the seminar, participating in it as an accomplice. I began to talk the talk.

I remember accompanying an ESL instructor from the community college to the trailer park where he gave classes. We stood in the grassy area in the middle of the park, looking out at the individual trailers, some with children and families outside them. The instructor was giving me the rundown on their living conditions and other problems. I was nodding my head, all the while gazing at the people who looked back at us. I remember ducking my head, painfully aware of my awkward position. Whose side was I on? In participating in this manner with the instructor, I was, as hooks (1989) says, "one with them in a fellowship of the chosen and superior, [it was] a gesture of inclusion in 'whiteness' " (p. 68), affirming that I had been assimilated. I felt uncomfortable, yet I participated, as in the graduate seminar, by betraying my anger and remaining silent, and by not challenging the discourse. In conversations with Hope City professionals, I had to choose my alignment in the power structure of the community—either with the leaders who were in positions to make policy, or with the disenfranchised Latino community.

Choosing to align myself with the dominant English-speaking leaders entailed sharing the same discourse and language to talk about the Latino community. To do this, I had to distance myself from the Latino community and the experiences I shared with them, and speak as the subject about the object. I could do this in the eyes of the dominant English-speaking community because I was formally educated and spoke English as well as they.

In this southern community, there were no other Chicanas/os in leadership positions. I had no one with whom to share a collective vision for the empowerment of "our" community. The ESL instructor and I spoke in a detached manner about the problems of "these people," as if I had not been socialized in a Latino family and immigrant community. I spoke as if Latino families and friends had not been the most important people in my private life. I silenced myself so that I could have further conversations with the community leaders who were the key to my accessing the educational institutions of the community. By participating in their discourse, I had to disengage myself from my experience as an intimate participant in Latino families and communities. The dominant discourse of difference was powerful, and my experiences were again nullified through my participation in detached and rational discussions of the problems of the "other."

My uncomfortable feelings soon turned to outrage and hurt. One particular discussion with a school principal startled me out of my perceived unproblematic role as a Chicana researcher. My advisor and I went to speak with the principal about my starting a mother/child class to teach children how to read and write in Spanish. The principal, who held blatantly racist views of Latino families, told us he would play the devil's advocate and point out some problems—for example, how were we going to get mothers to come? He went on to say that we had to understand the Hispanic family. The man, he said, dictates, and the woman is subservient: "The man will not let her out of the house. They do not care about education and so it's hard to get the mothers to come to the school." An ESL teacher who was also in the room explained that these were poor people, blue-collar workers who did not have education themselves. I later responded angrily in my field notes:

> How dare you say this to me. How is it that you are telling me what Latino families are like. I was so insulted. They were talking about my "raza" so negatively as if I were not Latina myself. This goes to show how easily I can "pass" and that in certain contexts, I am not identified as one of "them." With this conversation as in others, I have felt that I have had to put on a different persona in order to play along with well meaning racist discourse. I have felt very uncomfortable talking to benevolent people about the "other," the exotic poor people who need our help. "Our" referring to my complicity as researcher. (Field notes, March 1994)

After that incident, I began to question my identity and my role as a Chicana researcher. It was evident that the dominant English-speaking community did not consider me a Latina, like the women we were discussing, but a middle-class, educated woman of Spanish descent. How was I to relate to this dominant discourse of difference and "othering?"

I looked to recent works on the researcher's role in disenfranchised communities in which the researcher shares the same cultural background as the research participants. Delgado-Gaitan (1993) and Delgado-Gaitan and Trueba (1991) write about an ethnography of empowerment, a framework that "provides a broad sociocultural premise and possible strategy for studying the process of disempowerment and empowerment of disenfranchised communities" (p. 391). This kind of ethnography is based on a Freirian notion of self-awareness of the social and cultural context of the nature of oppression suffered by disempowered people (Delgado-Gaitan & Trueba, 1991). Such a framework calls for "the construction of knowledge through the social interaction between researcher and researched with the fundamental purpose of improving the living conditions of the communities being researched" (Delgado-Gaitan & Trueba, 1991, p. 392). Delgado-Gaitan (1993) emphasizes that the researcher shapes the research participants and their environment while, at the same time, the researcher is also shaped by the participants and the dynamics of their interactions. Delgado-Gaitan's (1993) own provocative story is of the transformation of her role with respect to her work on literacy practices in the homes and schools of a Latino community. As the parents mobilized to effect changes in the school, Delgado-Gaitan redefined her role as researcher to become involved as facilitator and informant in the process of community empowerment. As a result of her own unique experiences, Delgado-Gaitan, a Latina herself, built upon the notion of making problematic her relationship with Latino communities. By doing so, she put into practice qualitative researchers' call for the reexamination of one's identity and place within the research context of privilege and power.

My story extends this notion by problematizing the relationship between the marginalized researcher and the majority culture. The internalization of oppressive discourses relating to one's own people, especially as a product of institutionalized education and university training, can lead to a disempowerment of the researcher and the research process. The analysis can be extended then to include the empowerment of the researcher and the role of the ethnographer's culture, self-identity, and her/his raced, classed, and gendered experiences in the research process. In my case, while I naively looked for ways in which I could help Latina mothers "empower" themselves (see Le Compte & de Marrais, 1992, for a critique on the discourse on empowerment), I failed to realize that I needed to help myself become empowered vis-à-vis the dominant, English-speaking community. I needed to examine my own identity in the particular cultural arena that formed the context for my research study. Not having done so, I could not engage in the process of constructing knowledge with the research participants. I needed first to ask myself, How am I, as a Chicana researcher, damaged by my own marginality? Furthermore, how am I complicit in the manipulation of my identities such that I participate in my own colonization and marginalization and, by extension, that of my own people—those with whom I feel a cultural and collective connectedness and commitment?

For these reasons, researchers must examine how their subjectivities and perceptions are negotiated and changed, not only in relation to the disenfranchised community as research participants, but also through interactions with the majority culture. In most cases, the latter are the people who espouse the dominant discourse of difference and "other," that is, the cultural views of Latino families as a "problem"—poor, disadvantaged, and language deficient. In Hope City, Latina mothers are constructed as "at risk" in the discourse of the dominant community (i.e., professionals in education, health, and social services) so that the ways in which they raise and educate their children are devalued (Swadener & Lubeck, 1995). It is this "at risk" and "problem" discourse that I was being pushed hard to legitimate in Hope City. Yet this discourse concerned my own rearing, my own family, my own mother, and my own beliefs and those of my community. Through my engagement in the majority culture's "Latinos as problem" discourse, I was further marginalized and encircled in my own guilt of complicity.

Identity, Tension and Power: Interpreting My Insider/Outsider Perspective

I find it useful to appropriate Delgado-Gaitan's (1993) insider/outsider concept and apply it in a different manner to my emerging and changing identity as a Chicana researcher. In the process of conducting her study, Delgado-Gaitan (1993) learned that a researcher initially could only be an outsider to the community of research participants, but that with insight, the researcher could foster relational and reflective processes with their participants and in time become an insider. What are the particular behaviors and/or characteristics of the researcher that can make her/him an insider to the community of research participants? In a general sense, it is the sharing of collective experiences and a collective space with the research participants, such that the researcher is gradually accepted as a member of that particular community. As researchers, we can be insiders and outsiders to a particular community of research participants at many different levels and at different times.

In my case, I had two layers of communities to penetrate, at least on different terms. From my perspective at the time, the irony was that I was becoming an insider to the "wrong" community—the dominant, English-speaking community of leaders with whom I felt no familial, historical, or intimate relation. I was, in fact, the outsider to the Latino community of this town, since I was not *of* their community and did not share in their everyday experiences (I did not live in Hope City). Further, I was being recruited by the institutional representatives to become an insider in the legitimization of the dominant discourse of Latinos as "problem" and "victim." The effects on me of participating in the dominant discourse in a detached manner through rational dialogue were powerful. Consequently, I had to step back and negotiate internally the ongoing recruiting efforts of the dominant, English-speaking community leaders to their discourses of difference.

I began my fieldwork on site at the beginning of the spring semester of the academic year. I discussed with my advisor how the White community might be cautious in talking with me about the Latino community, since I might be perceived as a member of this community. As I stated earlier, my advisor and I were soon proven wrong. The White community leaders were eager to talk to me about their perceptions of Latino families.

I had worked hard all semester to gain access to the Hope City Latino community and to find a niche in which to practice my profession of "maestra" (teacher), and to do research as well. My diligence paid off in that many opportunities were opened for me by English-speaking community leaders. I had received invitations to teach ESL and literacy in the churches (both the Catholic and Methodist churches), the elementary school, the community college, and the health department.

I decided to dedicate my time to teaching ESL to adults at the community college, a job in which I not only had experience but that I also thoroughly enjoyed. At the end of the semester, I looked to see what my story in terms of my research had been thus far. I had written in my field notes about my uneasy and uncomfortable feelings as I had conversations with English-speaking community leaders. Interestingly, I had also recorded my feelings of awkwardness when I talked to Latinas/os as a researcher researching "them." I was unconsciously documenting the power relations that defined the research context of which I, the dominant community leaders, and the Latino immigrant community each formed a part. Roman and Apple (1990) emphasize that a crucial task for the ethnographer should be the "elaboration of the structural power relations that formed the basis for conducting the field research and the study" (p. 60). The documentation of my feelings of anger and awkwardness formed the basis for the elaboration of my identity as a Chicana researcher in the community's power structure.

The power play in the recruitment efforts of the White power structure, and later in their efforts to appropriate me, was clearly evident. To recruit me to their discourse and narratives of difference, the community leaders had to view me as equal with them in the power structure. They appropriated my persona and appeared, at least initially, to welcome me as an equal.

I later understood this welcome to be a form of colonizing. They appropriated my persona by presuming shared assumptions of a body of experiences. For example, a community college instructor warned me about the dangers of the trailer park, implying that I shared his fear of poor people and of people of color. The community leaders also treated me as an equal by talking about Latinos as the "other" and including me in the distanced and detached conversations about the "problems of Latinos." Sharing our detached, rational observations of Latinos made me seem objective and scientific, and seemed to put us on equal footing with each other and in a superior position to the Latino community.

I felt powerful because I could discuss "their" problems. I was even in a position to negotiate power with the elementary school principal when I proposed Spanish tutoring classes for young children and their mothers. Not only did my credentials give me leverage in these negotiations, but my professional identity and language also met the criteria for inclusion and commonality with the institutional representatives. In more ways than one, I found it easier to be an insider to the community of dominant English-speaking leaders than to the Latino community.

The powerholders' recruiting efforts were intense precisely because they had a lot at stake in interpreting, structuring, and legitimating their cultural constructions of difference and diversity. The schools and agencies were interpreting Latino "cultures" and child-rearing practices. They were structuring the relationships between the Latino and English-speaking communities through the mediating force of agency bureaucracies (see Adkins, Givens, McKinney, Murillo, & Villenas, 1995). And, they were legitimating the "at risk" and "problem" discourses.

Undoubtedly, as a "Hispanic" professional, I served to legitimate the "at risk" discourse and the definition of Latino child-rearing as a "problem." Sleeter (1995) argues that "the discourse over 'children at risk' can be understood as a struggle for power over how to define children, families, and communities who are poor, of color, and/or native speakers of languages other than English" (p. ix).

In later months, community leaders called on me to speak about and for the Latino community. In their eyes, I was the "expert" on the educational experiences of Latino families, not because I had begun talking with Latina mothers and could possibly articulate their points of view, but because I was seen as the professional who possessed formal education, teaching experience, and spoke both Spanish and English. Indeed, they would introduce me not only by name, but also by my academic credentials and past teaching experience. On one occasion, I was asked to speak to a group of community leaders from various social service agencies about Latino families and their educational needs. I chose to speak about the strengths of language and literacy socialization in Latino families. On another occasion, I was asked to translate for and represent the Latinas from my ESL class at a meeting to organize a county chapter of a council for women. At yet another meeting, called by the county migrant education office, about one hundred Latino parents met in the elementary school cafeteria where I spoke to them about strategies to help their children in school. On all of these occasions, I was serving as the broker for and the link to the Latino community for the professional community leaders. They called on me to participate in meetings and to give presentations. The stakeholders of this community clearly felt an urgent need to co-opt certain people, such as myself and other English-speaking town leaders, to represent the Latino community. It was as if in doing so, they did not have to handle the raw material. The Latino community was too foreign, too different, too working class, too brown; so they appropriated me, Sofia, the preprocessed package, wrapped in formal education and labeled in English.

Of course I did not want to be associated with the dominating power structure in the eyes of the Latino community. I had qualms about being perceived as the imperialist researcher. I felt tension with the Latino community when I was in my role as researcher, and when they saw me in company and complicity with the community leaders. I am reminded of two situations in which I felt these tensions most acutely.

It felt normal and comfortable, for example, when I visited Tienda Adrian (Adrian's Store), a Latino food store, with my husband and children. We spoke with the store owners in Spanish, asking about the town. However, the following week I felt uncomfortable when I revisited Tienda Adrian with my advisor and approached the store owners cloaked in my university researcher role to ask about the town. Similarly, I felt the tension of power in my researcher role when I began formal interviews with the women in the Latino community. The interviewing situation was uncomfortable for me, in contrast to the times we had engaged in informal talks about raising and educating children in Hope City.

I felt the tension of power and complicity even more directly when I engaged in social interaction with an English-speaking institutional representative and a Latina client at the same time. I felt this more acutely when service agency providers used English to talk about Latina clients in their presence. The Latina clients, who, for the most part, were new arrivals in Hope City, could not speak English. One particular service provider had the habit of introducing me to a Latina client and then giving me her personal life history right in front of her. In these situations, power was wielded through language, and English became the language of exclusion. The women's personal lives were presented to me like an open book in a language that they did not understand. In having to respond in English to the service provider, I was self-conscious and awkward about the exploitation and "othering" of the women. I did not want to be complicit with the "colonial administrator," but I was unaware that this was how I was being positioned.

My feelings of complicity and guilt, however, led me to engage in small spontaneous subversive strategies and acts of resistance. Any time a community leader spoke in English about a Latina client in her presence, I translated. Sometimes I would change the meanings somewhat so as not to cause embarrassment or hurt. On one occasion, for example, I said, "He's saying that you had gone through some rough times," even though the service agency provider said that she had had a nervous breakdown and had psychological problems. I began to translate into Spanish everything I said to community leaders when Latinos were present.

I also brought politics and subversion to the meetings at which I spoke for the community leaders. I did not always say what they wanted to hear, stirring controversy at one meeting and causing some Whites to react defensively at another. At one meeting at the elementary school, I disrupted the discourse of dominance by not accepting the seat they had saved for me in the front of the room facing the Latino audience. Instead, I took a seat among some Latino friends.

As an ESL instructor, a "maestra," in the Latino community, I am more active in dialogue and discussions with my Latino students than with the community of school and agency professionals. In being able to name and identify the situatedness of my identities, I am beginning to react to my positioning and act towards a transformation of my identity and role as a Chicana educational researcher in a Latino community.

Negotiating Identities: Toward New Discourses

I am in the process of my own learning, and it is not my goal to arrive at a final resolution. Rather, I am in continual discovery. Identity and self are multiple and continually remade, reconstructed, reconstituted, and renewed in each new context and situation (Stone, 1992). When I left Los Angeles to attend graduate school in the South, I also left behind identities formed against the backdrop of a segregated city and against a historical context of the racial subordination and conquest of Native and Mexican peoples. In my limited and segregated experiences, I only knew Whites as living the middle-class lifestyle, and rarely as working-class people. I defined myself and was defined by this historical relationship.

In North Carolina, at first I believed I had encountered a place where a historically embedded antagonism did not exist between Mexicans and European Americans, as it exists in the Southwest. There is no territorial Alamo to remember, nor a U.S.-Mexico treaty that appropriated one-third of Mexico's land. I seemed to have forgotten the history of the genocide of American Indians and of the slavery and segregation of African Americans. Nevertheless, I believed space existed in which I could enter into new relationships with the majority culture and define new grounds and new terms. Because of this belief, I found it painful to go into the town where I was to conduct my research project, a town where a new immigrant community of Latinos were the objects of oppressive discourses. The old relationships and identities formed against these discourses were being re-inscribed in me. In confronting these oppressive discourses of difference, I experienced domination and oppression, and was a party to the exercising of them.

This story demonstrates that some Chicanas/os do not move from marginalization to new positions of privilege associated with university affiliation, as if switching from one seat to another on the bus. We do not suddenly become powerful in our new identities and roles as university researchers. We do not leave one to get to the other. As Chicanas/os and ethnographers of color, we carry our baggage with us—a baggage of marginalization, complicity, and resentment, as well as *orgullo* (pride) and celebration. These are not easily cast away. No doubt it is not too difficult to embrace whole-heartedly the privileges of upward mobility, but to many of us the costs are great. Just as becoming raceless was a strategy for Black adolescents who, in Fordham's (1988) study, had to unlearn their racial identities and cultural behaviors in order to make it through high school and beyond, so must some Chicanas/os do the same. As bilingual, tricultural peoples, we "continually walk out of one culture and into another" (Anzaldúa, 1987, p. 77). In Anzaldúa's images, we are straddling multiple worlds, trying to break from colonized identities formed against White supremacy and male dominance and to form a new consciousness: "I am in all cultures, at the same time" (p. 77). We learn to tolerate contradictions and ambiguities of identities and to "seek new images of identities, new beliefs about ourselves" (p. 87).

While I recognize that part of my ongoing process is seeking, forging, and negotiating new images and identities, I am also raging against postmodern renderings of the White middle-class "discovery" that politically and socially situate the ethnographer as synonymous with colonizer, imperialist, and privileged researcher. In this view, it does not matter whether we are Chicanas/os or middle-class White male ethnographers. In the name of a postmodern understanding of identity and privilege, I am led to believe that I am now the same "researcher as colonizer," that I am now privileged, and that I share the same guilt for the same exploitation of the less privileged research participants. In a sense, I was not only being recruited to legitimate the majority culture's discourse of "Latinos as problem," but I am also symbolically being co-opted to legitimate academia's declaration of the postmodern ethnographer as the socially and politically privileged colonizer. In both instances, I am being co-opted to be like the colonizer, the oppressor, in ways that ignore my own struggle as a Chicana against subjugation and marginalization.

Thus, while I recognize my contradictory position and privilege (that come from university affiliation), and while I would gladly serve as a facilitator and translator for the voices of the Latina mothers of a small rural town in North Carolina (if they would have me), I must also see myself as going beyond the role of facilitator. I must see my own historical being and space. I must know that I will not "mimic the colonizers" (Perez, 1991, p. 177) and call myself the ethnographer/colonizer, for this insults my gendered, racial memory.

As I look back on my experience in the graduate seminar, I know that in the future I will not be silent, just as I could not be silent any more in the face of the dominant community's attempts to recruit me to their discourses about the Latino population in Hope City. I cannot continue to pretend that as a qualitative researcher in education, I am distanced from intimacy, hope, anger, and a historical collectivity with Latino communities. For these reasons, I cannot be neutral in the field, because to be so is to continue to be complicit in my own subjugation and that of the Latino communities. To take on only the role of facilitator is to deny my own activism. I must recognize that my own liberation and emancipation in relationship with my community are at stake, and that continued marginalization and subjugation are the perils.

I did not seek these confrontations and realizations. They came upon me while I was turned the other way, disengaging myself from the intimacy of Latina sisterhood. They came upon me as I convinced myself that I had to be careful because I was the privileged and thus the colonizer. I was attuned to seeking to reform my relationship with the research participants and to promote their empowerment, without realizing that *I* was being worked on and commodified, that *I* needed to be empowered. I suddenly found myself complicit in my own subjugation, vis-à-vis the dominant public discourse.

In the meantime, I find hope in Fine's (1994) narrative of the way her Latina niece, who was adopted into her middle-class Jewish family, moved in and out of identities as she fought a criminal case for sexual assault. Fine writes:

> Jackie mingled her autobiography with our surveilled borders on her Self and the raced and gendered legal interpretations of her Other by which she was surrounded. She braided them into her story, her deposition. . . . She slid from victim to survivor, from naive to coy, from deeply experienced young woman to child. In her deposition she dismantled the very categories I so

worried we had constructed as sediment pillars around her, and she wandered among them, pivoting her identity, her self representations, and, therefore, her audiences. (1994, p. 71)

Herein I find the key: to resist "othering" and marginalization is to use our multiplicity of identities in order to tolerate and welcome the contradictions and ambiguities, as Anzaldúa (1987) writes, so that in our quest for liberation, we also dismantle the categories and the conquering language of the colonizer. In this manner, we "work the hyphen between Self and Other," as Fine (1994, p. 72) challenges us to do, yet we work from within ourselves as the Self/Other, Colonizer/Colonized ethnographer.

Thus, it is important to continue theorizing on the researchers' multiplicity of identities and the implications of this for qualitative research in education. As members of marginalized groups assume more privileged positions in the educational socioeconomic structures of hierarchy, people who were once merely the exotic objects of inquiry are now the inquirers—the ones formulating and asking the questions. As some enter the ranks of teachers, administrators, and scholars, we are becoming the enforcers and legitimators as well as the creators of official knowledge. Hence, as qualitative researchers in the field of education, we need to explore and understand the dilemmas created for Chicanas/os, African Americans, Native Americans, and scholars from other disenfranchised groups vis-à-vis the majority culture. We scholars/activists of color need to understand the ways in which we manipulate our multiple, fluid, clashing, and colonized identities and how our identities are manipulated and marginalized in the midst of oppressive discourses. Luke and Luke (1995) argue, "Only by describing and understanding how power works in oppressive social formations, how identity is shaped both through contestation and collusion with oppressive regimes of control, is it possible to lay down a systematic knowledge of marginal identities" (p. 376).

Further studies are also needed that capture the intricacies of marginalized teachers and scholars who are teaching and researching their own communities. Watson-Gegeo (1994) introduces a collection of articles that illuminate important questions dealing with "minority" teachers teaching "minority" students.[5] These excellent studies encourage further probing of the questions of resisting, negotiating, and tolerating identities in a context of power and privilege—in other words, to pay close attention to how we manipulate our identities and how our identities are manipulated by others. We need to see how Latino ethnographers, for example, become commodified in the process of research. At the same time, we also need to examine the gender, race, and class dynamics created in the university setting, where for example women of color, who are professors, and middle-class White students come together (see Vargas, 1996). These are critical questions that need further exploration.

Conclusion

This story is an attempt to untangle my own multiplicity of identities played out in the terrains of privilege and power in ethnographic research. With the new generation of "native" ethnographers, including myself, increasingly working within and writing about our own communities, we are beginning to question how our histories and identities are entangled in the workings of domination as we engage the oppressive discourses of "othering." In my case, while researching in a rural town in North Carolina, I had to confront both my own marginalization and my complicity in "othering" myself and my community, as I encountered the discourse that identified Latino family education and child-rearing practices as "problem" and "lacking."

At a time when qualitative researchers in education are questioning their own privilege in relation to the research participants, the "we" in the literature needs to be re-theorized. My identity/role as a Chicana ethnographer cannot be collapsed in terms of "privileged" researcher in the same manner that other ethnographers are privileged in their relationships with their research participants. In failing to address the ways in which the ethnographer can be damaged by her/his own marginalization in the larger society, the literature has created a "we" that does not include my experience in the field as a Chicana ethnographer.

What might this story teach majority-culture ethnographers of education so that they too move beyond the "researcher as privileged" dilemma? I believe they also can confront their own multiplicities of identity and histories of complicity and mark the points of their own marginalization. Rosaldo (1989) and Patai (1991) write that ethnographers cannot escape their complicity in exploiting the "researched," yet I still need to ask, What is the nature of the space that I have found, and what are the possibilities for the Latino community in Hope City, North Carolina? My space is a fluid space of crossing borders and, as such, a contradictory one of collusion and oppositionality, complicity and subversion. For "Hispanos" in Hope City, surrounded by a historically violent and entrenched biracial society in which one is either Black or White, emancipatory possibilities lie in the creation of a dignified public space where they can negotiate new identities and break down the biraciality. Likewise, my challenge to majority-culture ethnographers is that they call upon their own marginalizing experiences and find a space for the emergence of new identities and discourses in the practice of solidarity with marginalized peoples.

My own journey moves me towards new transcendent discourses that are transformative and emancipatory. I hope to be, in Olson and Shopes's words, a "citizen-scholar-activist(s) rooted in the community" (cited in Van Galen & Eaker, 1995, p. 120). Recognizing our multidimensional identities as colonizers, colonized, neither, and in-between, we *camaradas* in struggle must work from within and facilitate a process where Latinas/os become the subjects and the creators of knowledge. My answer to the ethnographer-as-colonizer dilemma is that I will not stop at being the public translator and facilitator for my communities, but that I am my own voice, an activist seeking liberation from my own historical oppression in relation to my communities. We *mojado* ethnographers look anxiously to learn about the rich diversity of Latino communities in the U.S., and in doing so, create our own rich diversity of models, paradigms, and languages as we cross between our communities and "the artificial borders into occupied academic territories" (E. G. Murillo Jr., personal communication, 1995).

Notes

1. "Chicano" and "Chicana" are self-identified terms used by peoples of Mexican origin. They are political terms of self-determination and solidarity that originated in the Chicano liberation movement of the 1960s.
2. "Hispanic" is a U.S. government term used to classify Spanish-speaking peoples of Latin America living in the United States. "Latino" refers to a collective community of Latin Americans. "Latino" is my chosen term, which I use interchangeably with the emic term "Hispano." I use "Latino" to refer to the very diverse Spanish-speaking community of Hope City (a pseudonym). North Carolina. "Latino" also refers to male members of the community,

while "Latin*a*" refers to the women. Members of the Latino community in Hope City usually refer to themselves in national terms: Mexican, Salvadoran, Guatemalan, etc. However, they have also adopted the term "Hispanos" to refer to themselves collectively as a community. It is also important to note that people self-identify differently. For this reason, when I refer to my friends, I use the various terms with which they identify themselves. Also, an "Indigenista" or "Mesocentric" (Godina, 1996) perspective has spurred interest among Latinos and peoples of indigenous ancestry between themselves and tribal Native Americans. In essence, through this movement we (including myself) are saying that we *are* Native American people.

3. "Aztlan" refers to the mythical origins and ancient homelands of the Aztec civilization. Over the last thirty years, Aztlan has been popularized by the Chicano liberation movement and is linked to the vast northern territories of Mexico that were invaded and annexed by the United States in 1848.
4. "Othering" refers to objectifying people who are different than the Western White self in a manner that renders them inferior.
5. This edited collection includes articles by Foster (1994) on the views of African American teachers who counter prevailing hegemonic beliefs about African American children in reform efforts to improve their achievement in schools; Watson-Gegeo and Gegeo (1994) on the ways in which a history of colonization and modernization in the Solomon Islands serves to keep teachers' cultural knowledge out of the classroom: and Lipka (1994), who examined how Yup'ik Eskimo teachers in Alaska face administrative barriers when working to include their language and culture in their classrooms.

References

Adkins, A., Givens, G., McKinney, M., Murillo, E., & Villenas, S. (1995, November). *Contested childrearing: The social construction of Latino childrearing.* Paper presented at the meeting of the American Educational Studies Association, Cleveland, OH.

Anzaldúa, G. (1987). *Borderlands/La frontera.* San Francisco: Aunt Lute Books.

Crapanzano, V. (1986). Hermes' dilemma: The masking of subversion in ethnographic description. In J. Clifford & G. Marcus (Eds.), *Writing culture* (pp. 51–76). Berkeley: University of California Press.

Delgado-Gaitan, C. (1993). Researching change and changing the researcher. *Harvard Educational Review, 63,* 389–411.

Delgado-Gaitan, C., & Trueba, H. (1991). *Crossing cultural borders: Education for immigrant families in America.* London: Falmer Press.

Ellsworth, E. (1989). Why doesn't this feel empowering: Working through the myths of critical pedagogy. *Harvard Educational Review, 59,* 297–324.

Fine, M. (1994). Working the hyphens: Reinventing self and other in qualitative research. In N. Denzin & Y. Lincoln (Eds.), *Handbook of qualitative research* (pp. 70–82). Thousand Oaks, CA: Sage.

Fordham, S. (1988). Racelessness as a factor in Black students' school success: Pragmatic strategy or pyrrhic victory? *Harvard Educational Review, 58,* 54–84.

Foster, M. (1994). The role of community and culture in school reform efforts: Examining the views of African American teachers. *Educational Foundations, 8*(2), 5–26.

Godina, H. (1996, April). *Mesocentrism: Teaching indigenous Mexican culture in the classroom.* Paper presented at the annual meeting of the American Educational Research Association, New York.

hooks, b. (1989). *Talking back: Thinking feminist, thinking Black.* Boston: South End Press.

hooks, b. (1990). *Yearning.* Boston: South End Press.

hooks, b. (1994). *Teaching to transgress: Education as the practice of freedom.* New York: Routledge.

Lather, P. (1991). *Getting smart: Feminist research and pedagogy with/in the postmodern.* New York: Routledge.

LeCompte, M., & de Marrais, K. (1992). The disempowering of empowerment: Out of the revolution and into the classroom. *Educational Foundations, 6*(13), 5–31.

Lipka, J. (1994). Schools failing minority teachers: Problems and suggestions. *Educational Foundations, 8*(2), 57–80.

Luke, C., & Luke, A. (1995). Just naming? Educational discourses and the politics of identity. In W. Pink & G. Noblit (Eds.), *Continuity and contradiction: The futures of the sociology of education* (pp. 357–380). Cresskill, NJ: Hampton Press.

Patai, D. (1991). U.S. academics and third world women: Is ethical research possible? In S. Gluck & D. Patai (Eds.), *Women's words: The feminist practice of oral history* (pp. 137–153). New York: Routledge.

Perez, E. (1991). Sexuality and discourse: Notes from a Chicana survivor. In C. Trujillo (Ed.), *Chicana lesbians: The girls our mothers warned us about* (pp. 158–184). Berkeley, CA: Third Woman Press.

Pratt, M. (1986). Fieldwork in common places. In J. Clifford & G. Marcus (Eds.), *Writing culture* (pp. 27–50). Berkeley: University of California Press.

Roman, L., & Apple, M. (1990). Is naturalism a move away from positivism? Materialist and feminist approaches to subjectivity in ethnographic research. In E. Eisner & A. Peshkin (Eds.), *Qualitative inquiry in education: The continuing debate* (pp. 38–73). New York: Teachers College Press.

Rosaldo, R. (1989). *Culture and truth: The remaking of social analysis.* Boston: Beacon Press.

Sleeter, C. (1995). Foreword. In B. Swadener & S. Lubeck (Eds.), *Children and families "at promise"* (pp. ix–xi). Albany: State University of New York Press.

Stone, L. (1992). The essentialist tension in reflective teacher education. In L. Valli (Ed.), *Reflective teacher education: Cases and critiques* (pp. 198–211). Albany: State University of New York Press.

Swadener, B., & Lubeck, S. (Eds.). (1995). *Children and families "at promise."* Albany: State University of New York Press.

Van Galen, J., & Eaker, D. (1995). Beyond settling for scholarship: On defining the beginning and ending points of postmodern research. In W. Pink & G. Noblit (Eds.), *Continuity and contradiction: The futures of the sociology of education* (pp. 113–131). Cresskill, NJ: Hampton Press.

Vargas, L. (1996, April). *When the other is the teacher: Implications for teacher diversity in higher education.* Paper presented at the annual meeting of the Eastern Communication Association, New York City.

Watson-Gegeo, K. (1994). Introduction: What's culture got to do with it? Minority teachers teaching minority students. *Educational Foundations, 8*(2), 3–4.

Watson-Gegeo, K., & Gegeo, D., (1994). Keeping culture out of the classroom in rural Solomon Islands schools: A critical analysis. *Educational Foundations, 8*(2), 27–55.

Weis, L. (1995). Identity formation and the process of "othering": Unraveling sexual threads. *Educational Foundations, 9*(1), 17–33.

I am indebted to George Noblit for the conversations that enabled me to tell this story. I also wish to thank Amee Adkins and Lynda Stone for their insights on the manuscript and to Bernardo Gallegos for his encouragement. The research project in Hope City was funded by the Frank Porter Graham Child Development Center, with partial funding by the North Carolina Humanities Council.

22

"Where Are You Really From?"

Representation, Identity and Power in the Fieldwork Experiences of a South Asian Diasporic

Marsha Giselle Henry

A substantial amount of literature explores the dilemmas faced by researchers using both qualitative research methods and a feminist approach (Bell et al., 1993; Coffey, 1999; Fonow and Cook, 1991; Gluck and Patai, 1991; Golde, 1970; Reinharz, 1992; Roberts, 1990; Stanley, 1983; Wolf, 1996). Feminist accounts of fieldwork have often been concerned with issues of representation, both of the researchees and the researcher, exposing some of the complications that arise when the researcher must make critical decisions about representing herself to her research participants (Abu-Lughod, 1988, 1990; Acker et al., 1991; Berik, 1996; Dossa, 1997; Kondo, 1986; Lal, 1996; Narayan, 1993; Ong, 1995; Patai, 1991; Reinharz, 1992; Schrijvers, 1993; Stacey, 1991). These accounts demonstrate that a fieldworker's identity *does* in fact impact upon the research process and product, challenging notions of researcher objectivity and neutrality. This article examines some of the issues raised in feminist research methodologies within the context of a first generation South Asian researcher's experiences.[1]

I contribute to some of the feminist accounts by complicating the processes of representation and the power and problem of naming; identity and its impact upon the research process; and the field as a place of complex power structures, which can produce questions that seem all too familiar. One of the questions raised in relation to representation, identity and the field is one that I have been asked virtually all my life, but which has different meanings in different contexts. My research participants often asked, 'where are you *really* from?', a question in the context of the feminist literature on methodology that has enabled me to analyse some of the difficulties and problems I faced in doing fieldwork. It has also enabled me to develop a different conceptualization of the research process and research participants. Finally, it has demonstrated some of the difficulties that our current and limited language of race, ethnicity and nationality pose for first generation South Asian researchers.

In this article, I examine specific themes in relation to my own research experiences after having grown up in Canada, and then later living and studying in Britain and conducting fieldwork in India. I locate these experiences within qualitative research literatures and suggest that the 'field' needs to be continually challenged and reconceptualized if feminist researchers are to be inclusive of all women's experiences, both as researchers and participants.[2]

Representation and the Power and Problem of Naming

In discussing some of the differences between researchers and research participants, Diane Wolf writes that:

> . . . our power and control offers us the choice to construct and (re)shape our selves to our subjects, playing on the different positionalities of the researcher and the researched. This is particularly the case when researchers are far enough from home that the researchers do not encounter many of their family members or friends, whereas our respondents are usually surrounded by kin and friends and cannot similarly withdraw, hide and alter aspects of their identity.
>
> (Wolf, 1996: 11)

Wolf's argument warrants discussion here, especially because there are at least two problems with her account in relation to my own research experiences. First, Wolf's quote suggests that the researched are somewhat unveiled and 'genuine' in their habitats, assuming that participants are open to the researcher's gaze and do not participate in the performative act of representing themselves. Parin Dossa, in her reflections on fieldwork, challenges the idea of the ethnographer as the 'quintessence of mobility, a status that makes them omnipotent "seers" ' (1997: 506). Participant accounts, like researcher accounts, are also contextually and historically specific, mediated versions of experience. Second, Wolf's statement assumes that representing oneself is a somewhat easy business in the researcher's country of residence and that dilemmas arise in research because of various points of difference in the field. While it is important to note that fieldwork is a particular process, it is, nevertheless, a process of representing oneself that is not entirely dissimilar to other processes that may take place in the fieldworker's home. By using examples from my own fieldwork, I want to illustrate some of the problems that I encountered in relation to the second point.

First, I want to discuss some of the uncertainty I have representing myself on a day-to-day basis in Canada. Growing up in a so-called multicultural environment, it might appear surprising to note that my representations changed dramatically from day to day and from my adolescent to adult years. My parents emigrated from Pakistan to Canada in 1965, first living in a predominantly Francophone region and then subsequently moving to the Anglophone west. Both my father and mother were born in pre-Independence India and lived in post-partition Pakistan; my mother's middle-class family had migrated from the state of Goa, and my father's Anglo-Indian, working-class family had moved from the Punjab. Because my father was 'white', and my parents were practising Catholics, they told me they left Pakistan as they felt a sense of religious and cultural marginalization after partition and they believed that neither Pakistan nor India offered a future for them. Of the three children, I was the only one born in Canada. As I was growing up, my parents and relatives always teased me, telling me that I was the 'true' Canadian in the family. This sense of 'outsiderness' was also reinforced by a comical story that was told by my father at various social gatherings to explain why I was such a 'Canadian' child. I was, according to him, not really theirs, but was found in some rubbish upon their arrival in Canada and they had charitably rescued me from a bin in a park. Despite some reinforcement of my authenticity as a 'Canadian', from my youngest days, I remember being asked the question, 'where are you from?', and when I said, 'Canada', the questions almost always continued, 'where are you *really* from?', 'where are you *originally* from?', 'where are your parents from?', or 'what are your origins?'. I distinctly remember that these questions were seldom asked of my white friends (even though they were all children of recent immigrants) and I grew accustomed to providing various stock answers. When I was young, I remember emphasizing my father's whiteness as a way of gaining acceptance with other children and I remember struggling to give a short and concise response to the question, 'where are you from?', Nevertheless, I have also always felt a responsibility to justify my 'Canadianness', while, at the same time and as an adult, feeling a political necessity to include 'Indianness' (or South Asianness) in my accounts of representation. However, the problem of owning and naming certain representations can be that purist stances of origin tend to serve the interests of dominant groups:

> Being easily offended in your elusive identity and reviving old, racial charges, you immediately react when such guilt-instilling accusations are levelled at you and are thus led to stand in need of defending that very ethnic part of yourself that for years has made you and your ancestors the objects of execration.
>
> (Minh-ha, 1989: 89)

In this way, I suggest that representing oneself at 'home' is a process that is located within complicated social and historical contexts.

While the questions did not stop upon arriving in England seven years ago, I found that many people accepted my representations more readily. I was not prepared for the importance of accent in the English context and did not expect that people would only hear the 'North Americanness' in my voice. I have spent a great deal of time battling with people over the distinctness of Canadian identity in relation to American identity, or justifying why it should be pronounced *Fried Green Tomatoes* [toh-may-tohes], rather than tomatoes [toh-mah-toes] after having various lessons in pronunciation and even hearing one account that I was not a native English-language speaker because I was not from England. However, I have had my accounts challenged by others and have been asked about my parents' origins, where I am *really* from and, in many contexts, my partner has developed a tendency to tune out whenever the pedigree questions surface at social gatherings. In many cases, people have assumed that my parents are migrants because they are familiar with Asian migration in England. Nevertheless, I have still encountered the questions, when 'white' friends have not. Someone I met recently questioned my identity by saying, 'you don't look Canadian', while my white partner's claim to being Canadian remained unchallenged. My feelings of dislocatedness have been reinscribed in the move to England, but the desire to be the same and simultaneously different remains:

> Completely dislocated, unable to be abroad with the other, the white . . . who unmercifully imprisoned me, I took myself far off from my own presence, far indeed, and made myself an object. What else could it be for me but an amputation, an excision, a haemorrhage that spattered my whole body with black blood? . . . I slip into corners, I remain silent, I strive for anonymity, for invisibility. Look I'll accept the lot, as long as no one notices me!
>
> (Fanon, 1990: 110–12)

But my paradoxical struggle for visibility and invisibility, despite my articulations of racial, ethnic and national identity, come from a place of privilege. That I came to England as a student, and not a labourer, that my Canadian passport receives little concern at immigration and customs and that people cannot always place where I am *really* from, allows me to occupy that in-between space of ambiguity, hybridity, fluidity:

> The claim to a lack of identity or positionality is itself based on privilege, on a refusal to accept responsibility for one's implication in actual historical or social relations, on a denial that positionalities exist or that they matter, the denial of one's own personal history and the claim to a total separation from it.
>
> (Martin and Mohanty, 1986: 208)

But there is no 'authentic' position from which to speak and to represent oneself, and I acknowledge that hybridity is performative in that I often choose to occupy this nether space, and that my class privilege offers me shelter and safety from violent challenges. As Visweswaran argues, 'the question "where are you from?" is never an innocent one, yet not all subjects have equal difficulty answering' (1994: 115).

I naively assumed that these matters would be less complicated when I began my fieldwork. On a trip in 1995, I had visited India for the first time as an adult and developed a personal and political interest in gender relations in South Asia. Having lived in Canada most of my life, I began to understand my parents' sense of identity, as well as their longings, desires and tastes and, more importantly, how these traces and memories were shaping and reshaping my own identity. While the main purpose of the trip was to attend a women's studies conference in Delhi, I took a side trip to the state of Goa to visit relatives and have a holiday. The social interactions I had with my female cousin in Goa revealed to me that all Indian women live at the intersections of many identities and experiences (patriarchal, familial, communal, social, moral and religious) with a great deal of ingenuity and do not inhabit easily or comfortably categories and roles expected of them. My cousin and my aunt, as well as the other women I met, did not exist as the western media often portrays them (as victims); instead they were strategically and creatively acting to increase their autonomy and agency while under social, cultural and religious constraints. This experience was the foundation upon which my academic interest in gender relations in South Asian contexts began to develop. This influenced my doctoral research project which is concerned with the popular representation of Indian women in Canadian, British and Indian newspapers and the representation of Indian women by a sample of Indian women themselves. The fieldwork involved in-depth interviews with small samples of women from the south of India.

When I went to India two years later to begin this research, I innocently believed that I would be accepted as a child of Indian parents, who had migrated to Canada some time ago. When asked where I was from, I told many of my participants that I was from Canada. When I did this, they almost certainly paused and looked quizzically at my features, . . . 'but where are your parents from?' they would ask and, when I would say, 'India' or 'Pakistan', they would sigh knowingly and say, 'I knew you looked Indian'. When I introduced myself as a child of Indian parents and stressed my parents' (and thus my own) 'Indianness' as an alternative way of representing myself. I was told that I was not really Indian as I had not grown up in India, nor did I really look Indian. Visweswaran writes that 'for someone who is neither fully Indian nor wholly American', the question 'where are you from?' can '[provoke] a sudden failure of confidence, the fear of never replying adequately' (1994: 115). From one day to the next, I felt confused about which approach I should use; both somehow seemed problematic and would leave sufficient space for questioning and challenging. I spent most mornings deciding to wear a salwaar kamiz only to end up being in the company of those wearing Western dress and feeling like an anthropological poser or, other days, showing up in a blouse and skirt and feeling very conspicuous amongst the saris. On one of my trips, I was told by some participants that I was fair-skinned and that it was not surprising that my father was Anglo-Indian. Another group of participants told me I looked like a typical Keralite, as my dark skin indicated. Even though I did not perceive these questions as racist. I remember feeling angry and frustrated when people challenged my representations, always probing and asking additional questions and then resigning themselves to some first impression.

Representation and identity have been one of the key 'dilemmas' for feminists engaged in cross-cultural fieldwork (Abu-Lughod, 1988, 1990; Acker et al., 1991; Berik, 1996; Kondo, 1986; Lal, 1996; Narayan, 1993; Ong, 1995; Patai, 1991; Reinharz, 1992; Schrijvers, 1993; Stacey, 1991). In several accounts marital status, dress and gender behaviour were of concern to many fieldworkers. Joke Schrijvers, in reflecting on her research with Sri Lankan women, writes that she presented herself as a married woman to her participants, but that eventually her two young sons, who accompanied her on her fieldwork trip, revealed to her participants that she was unmarried to her current partner. Consequently, Schrijvers revealed 'all' and informed her participants that she was in fact divorced and that her present partner was not the father of her two sons. To her surprise, her marital status, which she had believed would make her less respected by her participants, created more opportunities for dialogue:

> Contrary to what we had been afraid of, our scandalous past did not damage our good reputation. Rather it helped us to be viewed as more or less 'normal' human beings, people who, just like most villagers, had undergone some serious difficulties in their personal lives . . . [i]mmediately after the news had spread through the village women started confiding in me, talking about their own family dramas they had so far kept silent about. We became much closer, and I did not have to rebel any longer against the unwelcome image of the lofty lady maintaining the family status.
>
> (Schrijvers, 1993: 149)

But other researchers feel it is necessary to preserve and maintain 'respectability' within the communities they research. Günseli Berik, in her research in rural Turkey, chose to conform to 'gender norm' by avoiding walking alone in the city streets, performing different greetings of affection and offering addresses of respect for different members of the family and, in general, she 'acquiesced to a subordinate role vis-a-vis men in the villages' (1996: 60). She felt that the 'cost of nonconformity' would have resulted in her not being able to interview women (1996: 65). From Berik's and Schrijvers's accounts, it is apparent that many difficulties arise in the course of conducting research in relation to how a researcher should represent herself to her participants both for the purpose of facilitating access to interview participants and keeping a check on power relations between participant and researcher.

These feminist accounts, alongside my own experiences, demonstrate the problems of naming and the power of others to name while challenging dominant ideas about representation in the field. Like Schrijvers, I was prepared to answer questions about my marital status from participants. However, the majority of them were unconcerned with this issue and, instead, were more often concerned with my 'authenticity', either as a South Asian or a Canadian.

Identity

The starting-point of critical elaboration is the consciousness of what one really is, and 'knowing thyself' as a product of the historical process to date which has deposited in you an infinity of traces, without leaving an inventory (Gramsci, 1971: 324).

How do identities affect research? How did my inability to name where I am *really* from (as if there is a truth to my origins) structure my interactions with participants? In Diane Wolf's account of fieldwork dilemmas, she suggests that:

> ... those who studied a group to which they belonged often claimed to have an advantage that led to a privileged or more balanced view of the people/society under study. This perspective includes arguments that native or indigenous researchers would offer a critique of colonialist, racist, ethnocentric, and exploitative anthropology, balance the distortions presented by white or Anglo researchers, creatively use their special standpoint or double consciousness, or be privileged to a more intimate view.
>
> (1996: 15)

While I am a diasporic,[3] I was not returning 'home' to do research.[4] Nevertheless, I did feel a sense of 'double consciousness' that allowed me to be both an insider and outsider simultaneously, 'moving between two worlds and identities, disrupting traditional anthropological boundaries between Self and Other' (Wolf, 1996: 17). However, some feminists have criticized such a pure bifurcation, suggesting that identity in the field is too complicated to exist as one or the other and that 'two halves cannot adequately account for the complexity of an identity in which multiple countries, regions, religions and classes come together' (Narayan, 1993: 673).

But, the question about where I am *really* from was often aimed at uncovering more than my national or ethnic identity. The question often spurred on other identity questions, especially in relation to class. For example, many participants, besides asking where I was from, wanted to know my parents' occupations and, in many cases, what they earned and owned. In asking where I was *really* from, my participants and others whom I spoke with during fieldwork did not only want to understand and position me in terms of my national identity, but the ways I could be placed in economic and material terms. Being seen as either Anglo-Indian, Goan, Indian or Canadian was so interconnected with class that it served to indicate my level of respectability and legitimacy as a researcher in India as well as how they should or could behave towards me.

Kirin Narayan argues that other factors, such as gender, class, sexual orientation, race and duration of contacts, may 'outweigh the cultural identity we associate with insider or outsider status' (1993: 672). Her critique of the entire insider-outsider paradigm traces the initial distinction between 'native' and 'real' anthropologist to colonialist times. She asks, how native is a native anthropologist and how foreign is one from abroad? She argues for a greater focus on the 'quality of relations' with those we represent in our texts and for the 'enactment of hybridity' in writing that 'depicts authors as minimally bicultural in terms of belonging simultaneously to the world of engaged scholarship and the world of everyday life' (Narayan, 1993: 671). Narayan argues that every anthropologist exhibits a ' "multiplex subjectivity" with many cross cutting identifications, such that each context may force us to choose or accept different facets of our subjectivity' (Narayan, 1993: 681). Furthermore, Aiwha Ong argues that 'ethnographic authority derives not so much from our position and embodiment as postcolonial analysts as from recognition of an inter-referencing sensibility that we share with less privileged postcolonial women' (1995: 367). Ong suggests that feminists should move from a politics of positionality to a politics of intercultural perception and interaction in ethnography where 'this common ground of a decentered cultural/political relationship to the West can foster a more equitable kind of listening and retelling' (1995: 367). In this way, my own struggles with representation and identity served as a resource and link to the research participants of this study, especially when I experienced some of the frustrations of having identities inscribed on me, despite efforts to mark out identities for myself.

What impact did the research process have on my identity? In a project that was centred around Indian women's accounts of their identity, their experiences of being daughters and of having daughters, it is interesting that the process should also reveal a great deal about myself. In constructing these women's lives, the process contributed to a reinscription of my 'multiplex subjectivity'. Often, in the process of 'storytelling', of giving accounts of their lives, it was not uncommon for my participants to construct me in particular ways, challenging my own hazy boundaries. While some of my participants would regularly make generalizations about Indian culture and seek a cultural handshake to confirm that I did have that particular insider knowledge, they also did precisely the opposite, suggesting that, as a westerner and foreigner, I could not possibly know anything other than media stereotypes when it came to Indian culture. For example, the women often sought a look of approval when they complained about men's lack of participation in household duties, but suggested that I would not fully understand family life in India because I had not grown up there.

While I have not found it any easier to describe where I am from, I suggest that my 'multiplex subjectivities' will be partially revealed through my representation of women participants in the final product:

> . . . it has become clear that every version of an 'other', wherever found, is also the construction of a 'self' and the making of ethnographic texts . . . is the constant reconstitution of selves and others through specific exclusions, conventions and discursive practices.
>
> (Clifford, 1986: 23–4)

The Field and Power Relations

Before doing fieldwork, I always imagined the field as a place that exists separately from 'home' and where I would have authority and legitimacy as a researcher. After reading feminist accounts of fieldwork, I assumed that I would need to be in constant check of the power that I held as a western researcher and would need to implement many techniques to minimize and compensate for it in the field. I had also assumed that I would be asking the questions, listening to the stories and that, continually, I would be representing, reconstructing and reflecting other women's lives. Later in the research process, I also assumed that the field would be a quasi-homecoming, that I might experience a small sense of belonging and gain some insight into my parents' identity and thus my own and possibly resolve my dilemmas of representation.

What I found was that the field is a complex site of power, one which could be conceptualized in a number of ways, either as a web, network or text of the bodies living in it (Foucault, 1980; Grosz, 1994). Dossa suggests that 'the ethnographic distinction between home and field is untenable' where field-workers conduct research in multiple 'homes' and 'fields' (1997: 506). Any polarization of the 'field' and 'home' is easily challenged by my experiences, as there are obviously continuities as well as discontinuities between the two places. I also learnt that, not only was my identity a complicated thing to represent, but my participants had multiple, and sometimes unrepresentable, identities. In addition, the participants often asked questions, listened to my storytelling and constructed and fashioned identities for me, processes which I suggest challenge the view that participants are unable to play on different positionalities.

Pat Caplan suggests that feminists, in relation to their research participants, should ask, 'who are we for them? who are they for us?' (1993: 178). Where a researcher is socially located and positioned vis-a-vis the researched plays a significant role in processes of representation and its role in power relations. Rajeswari Sunder Rajan writes about the politics of location stating that, 'location is not simply an address. Rather, one's affiliations are multiple, contingent and frequently contradictory' (1993: 8). But the location and position of the researcher are important to understanding the nature of power in the research process. As Rajan notes,

> as a postcolonial feminist in India I undeniably have an institutional status that affiliates me with the academy in the west; at the same time I do not have a share in all the privileges of that 'other' place—especially and above all, that of the distance that provides the critical perspective of 'exile'. . . . My intention is not to claim for myself 'marginality'—it's a dubious privilege in any case—but to show that location is fixed not (only) in the relative terms of centre and periphery, but in the positive (positivist?) terms of an actual historical and geographical contingency.
>
> (1993: 8–9)

If feminists take into account the way in which their positions are reflected in the kinds of projects and perspectives they can adopt, a reflective and critical forum can be established. Because the researcher's life, politics and relationships become part of fieldwork, positionality and location cannot be ignored in reflections on process Patricia Zavella suggests that locating ourselves as positioned subjects and drawing on these social locations as a source of data are important for feminist research (1991).

In Dorinne Kondo's methodological accounts, she suggests that her participants asserted power over her during the research process, engaging in ' "symbolic violence" trying to dominate the anthropological encounter' and, in this way, research participants cannot be seen as only objects, but as active subjects, who have the power 'to shape and control the ethnographer and the ethnographic encounter' (1986: 80). This is true of my research experience, where I often felt that the actions of my participants were not just inhibiting access to certain people or sources of data, but were actually transforming the whole project. Some scholars have suggested that the issue of power in the research process is complicated, but that research participants generally do not have the institutional power that researchers do:

> Yet to claim complete powerlessness on behalf of the researcher seems disingenuous. It is clear that subjects can resist and subvert the researcher's efforts, making some interviews difficult or even impossible. But it is important to differentiate between the power plays during the micro-processes of interpersonal dynamics, which may render the researcher quite helpless, and her locationality and positionality within a global political economy. In other words, the powerlessness a researcher may feel when her subjects won't talk to her or won't share the full story does not mean the researcher is a powerless person.
>
> (Wolf, 1996: 22)

However, I suggest that the field is a richer site if participants are conceptualized as agents, rather than purely as victims of the research process. I do not claim that, as a researcher, I had no power at all, nor that feeling powerless always correlates with being powerless.[5] Nor do I claim that the question, 'where are you from?' travels with the same meanings, since it clearly has multiple meanings across location and time. I suggest that feminist fieldwork methodologies need to account for some aspects of the researched and researcher's multiplex subjectivities, challenging any uniform idea of the researcher and conceptualizing the field as a site of complex power relations.

On a personal, political and professional note, my fieldwork experiences have helped me to articulate some of the daily struggles I have experienced in Canada, England and in India. In the words of bell hooks:

> I have been working to change the way I speak and write, to incorporate in the manner of telling a sense of place, of not just who I am in the present but where I am coming from, the multiple voices within me . . . [w]hen I say then that these worlds emerge from suffering, I refer to the personal struggle to name the location from which I come to voice—that space of theorising.
>
> (1989: 16)

There is a tendency in feminist methodology to spend countless hours reflecting on these issues, perhaps at the expense of actually doing and completing feminist research. As Jayati Lal notes in her chapter on fieldwork, in an era of rampant reflexivity, just getting on with it may be the most radical action one can take (1996: 207).

Conclusion

In this article, I have discussed some of the debates in feminist methodology, focusing on ethnographic research, and situated some of my fieldwork experiences within the discussions concerning representation, identity and fieldwork. I have shown that some of the categories and labels that fieldworkers have available to them for representing and identifying themselves are problematic, especially for South Asian diasporics. How can a researcher who exists on both the 'inside' and 'outside' of South Asian cultural identities simply label and name herself? Or occupy positions of power and privilege in the 'field'?

The issue of representation is important both during and after conducting fieldwork. While emancipatory, participatory and reciprocal methods may have informed or been applied to the process of research, this does not ensure that the written representations will reflect 'equal' participation. In addition, final texts are always mediated accounts, with the researcher's own interpretation woven into the words. As Diane Wolf argues, representation in the final product does not necessarily challenge inequalities between the researcher and participants, as may be possible during the research process:

> Whereas experimenting with strategies of representation has produced some alternatives, it is doubtful that these forms of representation are distinctly different from others, since the end product does not necessarily appropriate less and does not shift the balance of power or the benefits.
>
> (1996: 34)

The power relations involved in representing other's experiences and voices cannot be avoided in qualitative research, even if they are accounted for. However, Jayati Lal argues that 'reflexivity [cannot be] an end in itself' and suggests that a 'reflexive and self-critical methodological stance can become meaningful only when it engages in the politics of reality and intervenes in it in some significant way' (1996: 207).

I suggest that the 'field' and 'fieldwork' need to be challenged and recon-ceptualized if research accounts are to be inclusive of all women's experiences, both as researchers and participants. If we, as researchers, recognize some of the problems with the labels that we use in representing ourselves, or the ones that are assigned to us in the field, it can help us to become aware of the ways in which we construct our participants. This may also enable us to recognize that names and positions in the research process are not static, but conditional, contingent and shifting. Research methodologies must account for the experiences of those female researchers who are not able to inhabit the 'native' and 'real' researcher categories, but who must carve out new, and perhaps messy, ways of being in the field. For South Asian diasporic and first generation researchers, this will hopefully lead to developing more complex ways of understanding both 'home' and the 'diaspora'.

Notes

1. The term 'first generation' is used throughout this article to refer to the first generation of a family born in the country of migration. For example, first generation Canadian refers to children of immigrant parents who are born and raised in Canada. Generally the term first generation refers to those who first emigrated.
2. Many thanks to Suruchi Thapar-Björkert for years of friendship and collaboration. This article would not have been possible without her intellectual and emotional support. Also, thanks to Joanna Liddle, Lynda Birke, Parvathi Raghuram, Nirmal Puwar, Jonathan Reinarz and two anonymous referees who provided valuable comments and suggestions.
3. According to Avtar Brah's definitions of diaspora (Brah, 1996).
4. For a good account of some of the complexities of 'insider' fieldwork see Panini, 1991.
5. Thanks to Caroline Wright for her comments on a draft version of this chapter and for emphasizing that having power and feeling powerful may be very different.

References

Abu-Lughod, Lila (1988) 'Fieldwork of a Dutiful Daughter', in Soraya Atorki and Camillia Fawzi El-Solh (eds) *Arab Women in the Field: Studying Your Own Society*, pp. 139–61. Syracuse: Syracuse University Press.

Abu-Lughod, Lila (1990) 'Can There be a Feminist Ethnography?', *Women and Performance* 5(1): 7–27.

Acker, J., Barry, K. and Essveld, J. (1991) 'Objectivity and Truth: Problems in Doing Feminist Research', in M. Fonow and J. Cook (eds) *Beyond Methodology: Feminist Scholarship As Lived Research*, pp. 133–53. Bloomington, IN: Indiana University Press.

Bell, Diane, Caplan, Pat and Karim, Wazir Jahan (eds) (1993) *Gendered Fields: Women, Men and Ethnography*. London: Routledge.

Berik, Günseli (1996) 'Understanding the Gender System in Rural Turkey: Fieldwork Dilemmas of Conformity and Intervention', in Diane Wolf (ed.) *Feminist Dilemmas in Fieldwork*, pp. 56–71. Oxford: Westview Press.

Brah, Avtar (1996) *Cartographies of Diaspora*. London: Routledge.

Caplan, Pat (1993) 'Learning from Gender: Fieldwork in a Tanzanian Coastal Village, 1965–1985', in Diane Bell, Pat Caplan and Wazir Jahan Karim (eds) *Gendered Fields: Women, Men and Ethnography*, pp. 168–81. London: Routledge.

Clifford, James (1986) 'Introduction: Partial Truths', in James Clifford and George Marcus (eds) *Writing Culture: the Poetics and Politics of Ethnography*, pp. 1–26. Berkeley: University of California Press.

Coffey, Amanda (1999) *The Ethnographic Self: Fieldwork and the Representation of Identity*. London: Sage.

Dossa, Parin (1997) 'Reconstruction of the Ethnographic Field Sites: Mediating Identities: Case Study of a Bohra Muslim Woman in Lamu (Kenya)', *Women's Studies International Forum* 20(4): 505–15.

Fanon, Frantz (1990) 'The Fact of Blackness', in David Goldberg (ed.) *Anatomy of Racism*, pp. 108–26. Minneapolis, MN: University of Minnesota Press.

Fonow, M. and Cook, J. (eds) (1991) *Beyond Methodology: Feminist Scholarship as Lived Research.* Bloomington, IN: Indiana University Press.

Foucault, Michel (1980) *Power/Knowledge: Selected Interviews and Other Writings, 1972–1977,* Colin Gordon (ed.) New York: Pantheon Books.

Gluck, S. and Patai, D. (eds) (1991) *Women's Words: The Feminist Practice of Oral History.* London: Routledge.

Golde, Peggy (1970) *Women in the Field: Anthropological Experiences.* Berkeley: University of California Press.

Gramsci, Antonio (1971) *The Prison Notebooks: Selections.* Quintin Hoare and Geoffrey Nowell Smith (trans and eds), New York: International Publishers.

Grosz, Elizabeth (1994) *Volatile Bodies: Toward a Corporeal Feminism.* Bloomington, IN: Indiana University Press.

hooks, bell (1989) *Talking Back: Thinking Feminist, Thinking Black.* Boston, MA: Southend Press.

Kondo, Dorinne (1986) 'Dissolution and Reconstitution of Self: Implications for Anthropological Epistemology', *Cultural Anthropology* 1(1): 74–88.

Lal, Jayati (1996) 'Situating Locations: The Politics of Self, Identity, and "Other" in Living and Writing the Text', in Diane Wolf (ed.) *Feminist Dilemmas in Fieldwork,* pp. 185–214. Oxford: Westview Press.

Martin, Biddy and Mohanty, Chandra (1986) 'Feminist Politics: What's Home Got to Do With It?', in Teresa de Lauretis (ed.) *Feminist Studies,* pp. 191–212. Bloomington, IN: Indiana University Press.

Minh-ha, Trinh (1989) *Woman, Native, Other: Writing Postcoloniality and Feminism.* Bloomington, IN: Indiana University Press.

Narayan, Kirin (1993) 'How Native is a "Native" Anthropologist?', *American Anthropology* 95(3): 671–86.

Ong, Aiwha (1995) 'Women of China: Travelling Tales and Traveling Theories in Postcolonial Feminism', in Ruth Behar and Deborah Gordon (eds) *Women Writing Culture,* pp. 350–72. Berkeley: University of California Press.

Panini, M. (ed.) (1991) *From the Female Eye: Accounts of Women Fieldworkers Studying Their Own Communities.* Delhi: Hindustan Publishing Corporation.

Patai, Daphne (1991) 'U.S. Academics and Third World Women: Is Ethical Research Possible?', in Sherna Berger Gluck and Daphe Patai (eds) *Women's Words: The Feminist Practice of Oral History,* pp. 137–53. New York: Routledge.

Rajan, Rajeswari Sunder (1993) *Real and Imagined Women: Gender, Culture and Postcolonialism.* London: Routledge.

Reinharz, Shulamit (1992) *Feminist Methods in Social Research.* New York: Oxford University Press.

Roberts, Helen (1990) *Doing Feminist Research.* London: Routledge.

Schrijvers, Joke (1993) 'Motherhood Experienced and Conceptualised: Changing Images in Sri Lanka and the Netherlands', in Diane Bell, Pat Caplan, and Wazir Jahan Karim (eds) *Gendered Fields: Women, Men and Ethnography,* pp. 143–58. London: Routledge.

Stacey, Judith (1991) 'Can There Be a Feminist Ethnography?', in S. Gluck and D. Patai (eds) *Women's Words: The Feminist Practice of Oral History,* pp. 111–19. London: Routledge.

Stanley, Liz (1983) *Breaking Out: Feminist Consciousness and Feminist Research.* London: Routledge.

Visweswaran, K. (1994) *Fictions of Feminist Ethnography.* Minneapolis, MN: University of Minnesota Press.

Wolf, Diane (ed.) (1996) *Feminist Dilemmas in Fieldwork.* Oxford: Westview Press.

Zavella, Patricia (1991) 'Mujeres in Factories: Race and Class Perspectives on Women, Work and Family', in Micaela di Leonardo (ed.) *Gender at the Crossroads of Knowledge: Feminist Anthropology in the Postmodern Era,* pp. 312–36. Berkeley: University of California Press.

23

White Like Me?

Methods, Meaning, and Manipulation in the Field of White Studies

Charles A. Gallagher

I came to my research project with the understanding that my racial background would be an asset. As a young white male from a working-class neighborhood I had been exposed to a raw, unadulterated, unapologetic kind of racism. The filtered and perfumed racism I encountered when I left my neighborhood and interacted with individuals from middle- and upper-middle-class backgrounds was made socially palatable by use of qualifiers, caveats, and appeals to meritocratic and individualistic principles. Being white and moving in different social circles has allowed me to sample (and at times be a part of) the way racism is expressed in different white communities. The "white stories" I heard growing up had, I was told, sensitized me to the ways of whites, which would inform and guide my research project. I thought I was uniquely positioned, a native son of white America, who could easily and readily chronicle the souls of white folks.

When I started my initial research on white identity construction by focusing on the way whites view themselves I did not need—or so I thought—to do much more than quickly gloss over how my social location might effect the interview process. I was trained to take into account the background characteristics of those we research and, to a lesser extent, the way the researcher's race, class, gender, and personal biography influences the research enterprise.

Reflecting on how personal biography influences the research process is a well-traveled road. But the development of the field of "white studies" has introduced new methodological terrain that has yet to be adequately mapped. If this line of research is to move from description to one concerned with rethinking and dismantling the way racial categories are constructed and made static, assumptions about access, rapport, and automatic insider status based on one's race need to be revisited and reconceptualized. In order for whiteness to be demystified and stripped to its political essence, our interviews must generate counternarratives of whiteness which give respondents the opportunity to rethink the white scripts, those "unquestioned assumptions" about race that are constantly being written, rewritten, and internalized.

I saw myself, at least in retrospect, as unburdened by my color because whiteness was the focus of my study, because I am white, and because I would be interviewing other whites about the meaning they attach to their race. In addition, the first phase of my research as an advanced graduate student involved interviewing white respondents from the metropolitan area in which I had been raised. I knew the stereotypes, economic profiles, and racial tensions which characterized my respondents' neighborhoods.[1]

There was a temptation to assume that I had access to respondents simply because of our skin color. Access to others because of one's race is often perceived as a methodological given. Describing how middle-class researchers use their own experiences as a template in which to bracket those they interview, Norman Denzin warns of the dangers of taking social location for granted in the interview: "They assume that all subjects will have a common perspective on such matters as annual income, patterns of sexual behavior, attitudes towards war, and so on: and they translate their stance on those issues into the interaction process, seldom questioning the legitimacy of their decision."[2]

It may be assumed that since the researcher and respondents are white and the interviews are about what whiteness means, the social biography and location of the researcher need not be scrutinized as critically as when, for example, a black researcher interviews Korean grocers in a black neighborhood or a self-identified Jewish researcher interviews members of Posse Comitatus. The legitimacy of one's role in the research process may be questioned, but because race and racial divisions are so central to the way we structure every aspect of our lives, the belief in a common perspective or narrative of whiteness may guide research assumptions and the interaction between respondent and researcher. One may be—as I initially was—lulled into the belief that the experiences of 200 million whites in the United States are linked by a common cultural thread because whites are the dominant racial group. However, while the majority of whites enjoy many privileges relative to other racial groups, one must nevertheless critically access where one's social location, political orientation, religious training, and attitudes on race fit into the research project.

Not only did I imagine myself having access to whites because I was white, but much of the literature on qualitative methods suggests that ascribed status should guide (at least in part) who one is able to study. John and Lyn Lofland, while cautioning researchers not to overemphasize the ascribed status of the interviewer, post this warning in their widely used qualitative methods textbook: "If you are black, studying Ku Klux Klan members and sympathizers will probably not be feasible. Nor are you likely to reach the desired 'intimate familiarity' if you are male and attempting to study a radical lesbian group."[3]

Providing an overview of how social location influences what researchers "see and do not see," John H. Stanfield II argues that "only those researchers emerging from the life worlds of their 'subjects' can be adequate interpreters of such experiences."[4] As a white researcher studying whites I saw myself situated squarely within the insider doctrine, which "holds that insiders have monopolistic or privileged access to knowledge of a group."[5] While inscribing myself within these interviews as a racial insider I was also able to maintain the role of the "objective" outsider. This methodological legerdemain could be maintained simply by embracing the neutral techniques of qualitative methods outlined in textbooks which define the field. I could embrace the role of detached dispassionate researcher-outsider with access to knowledge "accessible only to nonmembers of those groups" while simultaneously being an insider because of my color.[6]

However, being an insider because of one's race does not mute or erase other social locations which serve to deny access, create misunderstanding, or bias interviews with those from the same racial background. Nor does perceiving or defining oneself as an outsider allow one to claim that one's research is value-free. Skin color does not necessarily allow one to automatically pass into and have access to individuals or communities because of shared ascribed characteristics.

"Being white," like being a member of any social group, has a host of contradictory, symbolic, and situationally specific meanings. As a northerner raised in the working-class section of a big city who now lives in the South, being white will not provide me with automatic cultural access to the whites I will be interviewing in rural southeast Georgia. How will my whiteness smooth over differences based on my age, gender, or presumed ethnicity in my interviews? Will my Yankee dialect and status as professor with an urban university affiliation position me as a cultural outsider? Will the perception that I am Jewish, and the racial confusion many have concerning this category, make me a "racial" outsider? The argument could be made (and I have been told this already) that even though most people view me as white I will still be viewed as an outsider here in Georgia. In either scenario, as a cultural and/or racial outsider, I will have to consider how my perceived characteristics may shape the interview.

[. . .]

Marking or Manipulating Whiteness: Resisting the Racial Template

The field of inquiry now defined as "white studies" has grown enormously in the last decade. A number of "white scholars" are examining the ways in which white identity intersects with the issues of class, gender, law, economics, and popular culture. Influenced by postmodern theories of deconstructionism, this nascent field of inquiry has taken it upon itself to strip away the subjectivity of whiteness and expose the relational and situational nature of white identity. This intellectual scrutiny has moved whiteness from being merely a backdrop in the discourse on racial identity formation to becoming the subject of study.

When I started my project in 1992 little empirical work had been done on how whites define whiteness, on the social and political situations which push whiteness to the fore-front as a social identity for whites, and on the way the construction of whiteness is linked to structural elements which shape those meanings. This is no longer the case. However, the systematic, empirically grounded gathering and telling of white people's narratives about their understanding of their race, as opposed to the way whites define the racial "other," is still relatively unexplored.

When I initially formulated the questions that would inform my data collection I was not aware just how much my research project was being manipulated by my own assumptions about whiteness. In an attempt to provide different measures of the same social phenomena I employed focus groups, in-depth interviews, and a survey. But using surveys to tap something as complex as how someone constructs their racial identity raised a number of thorny issues. Could I examine whiteness so as to capture the social complexities and varied cultural nuances which define racial categories by using a questionnaire? Could racial identity be conceptualized as a temporally static and discreet category, like height, weight, or income? Could I, as I was instructed at one point, create a "white index" using factor analysis which would rank on a single scale the "whiteness" of one respondent relative to another? If I did not produce data that could stand up to at least a test of Chi-square would I be left, as I was told, with "only stories" about whiteness based on my focus groups and interviews which could not, by themselves, stand up to peer review?

After much deliberation and pretesting, my position was that by their very design, surveys could neither tap nor measure how, why, or to what extent whites come to understand the complex, contradictory, and subtle ways whiteness is articulated. A mixed methodological approach allowed me to use the cultural expressions of whiteness voiced by respondents in my interviews to frame and complement the survey questions. This allowed me to examine the underlying ideological and structural influences that mediate the process of white racial identity formation.

My struggle to create a methodological approach that included both rich textured accounts of the *meanings* whites attached to their racial positions and surveys that allowed for some generalizability beyond my population masked the more pressing ethical and political concerns that became apparent in subsequent interviews. As is the common practice in survey research, my questions were drawn from existing studies that purported to tap the attitudes of whites. The final survey questions and semistructured interview guide were drawn from "commonsense" notions about whites derived from surveys, popular opinion polls, social science research, the input of my committee members, and what I perceived to be the issues that shape white identity construction.

The resulting white template I designed, and which guides much of the research on race relations, is based on a priori assumptions about how social scientists understand and define white attitudes, white fears, and white culture. These survey-generated beliefs become the white attitudinal baseline which influences how researchers in other fields structure their interview guides and data matrices, or redesigned their survey questions. If white identity is conceptualized only in oppositional terms, alternative narratives of whiteness cannot emerge in the interview.

A portion of my survey and interview schedule have been included in Appendix 1 and 2. The overwhelming majority of questions in Appendix 1 reflect an early and (in retrospect) rather simplistic understanding of how and why whites attach meaning to their race. My survey questions tap a narrow version of whiteness that frames racial identity construction only in opposition to racial minorities. However, the open-ended questions in the survey did sensitize me to issues of identity construction which had not been adequately addressed in the literature. Not all whites construct their racial identity in opposition to blacks, Asians, or Latinos, nor did whiteness serve as a proxy to a reactionary worldview. These expressions, which challenged the "commonsense" literature on whiteness, became the basis for questions I would later ask in my focus groups and interviews. While relatively unstructured, my interview schedule reflects an approach to whiteness that attempts to capture whiteness as being constructed in oppositional and cultural terms. I believe the field of white studies is moving to a more nuanced yet critical understanding of white identity construction. The view that "Whites' "consciousness" of whiteness is predominately unconsciousness of whiteness"[7] or the that "Transparency, the tendency of Whites to remain blind to the racialized aspects of that identity, is omnipresent"[8] is no longer a sustainable narrative in the wake of racial identity politics. The view of whiteness as invisible will be supplanted by a theoretical approach to whiteness that will, as Henry Giroux argues, mark "whiteness as a form of identity and cultural practice" which "makes the distinction between 'whiteness' as a dominating ideology and white people who are positioned across multiple locations of privilege and subordination."[9] The idea of whiteness is being constructed, reinterpreted, and molded by whites for whites as a cultural product understood in ways other than being in opposition to nonwhites.[10]

Researching Whiteness as an Antiracist Project

In almost all my focus groups I asked or respondents offered their views on affirmative action. Respondents who had been reticent throughout the focus group discussion suddenly came to life, arguing forcefully about the need for, or more often the inherent unfairness of, affirmative action. In many interviews this topic was a turning point. Many whites took the opportunity to articulate a narrative of their whiteness that was based on victimization.[11] This conversation often led to a discussion about welfare, multiculturalism, and downward economic mobility because the labor market now preferred blacks and Asians to whites. The laments, outrage, and pent-up guilt about this topic were fascinating, sociologically rich, and deeply troubling.

But what if, after these issues had been exhausted, I had asked my focus groups to consider another scenario? What if they had been provided with a number of social facts about the relative social standing of whites compared to other racial groups in the United States? How might whites define themselves if it was demonstrated that racial discrimination in the labor market is unquestionably still a sorting mechanism that privileges whites, that whites are twice as likely to graduate from college as blacks, that the face of welfare in the United States is white, that almost every socioeconomic measure—from infant mortality, to home ownership rates, to the accumulation of wealth—favors whites over blacks, Latinos, or many Asian groups?

If the belief that whites are losing out to blacks or Asians was refuted in the interview and whites had a chance to articulate an identity that could not be based on victimology, what would that white racial identity look like? Would there or could there be a white racial identity that was not merely "a politically constructed category parasitic on blackness"?[12] My experiences suggest that when white respondents are given counterarguments that demonstrate that racial inequality still exists they *modify* many of their positions.[13]

While critical of my own work for bracketing a narrative of whiteness within a reactionary and conservative framework, Henry Giroux asks how, as antiracist researchers and educators, we might provide: "the conditions for students to address not only how their 'whiteness' functions in society as a marker of privilege and power, but also how it can be used as a condition for expanding the ideological and material realities of democratic public life."[14]

The conditions required to think ourselves out of an oppositional understanding of whiteness means breaking the racial template which seduces researchers into asking questions which merely reproduce a "commonsense," neoconservative definition of whiteness and race relations based on whites' perceived marginalization. Those who wish to "abolish the white race" or define whiteness *only* as a source of power equally shared by all whites, level the social, political, and economic differences among whites while creating a simple racial dichotomy which is easily and routinely manipulated politically.[15]

Data does not "speak for itself " nor does it "emerge" in a vacuum. Who we are (and appear to be in a specific context) influences the questions we ask, the responses we get, and the scholarship we produce, which is reproduced by yet another cohort of graduate students. Some of this scholarship finds its way into *Newsweek*, the *Wall Street Journal*, or as a discussion topic on *The Oprah Winfrey Show* or *Montel*, where it becomes part of our collective understanding of race relations. I was reminded of this trickle-down understanding of race relations by a white male in a focus group. He insisted that Rodney King was a threat to the police officers who savagely beat him because he kept moving when he was on the ground. "If you want to know what is really going on," he told the group, "You gotta watch Rush [Limbaugh]."

Unfortunately, the counternarratives that might challenge the existing racial status quo go in large part unexplored. A colleague from a working-class background who was familiar with my work told me the purpose of my project was to demonstrate that working-class whites are racist. I would, as others had done before, paint a portrait of working-class whites as racists. This was not my intention, although his prediction was fairly accurate. I was steered toward a version of whiteness that had been framed by the narrow binary ways in which many researchers choose to explore racial identity construction and had accepted the script that had been provided to my respondents.

Beyond White Essentialism

An agitated white male in a focus group, typical of many I interviewed, complained that whites are the new minority group in the United States. Talking about the treatment of blacks, Mike explained to me: "It's not like they're discriminated against anymore, it's like the majority is now the minority because we are the ones being discriminated against because we are boxed in. We can't have anything for ourselves anymore that says exclusively white or anything like that. But everyone else can. You know what I mean."

Throughout my research white respondents generally embraced the belief that the U.S. class system was fair and equitable. Most respondents argued that those who delay gratification, work hard, and follow the rules will succeed, irrespective of color.[16] Many white respondents felt the leveled playing field argument has rendered affirmative action policies a form of reverse discrimination and source of resentment. Jennifer Hochschild calls this "whites' quandary." "Whites are more sure that discrimination is not a problem," that blacks can succeed, that self-reliance pays off, that blacks now "control their own fate" *and* whites feel that their life chances have eroded.[17] This was how my respondents were able to define themselves as victims. As the above quote by Mike explains, it is whites who are "now the minority." Like the white stories I outlined earlier, the whites-as-victim perspective can be added to the ever-growing list of those situations, attitudes, or injustices that make up the "white experience."

Like many other young whites from modest backgrounds, Mike defined himself as the racial "other." He viewed himself as lacking agency in a world where he was marginalized because of his race. This perception lends itself to the development of defensive strategies based on an essentialist understanding of whiteness. What, many of my respondents asked me, would blacks do if we wore a "It's a white thing. . . . You wouldn't understand" t-shirt? My point here is not to examine whether whites can be the subaltern, the racial outsider in a white society, or the other "other." My question concerns the shift from a racial identity that is invisible to one made explicit and the way this process may essentialize whiteness. Michael Omi and Howard Winant explain that "a racial project can be defined as racist if and only if it creates or reproduces structures of domination based on essentialist categories of race."[18] While ostensibly concerned with social justice and racial equality it is unclear to what extent white studies, as a racial project, can embrace an antiessentialist epistemology or methodology.

Much of the work being done in white studies embraces an essentialist standpoint in two ways. First, we have allowed a narrative of whiteness to emerge which has been molded by a reactionary political and cultural climate with a vested interest in defending the racial status quo. We might challenge the tendency for white respondents to validate and justify white privilege by inverting the questions we ask, so that respondents are forced to think of the structural advantages that accrue to them because of their skin color. How might a white informant respond to the question that requires him or her to consider how a fifty-year-old, white-collar black or Asian woman might view their whiteness? Do we ask questions which challenge our respondents to think about race as a political category, or do we reproduce, normalize, and continue to make whiteness invisible by uncritically validating the version of whiteness we expect to hear? White studies is in a position to explore counternarratives of racial identity construction which imply that whites have agency in the way they define themselves, and suggest that they might take responsibility for, or at least have a fuller understanding of, racial privilege in the United States.

This is of course a double-edged sword. To not talk about the ways in which whiteness retains its invisibility and hence its power is to "redouble its hegemony by naturalizing it."[19] However, to talk about whiteness as a visible, meaningful identity with definable particularizing qualities, is to treat this category as if it were real. It is unclear at the time of this writing whether "white studies" will embrace a critique of whiteness that challenges racial hierarchy through an explicit antiessentialist discourse, or whether it will become the vehicle through which a sophisticated, critical essentialism is articulated.

Appendix 1

Survey Given to 514 Students at a Large Urban University

The entire original survey was thirteen pages. For this publication I have only included those questions that explicitly address white identity construction. Questions on race and residence, standard background variables, social networks and race, interracial dating, social distance scales, and the strength of ethnic identity measures have been omitted.

For a complete copy of the survey please contact me at: The Department of Sociology, Georgia State University, Atlanta, GA 30303–3083, or cgallagher@gsu.edu.

1. What is your racial/ethnic background?_____

2. What percentage of the U.S. population is:
    White   _____   %
    Black   _____   %
    Asian   _____   %
    American Indian   _____   %

3. Think for a moment about the neighborhood or area where you were raised. When I am in the area where I was raised: (check one)
    _____ I sometimes think about my race
    _____ I often think about my race
    _____ I never think about my race

If you answered "sometimes" or "often" what are the situations that make you think about your race?

_____

_____

If you answered "I never think about my race" what kinds of events in your neighborhood would make you think about your race?

4. When I was in high school: (*check one*)
   _____ I sometimes thought about my race
   _____ I often thought about my race
   _____ I never thought about my race

If you answered "sometimes" or "often" what were the situations that made you think about your race?

_____

_____

If you answered "never" why might that be the case?

_____

_____

5. In the course of my school day at Urban University:
   _____ I sometimes thought about my race
   _____ I often thought about my race
   _____ I never thought about my race

If you answered "sometimes" or "often" what were the situations that made you think about your race?

_____

_____

6. In the course of your school day at Urban University in what situations are you likely to think about your race? (check all that apply)
   _____ on public transit
   _____ in the dorms
   _____ in the classrooms
   _____ in Student Activities Center
   _____ in the library
   _____ driving to Urban University
   _____ dealing with the administration (bursar, financial aid)
   _____ when I am a numerical minority in a class
   _____ when I am interacting with students from different racial backgrounds than my own
   _____ parking off campus
   _____ when I interact with faculty
   _____ at fraternity/sorority parties

_____ staying late on campus
_____ sporting events
_____ eating lunch on campus
_____ being approached by the homeless

7. What other Urban University situations or specific encounters on campus are likely to remind you of your race?

_____

_____

8. Are there any situations on campus that you find threatening?

_____

_____

9. What percentage of the Urban University population is:
   White_____%
   Black_____%
   Asian_____%
   Other_____%

10. Do you think more about your race since attending Urban University?
    _____ yes_____ no_____ no opinion

Appendix 2

Focus Group and Individual Interview Schedule

1. General background questions: age, place of birth.
2. Where were you raised? What was your neighborhood like? Was it integrated?
3. How would you define your class background?
4. What was the class background of the family in which you were raised?
5. How do you define yourself ethnically?
   What is it—single, multiple, hybrid, symbolic?
   What meaning do you or does your family attach to your ethnicity?
   Are these things ethnically important: holidays, food, dating, neighborhood dynamics?
6. What does it mean to be white in the United States in 1999?
7. Are you conscious of being white? When?
8. In what situations do you think about being white?
9. What would you define as white culture?
10. Why do some whites feel threatened about the current state of race relations?
11. How is being white different from being black or Asian?
12. How is being white similar to being black or Asian?
13. What objects would you place in a museum of white history?
14. Define yourself politically.
15. What does that mean?
16. Once again, what does it mean to be white?

Notes

I would like to thank France Winddance Twine for editorial guidance and comments on earlier versions of this chapter.

1. See Charles A. Gallagher, "White Reconstruction in the University," *Socialist Review* (1995) 94 (1/2): 165–88.
2. Norman Denzin, *The Research Act: A Theoretical Introduction to Sociological Methods* (Englewood Cliffs, N.J.: Prentice Hall, 1989).
3. John Lofland and Lyn H. Lofland, *A Guide to Qualitative Observations and Analysis*, 2d ed. (Belmont, Calif.: Wadsworth, 1984).
4. John H. Stanfield II, "Ethnic Modeling in Qualitative Research," in *Handbook of Qualitative Research*, edited by Norman Denzin and Yvonna Lincoln (Thousand Oaks, Calif.: Sage, 1994).
5. Maxine Baca Zinn, "Field Research in Minority Communities: Ethical, Methodological, and Political Observations by an Insider," *Social Problems* (1979) 27 (2): 209.
6. Ibid.
7. Barbara Flagg, "Transparently White Subjective Decision Making," in *Critical White Studies: Looking Behind the Mirror* edited by Richard Delgado and Jean Stefancic (Philadelphia: Temple University Press, 1997), p. 220.
8. Ian F. Haney López, *White by Law: The Legal Construction of Race* (New York: New York University Press, 1996), p. 157.
9. Henry A. Giroux, "White Squall: Resistance and the Pedagogy of Whiteness," *Cultural Studies* (1997) 11 (3): 383.
10. See Ashley W. Doane, Jr., "Dominant Group Ethnic Identity in the United States: The Role of 'Hidden' Ethnicity in Intergroup Relations," *Sociological Quarterly* 38 (3): 375–97.
11. See Charles A. Gallagher, "Redefining Racial Privilege in the United States," *Transformations* 8, no. 1 (spring 1997): 28–39.
12. Cornel West, "The New Cultural Politics of Difference," in *The Cultural Studies Reader*, edited by Simon During (New York: Routledge, 1993), p. 212.
13. Paul M. Sniderman and Thomas Piazza, *The Scar of Race* (Cambridge: Harvard University Press, 1993). Sniderman and Piazza found that whites were quite willing to change their minds about racial policy issues when presented with a counterargument.
14. Henry A. Giroux, *Channel Surfing: Race Talk and the Destruction of Today's Youth* (New York: St. Martin's Press, 1997), p. 108.
15. See *Race Traitor*, edited by Noel Ignatiev and John Garvey (New York: Routledge, 1996).
16. See Charles A. Gallagher, "White Racial Formation: Into the Twenty-First Century," in *Critical White Studies: Looking Behind the Mirror*, edited by Richard Delgado and Jean Stefancic (Philadelphia: Temple University Press, 1997).
17. Jennifer L. Hochschild, *Facing Up to the American Dream* (Princeton: Princeton University Press, 1995), p. 68.
18. Michael Omi and Howard Winant, *Racial Formation in the United States: From the 1960s to the 1990s* (New York: Routledge, 1994), p. 71.
19. Cited in David Roediger, *The Wages of Whiteness: Race and the Making of the American Working Class* (New York: Verso, 1991), p. 1.

24

The Power to Know One Thing Is Never the Power to Know All Things

Methodological Notes on Two Studies of Black American Teachers

Michèle Foster

In a 1988 novel by Gloria Naylor, a well-educated young man known only as "Reema's boy" returns home from across the river where he had gone to be educated to conduct research among his own people on Willow Springs, a coastal sea island that, according to Naylor, belonged neither to Georgia nor South Carolina. Armed with notebooks and a tape recorder, the indispensable instruments of an anthropologist, Reema's boy begins questioning relatives and neighbors about a commonly used phrase.

> And when he went around asking about 18 & 23, there weren't nothing to do but take pity on him as he rattled on about "ethnography," "unique speech patterns," "cultural preservation," and whatever else he seemed to be getting so much pleasure out of while talking into his little gray machine. He was all over the place—What 18 & 23 mean? What 18 & 23 mean? And we told him the God-honest truth: it was just our way of saying something. Winky was awful, though, he even spit tobacco juice for him. Sat on his porch all day, chewing up the boy's Red Devil premium and spitting so the machine could pick it up. There was enough fun in that to take us through the fall and winter when he had hauled himself back over The Sound to wherever he was getting what was supposed to be passing for an education. And he sent everybody he'd talked to copies of the book he wrote, bound all nice with our name and his signed on the first page. We couldn't hold Reema down, she was so proud. It's a good thing she didn't read it. None of us made it much through the introduction, but that said it all: you see, he had come to the conclusion after "extensive field work" (ain't never picked a boll of cotton or head of lettuce in his life—Reema spoiled him silly), but he done still made it to the conclusion that 18 & 23 wasn't 18 & 23 at all—was really 81 and 32, which just so happened to be the lines of longitude and latitude marking off where Willow Springs sits on the map. And we were just so damned dumb that we turned the whole thing around.
>   Not that he called it being dumb, mind you, called it "asserting our cultural identity," "inverting hostile social and political parameters." 'Cause, see, being we was brought here as slaves, we had no choice but to look at everything upside-down. And then being that we was isolated off here on this island, everybody else in the country went on learning good English and calling things what they really was—in the dictionary and all that—while we kept on calling things ass-backwards. And he thought that was just so wonderful and marvelous, et cetera, et cetera . . . Well, after that crate of books came here, if anybody had any doubts about what them developers were up to, if there was just a tinge of seriousness behind them jokes about the motorboats and swimming pools that could be gotten from selling a piece of land them books squashed it. The people who ran the type of schools that could turn our children into raving lunatics—and then put his picture on the back of the book so we couldn't even deny it was him—didn't mean us a speck of good. (Naylor 1988, 7–8)

For those of us doing research in our own communities, this excerpt from Naylor's novel should serve as a cautionary tale. Increasingly, those undertaking fieldwork and conducting life-history research are insiders, members of the subordinate groups they have chosen to study. Social science reveals a growing trend toward "native anthropology" and other insider research, studies by ethnic minorities of our own communities.

Despite this trend and a large literature on ethnographic and anthropological method that treats the involvement, role, and stance that researchers adopt vis-à-vis the communities they are studying, most of these references—contemporary work as well as that from earlier periods—deal with research conducted among others whether the others are the "natives" in "exotic" communities in United States society or abroad. This is not surprising. Traditionally, anthropologists have studied "the other." Thus, anthropology, even as it has promoted cultural relativity, was conceived and nurtured in a colonial world of haves and have-nots, powerful and powerless, self and other. As the ethnographic method became more commonplace and studies grew to include more complex industrial and postindustrial societies like the United States, the power relationship between researcher and researched remained unaltered. For the most part, this research has also been dichotomized, with the self studying the other, the powerful the powerless, the haves the have-nots. However, a distinctive hallmark of the newer literature in ethnographic theory and method, including recent work in education, is its self-conscious examination of the subjective nature of the research endeavor.

Presently it is widely acknowledged that all researchers are influenced by their particular perspectives. But what about the perspectives of ethnic minorities? In what ways do our experiences inform out research endeavors? Many of us are first socialized into the values, norms, and communication standards of our home communities and later, after many years of education, into those of the mainstream culture. Moreover, the subordinate position assigned to our communities in the American social order forces us to see ourselves through others' eyes. This means that we are more likely to understand, if only through our own lived experiences, what it means to be marginalized.

Crossing the cultural borders into the mainstream is often fraught with contradictions. In matriculating into the dominant culture, we are instructed in different paradigms, tutored in new world views, and trained in correct "ways of knowing." Years of schooling teach us to rename, recategorize, reclassify, and reconceptualize our experiences. Like the transition to English, the transition to dominant ways of thinking, valuing, and behaving is often complete and one-way. New values implanted, new voices acquired like the fictional character in Naylor's account; or, like the unfictitious Richard Rodriguez (1982), we may have forfeited the ability to communicate appropriately, may have renounced community belief systems, or embraced an ideology no longer in accord with that of our communities.

But these experiences also contain the potential for developing multiple perspectives that can be brought to bear on our research endeavors. Noted Black feminist bell hooks (1984) maintains that including the experiences of those who have lived on margin and in the center not only can enrich contemporary paradigms but can also invigorate progressive movements as well.

This essay is concerned with the problems and the possibilities that obtain when researcher and researched are members of the same cultural and speech community. It is written from the vantage of a Black woman with eight years' experience conducting ethnographic and life-history research in the Black community. Drawing on my personal autobiography as well as on firsthand experiences accumulated in two separate studies as a researcher studying the lives and practices of Black teachers, this chapter examines some of the political conflicts in which I have become entangled, the methodological dilemmas and ethical issues I have grappled with, and the multiple and often conflicting roles I have had to adopt in order to accomplish my research. The goal of this essay is twofold: first, to compare the competing mainstream and Black value systems at work in my own background and which frequently marked the research settings and resulted in political struggles; and second, to demonstrate the positive effect that a shared identity can have on establishing rapport and recovering authentic accounts, but also to illustrate that even members of the same speech and cultural community are differentiated by other equally important characteristics that make the researcher both an insider as well as an outsider.

Problem, Theory, and Method

A review of the sociological, anthropological, and first-person literature on teachers convinced me that African-American teachers had largely been ignored by the literature; where they had been portrayed, except in a few instances, it had generally been in a negative not a positive light. Most of the negative portrayals of African Americans were written by outsiders and at a time when the rhetoric of equal opportunity made attacks on segregated schools with all their attendant shortcomings, including Black teachers, legitimate targets. These findings seemed to endorse Du Bois's (1945) comment that because the fates of Black teachers have been so entangled with the maintenance of segregated schools for Black pupils, it has been difficult to attack segregated schools and at the same time to commend and respect Black teachers.

To my surprise, when Blacks wrote about Black teachers, their descriptions were considerably more flattering and well balanced than those penned by Whites. Finally, though I found several historical accounts that chronicled the fight undertaken by the Black community to secure Black teachers for its children, accounts written by Black teachers themselves, either historic or contemporary, are relatively rare.

The preponderance of negative portrayals of Black teachers written by outsiders, the contrasting more flattering and well-balanced insider descriptions, and the paucity of Black teachers telling their own stories convinced me of the need to augment the literature of Black teachers speaking in their own voices. Voice is a multifaceted concept. On one hand, it may be understood simply as words; on the other the concept of voice can extend beyond mere words to include perspectives and particular orientations. Consequently in developing my research strategy, I had to deal with several other issues—the choice of subjects, the definition of the problem, the source of the analytic categories employed, and the appropriateness of theories applied to interpreting the words—all essential to the concept of voice.

My first consideration was developing a process that would enable me to study those Black teachers whose practice could typify what the Black community thought best about its teachers. To this end, I developed "community nomination," a term and method of selecting the teachers designed specifically for this study. Community nomination builds on the concept of "native anthropology" developed by Jones (1970) and Gwaltney (1980, 1981) in order to gain what anthropologists call an "emic" perspective, an insider's view—in this case the Black community's perspective of a good teacher. Teachers selected by this method were chosen though direct contact with Black communities. African-American periodicals, organizations, institutions, and individuals provided the names of the teachers.

Another consideration was deciding among the various theoretical orientations. My graduate training had been in the traditions of phenomenology, African-American anthropology and sociolinguistics, and the related field (ethnography) of speaking. Each of these perspectives and a more recent interest in critical theory influenced my understanding and approach to the topic. At the same time, I was mindful of hooks's (1984) caution that just because individuals are unable to articulate a particular position is not evidence per se of their never having embraced it. Her admonition, coupled with my own desire to preserve the authenticity and integrity of the teachers' experience, inclined me to search for explanations that would enable me to meld their interpretations with the theories that guided my work.

Researcher as Subject

The process of the research as well as the subjective experiences of the researcher are currently the subject of intense debate (Peshkin 1988; Lather 1991). In my case, these are important considerations. In a number of respects, my experiences are not unlike those of the teachers whose lives and practices form the basis of my inquiries. Like them I have been a teacher for most of my professional life. And though younger than some, what we all have in common is having belonged to the generations that came of age during the period when separate but equal was a controlling principle of American society.

It was within my family and local community that I learned my first lessons about simultaneously being an insider and an outsider. My family also made sure that I understood the need for individual and collective struggle against the structures of racism. Being both an insider and outsider in the small, predominantly White, New England community where my family have lived since 1857 necessitated not only that I understand mainstream Anglo values but also become proficient in its norms and behavior. It was not only household and community circumstances that dictated these lessons but also my family's expressed desire for me to prepare myself to take advantage of the improved opportunities for Blacks they believed were on the horizon. At the same time, however, my family wanted me to have a strong racial identity, to feel at ease and be a part of the Black community in which we spent the most significant portion of our social lives. Consequently, they expected me to recognize when the values of the separate but overlapping community were at odds and, depending on the context, to demonstrate appropriate behavior. Whether taught explicitly by pointing out where specific transgressions had occurred or more indirectly through family stories, the training was unambiguous and the lessons to be learned unequivocal. For instance, because of my early school success and the prospect of a favorable future in academic pursuits, my mother made sure I internalized the lesson that, while scholarly pursuits were important, they were not more important nor were they to override competence in social interaction. One could never retreat to solitary activities if others desired social interaction; to do so was considered rude and self-centered. Another lesson drilled into me was the community prohibition against self-aggrandizement, a behavior commonly associated with the White community, which my family scorned. It was not uncommon to hear the sarcastic retort "That's damn White of you" addressed to someone for calling attention to some act that was generally expected of them. Correspondingly, it was not unusual for a person who had been complimented for some personal achievement to minimize its importance by responding that "White folks raised me."

In order to establish the fact that our family was both insider and outsider, and to reinforce a responsibility to fight any injustice, my grandmother told many stories. One of her favorites described an incident that occurred when my uncle was a teenager. While walking with friends on the way home from school one day, he was verbally attacked by a group of out of towners, who were in town to work on a construction project. A person who rarely tolerated insults of any kind, my grandmother insisted that the town fathers take action. The mayor, along with other city officials, responded by demanding that the crew leave town "by sundown." Outsiders, they insisted, could not harass any of the townspeople.

While this story can be read as an acknowledgement of my family's insider status, my grandmother told others that it highlighted the family's standing as outsiders. In one story, my grandmother recalled the fierce battle she had undertaken to ensure that my mother and uncle were placed in the high school's college preparatory program instead of the vocational track deemed more suitable to the employment prospects for Negroes. Accompanying my grandmother's stories were my grandfather's anecdotes of his early involvement in founding the Brotherhood of Sleeping Car Porters, one of the first unions to wage a collective struggle for fair treatment of Black workers.

While the perception of limited opportunity can result in developing an oppositional frame of reference with respect to academic achievement (Ogbu 1988, 1989, 1991) or in developing a raceless persona in order to achieve academically (Fordham 1988), my family's response to limited opportunity was to excel in spite of the limitations and to maintain strong cultural and political affiliations and ties to the Black community in the process. In other words, my family strove to make sure that I would develop what Du Bois (1903) referred to as a double consciousness, an awareness of who I was and what I was capable of achieving regardless of the prevailing beliefs of society.

Unwittingly, with its explicit teaching and unambiguous expectations, my Catholic schooling bolstered my family's teaching. Not until college—the locus of my initial socialization into the bourgeois tradition of academia and the culture of the academy, a process that continued in graduate school—did the ambiguities become prominent. Attending a college with fewer than thirty Black students and living away from the confines of family and community obscured the separation between the two worlds. Concomitantly, the coaching that had previously been available about how to negotiate both worlds became more sporadic and less explicit.

After completing college and relocating to Roxbury, Boston's Black community, I began a twenty-year career as a professional educator. Several years as a substitute teacher in the Boston public schools (where, prior to desegregation Black teachers were unilaterally assigned to de facto segregated schools) and a subsequent position as a director of METCO (a voluntary urban-suburban desegregation program that bused Black students to predominantly White suburban school districts) cast me into the role of outsider once more. Most of the substitutes assigned to all-Black schools found it difficult if not impossible to teach in them. Like the students they served, these schools were considered undesirable. Consequently, the students in the schools to which I was assigned typically saw a procession of substitutes, many who endured only one day, others who vanished by recess. Unlike these substitutes, by revisiting and recovering the belief systems, values, and behaviors learned in my childhood, I not only survived but thrived in these schools.

One of my major responsibilities as a METCO director was serving as a cultural broker, which primarily entailed simultaneously interpreting between White suburban teachers and urban Black students. One task was helping White teachers, many of whom were considered effective with White students and appeared to encounter few serious difficulties teaching them, learn how to interact successfully with Black students participating in the METCO program. This task was matched only by the equally difficult one of trying to convince the Black students that they should cooperate with their teachers. My efforts at cultural brokering were only partially successful. Although teachers and students gradually expanded the meanings they attached to specific behaviors, rarely did these expanded interpretations produce any adjustments in their behavior.

Returning to graduate school, I resumed my struggle with the culture of the academy. One of my principal frustrations was the lack of fit between my experiences and the germinal theories being taught in graduate school. African-American conceptions, values, or belief systems rarely figured into analyses or solutions. My insights into characteristics that differentiated the Black and White communities had no forum in the graduate school classroom, nor did the considerable personal information I had accumulated about how to teach Black students. Consequently, I was left alone to try to reconcile what I was learning in graduate school with my own lived experiences. In her forthright discussion about the formulation and distribution of a particular perspective as if it were universal, Smith (1987) writes:

> The forms of thought we make use of to think about ourselves and our society are part of the relations of ruling and hence originate in positions of power. These positions are occupied by men almost exclusively, which means that our forms of thought put together a view of the world from a place women do not occupy. The means that women have had available to them to think, imagine and make actionable their experience have been made for us and not by us. It means that our experience has not been represented in the making of our culture. There is a gap between where we are and the means we have to express and act. It means that our concerns, interests and experiences forming "our" culture are those of men in positions of dominance whose perspectives are built on the silence of women (and of others). As a result the perspectives, concerns, interests of only one sex and one class are directly and actively involved in producing, debating, and developing its ideas, in creating its art, in forming its medical and psychological conceptions, in framing its laws, its political principles, its educational values and objectives. (19–20)

Though in this passage Smith is referring to the absence of women in the construction of the culture, her words apply to the experiences of other subordinate groups as well. Her words represent the voicelessness I felt in graduate school, where faculty strove to ground me in the particular understandings and knowledge that they assumed were generalizable to everyone, a phenomenon that others have described (Murrell 1991). Despite my determination to maintain my racial identity and cultural behaviors, the faculty also undertook with the assistance of my peers to indoctrinate me into a distinctive mind set and, by altering my manner and deportment, to align my behavior more closely with that expected of academics. As typifies the middle class, the power exerted in the academy was hidden, concealed from view (Delpit 1988).

Regardless of academic potential, failure to conform to middle-class norms exacts severe penalties, including exclusion from the "star system," a process whereby early in their graduate education particular individuals are marked for distinguished achievements. Admission into the star system depends principally on the level of comfort and familiarity potential stars communicate to their sponsors, and only secondarily on talent and persistence (Carter 1991). Denied admission to the star system cast me once again into the role of outsider.

The Studies

As mentioned earlier, this chapter draws on my own experiences conducting research in two separate studies on the lives and practices of Black teachers. While both studies are similar with respect to subject matter, there were important differences pertaining to methodology and context. In the first one, I undertook a study of the practice of one Black teacher, whom students had consistently rated as an "ideal type." The dominant approach to gathering data was ethnography—principally sociolinguistic behavior—with only a secondary focus on life history. As I reviewed the notes from informal conversations and the transcripts of the more formal interviews undertaken with this teacher, it became increasingly apparent the extent to which the teacher's philosophy of teaching and her pedagogy had been influenced by and was grounded in her social and cultural experiences in the Black community. Interested in comparing this teacher to others, I expanded my research to include a larger, more geographically diverse and age-stratified group. In this way, the second research project, a life-history study of Black teachers, grew out of the first. While this decision moved me beyond the idiosyncratic nature of a single case study, it shifted the primary focus of investigation from behavioral and sociolinguistic data to information collected in face-to-face interviews. Thus while the subject matter in both studies was similar, the primary method of data collection in the first study emphasized observation over interviews and the second study emphasized interviews, with observations playing only a secondary role. Using Goodson's (1988) analysis of studies of teachers, it is possible to characterize my two studies as emphasizing varying degrees of focus on the "song" or the "singer." Since the research context was a critical variable that both influenced the course of my research and shaped my relationships with the teachers, the next section characterizes the settings.

Setting I: Regents Community College

I undertook the first study at Regents Community College in Massachusetts, a predominantly Black community college in the Northeast, where I had once been on the faculty. It is beyond the scope of this paper to describe in great details demographics and setting. A task that is undertaken elsewhere (Foster 1987, 1989). What is important to advancing this chapter is addressing the political situation at the college and providing a brief explanation of the two competing value systems that were at work there.

Founded in 1973 during a period of considerable community activism, the College was the fifteenth community college to be charted by the State Board of Regents. Its founders envisioned it as a Black college with a unique mission: to serve the underprepared students from the local Black community, a task which the other community colleges had neglected. From its inception, Regents was plagued by a series of problems, a succession of presidents and administrators, three temporary sites, high turnover rates among faculty, and, most important, a marked tension between Black and White faculty over the best way to educate its students.

Most often these conflicts arose because Black and White faculty held different ideas about what were appropriate goals for students. In an example from the college's early history, a group of Black faculty, seeking to establish a comprehensive writing program, forced the English department chair, a White woman, to resign for her comment that "their [Black students] was quaint and shouldn't be changed." Although some Black faculty conceded that the chair's comments could have indicated an acceptance and valuing of Black students' language, they were outraged by her suggestion that the Black students did not need to command standard American written English. In a controversial essay, Delpit (1988) provides a detailed analysis and clarification of both points of this controversy.

At the time of my study, an external grant whose overarching goal was to improve teaching and learning, but which was specifically designed "to train teachers to understand students' use of language and other culturally learned behaviors," was underway at Regents. Through a set of training sessions, workshops, and discussions led by experts, the project aimed to introduce the participants to anthropological research techniques through which they might learn how their students as well as they themselves behaved and used language in and outside the classroom. Because I was Black and knowledgeable about the issues the project sought to address, its director, a White woman, had enlisted my support. And although an outsider at the time, the director was aware many faculty still perceived me as an insider.

During the year that the project was begun the tensions between Black and White faculty reached a boiling point. Many Black faculty members were irritated because they believed White faculty were gaining too much power in the college. Two factors—subtle changes taking place in faculty composition and changes in the faculty leadership—lent support to their perception. Though the absolute number of Black faculty had remained constant, over the two preceding years the percentage of Black faculty had dropped from 38 to 33. The fact that the faculties at the other community colleges in the state were overwhelmingly White made the increasing numbers of White faculty at Regents an especially sore point among Black faculty. At the same time two organizations—the Faculty Union and the Faculty Assembly, part of the college's governance structure—were scheduled to merge. Historically there has been a division of power based on race with respect to faculty leadership. Almost without exception, the Faculty Union leadership had been White and the Faculty Assembly leadership Black. Prior to the merger, the faculty had participated sporadically and rather unsuccessfully in both organizations. For some, then, merging the two organizations seemed a logical solution in a college where faculty were already overburdened. For others, however, the merger represented another attempt by White faculty to dominate the college. All of these factors coupled with the fact that all except one of the project trainers was White fueled the discontent of the Black faculty. Taken together, these facts suggested, if not a diminishing role for Blacks, an increasing one for Whites. The result was that the project became the flashpoint for increased hostilities between White and Black faculty.

From the beginning, the project was embroiled in controversy, the faculty divided over its merits. Faculty, both Black and White, gave similar reasons for refusing to participate. The reasons ranged from the irrelevancy of anthropology over politics in determining power relations and thus education, to the belief that class content—the subject matter taught—was more critical than the process used to teach it. But, for Black faculty especially, the project became entangled in the larger political issues that gripped the campus.

In order to accomplish the project, a series of workshops and seminars was undertaken with the expectation that the faculty would modify their classroom practices. Although fifty faculty, staff, and administrators participated in at least one of the activities, and while a fourth of these participants were African American, the large majority of those who actively participated and all of those that undertook major curricular changes were White.

Consequently, despite the fact that the project's stated goal was improving the education students received and involving faculty in curricular reform by providing release time—goals that the majority of Black faculty deemed inherently worthwhile—many were overtly hostile to the project and its director.

From the beginning the director was on the defensive. One of the first people to challenge the project was Ms. Morris, the teacher I was studying, who demanded that the director explain how "the study of primitive people"—the definition of ethnography she had read in the dictionary—had anything to with teaching Black students. Other Black faculty questioned what Whites could tell them about their own language and culture, which they believed they shared with the students.

Initially I tried to encourage Black faculty participation. Trying to persuade some Black faculty who were not involved in the project to reap some of its benefits became a personal goal. But despite my efforts, Black faculty remained distant. Part of the problem stemmed from the different value systems that were manifest in different styles of communication, which could be detected in the different patterns of interaction and which reflected the typical patterns for Black and White faculty. One of the major differences was Ms. Morris's use of more official channels as contrasted with my dependence on the more informal networks at the college. Although specific rules controlled routine tasks like xeroxing, securing library materials, and other bureaucratic matters, following the guidelines did not guarantee that tasks would be completed. The prevailing but unofficial culture of the school dictated using informal channels to get the tasks accomplished. Related to this was the director's tendency to avoid confrontation, which she did by conducting most of her communication, whether official or personal, by written channels. In contrast, the preferred style of African-American faculty, also my own, was to confront problems as they arose using written correspondence only to arrange face-to-face meetings. Despite the frustration, inconvenience, and roadblocks they faced in getting tasks accomplished and engaging in fruitful interactions, for the most part White faculty declined to take up unfamiliar ways of behaving. Ultimately, the escalating conflict within the project, a microcosm of that extant in the larger college, threatened to jeopardize my relationships with Black faculty and to derail and compromise my study, so I severed my affiliation with the project.

The irony of this project was that while faculty were attempting to understand the community-oriented participation of Regents's Black students, they were unable or perhaps unwilling to recognize the community norms and preferences of Black faculty colleagues. To be sure, the faculty and the researchers associated with the project wanted to understand the effect of cultural diversity on teaching and learning. Unwilling to engage in critical dialogue with Black and other faculty of color, however, they incorrectly assumed they could gain access to this cultural knowledge without seeking authentic renditions of that knowledge.

Setting II: The Construction of Black Teachers' Life Histories

In February of 1988, the active phase of my second research project, a life-history study of Black teachers, began with the interview of my first informant. Unlike the study at Regents, the teachers who participated in this second study resided in many regions of the country. Although all of the teachers I contacted agreed to an interview, there were long periods between initial written contact, subsequent phone conversations, and visits to interview the informants. One of my greatest fears was that when I arrived in an unfamiliar city, the teacher would not be there.

Eager to secure cooperation, but realizing that my informants were being confronted with a complete stranger, I claimed insider status, making sure from the outset to emphasize our shared characteristics in my initial letter and subsequent phone conversations. Whether claiming insider status minimized the social distance and ultimately influenced the informants' decision to participate is unclear. Most were flattered to have been selected to be interviewed; only once was an interview refused and then because of illness. John Gwaltney (1980), an African-American anthropologist who conducted a major life-history study of African Americans, discussed the willingness of his narrators who knew he was a "native" to assist him with his life-history project. My own experiences paralleled those reported by Gwaltney. Without exception, all of the teachers I sought to interview cooperated with my efforts. This generosity was exceptional since all of the arrangements for interviews had been made by letter and telephone.

Arranging and negotiating the details of my interview and visit provided me with some insights regarding the extent to which the teachers accepted my claims of insider status. Two-thirds of the teachers invited me into their homes to conduct interviews, a fact that seemed to acknowledge my claims of insider status. A few picked me up at my hotel, some had their friends drive me to the airport, and at least one insisted that I sleep in a spare bedroom rather than waste money on a hotel. In these informal settings, I interacted with the participants and their families, frequently accompanying and participating with them in activities within their communities. It is possible to interpret these courtesies as mere instances of hospitality; however, in retrospect I believe that they probably served a dual purpose. Watching me interact with family, friends, and other community members allowed them to observe my behavior and assess for themselves whether my claims of insider status were warranted.

My experiences during my first visit with Miss Ruthie illustrate this dual purpose of hospitality and testing that I was subjected to. When I arrived on Pawley's Island, a small community not far from Charleston, South Carolina, I called Miss Ruthie to find out how far my motel was from her house. "Just up the road," she assured me.

"About a mile?" I asked.

"About a mile," she replied.

Not wanting to be late, I set out at 7:30 the next morning to reach her house in time for our 9 o'clock appointment. The walk along the highway toward her house seemed interminable. Only when I arrived and was greeted by the teacher and two of her friends, who laughingly told me that they "didn't expect a city slicker to be able to make it," did I discover that the distance I had walked was over three miles. Once I had passed this initial test, Miss Ruthie and other members of the community were extremely hospitable, though I was mindful of their continuing scrutiny of my behavior. What I have concluded from this and other encounters is that invitations into their family and community worlds represented an attempt to tip the power balance in their favor.

A third of the participants suggested a more neutral location for the interviews, usually their school, but in some cases my hotel room. Often, but not always, after the initial interviews were over the teachers suggested that the next interview be held at their homes. This happened frequently enough to suggest that these teachers had felt at ease during our first meeting. Whether the interviews took place in homes or a classroom, a meal eaten at home or in a restaurant often preceded the interview.

My claims of insider status notwithstanding, a number of my interviewees were surprised to discover I was Black, claiming that I didn't sound Black over the telephone. Sometimes merely discovering that I was Black modified their expectations of the interview that was to take place. In other cases, teachers seemed genuinely pleased when they saw I was Black. But they gave no overt indication that they expected that our shared background might shape or influence the interview. Ella Jane was one teacher whose expectations were immediately altered when we met. Like all of the other narrators, she had never seen me before we met at her East Texas elementary school at the close of the school day. As soon as she saw I was Black, she excused herself to telephone her husband. When she returned, she explained she had telephoned to tell him she would be later than expected. "As I saw you were Black, I knew the interview was going to be a lot longer than I thought. White folks want to interview you, but they really don't want to hear all that you have to say."

Miss Ruthie, an eighty year old woman who had taught over fifty years in a one-room schoolhouse, had previously spoken with a number of other interviewers. Nonetheless, she was delighted to discover I was Black because as she said, "I've been waiting a long time for somebody Black to come and hear my story."

From my perspective these initial, overt markers of acceptance were insufficient evidence that the conversations were authentic candid versions of my narrators' lives. Therefore, I paid close attention to the ways in which the teachers used language throughout the interviews. Though I did not transcribe the tapes myself, I spent many hours reviewing them because my training in sociolinguistics had taught me that in order to understand completely what was being conveyed I needed to attend to attend to not only what was being said but also the manner in which it was said. Listening to the tapes revealed a consistent pattern. Early in the interviews, the discourse patterns were those of standard English. As the interviews progressed, the language shifted from standard English to include more markers of Black English. There were many morphological, intonational, and discourse features of Black English later in the interviews, suggesting that my insider status was being negotiated throughout the course of the interviews.

There were other characteristics that separated me from individual narrators, making me an insider and outsider in ways that were intricate and intertwined. I was a northerner when I interviwed southerners, an urban resident when I talked with rural residents, a younger person when I conversed with older teachers, a woman when I interviewed men. Often I was positioned as an outsider on several dimensions simultaneously. These characteristics shaped the interviews in some immediately obvious and less obvious ways. Consider the dimension of generation. Because I had lived through the turbulent time of the 60s, it was easier for me to identify emotionally with the racial struggles of the teachers who came of age during the same period. Conversely, although I had read a lot about the struggles of Blacks during the 20s, 30s, 40s, and 50s, and heard about them from my grandparents who experienced them firsthand, my emotional responses were muted compared to those I'd experienced when interviewing my age mates. This generational disjunction affected my interview with Miss Ruthie, a teacher born at the turn of the century. Throughout her interview she repeated her assertion that during the first and second decades of the twentieth century when she had attended Avery Institute, a private normal school founded by the American Missionary Association, the students regularly put on Shakespeare plays. At first, I missed the significance of her statement. It was only after reviewing the tape several times and hearing her repeat the claim in marked intonation that I understood its importance in her own mind. Not until I had read several books on the education of Blacks in the South, however, did I understand the historical significance of her assertion. What I discovered as I read these accounts was her attempt to convey that she considered the classical and liberal arts education received at Avery Institute to have been a challenge to the social order of the time, schooling that typically consisted of vocational training advocated by Washington and supported by the larger White educational establishment of the time (Anderson 1988). What this experience taught me was that my own outsider status, the result of generational differences, made it difficult for me to perceive easily or appreciate fully the significance of the racial struggles waged by some of the older teachers whose eras I had not experienced.

A comparison of the interviews of men with those of women also provided evidence that the connections that emerged from race were easily overshadowed by those of gender. The interviews with men showed sharply divergent turn-taking patterns compared to those conducted with the women. When I spoke with women, the talk was more conversational. Turn-taking exchanges were more balanced and there were many more instances of overlapping speech to mark comembership. In contrast, in the interviews with men there were considerably fewer occurrences of overlapping speech, and the turn-taking patterns were more asymmetrical, with men speaking for much longer stretches at a time.

The Power to Know

I undertook this research in order to recover part of the cultural knowledge and history of the Black community. By using the personal histories and personal experiences of members of the Black community and framing them in theoretical and conceptual perspectives that gave voice to their realities, it was my hope to contribute to a more complete understanding and empowerment of Black communities and that the work would become part of the collective memory of the Black community as well as part of the scholarship studied within the academy.

Even though there is a substantial and steadily accumulating body of research written by African-American scholars from an African-American perspective, it is too often the case that this work is marginalized from mainstream academic discourse. Let me cite a personal example. My early work on the performative aspects of "sharing time" (Foster 1982) and my subsequent work on the Black tradition of performance that undergirded the study of a successful Black teacher at Regents (Foster 1986, 1987, 1989) (reported earlier in this chapter) remain largely overlooked in scholarly considerations in favor of alternate, more mainstream, and Eurocentric explanations, despite the fact that West (1985) has identified the Black tradition of performance as one of the organic intellectual traditions in African-American life. It was only when the teacher in the Regents study authenticated her reliance on the Black traditions of preaching and performance and the students confirmed its significance that I felt that I had adequately captured her perspective and consequently that this theoretical perspective had merit as an analytic construct able to represent the organic intellectual tradition of contemporary African-American life.

I am convinced that the teachers' acceptance of me as an insider influenced their willingness to participate and shaped their expectations and responses. At the same time, I know that my claims to insider status were continuously tested and renegotiated, and that differences of gender, generation, and geography produced varying degrees of solidarity. Consequently, I make no claim that the information acquired through interviews and observations is absolute. Nor do I claim that the interpretations I have brought to bear on them are the only ones possible.

Research conducted by insiders cannot capture the total experience of an entire community. But neither can research conducted by outsiders. We must be mindful of this fact for, as the title of this paper attests, no one commands the power to know all things.

There were many times when I interacted with my subjects that I heard my own voice in theirs, voices that had waged a continuing struggle against an analysis of their lives imposed by outsiders; voices that had struggled to be heard among the echoes of dissonant interpretive frames seeking to reorder their realities to conform to an external agenda; voices that reflected the complexities of their lives unacknowledged by liberals, conservatives, or progressives speaking from their various camps, but seeking to appropriate them nonetheless. Research undertaken by scholars of color can be revisionist: it can offer new if disturbing insights, alternative and disquieting ways of thinking, can be a means of creating new paradigms and expanding existing ones, and can result in a much needed dialogue between scholars of color and their White peers. Regrettably, it is still the rule rather than the exception to distort and to exclude the realities and to subjugate the voices of people of color to further prevailing paradigms so as to fit the requirements of a caste society.

References

Anderson, J. (1988). *The education of Blacks in the South, 1860–1935.* Chapel Hill: University of North Carolina Press.

Carter, S. (1991). *Reflections of an affirmative action baby.* New York: Basic Books.

Delpit, L. (1988). The silenced dialogue: Power and pedagogy in educating other people's children. *Harvard Educational Review* 58 (3): 280–98.

Du Bois, W. E. B. (1903). *The souls of Black folk.* Greenwich, CT: Fawcett.

Du bois, W. E. B. (1945). The winds of time. *Chicago Defender* (13 October), 13.

Fordham, S. (1988). Racelessness as a factor in Black students' success: Pragmatic strategy or Pyrrhic victory? *Harvard Educational Review* 58 (1): 29–84.

Foster, M. (1982). Sharing time: A student-run speech event, ERIC Document Reproduction Service No. ED 234 906.

Foster, M. (1986). Folklore and performance theories: Models for analyzing classrooms. Special qualifying paper. Cambridge, MA: Harvard Graduate School of Education.

Foster, M. (1987). It's cookin' now: An ethnographic study of the teaching style of a Black teacher in an urban community college. Ph.D. dissertation, Harvard University.

Foster, M. (1989). It's cookin' now: A performance analysis of the speech events of a Black teacher in an urban community college. *Language in Society* 18 (1): 1–29.

Goodson, I. (1988). Teachers' lives. *Qualitative Research in Education: Teaching and Learning Qualitative Traditions.* Proceedings from the second annual conference of the Qualitative Interest Group. University of Georgia, Athens, GA.

Gwaltney, J. (1980). *Drylongso: A self-portrait of Black America.* New York: Random House.

Gwaltney, J. (1981). Common sense and science: Urban core Black observations. In D. Messerschmidt, ed.,

Anthropologists at home in North America: Methods and issues in the study of one's own society, 46–61. New York: Cambridge University Press.

hooks, b. (1984). *Feminist theory: From margin to center.* Boston: South End.

Jones, D. (1970). Toward a native anthropology. *Human Organization* 29 (4) (Winter): 251–59.

Lather, P. (1991). *Getting smart: Feminist research and pedagogy within the post-modern.* New York: Routledge.

Murrell, P. (1991). Cultural politics in teacher education: What is missing in the preparation of minority teachers? In M. Foster, ed., *Reading on equal education, Volume 11: Qualitative investigations into schools and schooling*, 205–225, New York: AMS.

Naylor, G. (1988). *Mama Day.* New York: Vintage.

Ogbu, J. (1988). Diversity in public education: Community forces and minority school adjustment and performance. In R. Haskins and D. Macrae, eds., *Policies for America's public schools: Teachers, equity and indicators*, 127–70. Norwood, NJ: Ablex.

Ogbu, J. (1989). The individual in collective adaptation: A framework for focusing on academic underperformance and dropping out among involuntary minorities. In L. Weiss, E. Farrar, and H. Petrie, eds., *Dropouts from schools: Issues, dilemmas and solutions*, 181–204. Albany, NY: State University of New York Press.

Ogbu, J. (1991). Low school performance as an adaptation: The case of Blacks in Stockton, California. In M. A. Gibson and J. U. Ogbu, eds., *Minority status and schooling: A comparative study of immigrants and involuntary immigrants*, 249–85. New York: Garland.

Peshkin, A. (1988). In search of subjectivity—One's own. *Educational Researcher* (October): 17–21.

Rodriguez, R. (1982). *Hunger of memory: The education of Richard Rodriguez: An autobiography.* New York: Godine.

Smith, D. (1987). *The everyday world as problematic: A feminist sociology.* Boston: Northeastern University Press.

West, C. (1985). The dilemma of the Black intellectual. *Cultural Critique* 1: 109–124.

25

Entering the Inquiry

Susan Talburt

A central portion of this book considers the constitution of academic practices in specific domains as three women, Julie Howard, Olivia Moran, and Carol Davis, create their relationships to their roles as faculty members.[1] Through interviews with them, their students and colleagues, classroom observation, and interviews and study of university policy and social life across campus, I seek to understand their academic work within the contradictory social and institutional space of Liberal U, the university at which they work. While some themes in this text resonate across all three women's academic lives, more typically they diverge, revealing problematics specific to each woman's institutional and social locations. As the following brief introductions suggest, the narratives that unfold in this text are unique in their combinations, recombinations, and elisions of aspects of the personal, political, and intellectual.

Julie Howard, a white full professor of religious studies, is a practicing Catholic who understands her life as a spiritual and intellectual journey. She has been at Liberal U for some twenty years and is well established in the field of contemporary American Catholicism. Much of her research is born of dilemmas she has faced as a feminist and a Catholic, a fact that positions her uncomfortably in a department dedicated to the secular study of religion. Her teaching is an effort to complicate students' understandings of religion, a goal she at times pursues through "objective," yet irreverent, pedagogy and at times through sharing her self and her experiences as Catholic, as feminist, and as a woman who has had breast cancer while inviting students' personal explorations into the classroom. Julie has infrequently *voiced* her sexuality in her professional life, although in the last few years—particularly after her mastectomy and decision not to wear a prosthesis—she describes herself as more visible as lesbian to colleagues and some students.

It was the end of June when I first went to meet with Julie Howard. She had given me clear directions into town and to her house. Flowers lined the sidewalk to the front door. "Come in." We shook hands and she directed me to her back porch, where we took the same chairs we would sit in until we moved to her living room in late fall. I was disarmed by the lack of small talk—no mention of the weather, no obligatory niceties. She seemed unconcerned with consent forms and logistics, reading quickly, listening politely when I interrupted her to explicate points. "That's fine," she said, scribbling her signature where I indicated. As she looked through forms, I noticed the seeming comfort with which she stretched out in her chair and wore her clothes, an untucked Liberal U T-shirt, shorts, and Reeboks. I found myself pausing for a moment to look at the place where her breast had been.

During this first interview, Julie spoke of disembodiments she has faced throughout her professional life, first as a female teaching in a papal seminary (Dr. J. Howard, the sign on her door said), then as a lesbian entering Liberal U's Department of Religious Studies in the mid-1970s, and finally, the summer before, after a mastectomy, as a woman who refused to wear the prosthesis she was told would make her look "normal," a decision she described as something of a re-embodiment. She explained how making visible her breast cancer has led her to rethink the concealment of her sexuality in her professional and parts of her personal life. She went on to tell stories of growing up in a religion in which girls were destined to become nuns or mothers, and the few who deviated from this rule were the "career gals." Her colleagues, she said, have thought of her as like a nun. When she turned to her work at Liberal U, Julie described her research as a process of thinking through and learning from questions she encountered in her lived experience. She spoke of maintaining privacy in her relations with students, listing what she does not reveal: where she lives, her telephone number, her religious beliefs, and her sexuality. At the same time, she spoke of pedagogical situations in which sharing her religious beliefs has been helpful and in which sharing her sexual orientation could be relevant.

I was struck by her seeming candor, surely not completely unguarded, but openly reflective, confident at times and at others floundering, "I don't know, I'll have to think about that some more." What had seemed initially to be a gruffness or bluntness was complicated by the vividness with which she depicted her experiences, her gentle rendering of the contradictions she has endured, and an unexpected moment when she said, "I'm looking forward to this, this year, and this interaction. I hope I'm the kind of person you want to do this."[2] After I left Julie that first day, I was rapt by her ability to paint complex portraits in words of the felt, thought, and lived. She had an irreverent streak that combined with an earnestness in reflection that engaged me in unexpected ways.

With the exception of a six-year relationship, she has lived alone during most of her twenty years in Oasis, immersed in intellectual and spiritual work, yet not isolated from a wide circle of friends. Her words in a conversation we had toward the end of our months together present some central aspects of Julie's life. We had been talking about feminism and the Catholic church when I asked, "You've often said that the Church is lifegiving for you despite the difficulties between feminism and the Church and what you value and what you care about, and I don't think I know in what ways it's lifegiving."

> I believe in God. Teresa de Avila is not something I teach, it's something I like. I mean the only thing in my life I would change right now—I would have cancer again, I would have that stupid relationship again—if I had a year to live from right now, the only thing I would do is try to deepen my prayer life. I have no other interest. I'm not interested in finding another partner, though it would be nice. If I don't, that's fine with me. I could write another book. If I don't, I don't care. I want my friends to remember me as kind and generous, and I would like to deepen my prayer life. So religion matters to me, and this is not the kind of place to admit that any more than it's a kind of place to admit being queer. . . . There are all these closeted parts of my life. I closet my belief, closet my sex, and somehow am supposed to clothe my body in a way that I might as well put it in a closet, to deny that I've had breast cancer. I mean, it's hard to say. I think if you don't believe in religious experience, it makes no sense whatsoever. And so I don't expect it to make sense, but I believe in God, and prayer is something I want to do. Church is one of the avenues that makes prayer possible in another way. Without it, I think I would be too inclined to just sit here by myself, in my little contemplative mode.

The links between her teaching and what she cares about, her involvement with a number of communities, her connection to spiritual and religious practices, the closeting of parts of her self, the sometimes contradictory dimensions in her life—resonated throughout our conversations and my fieldwork as I learned of her relations to Liberal U, her department, her students, and the subjects she studies, and as she spoke of the meanings of cancer in her life.

Olivia Moran, a white associate professor of English, is in her second year at Liberal U. Specializing in feminist theory and lesbian studies, she is an academic "star" whose intellectual project is to debunk the category lesbian yet whose success is due to her work in lesbian studies. She thus lives an interesting contradiction, being known and in some ways hired for her work in what she calls "the commodified category" of lesbian theory, yet using the premises on which she is called to speak to challenge the category. Similarly, much of Olivia's teaching centers on denaturalizing the given, be it social categories or the organization of knowledge; in this spirit, she does not self-announce in her classes. Although she eschews connections between sexuality and her roles as faculty member, her relations with colleagues and understandings of her work in the department are mediated by her sexuality and area of scholarship.

I went to meet Olivia Moran the afternoon of the same day I first met Julie. As I turned the corner of the hallway to her office, I found her standing in the hallway chatting with her colleague Karen. After we exchanged greetings and banter, I walked with Olivia to her office, a place that fascinated me throughout our time together. Each time I came in, some things remained the same, but others changed. I wrote afterward in my research journal: "It's messy—a pile of books and papers on the floor, a tipped over lawn flamingo in the middle of them. A slinky on her desk. Bookshelves filled with small plastic super-hero-looking things and other assorted toys. Maybe showing something to those who come in, but I'm not sure I can read the message." I remember feeling a little like I had after reading Virginia Woolf's *Jacob's Room*, unsure who Jacob was but very aware of his room. In another survey, I recorded the following: "Full coke cans, orange wig, ad for her latest book, an old lunch box, a Schwarzenegger doll that throws barbells, Barbie cards strewn on the floor, a *PMLA* wrapper." At one point during the semester, the plastic pink flamingo had something that looked like someone's tenure review file underneath it.

On our first meeting, Olivia had just finished teaching a summer session class and seemed anxious to get out of her office, so we went in her sportscar for beers at a bar on the edge of campus. After we sat down, I handed her the consent form to look over, which she glanced through and proceeded, quite eloquently, to deconstruct. I initially was somewhat alarmed, not by what she was saying but by *the fact that she was saying it*; it seemed incongruous, inappropriate to acknowledge the falsity of the contract in the context of a research relationship. As I listened to her, I found myself wishing I could be taping her words; ironically, it was not until she had signed the now-acknowledged-as-meaningless consent form that I was able to audiotape. Her voiding the consent form of meaning yet willingly signing it, had the discomfiting effect, I think, if not exactly of reorganizing our positions in relation to each other, then forcing a recognition of my dependence on her. It was Olivia's first performative interview act, one of a series to which I would become accustomed. Her performances had the effect of creating a tacit yet (I think) shared acknowledgment of the constructed nature of research relationships and something of a reconstruction of ours. For example, Olivia seemed intrigued that I didn't often refer to my interview guides during our time together, and would sometimes ask what question we were on. I explained that they were groups of topics that we were indeed addressing, but that I preferred to talk through a mix of what was important to her and what was important to me—and did not want to be bound by prescripted questions. Performing the impossibility of *sustained* natural conversation in interviews, she took from time to time to saying things such as, "So are we on clump number one or clump number two?" On one occasion, in one of our last interviews, Olivia read a question from my paper upside down and proceeded to answer it, performing yet another strangely disconcerting commentary on dialogue, power, and control in interview relationships.

During our first meeting, Olivia spoke of her understandings of identity, of academia as a space that allows her her own timetable to ask and answer her questions, and of becoming a smaller fish in a bigger ocean with her upwardly mobile move the year before to Liberal U. She spoke of her preference for questioning the category lesbian rather than assuming it, her rejection of self-announcing her sexual orientation, and her dissatisfaction with lesbian communities and political activism. She located her academic work as political, suggesting that her research "infected" classrooms by introducing new questions and that her performance of "unscripted" pedagogical acts had the potential to challenge aspects of processes of teaching and learning. She spoke of her field, positioning herself in feminist and psychoanalytic traditions and in lesbian studies and rejecting alignments with gay men. As was reiterated throughout our subsequent meetings, our conversation remained primarily in the domain of the professional, with only occasional talk of Olivia's family of birth, her life with her partner, or her circles of friends. The themes that would become salient in her presentation of self and in her actions were bound up with Olivia's performance of questioning as a means to change: questioning a category of sexual identity she doesn't believe is meaningful, questioning the roles of teachers and students and naturalized orders of knowledge in her teaching, and questioning the category of "lesbian theorist" and the "discipline" of gay and lesbian studies in her work in the English department.

I was drawn into conversation with Olivia in ways different than I had been with Julie. Julie had affected me on a personal level; Olivia struck me as an intellectual puzzle. Several months later, a colleague of Olivia's said of meeting her years ago: "She's all very much there, but she's inaccessibly there, so it was both intriguing, but. . . . She's there, she's funny, she's engaged, but you're not necessarily sure who she is even then. She can talk, I mean she can perform, she can perform her presence, but you're not sure who she is. And she's smart as shit, and she's really happy in demonstrating that, and you're just like, oh my God, you know, blown away by it." As I came to understand over time, the dynamic speaker, teacher, and thinker was in many ways performing a questioning of an essential "self."

Carol Davis, in her fifth year as an assistant professor of journalism, has expertise in newspaper journalism, media history, and cultural studies. Carol is African-American, hired through an affirmative action program that had the effect of undermining her scholarly abilities and constraining colleagues' understandings of her areas of expertise. Hypervisible because of her blackness in a white institution, Carol lives in a tenuous relationship with some members of the African-American community because she is lesbian and her partner is white. As she defines her roles as faculty member, she does so primarily in relation to her race and gender, struggling with issues of authority with colleagues and students. Her race obscures her lesbianism, rendering it inscrutable to others, despite the fact that she is "out" to her colleagues and at times to students.

Carol had been away during the summer, having just returned to Oasis from a year at another institution. On the phone she had described herself as "having her teeth a bit more on edge than usual" as she braced herself for another year at Liberal U. I appeared at her office a week before the semester began. The Journalism area felt orderly—carpeting, quiet corridor, names on doors. Carol smiled, invited me to sit down, and did the perfunctory pardoning of the mess on her desk. Except for a few papers and journals to one side, it wasn't messy. She was wearing shorts and a short-sleeved button-down shirt with a pattern of donkeys and black boys that said "real native entertainment" under each picture. Throughout our time together, I often thought that her office looked like an office "should": two awards she has received hang on a bulletin board over her desk, her diploma sits to a side, books on the media, women, and African-Americans line the bookshelves, a poster about African-American women fills the wall behind her head.

Carol attended to the consent form, expressing interest in talking organizationally of various aspects of the study and fashioning a tentative calendar of interviews and observations, one that would prove annoyingly difficult to keep. We then began our first audiotaped conversation, which would introduce me only schematically to the complexities of her experiences in her academic life due to her race, gender, and sexuality. She described her decision to enter academia as rooted in her developing political consciousness and intellectual interests. Based on her experience in newsrooms, she became increasingly concerned with issues of gender and race in the practice and consumption of media, as well as with disrupting commonsense journalistic practices, such as subverting market-based assumptions in news coverage, questioning objectivity in reporting, and rethinking the journalistic canon of "newsworthiness." She entered academia with a belief that a position from the "outside" would be more efficacious in effecting change. She turned to describe her first job at a four-year college, at which, as the first black female faculty member at the college, she walked into a minefield of expectations for the roles she would take on, primarily that of "black mother" to students. She was not "out" at her first job, a fact she says complicated her relations to the small core of African-Americans, who moved between knowing and not knowing. The difficulties she had negotiating others' knowledge/ignorance precipitated her decision to be "clear" when she was invited to interview for the position at Liberal U. She described being "awkwardly" hired there under a special affirmative action line—the first person of color in the School of Journalism—and expected to "embody all their diversity" through research, work on the curriculum, and student advising. As she spoke of multiple expectations that circulate around her race and gender, Carol included difficulties she has had in classrooms, as students sometimes challenge her "authority" because she is young-looking, African-American, and female.

Our first interview introduced some themes that would resurface over the next months, such as the raced, gendered, and sexualized otherness(es) that often define(s) her interactions with colleagues and students. Carol hinted at the projects of her research and teaching, her status as valued yet devalued commodity in her department, and her mobile affinities within the university. However, it was not until subsequent interviews that she would speak of her intellectual positioning in her field or department as she gains credibility through historical work and loses credibility in some spheres for what is seen as more speculative, politicized work that draws from cultural studies. In later interviews, she would speak of the tactics she has used to survive in predominantly white environments and to gain authority in her department. She would also speak of the ways the salience of her race erases both her sexuality and her professional expertise; she is granted provisional authority in her department in issues of race and gender, but not in the history of journalism. Like most, but not all of our interviews, the first interview stayed within the frame of the expected. There is something deceptively "clear" about Carol; as she spoke, she did not wander from topic to topic but focused on particular themes. She had a tendency to make a point, follow it with a narrative example, and offer analysis of the situation she had described (a journalistic habit?). The linearity of her talk often belied her complex understandings of the intersections of academic politics and the politics of race, gender, and sexuality; it was only by unsmoothing the lines myself that I was able to locate the nuances of her understandings. There is a similar clarity in her teaching that appears to simplify the complex; yet, understood in the context of her goals and the interpersonal dynamics of her classrooms, her pedagogy retains much of the complexity of her understandings. As I began my interactions with her, I was absorbed by her narratives, yet unable to move beyond them as transparent texts. I carried my naive readings into her classrooms, which initially dissatisfied me as unexciting, traditional, and authoritative. It was not until I began to reorganize her transparent texts and to juxtapose them to the texts of her classrooms that I began to listen to the complexities underlying Carol's practices.

On leaving her office after our first meeting, I wrote of her situation in her department, imagining colleagues' responses to her: "She strikes me as an 'acceptable black.' She's well-spoken, articulate, uses 'standard English' and doesn't slip into jargon or threatening dialects. . . . She's not scary in appearance, either as black or as lesbian—autonomous body movement but not dykey." Hers is an interesting acceptability, however, for she tactfully reminds spectators that she will not accept the status of "real native entertainment"—or "higher educational entertainment," as Hazel Carby[3] has said—that they might ascribe to her.

As may be imagined through these brief introductions, Julie, Olivia, and Carol each complicate the meanings *lesbian* and *academic* can carry. Coming to know them as I did demanded that I rethink the meanings of voice, visibility, knowledge, and practice. I have not always been able to resolve the relations of these terms neatly, and have become convinced that the lack of resolution constitutes the importance of this inquiry. Each woman's opening words in our first interviews begin to suggest the impossibility of fixing the meanings of *lesbian* and *intellectual,* and of voice and visibility in practice. I began each interview by asking, "Could you talk to me a little bit about your decision to participate in this project?"[4]

JULIE. I think I told you on the phone I had breast cancer last summer, had a mastectomy, and there was something about the whole process of getting a prosthesis—they start early. A friend of mine took me over to a place called Beautiful Creations. It was awful. I spent the entire time in that place crying, and I think said "Fuck" about five hundred and fifty times. And my friend kept saying to this nurse person, "She's not usually like this, she's not usually like this." But I just didn't want to do this, I didn't want to hide this, but I actually went to Vermont—about six weeks after surgery last summer—and I wore this goddamn bra with a fake boob. I was traveling with this good friend of mine who thought this was really nifty, but I felt worse and worse and worse about it, and I came home and took the whole contraption and put it in the garage and said, "Screw it, I'm not ever wearing this again." And the more I started thinking about that experience, in terms of hiding, the more I began to think about closets. . . . I was in a reading group, we were reading *Epistemology of the Closet.* I had sort of been thinking about it anyway, and lately I had been much more comfortable, I think, with being more, I don't know, being more dykey looking, kind of out in the department. Part of this is because of a friend in another department who's been, I call her my fairy godmother, and part of it is because I have a young colleague in the department now who's gay and who started taking me to gay/lesbian faculty cocktail parties which I had never gone to before. My life has been very, very different because of these people. And because of cancer. So anyway, I'm going to write an essay about being queer and about not wearing a prosthesis, and so in the context of thinking about that project. . . . The person who got me in touch with you to begin with told me it might help me think about some of the issues I want to bring up in the essay. So I think that was what piqued my interest. . . . I'm a scholar-writer, if I can't get something out of what I'm doing, I don't really want to do it. A lot of my work very much is tied up with certain kinds of things I do or think. I write about contemporary issues for the most part. If I were just doing this and I were not somehow going to get something out of it for my own writing, I wouldn't do it. . . . Since I'm going to be writing about myself as a lesbian, I thought, why not? It would kind of be interesting. I think it'll be a whole new experience level for me, too, to think about this aspect of myself in ways that are much more overt and connected with a whole lot of different things. I feel like an evolving person on this particular plane.

OLIVIA. Actually, I was intrigued by the way you had formulated this, and I was really curious to see how it played out, particularly around the identification of people in a particular identity category, which I actually don't take too seriously. So I was curious to see how this would play out—I had a kind of intellectual curiosity about what you were going to do with this. And I was also interested to see how your ideas about this would change as you talked to three disparate people, . . . so that's, it's kind of an intellectual, intriguing interest. . . . I see it [invoking a category of identity] as a way of starting, I'm not sure that's where you're going to end up. So, that's what I'm interested in watching, is the process, I'm interested to see where you're going to get with this, because if you're going to do what you propose, which is to look at the work that the three of us do, to watch us teach class, and to watch us behave, I'm wondering how much that category is going to actually define much of anything or whether it defines things we don't know it's defining—which would be equally useful to know, for me. Or, in which case, we might want to alter or redefine that category in other ways. So, in any case, it seemed to me sort of an evolutionary, progenitive project, and that's why I was kind of interested in it. . . . It's like who knows, I might find something out about myself, too. I don't know, but I was curious to see what would happen here.

CAROL. I've been through this process [participating in a research project] before. On the one hand, the process last time was time consuming, but I found it insightful for myself in a lot of ways, to talk through some of the things I had been thinking but perhaps hadn't expressed verbally, put into context some of the political issues in the academy that I had been feeling. And so, from a personal stand-point I knew it wouldn't be an ordeal or an unpleasant experience and that it could certainly be positive. And, I guess there were some small altruistic reasons, I'm close enough to having been a graduate student myself to know how hard it is, you know, and I did some ethnographic work in graduate school, . . . and so I wanted to help another graduate student whom Karen spoke very highly of. Karen said something like this, "Now this isn't your basic stupid graduate student." You know, Karen can be very blunt. She said, "You know, she's very bright and I think you'll like her." So I guess there were a variety of factors. It wasn't something I agonized over, I talked to you, I saw your stuff, I said okay. It was a simple straightforward decision. You know, this is sort of part of the job, helping facilitate people's research, particularly if you find the person interesting and the project interesting, that's part of being an academic, being a scholar. Wanting to help a feminist, a lesbian, get her work done, that becomes part of it also. I joked with Karen about how I'm becoming this big object of study, but in a lot of respects I'm used to that as a black lesbian. As a black woman, I've been scrutinized in so many ways for so long in every aspect of my professional life, my adult life really, that it's become par for the course, that there's some reason why somebody finds me interesting. Sometimes it's an exploitive kind of situation, sometimes it's very problematic, but there are times when it's important. There aren't a lot of black women in the academy, and our perspectives are very unique, and I think very much imbued with the politics of race and gender and sexuality and so forth, not only in higher education but also in national discourse, so we, I think it's important for us to put that out there. And in a lot of ways this is a lot easier than my writing an article about my personal experiences.

Each woman's presentation of self, her interests or struggles, whether inflected with the personal, the intellectual, or the political, immediately decenters any singular perspective about how sexuality operates in academic lives. *Lesbian* is present (it was the premise of our coming together), yet is not central. Personal experience, scholarship, cancer, and unconcealment are bound up with structures of the closet and a desire to explore those structures; intellectual curiosity (or perhaps "project" would be a better word) in how the category *lesbian* might (d)evolve in the course of the study form a basis for interest; race, gender, and sexuality, but most saliently race and gender, create a set of experiences and a specific perspective that desires to be voiced. Although it would be reductive to align the women's words with social and intellectual developments of the past several decades by saying that they "represent" specific strands of thought, the themes that emerge in their opening words point to some of the tensions that structure discourse around lesbian academics: the relations of the personal to the intellectual, of a social category to one's actions and sense of self-identity, and of individuals to institutions.

Narrative Knowing as Practice

As I have said, it is difficult to know what meanings *lesbian* carries and what it means to be seen or heard. In discussing concepts that are impossible to stabilize, I find that I implicitly define them in my textualization. I do so with the hope that my text offers a means to learn from and about lesbian academics' practices that will open categories and terms such as *lesbian, knowledge,* and *identity* and their interrelations to multiple interpretations. Despite the awkwardness of invoking a category whose meanings at once seem over-determined and at other moments elusive, I try to speak beyond it.[5] I am made hopeful by Gayatri Spivak's contention that representation necessitates a degree of essentializing, a tactic that can be deployed to strategic ends.[6] . . .

[. . .]

At professional meetings I have received queries about my "identity" that reveal desires to know whether my dwelling in the categories "lesbian" and "academic" defines me as an "insider" relative to Julie, Olivia, and Carol or as implicated in the subject of research. As I have explained, I began with ambivalences and curiosities about such issues as the meanings lesbian can have in intellectual and academic practice, the efficacy of "coming out" to colleagues and students, how one defines research interests, and how institutional and social structures affect one's actions. The women's initial descriptions of their reasons for agreeing to participate in my research—Julie's seeking to uncover meanings of lesbian in her life, Olivia's denial of them and curiosity to see what would happen to the category lesbian during my inquiry, and Carol's desire for the representation of a black lesbian voice—reveal contradictory commitments that drew simultaneously on my humanist and poststructuralist assumptions and on my ambivalences and wonderings about living in categories. There is a persistent irony that, despite our shared skepticisms of the category, sexuality served as the premise of our coming together. Living in a marked category of sexuality does not confer privileged access to or automatic understandings with another person. Whatever understandings are formed among participants in inquiry or by the researcher are provisional, made possible by the intermingling of time and space. The intersections and points of departure among us put into question assumptions that there are easy "insider" relationships among lesbian researchers and participants in fieldwork, just as my ongoing ambivalences call into question whether a researcher can have a single "position" in relation to her inquiry. Throughout the inquiry, I have found it at once freeing in some ways and troubling in others, and resonant with much of my own experience, to think that intellectual and lesbian may be constructs with few affinities or points of connection. As I have considered the implications of my interpretations, I have been mindful of the gains that have been made through identity politics in certain contexts, yet concerned that an emphasis on identity forecloses possibilities of understanding and changing human relations in ways that allow us to exceed the given. By placing ourselves and others in research within boundaries of identity, we reify ourselves, those who participate in research, and the questions and purposes that evolve in the process of inquiry. Queer research may be less about who researches whom or what is researched than about what is and what can be done with the research. [. . .]

Notes

1. The names of all participants in the study, as well as institutional and geographic names, are pseudonyms.
2. In transcribed text from interviews or classroom scenes, slashes / / appear to indicate that a word or words were inaudible in transcription. A word or words appearing inside slashes indicates my best guess, based on partial audibility or my recollection of the interview. Brackets denote the addition of my words to the text, usually for clarification. A three-em dash denotes something I have omitted, such as the title of a book or article that one of the women has written, usually for the sake of confidentiality. Ellipses indicate text I have omitted, a phrase (. . .) or (a) sentence(s) (. . . .) that may be redundant, do not enhance clarity or understanding, or represent an interruption (a phone call or person stopping by an office).
3. Hazel Carby, "Politics of Difference," 84.
4. Over six months, I conducted seven interviews lasting an average of two hours with Julie and Carol, and six with Olivia. The interviews could be described in social scientific terms as semistructured. I began with the same interview guide for all three women and constructed subsequent guides with their specific concerns in mind. I made a point of asking a "core" of common questions, such as the ways they negotiate their sexuality with colleagues and students, their conceptions of themselves and goals as researchers and teachers, the connections they experience between their research and pedagogy, the types of professional service in which they are engaged, and their views of their disciplines, departments, and university. As the women's particularities emerged, the interviews became specific to their situations. For example, Julie and I spoke about the ways her cancer had affected her understandings of what it has meant to hide her sexuality; Carol and I spoke of the polite racism she faces and how her race obscures her sexuality for her colleagues; Olivia and I spoke of how her stature in lesbian studies turns her into a commodity. Although my interview guides were based in the logic of fieldwork, our interviews frequently took other courses, cycling away from and back to topics on the guides (see Hammersley and Atkinson, *Ethnography: Principles in Practice*, on flexibility in interviewing). There were times when the interviews began with spontaneous discussion of something that had occurred in class that day, or when they deviated completely from the expected. Although the origin of the interviews lay in my questions, they evolved through the negotiation that characterizes conversations (see, for example, Clandinin and Connelly, "Personal Experience Methods"). However, as evidenced in my interactions with Olivia, there was not symmetry in the interview relationships, though the asymmetry differed from that typically documented in the research literature, which preoccupies itself with researchers' power over participants, or with differential social positions, in which the researcher is in or from a "more powerful" position than the researched (see, for example, the essays in Gitlin, ed., *Power and Method*).
5. See James Sears, "Researching the Other," for a lucid description of the "conceptual difficulties in defining people on the basis of 'sexual orientation' " (150) and the damages of "validat[ing] spurious categories that become the very engines of oppression" (151). While I relied on self-identification as lesbian, I do not mean to suggest any meanings inhere in that term nor that "lesbian" must be a central organizing category for one's life or work.
6. Gayatri Spivak, "Post-Colonial Critic," 109.

References

Carby, Hazel. "The Politics of Difference." *Ms.*, July/August 1990, 84–85.

Clandinin, D. Jean, and F. Michael Connelly. "Personal Experience Methods." In *Handbook of Qualitative Research*, edited by Norman K. Denzin and Yvonna S. Lincoln, 413–427. Thousand Oaks, Calif.: Sage, 1994.

Gitlin, Andrew, ed. *Power and Method: Political Activism and Educational Research.* New York: Routledge, 1994.

Hammersley, Martyn, and Paul Atkinson. *Ethnography: Principles in Practice.* 2nd ed. New York: Routledge, 1995.

Lather, Patti. *Getting Smart: Feminist Research and Pedagogy with/in the Post-modern.* New York: Routledge, 1991.

Sears, James. "Researching the Other/Searching the Self: Qualitative Research on [Homo]sexuality in Education." *Theory into Practice*, 31, no. 2 (1992): 147–156.

Spivak, Gayatri Chakravorty. *The Post-Colonial Critic: Interviews, Strategies, Dialogues.* Edited by Sarah Harasym. New York: Routledge, 1990.

26

Learning from Kids

Barrie Thorne

> A different reality coexisted beside my own, containing more vitality, originality, and wide-open potential than could be found in any lesson plan. How was I to enter this intriguing place, and toward what end would the children's play become my work?
> —Vivian Gussin Paley, "On Listening to What the Children Say"

When I first entered the Oceanside fourth/fifth-grade classroom as a note-taking visitor, I thought of myself as an ethnographer with an interest in gender and the social life of children. Beyond that, I had not given much reflection to what I was bringing to the research. But I slowly came to realize that within the ethnographer, many selves were at play. Responding to our shared positions as adult women and as teachers, I easily identified with Miss Bailey and the other school staff. Being around so many children also stirred my more maternal emotions and perspectives. (When I started the fieldwork, our older child was in preschool, and by the end of the year I was pregnant with a second child.) Occasionally I felt much like the fourth- and fifth-grader I used to be, and the force of this took me by surprise. This jangling chorus of selves gave me insight into the complexity of being an adult trying to learn from kids. Hearing first one, then another, of these different selves, or types of consciousness, helped shape what I discovered and how I put my ideas together.[1]

Like Westerners doing fieldwork in colonized Third World cultures, or academics studying the urban poor, when adults research children, they "study down," seeking understanding across lines of difference and inequality. When the research is within their own culture, the "studying down" comes swathed in a sense of familiarity. Despite their structural privilege, Western ethnographers who enter a radically different culture find themselves in the humbling stance of a novice. But it is hard to think of one's self as a novice when studying those who are defined as learners of one's own culture. To learn *from* children, adults have to challenge the deep assumption that they already know what children are "like," both because, as former children, adults have been there, and because, as adults, they regard children as less complete versions of themselves. When adults seek to learn about and from children, the challenge is to take the closely familiar and to render it strange.

Adrienne Rich has observed that power seems to "engender a kind of willed ignorance . . . about the inwardness of others."[2] To gain intersubjective understanding, ethnographers who "study down" often have to confront and transcend their own images of the devalued "Other."[3] Adults who study children of their own culture may encounter similar, although perhaps less conscious, barriers of consciousness. These barriers are rooted, perhaps paradoxically, in differences of power and in the fact that identifying with children may evoke the vulnerable child within each adult. The clinician Alice Miller describes deeply unconscious processes that may lead parents, who are threatened by their own sense of vulnerability, to deny their children's separate capacities for knowing and feeling.[4] Adult interest in controlling children may be driven, in part, by fear of their own sense of uncertainty and absence of control.

In my fieldwork with kids, I wanted to overcome these barriers and to approach their social worlds as ethnographers approach the worlds of adults: with open-ended curiosity, and with an assumption that kids are competent social actors who take an active role in shaping their daily experiences. I wanted to sustain an attitude of respectful discovery, to uncover and document kids' points of view and meanings.[5] To adopt that basic stance means breaking with an array of common adult assumptions: that children's daily actions are mostly trivial, worthy of notice only when they seem cute or irritating; that children need to be actively managed or controlled; that children are relatively passive recipients of adult training and socialization.

As I argued in the preceding chapter, asking how children are socialized into adult ways, or how their experiences fit into linear stages of individual development, deflects attention from their present, lived, and collective experiences. Moving back a step, one can see "socialization" and "development" as perspectives that many parents, teachers, and other adults *bring* to their interactions with children.[6] As mothers and teachers of young children, women, in particular, are charged with the work of "developing the child."[7] But children don't necessarily see themselves as "being socialized" or "developing," and their interactions with one another, and with adults, extend far beyond those models. In my fieldwork I wanted to move beyond adult-centered, individualized frameworks and learn about the daily lives of children, especially what they do together as "they mutually build social occasions and activities in each others' presence"—to quote Matthew Speier.[8]

When I started observing in the Oceanside School, I set out to learn about gender in the context of kids' interactions with one another. I began to accompany fourth- and fifth-graders in their daily round of activities by stationing myself in the back of Miss Bailey's classroom, sitting in the scaled-down chairs and standing and walking around the edges, trying to grasp different vantage points. I was clearly not a full participant; I didn't have a regular desk, and I watched and took notes, rather than doing the classroom work. As the kids lined up, I watched, and then I walked alongside, often talking with them, as they moved between the classroom, lunchroom, music room, and library. At noontime I sat and ate with the fourth- and fifth-graders at their two crowded cafeteria tables, and I left with them when they headed for noontime recess on the playground. Wanting to understand their social divisions and the varied perspectives they entailed, I alternated the company I kept, eating with different groups and moving among the various turfs and activities of the playground.

In Ashton, the Michigan school, I also followed the kids' cycle of activities, but I stuck less closely to one classroom and its students. I observed in a kindergarten and in a second-grade classroom, and I spent a lot of time in the lunchroom and on the playground mapping all the groups and trying to get an overview of the school and its organization.

Looking back on my presence in both schools, I see how much I claimed the freelancing privilege of an adult visitor. I could, and did, come and go, shift groups, choose and alter my daily routines. Unlike the kids, I was relatively, although not entirely, free from the control of the principal, teachers, and aides. Without a fixed, school-based routine, I also had more spatial mobility than the teachers and aides. My spatial privileges were especially obvious during severe winter days in Michigan, when the Ashton students, even if they wore skimpy clothes and had no mittens or gloves, were forced to stay outside for forty-five minutes during the noontime recess. While some of the kids stood shivering near the school, I was free, although I usually resisted the temptation, to go into the warm building.

I entered students' interactions to varying degrees. In teaching settings like classrooms and the Oceanside music room and auditorium, I felt most like an observer. In the lunchrooms where I was more visually separate from other school-based adults since teachers ate elsewhere and aides were on patrol, I joined more fully in kids' interactions by eating, conversing, and sometimes trading food with them. On the playgrounds I usually roamed and watched from the margins of ongoing activities, although I often talked with kids and sometimes joined groups of girls playing jump rope and games like "statue buyer." Whether on the margins or joining in, I was continually struck by kids' forms of physicality and by the structures of authority that separate them from adults.

Kids' Physicality and Imagination

When I began my concerted effort to spend time with kids, I felt oversized, like a big Alice or Gulliver trying to fit into a scaled-down world. Schools are furnished for two sizes: smaller chairs, desks, and tables: and adult-sized chairs and desks, at which kids can sit often only with special permission. Staff bathrooms have big toilets and sinks, and the separate children's bathrooms have smaller toilets and sinks. I knew I had crossed more fully into kids' spaces when the sense of scale diminished, and I felt too large.

Watching kids day after day, especially on the playground, I was struck by other differences of physicality: their quick movements and high levels of energy, the rapidity with which they formed and reformed groups and activities. Public schools are unusually crowded environments, which intensifies the sense of chaos; the playgrounds were often thick with moving bodies. At first I felt like a sixteen-millimeter observer trying to grasp the speeded-up motions of a thirty-six-millimeter movie. One of the teachers told me that groups of children reminded her of bumblebees, an apt image of swarms, speed, and constant motion.

After I had observed for several months, I saw much more order in the chaos, and I developed strategies for recording rapidly shifting and episodic activity.[9] For example, when I entered the playground, I went on an initial tour, making an inventory of groups and activities. Then I focused on specific groups or individuals, sometimes following them from one activity to another, or from formation to dispersal. I tried to spend time in all the playground niches, including basketball courts, bars and jungle gyms, swings, the varied activities (foursquare, zone dodgeball, handball, jump rope, hopscotch, tetherball) that took place on the cement near the buildings, wandering groups, chasing scenes, large playing fields where, depending on the season, games of baseball, soccer, kickball, and football took place. There were also sites unique to each school: at Oceanside, "the tires," a climbing and swinging structure made of big rubber tires, and "the hill," a small rise of grass; and at Ashton, the school steps, where kids hung out and talked.

I was struck not only by kids' rapid movements but also by their continual engagement with one another's bodies—poking, pushing, tripping, grabbing a hat or scarf, pinning from behind. Since adults in our culture experience such gestures as invasions of personal space (notably, kids never poked, pushed at, or pinned me from behind), I initially interpreted these engagements as more antagonistic than, I realized over time, the kids seemed to experience or intend. Trying to sort out playful from serious intent alerted me to the nuances of kids' meanings *and* to my personal readiness to look for trouble, a readiness magnified by my outlooks as a teacher and a mother.

I came to relish kids' playful uses of their bodies, their little experiments in motion and sound, such as moving around the classroom with exaggerated hobbling or a swaggering hula, bouncing in a chair as if riding a horse, clucking like hens or crowing like roosters, returning to a desk by jerking, making engine noises, and screeching like the brakes of a car. They wrote on their bodies with pencil and pen and transformed hands into game-boards by writing "push here" across their palms. They held contests to see who could push their eyeballs farthest back and show the most white, or hold their eyes crossed for the longest time. Sometimes these performances were private, at other times, constructed with dramatic flair and a call for an audience.

These moments struck me as little oases of imagination in dryly routinized scenes. They led me to reflect on growing up as a process of reigning in bodily and imaginative possibilities, a perspective shared by nineteenth-century romantic poets like Words-worth, and by recent social critics like Edith Cobb, Vera John-Steiner, and Ernest Sch-achtel. These writers argue that children are more sensuous and open to the world than adults, and that adult creativity hinges on overcoming repression and gaining access to the child within.[10] This idealization of children contrasts with the idealization of adults built into many versions of the "socialization" and "development" perspectives. In assuming exaggerated dichotomies and casting value primarily in one direction, both views are limited.

Getting Around Adult Authority

My greater size; my access to special relations with the principal, teachers, and aides; and my sheer status as an adult in an institution that draws sharp generational divisions and marks them with differences in power and authority, posed complicated obstacles to learning from kids. I knew that if I were too associated with adult authority, I would have difficulty gaining access to kids' more private worlds. Nor did I want the tasks of a classroom or playground aide. The practical constraints of keeping order and imposing an agenda would, I quickly realized, run against the open-ended curiosity and witnessing that ethnography requires.

I entered the field through adult gatekeepers. A friend introduced me to Miss Bailey, the fourth/fifth-grade Oceanside teacher, and she, in turn, agreed to let me observe in her classroom, as did Mr. Welch, the school principal, who asked only that I not "disrupt" and that I report back my findings. My more formal entry into Asthon School, via the district Title IX office, seemed to make the Ashton principal a little nervous. But Mrs Smith, the kindergarten teacher, and Mrs. Johnson, the second-grade teacher, seemed at ease when I was in their classrooms, and I had ample latitude to define my presence to the students of both schools.

In both schools I asked kids as well as staff to call me by my first name, and I called the staff by their first names when we spoke directly with one another. But when I talked with kids, and that's where I did most of my talking as well as watching, I joined them in using titles to refer to the teachers and principals. Everyone called the Ashton lunchroom aides by their first names. In my writing, I follow the kids' use of titles or first names; the actual names, of course, have all been changed.

On the playgrounds kids sometimes treated me as an adult with formal authority. Calling "Yard duty, yard duty!" or "Teach-er!" they ran up with requests for intervention—"Make Ralph give me back my ball"; "Burt threw the rope onto the roof." I responded by saying, "I'm not a yard duty," and usually by refusing to intervene, telling those who asked for help that they would have to find someone who was a yard duty, or handle the situation by themselves.

I went through the school days with a small spiral notebook in hand, jotting descriptions that I later expanded into fieldnotes. When I was at the margins of a scene, I took notes on the spot. When I was more fully involved, sitting and talking with kids at a cafeteria table or playing a game of jump rope, I held observations in my memory and recorded them later. I realized that note-taking had become my special insignia when the fourth-grader who drew my name in the holiday gift exchange in Miss Bailey's class gave me a new little spiral notebook of the kind I always carried around. As I opened the gift, the kids speculated about how many notebooks I had filled by then. They also marveled at my ability to write without looking.

This continual scribbling invited repeated inquiries about my presence and purpose. Again and again, in classrooms and lunch-rooms, and on the playgrounds, kids asked me why I was taking notes. "What's that? What're you doing?" "You still takin' notes?" Sometimes they prefaced inquiry with a guess about my purpose: "You writin' a book on us?" "You spying on us?" "Is it like being a reporter?" "You're gonna have a big diary!" "You gonna be a writer?" "What are you sposed to be?" (Questions about what I was "gonna" or "sposed to be" startled me into realizing how much kids are encouraged to cast life in the future and subjunctive tenses.)

Responding to these queries. I tried to be as open and straightforward as I could. But I ran into gaps of understanding. The kids' responses clued me into the drawbacks of some of my explanations. During one of my first forays on the Oceanside playground, a boy came over and asked, "What ya writing?" "I'm interested in what you children are like," I responded; "I'm writing down what you're doing. Do you mind?" He warily edged away. "I didn't do anything," he said. Another of my early explanations—"I'm interested in the behavior of children"—also brought defensive responses. I came to see that verbs like "doing" and "behaving," which figure centrally in the language of social science, are also used by adults to sanction children. The social sciences and child-rearing are both practices geared to social control.

The kids seemed to understand more fully when I explained that I was interested in the ways that they "play" or "what it's like to be a kid." But when I elaborated. I ended up feeling irrelevant and long-winded. For example, during one Oceanside recess as I crouched, watching and scribbling, on the sidelines of a basketball game, a girl came up and asked, "What are you doing?" "A study of children and what they play." "Do you wanna be a teacher?" she asked. "I am one. I teach sociology, ever hear of that?" "No." "It's the study of people in groups." "Well, good-bye," she said, running off.

Sometimes the kids played with the dynamics of my constant written witnessing. When they asked to see my notes, I showed them, privately feeling relieved that they found my scribbles mostly indecipherable. Occasionally kids calibrated behavior and its instant representation by telling me what to write down. "Why don't you put that John goes over and sharpens his pencil," said a fifth-grader, pointing to a boy in motion. On another occasion, a boy I'll call Matt Washburn hovered by my notebook and said, "Write down: 'My best kid is Matt Washburn.' "

One girl who asked if I was "taking down names" voiced what seemed to be their major fear: that I was recording "bad" behavior and that my record would get them into trouble. I assured them again and again that I would not use their real names and that I would not report anything to the teachers, principal, or aides. But of course what I wrote was not under their control, and, like all fieldworkers. I lived with ambiguous ethics. I guarded the information from local exposure, but intended it, with identitites disguised, for a much larger audience. I was the sole judge of what was or was not reported and how to alter identifying information. My fieldnotes and later writing from this project feel less guilty than the information I gathered as a participant-observer in the draft resistance movement of the late 1960s.[11] This is partly because information about kids and their doings seems much less consequential than information about adults, especially adults acting in a risky public arena. But of course that perception comes from adult consciousness, not identification with kids' sense of risk.

Although a note-taking adult cannot pass as even an older elementary school student, I tried in other ways to lessen the social distance between me and the kids.[12] I avoided positions of authority and rarely intervened in a managerial way, and I went through the days with or near the kids rather than along the paths of teachers and aides. Like others who have done participant-observation with children, I felt a little elated when kids violated rules in my presence, like swearing or openly blowing bubble gum where these acts were forbidden, or swapping stories about recent acts of shoplifting. These incidents reassured me that I had shed at least some of the trappings of adult authority and gained access to kids' more private worlds. But my experiences with adult authority had a jagged quality. Sometimes I felt relatively detached from the lines of power that divide kids and adults in schools. At other times I felt squarely on one side or the other.

I tried to avoid developing strong allegiances with the school staff and to build up loyalty to the kids, a strategy resembling that of ethnographers who want to learn about the experiences of prison inmates or hospital patients and therefore avoid obvious alliances with the wardens or medical staff. But I was tethered to adults by lines of structure and consciousness. My presence in both schools was contingent on the ongoing goodwill of the adult staff, which made me susceptible to their requests. When Miss Bailey asked me to help a student who was having trouble in math, or when Mrs Johnson asked me to help the second-graders as they crafted dolls out of corncobs, I couldn't refuse, and I shifted with ease into the stance of an overseeing adult. Luckily, such requests were relatively rare because of my erratic schedule and because the teachers knew I was there to observe and not to help out in the classrooms.[13]

Although the teachers made few formal demands that drew me into their orbits of authority, they sometimes turned to me for a kind of adult companionship in the classrooms. While the students were seated, I usually stood and roamed the back, while the teacher often stood in front. That arrangement spatially aligned me with the teacher, and it was easy for our adult eyes to meet, literally above the heads of the kids. When something amusing or annoying happened, the teacher would sometimes catch my eye and smile or shake her head in a moment of collusive, nonverbal, and private adult commentary. During those moments, I felt a mild sense of betrayal for moving into allegiance with adult vantage points and structures of authority.

When physical injury was at stake, my intervening adult-parental-teacher sides moved to the fore. One day just before recess a physical fight broke out in Miss Bailey's fourth/fifth-grade classroom, and the substitute teacher and I rushed to pull the antagonists apart. When I was observing on the Oceanside playground, a girl fell off the bars to the ground. Several other girls rushed toward her, one calling "Get the yard duty person! She can't breathe!" I ran over and asked the girl lying on the ground if she was hurt. An official "yard duty person" joined us, and she and I walked the injured girl to the office.

I could usually rely on playground aides to be on the lookout and to handle scenes of physical injury. It was harder for me to stay detached when kids hurt one another's feelings, and I sometimes tried to soothe these situations. For example, when Miss Bailey's students were drawing pictures at their desks, several girls talked about their summer plans. Jessica said she and her sisters and brother were going to Texas to see their mother. Sherry asked, "Why did your mother leave you?" Jessica replied. "She wanted to marry a guy, but they had a fight and she didn't." Almost simultaneously, Nancy spoke up, "She left because she didn't love you." Jessica blushed, and I resonated with her stung feelings. Feeling quite maternal, I tried to comfort Jessica by putting my arm around her and saying, "I'm sure it was hard for your mother to leave."

The teachers, principals, and aides generally assumed I was a colleague who would back up their rule. But I was primarily interested in the ways kids construct their own worlds, with and apart from adults. The official agenda of the schools—the lessons, the rules, the overtly approved conduct—seemed like cement sidewalk blocks, and the kids' cultural creations like grass and dandelions sprouting through the cracks. I watched eagerly for moments of sprouting and came to appreciate kids' strategies for conducting their own activities alongside and under the stated business of the hour.[14]

The Underground Economy of Food and Objects

From my position in the back of Miss Bailey's classroom, which gives a very different perspective than the front, I could see what went on when desktops were raised, presumably on official business. Some kids had customized their desks by taping drawings or dangling objects from the inside top. In addition to official school artifacts like books, papers, rulers, pencils, and crayons, the desks contained stashes of food, toys, cosmetics, and other objects brought from market and home. These transitional objects, most of them small and pocketable, bridge different spheres of life. They also provide materials for an oppositional underlife often found in "total institutions," or settings like prisons and hospitals where a subjected population is kept under extensive control.[15] Although schools maintain far less control than prisons, students have little choice about being present, and members of a smaller, more powerful group (the staff) regulate their use of time, space, and resources. Like prison inmates or hospital patients, students develop creative ways of coping with their relative lack of power and defending themselves against the more unpleasant aspects of institutional living.

Some of the objects that kids stash and trade, like "pencil pals" (rubbery creatures designed to stick on the end of pencils), rabbit feet, special erasers and silver paper, could be found in the desks of both boys and girls. Other objects divided more by gender. Boys brought in little toy cars and trucks, magnets, and compasses; and girls stashed tubes of lip gloss, nail polish, barrettes, necklaces, little stuffed animals, and doll furniture. Patterns of trade marked circles of friendship that almost never included both girls and boys. The exception was a flat pink and yellow terri cloth pillow that Kathryn, the most popular girl in Miss Bailey's class, brought in to cushion her desk chair. Invested with the manna of Kathryn's popularity, the pillow traveled around the entire room; girls and boys sat on and tossed it around in a spirit more of honoring than teasing.

Ashton School felt like a much harsher environment than Oceanside School, in part because of the difference in weather (California was spared the cold winter of Michigan), but also because Ashton had strict rules against kids bringing objects from home. Even when it was raining, Ashton students were not allowed to carry umbrellas onto the playground, and if aides spotted any personal toys or objects, they immediately confiscated them. As a result, the school had an impoverished underground economy. (School staff might describe this differently, as eliminating distractions and maintaining order.) I saw a few sneaky sharings of food, lip gloss, and, on one occasion, a plastic whistle, but nothing like the flourishing semi-clandestine system of exchange at Oceanside School.

In subsequent chapters I return to the significance of material objects in kids' social relations, as a focus of provocation and dispute, as a medium through which alliances may be launched and disrupted, as sacraments of social inclusion and painful symbols of exclusion, and as markers of hierarchy.[16] But here I want to highlight the relatively secret and oppositional nature of these objects and their negotiation and exchange. Students are not supposed to eat, play with toy cars, or rub pink gloss on their lips in the middle of an arithmetic or social studies lesson. But I saw them do all these things, creating their own layers of activity and meaning alongside, or beneath, the layers they shared with the adult school staff.

When kids invited me to participate in their secret exchanges, I felt pulled between my loyalty to them and my identification with and dependence on the teacher. During a social studies lesson, the fourth/fifth-grade students were supposed to be drawing pictures of early California missions. As Miss Bailey helped someone in another part of the room. I wandered to a corner where Jeremy, Don, and Bill leaned over and loudly whispered behind their raised desktops. Jeremy asked Don, "What's your middle name?" Don replied, "Top secret." Bill chimed in, "Porkchop." Don, who was taking pins from a box in his desk and sticking them through an eraser, responded. "Porkchop! I have two nicknames. Dog and Halfbrain." Jeremy reached for some pins from Don's desk and fashioned an X on his pencil eraser. Bill played with an orange toy car, making "zoom" noises as he scooted it into Jeremy's open desk. Jeremy took out an almost-finished bag of potato chips, held it out to Don, and shook a few into his hands. Bill held out his hand, but Jeremy ignored the gesture. "Give me one." Bill said. "No, you're too fat; you should be on a diet." "I am on a diet," Bill said as Jeremy shook a few chips into his hands." "Give Barrie some," Bill said. Jeremy turned (I was sitting behind him) and asked, "Do you want some?" "Yes," I said and held out my hand as he shook a few chips into it. All of this forbidden activity went on behind the screen of the open desktops. Jeremy grinned, and I grinned back, feeling conspiratorial as I quietly munched the chips.

When I sociably interacted with a group of kids during work time, Miss Bailey sometimes noticed and told them to get back to work. This made me feel a trifle guilty since I realized that she suspected I was undermining rather than affirming—or even taking a neutral relationship to—classroom order. I noticed that Miss Bailey always refused when her students offered loans or gifts and the particularized, nonprofessional relationships they entail. But, seeking closer, more lateral ties, I accepted offers of potato chips, a cookie, a nickel; and I occasionally gave kids pencils and small change, which we called loans, although they were never returned. Once Miss Bailey saw me give a pencil to Matt when he asked if I had an extra one. She firmly told him to return the pencil to me and to get his own. I understood her actions; as a teacher, she tried to maintain social distance and a guise of universalistic treatment, and when I teach, I do the same thing. The kids called her "Miss Bailey," while I asked them to call me by my first name, another set of disparate practices that set me apart from the teacher.

I came to realize that within the classroom, the teacher and I were working at cross-purposes. Miss Bailey had lessons to teach, authority to maintain, the need to construct and display an orderly classroom. I was a kind of sideline booster, rooting for the moments when kids brought out their own artifacts and built their own worlds of talk and interaction.

I had an observational feast on a day when there was a substitute teacher who "couldn't keep control," in the words of a disgusted bilingual aide who came for several hours each day. The kids made lots of noise and ran boisterously about; a group of them talked loudly about who had beat up whom in the third grade, and who could now beat up whom. They brought out objects that were usually kept relatively under cover—a skateboard magazine, a rubber finger with a long nail, bags of nuts and potato chips—and openly passed them around. As the kids walked out the door for lunch, Jessie, one of the girls who had joined in the talk about fighting, got into an angry fist fight with Allen. This was the one fight where I intervened; the substitute teacher and I jointly worked to separate their flailing bodies. In the lunchroom Jessie retreated to sit with a group of girls, and talk about the fight went on for the rest of the day. After lunch a row of girls sat on the radiator and threw an eraser at several boys, who threw it back in an improvised game of catch. Another group went to the blackboard and drew hearts encircling different boy-girl paired names.

Mr. Welch, the principal, came in once and told the class to behave, but the effect was short-lived, and the substitute teacher seemed resigned to the chaos. I observed for three hours and that night typed up eleven single-spaced pages of notes, rich with descriptions of gender boundaries and antagonism, sexual idioms, interactions among boys and among girls, and crossing between same-gender groups. When I returned to the classroom two days later, Miss Bailey lamented the students' "sub behavior." Her managerial low was my highpoint of juicy witnessing.

Tugs of Memory, and the Child Within

When I colluded with the kids in breaking rules, especially when the teacher was watching, I remembered how it felt to be caught in similar situations in my own elementary school days. In the spring just after the buzzer rang at the end of an Oceanside school day, Miss Bailey called out across the room, "Barrie, Mr. Welch wants to talk with you." Several kids picked up the ominous connotations and called around the room, "Mr. Welch wants to see Barrie!" For a moment, I felt like a child being brought to task, and the class laughed with a similar reaction. Mr. Welch, it turned out, wanted me to tell him how my research was going, an inquiry that drew my adult self back to the fore.

Tugs of memory pulled on other occasions as well, especially during the first few months of fieldwork. When I began observing, I also began a chain of remembering. There was a close familiarity with the scaled-down desks and tables, the blackboards and stylized graphics on classroom walls, the sight of worn-out red rubber kickballs and dirty jump ropes, smells of wax in the hallways and urine in the girls' bathroom, the loud buzzers that govern so many local routines, the lining up, the clatter of voices in the cafeteria, and the distinctive sing-song tones of teachers. Varied sights, smells, and sounds brought me back to the Woodruff School in Logan, Utah, in the early 1950s.

Memories of my own experiences in fourth and fifth grades scatter through my field-notes, especially when a specific girl (boys didn't evoke such remembering) reminded me of a vivid figure from my own childhood. Three of the girls in the Oceanside fourth/fifth-grade classroom continually evoked my memories of, and feelings about, specific girls from my past: the most popular girl; a girl who was quiet, whiny, and a loner; and a girl who was unkempt, smelled, and was treated as a pariah. When I made these associations, the names of their 1950s doubles came immediately to mind.

After a few days of observing, I had figured out that Kathryn was the most popular girl in the classroom. Her cute face, stylish curly brown hair, nice clothes, and general poise and friendliness were easy to notice, and she received a lot of deference from both girls and boys. In situations where individual privileges were granted, for example, to choose and touch bowed heads in games of "seven-up" or to hand out balls in preparation for recess, Kathryn got more than her share. Miss Bailey often chose Kathryn to run errands to the main office or to do other tasks that marked out favored students. After a few weeks at Oceanside. I realized that my fieldnotes were obsessed with documenting Kathryn's popularity. "The rich get richer," I thought to myself as I sorted out yet another occasion when Kathryn got extra attention and resources. Then I realized the envy behind my note-taking and analysis and recalled that many years ago when I was a fourth- and fifth-grader of middling social status. I had also carefully watched the popular girl, using a kind of applied sociology to figure out my place in a charged social network.

In the course of my fieldwork, I felt aversion rather than envy toward Beth, a quiet fourth grader, who continually asked me to sit by her at lunch. Initially I was glad for an invitation. But when I discovered that Beth had few friends, that sitting with her, rather than, say, next to Kathryn, brought minimal social yield, and that Beth also wanted me to stick by her on the playground, I felt, as I wrote in my fieldnotes, associating to my own elementary school past, "as if Beatrice Johnson had me trapped." When Beth requested my company, I began to respond vaguely ("maybe"; "we'll see"), much as I had in fifth grade when I felt Beatrice was trying to cling to me and I didn't want her social encumbrance.

Rita, another girl in the present who evoked strong memories from my own past childhood, was from a family with thirteen children and an overworked single-parent father (Jessica, who told the story of their mother's departure, was Rita's sister). Rita, who took care of her own grooming, had tangled hair and wore dirty, ill-fitting, and mismatched clothes; she seemed withdrawn and depressed. The first time I came close to Rita, leaning over to help her with work in the classroom, I was struck by the smell. I wrote in my fieldnotes:

> Rita's hair was quite dirty, greasy at the roots, and it smelled. There was dirt on her cheek, and her hands were smudged. She wore the same clothes she had on yesterday: a too small, short blue nylon sweater with white buttons and dirt on the back, and green cotton pants that didn't zip

right. Leaning over and catching the scent of her hair. I thought of Edith Schulz, whom we all avoided in the fifth grade. I remember Edith, whose parents were immigrants from Germany, wearing a cotton sleeveless blouse and dirndl skirt in the dead of winter. The smell, the incongruous clothing—the signs, I now see, of poverty—set her apart, like Rita; both were treated like pariahs.[17]

In such moments of remembering I felt in touch with my child self. I moved from the external vantage points of an observer, an adult authority, and a "least adult" trying to understand kids' interactions in a more open and lateral way, to feeling more deeply inside their worlds. This experience occurred only when I was with girls. With boys, my strongest moments of identification came not through regression to feeling like one of them, but from more maternal feelings. Sometimes a particular boy would remind me of my son, and I would feel a wave of empathy and affection. But I generally felt more detached and less emotionally bound up with the boys.

Joel, a boy who was socially isolated and overweight, often tried to tag along with me, seeking my company and cover. After several lunchtimes spent talking with him, I made excuses to give myself more room to wander, excuses like those I offered to Beth. But I staved him off without the edge of annoyance, anchored in memories of Beatrice Johnson, that I felt with Beth. The differences in my responses to girls and to boys led me to ponder the emotional legacy of my own gender-separated elementary school years.

I felt closer to the girls not only through memories of my own past, but also because I knew more about their gender-typed interactions. I had once played games like jump rope and statue buyer, but I had never ridden a skateboard and had barely tried sports like basketball and soccer. Paradoxically, however, I sometimes felt I could see boys' interactions and activities more clearly than those of girls; I came with fresher eyes and a more detached perspective. I found it harder to articulate and analyze the social relations of girls, perhaps because of my closer identification, but also, I believe, because our categories for understanding have been developed more out of the lives of boys and men than girls and women.

Were my moments of remembering, the times when I felt like a ten-year-old girl, a source of distortion or insight? Both, I believe. The identification enhanced my sense of what it feels like to be a fourth- and fifth-grade girl in a school setting. I lived that world in another time and place, but the similarities are evocative. Memory, like observing, is a way of knowing and can be a rich resource.[18]

But memories are also fragile and mysterious, continuously reconstructed by the needs of the present and by yearnings and fears of the past. Memories can distort as well as enrich present perceptions. Beth was a different person, in another time and place, than the Beatrice that I recalled, and no doubt had mentally reworked and stereotyped, from my childhood. When my own responses, like my obsession with documenting Kathryn's popularity, were driven by emotions like envy or aversion, they clearly obscured my ability to grasp the full social situation. As Jennifer Hunt has observed, in the course of field research, unconscious processes may both enhance and interfere with empathy.[19]

As I got in touch with the effects of memory and emotion, I altered my strategies for observing. My memories evoked the standpoint of a girl in the middle of the social hierarchy, who envied those above, who was susceptible to but used strategies for avoiding the claims of someone below, and who felt contaminated by a girl on the margins. During my months in Miss Bailey's classroom I thought a lot about those experiences, and I worked to see kids' interactions from other, and varied, perspectives. Instead of obsessing over Kathryn and avoiding Beth or Rita, I tried to understand their different social positions and experiences, and those of other girls and boys. This emphasis on multiple standpoints and meanings came to inform my understanding of gender.

Before I turn to to the topic of gender, I want to mention one final paradox in this particular relationship between the knower and those she sought to know. I like to think of myself as having hung out in classrooms, lunchrooms, playgrounds, relating to kids in a friendly and sometimes helpful fashion, and treating them, in my analysis and writing, with respect. But, like all fieldworkers. I was also a spectator, even a voyeur, passing through their lives and sharing few real stakes with those I studied. Several kids asked me if I was a spy, and, in a way, I was, especially when I went in search of the activities and meanings they created when not in the company of adults. Schools are physically set up to maximize the surveillance of students, with few private spaces and a staff who continually watch with eyes that mix benign pedagogical goals, occasional affection, and the wish to control. Kids sometimes resist this surveillance, and I wanted to observe and document their more autonomous collective moments. But in the very act of documenting their autonomy, I undermined it, for my gaze remained, at its core and in its ultimate knowing purpose, that of a more powerful adult.[20]

On the other hand, "adult," like "child," is too unitary a category. A growing sense of multiplicity and context brought me to question the use of dualistic frameworks not only for understanding gender, but also for understanding categories related to age. The dichotomy between "adult" and "child" is not a given of biology or nature; chronological and developmental age are complex continua, with enormous variation between and among five-, twelve-, and thirty-five-year-olds. People often negotiate the use of labels like "child," "teen," and "adult." However, we mark and reinforce an "adult/child" dualism—we produce categories like "the adult" and "the child"—through cultural practices such as channeling young people into elementary schools where five- and eleven-year-olds are cast together in the position of students and subordinates, with adults on the other "side" (a boundary I continually encountered in my efforts to lessen social distance between me and the kids).

[. . .]

Notes

1. For interesting essays on uses of the self and personal experience in doing social science, see Susan Krieger, *Social Science and the Self: Personal Essays on an Art Form.*
2. Adrienne Rich, *Of Woman Born: Motherhood as Experience and Institution*, p. 50.
3. James Clifford and George E. Marcus, eds., *Writing Culture: The Poetics and Politics of Ethnography*; Frances E. Mascia-Lees et al., "The Post-modernist Turn in Anthropology: Cautions from a Feminist Perspective."
4. Alice Miller, *The Drama of the Gifted Child.*
5. Vivian Gussin Paley, a teacher who taped and then wrote about her interactions with young children, describes a similar effort of consciousness. See Paley, "On Listening to What the Children Say."
6. Speier, "The Adult Ideological Viewpoint in Studies of Children," p. 185.
7. Dorothy E. Smith, *The Everyday World as Problematic*; and Valerie Walkerdine, *Schoolgirl Fictions.*
8. Speier, "The Adult Ideological Viewpoint in Studies of Children," p. 172.
9. Nancy Mandell ("The Least-Adult Role in Studying Children") describes a similar shift of consciousness in her observations in a preschool.
10. In *The Prelude: Or Growth of a Poet's Mind*, William Wordsworth wrote about the creative power that comes from reliving childhood experience, with the outer world "striking upon what is found within." Examining the biographical experiences of creative people, Edith Cobb (*The Ecology of Imagination in Childhood*) and Vera John-Steiner (*Notebooks of the Mind: Explorations of Thinking*) argue that adult creativity is nurtured by access to

the child within. In a contribution from psychoanalytic theory, Ernest G. Schachtel (*Metamorphosis*) contends that children have unique access to sensory experience.

11. The ethical dilemmas of my fieldwork in the draft resistance movement are explored in Barrie Thorne, "Political Activist as Participant Observer: Conflicts of Commitment in a Study of the Draft Resistance Movement of the 1960s."

12. Mandell ("The Least-Adult Role in Studying Children") writes about her efforts to create a position of "least adult" in a preschool; similar strategies are reported by Corsaro (*Friendship and Peer Culture*) and by Bronwyn Davies (*Frogs and Snails and Feminist Tales: Preschool Children and Gender*). Gary Alan Fine, who was a participant-observer with ten- to twelve-year-old boys on Little League baseball teams, and Barry Glassner, who observed in an elementary school, tried to hang out, mixing friendliness with minimal authority (Gary Alan Fine and Barry Glassner, "Participant Observation with Children: Promise and Problems"). All these observers avoided intervening and disciplining, except when there was a chance of serious physical injury. For a review of these and other discussions of participant-observation with children, see Gary Alan Fine and Kent L. Sandstrom, *Knowing Children: Participant Observation with Minors.*

13. Corsaro (*Friendship and Peer Culture*), Mandell ("The Least-Adult Role in Studying Children"), and Fine and Glassner ("Participant Observation with Children") also describe their efforts to contain adult requests for help. These requests exemplify a recurring feature in our culture's organization of children's worlds: a low ratio of adults to children and an assumption that more adult hands are always welcome, and will readily be made available, in the managerial tasks.

14. Bronwyn Davies (*Life in the Classroom and Playground: The Accounts of Primary School Children*) also discusses the dual agendas of classrooms—one set by the teacher and another, running parallel and sometimes contradictory or complementary, set by students. Also see Philip A. Cusick, *Inside High School.*

15. Erving Goffman, *Asylums*. Corsaro (*Friendship and Peer Culture*) describes processes of sharing and dispute among preschool children who smuggled in forbidden objects from home.

16. For further analyses of ritualized exchanges among children, see Tamar Katriel (" '*Bexibudim!*': Ritualized Sharing among Israeli Children"), who observed stylized sharing of treats by children on the way home from school, and Elliot Mishler, "Wou' You Trade Cookies with the Popcorn? Talk of Trades among Six Year Olds."

17. Social class was more inscribed in the appearance of girls than of boys. In both schools boys wore mostly T-shirts and solid-colored jeans or pants, whereas girls' clothing range more widely in design, fit, materials, and colors, and hence could go more easily awry. Furthermore, standards of grooming are also more exacting for girls than for boys. Girls from more impoverished backgrounds, like Rita and Jessica, wore mismatched patterns and fabric, and pants whose seats bulged out from wear. In contrast, girls from more affluent families, like Kathryn, wore well-matched "outfits" (the word itself is telling.)

18. In several evocative studies, adult women have drawn on their own memories as a research tool for learning about experiences of girlhood in a patriarchal culture. See Walkerdine, *Schoolgirl Fictions*, and Frigga Haug, *Female Sexualization: A Collective Work of Memory*, which explains an interesting methodology of collective "memory-work."

19. Jennifer C. Hunt, *Psychoanalytic Aspects of Fieldwork.*

20. Walkerdine (*Schoolgirl Fictions*) analyzes the "adult gaze" in teaching and in research with children.

References

Clifford, James, and George E. Marcus, eds. *Writing Culture: The Poetics and Politics of Ethnography.* Berkeley: University of California Press, 1986.

Cobb, Edith. *The Ecology of Imagination in Childhood.* New York: Columbia University Press, 1977.

Corsaro, William A. *Friendship and Peer Culture in the Early Years.* Norwood, N.J.: Ablex Publishing, 1985.

Cusick, Philip A. *Inside High School.* New York: Holt, Rinehart and Winston, 1973.

Davies, Bronwyn. *Frogs and Snails and Feminist Tales: Preschool Children and Gender.* Boston: Allen and Unwin, 1989.

——— . *Life in the Classroom and Playground: The Accounts of Primary School Children.* Boston: Routledge and Kegan Paul, 1982.

Fine, Gary Alan, and Barry Glassner. "Participant Observation with Children: Promise and Problems." *Urban Life* 8 (19879): 153–174.

Fine, Gary Alan, and Kent L. Sandstrom. *Knowing Children: Participant Observation with Minors.* Newbury Park, Calif.: Sage Publications, 1988.

Goffman, Erving *Asylums.* Garden City, N.Y.: Anchor Books, Doubleday, 1961.

Haug, Frigga, ed., *Female Sexualization: A Collective Work of Memory.* London: Verso, 1987.

Hunt, Jennifer C. *Psychoanalytic Aspects of Fieldwork.* Newbury Park, Calif.: Sage, 1989.

John-Steiner, Vera. *Notebooks of the Mind: Explorations of Thinking.* New York: Harper and Row, 1985.

Katriel, Tamar. " '*Bexibudim!*': Ritualized Sharing among Israeli Children." *Language and Society* 16 (1987): 305–320.

Krieger, Susan. *Social Science and the Self: Personal Essays on an Art Form.* New Brunswick, N.J.: Rutgers University Press, 1991.

Mandell, Nancy. "The Least-Adult Role in Studying Children." *Journal of Contemporary Ethnography* 16 (1988): 433–467.

Miller, Alice. *The Drama of the Gifted Child.* New York: Basic Books, 1983.

Mishler, Elliot. "Wou' You Trade Cookies with the Popcorn? Talk of Trades among Six-Year-Olds." In *Language, Culture, and Society,* ed. O. Garnica and M. King, 221–236. Oxford: Pergamon, 1979.

Paley, Vivian Gussin. "On Listening to What the Children Say." *Harvard Educational Review* 56 (1986): 122–131.

——— . *Boys and Girls: Superheroes in the Doll Corner.* Chicago: University of Chicago Press, 1984.

Rich, Adrienne. *Of Woman Born: Motherhood as Experience and Institution.* New York: Bantam.

Schachtel, Ernest G. *Metamorphosis.* New York: Basic Books, 1959.

Smith, Dorothy E. *The Everyday World as Problematic.* Boston: Northeastern University Press, 1987.

Speier, Matthew. "The Adult Ideological Viewpoint in Studies of Childhood." In *Rethinking Childhood,* ed. Arlene Skolnick, 168–186. Boston: Little, Brown, 1976.

Thorne, Barrie. "Political Activist as Participant Observer: Conflicts of Commitment in a Study of the Draft Resistance Movement of the 1960s." *Symbolic Interaction* 2 (1978): 73–88.

Walkerdine, Valerie. *Schoolgirl Fictions.* New York: Verso, 1990.

27

Teacher–Researcher Collaboration from Two Perspectives

Polly Ulichny and Wendy Schoener

This article tells the story of qualitative research that evolved into a collaborative project between the two of us: Wendy, a teacher, and Polly, a researcher. Collaboration for us came to mean determining mutual goals for the research, sharing responsibility for the research product, and building a trusting relationship that permitted interdependence and mutuality between teacher and researcher.

This story is told from both of our perspectives. Polly details the process of establishing rapport in qualitative research and describes the elements of discourse and relationship that contributed to an evolving collaboration between the researcher and the teacher. She frames her understanding of conducting collaborative qualitative inquiry within a feminist methodology. Wendy describes her journey through the project, from the misgivings and fears that surrounded her initial participation in the "researcher's project" to her insights and professional development as an English as a Second Language (ESL) instructor and teacher-researcher.

Collaborative Research and the Role of Rapport

Traditional qualitative research acknowledges the centrality of rapport between researcher and informant. Most references to establishing rapport discuss the need to establish trust in the field with informants, and at the same time to remain detached and "neutral" in order to avoid biasing the data collected. The title of Agar's text on ethnographic methods, *The Professional Stranger* (1980), captures the role that many mainstream qualitative researchers advocate for students of ethnography or in-depth interviewing methodologies. Glesne and Peshkin (1992, p. 98) illustrate the advice most textbooks and manuals give to novices in qualitative research methods:

> When a distinction between rapport and friendship is made in qualitative literature, the overwhelming tendency is to warn against forming friendships because of the hazards of sample bias and loss of objectivity. These hazards are linked to over identification, also called "over-rapport" and "going native" (Gold, 1969: Miller, 1952; Shaffir, Stebbins, & Turowetz, 1980; Van Maanen, 1983).

Recently, however, feminists, critical ethnographers, and postmodern qualitative researchers have critiqued the traditional, detached stance of conducting participant observation precisely because it leads to objectifying and "othering" the informant of the research while hiding the identity of the much implicated researcher (Fine, 1994; Lather, 1991; Lincoln, 1995; Lykes, 1989; Oakley, 1981; Reason, 1994; Reinharz, 1984; Van Maanen, 1988).

A simple schematic delineates the possible research stances available to qualitative researchers along two continua—one of action and one of relationship:

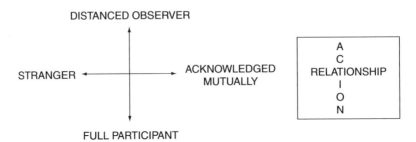

Figure 1

The action continuum ranges from distant observer—the researcher as a potted plant or fly on the wall observing social behaviors without any participation in the activity underway—to complete involvement—experience of and coparticipation in the events of the field. The relationship continuum offers the researcher a range of connections to informants in the field, from relative stranger to acknowledged mutuality as friends, confidants, facilitator-facilitated, or even informal therapist and client.[1]

The informants in qualitative research have similar continua along which they may situate themselves. The action dimension for them, however, refers to the research project and not to engagement in the field under study. As the informants become more engaged along either the action or relationship continuum, the research project is transformed into one of collaboration.

As with descriptions of possible researcher relations in the field, the literature on collaborative research offers an array of definitions for what is considered collaborative. These range from inviting informant input into the researcher's research questions or process, to requiring, in the case of some action research advocates, that the researcher investigate only what the host or informant community defines as the research focus (Oja & Smulyan, 1989; Reason, 1994; Reinharz, 1992; Stenhouse, 1975). As mentioned above, our definition of collaboration extends beyond the process of determining the focus of the research to creating a mutuality and interdependence between teacher and researcher in all phases of the research project. By mutuality we mean that the relationship that evolved between us was one of equal status based on mutual respect and concern. Since we each provided unique contributions to the project, interdependence meant that data collection, interpretation, and even communication of the results were activities we jointly participated in, albeit with differing contributions based on our roles, which we explain in detail below.

Relatively little has been written from the standpoint of the researched participant on the nature of relationship and involvement in the research process (see Florio and Walsh, 1981, and Florio-Ruane and Dohanich, 1984, as exceptions). The more voluminous literature that discusses the benefits and pitfalls of collaborative research comes, not surprisingly, from the researcher side of the interaction (Campbell, 1988; Gibson, 1985; Jacullo-Noto, 1984; Johnston, 1994; Reinharz, 1984; Wallace & Louden, 1994). Much of it discusses the difficulties of collaboration and the challenge of producing research that benefits the teacher participants in the collaboration. Florio-Ruane (1991), for example, tells of the disappointing reaction that teacher collaborators had to the researchers' final report of a lengthy joint investigation of writing instruction:

> When we showed our teacher informants the technical report we had produced, . . . we were a bit nervous. We hoped at best to interest the teachers, at worst, not to offend them. . . . We were not at all prepared for their response. The teachers read our text carefully . . . [and] returned with little to say. Too polite to admit it, we later learned that they had found the report, not offensive, but frankly, dull and disappointing. They wondered that we had spent so much time with them and their students and noticed so little of what they thought important. . . . Additionally, our antiseptically third person accounts disappointed the teachers because they left out personal details of what we as researchers had learned or felt while sharing the classroom with them for a year. (p. 8)

Because of this disjuncture, some have claimed that the foundation of teacher-researcher collaboration is exploitation of teachers (Ladwig, 1991), and others have advocated that the academic researcher be replaced by teachers who investigate their own practice, thereby not only permitting the teacher's voice to be heard, but also to establish a new set of parameters defining teacher knowledge (Berthoff, 1987; Cochran-Smith & Lytle, 1990). We are sympathetic to both of these positions, but we take them as cautions rather than blueprints for conducting research on teaching. Researchers and teachers often see things from different perspectives, and it is true that the researcher's perspective has been the more credible in academic settings. But rather than eliminating the researcher from the enterprise of creating knowledge about teaching, the model we present is one in which both teacher and researcher have a voice, because in our study, we have profited from a successful collaborative effort that has provided knowledge that we both value. Neither of us on our own would have been able to produce the study that emerged through our collaboration.

Our presentation here describes the evolution of this collaborative research project in the voices of both the researched and the researcher. We describe the conditions that existed for each of us upon entering this study, and how they affected our respective expectations of the research process and its outcomes. As the study evolved, so did our positions along the continua of action and relationship. How we managed the shifts, what they felt like for each of us, and how they determined the direction of the research itself are the subjects of this article. Our intention here is not to prescribe a particular method of collaborative research, even though the results of this project, both in substance and process, were valued by both of us. We found that the detached position of participant-observer in a qualitative single-subject case study is not desirable, and may not even be feasible. To make our case, we present a two-part narrative in which we chronicle how recognizing and dealing with whole persons in the research endeavor affected both of us, as well as the results of the research. While a prescription for relationships in the field is neither possible nor desirable, researchers and informants cannot escape the fact that, whatever their nature, relationships do exist and therefore require the attention of both researchers and researched.

Polly: Purposes of the Study

From my researcher's point of view, this project had two sources. First, as an educator interested in teaching and learning among diverse populations, I wanted to investigate how a teacher manages to instruct students from diverse cultures and linguistic backgrounds, students who presumably construct academic knowledge differently. I wanted to look at a "successful" resolution of these differences, and therefore chose to study an adult ESL classroom.

My experience in K-12 public school settings with ESL students, as a staff development instructor, researcher, and coordinator of an ESL teacher certification program, informed me of widespread teaching and learning that was less than ideal. This was due to many factors, including marginalization of ESL populations within the schools, a general lack of relevant training and experience among teachers assigned to ESL classes, and a common practice of pullout ESL instruction. My experience with adult ESL classes, which students attended voluntarily, was quite the opposite. Teachers in these classrooms were specially trained, and the students, who were eager to learn, rarely experienced misunderstandings and cultural mismatches that interfered with their learning. This seemed quite different from numerous examinations of K-12 classrooms, where culture and language differences between students and teachers caused widespread school failure (Cummins, 1986; Delpit, 1988; Heath, 1983; Nieto, 1994; Ogbu & Matute-Bianchi, 1986; Philips, 1972).

I was also interested in discovering how a teacher manages to interpret and respond to diverse learners, particularly when, at best, very few of them share common assumptions or a common language. Although most qualified ESL teachers speak another language, it is inconceivable that one would speak all the languages of the students she teaches in multilingual ESL classes. Much has been written about how an ESL teacher *should* teach linguistically and culturally diverse students, but very little research has investigated exactly how a teacher goes about it: how she plans, implements, and accommodates her instruction to meet the diverse and often extreme needs of her students (Ulichny, 1996). Thus, my reason for conducting this research was to examine closely an ESL teacher's practice by observing, audio-taping, and carrying out a discourse analysis of the classroom interaction.

Second, although I had embraced ethnography as a way of deepening my understanding of face-to-face interactions among linguistically diverse speakers, my initial experiences in the field were less than satisfactory. It seemed to me that understanding the context of the interactions and how they developed over time among the participants offered a deeper, and hence better, explanation of interactions than merely examining carefully transcribed linguistic data (Corsaro, 1981; Hymes, 1980; Watson-Gegeo & Ulichny, 1988). Nevertheless, one particular instance left me with serious questions about my role and responsibilities to informants of ethnographies.

Fieldwork Disaster

I had negotiated entry into a college level ESL classroom through the teacher I wanted to investigate. I explained one of my purposes to her—to undertake a discourse analysis of the classroom interaction in order to explore how teaching and learning happens in an ESL environment—and she agreed to have me attend her classes weekly, talk informally to both her and the students as time permitted, and to tape-record interactions. I further explained to her that I had no preconceived notion of the categories I would be looking at. Rather, as an ethnographer, I was committed to letting the data drive my questions and the explanations for the interactions I observed. Within three weeks, however, I sensed a growing tension that eventually resulted in my leaving the class prematurely. Although the teacher never really asked me to leave, when the discomfort with my tape-recording caused her to suggest that I might be "stealing" her method, I offered to disband my study, and she readily agreed.

As I reflected on what the teacher's reasons might have been for wanting me to discontinue my observations and recordings of her classroom, I came to understand how naive my researcher's stance had been. My silent observations, private field notes, and analyses seemed to make this teacher extremely uncomfortable. It wasn't that I had criticized what I was seeing in her classroom; the very fact that I was there offered her a different vantage point from which to view her own practice. Furthermore, I left each lesson I attended with a record of the interaction and provided no accounting for it. Through my silent observations she viewed herself as she thought I must see her—conducting a less-than-perfect lesson and making mistakes. The more uncomfortable she became with her own practice, the more critical she was of her interactions with the class, and the more intolerable my silent scrutiny became.

Eventually, I abandoned my ethnography with the disconcerting feeling that I had somehow violated the principle that had drawn me to it in the first place—respect for the whole person within the context of practice. What right did I have as a researcher to interfere in her relationship with her students and her practice? None, I concluded. But I also concluded that remedying the situation in future studies would require some action, rather than the non-action I had negotiated in this study.

In order to understand what action would be necessary to put at ease a research subject who was undergoing close scrutiny of her professional behavior, I considered aspects of the research situation that may have led to the disaster. I believe four features of the teacher-researcher relationship, enumerated below, serve to exacerbate teacher discomfort.

1. Invasive Design

My reflection on this situation led me to a number of insights about the design of participant-observer research. A qualitative single-subject case study of a professional practice can be a very invasive design. While the researcher is not manipulating the setting by imposing experiments or contrastive experiences, in-depth observations of one person's practice for the purpose of analysis intrudes on a most intimate component of the informant's identity—the relationship between personal and public identities in one's practice. In multi-site studies or institution-wide investigations, the same degree of invasiveness may not be present. Observing many subjects engaged in similar behaviors focuses the researcher's attention on aspects of the social context and regularities of practices. Observing a single subject, however, shifts that attention to the way that a particular individual enacts her profession and why. I don't believe my initial negotiation into the teacher's classroom, which merely asked her to allow me to sit in and tape-record some lessons as a basis for a written report on an as yet unidentified question, prepared her for the feeling of intrusion into her secrets that she would experience.

2. Doubtful Benefits of the Research to the Informant

The potential benefits of the research to the practitioner are remote, because the ethnographer enters the field without a clear research question and with no prediction about the results of the study. Given the intimate view that the informant permits the researcher, shouldn't the subject expect something positive to emerge from the experience? For a practitioner, something positive usually means an enhancement of her own practice. Feeding back insights gained from the research is normally what the researcher expects to give back to the field. Current textbooks that introduce researchers to qualitative methods underscore the importance of payback, and suggest that researchers either give of their time (often difficult in the midst of a demanding academic life) or offer information gleaned from the study that would "improve" the field (Bogdan & Biklen, 1992; Ely et al., 1991). Ethicists and feminist social science researchers have gone further, suggesting that information about informants belongs to the informants as much as, if not more than, to the researcher (Deyhle, Hess, & LeCompte, 1992; Lather, 1991; LeCompte & Preissle, with Tesch, 1993; Lincoln, 1995). However, it is common knowledge among both researchers and teachers that the reports researchers produce rarely find their way into schools and classrooms (Cochran-Smith & Lytle, 1993). As Cochran-Smith and Lytle (1993) claim, "[researchers] fault teachers for not reading or not implementing the findings of [their] research even though teachers often view these findings as irrelevant and counterintuitive" (p. 10). The abstractions researchers struggle to produce seem removed from day-to-day experience and provide little direction for dealing with particular students and situations (Bickel & Hattrup, 1995).

On the other hand, practitioners who undergo the researcher's scrutiny are likely to be interested in the individualized feedback a participant-observer can provide, especially if the researcher presents herself as a nonjudgmental seeker of new knowledge. In the early stages of fieldwork, this request for feedback, whether explicit or implicit, can be difficult to manage. In my own experience, striving for neutral language to describe behaviors and censoring interpretation as much as possible in the data collection process made it difficult to say anything worthwhile to the practitioner about her work. The level at which I was operating—*what's going on here?*—would seem completely trivial to the practitioner, who is more interested in knowing *what does what's going on here mean for me and my students?* In reality, however, the participant observer is less likely to be able to answer that question during the initial stages of fieldwork than is the practitioner herself, a point to which I will return later.

3. Researcher as Critical Evaluator and the Issue of Trust

The third feature that can lead to teacher discomfort, a feature related to the previous two points, is the fact that the participant observer is obtrusive in the field. In spite of assurances and precautions to the contrary, the researcher alters the context of the situation by her very presence (see Labov, 1972, p. 209, for a discussion of this issue, which he has labeled the "observer's paradox"). Teachers are normally accustomed to being scrutinized by two types of observers—supervisors and apprentices. In both cases, but particularly in that of the supervisor, the object of the scrutiny is to judge the teacher's performance of professional duties. When teachers experience a researcher's intrusion into their profession and no feedback is forth-coming, they are likely to interpret the silence around issues of practice as implicit criticism. A reasonable inference from an observer's silence, then, is negative evaluation of practices.

This presumed critical stance of the researcher leads to the lack of trust that teachers often exhibit towards researchers. This distrust emerges, in my experience, from the distanced stance of the silent researcher-observer. Even though the process of conducting field research is intended to be nonjudgmental, the researcher needs to work to achieve this position, particularly in ethnographies of familiar settings and social institutions. Even though the researcher pushes beyond her initial judgements to achieve a deeper understanding of the informants in their contexts, the ultimate goal of educational research is to provide information that can promote better educational experiences for all. Thus, the educational researcher is likely to have an opinion about good and bad practices and is, furthermore, expected to discuss education in evaluative terms. It is doubtful, then, that the assurance of nonjudgmental research can be upheld.

Discussions of ethics and of the researcher's responsibilities to the field deal with this delicate contradiction by advocating anonymity in the reporting of research (Agar, 1980; Bogden & Biklen, 1992; Deyhle et al., 1992; Glesne & Peshkin, 1992; LeCompte et al., 1993; Stainback, 1988). This is intended to protect the informants from disapproving readers, as well as from identification by those who may influence their lives and livelihoods. Anonymity can protect them from the former, but it is unlikely to be totally successful in protecting them from the latter. It has been my experience that the informants of intensive qualitative research projects are far more concerned with what the researchers/ experts think about them than with what anonymous readers of a scholarly journal will think. Anonymity as a protective device means little since it cannot be applied in the face-to-face encounters with the researcher.

A second source of informants' distrust—which was true in my particular case—comes from a history of research abuses in the university town in which the study was conducted. A particularly virile "town-gown" antagonism exists in educational settings that have been the targets of negative research reports. Less destructive, but nonetheless damaging to the teacher-researcher relationship, are the many examples of "rip-and-run" research, where both qualitative and quantitative researchers leave the field to publish their studies and are never heard from again by their hosts. Both the personal and professional contexts of conducting intensive observational research make for an uneasy alliance in the qualitative single-subject case study research design.

4. Power and Knowledge Differential

Finally, perhaps the most critical feature of the teacher-researcher relationship, and the feature underlying all that I have described so far, is the power/knowledge differential between researcher and teacher. Within the dyad, the researcher has more power while the teacher has more knowledge. This creates a contradiction in the research process that requires resolution.

The power of the researcher derives from the differential status that the wider academic community gives to the researcher's work—producing knowledge about teaching—versus the status accorded to the teacher. In the educational context, the researcher's version of a classroom or instructional practice is seen as more "objective" and convincing than the teacher's version. There is an assumption that the researcher, through rigorous methods, can see more, and more accurately, than the teacher. Moreover, with respect to the wider issues under investigation in the project, the researcher is believed to know more than the teacher. Power chits in the educational world are accumulated on the basis of the size of one's knowledge base within a formal, academic context. Thus, the researcher *appears* to the outside world as the more credible knower, which implies a knowledge of what should and shouldn't be done in the educational setting. Finally, through writings and public presentations, the researcher has access to a wider audience than the teacher. The written words of professionals in their scholarly formats establish generalized knowledge. It is difficult for informants of the particular to compete (Cochran-Smith & Lytle, 1990).

While the power and the knowledge appear to reside with the researcher vis-à-vis the broader educational community, it is, however, the teacher who has the most knowledge of the setting under investigation. The teacher knows what happens in her own classroom and why it happens more intimately than the researcher. The tension that results from intimately knowing one's own classroom, yet feeling that one's knowledge can legitimately be challenged by the researcher, creates a vulnerability that may shake a teacher's confidence in both teaching and knowing how to teach. This is, in essence, the wedge that inserts itself in the practitioner's concept of self as a professional. It separates professional practice from the professional and, hence, alienates the person from her work activity.

These aspects of the relationship between researcher and teacher evince the need to establish the teacher as the primary knower in the research project. As a result of that adjustment in the design and, therefore, in the relationships in the field, the power differential that exists between researcher and researched might also be diminished.

Wendy: To Engage or Not to Engage in the Research

I had been teaching ESL at the university level for just over a year when my office mate, Polly, asked me a favor. She was teaching graduate courses at the same school, and we knew each other, though not well, through the forced acquaintance of shared offices at the university. The favor had to do with the other part of her life—completing a research project on ESL teachers. My sincere impulse was to say no, thank you. A whole school semester? My blood pressure rose when supervisors came in to observe for a mere twenty minutes.

Nevertheless I said yes, though with misgivings. My primary motivation was, as I told her, to learn something about how to teach. I imagined that Polly would work as a supervisor in observing my teaching, with the object of making sure nothing was going too wrong and perhaps offering suggestions to improve my classroom work. My secondary motivation was to avoid disappointing the director of our center, who was always enthusiastic about teachers' involvement in research.

A researcher, for me, was simply and inevitably the stranger, the distant observer. Distance and nonaffiliation were required, I felt, to achieve the objectivity needed in research. I supposed that Polly's observations would give her the opportunity to discover problems that would be hurtful to hear about, and that she was honor-bound to reveal this hurtful news publicly, while preserving my anonymity.

I was concerned about how I could avoid feeling paralyzed in my practice if Polly gave me feedback that I was doing poorly. I was aware of the crisis of confidence in the teaching profession, that is, the public emphasis on "accountability," which suggested that teachers had somehow been less responsible than they should for student learning. I was also not very self-confident. I perceived that there were legitimate conflicting viewpoints on teaching ESL, and yet also believed that if I were a smarter person, I would have already learned the "right" answers to my teaching problems from existing research. I did not know Polly's orientation in this contentious area of education, but I did know that she was a researcher and that researchers had access to specialized knowledge frequently not available to practitioners. I decided I could resolve my predicament by preparing "extra hard" for the class she observed.

I did not express these views directly to Polly because I could not blame her for simply fulfilling her function as researcher, but I did verbalize them with peers, who agreed with me. I discussed the proposed project with one of the other teachers Polly hoped to observe, and this teacher's fearfulness about possible outcomes confirmed my own. We joked nervously about how Polly would inevitably compare us and then decide which one was better. If we were lucky, we reasoned, we would never find out her conclusions. Then, right before the new semester began, I learned that the two other teachers Polly had asked to participate in the project had said no and that my class would be the sole focus of her work. While this meant that I would not be compared with my colleagues, I imagined that the intensified focus on my teaching would yield its own dangers. Perhaps I would seem less talented under the close examination she would now have time to do.

There was nothing Polly could have said before we worked together to dispel my fears. She had been her usual approachable self through our initial negotiation for the project, the same friendly office mate that I had known for a semester. But her simple suggestion that we step into roles of observer and observed was enough to make me feel more wary. I imagined that the research situation could degenerate over the semester and leave me wishing I had never revealed myself. In the past, my anxiety about classroom observers had been visible enough to register with my students. What if I made my own students anxious by putting myself in a difficult position? Even without a watchful presence in my classroom, I regularly had moments of feeling that other teachers (and certainly researchers) would know intuitively how to do my work better than I did.

Over semester break, I prepared for the class Polly would observe, a noncredit ESL reading class recommended to students who were considered not yet ready for mainstream freshman courses. All the while I anticipated her reaction to my plans. Were the lessons too simplistic? Too demanding? I imagined both criticisms applying to the same lesson. I was working with a colleague to design a course based on individual chapters from college texts used on campus: a chapter on the family from a sociology text, one on language acquisition from a psychology text, another on developing world economies from an economics text, and one on Mendel's early genetic research from a biology text. We were doing this partially in reaction to the fact that the previous semester's course, based on social movements of the 1960s, had seemed to interest the students a good deal less than it had interested us. We were hopeful that changing topics and offering readings from a variety of sources would at least interest some of the students some of the time. Still, I would be trying an entirely new and different course in front of someone whose sympathy was hardly guaranteed, in my eyes, by virtue of her role.

Polly: Adjustments to the Method

At the end of my negative field experience, I decided to establish a research stance that would not be distant from and seemingly critical of a teacher's practice. After several months, I reinitiated negotiations with three ESL teachers at my university, thinking that observing three teachers instead of one might make them feel less threatened, as I would spend less time in each individual's classroom. I explained my intent—to study classroom interaction—and told them I wanted to minimize the discomfort that my presence might cause by speaking openly with each of them during the course of the study. Two of the three felt uncomfortable about having a researcher in their classrooms because both were trying out a new syllabus and were unsure about the results. They did not want to be observed as they worked through potential problems. Only one of the teachers, Wendy, agreed to have me study her class, and yet, as I discovered later, she was less than enthusiastic about my presence. What she indicated at the time, however, was that she was enthusiastic about participating in the study because she "thought she would learn something from it to improve her teaching." This added to my fears: I was already concerned about building trust; now I had to be concerned about what benefit the research might have for Wendy.

Wendy and I shared an office at the same university because we had schedules that rarely coincided. We also taught in different programs and had minimal knowledge of each other's work. Thus, although we shared our work space, we had not established much of a relationship prior to my entering the field of her classroom. The shared office might be an advantage. I reasoned, since we would have some opportunity to discuss the research and the classroom informally if we chose to. On the other hand, having to deal with each other in and out of the classroom might make us even more self-conscious. It was clear she expected me to give her feedback about her teaching. Would I have anything significant to tell her? And, more importantly, how would I handle situations in which my understandings of her practice were not positive? A researcher who has the luxury of observing interactions without the pressure of decisionmaking can see things that might be uncomfortable to report back to the teacher. This is particularly true when the researcher slows down the transcription process. Her privileged position allows her to listen carefully and reflect on what is happening at any given moment. For example, I might understand a student's question or contribution differently, not right or wrong, from the teacher, and see how the teacher may have misread or inadvertently silenced a student who was attempting to participate. While it might be useful for a teacher to be aware of such situations, a researcher-observer could easily jeopardize her relationship in the field if she communicated this information without sufficient regard for the teacher's self-esteem.

Erickson (1986) has illustrated this difficult situation in the form of a two-by-two matrix. Researchers can communicate news to their informants that is either known or unknown, good or bad. The good news is easy to hear, especially when it is unknown to the subject. It is the kind of information that overcomes the lack of trust an informant can experience. Known bad news is somewhat easy to hear and, with careful attention to the teacher's vulnerable position, can be shared in a way that does not undermine the fragile trust between researcher and informant. The greatest problem occurs in communicating bad news—what the researcher's privileged position reveals that has escaped the practitioner's awareness. At the beginning of this research endeavor, I had no experience and little confidence in being able to deal with that area.

GOOD NEWS   BAD NEWS

	GOOD NEWS	BAD NEWS
KNOWN	EASY TO HEAR	RELATIVELY EASY TO HEAR
UNKNOWN	GREAT TO HEAR	HARD TO HEAR

Figure 2

Just before I entered the field, but after I had negotiated entry into Wendy's classroom, I reached a solution, after consulting with Morimoto (personal communication, 1988), to my dual dilemma of dealing with feedback and establishing Wendy as the primary knower of the classroom meanings. I decided to let the seeing come from her, that I would access her knowledge and simultaneously reduce my power by taking a back seat in the interpretation of what transpired in the classroom. By doing so, I hoped the research would also be more likely to produce benefits that Wendy desired. This did not mean that I was eliminating the possibility of sharing bad news with Wendy, but rather that its introduction would come from her rather than from me. In the words of Morimoto (personal communication, also stated in Morimoto, Gregory, & Butler, 1973), researchers can most benefit a teacher when they lend an ear, not a remedy. What teachers need is the time and space to reflect on their practice so they can come up with their own solutions to problems.

Borrowing a method developed by Erickson and Shultz (1982), I decided to tape-record the classroom interactions I observed and subsequently interview Wendy about them, using the tapes as a stimulus for her recall. Contrary to recommendations for doing qualitative research. I would put off taking detailed field notes and carrying out an ongoing analysis of the classroom data, preferring to follow Wendy's lead. With my major difficulty resolved in this adjustment to the design. I was left with only one last hurdle: convincing Wendy to spend even *more* time on what was essentially *my* research project. I presented the idea, which I framed by relating my uneasiness with conducting single-subject observational research. It was my intention to impose my views on the research as little as possible, which was a very naive plan. I had justified my removal on the action continuum, but I had not anticipated the effects of this design on the relationship continuum.

When I asked Wendy to meet with me weekly to discuss the tapes, she expressed her reluctance. Too many of her waking hours were already dedicated to her profession and she felt that she needed to protect her minimal free time. I offered to meet her at her convenience in a non-work setting, and persuaded her to try it on a biweekly basis. If at any point she thought it was too time consuming or not useful, she could call an end to the interviews.

Wendy: Reactions to the Adjustment

Before the semester started, Polly proposed that we meet weekly to discuss the class, in language that should have reassured me. She told me in several ways that she wanted to understand the classroom interaction from my point of view and that she had something to learn from me. But my general feelings about research were fatalistic enough then that I did not see the value of such work; it simply represented another risk. My first response to this request was that I didn't have the time for such interviews, which was true. I was the only full-time teacher on campus who had sixteen teaching hours per week. I made assignments at a rate that left me with stacks of papers to grade each week. But my greater fear, without doubt, was of the additional anxiety such meetings would cause. I told Polly I didn't have time to be so involved, rather than admitting to patent cowardice, but we negotiated. In the end, I agreed to less frequent meetings and the option to discontinue altogether if I wished. The problem of demands on my time had been addressed; the problem of risk had not been because I had not raised it.

Polly: Doing the Research

Wendy and I began the project wary of each other's reaction to our individual practices. I was concerned that I would make her feel uncomfortable or, worse, invalidated. Nonetheless, we began meeting every other week for several hours to listen to and comment on the audio tapes of the class. I tape-recorded each of these sessions, which included pieces of classroom interaction, and transcribed them. The following comments on the nature of the talk and its development are based on these data.

In the first interview we mainly listened to the tape and had short discussions of what Wendy found interesting. She framed most of what she chose to discuss in terms of crisis management in the classroom. She pointed out weaknesses in the way things were going and talked about how she might improve them. Attached to that were longer, free-flowing segments in which Wendy discussed why addressing the weaknesses was difficult, if not impossible. She seemed to me to be critical of her teaching. Her initial remarks after stopping the tape were prefaced with a version of "I could have done that better." In fact, in the first interview session, she did not stop the tape even once to comment on something positive. In addition to being critical, however, her talk demonstrated that she thought deeply about how to teach her classes. Her negative judgment made me wonder if it was a reaction to what she thought I must be thinking. If she pointed to the flaws, I would not have to. But her voluminous comments on the context of the classroom, student backgrounds, and reflections on practice encouraged me to think that the interviews might, in fact, be useful for her to consolidate her thinking. In a Vygotskyan sense, she was problematizing her practice, making it richer and truly complex through the talk. Reifying her practice at this reflective level seemed to hold her interest. I was not aware of struggling to keep the talk going, and we were both surprised when two hours had slipped by without our noticing the time.

The following example from that first interview demonstrates Wendy's tendency towards negative self-appraisal, as well as her deference to my more power-imbued understandings:[2]

(Wendy turns off the tape to comment.)

Wendy: Oh . . . uhm . . . a couple of things. Ugh! Do I really sound like that? My voice sounds ten octaves higher than what I think.

Polly: Tapes tend to do that, but I think that it sounds higher because you [normally] hear [your voice] in the cavity of your own head.

Wendy: I don't want . . . I'm so aware of not wanting to sound like a nursery school teacher (uh hm) with them. So it strikes me to hear my voice so high. I had a couple of other . . . I don't know actually. I'm almost more interested in hearing what you think about a couple of things. I wonder about sometimes simplifying things so much that I might not say precisely what I want to say.

Polly: Like what?

Since I was particularly sensitive to her negative feelings about her practice during the first listening session, I tried to curb them. I sometimes offered an explanation that was less negative than her own, as in the case of her voice in the example above, or rephrased her concerns in the form of dilemmas she was facing. This seemed to me to take the focus off of conducting a lesson badly and put it on the pressures that she felt caused her to respond in practice in a less than desirable way. By directing the talk to dilemmas and probing them with Wendy, I was not the passive listener I had intended to be. I introduced topics of discussion by naming dilemmas that previously had not been part of Wendy's meaning-making of her teaching practice. What was intended to be a mitigating contribution on my part turned out to be a significant role in introducing the essential themes of the analysis:

(Wendy has just commented negatively on her tendency to oversimplify text ideas for the students.)

Polly: Do you have any sense of why you do that? I mean is it . . .

Wendy: I guess it's my way of compensating for thinking that even the way I do it . . . Oh how can I put it? Even the way I do it is gonna be pretty hard for some people and so predigesting it, simplifying it very drastically, is a way of not frightening those people. At the same time, what am I there for except to present something that's a little bit tough.

It seemed from Wendy's responses to my comments that she frequently interpreted them in evaluative terms. She heard them as suggestions for action, as well as frameworks for interpreting her classroom activities. During the interviews, I frequently stated that I was not evaluating her teaching or advocating for a particular practice over another:

Polly: You keep mentioning the schedule. Where does that come from?

Wendy: I know, I know uhm maybe it's not that important.

Polly: I mean I don't know, but it's something (uh hum) that you've mentioned several (uh hum) times about getting through the material and staying on schedule.

Wendy: Yah, yah, it's that I don't . . . I think for one thing, in spite of the fact that we haven't gotten very far in this chapter . . . maybe it's just my sense but I kind of feel that we've started to beat [the family chapter] to death and that it might be just as well to go on to the next thing. But I do that to myself a lot actually (uh hm). I'll think, oh boy, they're not ready and I really underestimated what it was going to take, and I'll put things off but I don't like it (laugh). You know it's kind of silly. I should really think about that.

Polly: So do you think, let me just play around with this, if you had a different kind of organization to your course, where every week you were working on a different reading and you were doing, I mean that's not a suggestion because you'd be throwing away all sorts of other advantages to this program, but would that allay your fears of getting through it faster? If you were not looking at the same content all the time?

We openly addressed Wendy's tendency to take all of my comments as suggestions. It became a topic of our talk as we explored the perceived differences in our power and knowledge bases. Although she persisted in hearing "suggestions" throughout the data collection period, she could also stand back and see what she was doing and take a more confident stance:

(We are trying to arrange my observations during the last weeks of the class. I asked when she will discuss the text reading next so I am sure to be present.)

Wendy: . . . .when is the next time [we discuss biology]? Probably Monday, with the film.
Polly: Oh, 'cause you're going to discuss *Raisin in the Sun* the whole time. You're going to see the second part of it?
Wendy: The film requires two hours.
Polly: Oh, so you'll just show it part on Wednesday and show it again on Friday.
Wendy: Maybe I *should* stagger it. Somehow. You're right. Maybe we shouldn't be away from biology that long. I have to think about that.
Polly: I didn't, I didn't suggest that. I'm just . . .
Wendy: No, I know. (We both laugh.) I know, but you're making me think, I should say.

My talk, particularly during the first interviews, indicated a desire to shed the authority, the "seer" role Wendy seemed willing to give me. I joined her talk about the complexities of teaching, as well as the fact that there were no easy, textbook answers to most of them. I also showed a preference for responding to her negative comments with probing questions. I neither acknowledged nor disclaimed her judgment by asking her for more information. As the interviews progressed, it became somewhat more comfortable for me to address the known bad news she brought up. I was careful, however, not to initiate a bad news topic that could have placed me in the unknown-bad-news box in Figure 2. If I did evaluate, I was generally positive in my assessment. I generally chose to voice only my positive assessments, of which there were many. During the initial phases of data collection, in particular, when Wendy and I were establishing our relationship and building trust, I chose to avoid commenting on my interpretations of classroom activities that seemed to limit student participation or show a misunderstanding of a student's meaning. I did not want to interfere with Wendy's interpretation of the classroom by steering the talk to mine. I planned to introduce my understandings, as necessary, in the discourse analysis of the classroom interaction that I intended to carry out after the conclusion of the class:

Wendy: ... Do you, do you get a feeling that, I mean it is kind of funny that I insisted on (laugh) having this done to myself in the time that I planned, but do you think that it seemed a little rushed?

Polly: No.

Wendy: 'Cause I don't want to give them that [impression].

Polly: No, I've seen three extremely well designed lessons that you've presented that began and finished within the time period. I mean (uh hum) for each of those different kinds of lessons you had an agenda and you carried it through and it was completed ... uhm ... I don't feel like it was either too rushed or too slow.

A form of interaction, that seemed to reduce the power differential by taking me out of the role of evaluator or expert, was matching stories. Some of the problems Wendy identified in her classroom were ones that I could relate to my own teaching. When she wondered, for example, if she had allocated turns at talk in a way that encouraged participation rather than squelched it, I offered parallel reflections that revealed my own dilemmas on this issue.

Perhaps the most significant step I took in my attempts to reduce the power and knowledge differential, however, was to directly address the issue of how I envisioned it. In a form of matching story I revealed my own reservations about how to successfully conduct this type of research, much in the same way Wendy was opening up to me about her teaching. As we see in the following excerpt, it allowed us to talk frankly about some of the issues that had festered undercover in my previous experience. I could make clear that I didn't view myself as any more of an expert on how to manage the dilemmas than she was:

Polly: (telling the story of being advised to listen as a researcher) ... she is sharing her experience and talking to me and I said I know I'll want to jump in and say "oh, why don't you do this and why don't you do that," because it makes me feel helpful, you know, in some way (uh hum) because then that way there's some kind of exchange going on. But I don't have any right answers, I don't think I know how to do something. I mean that's precisely my point is that there is no expert knowledge about how to do these things. It's all by the seat of your pants and putting together your experience with what you think is going on and your background, whatever ... And [Morimoto] said if you just listen and you give that attention ... she's the expert of her expertise and what [conclusions] she draws, that's what you can give her (uh hum). And he said that's what you can (yah) give, attention, so that she can find out her own understanding (uh hum). And that made so much sense to me, I mean I just felt that unlocked it (uh hum). But I think that that's exactly what, you know, if you get anything out of this (uh hum) that's what it's going to be. It's all from you (uh hum).

Wendy: These dialogues are different from going home and thinking why do I do this (uh hm). It's so much personality too, you know. I mean I'm the first person who, when it comes time to make a decision, my first feeling is I'm going to make the wrong one (laugh) or it's not going to be good (laugh). So I think if I have that a little bit I can't reassure myself as much as you can assure me that well, gee, this is complicated or how many things go on (uh hm) and that puts a different face on things, it's interesting.

In spite of the fact that I had intended to be a good listener, which in my mind meant letting Wendy do all the talking, I had unconsciously taken an active role in the initial interviews. When I transcribed the interviews, I was very uncomfortable with the amount of substantive talk in which I had engaged. Nearly all the discussions of interview technique cautioned against this type of interaction, claiming it would either unduly influence the interviewee or shut down her opportunity to communicate (Davis, 1984; McCracken, 1988; Seidman, 1991). In an examination of the transcripts, however, Wendy seemed more encouraged to speak freely about her reflections on her teaching as a result. I believe that the initial establishment of a more mutual relationship during our talks was crucial to the success of the interviews. As a result of my greater participation in the talk, we advanced significantly along the relationship continuum in our first meetings, which made Wendy a more open and willing participant in the interviews. This type of interview technique, which involves greater interviewer disclosure, has been promulgated by some, but not all, feminist researchers. Oakley (1981), for example, suggests that the feminist researcher has an obligation to participate openly in talk with her subjects. To do otherwise is to use subjects as distanced objects to be merely studied.

The other caution of the methodologists, that too much talk by the interviewer would unduly influence the interviewee, was more probably the case. As I mentioned earlier, assuming I would take a back seat to the analysis was a naive position on my part. By naming dilemmas, recapitulating what I thought Wendy was saying, adding my own stories to confirm her experience, and complimenting her efforts, I was very influential in shaping the direction of the interview talk. I helped lay the terrain for reflective problem-solving, and Wendy began to use our sessions to do just that.

By adjusting my relationship in the field to a more collaborative stance by reducing the social distance that traditionally exists between researcher and teacher, I also got more involved in the activity of Wendy's teaching. Throughout her reflections and problem-solving, I functioned as a friend/counselor, ready to listen and to offer my reflections. As Wendy describes it, our talk was instrumental in the changes she underwent during this study and later. I had moved, therefore, along the action continuum from mere observer to active participant in the reflective process.

Wendy: Doing the Research

Polly and I both put great effort into making the first interviews succeed. I offered the thoughts I had about the classes we reviewed as frankly as possible. Dissembling and defensiveness seemed unfair when Polly showed such interest and never gave me reason to feel defensive. We also made the interviews partly a social time in which we could get to know each other better. But while we both made efforts, Polly shouldered the larger burden of making the first meeting work. She had to re-negotiate virtually all of my ideas about researchers' and teachers' roles, and the goals of the project. Early interview transcripts indicate a degree of vulnerability on my part that surprised even me when I read them several weeks into the project. My talk was filled with doubts and criticisms of my work as a teacher. I was, as Polly imagined, trying to outrace her in finding my errors so that I would not have to hear them from her. I felt that, at any rate, being critical of practice was what we were supposed to do in research, however collaborative.

Polly responded in ways that blunted my worst fears. In the first of these moves, she made it clear that she was working with me as a colleague, not a supervisor, and she genuinely wanted to know how I saw my practice. I sometimes criticized my practice in the areas where I felt vulnerable—wondering, for example, why I could not glibly make up good definitions when students asked about unfamiliar vocabulary. That I chose this rather superficial issue underlines the anxiety I felt about Polly's evaluation of my performance. In response to such a trivial concern, Polly honestly said that she knew these issues made one feel vulnerable, but that she did not regard them as important problems in practice. In addition, she shared with me her own uncertainties about how to do her research, relating a talk she had had with an advisor who had suggested that a researcher needs to simply listen to a teacher/informant, and that this would offer the teacher a forum for finding her own solutions. At the time, the very idea that Polly dealt with uncertainty, too, came as a revelation and had a moderate leveling effect on the vast differences I imagined between us. Such reassurances occurred frequently in the first few weeks of our project, as Polly acted consistently on her belief that the person with more power must work to level the differences felt by those with less.

Outside of the interviews, Polly conveyed enthusiasm and warmth. More than in the past, we shared anecdotes from our teaching and our everyday lives when we crossed paths at the office. Polly once recounted her stepdaughter's having referred to me as "Polly's teacher," to which she replied that I *was* her teacher, not in the sense of her teacher/informant, but in the sense that I was teaching her things. These early interactions brought more clarity to the abstraction of Polly's wanting to hear my point of view, and I grew to give this notion some credence.

In the weeks of interviews that followed, I gradually became more confident and far more eager to talk about what had happened in class and the issues about which I had thought. My own talk took up a great deal more interview time, frequently interrupting Polly's. Her handling of our conversations affirmed my treatment of the interviews as my time to talk. Her questions were straightforward: "How many of [the students] do you think have any knowledge of biology at all? I mean, do you feel like . . . their background knowledge in biology is weaker than it was in, say, in psychology or economics or sociology?" In the transcripts, my answers to such questions, and my digressions from them, frequently ran three-quarters of a page. I began to look forward to sessions with Polly; my lack of time was no longer an issue. To my friends, I described my sessions with Polly as "therapy for teachers."

Although reluctant to be cast as my teacher. Polly made it possible for me to learn from our project in a manner similar to that observed by Schön (1983) in his research on training in professional schools. Schön notes, in the cases of both the architect and the psychotherapist studied, when the professor sees a student "stuck" in practice, the professor "attributes the student's predicament to his/her way of framing the problem" (p. 129) and helps the student to reframe the problem. While Polly always insisted that she did not have the answers to what I should do in my practice, she did offer a new, more distanced, and ultimately more merciful framing than my own of my practice: it was not, she argued persistently, that I "didn't have the right answer," but that teaching was rife with dilemmas that one managed as best one could. As our mutual trust deepened, our talks delved into the attitudes and beliefs I brought to my teaching, the institutional context in which I worked, and even the life history that led me into my career. Our talks helped me see that all of these factors contributed to how I framed and attempted to resolve problems in my teaching. By articulating my beliefs about what needed to happen in my class. I began to affirm the way I thought and to criticize constructively less superficial aspects of what I was doing.

Through this "therapy" process, I began to articulate a sequence of changes that I wanted to make in my teaching. Some problems could be solved quickly (such as allowing oral rehearsal time in small groups when students were still struggling with the material); others required a change in the syllabus and a new start (which I will discuss later); others I wryly called the "congenital" problems, those that hung on my own personality. This framework helped me to see that the fruit of my work with Polly could, and had to, extend beyond the semester; she was not expecting me to solve all my issues in the following weeks, nor was I.

Among my congenital problems was my tendency to "do the work" for the students, as we put it in interview shorthand: I favored making the work of comprehending the text easy for them (by offering a substantial foundation for that comprehension myself) rather than difficult (by letting them grapple with text) in the hope of helping them believe that they could produce what I modeled. The problem was that my ultimate goal for the course—for students to engage in what we called "seminar talk" based on texts—was defeated by my own methods. I sacrificed opportunities for students to struggle to make meaning because I did not want them to feel frustrated in their attempts to understand text. Students' frustration seemed to me proof of a teacher's failure to recognize their needs and lend help; it was the emblem of inexperienced teaching. Still, how would we get from struggle-free learning to seminar talk?

The real power of seeing my issues through the lens of Polly's interpretations was that I could get a little healthy distance from them. I could begin to say about myself, I do X, with these positive and negative results; I could change in these ways. A far cry from my embarrassed, somewhat helpless affect in our first talks.

But more pertinent than my own improved comfort was the accompanying higher level of clarity about my teaching practice, and how that clarity helped me to work with my own students. After discussing issues with Polly, solutions of startling simplicity came to my mind. I decided, for example, to provide for a more even share of turns per student, even though it meant violating other precepts of mine, such as not pressuring quiet students to speak and not interrupting the more willing speakers.

Also, Polly and I noticed the range of responses I got when I asked students only one broad question about a topic (Why are some countries rich and some poor?), rather than many questions, and I started thinking about using more such "key questions." I continued to grapple with the feedback I got from the class: questions that invited students to talk about their experience provoked answers that revealed their capacity for defining and analyzing. But, questions that asked them to apply what they knew to a text were not as successful in bringing out that same capacity. They were capable, for example, of explaining causes of poverty in their own countries but less able to see where the arguments of the economics reading differed from their own. I could not readily assign causes to these areas of difficulty: were students confused by the text or less interested in text than in sharing their own ideas? Were the stakes too low for any individual to struggle through a critical reading of the text? As Polly observed, the higher stakes involved in arguing for the correctness of their answers to test questions had inspired many students to work carefully at articulating their interpretations of text.

Polly: The Place of an Independent Analysis and Unknown Bad News

The place of the researcher's independent analysis of the classroom data and how to broach the topic of unknown bad news are two remaining issues related to the emergent collaborative research we conducted. In our collaboration, the two were related.

While we both valued the richness of the reflective talk that took place during the interviews, as a discourse analyst I also valued the information a micro-analysis of the classroom interaction would provide. In many ways, Wendy's reflective analysis of the interaction, as well as the naming of her dilemmas, directed the micro-analysis. I chose to examine with an independent analytical lens passages of interaction that exemplified the development Wendy chronicled in our talks. I hoped to discover, in the talk itself, elements that confirmed her judgments and intuitions about the class. In addition, I expected my analysis to shed some light on events in the classroom that continued to perplex Wendy. I did wonder privately, and in conversation with Wendy, however, if that level of analysis would be useful or even interesting to Wendy.

Themes emerged from the micro-analysis similar to those Wendy had laid out. The analysis also provided more subtle information about how she managed to teach a group of students with diverse English ability and cultural differences. In other words, while she could name her dilemmas during the reflective stimulated-recall discussions, the discourse analysis indicated how she actually managed them. Some of this information was new to Wendy.

I first shared my interpretations with Wendy in conversation and later in writing. The analysis provided an in-depth look at what a teacher actually does during a class, and revealed how she interprets the class's contributions and what "in-flight" decisions she makes on that basis (Ulichny, 1996). There was one instance, however, in which the analysis provided what I worried would be the unknown bad news normally so difficult to convey. In the final stages of analysis, which took place during the writing of the research report. I discovered, contrary to Wendy's assumptions at the time of the occurrence, that the students had, in fact, progressed in their ability to understand and discuss expository text. I also discovered that Wendy's management of the classroom discourse prevented the students from displaying the ability effectively. I believe, however, that the strength of our relationship and the shared goal of making the research project useful first and foremost to Wendy helped us progress through the analysis.

Wendy: Reacting to the Research Report

Though I eagerly anticipated reading Polly's written report, which contained a micro-analysis of the classroom talk, enriched by information gained during our taped conversations, I sensed that it might not always feel comfortable to see my semester reflected back at me alone. Ever since those early interviews. I had not imagined that Polly would write anything like the reports we had shuddered at during our talks—reports that were harshly critical of teachers or that failed to take into account why they behaved the way they did. Still, she would be writing for an intended audience much larger than me. Unlike the interviews, the report could not focus so intensely on my possible reactions and hurt feelings.

I did feel sheepish reading parts of the report—but not because of how Polly expressed her findings. Instead, I cringed a little at the difference between my best guiding intuitions applied during that semester and ways I now made sense of teaching—knowledge I gained from the project. I read certain ideas I had stated with conviction and wondered how I could have been so narrow in my thinking. I winced at my awkward phrasings in the interview transcripts, frankly doubting Polly's earlier comment to me that everyone's conversations sound incoherent in transcription.

Writing obliged Polly to use phrases she did not have to when speaking directly with me (reporting, for example, that "to Wendy's mind" a particular event meant X), and this caused me to think more about some of the areas in which she might well have disagreed with my interpretations but had chosen not to say so. As I had initially suspected, the micro-analysis revealed information about some of the difficult periods in the semester. In the last part of the course, the class and I studied the biology chapter I had selected, which proved to be the most problematic part of the course. I had never taken a college-level biology course myself, and I had seen during my planning that most of the chapters in the text, including those on cell physiology, were beyond my ability to teach. I had chosen the chapter on the Mendel flower experiments, basically a narrative, because I understood it best. Choosing readings on subjects in which the teacher has no college-level experience may seem quite foolhardy, but I had chosen them knowing that there is a movement in ESL that encourages just that. The ESL teacher, so the argument goes, "remains the language expert" in this situation while her students are "the sources of information from the various disciplines" (Braine, 1988, p. 702).

During this part of class, activity bogged down in ways that I did not understand clearly. Polly listened sympathetically to my concerns about the torpid pace of the class and the seeming regression of some students. Was this text really more difficult than the others? Was their background in biology possibly weaker than it had been in the other subjects? Had my other, competing commitments taken up so much time that I was inadequately prepared? With final exams on the horizon, had students simply stopped working on this not-for-credit course?

My own lack of background in this area caused me difficulties I had not anticipated, and student "sources of information" on biology never materialized in this class. Interestingly, a graduate student in biology attended the other section I taught, an unusual situation that reflected his difficulties functioning in English. While his knowledge of biology was infinitely superior to mine, even he was not in a position to save me from my own reading. He could clarify minor uncertainties I had, for example about vocabulary, but this barely addressed the difficulties I had in teaching an unfamiliar subject area. This left me questioning the assumptions of teaching across the curriculum: despite predictions, an excellent student source in biology and a teacher clearly proficient in English had added up to a whole far less than the sum of the parts.

I felt that if the material were less difficult for me, it would be for the students, and that they knew this, too. I realized that I was uncertain at best whenever students asked me questions outside of the text ("Is the 'pollinate' . . . for the flower or for the animals?" My answer: "Only flowers, I think. And maybe other plants. Maybe other plants.") My attempt at a pep talk yielded the information that the students thought the text was hard.

I chose to revert to very simple work with the Mendel text, asking questions designed to prompt student paraphrasing of the text, virtually sentence-by-sentence. After many weeks during which students had seemed better equipped to negotiate meaning, I was back to "doing the work" for the class. They had been successful earlier because they had been working on easier materials, I concluded. I was discouraged by my backtracking, but it seemed necessary. The semester ended with my regretful declaration to Polly that perhaps students did not think the course had helped their reading skills very much.

During the summer, Polly and I talked about her analysis of the tapes from this part of class. Her analysis revealed something that I had not really suspected at the time: the students had learned a great deal about how to participate in class and draw meaning from text, but they had probably been confused by my downshifting to simple questions and requests for paraphrasing. There were times on the tapes, Polly reported, when a student offered a correct answer that I did not recognize as such, since I was relying on students to focus on the same bit of text that I myself was using. My requirement that students go through the text with me in locating answers had been an impediment to class work rather than a support for dealing with "hard" text. In other words, the students were demonstrating more skill in handling the Mendel reading than I was.

It is true that I had a little distance from the course by the time Polly told me this news: the semester was over, the students had done well on a final test, and I was on to planning a completely different reading course for the next semester. But, my warm reception of this information indicates more than anything else the value of Polly's and my work on our relationship in the project. I was more rueful than embarrassed at Polly's revelation and what it said about my own tactical errors. I felt cheered by the thought that the students had learned much more than we had thought. Polly also pointed out that these findings supported my decision not to teach subject material with which I was not familiar. My trust in the project already established, I was able to hear in her words the useful information they conveyed.

After reading the whole report, I felt very much respected in Polly's analysis. She had written with care and sympathy about every factor in my thinking and teaching experience that might explain some of my less felicitous choices. Also, she gave me the opportunity to respond to anything I wanted, and she added my comments to the report, as well as a long letter I had written about the effects of the project on me.

However, beyond my positive response to the written report lay the immense detail and the observer's perspective from which to draw important conclusions. The intensive work of the micro-analysis yielded the most thorough review of a course that I suppose I will ever have. It helped me appreciate, in a very different way than did the rest of our work, the intricacy of ESL teaching and learning. It crystallized my understanding of the unintended effects of the various strategies I employed. For example, the discourse analysis revealed the quick "on-line" decisions I made unconsciously in class. Polly spoke about the "fine tuning" of my practice; in close parallel, Schön writes of a "knowing-in-practice [that] tends to become increasingly tacit, spontaneous, and automatic, thereby conferring on [the practitioner and clients] the benefits of specialization" (Schön, 1983, p. 60). Polly pointed out many instances of such knowing, for example, my quickly cycling through questions designed to get at where students were troubled. While the questions depended upon the subject at hand, analysis revealed that they always functioned as a systematic probe: was unfamiliar vocabulary causing a problem, or was it disagreement with the text or a cultural misunderstanding?

Reading the report brought to mind, again in highly significant detail, ideas for how I might do better. It helped me to see with much greater clarity what strategies students employ in learning and how I might encourage the most constructive of these.

Polly: The Researcher Concludes

The form of collaborative action research that emerged in this project grew out of my concerns about controlling the damage that a researcher can inflict as a result of the higher status normally accorded her role as compared to a teacher's. It also developed from the way Wendy and I naturally evolved in our working relationship. This evolution was unpredictable at the start of the project and no doubt was greatly influenced by our respective personalities, interests, and interactive styles. I believe, however, that an essential ingredient to forging that relationship was overtly paying attention to it, voicing the difficulties inherent in teacher/researcher relationships, and, on my part, constantly monitoring how we were doing on that account. I have come to understand that wishing power and status differentials did not exist between researcher and informant is not enough to reduce them. Active participation in creating mutual structures in the research is required. These structures need to be created not only in the research design, but also in the everyday interaction that takes place between researcher and participants in the field.

This is not to say that researcher and teacher need to do everything together to create mutual structures in the research. Not only is this unrealistic, it is probably not desirable. There are different roles that each of the participants needs to assume during the project. Wendy needed to focus her energies on her teaching and I on the contribution this study would make to understanding teachers' practices in multilingual, multicultural classrooms. Acknowledging this difference helped give me license to talk about Wendy, not only to talk with her. The "covenantal" that guided my research, however, required that in talking about her I acknowledge the special responsibility I accrued towards her as a result of our relationship (Deyhle et al., 1992).

While Wendy and I had different agendas for the research on one level, we also shared a joint commitment—to further our collective knowledge about the complexity of the teaching task. We both saw this as a needed corrective to methodology handbooks and teacher manuals that reduce the work of teaching to scripts and strategies.

What emerged for us was a way of realizing that commitment can be expressed as a feminist approach to doing qualitative single-subject case studies (or any ethnographic work, for that matter, although the parameters of relationship will obviously change with increased numbers of participants). While there is no one definition of feminist research methodology, I agree with Reinharz's (1983) description as summarized by Neilson (1990). She describes it as "contextual, inclusive, experiential, involved, socially relevant . . . open to the environment, and inclusive of emotions and events as experienced" (p. 6). Moreover, most feminist researchers would agree with Roman (1992) that they are unified in rejecting "the subject-object dualism, or what feminist philosopher of science Harding (1986, 1987) calls, 'objectivism.' By objectivism, Harding means the stance often taken by researchers in attempts to remove, minimize, or make invisible their own subjectivities, beliefs, and practices, while simultaneously directing attention to the subjectivities, beliefs, and practices of their subject as the sole objects of scrutiny" (p. 556).

The feminist methodology that I engaged in to investigate my original question involved a number of precepts. The first one involved paying primary attention to the relationship and connection between people involved in the research. The report to an external audience was of secondary importance. In the end, we were both pleased with the results of the research as well as with our relationship. Had the data revealed a story that was critical of Wendy's teaching, or had I observed lessons and discovered mostly what was going wrong in the teaching and learning, I would not have published this account. The addition of this study to the published accounts of classroom research would not, in my opinion, have warranted the damage to Wendy's professional persona that publication would have entailed.[3] This is quite different from many ethnographies of classrooms that focus on what *could* be, under better circumstances, and often concentrate on the defects of the context under investigation.

I feel that my attention to going through or beyond the disaster tales that Wendy was anxious to lay out actually improved the results of this analysis. My ethic of relationship forced me to push the analysis to deeper levels in order to find significant patterns that explain both the interview and classroom data.

A second precept underlying the methodology was an interest in incorporating voices of traditionally unheard, undervalued members of the educational community into published research. The academic community of education professors and researchers has consistently ignored and undervalued the perspective of teachers in attempting to understand social context and cognition in schools. Valuing a teacher's voice raised my awareness of the wealth of information and insight that is untapped by most educational research.[4]

A third precept of my methodology was paying attention to power differences and leveling them when they appeared. This included the empowerment of the informant and her subjectivity. By this I mean that Wendy's interpretation of the classroom was the springboard from which I began my micro-analysis of the discourse. Her meanings and her subjectivity were, therefore, incorporated into the account of the classroom. Wendy's intimate involvement in providing the interpretation of the classroom activities altered the underlying priority of the researcher: as we conducted the study, we were both more interested in making the immediate situation—Wendy's classroom—the primary beneficiary of our activity, rather than the academy.

I shifted my attention from the eventual results of the research to the process of conducting it. This move made entry more acceptable to both of us and eased our dealing with the unknown bad news that emerged. Since all information we learned from the project was intended to support Wendy's instructional practice, it was easier to discuss bad news, even unknown bad news, without it being perceived as a researcher's exposé of problematic interactions. By discussing problems with the priority of instruction in mind, Wendy felt less vulnerable than she had imagined she would by a published report of a less-than-perfect practice.

Another underlying precept of the methodology was the transformational characteristic of the research. It was not a hands-off, neutralized view of a teacher and her classroom. With Wendy's implicit permission, we both engaged in change. Empowerment of the teacher was the precondition, as well as the outcome, of the transformative process.

Finally, we experienced, as a result of how we engaged in this project, an extension of the traditional boundaries of research. As our friendship, which began through the research, developed, the boundaries of public and private space blurred. In addition to our interviews there was a great deal of off-record talk. Some of this talk also, inevitably, became data for the analysis.

What resulted from this purposefully collaborative and feminist methodology was a way of conducting research that does not fit the usual description of participant observation. A more accurate term for it—Temporary Affiliation—was coined by Reinharz (1984). She describes this method as one of experiencing the subjects' world first hand. While I was not a coteacher with Wendy, we coconstructed the reflective environment that provided much of the data. Reinharz calls this "affiliation" to underscore the making of personal commitments to people in the field, which more adequately describes our involvement, although our continued involvement in each other's lives years after the research project causes us to question the notion of *temporary* affiliation. Can partners in intense action and relationship in the field ever lose their affiliation with one another?

Wendy: The Teacher Concludes

My teaching and my views on teaching have changed markedly as a result of this project. I have abandoned the idea that I can give students a taste of many subject areas and choose materials for single-theme courses from areas with which I have only passing familiarity. My reading courses, since working on the project, have been grounded in American studies, English literature, and history, areas I know best. With another teacher, I have developed a course on the 1920s and 1930s in U.S. history. Another course features novels and autobiography by immigrants, Native Americans, and African Americans, and focuses on the possibility (important to my students as much as to me) of personal growth resulting from adversity. I have decided that my goal of giving students the opportunity to participate in text-based, classroom talk should take priority over other criteria, such as a selection of readings from "across the curricula." I exercise a more practiced eye in choosing texts by using readings that in some way parallel students' realities. I define the success of my classes in terms of full, articulate student participation. I act on greater faith that students can struggle together with text and direct our discussion if I give them the opportunity. I find ways of allowing the class itself to establish some shared understanding of texts without dragging students through the detailed "quiz-show" questions I had previously employed in teaching less familiar subject matter.

All of these tactical changes in my teaching have helped to produce courses closer to my ideal. If I were asked to identify the most important shift in my practice after this project, however, I would probably point to my willingness to share my own dilemmas with students, as Polly had with me. When composition students clamored for more intensive grammar correction ("Tell me every mistake I make"), I was not sure what course of action I thought best. But rather than hide my concerns from students and pick a strategy on my own, I suggested we experiment with different forms of feedback on their papers. One involves smattering student papers with symbols indicating every grammatical error I find; the other provides in letter form comments on and examples of a few types of errors found in a given composition and invites the writer to find more instances of such errors in the same paper. Then I polled the students themselves on their preferences: almost unanimously they decided the focus on fewer errors was more helpful. One student confessed that she treated the draft with many corrections as a secretarial exercise in which she decided on and plugged in correct answers without even rereading her draft. In such moments I am impressed again and again at the seriousness students display toward their endeavors: they are looking for situations in which they know they are truly engaged and learning.

This shift in my view of teaching reflects the two professional stances described by Schön: the defensive "expert" stance and that of the "reflective practitioner." The first feels she is "presumed to know and must claim to do so," either hiding or ignoring her own uncertainty. The second feels that she might not be the only one to know something relevant to the situation and that her "uncertainties may be a source of learning" (Schön, 1983, p. 300). In my experience, it is only by shedding the "expert" attitude that a teacher has the opportunity to treat relationships with students as real ones in which "right" answers are no longer the primary focus.

The psychological benefits of the project have proven nearly incalculable. When I started our work I did not believe that it could be collaborative at all, because I did not understand that my own, sufficient role was to do what I did. Instead I felt I was failing to do my share because I could not do Polly's part. Her task in the early weeks lay in convincing me that we each had something to contribute. I also believed that I was the wrong teacher for the right project: I recognized that I was often hurt, even by opinions I did not respect. I was not sure I could withstand the effects of having someone whose opinions I respected find fault with my professional performance. My own research experience with observing other ESL teachers, accrued since the end of this project, has helped me to see that most teachers, however excellent, experience the same sense of vulnerability that I did in research situations. Whatever their particular personalities, they, too, are subject to the effects of their marginal status in the university, the common perceptions of the hierarchy in which teachers and researchers are placed, and their lack of opportunity to see other teachers confronting the same dilemmas. Another positive result of my work with Polly is a "shifting of the debt," where I pay her back with my support of the talented teachers whose classrooms I observe.

Polly would argue that the learning I managed in her project came not from her but, as Morimoto predicted, from me. I am nevertheless grateful that she was there while I learned it and that we continue the rich dialogue that began with our project. I know now that I cannot divorce who I am from how I teach, but that something constructive can be made of this situation. And I have learned that I will always have dilemmas in my profession and that my greatest possibilities lie in paying attention to them.

Notes

1. The schematic presented here seemingly offers a static view of relationship and action possibilities. The reality of field work, however, is dynamic. The evolution of a research project often involves shuts over time along these continua.
2. The transcripts are minimally edited to ease reading. Some hesitations and false starts have been eliminated and bracketed words inserted or substituted to make the meaning clearer. Both Wendy and I gave agreement feedback (uhm hmm) at regular intervals throughout the interviews. These are inserted in the conversation when they occurred. Punctuation in the transcripts respects conventions of written language. It is not intended to signal prosodic information. However, the following notations signal aspects of speaker performance: . . .—pause or hesitation: []—candidate hearings of unclear utterances.
3. Cazden (personal communication) tells the story of early work on classroom discourse in which researchers

revealed to a participating teacher that she tended to favor the White students in her class with nonverbal cues such as eye-contact and body positioning. The teacher was so distraught at the thought of being racist in her instruction that she wanted to quit teaching.

4.   Subsequent work in which I have been involved has focused on this point. A growing national network of urban teachers has been conducting research in their classrooms and disseminating this information as part of the Urban Sites Network of the National Writing Project. University-based researchers are primarily consultants in the research undertakings of the teachers (Muncey, Uhl, & Nyce, 1994: Peterson, Check, & Ylvisaker, 1996).

References

Agar, M. (1980). *The professional stranger.* New York: Academic Press.

Berthoff, A. (1987). The teacher as researcher. In D. Goswami & P. R. Stillman (Eds.), *Reclaiming the classroom: Teacher research as an agency for change* (pp. 28–38). Upper Montclair, NJ: Boynton/Cook.

Bickel, W. E., & Hattrup, R. A. (1995). Teachers and researchers in collaboration: Reflections on the process. *American Educational Research Journal, 32*(1), 35–64.

Bogdan, R., & Biklen, S. (1992). *Qualitative research for education: An introduction to theory and methods* (2nd ed.). Needham Heights, MA: Allyn & Bacon.

Braine, G. (1988). Two commentaries on Ruth Spack's "Initiating ESL students into the academic discourse community: How far should we go?" *TESOL Quarterly, 22,* 700–708.

Campbell, D. (1988). Collaboration and contradictions in a research and staff development project. *Teachers College Record, 90*(1), 99–121.

Cochran-Smith, M., & Lytle, S. L. (1990). Research on teaching and teacher research: The issues that divide. *Educational Researcher, 19*(2), 2–11.

Cochran-Smith, M., & Lytle, S. L. (1993). *Inside/outside: Teacher research and knowledge.* New York: Teachers College Press.

Corsaro, W. A. (1981). Communicative processes in studies of social organization: Sociological approaches to discourse analysis. *Text, 1*(1), 5–63.

Cummins, J. (1986). Empowering minority students: A framework for intervention. *Harvard Educational Review, 56,* 18–35.

Davis, J. (1984). Data into text. In R. F. Ellen (Ed.), *Ethnographic research: A guide to general conduct* (pp. 295–318). London: Academic Press.

Delpit, L. (1988). The silenced dialogue: Power and pedagogy in educating other people's children. *Harvard Educational Review, 58,* 280–298.

Deyhle, D. L., Hess, A. G., Jr., & LeCompte, M. D. (1992). Approaching ethical issues for qualitative researchers in education. In M. D. LeCompte, W. L. Millroy, & J. Preissle (Eds.), *The handbook of qualitative research in education* (pp. 597–642). San Diego: Academic Press.

Ely, M. et al. (1991). *Doing qualitative research: Circles within circles.* Bristol, PA: Falmer Press.

Erickson, F. (1986). Qualitative methods in research on teaching. In M. C. Wittrock (Ed.), *Handbook of research on teaching* (pp. 119–161). New York: Macmillan.

Erickson, F., & Schultz, J. (1982). *Gatekeeping in counseling interviews.* New York: Academic Press.

Fine, M. (1994). Working the hyphens: Reinventing self and other in qualitative research. In N. K. Denzin & Y. S. Lincoln (Eds.), *Handbook of qualitative research* (pp. 70–82). Thousand Oaks, CA: Sage.

Florio, S., & Walsh, M. (1981). The teacher as colleague in classroom research. In H. T. Trueba, G. Guthrie, & K. A. Au (Eds.), *Culture and the bilingual classroom* (pp. 87–101). Rowley, MA: Newbury House.

Florio-Ruane, S. (1991). *A conversational interpretation of teacher/researcher collaboration, George Mason University.* Manassas: Fairfax County, Virginia, Public Schools.

Florio-Ruane, S., & Dohanich, J. (1984). Communicating the findings: Teacher/researcher deliberations. *Language Arts, 61,* 724–730.

Gibson, M. A. (1985). Collaborative educational ethnography: Problems and profits. *Anthropology and Education Quarterly, 16,* 124–148.

Glesne, C., & Peshkin, A. (1992). *Becoming qualitative researchers: An introduction.* White Plains, NY: Longman.

Gold, R. (1969). Roles in sociological field observations. In G. McCall & J. L. Simmons (Eds.), *Issues in participant observation: A text and reader* (pp. 30–39). Menlo Park, CA: Addison-Wesley.

Harding, S. (1986). *The science question in feminism.* Ithaca, NY: Cornell University Press.

Harding, S. (1987). Introduction: Is there a feminist method? In S. Harding (Ed.), *Feminism and methodology* (pp. 1–14). Bloomington: Indiana University Press.

Heath, S. B. (1983). *Ways with words: Language, life, and work in communities and classrooms.* Cambridge, Eng.: Cambridge University Press.

Hymes, D. H. (1980). *Language in education.* Washington, DC: Center for Applied Linguistics.

Jacullo-Noto, J. (1984). Interactive research and development: Partners in craft. *Teachers College Record, 86,* 208–222.

Johnston, S. (1994). Is action research a "natural" process for teachers? *Educational Action Research, 2*(1), 39–48.

Labov, W. (1972). *Sociolinguistic patterns.* Philadelphia: University of Pennsylvania Press.

Ladwig, J. G. (1991). Is collaborative research exploitative? *Educational Theory, 41,* 111–120.

Lather, P. (1991). *Getting smart: Feminist research and pedagogy with/in the postmodern.* New York: Routledge.

LeCompte, M. D., & Preissle, J., with Tesch. R. (1993). *Ethnography and qualitative design in educational research* (2nd ed.). New York: Academic Press.

Lincoln, Y. S. (1995, April). *Standards for qualitative inquiry.* Paper presented at the annual meeting of the American Educational Research Association, San Francisco.

Lykes, B. (1989). Dialogue with Guatemalan women. In R. Unger (Ed.), *Representations: Social construction of gender* (pp. 167–184). Amityville, NY: Baywood.

McCracken, G. (1988). *The long interview.* Beverly Hills. CA: Sage.

Miller, S. M. (1952). The participant observer and "over-rapport." *American Sociological Review, 17,* 97–99.

Morimoto, K., Gregory, J., & Butler, P. (1973). Notes on the context for learning. *Harvard Educational Review, 43,* 245–257.

Muncey, D., Uhl, S., & Nyce, J. (1994). *An evaluation of the Urban Sites network* (Evaluation report submitted to the DeWitt Wallace-Reader's Digest Foundation). New York: Urban Sites Network of the National Writing Project.

Neilson, J. M. (1990). Introduction. In J. M. Neilson (Ed.), *Feminist research methods: Exemplary readings in the social sciences* (pp. 1–37) Boulder, CO: Westview Press.

Nieto, S. (1994). Lessons from students on creating a chance to dream. *Harvard Educational Review, 64,* 392–426.

Oakley, A. (1981). Interviewing women: A contradiction in terms. In H. Roberts (Ed.), *Doing feminist research* (pp. 30–61). Boston: Routledge & Kegan Paul.

Ogbu, J. U., & Matute-Bianchi, M. E. (1986). Understanding sociocultural factors: Knowledge, identity, and school adjustment. In California State Department of Education Bilingual Education Office (Ed.), *Beyond language: Social and cultural factors in schooling language minority students* (pp. 73–142). Los Angeles: California State University, Evaluation. Dissemination and Assessment Center.

Oja, S. N., & Smulyan, L. (1989). *Collaborative action research: A developmental approach.* London: Falmer.

Peterson, A., Check, J., & Ylvisaker, M. (Eds.). (1996). *Cityscapes: Eight views from the urban classroom.* Berkeley, CA: National Writing Project.

Philips, S. U. (1972). Participant structures and communication competence: Warm Springs children in community and classroom. In C. Cazden, D. Hymes, & V. P. John (Eds.), *Functions of language in the classroom* (pp. 161–189). New York: Teachers College Press.

Reason, P. (1994). Three approaches to participative inquiry. In N. K. Denzin & Y. S. Lincoln (Eds.), *Handbook of qualitative research* (pp. 324–339). Thousand Oaks, CA: Sage.

Reinharz, S. (1983). Experiential analysis: A contribution to feminist research. In G. Bowles & R. D. Klein (Eds.), *Theories of women's studies.* London: Routledge & Kegan Paul.

Reinharz, S. (1984). *On becoming a social scientist* (2nd ed.). New Brunswick, NJ: Transaction.

Reinharz, S. (1992). *Feminist methods in social research.* New York: Oxford University Press.

Roman, L. G. (1992). The political significance of other ways of narrating ethnography: A feminist materialist approach. In M. D. LeCompte, W. L. Millroy, & J. Preissle (Eds.), *The handbook of qualitative research in education* (pp. 555–594). New York: Academic Press.

Schön, D. A. (1983). *The reflective practitioner.* New York: Basic Books.

Seidman, I. E. (1991). *Interviewing as qualitative research.* New York: Teachers College Press.

Shaffir, W. G., Stebbins, R. A., & Turowetz, A. (1980). *Fieldwork experience.* New York: St. Martin's Press.

Stainback, S. B. (1988). *Understanding and conducting qualitative research.* Dubuque, IA: Kendall/Hunt.

Stenhouse, L. (1975). *An introduction to curriculum research and development.* London: Heinemann.

Ulichny, P. (1996). What's in a methodology? In D. Freeman & J. C. Richards (Eds.), *Teacher learning in language teaching* (pp. 178–196). Cambridge, Eng.: Cambridge University Press.

Van Maanen, J. (1983). The moral fix: On the ethics of fieldwork. In R. Emerson (Ed.), *Contemporary field research* (pp. 269–287). Boston: Little, Brown.

Van Maanen, J. (1988). *Tales of the field: On writing ethnography.* Chicago: University of Chicago Press.

Wallace, J., & Louden, W. (1994). Collaboration and the growth of teachers' knowledge. *Qualitative Studies in Education, 7,* 323–334.

Watson-Gegeo, K. A., & Ulichny, P. (1988). *Ethnographic inquiry in second language acquisition and instruction* (Working Paper) Manoa: University of Hawaii at Manoa, Department of ESL.

28

Writing the "Wrongs" of Fieldwork
Confronting Our Own Research/Writing Dilemmas in Urban Ethnographies

Michelle Fine and Lois Weis

Inspired by Laurel Richardson's (1995) call for "writing stories," the authors of this essay struggle with how to produce scholarly texts drawn from narratives of over 150 poor and working-class men and women—White, African American, Latino, and Asian American. They unveil a set of knotty, emergent ethical and rhetorical dilemmas they have encountered in their attempt to write for, with, and about poor and working-class informants at a time when their lives and moralities are routinely maligned in the popular media; when the very problematic policies that may once have "assisted" them are being abandoned; and when the leverage of and audience for progressive social researchers and policy makers has grown foggy, and weak in the knees. Writing with a desire to create a conversation about ethics, writing, and qualitative research, the authors worry about the contemporary role of qualitative social researchers.

As critical ethnographers, we have explored the perspectives that working class and poor adolescents hold about the relationships between the economy, education, families, and political action. Our major works, *Working Class Without Work* (Weis, 1990), *Between Two Worlds* (Weis, 1985), *Framing Dropouts* (Fine, 1991), *Disruptive Voices* (Fine, 1992), and *Beyond Silenced Voices* (Weis & Fine, 1993) all hold as central the social analyses narrated by low-income and working-class adolescents and young adults.

With the support of the Spencer Foundation, we are currently expanding our research to include the perspectives and practices of Latino, African American, and White young adults, ages 23 to 35, as they narrate their educational, familial, and economic biographies and project and enact their parental involvements within their communities, churches, and children's schools. Specifically, we have interviewed 150 individuals across racial and ethnic groups (men and women) in Buffalo and Jersey City, and have conducted focus group interviews with specified populations in each city to probe further their perspectives and practices, unearthing at once their despair about and envisioned opportunities for individual, community, and social change. We thus far have conducted group interviews with African American welfare- and nonwelfare-receiving mothers; Latina mothers who are probing the meaning of workfare programs in Jersey City; African American men who see the church as a way of envisioning both self and community differently from what they see as the dominant society's definition; White women who, although caught in patriarchal working-class communities, both push and accept the limitations of their female bodies and selves; and White men who patrol the borders of White masculinity, desirous of keeping all others out of what they see as their rightful position. We have assembled a rich array of interview material that will enable us both to narrate the experiences of the poor and working class during the 1980s and 1990s and to press carefully into the policy realm given our findings. We have met with and are interviewing a broad range of policymakers in both cities to explore fully the situated nature of our findings, as well as to affect broader social policy. We have testified and written Op Ed pieces on local and State policies as they affect constituents (e.g., vouchers and school takeover in Jersey City, welfare reform) and intend to do more (Weis & Fine, 1995).

Perhaps the most arrogant way to think about our project is that we aim to produce a biography of the Reagan–Bush years, as narrated by poor and working-class young adults in urban America; a more modest description would suggest that we are engaged in a two-city community study that, through the oral life histories of poor and working-class White, African American and Latino young adults, unravels the transformations in urban economic, racial, social, and domestic relations that have transpired over the past 20 years.

We are two Jewish White woman academics, trained well in the rigors of social psychology (Michelle) and sociology (Lois), experienced in the complexities of critical ethnography, who, with generous support from the Spencer Foundation and the assistance of extremely talented graduate students, are eager to traverse the borders of research, policy, activism, and theory, and are worried about what it means to do "critical work" in our provincial urban backyards just when the Right has cannibalized public discourse and when the academy has fractured amid poststructuralism and identity politics. This article may be conceptualized as an early "coming out" about some of the methodological, theoretical, and ethical issues that percolate from our field-work, keeping our e-mail bills high, our nights long, our essays delayed, and our commitments to social change *and* social theory swirling in ambivalence.

With this article we hope to pry open a conversation in need of public shaping. Many of the friends and colleagues with whom we have discussed some of these research/ethical dilemmas say they are relieved that someone is "saying aloud" this next generation of methodological and conceptual troubles. And yet answers evade us. With this writing we wedge open this conversation that we presumably needed, hoping that colleagues working ethnographically "in our own backyards" will engage with us in excavating the next generation of always tentative resolutions. As we write, we straddle the semifictions of empiricism and the intellectual spheres of critical theory, feminism, and poststructuralism; as we read and hear our friends (and ourselves) pleading for researchers to be critical and self-reflexive, we note that many of these same friends have long stopped collecting data; as we consume the critical literature on race and gender and ask our informants to talk about both, they keep responding, "Really I'm Black, why do you keep asking?" or, "A woman—what do you think?" We write in that space between despair and hope because we hear much of the former from our informants and whispers of the latter from the same and because that is the space within which we can live. Yes, structures oppress, but we *must* have hope that things can be better.

We speak now because we worry that many of us are simply studying the apocalypse to cope with it, as one more piece of the sky falls. This article represents a concrete analysis in the midst of what Michelle has called "working the hyphen."

> Much of qualitative research has reproduced, if contradiction-filled, a colonizing discourse of the "Other." This essay is an attempt to review how qualitative research projects have *Othered* and to examine an emergent set of activist and/or postmodern texts that interrupt *Othering*. First, I examine the hyphen at which Self-Other join in the politics of everyday life, that is, the hyphen that both separates and merges personal identities with our inventions of Others. I then take up how qualitative researchers work this hyphen ... through a messy series of questions about methods, ethics, and epistemologies as we rethink how researchers have spoken "of" and "for"

> Others while occluding ourselves and our own investments, burying the contradictions that percolate at the Self-Other hyphen. (Fine, 1994, p. 70)

This article, then, offers up our questions/dilemmas/concerns as we grapple with what it means to be in the midst of a study that attempts to work across many borders, always searching for ways to "work the hyphen." We take our cue from Richardson (1995, p. 191), who invites what she calls "writing-stories":

> With the poststructural understanding that the social context affects what we write, we have an opportunity—perhaps even an ethical duty—to extend our reflexivity to the study of our writing practices. We can reflect on and share with other researchers what I think of as writing-stories, or stories about how we came to construct the particular texts we did. These might be of the verification kind, or they might be more subjective—accounts of how contexts, social inter-actions, critiques, review processes, friendships, academic settings, departmental politics, embod-iedness, and so on have affected the construction of the text. Rather than hiding the struggle, concealing the very human labor that creates the text, writing-stories would reveal emotional, social, physical, and political bases of the labor.

Echoes (and Aches) in Our Head

On community. Perhaps our most vexing dilemma at the moment concerns the question "What constitutes community?" How do we write about communities in which we find little sense of shared biography or vision? We write "as if" the contours of geography or a standard metropolitan statistical area adequately define the boundaries of these two "communities." Coherence organizes life within, whereas difference defines life between.

And yet we recognize from our theoretical interests, confirmed by the narratives we've collected, that piercing fractures define life within communities and some pronounced similarities emerge across the two cities. Internal geographic coherence seems a naive fiction, whereas blunt cross-community contrasts seem deceptively polarized.

Simple demographic fractures, by race/ethnicity, gender, class, generation, and sexuality marble inside each city. Within local neighborhoods or racial/ethnic groups, gender, sexuality, and generational divisions boldly sever what may appear at first glance to be internal continuities.

For instance, within presumably the same community, African Americans will refer to local police with stories of harassment and fear, whereas Whites are far more likely to complain about a rise in crime and brag about a brother-in-law who's a cop. Parallel dynamics can be found in both Jersey City and Buffalo.

Likewise, from within the same households we hear White working-class women describe growing up in families with much childhood exposure to alcohol and abuse, whereas comparably situated White men—raised in the very same homes and neighbor-hoods—are virtually silent on these topics. Again, the parallels across the two cities have been striking.

Jersey City Whites describe "good old days" of economic security and pine for the day when they'll be moving to Bayonne, whereas African Americans harbor few wistful memories of good old days and try to avoid "getting stopped at red lights" in Bayonne, lest their stay be extended beyond what they expected.

At historic moments of job security and economic hard times, the presumed harmony of working-class/poor communities is ravaged by interior splits, finger pointing, blame, and suspicion. Coalitions are few, even if moments of interdependence for survival are frequent. Within homes, differences and conflicts explode across gender and generations. A full sense of community is fictional and fragile, ever vulnerable to external threats and internal fissures. A sense of coherence prevails only if our methods fail to interrogate difference. And at the same time, commonalities *across* cities—by demography and biography—are all the more striking.

So, for the moment in our writing, we script a story in which we float a semifictional portrait of each community, layered over with an analytic matrix of differences "within." For our analysis—within and between cities—we delicately move between coherence and difference, fixed boundaries and porous borders, neighborhoods of shared values and homes of contentious interpretations.

On "race." As with community, race emerges in our data as both an unstable and an enduring aspect of biography. Gates (1985) has written beautifully about race, always using quotes; Dyson (1993) argues against narrow nationalistic or essentialist definitions for either skin color or language; Hall (1981) narrates the contextual instability of racial identities. Like these theorists, our informants are sometimes quite muddy, other times quite clear, about race. Indeed, some of our informants, like the one below, suggest that race constitutes inherently undefinable territory. This is not a narrative of denial as much as it is one of complexity.

Question: Your dad?

Answer: Yes, my dad was the craziest Puerto Rican you had ever seen in the 70's. Oh my Lord.

Q: What is your mom's background?

A: Mom, Mom was raised Catholic, but in my mother's days, when an Irish and German woman went with a Chinese guy, in those days that was like, oh no, no that cannot happen. My grandfather had to drop his whole family for my grandmother, so they could be together. Everybody disowned him in this family.

Q: Because he married a—

A: Yeah, he married my grandmother.

Q: What about your mom's side?

A: That is my mom's side.

Q: What about your grandfather's side?

A: My grandfather, he was in Vietnam, World War II, oh, I forgot the name. It was a very big war, that I know.

Q: Korean War?

A: Yeah, something like that, I just can't remember what it was. Yeah, he had honors and everything my mother told me.

Q: So you looked very different?

A: Yeah, I'm a mixture.

Q: You have Chinese blood?

A: Right. I got Irish and German, I got Puerto Rican and Italian, I have a lot. I'm a mixed breed.

Q: I was wondering. The first time I saw you I thought you were from the Middle East.

A: From the Middle East?

Q: Yeah.

A: Oh, golly gee, no. I'm, like, really mixed. I'm like everything. I got all these different personalities that just come out all the time. I swear to God. No lie. No lie.

When we began our interviews in Jersey City and Buffalo, we were well influenced by poststructural thinking on questions of race. With Hall (1981) particularly in mind, and willing to acknowledge the artificiality, the performances, and, indeed, the racist roots of the notion of race (1/32nd drop of blood, etc.), we constructed an interview protocol that generously invited our informants to "play" with race as we had. So we asked them, in many clever ways, to describe time-/context-specific racial identifications—when they fill out census forms, walk through supermarkets, when alone or among friends. By the third hour, informants of color, trying to be polite, grew exasperated with these questions. White folks were sure we were calling them racist, or they went on about being Irish, Italian, human—never White. Needless to say, the "playfulness" of the questions didn't work.

We don't mean to retreat now to a simplistic formulation by which we declare that race is more "real" than critical race theory suggests. Indeed, our data give much support for reasserting a floating sense of race—one always braided with gender, generation, biography, and class. Yet, reading the narratives, it's hard to miss entrenched, raced patterns of daily life. Most White respondents *say* they don't think much about race; most people of color wish they weren't reminded of their race—via harassment, discrimination, and on-the-street stares—quite so often. Many argue that race *shouldn't* make much of a difference. Yet the life stories as narrated are so thoroughly raced that readers of the transcript can't not know even an "anonymous" informant's racial group. Personal stories of violence and family structure, narrative style, one's history with money, willingness to trash (and leave) men and marriages, access to material resources, relations with kin and the State, and descriptions of interactions with the police are all profoundly narrated through race, fluid though it is.

Race is a place in which poststructuralism and lived realities need to talk. Race is a social construction, indeed. But race in a racist society bears profound consequence for daily life, identity, social movements, and the ways in which most groups "other." Du Bois noted that race was the dividing line for the 20th century. He may have been a two-century prophet.

But how we write about race in our work worries us. Do we take the category for granted, as if it were unproblematic? Do we problematize it theoretically, well knowing its full-bodied impact on daily life? Reflecting on our writings thus far, we seem to lean toward theorizing for and about Whites who deny they have a race, whereas we offer much more open latitude around the voices of people of color who articulate their thoroughly embodied experiences within race. We try to construct theoretical structures of racial formations, borrowing from Omi and Winant (1986), recognizing that Whiteness requires—indeed, creates—Blackness in order to see the self as moral, hard working, family-oriented, a good citizen. We give lots of room to those who define themselves with multiple roots and at varied hyphens. We envy and resent colleagues who have stopped collecting data because they have done such a marvelous job of complicating that which actually doesn't feel so complicated to our informants. Yes, race *is* a social construction, but it's so deeply confounded with racism that it has enormous power in people's lives. We can't simply problematize it away as if it does not really exist. To the informants with whom we spoke, race does exist—it saturates every pore of their lives. How can we destabilize the notion theoretically, while recognizing the lived presence of race?

Here are some trivial but telling examples. One problem that may appear, at face value, to be a "sampling problem" related to race, involves our struggle to find "equally poor" and "equally working-class" African American, Latino, and White young adults in both cities, so that comparisons by race/ethnicity would not be compounded by class. Guess what? The world is lousy with confounds. Although we found poor and working-class Whites, the breadth and depth of their cross-generational poverty was nowhere near as severe as in the African American sample.

White informants were sometimes as well off as, but were more often slightly worse off than, their parents. But—and here's the *unacknowledged* impact of 1940s' and 1950s' U.S. federal subsidies for the White working class/middle class—these young adults often had access to a small house or apartment that their parents were able to buy, a small nest egg of cash the family had squirreled away, or a union-based pension that Dad had saved up. In contrast, our African American and Latino informants are in very tough financial straits but are not, for the most part, worse off than their parents. Their parents rarely had a home, a small stash of monies, or pensions that they could pass on. Further, some of our African American and Latino informants who have amassed small amounts of capital over time lost it at some point when someone in the extended family had a health crisis, a housing crisis, or a problem with the law.

Despite our meticulous combing of raced neighborhoods, our ambitious search for sampling comparability lost, hands down, to the profound "lived realities" of multigenerational poverty disproportionately affecting poor and working-class families of color. What may appear to be a methodological problem has been revealed as constitutive of the very fabric of society. Problematizing race alone does not help us confront the very real costs and privileges of racial categorization.

"*Bad data.*" Moving from worries of epistemology to worries about data, we excavate more headaches:

Q: Do you feel that your word is not trusted, that you need someone else to say, you need a lawyer or psychiatrist to say everything is okay now?

A: Because of DYFS [Division for Youth and Family Services], yes.

Q: But you can't have . . .

A: They won't, yeah. They won't just take you for your word, no. You need to have.

Q: You need to have somebody else say that for you?

A: Yes. DYFS, yes.

Q: How would DYFS treat your kids, though?

A: Because when you get child, they say I put their life in danger, because I did, but I was . . . I was in jail, I was in the psychiatric ward. They had to do the best interest for the children, I couldn't take care of them at the time.

Q: Oh, so DYFS took your kids?

A: Yeah, so DYFS gave them to their father. I'm in court now.

Q: At least it's not foster care, though.

A: That's what I said. They're with family. They might hate it there, they can't stand it. My kids say that they're treated worse.

Q: They hate their father?

A: No, they don't hate their father, they hate their grandmother, they hate their mother-in-law, they hate their grandmother. They don't like their grandmother.

Q: George's mother?

A: Yeah, they don't like their aunts, their uncles.

Q: They are a lot of Puerto Ricans?

A: They're all Puerto Ricans, but my kids were always like the outcasts because the didn't like me so my kids, my kids, I mean, George was 7 years old, 7 years or George's life, George had to have seen his grandmother six times. Nicole, in the 3 years of her life, never seen them. You know, my kids got dumped into a family that they know nothing about.

What does it mean to uncover some of what we have uncovered? How do we handle "hot" information, especially in times when poor and working-class women and men are being demonized by the Right and by Congress? How do we connect troubling social/familial patterns with macrostructural shifts when our informants *expressly don't* make the connections? The hegemony of autonomous individualism forces a self-conscious theorizing of data—especially "bad data"—well beyond the consciousness expressed by most of our informants. So, for instance, what do we do with information about the ways in which women on welfare virtually have to become welfare cheats ("Sure he comes once a month and gives me some money. I may have to take a beating, but the kids need the money.") to survive? A few use more drugs than we wish to know; most are wonderful parents but some underattend to their children well beyond neglect. These are the dramatic consequences, and perhaps also the "facilitators," of hard economic times. To ignore the data is to deny the effects. To report the data is to risk their likely misinterpretation.

In a moment in history when there are few audiences willing to reflect on the complex social roots of community and domestic violence and the impossibility of sole reliance on welfare, or even to appreciate the complexity, love, hope, and pain that fills the poor and working class, how do we display the voyeuristic dirty laundry that litters our database? At the same time, how can we risk romanticizing or denying the devastating impact of the current assault on poor and working-class families launched by the State, the economy, neighbors, and sometimes kin?

Because of our early questions about both perspectives and representations, the interview schedule was originally created using input from a group of activists and policy makers of varying racial and ethnic backgrounds from Jersey City and Buffalo who were working with the research teams. Many questions were inserted to satisfy local concerns, for example, questions about police harassment, welfare reform and its effects on children born to women on welfare, state takeover of school, and so on. Nevertheless, with data collection over and analysis now under way, we continue to struggle with how best to represent treacherous data—data that may do more damage than good, depending on who consumes/exploits them, data about the adult consequences of child physical and sexual abuse, data suggesting that it is almost impossible to live exclusively on welfare payments (encouraging many to lie about their incomes so that they feel they are welfare cheats), data in which White respondents, in particular, portray people of color in gross and dehumanizing ways, and data on the depth of violence in women's lives across race/ethnicity.

We spend much time reading through the *Handbook of Qualitative Research* (Denizen & Lincoln, 1994), Gregory's (1993) ethnographies of Queens, Scheper-Hughes's (1992) analysis of mothering in poverty-stricken communities of Brazil, Connell's (1994) representations of White male identity formation in Australia, M. E. Dyson's *Reflecting Black*

(1993), and rereading Gwaltney's *Drylongso* (1980) and Ladner's *Tomorrow's Tomorrow* (1971) to reflect on how to best write authentically and critically about the narratives offered, in ways that serve communities, theory, and public policy. We present these as dilemmas with which all field-workers must currently struggle. There is nothing straight-forward or objective about reporting *or* withholding these data. Each strategic decision of scholarship bears theoretical, ethical, and political consequences.

On the mundane. Sticking with dilemmas of data, we turn now to questions about mundane details of daily life.

> Well, I take . . . I get $424 a month, okay? And I get $270 in food stamps, so I take . . . there's four weeks to a month, so I take . . . I take the $270 and I divide it by four. And that's what I spend on food. It's just me and my daughters. And my oldest don't eat that much and I don't eat . . . I only eat once a day. I only eat dinner. I'm not hungry in the morning and I don't have breakfast. I have a cup of coffee or hot chocolate. My little one is the one that eats a lot. And whatever I don't . . . like I spend $65 a week in food. I go and I buy meat every day and I buy their breakfast, their lunch, her snacks for school. And whenever I can . . . I work at night . . . I work . . . if I get a call I go and clean somebody's house. I do that. Their father gives me money, you know. So I do whatever I . . . you know, whatever it takes, you know? Shovel your snow . . . [laughs] I don't care. You know, to me money's money, as long as your kids got what they need. But basically their father helps me the most. You know, he'll come in . . . oh, my dad does this, too, and I get really pissed off at him. He'll come in and he'll start looking through my cabinets and in my refriger-ator, and my closet. "Well, what do you have here?" And it's like, "I'm fine. Johnny's coming over later." "No! Blah, blah, blah." And he'll go out and he'll come back with food, and their father's always coming in looking through the refrigerator, and things like that, you know? I always . . . my kids have food, so that's good, you know? They never go hungry. You know, I . . . I hate to say this, but if I had . . . I mean, if it came to where my kids were gonna go hungry, I'd sell my body. To hell with that! My kids ain't gonna starve, you know? I'd do what it takes. I would give two shits. People could . . . my friends could tell me whatever they wanted. I have a . . . I have two friends that sell their bodies for money for their kids. And thank God, I have to knock on wood, I never had to do that. But I mean, if I had to, I would. If that's what it took to feed my kids . . . I mean, if their father . . . a lot of people that are on welfare have husbands worth shit. They don't care. If they had a father, but I guess that's, if that's what it took . . . I would try every aspect before doing that. But if that's what it really took to feed my kids, that's what I would do. I would do whatever it takes to feed and clothe my kids, you know, and put a roof over their head. I wouldn't care what the hell it was. I guess that's what I would do, you know?

These are the dull and spicy details of negotiating daily life in poverty. When we (researchers) listen to and read narratives, we tend (with embarrassment) to be drawn to—in fact, to *code for*—the exotic, the bizarre, the violent. As we reflect, though, we nevertheless feel obligated to explore meticulously the very tedious sections of the tran-scripts: those sections not very sexy, exciting, or eroticizing, like when the informants walk their kids to school, read the newspaper in horror, turn on the television for a break, look for a doctor they can trust, hope their children are safe on the way home from school. These rituals of daily living—obviously made much more difficult in the presence of poverty and discrimination, but mundane nonetheless—are typically left out of ethno-graphic descriptions of life in poverty. They don't make very good reading, and yet are the stuff of daily life. We recognize how carefully we need to *not* construct life narratives spiked only with the hot spots . . . like surfing our data for sex and violence.

On safe spaces. In contrast to bad—or even mundane—data, over time we have col-lected data on those contexts carved out by young adults in which they try to survive, with sanity, the depletion of the public sector. These are data on "safe spaces" that young adults have created to make sense of the insane worlds in which they live. Some of these safe spaces don't actually appear (to us) to be so safe or legal. Others are private and serene, filled with the incense of spirituality, belief in God, the language of social movements and nationalism, the daily coalitions of cross-racial/ethnic people trying to keep their neighborhoods safe. These spaces are delicious and fragile, but not entirely open to surveillance. They seek to be private.

In our first Spencer study, we heard from young women and men who survived in the working-class and poor segments of our society, how they viewed economic opportunities, how they would spin images of their personal and collective futures, especially as related to the power of schooling, how they conceptualized the shrinking public sector, economy, labor, and the military, and how they reflected upon progressive social movements that have historically and dramatically affected their ancestors' and their own chances in life. With respect to policies allegedly written for the poor and working class, our data enable us for the first time to hear from them. We have discovered pockets of possibility excavated by these young men and women, pockets that we desperately need to explore further. Amid their despair lies hope, and hope is cultivated in these safe spaces.

It would be profoundly irresponsible to argue that these working-class and poor women and men are simply depressed, despairing, and isolated, with no sense of possibility. As much as our individual interviews did suggest this at times, our focus groups alerted us that much else is happening. These young women and men are "homesteading"—finding unsuspected places within and across geographic communities, public institutions, and spiritual lives—to sculpt real and imaginary spaces for peace, struggle, and personal and collective identity work. These spaces offer recuperation, resistance, and the makings of "home." They are not just a set of geographic/spatial arrangements, but theoretical, analytical, and spatial displacements—a crack, a fissure in an organization or a community. Individual dreams, collective work, and critical thoughts are smuggled in and then reimagined. Not rigidly bounded by walls/fences, these spaces often are corralled by a series of (imaginary) borders where community intrusion and state surveillance are not permitted. These are spaces where trite social stereotypes are fiercely contested. That is, these young women and men—in constantly confronting harsh public representations of their race/ethnicity, class, gender, and sexuality—use these spaces to break down these public images for scrutiny and invent new ones.

These spaces include the corners of the African American church, where young men huddle over discussions of how to "take back the streets" to "save the young boys"; the Lesbian and Gay Center, carved out quietly by working-class late adolescents and young adults who are seeking identities and networks when their geographic and cultural contexts deny them sexual expression; the Headstart and Effective Parenting Information for Children (EPIC) programs in which poor mothers, and sometimes fathers, come together to talk over the delights and minefields of raising children in a culture permeated with racism and decimated by poverty; the cultural arts programs where men and women join self-consciously across racial and ethnic borders to create what is "not yet," a space, a set of images, a series of aesthetic products that speak of a world that could be.

Spaces such as these spring from the passions and concerns of community members; they are rarely structured from "above." They may be a onetime fiction, transitory or quite stable. They can be designed to restore identities devastated by the larger culture or they may be opportunities to flirt with identities and communities rejected by both mainstream culture and local ethnic groups. These spaces provide rich and revealing data about the resilience of young adults without denying the oppression that threatens the borders and interiors of community life amid urban poverty.

These "free spaces" (Boyte & Evans, 1992) are rarely studied by social scientists. We typically enter people's lives and communities and ask them the questions that titillate us, creating "unfree spaces." As Keith and Pile (1993) argue, by asking questions of "arbitrary closure," social scientists fail to see the world as it unfolds and is reshaped by community members across "spacialities" and time. Typically, social sciences fix (our) gaze on public (or private) programs that are offered to low-income adults. Then we collect evidence of their noninvolvement—laziness, resistance, helplessness. But we now know, as Brice-Heath and McLaughlin (1993) have documented, that there is a rich underground to community life that is vibrant and fundamentally self-created. These are spaces designed by and for community, into which we, after 3 years of interviewing in Buffalo and Jersey City, have been invited. They may be transitory, healing, and mobilizing. They may be official or absolutely ad hoc. They may be a way to reconstitute traditional culture, racial, gender, or sexual identities, or they may be contexts in which individuals cross borders of race, ethnicity, gender, and sexuality to find a small corner in which to breathe in peace. These free spaces, of which we have only glimmers, have raised questions that need attention. When should these data about private/free spaces float into public view? Does the public/private distinction need to be problematized, as Gubrium and Holstein (1995) have argued?

Foucault (1979) has written on the invasive stretch of surveillance, typically pointing at state institutions. Here we deploy the same notion to self-reflexively point at ourselves, social scientists, surveilling the safe cubbyholes of community life. Legitimately one may ask (and some have) whether we have any business floating through, writing about these sequestered quarters. Do our Whiteness, our femaleness, our class status, our staccato appearances adversely affect or interrupt the music of life within free spaces? Does our social scientific voyeurism shatter the sanctity of that which is presumably (although recognizably *not*) free?

We respond to this question, for the moment at least, by presenting two different incidents. One occurred in a basement office in which New Jersey community activists meet to discuss local politics. We were welcomed for the initial interview, but the notion of our sustained presence clearly provoked discomfort. Not asked to return, we left. Elsewhere, and surprisingly more typically, we have been invited into spaces in which members, directors, and others indicate they are eager for documentation, anxious for others to know who they really are, what functions the programs serve, how deeply spiritual and religious "those teenage mothers" can be, how organized and supportive "those gays and lesbians" are. In these latter cases, informants have welcomed us into their spaces to exploit our capacity and willingness to write and to testify to those aspects of community life that the straight media ignore, that trenchant stereotypes deny, that mainstream culture rarely gets to see. Our rights, responsibilities, and relationships influence how (and if) we have access to these spaces.

There is another version of social science surveillance that has recently haunted us, and that is the process by which social scientists—in this case, feminist social scientists—reframe private experiences as social troubles. Taking the lead from Mills (1959) and many since, we see it as our responsibility to move from narratives to theories of social dynamics that operate amid macrostructures, relationships, and communities to produce life as lived, even if this is not life as analyzed in the narratives of our interviewees.

Take the case of domestic violence, particularly among White working-class women, those still in what are considered stable, intact marriages but who are nevertheless being beaten at rates comparable to the women more explicitly living in less stable home environments. We have accumulated substantial evidence to suggest that women in both kinds of environments experience extraordinarily high levels of domestic abuse, and yet women in the seemingly stable homes rarely talk about it, refuse to critique the violence, and rarely question the role of men or their actions. They wouldn't call it abuse—should we?

In this work, we have been collaborating with two students, Amira Proweller and Corrine Bertram, on a domestic violence paper centered on the voices of brutalized and silenced working-class White women. Now what? Is this just a theoretical exercise in which we report narrations of denial? Or do we theorize *over* their voices, giving us little reason for collecting their stories?

There are lots of academics writing about these things, but few are really grappling with trying to meld *writing about* and *working with* activists within these communities (for such work, see Austin, 1992; Lykes, 1989, 1994; Weiss & Greene, 1992). We try to work with communities and activists to figure out how to say what needs to be said without jeopardizing individuals or presenting a universal problem as though it were particular to this class. And yet, cracking their silence—especially among White working-class women who are exceedingly reluctant to discuss or reveal, lest the ideology of domestic family life crumble and their role as savior of the family be exposed—is a feminist and intellectual responsibility fraught with dilemmas.

On self-reflexivity. We have certainly read much, and even written a fair amount, about researchers' subjectivities (Fine, 1994). Our obligation is to come clean "at the hyphen," meaning that we interrogate in our writings who *we* are as we coproduce the narratives we presume to collect. It is now acknowledged that we, as critical ethnographers, have a responsibility to talk about our own identities, why we interrogate what we do, what we choose not to report, on whom we train our scholarly gaze, who is protected and *not* protected as we do our work. As part of this discussion, we want to try to explain how we, as researchers, (can) work *with* communities to capture and build upon community and social movements. In other words, we will put forward parts of our ever-evolving political agenda, sharing the kinds of scholarship/action upon which we are focusing. We draw from our past work to illuminate what's possible "at the hyphens" of researcher and researched (Fine, 1994), and what feels impossible.

Thus far, in Jersey City and Buffalo, we have been able to document how state policies and local economic/social shifts have affected young women's and men's belief systems, world views, and social consciousness. Through individual interviews we have gathered much of these data. Through the focus groups (e.g., in the Lesbian and Gay Club, the African American and White churches, the EPIC parenting group, the Latina homeless shelter, the Pre-Cap college prep program for young adolescents), we have been able to encourage settings in which our interviewees have begun to weave together analyses that weren't entirely formed, to begin to piece together their commitments, for instance, to the "next generation of African American boys," or to "practice the ways of grandmother" around Latina spiritual rituals. Sister Kristin from the York Street Project and Dolores Perry from Head Start have both invited us to work more closely with groups of women and men in their programs, running focus groups that would raise questions, press issues, and help the participants reshape programs. In the EPIC group, we were told that the engagement of several members increased due to our kind of individual and group work. Indeed, Lois Weis was asked to facilitate an EPIC group on a long-term basis. The group interviews offered these women a way of piecing together the strengths of their lives, encouraging forward movement as they were raising their families in the midst of poverty.

Further, throughout the course of our 3 years of research, we have moved across the researcher-researched hyphen to apply our work toward support of local policy and community efforts. Michelle Fine has testified at state hearings on the state takeover of the local schools, advocating with community groups that the state remain in control until local participation can be encouraged and sustained. Research assistant Mun Wong coordinated a project among women on welfare who were eager to document the differential supermarket prices of similar items at different points in the month and in different markets in the community. We have provided census and qualitative data to city council members from the Latino community. Lois Weis supplied testimony in support of continual funding for EPIC and will be trained as an EPIC facilitator. Across communities, numerous conversations have taken place with key policy makers on a number of issues arising from our data.

We take for granted that the purpose of social inquiry in the 1990s is not only to generate new knowledge but to inform critically public policies, existent social movements, and daily community life. A commitment to such application, however, should not be taken for granted. This is a(nother) critical moment in the life of the social sciences, one in which individual scholars are making moral decisions about the extent to which our work should aim to be useful. Distinct camps are lining up with arrows poised.

We have colleagues who embrace the commitment to application, as we do, even if some think it is naive to imagine being able to infiltrate current policy talk on life within poor and working-class communities. Other colleagues have long seen their own scholarship as explicitly aimed toward political and social change (see Gittell, 1990, 1994; Lykes, 1989, 1994; Mullings, 1984; Piven, Block, Cloward, & Ehrenreich, 1987; Piven & Cloward, 1971, 1977; Powell, 1994). And we hear a growing chorus of colleagues who presume that if you are interested in policy and/or social practice, your data are thereby less trustworthy. This latter position was in retreat for perhaps a moment in time, but it seems to be returning to the academy in well-orchestrated volume. We do, of course, reject this position, but would ask again that academics who see this work as deeply nested in community life (recognizing that the notion of community is up for grabs) come together to argue cogently our responses to the following questions: Is this science? Is *only* progressive work biased? Is this politics or policy? And, to probe fundamentally, where are the sites of intellectual leverage by which our work can begin to fissure public and political discourse? That said, we take our responsibilities to these communities seriously, and are educating our graduate students to work with—not on or despite—local community efforts.

Throughout the design, the doing, and the interpretation of our fieldwork, we talk and write about the anxieties (many of which are represented in this article), struggles, passions, and pains. But we ask now, *how much* of our relatively privileged lives do we insert into essays when we chronicle lives under assault from the economy, the state, and within communities and even homes? Yes, *we* write the stories, we determine the questions, we hide some of the data, and we cry over interviews. But self-conscious insertion of self remains an exhilarating, problematic, sometimes narcissistic task. What more can we say than that we are two White Jewish women deeply committed to a better world? The poststructuralist question of "who are we?" is an important one indeed, but what does that mean as we weave together lives of passion, pain, and assault? A narcissistic look at self seems misplaced here. Whiting ourselves out seems equally wrong-headed.

So, in whose voice? Mark, a White working-class informant, tells us:

> It goes into another subject where Blacks, um, I have nothing against Blacks. Um, whether you're Black, White, you know, yellow, whatever color, whatever race. But I don't like the Black movement where, I have Black friends. I talk to them and they agree. You know, they consider themselves, you know, there's White trash and there's White, and there's Black trash and there's Blacks. And the same in any, you know, race. But as soon as they don't get a job, they right away call, you know, they yell discrimination.

In whose voice do we write? Well, of course, our own. But we also present long narratives, colorful with/from informants in our scholarly and more popular presentations, essays, and articles. Some of these narratives, particularly from "Angry White Men," contain hostile or grotesque references to "others"—people of color, police, men on the corner. As theorists, we refrain from the naive belief that these voices should stand on their own, or that voices should survive without theorizing. However, we also find ourselves *differentially theorizing and contextualizing* voices. That is, those voices that have been historically smothered—voices of White women, and men and women of color—we typically present on their own terms, perhaps reluctant, as White academic women, to surround them with much of our theory. And yet, when we present the voices of White men who seem eminently expert at blaming African American men for all their pain and plight, we theorize generously, contextualize wildly, rudely interrupting them to reframe them.

Is this an epistemological double standard in need of reform, or is it a form of narrative affirmative action, creating discursive spaces where few have been in the past? Hurtado and Stewart (in press), in a new and fascinating essay on Whiteness and feminist methods, argue that feminist scholars should self-consciously *underplay* (i.e., not quote extensively) hegemonic voices in their essays and relentlessly create textual room for counterhegemonic narratives. Although we agree, we also think it is vitally important to critically analyze what it is White men are saying about us, about themselves, about economic and social relations. To do this, we interpret their words, their stories, their assertions about others.

All of this raises what we have come to think of as the "triple representational problem." In our texts we ponder how we present (a) *ourselves* as researchers choreographing the narratives we have collected; (b) the *narrators*, many of whom are wonderful social critics, whereas some (from our perspective) are talented ventriloquists for a hateful status quo; and (c) the *others* who are graphically bad-mouthed by these narrators (e.g., caseworkers blamed by women on welfare for stinginess; African American men held responsible for all social evils by White men; police held in contempt by communities of color that have survived much abuse at the hands of police). Do we have a responsibility to theorize the agency/innocence/collusion of these folks, too? When White men say awful things about women of color, do we need to re-present women of color, denounce and re-place these representations? If not, are we not merely contributing to the archival representations of disdain that the social science literature has so horrifically chronicled?

Because all of these groups deserve to be placed within historical and social contexts, and yet power differences and abuses proliferate, how do theorists respect the integrity of informants' consciousness and narratives, place them within social and historical context, and yet not collude or dignify this perverse denigration of people of color? In what seems like too shallow a resolution, we have diversified our research teams, hired local activists and community members when appropriate to consult with us on design and interpretation, and read endlessly in an effort to get out of these boxes. However, these issues are *not* being raised by those in the field. We notice, perhaps defensively, that many of our friends and colleagues who now write on critical ethnography are writing about theory and methods, but not through data. Critical work on representations, poststructuralism, and ethnography has taken many of our once-in-the-field colleagues up and out, looking down now (as we have been wont to do) on a set of dilemmas that have nasty colonial pasts and precarious futures. Those of us still in the field, on the ground, so to speak, worry through this set of issues in highly concrete ways. We worry with no immediate resolution and only rare conversations. We know, though, that these points must be considered.

There are no easy answers to these dilemmas. In each of the essays we have produced thus far, we have tried to contextualize the narratives as spoken within economic, social, and racial contexts so that no one narrator is left holding the bag for his/her demographic group, but there are moments within the narratives when "others"—people of color, case workers, men, women, the neighbor next door—are portrayed in very disparaging ways. We also struggle with *representation,* working hard to figure out how to represent and contextualize our narrators, ourselves, and the people about whom they are ranting. Under the tutelage of historians Scott (1992) and Katz (1995) and psychologist Cross (1991), we try to understand how and why these categories of analysis, these "others," and these accusations are being cast at this moment in history, and who is being protected by this "scope of blame" (Opotow, 1990). At times, however, audiences have nevertheless been alarmed at the language in our texts, at the vivid descriptions and the portraits. We are working on these issues, and welcome help from others who are also struggling with both theory and empirical data.

When method and voice meet. We have noticed in the midst of analysis that the data produced vary by method collected. Methods are not passive strategies. They differentially produce, reveal, and enable the display of different kinds of identities. To be more specific, if individual interviews produce the most despairing stories, evince the most minimal sense of possibility, present identities of victimization, and voice stances of hopelessness, in focus groups with the same people the despair begins to evaporate, a sense of possibility sneaks through, and identities multiply as informants move from worker to mother, to friend, to lover, to sister, to spiritual healer, to son, to fireman, to once-employed, to welfare recipient. In the context of relative safety, trust, comfort, and counterhegemonic creativity offered by the few free spaces into which we have been invited, a far more textured and less judgmental sense of self is displayed. In these like-minded communities that come together to trade despair and build hope, we see and hear a cacophony of voices filled with spirit, possibility, and a sense of vitality absent in the individual data.

We make this point because we have stumbled again upon an issue that may appear to be methodological but is deeply substantive and ethical. Both psychology and education have depended religiously upon methods of individual surveys, interviews, observations, and so on, at the cost of not seeing or hearing collectives. If, as we postulate, collectives are more likely to generate stories of possibility and hope, then perhaps we have a social science, painted in despair, that is as much a methodological artifact as it is a condition of daily life in poor communities.

On a disappearing public sphere. Tamara explains:

I didn't want to be with the father of my children anymore. And at that time he really gave me a lot of headaches. "If you don't stay with me, then I'm not gonna help you with the kids." Which he really didn't do, which I'm thankful. But I just figured, "Well, the hell with it. Then I'll work . . . get the welfare." Because I pay $640 for this apartment. That's a lot of money for a two-bedroom apartment, you know? And the welfare only gives me $424, so I have to make up the difference. And plus I have a telephone, you know. I have cable for my daughters, you know. And it's just a lot of money. And I figure, you know, I figured, well, I couldn't make it on my own. I wasn't making enough to make it on my own back then, so I had to go on welfare. So I did it, and it was . . . I didn't like it. I didn't like sitting there. I didn't like the waiting. I didn't like the questions they asked me, you know?

Q: What kind of questions did . . .
A: Well, they asked me if I was sexually active, how many times I went to bed with him, you know? And I told the guy, "I'm sorry, but that is none of your business" and I refuse to answer the questions. Because to me, well what, they ask you if you, he asked me if I slept with Black men or White men, Puerto Rican men. What was my preference. And to me that was the questions . . .
Q: Was this on a form, or he . . .
A: No, he was just asking questions, you know? And I refused to answer them, you know. And he kind of like got upset. "We have to ask you this." I was like, "bull-shit." You know, they just wanted to, they asked, he asked me how many times I had sex in a day, and just really, you know, if I douched, if I was clean, if I took a shower. I don't think these are any of your business, you know? I take a shower every night and every day, you know? I think those are stupid questions he asked. I was, he asked me how many men I had in my life that I had, you know, if I have more than one man. And I turned around and told him, "I'm not your mother." I never heard of questions like . . . [laughs]
Q: Neither have I. [laughs]
A: They asked the weird questions.
Q: So, how, what was the procedure like?
A: It was embarrassing. Like, with Medicaid, for kids it's good. For kids, you know, you can go anywhere you want with the Medicaid. You can go to the doctors for kids. You know, they pay for braces. When it comes to an adult, I was going to, I was hemorrhaging. I was going to a doctor. I'd been bleeding since December, okay, and they're telling me, I've been going to a gynecologist through the welfare. "It's normal, it's normal. Don't worry about it. It's normal." So last week I was getting ready, for the past week I was feeling really dizzy and really weak, and I said the hell with it. Let me go see a gynecologist. And I paid her. Thank God, you know, the Medicaid took care of the hospital. But I had to pay her $700 for the procedure that I had to have done. [laughs] I had to do it. It was either that or bleed to death, you know. [laughs] But a lot of doctors, I asked her, because she used to take Medicaid. And I asked her, "Why don't you, you know, take Medicaid anymore?" And a lot of doctors that don't, doctors tell you because they don't pay them. She said she's been waiting for people that were on Medicaid to get paid for two years, three years, bills that's how old the bills are and she's still waiting to get paid.

For the past 3 years we have collected data on communities, economic and racial relationships, and individual lives deeply affected by public policies and institutions that rotted many years before. And yet these very same public policies and institutions about which we have deeply incriminating data are today disappearing, yanked away from communities as we write. Public schools, welfare, social services, public housing—defunded. Positioning a critique of the public sphere as it evaporates or, more aptly, as it has disappeared, seems an academic waste of time; worse, it anticipates collusion with the Right.

Our responsibility in this work, as we see it (and if it is doable), is *not* to feed the dismantling of the State by posing a critique of the public sector as it has been, but instead to insist on a State that serves its citizenry well and equitably. That is, social researchers must create vision and imagination for what could be, and demand the resurrection of a public sphere that has a full and participatory citizenship at its heart. Then we can layer on the critiques of what has been. That said, it's not so easy when Speaker of the House Newt Gingrich is just waiting to use our narrative words to do away with welfare; when Brett Schundler, mayor of Jersey City, is foaming at the mouth to get voucher legislation passed in a city in which public schools enjoy little or no positive reputation; when conservative theorists and writers George Gilder and Charles Murray will gleefully abduct our phrases as they paint poor women as lazy and irresponsible. Creating a safe space for intellectual, critical, and complicated discussion when the Right has shown such acute talent at extracting arguments that sustain the assault may be a naive, but worthwhile, wish.

Responsibilities for our writing. We watch the apocalypse and write about it. What is the relationship between what we see, the outrage we gather and feel, the relatively fame texts we produce, and our audiences, many of whom are alternately too depressed or too cynical to be mobilized? We feel the weight of academics; that is, as public intellectuals, we need to tell the stories from the side of policy that is never asked to speak, to interrupt the hegeomony of elite voices dictating what is good for this segment of the population. And yet we feel the need to document the pain and suffering in these communities and the incredible resilience and energy that percolates. It is important to note, therefore, another underground debate within community studies, the tension between representing historically oppressed groups as victimized and damaged *or* as resilient and strong. This may seem an artificial and dangerous dichotomy (we think it is), but we have encountered colleagues within feminism, critical race theory, poverty work, disability studies, and—most recently—queer theory arguing these intellectual stances, with these two "choices" carved out as the (presumably only) appropriate alternatives.

We share the worries, but worry more about the fixed choices that are being offered. Simple stories of discrimination and victimization, with no evidence of resistance, resilience, or agency, are seriously flawed and deceptively partial, and they deny the rich subjectivities of persons surviving amid horrific social circumstances. Equally dreary, however, are the increasingly popular stories of individual heroes who thrive despite the obstacles, denying the burdens of surviving amid such circumstances.

We lean toward a way of writing that spirals around social injustice and resilience, that recognizes the endurance of structures of injustice and the powerful acts of agency, that appreciates the courage and the limits of individual acts of resistance but refuses to perpetuate the fantasy that victims are simply powerless and collusive. That these women and men are strong is not evidence that they have suffered no oppression. Individual and collective strength cannot be used against poor and working-class people as evidence that "Aha! See, it's not been so bad!" We need to invent an intellectual stance in which structural oppression, passion, social movements, evidence of strength, health, and "damage" can all be recognized without erasing essential features of the complex story that constitutes urban life in poverty.

We take solace in the words of many of our African American male informants, drawn from churches and spiritual communities, who testify, "Only belief and hope will save our communities. We have come a long, long way . . . and we have much further to go. Only belief will get us through." Amid the pain and despair, hope survives. This, too, is a big part of community life, rarely seen in the light of day. It is time to recognize the full nature of community life.

Full Circle

Coming full circle, we are still a couple of White women, a well-paid Thelma and Louise with laptops, out to see the world through poor and working-class eyes through the words and stories that we collect across and within communities. We work with activists, policy makers, church leaders, women's groups, and educators in these communities to try to figure out how best to collect data that will serve local struggles, rather than merely to document them. We are surrounded by wonderful students of all races/ethnicities, languages and sexualities, and come to few conclusions with any illusion of consensus. We draw upon community activists and policy makers to help us invent survey questions and interpret the data; we use our data to write up "evaluations" for community programs surviving on shoestring budgets. We write through our own race and class blinders, and we try to deconstruct them in our multiracial and multiethnic coalitions. Decisions about design, sampling sets, interview schedule, interpretation, representation, and dissemination of findings have been developed, clumsily but broadly, through an open process among the members of the research team, with consultation from community members. Questions have been added and omitted by research assistants and community members. Phrasing of questions concerning social class, language, neighborhood violence, and childhood abuse have been best articulated by people who know community life, needs for privacy, and acceptable places for inquiry. Researchers can no longer afford to collect information on communities without that information benefiting those communities in their struggles for equity, participation, and representation. Although such collaborations are by no means easy (see Fine & Vanderslice, 1992), they are essential if social research is to serve the public good.

At base we are trying to work the hyphens of theory and research, policy and practice, Whitenesses and multiracial coalitions, and at this moment in history we find few friends who don't demand that we choose one side of each dichotomy and stake it out! Our commitments to "floating across" satisfy few. Policy makers want clear (usually victim-blaming) descriptions of social problems. Communities would prefer that we keep dirty laundry to ourselves. Some academics think we should stay out of policy talk and remain "uncontaminated" by local struggles. More than a few Whites see us as race traitors, whereas a good number of people of color don't trust two White women academics to do them or their communities much good.

In lame response to colleagues and graduate students, we are trying to build theory, contextualize policy, pour much back into community work, and help to raise the next generation of progressive, multiracial/ethnic scholars. We try to position ourselves self-consciously and hope that our colleagues who are engaged in critical work and still plowing the fields for data will enter with us into this conversation about writing the wrongs and rights in the field. When ethnography came "home," informants moved next door and read our books. Academics were reluctant, remiss, too arrogant to clear up some of these questions of ethics, methods, and theory. Many of our colleagues, on both the Right and Left, have retreated to arrogant theory or silly romance about heroic life on the ground. Others meticulously and persuasively deconstruct the very categories we find ourselves holding on to in order to write a simple sentence about community life. We toil on, looking for friends, writing for outrage, searching for a free space in which social research has a shot at producing both social theory and social change as the world turns rapidly to the Right.

Note

Author's Note: This article is an analysis based on data collected with the generous support of the Spencer Foundation. Address all correspondence to Michelle Fine, Ph.D. Program, Social-Personality Psychology, City University of New York Graduate School and University Center, 33 West 42nd Street, New York, NY 10036, telephone (212) 642–2509.

References

Austin, R. (1992). "The Black community," its lawbreakers, and a politics of identification. *Southern California Law Review, 65*, 1769–1817.

Boyte, H. C., & Evans, S. M. (1992). *Free spaces: The sources of democratic change in America*. Chicago: University of Chicago Press.

Brice-Heath, S., & McLaughlin, M. (Eds.). (1993). *Identity & inner-city youth: Beyond ethnicity and gender*. New York: Teacher's College Press.

Connell, R. W. (1994). *Knowing about masculinity, teaching the boys*. Paper presented at the 1994 conference of the Pacific Sociological Association, San Diego, CA.

Cross, W. E., Jr. (1991). *Shades of Black: Diversity in African-American identity*. Philadelphia: Temple University Press.

Denizen, N. R., & Lincoln, Y. S. (1994). *Handbook of qualitative research*. Thousand Oaks, CA: Sage.

Dyson, M. E. (1993). *Reflecting Black: African-American cultural criticism*. Minneapolis: University of Minnesota Press.

Fine, M. (1991). *Framing dropouts: Notes on the politics of an urban public high school*. Albany, NY: State University of New York Press.

Fine, M. (1992). *Disruptive voices: The possibilities of feminist research*. Ann Arbor: University of Michigan Press.

Fine, M. (1994). Working the hyphens: Reinventing self and other in qualitative research. In N. R. Denizen & Y. S. Lincoln (Eds.), *Handbook of qualitative research* (pp. 70–82). Thousand Oaks, CA: Sage.

Fine, M., & Vanderslice, V. (1992). Qualitative activist research: Reflections in methods and politics. In F. B. Bryant, J. Edwards, R. S. Tindale, E. J. Posavac, L. Heath, E. Henderson, & Y. Suarez-Balcazar (Eds.), *Methodological issues in applied social psychology: Social psychological applications to social issues* (Vol. 2, pp. 199–218). New York: Plenum.

Foucault, M. (1979). *Discipline and punish*. New York: Random House.

Gates, H. L., Jr. (1985). *"Race," writing, and difference*. Chicago: University of Chicago Press.

Gittell, M. J. (1990). Women on foundation boards: The illusion of change. In *Women and foundations/corporate philanthropy*. New York: CUNY.

Gittell, M. J. (1994). School reform in New York and Chicago: Revisiting the ecology of local games. *Urban Affairs Quarterly*, 136–151.

Gregory, S. (1993). Race, rubbish, and resistance: Empowering difference in community politics. *Cultural Anthropology, 8*(1), 24–48.

Gubrium, J. F., & Holstein, J. A. (1995). Qualitative inquiry and the deprivatization of experience. *Qualitative Inquiry, 1*, 204–222.

Gwaltney, J. L. (1980). *Drylongso: A self-portrait of Black America*. New York: Random House.

Hall, S. (1981). Moving right. *The Socialist Review, 55*(1), 113–137.

Hurtado, A., & Stewart, A. J. (in press). Through the looking glass: Implications of studying Whiteness for feminist methods. In M. Fine, L. Powell, L. Weis, & M. Wong (Eds.), *Off/White*. New York: Routledge.

Katz, M. (1995). *Improving poor people*. Princeton, NJ: Princeton University Press.

Keith, M., & Pile, S. (Eds.), (1993). *Place and the politics of identity.* London: Routledge.

Ladner, J. A. (1971). *Tomorrow's tomorrow: The Black woman.* Garden City, NY: Doubleday.

Lykes, M. B. (1989). Dialogue with Guatemalan Indian women: Critical perspectives on constructing collaborative research. In R. K. Unger (Ed.), *Representations: Social constructions of gender* (pp. 167–185). Amityville, NY: Baywood.

Lykes, M. B. (1994). Speaking against the silence: One Maya woman's exile and return. In C. E. Franz & A. J. Stewart (Eds.), *Women creating lives: Identities, resilience, and resistance* (pp. 97–114). Boulder, CO: Westview.

Mills, C. W. (1959). *The sociological imagination.* New York: Oxford University Press.

Mullings, L. (1984). Minority women, work and health. In W. Chavkin (Ed.), *Double exposure: Women's health hazards on the job and at home* (pp. 84–106). New York: Monthly Review Press.

Omi, M., & Winant, H. (1986). *Racial formations in the United States.* New York: Routledge.

Opotow, S. (1990). Moral exclusion and injustice: An introduction. *Journal of Social Issues, 46*(1), 1–20.

Piven, F. F., Block, F., Cloward, R. A., & Ehrenreich, B. (1987). *The mean season.* New York: Pantheon.

Piven, F. F., & Cloward, R. A. (1971). *Regulating the poor: The functions of public welfare.* New York: Pantheon.

Piven, F. F., & Cloward, R. A. (1977). *Poor people's movements: Why they succeed, how they fail.* New York: Pantheon.

Powell, L. (1994). Interpreting social defenses: Family group in an urban setting. In M. Fine (Ed.), *Chartering urban school reform: Reflections on public high schools in the midst of change* (pp. 112–121). New York: Teachers College Press.

Richardson, L. (1995). Writing-stories: Co-authoring "The Sea Monster," a writing-story. *Qualitative Inquiry, 1,* 189–203.

Scheper-Hughes, N. (1992). *Death without weeping: The violence of everyday life in Brazil.* Berkeley: University of California Press.

Scott, J. W. (1992). Experience. In J. Butler & J. W. Scott (Eds.), *Feminists theorize the political* (pp. 22–40). New York: Routledge.

Weis, L. (1985). *Between two worlds: Black students in an urban community college.* New York: Routledge.

Weis, L. (1990). *Working class without work: High school students in a deindustrializing economy.* New York: Routledge.

Weis, L., & Fine, M. (Eds.). (1993). *Beyond silenced voices: Class, race, and gender in United States schools.* Albany: State University of New York Press.

Weis, L., & Fine, M. (1995). *Voices from urban America: Sites of immigration and spaces of possibility.* Spencer grant proposal; submitted to and funded by The Spencer Foundation, Chicago, IL.

Weiss, H. B., & Greene, J. C. (1992). An empowerment partnership for family support and education programs and evaluations. Cambridge, MA: Harvard Family Research Project. *Family Science Review, 5*(1,2).

Section Four
Reflexive Writing Exercises

29

Reflexive Writing Exercises

Wendy Luttrell

The nature of reflexive writing is different from what you may be used to; it is meant to capture your thinking process while you are engaged in it. Reflexive writing can vary in length, form, and content, but its purpose is to make your thinking visible. Reflexive writing goes by various names, including memos, notes-on-notes, journal entries, free-writes, and "sampler" writing (DeVault, this volume). By whatever name—I'll use *memo*—three things are important.

Write for yourself. In these writings you are in conversation with yourself about your evolving ideas, associations, and feelings. Don't be afraid to connect your personal experience (including "fringe-thoughts," "snatches of conversation over heard on the street," and "dreams") to your writing (C.W. Mills, this volume: 140). Remember that you are writing to extend your thinking without worrying about drawing conclusions or making an argument. This will come later.

If you share your writings with others as part of a writing group or interpretive community (as I encourage you to do), be prepared to specify the kind of feedback you are looking for. The types of feedback offered by Elbow and Belanoff (this volume) provide good options. Their "summary and say back" type of feedback, where you invite listeners to say back what they hear so that you can reply with a restatement of what you wish to convey, is particularly useful for memos written at early stages of your research.

Establish a regular writing practice and ritual that works for you. Make a schedule and plan to write *at least* once a week. Writing is like exercising; you might not feel like doing it, but once in motion it feels good. And when you are done, you are glad you did it. Like exercise routines, writing routines change over the course of time and in accordance to your specific goals, available resources, and demands in your life. Learn to set your own writing stride and to trust your process. One of my doctoral mentors gave me invaluable advice while I was writing my dissertation. With two small children, one three and the other an infant, I had limited and inconsistent hours for writing each day. I worried that I would be unable to pick up quickly enough on my train of thought. He suggested two things: first, that I keep a journal next to my bed to scribble down thoughts that inevitably came to me in the middle of the night; and second, that at the end of each day, I should type three key words on a blank page that would jumpstart my thinking the next day. Rather than spending time reading over what I had written the day before, I should practice moving forward, starting with my thoughts about those three key words.

Overall, my take-home message about establishing a writing routine is that practice makes practice, not perfect. Many of my students have taken special comfort in Anne

Lamott's (1995) wonderful chapters, "Shitty First Drafts" and "On Perfectionism," in her book about the writing process, *Bird By Bird: Some Instructions on Writing and Life*. And others have appreciated the structure offered by Eviatar Zerubavel's (1999) book, *The Clockwork Muse*.

Develop a system for organizing your memos. Think of your memos in the same way you would think of other data you are collecting. Put a date on everything you write, and I advise students to give each memo a title as this can help to crystallize your thoughts. Arrange your memos into topical "files" as C. W. Mills suggests (in computer-language, "folders"). Be sure to take time to regularly review your memos and rearrange them into new "folders" as your thinking evolves. This practice enables you to chart your intellectual development.

In many cases, memos will be integrated into a research proposal, a first draft of a completed data analysis, or a publication. Charmaz (this volume) provides such an example, showing how the memo she wrote appeared in the published version of her research.

These reflexive writing exercises need not be followed sequentially, as qualitative research is not a linear process. They are presented as topics important for developing a reflexive practice.

Memo on Researcher Identity

The purpose of this memo is to begin a conversation with yourself about the personal relevance of the research you are planning and why you care about it. To help you get started, answer the following questions:

- What are your passions? What makes you care about the topic or the people, places, or things that you wish to study?
- What *presumptions* and beliefs do you hold about the topic, people, place or things? What are your assumptions and beliefs based on?
- What is currently *preoccupying* your mind as you begin your research?
- What are your *predilections* and preferences as a researcher?

Memo on Identity and Social Categories

The way we describe ourselves and others involves theoretical as well as rhetorical consideration.

Patricia Williams (1991) concludes her book, *Alchemy of Race and Rights*, with a short piece, "A Word on Categories."

Using her self-description as a guide, write 7–10 lines in which you describe yourself.

> While being black has been the most powerful social attribution in my life, it is only one of the number of governing narrative or presiding fictions by which I am constantly reconfiguring myself in the world. Gender is another, along with ecology, pacifism, my peculiar brand of colloquial English and Roxbury, Massachusetts. The complexity of role identification, the politics of sexuality, the inflections of professionalized discourse—all describe and impose boundary in my life, even as they confound one another in unfolding spiral of confrontation, deflection and dream. (256)

Williams continues to discuss her decisions on other categorical terms:

> A final note about some of my own decisions on categories: I wish to recognize that terms like "black" and "white" do not begin to capture the rich ethnic and political diversity of my subject. But I do believe that the simple matter of the color of one's skin so profoundly affects the way one is treated, so radically shapes what one is allowed to think and feel about this society, that the decision to generalize from such a division is valid. Furthermore, it is hard to describe succinctly the racial perspective and history that are my concern. "Disenfranchised" will not do, since part of my point is that a purely class-based analysis does not comprehend the whole problem. I don't like the word "minority" (although I use it) because it implies a certain delegitimacy in a majoritarian system; and if one adds up all the shades or yellow, red, and brown swept over by the term, we are in fact not. I prefer "African-American" in my own conversational usage because it effectively evokes the specific cultural dimensions of my identity, but in this book I use most frequently the term "black" in order to accentuate the unshaded monolithism of color itself as a social force. (256–257)

Think about the social categories related to your research topic and/or research participants. Write a memo (2–3 pages) that specifies the terms you are using and why you have chosen to use them.

Memo on Coming to Your Questions

This memo gets you started thinking about what you already know about your topic and what you want to know more about.

Think of your research topic as having both breadth and depth. Sketching the topic in terms of breadth, you may identify particular aspects of the content and/or context that you want to learn more about: missing pieces of the puzzle. Sketching the topic in terms of depth, you may wish to identify different levels or perspectives that require further investigation and alternative stances that you want to take in your research.

End the memo with a provisional statement of your research question(s) that identifies a setting and a cast of characters.

The following strategies may also be useful in crafting a memo about your research questions:

- Make a chart of your topic

Two or three things I know for sure	Where I got these ideas	How I might be Wrong	What I need to know	My rationale for my choices

- Ask someone to interview you about your topic. Your interviewer should probe you about what you think is going on, why, and where your ideas come from (personal experience, other research, etc.). Audio record the conversation and use it to write your memo.
- Complete the following sentences as a way to take an inventory of what you know about your topic:

The main way that my research topic draws on my own experience is _____
One thing I'm sure of about my topic is _____
I would be really surprised if, as a result of the research I learned _____
The biggest assumption I am making in my research is _____
What excites me most about this topic is _____
The main thing I am unclear or unsure about is _____

Memo Using the 100-Word Strategy: Three Versions

I've heard it said that Abraham Lincoln once wrote to a friend that he was sending a long letter because he didn't have time to write a short one. Taking this piece of wisdom to heart, you may have to draft longer versions before you can arrive at a shortened one. I advise students to use the "hundred word strategy" to boil down and refine their thinking.

In *100 words or less*—explain *why* your topic matters.
Write three different versions:

- *Version #1:* Why does this topic matter to you?
- *Version #2:* Why does it matter to the participants of your study?
- *Version #3:* Why does it matter to the field of education?

Memo on Key Words

Looking back on your previous memos, pay attention to key words, phrases, or concepts that you are relying on to explain what you know and think is going on. As C. W. Mills (this volume) suggests, look up synonyms for these key terms in dictionaries as well as technical books so you are aware of different connotations of the word/terms. Raymond Williams's (1983) *Key Words: A Vocabulary of Culture and Society* and Thomas Schwandt's (2001) *Dictionary of Qualitative Inquiry* are both great resources for this. Write a memo that discusses these terms and why they are relevant to your topic.

Memo on Getting a Comparative Grip

> The search for comparable cases, either in one civilization and historical period or in several, gives you leads. . . . That is so even if you do not make explicit comparisons.
> C. W. Mills (this volume: 144)

Identify other institutional settings, regions of the world (past and present), or events that may correspond or have parallels with the phenomenon you wish to study. Write about how these may or may not compare.

Memo on Who's Missing?

One of the biggest decisions you will make as you develop your research topic, is who to include and exclude from your investigation. Marj DeVault (this volume) offers many wise strategies for designing inclusive research projects.

For this memo, describe the composition of the group and the setting you wish to study. What is your rationale for wanting to investigate this particular group? Once finished, reread your memo and ask yourself: Who's missing? Why? How, if at all, is this relevant to your investigation?

Memo on Autobiographical Connections

What aspects of your biography, including your social and intellectual background, are consequential for your research topic or for the people, place, or things that you wish to study? Autobiographical writing can serve multiple purposes: to help researchers more closely examine social position and related perspectives; to gain clarity and insight about their assumptions; and to identify emotions that may be driving or thwarting their projects, to name a few.

To help get you started thinking about your intellectual background, you might consider writing a memo about a turning point in your thinking—a life experience, a book you read, a movie you saw, a course you took, or teacher you had. Tell what happened and how it changed your perspective.

Think of your personal connections to your research as a work-in-progress where you will continue to add memories, reflections, associations, and life events that relate to your topic, or the people, places or things you encounter (you may wish to make a "folder" dedicated to these autobiographical connections).

You don't need to share what you write with anyone; but if you do, be sure you are comfortable making it public. The point of telling about yourself is not to self-disclose for its own sake. Finally, take time to read how other scholars have written about themselves in relation to their research. The readings in *Section Three* are a good place to start.

Memo on Audiences: Two Versions

Our writing is always in conversation with an audience (both real and imagined). How we envision this audience—as friend or foe; attentive or impatient; lay or academic—shapes how and what we allow ourselves to write.[1]

- Imagine a sympathetic audience for your topic. Describe them. Why are they sympathetic?
- Imagine a hostile audience for your work. Describe them. Why are they hostile, and what are their concerns?

Memo on Ethical, Moral, and Political Guidelines

Develop your own set of ethical, moral, and political considerations that guide your research. Explain concrete steps you will take to address dilemmas.

Ethical/Moral/Political Guidelines	Possible Dilemmas	Steps I will Take

Memo on Concretizing Your Questions

You can't study everything interesting about your topic. Formulating *researchable* questions means making choices. Compose three or four main questions. Consider how these questions are related. It is helpful to think about the distinction between your research *topic* and more specific research *questions*. For example, a topic of study might be: "the school to prison pipeline" (i.e. racial inequality in school discipline and punishment). *Researchable questions* about this topic define the "slice" and scope of the phenomenon you wish to investigate. You might focus on questions about process—how do school labeling practices and the exercise of rules operate to criminalize black male youth? (e.g. Ferguson, this volume). Alternatively, you might focus on context—how does school mission and organization shape school disciplinary codes, school labeling practices and the exercise of rules? Or you might ask about the meaning that school labeling practices, and the exercise of rules have for black male youth. Your questions tack back and forth between theoretical concerns (i.e. what you want to know), practical issues (how you can best investigate this), research relationships (access, your point of entry), and so forth. Remember that "God is in the details"; your questions will become more refined the more you develop your plans.

Filling out the following matrix can help you get started.

What questions are most central to my study?	Why do I need to know this?	What kind of data will answer the questions?	How will I collect this data?	Where?	With Whom?

Memo on Using the Literature: Seven Levers

Had I enough space in this volume, Howard Becker's (1986) chapter, "Terrorized by the Literature," would surely have been included. He laments that students are all too often taught to *fear* rather than effectively *use* the literature in graduate school. He suggests a different way of thinking by comparing the woodworker with the researcher. The woodworker designs and makes a table using pre-cut lumber and prefabricated parts (e.g., drawer pulls and turned legs) that others have already produced. But the woodworker puts the pieces together in his or her own distinct way. Similarly, a researcher designs a project that uses the literature as pieces and parts that are already available and puts them together in the service of the researcher's own agenda and argument. And this is the best reason for knowing the literature—not as a means to prove oneself, but as a means to know what concepts and procedures are available so as not to waste time or reinvent the wheel.

If there were space, I would have also included Sarah Delamont's (1992) "Tales, Marvellous Tales: Recognizing Good Fieldwork and Reading Wisely." She introduces three different kinds of reading. First is reading *around* your topic, which should include "any kind of text [*that*] may be relevant: journalism, poetry, drama, comics, anything" (12). Second is reading *in contrast* to your topic. For example, say you are studying women scientists and engineers in higher education. To read in contrast, you would seek out research about men in "female" professions or women navigating male-dominated professions outside of education, like policing. The third is reading for *analytical and theoretical categories*. Delamont suggests that this reading is what separates the journalist from the social analyst.

To help you use, rather than fear, the literature related to your topic I suggest the following levers or handles:

- What are the best three things you have read about your topic (these can be empirical studies, theoretical pieces, or literature)? Write a memo explaining why these are the best.
- Identify a body of related empirical work on your topic and discuss "your take" on

this material. You may want to identify the enduring debates that have guided these studies, or you may want to identify "gaps."

- What are the dominant questions that have been asked and answers that have been provided in research about your topic? For example, Howard Becker (1986) suggests that students find the "ideological hegemony" (147) of the literature related to their topic. In my research on pregnant teens I found that "deviance" questions were hegemonic, meaning that the questions considered most worth asking was, "Why would girls do a wrong thing like that?" And the favored way of answering the question was to find a psychological trait or social attribute to differentiate girls who get pregnant from girls who don't. I wanted to shift the terms and ask what meaning girls made of their pregnancies.

- Identify an "exemplar" related to your topic—a work of scholarship that can serve as a touchstone (it need not be about your exact topic, but related to it). Explain why this work of scholarship is your touchstone. What are the elements of this work that you want to uphold in your own research?

- The concept of "bodies of literature" is misleading. These pre-formed entities are not out there waiting to be discovered or uncovered—they are self-constructed categories. Select an array of authors that you want to put into conversation with each other. Imagine you are inviting them to your home for dinner, and "introduce" them to each other and why you have brought them together for the evening.

- Write an "open letter" to a scholar/practitioner/activist/policy maker you admire and has profoundly influenced the way you think about your research. What do you want to say to this person about how her or his ideas, activities, commitments, and beliefs have inspired you? Or left you curious about something? Or made you skeptical? Or pushed you into thinking differently?[2]

- Select a book or article related to your research. Write a memo that describes the author's research design. Feel free to use quotes from the book. Be sure to address as many elements of reflexive research design that you can: goals, research relationships, research questions, knowledge frameworks; inquiry frameworks, including the specific *little-m methods* (description/justification of the research site or setting; sampling; data collection strategies, data analysis strategies, any protocols used); and strategies to ensure validity.

Memo on Pre-Observation Practice

As reflexive qualitative researchers, what we see depends on how we filter or select what we see. What we see also depends on *how* we look—how we open ourselves to the acts of seeing. The following exercises invite you to practice "seeing" from two different angles.

- *Researcher Gaze*: Try fixing your gaze on an everyday object—a kitchen pot, a piece of furniture, a computer—something in everyday use. Observe it. Describe the external details of the object and how it is used. Sketch it, map it, or photograph it. Start thinking deeply about the object. Is there a history to it? Who is its creator or owner? What does it say about the person who uses it? The person who made it? How are you positioned to see the object? What did you already know? Why did you choose it? Write a memo that offers an interpretation of the object in use.

- *Recalling a Sense of Place*: We carry our sense of place, our personal geography into our fieldwork. Before we research a setting it is important to retrieve and record our own internal landscape and make it explicit to ourselves. What images do we remember from a particular landscape? What details do we recall and why do these details, images, sensations return to us—why these and not others?

Choose a place that brings back a rush of sensory details: sights, sounds, smells, textures, and tastes. Describe this spot, and as you think about the specifics of this place, its details and sensation, see if you retrieve a dominant impression, a cluster of images, or some person connected to the memory. Write a memo with as many details as possible.

Memo on Pre-Interviewing Practice

This writing exercise is to help you prepare to write reflexive memos about the interview process.

- Develop a set of interview questions about your topic that you will use to ask someone you already know who shares an interest in or knowledge about your concerns. Explain the purpose of your study and ask the person whether they are willing to be audio recorded. Remind your interviewee that the interview is for your practice only. As soon after the interview as possible, while your memory is fresh, write up your notes about the interview. Describe your overall impression, and take note of which questions seemed to fall flat, and which evoked the most response or generated the most interest. Write a memo that summarizes these points.
- After listening to the tape several times, make a list of points about which you think need more clarification, questions you wish you had asked, and issues you would want to pursue. Then transcribe the most interesting parts of the interview—at least 5 pages. Spend time re-reading the transcript and write a memo about it. Why have you selected these parts? Are they related? If so, how? Is there a theme or a trend or a key distinction that has grabbed your attention? Explain how your particular values, expectations, assumptions, and interests influence what parts you selected and why these stood out to you.
- Finally, write a letter to the interviewee/narrator that summarizes what you learned from the interview.[3] Do not use any of the narrator's own words, only your restatements. When, and if you use any disciplinary concepts or terms that you think the narrator will not understand (i.e. "jargon"), be sure to translate these into lay language.

Memo on Establishing Your Criteria for Validity

Qualitative researchers need to be keenly aware of and transparent about how they arrive at their interpretations and conclusions. In designing your research, there are things you can anticipate ahead of time that will enhance your ability to make knowledge claims. As I discussed in the description of my Reflexive Research Design Model (161), you will need to make explicit your own criteria for what ensures validity, based on your research paradigm and epistemological stance.

- Write a memo that describes everything you will do in your research (from sampling, to data collection and analysis, to writing) that will establish the validity of your conclusions. Brainstorm all possible strategies, and then consider which of these are feasible and most relevant to your study.
- Write another memo that describes the biggest *strength* and *limitation* of your research design.

Memo on Writing in Different "Voices": Three Versions

Qualitative researchers have developed numerous strategies for listening to their research participants' voice(s)—during the interview and while interpreting it.[4] The reflexive practitioner also develops strategies for his/her voice to represent participants' words and experiences. For example, Michelle Fine (1992) distinguishes between using a "ventriloquist" (speaking for) compared to an "activist" (speaking with) voice. Susan Chase (this volume) distinguishes between three researcher voices—"authoritative, supportive, and interactive." And Lawrence-Lightfoot and Davis (1997) refer to five different researcher voices: "voice as witness" (the discerning observer); "voice as interpretation" (the researcher's attempt to make sense of the data); "voice as preoccupation" (the theoretical and intellectual assumptions that are embedded in the researcher's discussion); "voice as autobiography" (the knowledge, wisdom and experience upon which the researcher draws to connect or identify with research participants); and "voice in dialogue" (when the researcher's voice is intermingled with the voice of the research participants, describing the evolving relationship). Developing your own voice as a researcher is about taking a stance, a perspective, a lens through which you represent what you have learned. A researcher's voice need not be singular.

The point of this memo is to practice writing with different voices. Think of a familiar story from your family life—a story that you have heard told several times (let's say, how your parents met, or something you did as a child in school, something your sibling did as a child). Write your memory of the event. Then craft a story in three different versions:

- *Version #1*: as if it were being told by a third-person narrator.
- *Version #2*: as if it were being told by one of the characters (e.g. you, a parent, a teacher, a friend, a sibling, etc.).
- *Version #3*: as if it were being used to illustrate a larger social, cultural, psychological or educational point.

Memo on Translating your Research Design into a Research Proposal

As noted in the *Introduction*, a research design is not the same as a research proposal. Your *proposal* makes an argument; it presents a case or justifies your study. This memo is to help you get started on developing an argument.

Before you begin, think about all the pieces of your design and how they align: goals, research question, knowledge framework, inquiry strategies, validity, and research relationships.

Then write a memo that addresses the following questions:

- What are we going to learn as a result of your study?
- Why is this worth knowing—why is it useful or meaningful, and to whom?
- What are the advantages of the design you propose? And what are the limitations?
- What steps have been taken to ensure that the study poses no serious ethical problems?
- How will you decide that your conclusions are valid?
- What will be the benefits of the study?

Notes

1. I thank Debby Saintil Previna for her suggestion that I expand the parameters of the many types of audiences we consider as we write (personal communication).
2. See Michael Burawoy's "Open Letter to C. Wright Mills" (2008) for an interesting example.
3. I am indebted to Sherry Deckman for the letter-writing part of this exercise.
4. Lawrence-Lightfoot and Davis (1997) draw attention to the subtle different between "listening to" actors' voices and "listening for" voice (1997: 99–103).

References

Becker, H. 1986. "Terrorized by the literature." In H. Becker *Writing for Social Scientists*. Chicago: University of Chicago Press: 135–149.

Burawoy, M. 2008. "Open letter to C. Wright Mill." *Antipode*, Vol. 40 (3): 365–375.

Delamont, S. 1992. "Tales, marvellous tales: recognizing good fieldwork and reading wisely." In S. Delamont, *Fieldwork in Educational Settings: methods, pitfalls and perspectives*. London: Falmer Press: 10–28.

Fine, M. 1992. *Disruptive Voices: the possibilities of feminist research*. Ann Arbor, Michigan: University of Michigan Press.

Lamott, A. 1994. *Bird by Bird: some instructions on writing and life*. New York: Anchor Books.

Lawrence-Lightfoot, S. and Davis, J. H. 1997. *The Art and Science of Portraiture*. San Francisco: Jossey-Bass.

Schwandt, T. 2001. *Dictionary of Qualitative Inquiry*. Thousand Oaks, London, New Delhi: Sage Publications.

William, P. 1991. *Alchemy of Race and Rights*. Cambridge, MA: Harvard University Press.

Williams, R. 1983. *Key Words: a vocabulary of culture and society*. New York: Oxford University Press.

Zerubavel, E. 1999. *The Clockwork Muse: the practical guide to writing theses, dissertations and books*. Cambridge, MA: Harvard University Press.

Recommended Readings

Behar, R. and Gordon, D. (eds.) 1995. *Women Writing Culture*. Berkeley, CA: University of California Press.

Charmaz, K. and Mitchell, R. 1997. "The myth of silent authorship: self, substance and style." In R. Hertz, *Reflexivity And Voice*. Thousand Oaks, CA: Sage.

Harraway, D. 2004. "There are always more things going on than you thought: methodologies as thinking technologies." In *The Harraway Reader*, London and New York: Routledge Press: 332–341.

Janesick, V. 1999. "A journal about journal writing as a qualitative research technique: history, issues, and reflections." *Qualitative Inquiry*, 5 (4): 505–524

Richardson, L. 1997. *Fields of Play: constructing an academic life*. New Brunswick, NJ: Rutgers University.

——. 2002. "Poetic representation of interviews." In J. Gubrium and J. Holstein (Eds.) *Postmodern Interviewing*. London: Sage Publications.

Richardson, L. and St Pierre, E. 2005. "Writing: a method of inquiry." In N. Denzin and Y. S. Lincoln (Eds.) *Sage Handbook of Qualitative Research*. Thousand Oaks, CA: Sage.

Van Manen, M. 2006. "Writing qualitatively, or the demands of writing." *Qualitative Health Research*, 16 (5): 713–722.

Special Issue: Portraiture Methodology. 2005. *Qualitative Inquiry*, 11 (1) 3–106.

Speed, J. 2005. "Writing as inquiry: some ideas, practices, opportunities and constraints." *Counselling and Psychotherapy Research*, 5 (1): 63–64.

Recommended Books on the Writing Process

Dillard, A. 1989. *The Writing Life*. New York: HarperCollins

Didion, J. 1976. "Why I write." *The New York Times Magazine*, December 5.

Elbow, P. 1973. *Writing Without Teachers*. New York: Oxford University Press.

—— . 1998. *Writing With Power: techniques for mastering the writing process*. New York: Oxford University Press.

hooks, b. 1999. *Remembered Rapture: the writer at work*. New York: Henry Holt.

Strunk, William, J. and White, E. B., illustrated by Kalman, M. 2005. *The Elements of Style Illustrated*. New York: Penguin Press.

30

Summary of Kinds of Responses

Peter Elbow and Pat Belanoff

Here is an overview of eleven different and valuable ways of responding to writing—and a few thoughts about when each kind is valuable. We will explain them more fully later and illustrate their use on sample essays. After you have tried them out, you can glance back over this list when you want to decide which kind of feedback to request.

1. Sharing: No Response

Read your piece aloud to listeners and ask: "Would you please just listen and enjoy?" You can also give them your text to read silently, though you don't usually learn as much this way. Simple sharing is also a way to listen better to your *own responses* to your own piece, without having to think about how others respond. You learn an enormous amount from hearing yourself read your own words—or from reading them over when you know that someone else is also reading them.

No response is valuable in many situations: when you don't have much time, at very early stages when you just want to try something out or feel very tentative, or when you are completely finished and don't plan to make any changes at all—as a form of simple communication or celebration. Sharing gives you a nonpressure setting for getting comfortable reading your words out loud and listening to the writing of others.

2. Pointing and Center of Gravity

Pointing: "Which words or phrases or passages somehow strike you? stick in mind? *get through?*" Center of gravity: "Which sections somehow seem important or resonant or generative?" You are not asking necessarily for the *main points* but rather for sections or passages that seem to resonate or linger in mind or be sources of energy. Sometimes a seemingly minor detail or example—even an aside or a digression—can be a center of gravity.

These quick, easy, interesting forms of response are good for timid or inexperienced responders—or for early drafts. They help you establish a sense of contact with readers. Center of gravity response is particularly interesting for showing you rich and interesting parts of your piece that you might have neglected—but which might be worth exploring and developing. Center of gravity can help you see your piece in a different light and suggest ways to make major revisions.

3. Summary and Sayback

Summary: "Please summarize what you have heard. Tell me what you hear as the main thing and the almost-main things." (Variations: "Give me a phrase as title and a one-word title—first using my words and then using your words.") Sayback: "Please say back to me in your own words what you hear me getting at in my piece, but say it in a somewhat questioning or tentative way—as an invitation for *me to reply* with my own restatement of what you've said."

These are both useful at any stage in the writing process in order to see whether readers "got" the points you are trying to "give." But sayback is particularly useful at early stages when you are still groping and haven't yet been able to find what you really want to say. You can read a collection of exploratory passages for sayback response. When readers say back to you what they hear—and invite you to reply—it often leads you to find exactly the words or thoughts or emphasis you were looking for.

4. What is Almost Said? What Do You Want to Hear More About?

Just ask readers those very questions.

This kind of response is particularly useful when you need to *develop* or enrich your piece: when you sense there is more here but you haven't been able to get your finger on it yet. This kind of question gives you concrete substantive help because it leads your readers to give you some of *their ideas* to add to yours. Remember this too: what you imply but don't say in your writing is often very loud to readers but unheard by you—and has an enormous effect on how they respond.

Extreme variation: "Make a guess about what was on my mind that I *didn't* write about."

5. Reply

Simply ask, "What are *your* thoughts about my topic? Now that you've heard what I've had to say, what do *you* have to say?"

This kind of response is useful at any point, but it is particularly useful at early stages when you haven't worked out your thinking yet. Indeed, you can ask for this kind of response even before you're written a draft; perhaps you jotted down some notes. You can just say, "I'm thinking about saying X, Y, and Z. How would you reply? What are your thoughts about this topic?" This is actually the most natural and common response to any human discourse. You are inviting a small discussion of the topic.

6. Voice

(a) "How much voice do you hear in my writing? Is my language alive and human? Or is it dead, bureaucratic, unsayable?" (b) "*What kind* of voice(s) do you hear in my writing?" Timid? Confident? Sarcastic? Pleading?" Or "What kind of person does my writing sound like? What side(s) of me comes through in my writing? Most of all, "Do you trust the voice or person you hear in my writing?"

This kind of feedback can be useful at any stage. When people describe the voice they hear in writing, they often get right to the heart of subtle but important matters of language and approach. They don't have to be able to talk in technical terms ("You seem to use lots of passive verbs and nominalized phrases"); they can say, "You sound kind of bureaucratic and pompous and I wonder if *you* actually believe what you are saying."

7. Movies of the Reader's Mind

Ask readers to tell you honestly and in detail what is going on in their minds *as* they read your words. There are three powerful ways to help readers give you this kind of response. (a) Interrupt their reading a few times and find out what's happening at that moment. (b) Get them to tell you their reactions in the form of a *story* that takes place *in time*. (c) If they make "it-statements" ("It was confusing"), make them translate these into "I-statements" ("I felt confused starting here about . . .").

Movies of the reader's mind make the most sense when you have a fairly developed draft and you want to know how it works on readers—rather than when you're still trying to develop your ideas. Movies are the richest and most valuable form of response, but they require that you feel some confidence in yourself and support from your reader, because when readers tell you honestly what is happening while they are reading your piece, they may tell you they don't like it or even get mad at it.

8. Metaphorical Descriptions

Ask readers to describe your writing in terms of clothing (e.g., jeans, tuxedo, lycra running suit), weather (e.g., foggy, stormy, sunny, humid), animals, colors, shapes.

This kind of response is helpful at any point. It gives you a new view, a new lens; it's particularly helpful when you feel stale on a piece, perhaps because you have worked so long on it. Sometimes young or inexperienced readers are good at giving you this kind of response when they are unskilled at other kinds.

9. Believing and Doubting

Believing: "Try to believe everything I have written, even if you disagree or find it crazy. At least *pretend* to believe it. Be my friend and ally and give me more evidence, arguments, and ideas to help me make my case better." Doubting: "Try to doubt everything I have written, even if you love it. Take on the role of enemy and find all the arguments that can be made against me. Pretend to be someone who hates my writing. What would he or she notice?"

These forms of feedback obviously lend themselves to persuasive essays or arguments, though the believing game can help you flesh out and enrich the world of a story or poem. Believing is good when you are struggling and want help. It's a way to get readers to give you new ideas and arguments and in fact improve your piece in all sorts of ways.

Doubting is good after you've gotten a piece as strong as you can get it and you want to send it out or hand it in—but first find out how hostile readers will fight you.

10. Skeleton Feedback and Descriptive Outline

Skeleton feedback: "Please lay out the reasoning you see in my paper: my main point, my subpoints, my supporting evidence, and my assumptions about my topic and about my audience." Descriptive outline: "Please write *says* and *does* sentences for my whole paper and then for each paragraph or section." A *says* sentence summarizes the meaning or message, and a *does* sentence describes the function.

These are the most useful for essays. They are feasible only if the reader has the text in hand and can take a good deal of time and care—and perhaps write out responses. Because they give you the most distance and perspective on what you have written, they are uniquely useful for giving feedback *to yourself.* Both kinds of feedback help you on late drafts when you want to test out your reasoning and organization. But skeleton feedback is also useful on early drafts when you are still trying to figure out what to say or emphasize and how to organize your thoughts.

11. Criterion-based Feedback

Ask readers to give you their thoughts about specific criteria that you are wondering about or struggling with: "Does this sound too technical?" "Is this section too long?" "Do my jokes work for you?" "Do you feel I've addressed the objections of people who disagree?" And of course, "Please find mistakes in spelling and grammar and typing." You can also ask readers to address what *they* think are the important criteria for your piece. You can ask too about traditional criteria for essays: focus on the assignment or task, content (ideas, reasoning, support, originality), organization, clarity of language, and voice.

31

"Joining In" and "Knowing the I"

On Becoming Reflexive Scholars

Rhoda Bernard, Cleti Cervoni, Charlene Desir, and Corinne McKamey

In the 2000–2001 school year the four of us were in the beginning stages of our doctoral studies, starting to frame our research interests; we hoped to become educational scholars, though none of us felt at home in the academy. We approached Wendy Luttrell to help us read and think more about ourselves as researchers and ethnographers. She agreed to sponsor our independent study group focused on researcher reflexivity.[1] At first we were tentative, not knowing exactly how to "think with" each other.[2] Over time, through a process of reading, taking notes, keeping journals, and writing autobiographical stories, we came to trust our own development as scholars, and to understand our research in new ways.[3]

Weekly, we met to discuss the readings. Imagining ourselves as ethno-tourists visiting geographic places far from our graduate school location in the northeastern U.S.: New Mexico (Krieger 1991), Cuba (Behar 1996), Morocco (Rabinow 1977), the Philippines (Rosaldo 1989). We read about emotions in fieldwork, researcher subjectivity, and took to heart Kleinman's and Copp's (1993) caution that the shift from a *thinking* researcher to a *thinking and feeling* researcher—would be difficult. Inspired by our readings, we decided to explore our own movements in and out of the academic culture, including the full range of emotions bound up in our effort to become "scholars." Two practices that we developed concurrently—"joining in" and "knowing the I"—served us well in this pursuit.

"Joining in" requires a particular orientation towards responding to others in a discussion; it means attending to the speaker and reflecting upon the associations and emotions that arise. We learned to hold ourselves back from jumping in to criticize, give advice, or problem solve. Instead, we sought to meet the speaker where she was in her thoughts, and allowed her the space to express her experiences, connections, and doubts rather than imposing our own. "Joining in," meant listening for emotions, bringing them inside our discussion rather than banishing them from our minds and consideration. Instead, we sought ways to use our emotions as objects of reflection. It was refreshing, and at times we felt naughty about giving ourselves permission to bring our experiences and emotions into "academic discussions."

Through this practice, we also began to engage the literature differently. We imagined ourselves conversing with the authors we were reading. Placing ourselves as interested partners within these exchanges allowed us to embrace, rather than fear, the task of "reviewing the literature" related to our respective fields of study.[4]

Charlene described our process in terms that drew upon West African tradition and that we came to embrace as our own.

In the West African tradition,
when a speaker wants to address the community, she says *Ago*, which means *I* am ready to
speak and the response from the community is *Ame*, *I* am ready to listen.
I joined these women to better understand our similarities as researchers in order to
understand myself.
I found myself saying *Ame—I* am ready to listen, *Ame—I* am ready to listen and their
response was **NO**—*Ago*—you are ready to speak, *Ago*—you are ready to speak.
We began to think back on what **we** had to give up for the spirit of the child to become a
woman of courage.
In order for us to begin in the present **we** had to walk in the past.
Our meaning making of ourselves would be our personal tool to reflect on the other.
We gave rise
to our university voice by being true to our personal voice
We gave rise
to our research voice by listening to our communal voice
We gave rise
to our scholarship by accepting the *I*
And *I*
say *AGO AGO AGO*
And they
say *AME AME AME*
And together
we proceed knowing the *I*

We searched for ways to speak and write about the "I" in our scholarship. Ruth Behar's
(1996) essay, "The Girl in the Cast," pointed us in one direction, as did her call for
researcher reflexivity that is not for a "decorative flourish" or "exposure for its own sake"
(14). In her essay, Behar describes how being in a body cast as a child physically and
psychologically paralyzed her two decades after it had been removed. Upon reflection,
Behar realizes that her present day anxiety about an upcoming research trip to her homeland of Cuba is connected to this past experience. We too realized that each of us, in our
own way, felt some paralysis around past experiences, and that writing about them might
help release their grip on our evolving researcher identities.

Our Stories

Killing the Slave Within: Charlene Desir

Two years before his death, Dieusel's family moved from Haiti to the U.S. in order to have
a better life. One spring day, Dieusel was playing with his friends near a lake. An older boy
had an inflatable boat and urged the two younger boys to go in. The boat sank; one boy
could swim, and Dieusel could not.

In the Haitian Vodoun tradition, many believe that heaven exists under water. Some
have said if one loses their life in water, it cannot be a simple death. Such a lost life can be a
sacrifice for spiritual enlightenment. There were no memorials for the Haitian boy. There
were no support counselors to help students in Dieusel's school make meaning of his

death. There were no school personnel to speak at Dieusel's wake. As a researcher in the school and a Haitian American, I stood and spoke for this boy. The school had lost a friend, a brother, and a son. Words came from somewhere deep within my soul and reignited my purpose in education.

A part of me—the part that trusts in justice, the part that holds hope—was dying. The only way that I could describe this internal demise was to go back and understand when the African became a slave. Now I was enslaved to institutions that were bigger than me. As a graduate student I was attempting to battle this. I faced my courses with the knowledge that I worked in a school system that did not know how to honor a young boy's life. I would honor this boy's life by killing the slave within my being that was taking away my trust in justice and hope. My work and my research would not simply be an analytic task.

To prepare, I faced that young girl within myself who was also neglected and undervalued. I had to wrestle with the contradictions of my academic socialization. In this process, with three white faces staring back at me, a veil was raised from my eyes. They gave me the liberty to express my pain and anger at modern slavery. And in that space I reclaimed my voice (Desir 2008).

Sacrificing the Cow: Corinne McKamey

A childhood memory:

> Every year, my family kills a cow to share with the men and their families who work on the farm. This tradition has been practiced for at least two generations. For some reason, one year my father wasn't there the morning of the cow slaughter. We got a frantic radio call up at the house right before we were leaving for school. "The cow is possessed, and the spirits are angry," the man said over the phone. It wouldn't die. Could Kenny please come to the corral and put the soul to rest?
>
> We—my father, brother, sister, and I—arrived at the corral to see several worried, pacing men. A shotgun was leaning against the fence, and the cow walked along the back part of the enclosure, clearly agitated, but not looking very harmed. "We shot the cow five or six times, right between the eyes, and she wouldn't go down!" Dad picked the gun up, aimed, and shot the cow twice in the side of the head. She went down fast. "You can't kill a cow by shooting it between the eyes," Dad explained to the astonished group. Ten minutes late to school, I reported in to the secretary, who knew my family through my grandmother. "I'm late because the cow wouldn't die," I said. She wrote up an excused absence and told me to get to class.

The group's response to this story overwhelmed me. Among other things, we talked about my efforts as a girl to hold both explanations for why the cow wouldn't die. By one account, guided by local knowledge of spirits, the spirit of the cow would not rest because my father wasn't present. By another account, informed by scientific knowledge, the head-on bullets served to lobotomize, but not kill, the cow. I moved between and accepted both interpretations.

It was transformative for me to write about and discuss this and other memories that I had previously assumed were not "academic," and therefore not part of my graduate student self. With the support of the group, I cast a wider intellectual net that could include personal feelings, knowledge, and experiences.

In my dissertation fieldwork, these insights prompted me to listen for the ways immigrant high school students negotiated multiple and often conflicting interpretations of school, and to be attentive to experiences and knowledge that might be unexpected in academic contexts. I became committed to studying and creating spaces in schools where students and teachers can together explore different ways of knowing.

Music is My Truth: Rhoda Bernard

> Lots of us get punished because somebody out there has made a decision that their truth is the truth. That is why I keep going back to art. It is the most direct form of truth each of us has, whether it is music or dance or decorating a home.
>
> "Diana," as cited in Krieger (1991, p. 212)

Music is my truth. When I was a child, music was safety. I spent countless hours on the backyard swing set, singing to the skies. Sometimes I would sing songs from the radio, songs from Broadway musicals, but most of the time I would make up songs as I went along. I sang about a life I yearned for—a happy, carefree life, away from neglect and abuse. Making this music, I tried to construct a new truth for myself.

Sharing my music with others enabled me to share myself with others. Bringing my emotions and experiences to my songs, I communicated my thoughts, feelings, and identity. Members of the audience would hear me sing and would tell me how they had come to understand me and to think about themselves. Putting myself into my music, I made powerful connections with my listeners. Today, as a professional musician, I find myself deeply moved by the mutual recognition that music makes possible.

At the group's suggestion, I started taking field notes about my gigs as a means to help me investigate this passion. After a performance at a Jewish assisted-living facility, I wrote:

> Jacob hummed along with me as I sang. He also would smile or chuckle at the jokes in the songs or at the jokes I made in Yiddish during the concert.
>
> Jacob smiled and told me in Yiddish that my songs touched his heart. He told me that my songs made him think of his childhood. He said that the music he heard today brought him back to his bube's [grandmother's] kitchen, where she would sing to him as he watched her prepare Shabbat dinner. Tears welled in his eyes as he sang a bit of "Oyfn Pripetshik" [a well-known Yiddish folksong] to me.
>
> This experience overwhelmed me. The ability to communicate so directly with other people is an incredibly satisfying part of performing this music. By singing these songs, I witness people opening themselves up to me and sharing their memories and emotions with me. The music is the vehicle for that connection.

I came to understand that my passion for music stems from the ways in which we make personal meaning of the music that we make or hear. Writing about memories of making music—from childhood to the present—and unraveling the layers of meaning that they hold for me helped me to clarify what I wanted to learn from other musician-music teachers. The power of personal meanings that we make of music—as performers and as audiences—and the mutual connections that are made, is a missing discourse in music education that I seek to fill (Bernard 2004).

Teori and Me: Cleti Cervoni

> When someone with the authority of a teacher, say, describes the world and you are not in it, there is a moment of psychic dis-equilibrium, as if you looked into a mirror and saw nothing.
>
> Adrienne Rich, "Invisibility in Academe"
> (Rosaldo 1989: xxi)

For some children, what they know and feel and what they understand from their everyday life has little value or meaning in their classroom. When I returned to school as a graduate student, it was after twenty years as a science educator. I had returned to school because I was puzzled about children's science learning and I wanted to become a more effective teacher. In my course work, I found myself continually trying to reconcile the theory that I was learning with my past experience as a teacher. In some classes that was easier to do than in others. At times I sat silent, hoping someone would ask me about what I was thinking.

> I see myself in the young second grader, Teori, who I have been interviewing. When I hear Teori talk about her mealworms and how she collects ladybugs in a jar in her yard, I see myself and I empathize with her interest in animals and her pure joy of interacting with living things. When the classroom teacher doesn't have time for her to explain her experiment, and she hides under the desk and cries, my heart breaks that her wonderful ideas aren't honored and asked about or scaffolded. We have let children think their ideas are less than because they are different from what we expect, or we don't know what to make of them, or it's time to move on to a new subject. Ruth Behar talks about displacement and how she often asks her informants things she couldn't ask her family. I now understand what she means. In my work with girls, I now ask them to tell me more and to elaborate on their thinking often using artifacts of science, like batteries and bulbs, or tadpoles as prompts. In doing so, I am more likely to hear their feelings both about science and how they make meaning of what the teacher has asked them to do.

In my work with the second-grade children, I realize I want to ask questions that were not asked of me in school, which left me feeling invisible and silenced. As a student, researcher, and teacher, I believe in the power of feelings and have changed the way I look at classroom science learning (Cervoni 2007). I now see that when children sit still, are quiet, it is not because they are not interested in the subject, but that the classroom environment, including the teacher's pedagogy, classroom peers, and materials may not be accessible or feel authentic to them. This disconnect has haunted me; but as I have begun to reconcile my own relationship with science and subjectivity, I have become committed to researching and developing instruction in school that encourages science learning in both subjective and objective ways.

Evolving Researchers

Ruth Behar (1996) writes, "The woman who forgets the girl she harbors inside herself runs the risk of meeting her again—as I did—in the lonely space of a house that is her own in name only" (134). For us, writing personal stories provided us a way to connect with our deeply held emotions, beliefs, and fears. By serving as witnesses to each other's growth, we transformed ourselves from outsiders looking in, to writing within and against the culture of academia. We immersed ourselves in deep conversations among us, a group of graduate students who felt marginalized by the academy. We sat around the table talking with each other, sometimes with much difficulty, and sometimes with so much ease that the hours flew by without our noticing. We learned much about who we are as people, who we are as graduate students, and who we are (and continue to be) as educational scholars.

Notes

1. The reading list included the following Behar, 1996; Kleinman, S., & Copp, S. (1993); Krieger, 1991; Luttrell, 2000; Lughod, 1993; Rabinow, 1977; Rosaldo, 1989.
2. Wendy Luttrell (2003) describes and models what she calls "thinking with" rather than "thinking about"—a rhythmic move between emotional engagement and analytic distance that she describes in her book *Pregnant Bodies, Fertile Minds*. We also found Elbow and Belanoff's way of responding to writing extremely useful in structure out discussion. We were also influenced by a presentation/demonstration by Annie Rogers, Mary Casey, and Katie Pakos of how they worked as an "interpretive community."
3. This independent study morphed into a writing group that has lasted over eight years. We attribute our success as doctoral students and researchers to our participation in this process.
4. We benefitted from reading "Terrorized by the Literature," in Becker (1986).

References

Becker, H. S. (1986). *Writing for Social Scientists: how to start and finish your thesis, book, or article.* Chicago: University of Chicago Press.

Behar, R. 1996. *The Vulnerable Observer: anthropology that breaks your heart.* Boston: Beacon Press.

Bernard, R. 2004. "A Dissonant duet: discussions of music making and music teaching." *Music Education Research,* 6 (3): 281–298.

Cervoni, C. 2007. "Beyond access: girls and school science." *Sextant.* Salem MA: Salem State College: 34–35.

Desir, C. 2008. "Understanding the sending context of Haitian immigrant students." *Journal of Haitian Studies,* 13 (2), 73–93.

Elbow, P. & Belanoff, P. 1999. *Sharing and Responding.* New York: McGraw-Hill.

Kleinman, S., & Copp, S. 1993. *Emotions and Fieldwork.* Newbury Park, CA: Sage.

Krieger, S. 1991. *Social Science & the Self: personal essays on an art form.* New Brunswick: Rutgers University Press.

Lughod, L. A. (1993). *Writing Women's Worlds: Bedouin stories.* Berkeley, CA: University of California Press.

Luttrell, W. (2000). "'Good enough' methods for ethnographic research." *Harvard Educational Review,* 70 (4): 499–523.

—— . (2003). *Pregant Bodies, Fertile Minds: gender, race and the schooling of pregnant teens.* New York: Routledge.

Rabinow, P. 1977. *Reflections on Fieldwork in Morocco.* Berkeley: University of California Press.

Rosaldo, R. 1989. *Culture and Truth.* Boston: Beacon Press.

Supplemental Readings

Becker, Howard S. 1986. *Writing for Social Scientists*. Chicago: University of Chicago Press.

——— . 1998. *Tricks of the Trade*. Chicago: University of Chicago Press.

Blauner, Bob. 1987. "A Problem of Editing 'First-Person' Sociology." *Qualitative Sociology* 10(1): 46–64.

Boyatzis, R. E. 1998. *Transforming Qualitative Information*. Thousand Oaks, CA: Sage Publications.

Brizuela, Barbara, Stewart, Julie Pearson, Carillo, Romina G., and Berger, Jennifer G., 2000. *Acts of Inquiry: Studies in Qualitative Research*. Cambridge, MA: Harvard Publishing Group.

Charmaz, Kathy. 2005. *Constructing Grounded Theory: A Practical Guide Through Qualitative Analysis*. London, Thousand Oaks, New Delhi: Sage.

Creswell, J. W. 1998. *Qualitative Inquiry and Research Design: Choosing Among Five Traditions*. Thousand Oaks, CA: Sage.

Devereux, George, 1967. *From Anxiety to Method in Behavioral Sciences*. Mouton & Co.

Ely, Margot, Vinz, Ruth, Downing, Maryann, and Anzul, Margaret. 1997. *On Writing Qualitative Research: Living By Words*. London: Falmer Press.

Ely, Margot with Argaret Anzul, Teri Friedman, Diane Garner and Ann McCormack Steinmetz. 1991. *Doing Qualitative Research: Circles Within Circles*. London: Falmer Press.

Emerson, R., Fretz, R. and Shaw, L. 1995. *Writing Ethnographic Fieldnotes*. Chicago and London: Chicago University Press.

Gitlin, Andrew. 1994. (Ed.). *Power and Method: Political Activism and Educational Research*. New York and London: Routledge

Glaser, B. 1992. *Basics of Grounded Theory Analysis: Emergence versus Forcing*. Mill Valley, CA: Sociology Press.

Glaser, B. and Strauss, A. 1967. *Discovery of Grounded Theory*. Chicago: Aldine.

Hesse-Biber, S., and Leavy, P. (Eds.) 2006. *Emergent Methods in Social Research*. Newbury Park, CA: Sage Publications.

Jessor, Richard, et al. 1996. *Ethnography and Human Development*. Chicago: University of Chicago Press.

Kleinman, Sherryl and Copp, Martha. 1993. *Emotions and Fieldwork*. Thousand Oaks, CA: Sage Publishing.

Krieger, Susan. 1991. *Social Science and the Self: Personal Essays on an Art Form*. Rugers, NJ: Rutgers University Press.

Langer, Susanne. 1976. *Philosophy in a New Key*. Cambridge: Harvard University Press.

Lawrence-Lightfoot, Sara and Hoffmann Davis, Jessica. 1997. *The Art and Science of Portraiture*. San Francisco: Jossey-Bass.

Lofland, John and Lofland, Lyn. 1995. *Analyzing Social Settings: A Guide to Qualitative Observation and Analysis*. Belmont, CA: Wadsworth.

Lykes, B. and Coquillon, E. 2007. "Participatory and Action Research and Feminisms: Towards Transformative Praxis." In S. Hesse-Biber (Ed.). *Handbook of Feminist Research: Theory and Praxis*. Thousand Oaks, CA: Sage Publications: 297–326.

McLeod, J. 2009. *Researching Social Change: Qualitative Approaches*. London: Sage Publications.

Marcus, George E. 1998. *Ethnography through Thick & Thin*. Princeton: Princeton University Press.

Maykut, P. and Morehouse, R. 1994. *Beginning Qualitative Research: A Philosophic and Practical Guide*. London: Falmer Press.

Maynes, M. J., Pierce, J. L. and Laslett, B. 2008. *Telling Stories: The Use of Personal Narratives in the Social Sciences and History*. Ithaca and London: Cornell University Press.

Merriam, Sharan B. 1997. *Qualitative Research and Case Study Applications in Education*. San Francisco: Jossey-Bass.

Miles, Matthew and Huberman, Michael. 1994. *Qualitative Data Analysis*. Thousand Oaks, CA: Sage Publications.

Mishler, Elliot. 1986. *Research Interviewing: Context and Narrative*. Cambridge, MA: Harvard University Press.

Morgan, David L. 1988. *Focus Groups as Qualitative Research*. Qualitative Research Methods Series, Volume 16. Newbury Park, CA: Sage Publications.

Moss, J. 2008. *Researching Education: Digitally – Visually – Spatially*. Sense Publishers, Rotterdam.

Moustakas, C. 1994. *Phenomenological Research Methods*. Thousand Oaks, CA: Sage Publications.

Naples, N. 2003. *Feminism and Method: Ethnography, Discourse Analysis and Activist Research*. New York and London: Routledge.

Patai, Daphne and Gluck, Sherna B. 1991. *Women's Words: The Feminist Practice of Oral History*. New York and London: Routledge.

Polyani, Michael. 1998. *Personal Knowledge: Towards a Post-Critical Philosophy*. London: Routledge. 1998.

Rabinow, Paul D. 1977. *Reflections on Fieldwork in Morocco*. Berkeley, CA: University of California Press.

Rabinow, Paul D. and Sullivan, William (Eds.). 1987. *Interpretive Social Science*. Berkeley, CA: University of California Press.

Reinharz, Shulamith. 1992. *Feminist Methods in Social Research*. New York: Oxford University Press.

Riessman, Catherine Kohler. 1993. *Narrative Analysis*. Newbury Park, CA: Sage Publications.

——— . 2008. *Narrative Methods for the Human Sciences*. Los Angeles, London, New Delhi, Singapore: Sage Publications.

Seidman, I. E. 1991. *Interviewing as Qualitative Research: A Guide for Researchers in Education and the Social Science*. Teacher College, Columbia University New York, NY: Teachers College Press.

Silverman, David. 1993. *Interpreting Qualitative Data: Methods for Analyzing Talk, Text and Interaction*. Thousand Oaks, CA: Sage Publications.

Shacklock, Geoffrey and Smyth, John. 1998. *Being Reflexive in Critical Education and Social Research*. London: Falmer Press.

Stake, Robert. 1995. *The Art of Case Study Research*. Thousand Oaks, CA: Sage Publications.

Strauss, Anselm and Corbin, Juliet. 1998. *Basics of Qualitative Research: Techniques and Procedures for Developing Grounded Theory*. Thousand Oaks, CA: Sage Publications.

Van Manen, Max. 1988. *Tales of the Field: On Writing Ethnography*. Chicago: University of Chicago Press.

——— . 1990. *Researching Lived Experience*. New York: SUNY Press.

Weis, L. and Fine, M. 2000. *Speed Bumps: A Student-Friendly Guide to Qualitative Research*. Teacher College, Columbia University New York, NY: Teachers College Press.

——— . 2004. *Working Method: Social Justice and Social Research*. New York: Routledge.

Weiss, Robert S. 1994. *Learning from Strangers: The Art and Method of Qualitative Interview Studies*. New York: The Free Press/Simon & Schuster.

Wetherell, M., Taylor, S. and Yates, S. 2001. *Discourse As Data*. Thousand Oaks, CA: Sage Publications.

Wolcott, Harry. 1990. *Writing Up Qualitative Research*. Thousand Oaks, CA: Sage Publications.

——— 1994. *Transforming Qualitative Data*. Thousand Oaks, CA: Sage Publications.

——— 1995. *The Art of Fieldwork*. Thousand Oaks, CA: Sage Publications.

——— 1999. *Ethnography: A Way of Seeing*. Walnut Creek, CA: AltaMira.

Permissions

Chapter 1
Bogdan, R. & Biklen, S. (1998). Foundations of Qualitative Research in Education: An Introduction. In *Qualitative Research for Education: An Introduction to Theories and Methods* (3rd ed., pp. 7–31). Upper Saddle River, NJ: Allyn and Bacon/Merrill Education, Boston, MA. Copyright © 1998 by Pearson Education. Reprinted by permission of the publisher.

Chapter 2
Banks, J. (1998). The Lives and Values of Researchers: Implications for Educating Citizens in a Multicultural Society. *Educational Researcher*, 27(7), 1998, 4–5, 8–13, 15–17. Reprinted by permission of the publisher.

Chapter 3
Becker, H. (1983). Studying Urban Schools. *Anthropology and Education Quarterly*, 14(2), pp. 99–108. Reprinted by permission of the publisher.

Chapter 4
Greene, J. (1990). Knowledge Accumulation: Three Views on the Nature and Role of Knowledge in Social Science. In E. Guba (Ed.), *The Paradigm Dialog* (pp. 227–245). Newbury Park, CA: Sage Publications. Reprinted by permission of the publisher.

Chapter 5
Sprague, J. (2005). Seeing through Science. In *Feminist Methodologies for Critical Researchers: Bridging Differences* (pp. 31–52). Walnut Creek, CA: Alta Mira Press. Reprinted by permission of the publisher.

Chapter 6
Smith, L.T. (2005). On Tricky Ground: Researching the Native in the Age of Uncertainty. In N. Denzin & Y. Lincoln, *The SAGE Handbook of Qualitative Research* (3rd ed., pp. 86–91, 96–100, 103–107). Beverly Hills, CA: Sage Publications. Reprinted by permission of the publisher.

Chapter 7
Haney, W. & Lykes, M. B. (2000). Practice, Participatory Research and Creative Research Designs: The Evolution of Ethical Guidelines for Research. In Torbert Sherman (Ed.)

Transforming Social Inquiry, Transforming Social Action (pp. 275–294). Norwel, MA: Kluwer Academic Publishers. Reprinted by permission of the publisher.

Chapter 8
Halse, C. & Honey, A. (2005). Unraveling Ethics: Illuminating the Moral Dilemmas of Research Ethics. *Signs: Journal of Women in Culture and Society*, 3(4), 2141–2162. Reprinted by permission of the publisher.

Chapter 9
Mills, C. W. (1959). On Intellectual Craftsmanship. In *The Sociological Imagination* (pp. 215–220, 232–238). London, UK: Oxford University Press. Reprinted by permission of the publisher.

Chapter 10
DeVault, M. (1999). From the Seminar Room. In *Liberating Method: Feminism and Social Research* (pp. 207–217, 228–230). Philadelphia, PA: Temple University Press. Reprinted by permission of the publisher.

Chapter 12
McDermott, R. P. & Varenne, H. (1996). Culture, Development, Disability. In C. Jessor and R. Shweder (Eds.), *Ethnography and Human Development* (pp. 101–126). Chicago: University of Chicago Press. Reprinted by permission of the publisher.

Chapter 13
Charmaz, K. (2000). Grounded Theory: Objectivist and Constructivist Methods. In N. Denzin & Y. Lincoln (Eds.), *The SAGE Handbook of Qualitative Research* (pp. 511–535). Thousand Oaks, CA: Sage Publications. Reprinted by permission of the publisher.

Chapter 14
Chase, S. (2005). Narrative Inquiry: Multiple Lenses, Approaches, Voices. In N. Denzin & Y. Lincoln (Eds.), *The SAGE Handbook of Qualitative Research* (3rd ed., pp. 651–679). Thousand Oaks, CA: Sage Publications. Reprinted by permission of the publisher.

Chapter 16
Luttrell, W. "Good Enough" Methods for Life-Story Analysis. In N. Quinn (Ed.), *Finding Culture and Talk* (pp. 243–268). Palgrave. Reprinted by permission of the publisher.

Chapter 17
Maxwell, J. (2005). Validity: How Might You Be Wrong? In *Qualitative Research Design: An Interactive Approach* (pp. 4–5, 105–114). Thousand Oaks, CA: Sage Publications. Reprinted by permission of the publisher.

Chapter 18
Mishler, E. G. (1990). Validation in Inquiry-Guided Research: The Role of Exemplars in Narrative Studies. *Harvard Educational Review*, 60, 415–442. Reprinted by permission of the publisher.

Chapter 19
Dodson, L. & Schmalzbauer, L. (2005). Poor Mothers and Habits of Hiding: Participatory Methods in Poverty Research. *Journal of Marriage and Family*, 67, 949–959. Reprinted by permission of Blackwell Publishing Ltd.

Chapter 20
Ferguson, A. A. (2001). Don't Believe the Hype. In *Bad Boys: Public Schools in the Making of Black Masculinity* (pp. 1–23). Ann Arbor, MI: University of Michigan Press. Reprinted by permission of the publisher.

Chapter 21
Villenas, S. (1996). The Colonizer/Colonized Chicana Ethnographer: Identity, Marginalization, and Co-optation in the Field. *Harvard Educational Review*, 66(4), 711–731. Reprinted by permission of the publisher.

Chapter 22
Henry, M. (2003). "Where Are You Really From?": Representation, Identiy and Power in the Fieldwork Experiences of a South Asian Diasporic. *Qualitative Research* 3(2), 229–242. Reprinted by permission of the publisher.

Chapter 23
Gallagher, C. (2000). White Like Me? Methods, Meaning, and Manipulation in the Field of White Studies. In F. Twine & J. Warren (Eds.), *Racing Research, Researching Race: Methodological Dilemmas in Critical Race Studies* (pp. 67–70, 80–92). New York: New York University Press. Reprinted by permission of the publisher.

Chapter 24
Foster, M. (1994). The Power to Know One Thing Is Never the Power to Know All Things: Methodological Notes on Two Studies of Black American Teachers. In A. Gitlin (Ed.), *Power and Method: Political Activism and Educational Research* (pp. 129–146). New York: Routledge. Reprinted by permission of the publisher.

Chapter 25
Talburt, S. (2000). Entering the Inquiry. In *Subject to Identity: Knowledge, Sexuality and Academic Practices in Higher Education* (pp. 24–34, 224–225). Albany, NY: SUNY Press. Reprinted by permission of the publisher.

Chapter 26
Thorne, B. (1993). Learning from Kids. In *Gender Play: Girls and Boys in School* (pp. 11–29). Copyright © 1993 by Barrie Thorne. Reprinted by permission of Rutgers University Press.

Chapter 27
Ulichny, P. & Schoener, W. (1996). Teacher–Researcher Collaboration from Two Perspectives. *Harvard Educational Review* 66(3), 496–524. Reprinted by permission of the publisher.

Chapter 28
Fine, M. & Weis, L. (1996). Writing the "Wrongs" of Fieldwork: Confronting Our Own Research/Writing Dilemmas in Urban Ethnographies. *Qualitative Inquiry*, 2(3), 251–274. Reprinted by permission of the publisher.

Chapter 30
Elbow, P. & Belanoff, P. (1999). Summary of Kinds of Responses. In *Sharing and Responding* (3rd ed.). New York: McGraw-Hill, Inc. Reprinted by permission of the McGraw-Hill Companies.

Index